EU SOCIAL AND EMPLOYMENT LAW

Policy and Practice in an Enlarged Europe

EU SOCIAL AND EMPLOYMENT LAW

Policy and Practice in an Enlarged Europe

PHILIPPA WATSON

*Barrister, Essex Court Chambers; Visiting Professor,
City Law School, London*

OXFORD
UNIVERSITY PRESS

OXFORD
UNIVERSITY PRESS

Great Clarendon Street, Oxford OX2 6DP
Oxford University Press is a department of the University of Oxford.
It furthers the University's objective of excellence in research, scholarship,
and education by publishing worldwide in

Oxford New York

Auckland Cape Town Dar es Salaam Hong Kong Karachi
Kuala Lumpur Madrid Melbourne Mexico City Nairobi
New Delhi Shanghai Taipei Toronto

With offices in

Argentina Austria Brazil Chile Czech Republic France Greece
Guatemala Hungary Italy Japan Poland Portugal Singapore
South Korea Switzerland Thailand Turkey Ukraine Vietnam

Oxford is a registered trade mark of Oxford University Press
in the UK and in certain other countries

Published in the United States
by Oxford University Press Inc., New York

First published 2009

British Library Cataloguing in Publication Data
Data available

Library of Congress Cataloging in Publication Data
Data available

Typeset by Cepha Imaging Private Ltd, Bangalore, India
Printed by the
MPG Books Group
in the UK

ISBN 978-1-90-450153-4

1 3 5 7 9 10 8 6 4 2

CONTENTS—SUMMARY

CONTENTS

Contents

PART VII EQUALITY OF TREATMENT: RACE

28. The Race Directive

PART VIII EQUALITY OF TREATMENT: RELIGION, DISABILITY, AGE, AND SEXUAL ORIENTATION

TABLE OF CASES

TABLE OF LEGISLATION

EU LEGISLATION

Treaties

INTERNATIONAL INSTRUMENTS

Council of Europe

ILO

UN

PART I

GENERAL

1

INTRODUCTION

Social and employment law and policy in the European Union has evolved **1.01**
spasmodically and in a piecemeal manner. When the European Union was
founded some 50 years ago as the European Economic Community, it had as its
objective to achieve and maintain peace amongst nations, which had been torn
apart by war during the previous half century, through economic union. The
heads of state and governments of the six founder Member States:

> Resolved by thus pooling their resources to preserve and strengthen peace and lib-
> erty and calling upon the other peoples of Europe who share their ideal to join in
> their efforts,
>
> Have decided to create a European Economic Community . . . (Preamble to Treaty
> establishing the European Economic Community).

An economic union was the means of achieving peace, not an end in itself. This
is often forgotten.

The evolution of social and employment policy turns on five pivotal points in **1.02**
time in the life of the European Union: The accession of the Denmark, Ireland,
and the United Kingdom in 1973; the drive towards the completion of the
internal market in the mid 1980s by the Delors Commission; the Maastricht
Treaty; the Protocol on Social Policy annexed to the Maastricht Treaty; the
Amsterdam Treaty, and the Lisbon European Council. Each of these five points
in time marked a move towards the creation of a Community social and employment policy.

The purpose of this book is to set out the law and policy as it has evolved since **1.03**
the European Economic Community was established by six Member States
in 1957 through its subsequent five enlargements to the European Union of
27 countries.

Community social and employment law and policy is characterized by a num- **1.04**
ber of unique features. In terms of governance, it has spawned techniques and

instruments, some of which have subsequently migrated to other areas of law and policy. The Community Charter of the Fundamental Social Rights of Workers was the first time use had been made of a Charter to express a solemn commitment of the Member States to commonly held values. It has subsequently been used in other areas of Community policy, notably energy. The Open Method of Co-ordination had its origins in European Employment Strategy. It was institutionalized by the Treaty of Amsterdam as the means by which the Common Employment Policy was to be formulated. In 1999 it was recognized as a general Community instrument of governance by the White Paper on Governance, and widely used in the implementation of the Lisbon Strategy.

1.05   The Treaty establishing the European Economic Community, signed on 25 March 1957 in Rome, and commonly referred to as the Treaty of Rome, made no reference to social and employment policy and few provisions in it dealt with the issue. The principle of equal pay for men and women was laid down not because the founder Member States believed that parity in pay was a morally or socially desirable objective, but for purely economic reasons. If some Member States provided for equal pay for equal work, and others did not, this could have prejudiced the attainment and functioning of the common market. Business, particularly in labour-intensive sectors, it was feared, might move to countries where there was a pool of cheap female labour, and those countries which did pay men and women on an equal basis could find themselves at a competitive disadvantage due to their higher payroll costs. France, which required equal pay for equal work on a national level, was particularly concerned that its businesses might be prejudiced, and it was thus at France's instigation and insistence that the principle of equal pay for men and women was laid down in Article 119, which subsequently became Article 141. It was not envisaged that the Community would implement that principle and thus no legislative competence was conferred on the Community institutions; the Member States were charged with achieving equal pay for men and women by 31 December 1963.

1.06   Apart from equal pay, no other specific social or employment policy was mentioned in the Treaty of Rome. It was assumed that economic prosperity would result in full employment and a progressive improvement in living and working conditions. The Community institutions were thus given no specific powers with respect to either social or employment policy. And it was not until 1997, by virtue of the Treaty of Amsterdam, that the Community, as a whole, was endowed with such powers, and social and employment policy became a shared competence.

1.07   Post-Amsterdam, social and employment policy have figured amongst the principal objectives of the Community and legislative competence of the

Community institutions has been enhanced to achieve these objectives. Article 2 EC states that the Community has as its task to promote within the Community a high level of employment and of social protection and 'the raising of the standard of living and the quality of life'. Article 3 provides that, for the purposes set out in Article 2, the activities of the Community shall include:

(i) the promotion of coordination between employment policies of the Member States with a view to enhancing their effectiveness by developing a co-ordinated strategy for employment;

(j) a policy in the social sphere.

The Treaty of Amsterdam marked a commitment on the part of the Community **1.08** towards employment policy. It was henceforth seen as a policy objective central to economic and monetary union. Title VIII of the EC Treaty, introduced by the Treaty of Amsterdam and entitled 'Employment' has six provisions— Articles 125–130, which make employment policy an integral part of Community activity. The impact of all Community policies on employment must be taken into account both at the point of formulation and at implementation. The Treaty does not envisage the creation of a common employment policy but rather the promotion of active co-operation between the Member States' national employment policies by taking initiatives, reporting on employment trends and prospects, undertaking research, and harnessing national employment policies to Community objectives. The diversity of national employment policies is respected but the Member States are encouraged to act within the parameters, and in furtherance of defined common objectives.

Title XI of the EC Treaty is entitled 'Social Policy, Education, Vocational Training **1.09** and Youth'. Chapter 1 sets out the 'Social Provisions'. If we understand social policy as meaning that policy which is designed to be addressed to the population at large as opposed to the economically active, it has to be said this chapter has been little used for that purpose. Most of the objectives set out therein and the measures adopted on the basis of its provisions (with or without necessary bolstering from the general law-making provisions of the Treaty) are concerned with the economically active, notably the working conditions of the employed.

The Treaty of Nice introduced few amendments into the social policy provisions **1.10** of the EC Treaty. The Treaty of Lisbon—as yet not ratified—will introduce a provision reinforcing the place of the social dialogue in the Community policy and legislative process and require the union to pay heed in the development and implementation of its policies and activities to the elimination of discrimination on the grounds articulated in Article 13 EC.

Community legislative initiatives in social policy, are largely driven by economic **1.11** considerations or the implementation on a Community level of global social standards to which the Member States have subscribed. We see this in Chapter 7

5

on Community disability law and policy. Even in those areas of social policy where the Community is empowered to adopt legislation, increasingly, and in deference to the principle of subsidiarity, the Community's efforts are of a directional nature: the Community assuming responsibility for engendering debate on issues of social policy common to all and indicating how those issues should be managed to attain optimal results, but leaving the realization of those results to the individual Member States. This exercise is carried out within the Open Method of Co-ordination discussed in Chapter 5.

1.12   The book divides into eight parts.

1.13   Part I deals with general issues. It explores the sources of Community social and employment law and policy. The primary source is obviously the EC Treaty itself, but as will be seen from Chapter 3, for many years the Treaty had no specific provisions empowering the Community institutions to act. The result of this was twofold. To develop law and policy the Community institutions relied heavily on soft law measures, there being no other viable means to engage in the field. Although not legally binding, and hence neither a source of rights nor obligations, these measures were not without effect. They could be used as an interpretative tool. More importantly, when the Community began to acquire legislative competence many soft law measures formed the basis for legislative instruments. Their presence in the corpus of Community policy facilitated their enactment into law. The Charter of Fundamental Social Rights for Workers, the first time in which a Charter was used to express commonly held values amongst the Member States, resulted in a detailed legislative programme. Since there were no specific legislative powers set out in the Treaty, legislation was made possible only by reliance on the Community's general law-making powers set out in Articles 94 and 308 EC. These required first that the proposed legislative measure be necessary to achieve 'one of the objectives of the Community' (Article 308) or in the case of approximation measures that they 'directly affect the establishment or functioning of the common market' (Article 94) and secondly a unanimous vote in the Council. The requirement of unanimity made legislation difficult to adopt and even when it was adopted it was of poor quality, in the sense that in order to secure agreement amongst the Member States many concepts were left undefined or inadequately defined. As a result legislation was difficult to interpret and apply. This led to numerous references for preliminary rulings to the European Court of Justice from courts and tribunals across the Community. The case law of the Court is thus an important source—and at times has been the sole source—of social and employment rights. For example, the right to equal pay, and the right to equality of treatment in the matter of occupational social security schemes, was established through preliminary rulings on references from national courts.

Chapters 4 and 5 discuss governance: how policy and law are made. **1.14**

In Part II a number of social policy issues on which the Community is currently **1.15**
active are addressed. It consists of four brief chapters on social security, combating social exclusion, disability, and corporate social responsibility.

Part III is devoted to a discussion of the common employment policy: how it **1.16**
evolved; the Treaty provisions post-Amsterdam, and how employment policy on
a Community level is created.

Part IV sets out employment rights which are classified as 'collective' since they **1.17**
are generally framed as rights given to the workforce as a whole. Their collective
nature does not mean that they do not confer rights; they do and often directly
effective rights on individuals within the workforce which may be enforced
by them before national courts.

For the purposes of this work, collective rights relate to situations experienced **1.18**
by the collectivity of the workforce due to changes brought about in their
working environment by the decision or circumstances of their employer.

Collective rights derive from legislation, collective agreements, and industry **1.19**
practice. They have as their objective the protection of the employee in circumstances which are largely out of his personal control and, as such, can only
exceptionally be waived or departed from even by agreement between the
employer and the employee.

By contrast, individual employment rights pertain to the contract of employ- **1.20**
ment or employment relationship and are the subject of negotiation between the
employer and the employee save in so far as they are laid down by legislation or
collective agreement and thus mandatorily applicable except where derogation
therefrom is permitted under the instruments by which they came into being.

Collective employment rights were amongst the first measures of the Com- **1.21**
munity to lay down common minimum standards in the employment sphere.
In historical terms they precede the regulation of individual employment
rights by some twenty years. They derive their origins from the Social Action
Programme of 1974. As such, along with the directives on equal pay, equal opportunities, and equal treatment for men and women in social security, they can
be said to constitute the first generation of social and employment rights in the
European Union.

Three of the directives discussed in Part IV deal with the rights of the workforce **1.22**
in the event of multiple redundancies; the transfer of ownership of an undertaking and the insolvency of the employer. The fourth bundle of collective rights
relates to the information and consultation of the workforce and derives from a

number of legislative instruments, some of which, although of fairly recent vintage, had their origins some decades before final adoption.

1.23 Much of this early legislation differs from measures concerning individual employment rights discussed in Part V, adopted following the Agreement on Social Policy enshrined in the Maastricht Treaty, which ultimately became, by virtue of the Treaty of Amsterdam, Title XI of the EC Treaty, tending to be less prescriptive, drafted in broad and general terms, and generally not conferring directly effective rights which can be relied upon by individuals.

1.24 The Collective Redundancies Directive (Chapter 11), the Transfers of Undertakings Directive (Chapter 12), and the Insolvency Directive (Chapter 13) had no specific legal basis in the EC Treaty. They were adopted under the general law-making powers conferred by Article 94 and 308. As we have explained above, these provisions can be invoked where measures are necessary for the functioning of the common market but where no specific legislative competence is given to the Community institutions in the EC Treaty. Such measures must be adopted on the basis of a unanimous vote in the Council of Ministers. The need to find a mutually acceptable common denominator has resulted in short and often loosely worded legislation which in turn has spawned a large and rich body of interpretative case law. The ECJ, faced with often skeletal and sometimes confusing legislative provisions, and culturally diverse business environments, has chosen a functional approach when applying the Directives, looking beyond the textual wording to their objectives and interpreting and applying them accordingly. The extensive case law has necessitated a number of amendments to these three Directives. The legislation on Collective Redundancies and the Transfer of Undertakings has been consolidated. The Insolvency Directive has been the subject of comparatively fewer references for preliminary rulings to the ECJ, with the result that the original Directive has been amended on only one occasion. The Information and Consultation Directives, being more recent, have been based in a number of specific Treaty provisions.

1.25 The objective of the Collective Redundancies Directive, the Transfer of Undertakings Directive, and the Insolvency Directive was to protect employees during periods of restructuring which it was believed would be necessary as the single market developed.

1.26 These Directives, for the most part, are an exercise in partial harmonization. They prescribe minimum standards. Many essential concepts are defined according to national law with the result that impact of the Directives may be variable throughout the Community.

1.27 Part V is concerned with individual employment rights, that is, rights which attach to individual employees in the circumstances to which they pertain. All of the legislation discussed in this section has its origins in the Charter of Fundamental Rights for Workers. It has been adopted over a period of some six years beginning in 1991 with the Terms of Employment Directive (Chapter 15). During this period we see a shift away from the use of the general law-making provisions as the legal basis for directives, as the Community begins to gain more specific law-making powers, beginning with the Single European Act, then the Agreement on Social Policy, and finally, following the Treaty of Amsterdam, Article 137 EC. This period also marks the beginning of the sharing of the legislative function with the social partners.

Three measures are based on Article 118a of the Single European Act 1987, now **1.28** incorporated into Article 137, which provided for the first time a legal basis for the adoption, by way of a qualified majority vote, of directives to encourage improvements, especially in the working environment, as regards the health and safety of workers. The Pregnant Workers Directive aims to protect the health and safety of workers during pregnancy, in the immediate aftermath of birth, and during breastfeeding (Chapter 17). The Young Workers Directive has, as its objective, the protection of young persons against economic exploitation and working conditions likely to harm their health, safety, and social development or to prejudice their education, if still in full-time schooling (Chapter 18). The Working Time Directive lays down detailed rules in relation to almost every aspect of working time (Chapter 22). Its validity was challenged by the United Kingdom, which argued that the Directive should have been based on either Article 94 or 308—both of which required a unanimous vote—rather than Article 118a as the Directive was not concerned with health and safety. This challenge was unsuccessful. The Court held that Article 118a should be interpreted broadly as embracing all aspects of health and safety in the working environment with 'health' being defined as referring to 'a state of complete physical, mental and social well-being'.

Two further measures were based on the Agreement on Social Policy and hence **1.29** therefore initially not applicable to the United Kingdom. Following a change of government in the United Kingdom, the Directives were extended to it in 1997. A third measure on fixed-term employment was adopted on the basis of Article 137(1) EC.

These three measures were the product of agreements between the social part- **1.30** ners, becoming part of the Community legal order by means of Council Directives. The Parental Leave Directive lays down minimum requirement for parental leave for the purpose of bringing up children and time off work for parents on the grounds of *force majeure*. Employees are given the right to a period of time, to be defined by the Member States, but which must be at least three months, to look after a child until a given age (again to be laid down by the

Member States) of up to eight years. Employment rights are maintained during leave and workers have the right to return to their jobs or similar jobs (Chapter 16). The Part-time Work Directive has four objectives: to remove discrimination against part-time workers; to improve the quality of part-time work; to facilitate the development of part-time work on a voluntary basis; and to contribute to the flexible organization of working time in a manner which takes account of the needs of employers and workers (Chapter 19). The Fixed-Term Employment Directive, adopted in 1999, has as its purpose the protection of workers on fixed-term contracts by (i) eliminating discrimination between those employed on fixed-term contracts and workers employed under contracts of indefinite duration doing comparable work and (ii) preventing the abusive use of continuous fixed-term contracts or employment relationships (Chapter 20).

1.31 Chapter 23 deals with posted workers, that is persons working outside their home Member State, in the context of a contract for the provision of services, on a temporary basis. This type of employment is, at present, the most common form of economic movement of persons within the Community. Posted workers do not enter the labour market of the Member State to which they are sent by their employer. In general, they remain subject to the employment laws of their home country. Posting on the scale on which it presently occurs is problematic. It may result in skills and labour shortages as workers leave their home state to perform service contracts elsewhere in the Community. Recipient Member States have the advantage of the availability of services at a competitive price but the disadvantages that such a challenge brings to the market position of the traditional home service provider. Posted workers may be paid less than the nationals of the host Member State whom they work alongside doing comparable tasks. This may affect the overall harmony of the workplace and lead to general unease in the host Member State where posted workers may be perceived as taking away employment from nationals. Issues surrounding posting began to arise in the early 1980s before the Court of Justice, which sought to balance respect for the right to provide cross-border services, by for example prohibiting the levying of social security contributions by the host Member State in respect of risks covered by the social security system to which the posted worker was affiliated in his home state, with the right of the posted worker to be protected. In 1996 the Posted Workers Directive was adopted to co-ordinate the laws of the Member State to lay down a core of mandatory rules on the minimum protection of posted workers. Workers are guaranteed the basic terms and conditions of employment prevailing in the Member States in which the work is to be performed. Problems, however, persist with increasing tension between Member States who are recipients of services and those which are service providers.

Parts VI, VII, and VIII are concerned with equality of treatment.   **1.32**

Part VI consists, of four chapters dealing with equality of treatment between men   **1.33**
and women with respect to pay, equal treatment in employment, social security,
and occupational pensions.

Parts VII and VIII discuss Article 13 EC and the legislation adopted to imple-   **1.34**
ment the objectives set out therein.

Two directives were adopted in 2000 to fulfil the objectives of Article 13.   **1.35**
The first, Directive 2000/43 implementing the principle of equal treatment
between person irrespective of racial or ethnic origin[1] (the 'Race Directive'), is
discussed in Chapter 28. The second, Directive 2000/78 establishing a general
framework for equal treatment in employment and occupation (the 'Framework
Employment Directive'),[2] is the subject of Chapter 29. Both Directives have
been the subject of a number of references for preliminary rulings to the ECJ
from national courts and tribunals in a number of Member States. The Court has
adopted a functional and broad approach to the Directives. Whilst refusing to
interpret key concepts in such as way as to extend the Directives beyond their
intended scope, it has looked to the risks or 'suspect classes' to define the persons
to whom the legislation applies. This approach reflects that of the Equality of
Treatment in Social Security Directive: what is protected is discriminatory treatment on specified grounds and thus protection may extend beyond the person
who actually has the characteristics which give rise to the discriminatory treatment to others who are disadvantaged by association with him or her.

Chapter 30 offers some conclusions and looks to current issues preoccupying   **1.36**
the Community and possible future developments.

---

[1] [2000] OJ L180/22.
[2] [2000] OJ L303/16.

2

SOURCES OF LAW AND POLICY

A. Introduction

2.01 Social and employment law derives from a number of sources, operating at different levels with the Community legal and political orders. The primary source of law and policy is the EC Treaty itself. In addition, and complementary, to the provisions of the Treaty, are the general principles of law of which, for the purposes of the present discussion, the most important are the principle of equality of treatment and the principle of proportionality. Subordinate to, and dependent upon, the Treaty and the general principles of law is secondary legislation. Finally there is soft law.

2.02 There are five types of legal instrument prescribed by Article 249 EC: regulations, directives, decisions, recommendations, and opinions. Regulations are of general application; they are binding in their entirety and are directly applicable in the sense that they enter into national legal systems without any need for implementing measures.[1] Directives are binding as to the result to be achieved by each Member State to which they are addressed; national authorities may choose the form and method by which they implement directives. Directives, in contrast to regulations are not directly applicable. They require transposition into national law. They can however have direct effect. This will be the case if their provisions are clear, unconditional, and leave no discretion as to their implementation to the Member States. Directive have horizontal direct effect only, in the sense that they create rights enforceable against the State or emanations of the State. In contrast to EC Treaty provisions and regulations they do not create rights as between private parties (vertical direct effect).[2] Decisions are binding on the persons or entities to whom they are addressed.

2.03   Further to these legally binding measures, there is a substantial body of soft law, non-binding measures which do not create justiciable rights but are not entirely without legal effect,[3] consisting, inter alia, of Resolutions, Recommendations,[4] Opinions, and two Charters: the Community Charter of Fundamental Social Rights for Workers[5] and the Charter of Fundamental Rights of the European Union.[6] Whilst the former is concerned exclusively with employment and social rights, the latter is much broader in scope. Charters are formal declarations but have no legal effect in themselves. There is a degree of overlap between the two Charters.

2.04   To these sources may be added international conventions which inform policy and law-making.

2.05   Although the case law of the ECJ is not strictly speaking a source of law since the jurisdiction of the Court is to ensure 'that in the interpretation and application of [the] Treaty the law is observed',[7] in the area of social and employment law it has proved to be a major, and at times the sole, source of many rights.

2.06   Each of these sources, and the role they have played in the development of social and employment rights, will be examined below.

---

[1] Case 230/78 *Eridania* [1978] ECR 2749 Judgment at para 25.

[2] Case 152/84 *Marshall* [1986] ECR 723 Judgment paras 15 and 16.

[3] '. . . rules of conduct which in principle have no legally binding force but nevertheless may have practical effects' Snyder in Dainith: *Implementing EC law in the United Kingdom* Chichester 1995 51–87 at 64.

[4] Recommendations may have interpretative value: Case 322/88 *Grimaldi* [1988] ECR 4407.

[5] [1989] OJ C248/1.

[6] [2000] OJ C364/1.

[7] Art 220 EC.

B. EC Treaty Provisions

Social and employment policy figures prominently in the statement of principles **2.07**
set out in Part I of the EC Treaty.

(1) Principles

Article 2 of the EC Treaty enumerates the social principles upon which it is based. **2.08**
These include:

(a) a high level of employment and social protection;
(b) equality between men and women;
(c) the raising of the standard of living and equality of life within the
Community;
(d) social cohesion and solidarity among the Member States.

Article 3 sets out how these principles are to be attained: **2.09**

(a) the promotion of the coordination between employment policies of the
Member States with a view to enhancing their effectiveness by developing a
coordinated strategy for employment;
(b) a policy in the social sphere comprising the European Social Fund;
(c) the strengthening of social and economic cohesion;
(d) a contribution to the attainment of a high level of health protection.

Article 3(2) further states that in all the above initiatives the Community shall **2.10**
aim to eliminate inequalities (it is not specified which type of inequalities are to
be eliminated) and to promote equality between men and women.

Effect is given to the principles set out in Articles 2 and 3, in Titles VIII and XI, **2.11**
which deal with employment policy and social policy respectively, and Articles
12 and 13 EC.

(2) Employment

Title VIII, entitled 'Employment', acknowledges the Community's role in the **2.12**
development of a skilled labour force responsive to economic change and in
fostering the alignment of the employment policies of the Member States with
the Community's economic objectives. The Title consists of six provisions
(Articles 125–130). These provisions institutionalize the work of the Community
in the employment field which began with the Essen European Council in
December 1994 and is described in Chapter 10.

The primary responsibility for employment policy rests with the Member States **2.13**
themselves. The role of the Community is to complement and coordinate the

efforts of the Member States in establishing employment policy so as to ensure that national employment policy reflects Community economic policy. The Employment Title is an example of 'soft law'. It creates no rights for legal or natural persons nor obligations for the Member States but is a tool for the promotion of Community objectives whilst respecting the principle of subsidiarity.[8]

(3) Social policy

2.14   Title XI is entitled 'Social Policy, Education, Vocational Training and Youth'. Chapter 1 sets out the Community's competence in the sphere of social policy.

2.15   Article 136 states that the Community and the Member States:

> . . . shall have as their objectives the promotion of employment, improved living and working conditions, so as to make possible their harmonization whilst the improvement is being maintained, proper social protection, dialogue between management and labour and the development of human resources with a view to lasting employment and the combating of exclusion.

2.16   These objectives are to be achieved by measures which take account of 'diverse national practices' and which maintain the competitiveness of the Community economy.

2.17   Inspiration for these objectives is stated to be drawn from the European Social Charter signed in Turin on 18 October 1961 and the 1989 Community Charter of the Fundamental Social Rights of Workers. Any measures implemented by the Community or the Member States must take account of the 'diverse forms of national practice' and 'the need to maintain the competitiveness of the Community economy'.

2.18   Article 140 enables the Commission, with a view to achieving the objectives of Article 136 and without prejudice to the other provisions of the Treaty, to encourage cooperation between the Member States and to facilitate the coordination of their actions in all social policy fields, particularly in matters relating to:

(a)   employment;
(b)   labour law and working conditions;
(c)   basic and advanced vocational training;
(d)   social security;
(e)   prevention of occupational accidents and diseases;
(f)   occupational hygiene;

---

[8]   See Kenner: 'The EC Employment Title and the "Third Way": Making Soft Law Work' (1999) 15/1 IJCLLIR 33–60; Biagi: 'The Impact of European Employment Strategy on the Role of Labour Law and Industrial Relations' (2000) 16/2 IJCLLIR 155–73 at 160–1.

(g) the right of association and collective bargaining between employers and
workers.

For these purposes, the Commission can act in close contact with the Member   **2.19**
States by making studies, delivering opinions, and arranging consultations.
In order to fulfil these tasks, the Commission can adopt decisions requiring
Member States to provide it with information.[9]

(4) Equal pay and equal opportunities

Article 141 provides for equal pay for men and women. Paragraphs 1 and 2 have   **2.20**
remained substantively unchanged since the original EEC Treaty:

1. Each Member State shall ensure that the principle of equal pay for male and
    female workers for equal work or work of equal value is applied.
2. For the purpose of this article 'pay' means the ordinary basic or minimum wage
    or salary and any other consideration, whether in cash or in kind, which the
    worker receives directly or indirectly in respect of his employment from his
    employer.

Equal pay without discrimination based on sex means: **2.21**

(a) that pay for the same work at piece rates shall be calculated on the basis of the
same unit of measurement;
(b) that pay for work at time rates shall be the same for the same job.

Article 141(4) acknowledges the right of Member States to maintain or adopt   **2.22**
positive discrimination measures:

> With a view to ensuring full equality in practice between men and women in work-
> ing life, the principle of equal treatment shall not prevent any Member States from
> maintaining or adopting measures providing for specific advantages in order to
> make it easier for the under-represented sex to pursue a vocational activity or to
> prevent or compensate for disadvantages in professional careers.

Article 142 provides that Member States shall endeavour to maintain the existing   **2.23**
equivalence between paid holiday schemes. Articles 143 and 145 impose various
reporting requirements on the Commission and give the European Parliament
power to request the Commission to draw up reports on particular problems.

Article 144 empowers the Council to assign to the Commission tasks in connec-   **2.24**
tion with the implementation of common measures, particularly as regards social
security for migrant workers.

---

[9] Joined Cases 281, 283, 285 and 287/85 *Germany and Others v Commission* [1987] ECR 3203.

(5) Equality of treatment

2.25 Article 12 prohibits any discrimination on the basis of nationality. It is expressed to apply 'without prejudice' to any special provisions contained in the Treaty.

2.26 Article 13 provides for the Council, acting unanimously on a proposal from the Commission, and after consulting the European Parliament, to take 'appropriate action' to combat discrimination based on sex, racial or ethnic origin, religion or belief, disability, age, or sexual orientation. This list of prohibited grounds for discrimination is exhaustive.

2.27 Article 13 is an empowering provision. It enables the Council to take appropriate action within the limits set down therein. It does not therefore have direct effect.[10] Moreover, the Council is entitled to act within the limits of the Treaty and 'within the limits of the powers conferred by the Community'.

2.28 In view of the potentially far-reaching consequences, economic and financial, which the prohibitions set out in Article 13 may have in horizontal relationships between citizens and in vertical relationships between public authorities and interested citizens, which inform national legislation in this area, caution has been urged in the interpretation and application of Article 13.[11]

C. Legislative Competence

2.29 Social and employment law measures derive their legal bases both in the specific legislative competence granted to the Community institutions in Articles 12, 13, and 137 EC, and the residual general law-making powers provided by Article 94 and 308 EC. Prior to the Single European Act, which amended the EC Treaty, to grant legislative competence in the field of health and safety, and the Agreement on Social Policy of the Maastricht Treaty, social and employment measures had to be based on the Community's general law-making powers, there being no other viable legal basis.[12] Since the latter required unanimity, measures based on them

---

[10] Case C-227/04 *Lindorfer* [2007] ECR I–6767 Opinion Advocate General Sharpston at para 65; Case C-411/05 *Palacios de la Villa* [2007] ECR I–8531 Opinion of Advocate General Mazak at para 36.

[11] Case C-13/05 *Navas* [2006] ECR I–9583 Opinion of Advocate General Geelhoed at para 50.

[12] Examples of measures which have been adopted on the basis of Article 94 include Directive 75/117 on the approximation of the laws of the Member States relating to the application of the principle of equal pay for men and women ([1975] OJ L48); Directive 77/129 on the approximation of the laws of the Member States relating to the safeguarding of employees' rights in the event of transfers of undertakings, businesses or parts of businesses ([1977] OJ L61). Directive 76/207 on the implementation of the principle of equal treatment for men and women as regards access to employment, vocational training, and promotion and working conditions ([1976] OJ L39) is based

were often long in the making and frequently somewhat skeletal, thus leading, in some cases, to many references for preliminary rulings to the ECJ.

(1) Specific law-making powers

Article 137

Article 137(1) provides that, with a view to achieving the objectives set out in **2.30** Article 136, the Community 'shall support and complement the activities of the Member States' in the following fields:

   (i) the improvement, in particular, of the working environment to protect workers' health and safety;
  (ii) working conditions;
 (iii) social security and social protection at work;
 (iv) the protection of workers where their employment contract is terminated;
  (v) the information and consultation of workers;
 (vi) the representation and collective defence of the interests of workers and employees including co-determination;
 (vii) conditions of employment for third country nationals legally resident in Community territory;
(viii) the integration of persons excluded from the labour market;
 (ix) equality of treatment between men and women with regard to labour market opportunities and treatment at work;
  (x) the combating of social exclusion;
 (xi) the modernization of social protection schemes.

Objectives (i) to (ix) are to be attained by means of directives but the power of the **2.31** Council to adopt such directives is subject to five principles:

(a) directives must be adopted in support of and to complement the activities of Member States (Article 137(1));
(b) directives 'must have regard to the conditions and technical rules obtaining in each of the Member States' (Article 137(2)(b));
(c) directives may not impose administrative, financial, and technical constraints in a way which would hold back the creation and development of small and medium-sized enterprises (Article 137(2)(b));
(d) directives must maintain the competitiveness of the Community economy (Article 136);

---

on Article 308 of the EC Treaty, as is Directive 79/7 on the principle of equal treatment for men and women in matters of social security ([1979] OJ L6).

(e)   directives must consist of 'minimum requirements for gradual implementation' (Article 137(2)).[13]

2.32   In the case of directives implementing objectives (i) to (ix) of Article 137, the Council is competent to act on the basis of a qualified majority vote in accordance with the procedure set out in Article 251 and after consulting the European Parliament and the Economic and Social Committee and the Committee of the Regions.

2.33   Unanimity is required for the adoption of measures concerning the following matters:

(a)   social security and the social protection of workers;

(b)   the protection of workers following termination of the employment contract;

(c)   the representation and collective defence of workers and employers including co-determination with the exception of matters relating to pay, the right to strike, and the right to impose lockouts;

(d)   conditions of employment for third country nationals legally resident in Community territory;

(e)   financial contributions for the promotion of employment and job creation, without prejudice to the provisions contained in the Social Fund.

2.34   Article 137 does not apply to issues relating to pay nor does it apply to a number of collective labour rights, the right to strike, the right of association, and the imposition of lockouts. Even if Community competence is excluded in these areas, with the result that Member States remain free to lay down conditions for the existence and exercise of these rights, they must ensure that their competence is exercised consistently with Community law, in particular the EC Treaty provisions. This principle, entrenched in Community law for some years, was articulated in the context of the right to engage in industrial action in furtherance of Community law rights in *Viking*[14] and *Laval*.[15]

Viking *and* Laval

2.35   Viking and Laval raised the issue of the extent to which collective industrial action could be used or could be restrained in order to enforce or ensure respect

---

[13] This is not to be interpreted as limiting Community competence to the lowest level of protection within the Member States. Article 137(2) means that standards set by directives are to be regarded as a floor rather than as a ceiling, leaving Member States free to provide a level of protection more stringent than that resulting from Community law: Case C-84/94 *United Kingdom v Council* [1996] ECR I–5755 at para 17; Case C-2/97 *IP v Borsana* [1998] ECR I–8597 at para 35.

[14] Case C-438/05 Judgment of 11 December 2007.

[15] Case C-341/05 Judgment of 18 December 2007.

for Community law rights. The right of establishment under Article 43 EC was in issue in *Viking*; *Laval* was concerned with the freedom to provide cross-border services pursuant to Article 49 EC.

Viking, a company incorporated under Finnish law, is a large ferry operator. One **2.36** of its vessels, the Rosella, plies the route between Talinn in Estonia and Helsinki in Finland. FSU is a Finnish union of seamen. The crew of the Rosella are members of the FSU. The FSU is affiliated to the International Transport Workers' Federation (ITF), which is an international federation of transport workers' unions. It groups together 600 unions in 140 different states. According to ITF policy, only unions established in the state of beneficial ownership of a vessel have the right to conclude collective agreements covering that vessel. This policy is enforced by boycotts and other forms of collective action.

Since the Rosella was registered under the Finnish flag, Viking was obliged under **2.37** Finnish law and the terms of a collective bargaining agreement to pay the crew wages at the same level as those applicable in Finland. Estonian crew wages are lower than Finnish crew wages. The Rosella was running at a loss as a result of direct competition from Estonian vessels operating the same route with lower wage costs. Viking sought to re-flag it in Estonia or Norway in October 2003 in order to be able to enter into a new collective agreement with a trade union established in one of those states. The ITF sent a circular (the ITF circular) to its affiliates asking them to refrain from entering into negotiations with Viking. On 1 May 2004 Estonia became a member of the European Union. Since the Rosella continued to run at a loss Viking pursued its intention to reflag the vessel to Estonia. Since the ITF circular remained in force, Viking brought proceedings to obtain its withdrawal. On a reference for a preliminary ruling from the Court of Appeal, England and Wales, the ECJ was asked whether Article 43 must be interpreted as meaning that collective action initiated by a trade union or a group of trade unions against an undertaking in order to induce that undertaking to enter into a collective agreement, the terms of which are liable to deter it from exercising freedom of establishment, falls outside the scope of that Article. Further questions asked essentially whether collective action such as that in issue in the main proceedings constitutes a restriction within the meaning of Article 43 EC and if so to what extent such a restriction may be justified.

Laval arose out of a dispute a Latvian company, which sent some 35 workers **2.38** from Latvia to work on building sites operated by its wholly owned subsidiary which were constructing a school in Vaxholm, a town north of Stockholm. The facts and proceedings are set out in detail in paras 23.93–23.103. Essentially the issue there was whether a trade union could engage in collective action to force the negotiation and agreement of a collective agreement on the pay and working conditions of the Latvian workers who had been posted to Sweden.

2.39 In both cases the Court rejected the argument of the Swedish and Danish governments to the effect that the right to take collective action in the context of negotiations with an employer falls outside the scope of Articles 43 and 49 EC since, pursuant to Article 137(5) EC, the Community has no power to regulate that right. The Court held that even though in areas in which the Community does not have competence to act, the Member States remain, in principle, free to lay down conditions for the existence and exercise of the rights in issue, they must nevertheless exercise that competence consistently with Community law:[16]

> . . . the fact that Article 137 EC does not apply to the right to strike or the right to impose lockouts is not such as to exclude collective action . . . from the domain of freedom to provide services.[17]

2.40 In *Viking* the Court made a similar ruling with respect to the right of establishment: the right to strike was not excluded from the sphere of the right of establishment:

> Consequently the fact that Article 137 does not apply to the right to strike or to the right to impose lock-outs is not such as to exclude collective action such as that in issue in the main proceedings from the application of Article 43 EC.[18]

2.41 Thus in so far as collective action, even if taken in accordance with national law and practice, prejudices the exercise of Community law rights, such as the right to provide or receive services or the right of establishment, it is unlawful.

2.42 The Court also rejected the further argument that the right to strike was a fundamental right and as such falls outside the scope of Articles 43 and 49 EC. It held that although the right to take collective action must be recognized as a fundamental right which forms an integral part of the general principles of Community law, it may be subject to some restrictions. As re-affirmed by Article 28 of the Charter of the Fundamental Rights of the European Union, it is to be protected in accordance with Community law and national law and practices. The fundamental nature of the right to take collective action is not such as to render Community law inapplicable to such action.

2.43 Thus in *Viking* the Court found that collective action, such as that in issue in the main proceedings, has the effect of making it less attractive or even pointless for Viking to exercise its right of establishment inasmuch as such action prevents

---

[16] Case C-120/95 *Decker* [1998] ECR I–1831 Judgment paras 22 and 23; Case C-446/03 *Marks and Spencer* [2005] ECR I–10837 Judgment para 29.

[17] *Laval* (see note 15) Judgment para 88.

[18] *Viking* (see note 14) Judgment para 42.

Viking from enjoying the same treatment in the host Member State as other economic operators established in that state.

In *Laval* where the issue was the extent to which the right to engage in collective **2.44** industrial action—in that case the blockading of a building site and associated secondary action—could be restricted by Article 49 EC the Court reasoned as follows: it began by stating that Article 49 EC applied to rules which were not public in nature but which were designed to regulate collectively the provision of services. It was thus applicable to trade unions. The right of trade unions of a Member State to take collective action to force the signing of a collective agreement by an undertaking established in another Member State constitutes a restriction on the freedom to provide services within the meaning of Article 49 EC, in that it makes it less attractive or more difficult for undertakings to provide services in the host Member State.

However, both the right to provide services under Article 49 EC and the right of **2.45** establishment in Article 43 EC may be subject to restrictions. In addition to the limitations on that right specified in that provision itself, restrictions on the freedom to provide services and the right of establishment may be justified by overriding reason of public interest but, if that is the case, any restrictions must be suitable for securing the attainment of the objective which it pursues and not go beyond what is necessary in order to attain it. The right to take collective action for the protection of workers of the host state against possible social dumping may constitute an overriding reason of public interest justifying a restriction on one of the fundamental freedoms of the Treaty. The protection of workers is an objective of public interest and so:

> . . . in principle, blockading action by a trade union of the host Member State which is aimed at ensuring that workers posted in the framework of a transnational provision of services have their terms and conditions of employment fixed at a certain level, falls within the objective of protecting workers.[19]

But although, in principle, the action taken by the trade union in the *Laval* case **2.46** could be a permissible restriction on the provision of services under Article 49, the Court ultimately found that it was not justifiable in that case given that the negotiations on pay which the trade union required the service provider to enter into were 'characterised by a lack of provisions, of any kind, which are sufficiently precise and accessible that they do not render it impossible or excessively difficult in practice for such an undertaking to determine the obligations with which it is required to comply as regards minimum pay'.[20] The implication here is that had the rates of pay which the service provider was being asked to give his posted

---

[19] Judgment para 107.
[20] Judgment para 110.

workers been ascertainable, the industrial action might have been justifiable even if it did restrict the provision of services. It was the open-ended nature of the objective of the industrial action which made it unjustifiable.

2.47   Likewise in *Viking* the Court held that:

> . . . as regards the collective action taken by the FSU, even if that action—aimed at protecting the jobs and conditions of employment of the members of that union liable to be adversely affected by the reflagging of the Rosella—could reasonably be considered to fall, at first sight, within the objective of protecting workers, such a view would no longer be tenable if it were established that the jobs or conditions of employment at issue were not jeopardised or under serious threat.[21]

2.48   Even if the jobs or conditions of employment of the FSU's members were liable to be adversely affected by the reflagging of the Rosella, it would have to be determined whether the collective action initiated by the FSU was suitable for ensuring the avoidance of such prejudicial consequences or whether the FSU had some other means at its disposal which were less restrictive of freedom of establishment and, if so, whether it had exhausted those means before initiating collective action.

2.49   In *Impact*[22] the ECJ maintained the line of reasoning it had developed in *Viking* and *Laval* and held that the reference to 'pay' in Article 137(5) must be interpreted as covering measures which amount to direct interference by Community law in the determination of pay within the Community:

> It cannot . . . be extended to any question involving any sort of link with pay; otherwise some of the areas referred to in Article 137(1) would be deprived of much of their substance . . .

> It follows that the derogation in Article 137(5) EC does not preclude the interpretation of Clause 4 of the framework agreement [on fixed-term work] as imposing on Member States the obligation to ensure that fixed-term workers are also guaranteed the application of the principle of non-discrimination in relation to pay . . . [23]

Article 141(3)

2.50   Article 141(3) gave the Community, for the first time, legislative competence in the sphere of equal treatment for men and women in pay and employment:

> The Council . . . shall adopt measures to ensure the application of the principle of equal opportunities and equal treatment of men and women in matters of employment and occupation, including the principles of equal pay for equal work or work of equal value.

---

[21] See note 14; Judgment para 81.
[22] Case C-268/06 Judgment 15 April 2008.
[23] Ibid Judgment paras 125–126.

Two points are worthy of note here: (a) the Council is empowered for the first **2.51** time to adopt legislation not only to ensure equal pay but also the equal treatment of men and women; (b) such equal treatment is to pertain to all matters of employment and occupation. The Treaty is silent on the meaning of 'occupation' but it can be assumed from the wording of Article 141(3) that it means all types of economic activity (ie, activity carried out for remuneration) other than employment.

Articles 12 and 13

Article 12 prohibits discrimination on grounds of nationality. It gives the **2.52** Council competence to adopt measures designed to prohibit such discrimination. Article 12 is subject to two limitations: (a) it applies without prejudice to any special provisions contained in the Treaty; and (b) it applies within the scope of application of the Treaty.

Article 13 empowers the Council to take 'appropriate action' to combat discrimi- **2.53** nation based on sex, racial or ethnic origin, religion or belief, disability, age, or sexual orientation. As with Article 12, the Council's powers to achieve these objectives are fettered in two respects: they must be exercised without prejudice to the other provisions of the Treaty and within the limits of the powers conferred on the Council by the Community. The first limitation simply indicates that Article 13, like Article 12, is a residual provision and must give way to other provisions of the Treaty dealing with discrimination. Thus, for example, in the case of a measure designed to combat discrimination between men and women in the field of pay or to achieve equal opportunities for men and women in employment, the most appropriate legal basis might be Article 141, considered below. Secondly, Article 13 is only applicable to the extent to which the Council has competence to act in the particular area in which it is sought to adopt anti-discriminatory measures.

Article 13 can be said to be reactive rather than proactive, in the sense that the **2.54** Council may act to combat discrimination, but no positive right to equality of treatment is granted in the same way as, for example, is the case with Article 12. Nor does it seem possible, as is the case with Article 12, for an individual to rely on Article 13 as a source of rights, as no obligations are imposed on either the Member States or the Community institutions. Article 13 is simply an empowering provision, enabling the Council to take action to combat discrimination. It cannot as such have direct effect nor can it preclude the application of a national measure which, for example, discriminates on the ground of age.[24]

---

[24] Joined Cases T- 219/02 and T-337/02 *Herrera* [2004] ECR II–1407 Judgment para 89; Case C-227/04 *Lindorfer* note 10 Advocate General Sharpston at para 65; Case C-411/05 *Palacios de la Villa* note 10 Advocate General Mazak at 36.

(2) General law-making powers

2.55 In addition to the legislative powers given to the Community in Article 137, the enactment of social policy measures is possible under the general law-making provisions of the EC Treaty contained in Articles 94 and 308.

2.56 Article 94 provides for the adoption of directives for the approximation of the laws, regulations, and administrative provisions of the Member States which directly affect the establishment or functioning of the common market.

2.57 Article 308 provides that if action by the Community should prove necessary to attain one of the objectives of the Community, and the Treaty has not provided the necessary powers, the Council shall, acting unanimously on a proposal from the Commission, and after consulting the European Parliament, take appropriate measures. Article 94 empowers the Council to issue directives for the approximation of national measures which directly affect the establishment or functioning of the common market.

2.58 These two provisions require the presence of two essential factors before they can be used as a legal basis for a Community instrument: first, the existence of a Community objective and, secondly, the necessity to enact measures on a Community level to fulfil that objective. Measures based on Article 94 or 308 require, for their adoption, a unanimous vote in the Council.

2.59 Article 95 is another possible, but much more limited, legal basis for social law measures. It provides that in order to establish the internal market the Council may adopt measures for the approximation of national laws which have as their objective the establishment and functioning of the common market. However, Article 95 does not extend to fiscal measures, to measures relating to the free movement of persons, nor to those pertaining to the rights and interests of employed persons.

D. The Community Charter of the Fundamental Social Rights of Workers[25]

2.60 The Community Charter of the Fundamental Social Rights of Workers was adopted by 11 Member States on 9 December 1989. The twelfth Member State, the United Kingdom, did not feel it was appropriate for it to be a party to the Charter since it was of the firm opinion that many of the matters addressed

---

[25] See paras 3.43–3.49.

therein were not within Community competence and were, therefore, a matter for regulation on national level by the Member States. The Charter is a declaration of rights of Community citizens. Although its title refers to 'workers', some of its provisions extend to groups, such as the elderly and the disabled, which may not be in employment.

Title 1 of the Charter sets out 12 fundamental rights relating to the free move- **2.61** ment of workers, employment and remuneration, improvements in living and working conditions, social protection, freedom of association and collective bargaining, vocational training, equal treatment for men, and women, the right of workers to information, consultation, and participation in the running of the undertaking in which they are employed, health and safety in the workplace, the protection of children and adolescents, elderly persons, and the disabled.

E. The European Union Charter of Fundamental Rights

The Charter of Fundamental Rights, adopted in December 2000, is not at present **2.62** legally binding but it may become so in the near future. It is not envisaged that it will be included within the Treaty of Lisbon but there will be a cross-reference to it giving it 'legally binding value and setting out the scope of its application'.[26] The United Kingdom has secured an 'opt out' from the application of the Charter to its territory and it is understood at the time of writing that a number of other Member States may seek to opt out of at least some of the provisions of the Charter.

Until it becomes part of the Community legal order the Charter has no formal **2.63** legal standing but it is 'apt to influence the interpretation placed on instruments of EU and national law'.[27] The provisions of the Charter reinforce some existing social and employment rights and in some cases grant new ones.[28]

The Charter sets out a wide range of social and employment law rights. Article 20 **2.64** provides that everyone is entitled to equal treatment before the law. Article 21 prohibits any discrimination based on many grounds such as sex, race, colour, ethnic or social origin, genetic features, language, religion or belief, political or other opinion, membership of a national minority, property, birth, disability, age, or sexual orientation. Article 23 provides for equality between men and women

---

[26] Brussels European Council 21/22 June 2007 Presidency Conclusions para 9.
[27] Ellis: *Anti-Discrimination Law* Oxford University Press 2005 at 328.
[28] See Hervey and Kenner (eds): *Economic and Social Rights under the EU Charter of Fundamental Rights* Hart Publishing 2003; Peers and Ward (eds): *The European Union Charter of Fundamental Rights* Hart Publishing 2004.

in all areas including employment work and pay. It adds that the '. . . principle of equality shall not prevent the maintenance or adoption of measures providing for specific advantages in favour of the under-represented sex'. Article 25 recognizes the right of the elderly to lead a life of dignity and independence. Article 26 states that the union recognizes and respects the right of persons with disabilities to benefit from measures designed to ensure their independence, social and occupational integration, and participation in the life of the Community. Everyone has the right to protection from dismissal for reasons connected with maternity, the right to paid maternity leave, and to parental leave following the birth or adoption of a child (Article 33(2)). Article 32 prohibits child labour and provides for the protection of young people at work. Article 30 provides for the protection against unjustified dismissal. Article 28 guarantees the right of collective bargaining and the right of workers to take collective action to defend their interests including the right to strike. Article 31 gives the right to working time rights. Workers' rights to information and consultation are guaranteed in Article 27. Article 34 acknowledges the right to social security benefits and social services.

2.65 The Charter applies only within the scope of Union law to the Community institutions and the Member States when they are implementing Community law.[29] To the extent that those are based on the Community Treaties they must be exercised and defined within the limits of those Treaties. The rights guaranteed by the Charter may be limited if the objectives and the general interest of the Union so require, or in case of the need to protect the rights and freedoms of others.

2.66 Any limitations on Charter rights are subject to the principle of proportionality.

2.67 The Charter may not be interpreted as restricting or adversely affecting human rights and fundamental freedoms set out in international law, agreements to which the Union, the Community, or all the Member States are a party, notably the European Convention of Human Rights.

F. General Principles of Law[30]

2.68 The general principles of law form part of the constitution of the Community. They bear a status equivalent to EC Treaty provisions but are not superior

---

[29] Art 51.

[30] Arnull: *The General Principles of EEC Law and the Individual* St Martin's Press New York 1990; Bernitz and Nergelius (eds): *General Principles of European Community Law* Kluwer 2000; Schermers and Waelbroeck: *Judicial Protection in the European Union* Sixth Edition Kluwer 2001 28–97; Tridimas: *The General Principles of EC Law* Second Edition Oxford University Press 2006; Usher: *General Principles of EC Law* Longmans 1998.

to them.[31] They perform a threefold function: they are a ground of review, an aid to interpretation, and a superior rule of law, breach of which may lead to the extra-contractual liability of the Community.[32] They are mainly used as a means of controlling the use by the Community institutions of the many powers granted to them and also the actions of the Member States in implementing Community measures[33] or exercising their rights of derogation.[34] In essence the general principles of law are a standard of review within the limits of which both the Community institutions and the Member States must act.

The general principles have been formulated by the Court of Justice pursuant to **2.69** its obligation under Article 220 EC to ensure observance of the law in the interpretation and application of the Treaty. They add flesh to the bones of Community law, which being expressed in a framework treaty, would, in their absence, have remained a mere skeleton of rules falling short of a proper legal order.[35]

The use of the general principles of law to control the legality of Community **2.70** actions can be traced back to a judgment of the ECJ in the mid-1950s in a staff case, *Algera*.[36] The ECJ believed it had to solve the dispute between the High Commission of the European Coal and Steel Community (ESCS) and one of its employees but found no means whereby to do so in the ESCS Treaty. It therefore looked to the legal systems of the six Member States of the ECSC for guidance:

> The possibility of withdrawing such measures is a problem of administrative law, which is familiar in the case law and learned writing of all countries of the Community, but for the solution of which the Treaty does not contain any rules. Unless the Court is to deny justice it is therefore obliged to solve the problem by reference to the rules acknowledged by the legislation, the learned writing and the case law of the Member States.[37]

It is clear from *Algera* that the general principles derive from the laws of the **2.71** Member States. This does not however mean that they must be defined in the provisions of each national legal system nor indeed that they should be specifically articulated at all. The concept of 'general principles of law' is indicative of

---

[31] Case 40/64 *Sgarlata v Commission* [1965] ECR 215.
[32] Tridimas: 'The Application of the Principle of Equality to Community Measures' in Dashwood and O'Leary (eds): *The Principle of Equal Treatment in EC Law* Sweet & Maxwell 1997 214–42 at 219.
[33] Member States are constrained by the general principles when they implement Community Measures. Case 5/88 *Wachauf v Germany* [1989] ECR 2609; Case C-84/95 *Bosphoros* [1996] ECR I–3953; Case C-292/97 *Karlsson* [2000] ECR I–2737.
[34] Case C-260/89 *Ellinki Radiophonia Teleoranni* [1991] ECR I–2925.
[35] Case C-411/05 *Palacios de la Villa* note 10 Opinion of Advocate General Mazak at para 85.
[36] Joined Cases 7/56 and 3–7/57 [1957–58] ECR 39.
[37] *Algera* Judgment p 55.

the ideas and principles underlying the legal systems of the Member States,[38] principles which are generally found in the legal systems of democratic nations.

2.72 They may not all be present in any given system nor may they be referred to in specific terms: differences in terminology and effect may prevail.[39] They have been described as 'commuters'. They travel from national legal systems to the Community legal systems as principles common to the legal systems of the Member States. They subsequently may travel back to those systems as principles whereby to govern the implementation and application of EC law on a national level.[40] Article 6(2) of the Treaty on European Union pledges the Union to respect the constitutional traditions of the Member States as 'general principles of Community law'.

2.73 Amongst the general principles in the area under discussion the most important are the principle of equality and the principle of proportionality.

(1) The principle of equality of treatment

2.74 The principle of equality of treatment finds specific expression in a number of Treaty provisions, notably Articles 12, 13, and 141[41] and in secondary legislation.

2.75 Whilst those provisions identify the specific criteria on which differentiation of treatment may be based (and the grounds on which such differential treatment may be justified) and may, potentially, be a source of substantive rights for the individuals concerned in the circumstances set out therein, the general principle of equality of treatment governs the exercise of Community competence and the means by which Member States transpose Community measures into their

---

[38] Herdegen: 'The Origins and Development of General Principles of Community Law' in Bernitz and Nergelius (eds) (see note 30 above) at 17. 'A perusal of the case law of the European Court of Justice reveals comparatively few clear statements of the methodological approach in developing and applying general principles of law . . . fairly little guidance as to the proper method of "discovering" general principles may be gleaned. This nurtures the suspicion that we are confronted with a process of judicial law-making guided mostly by common sense rather than a hermeneutical process informed by a generally accepted methodology.' See also Ellis (see note 27 above) at 317.

[39] 'The fact is indeed the general principles of law, however new they may sometimes appear in their implementation, are also the very incarnation of legal traditions, as the values they represent find often their origin in the written or unwritten laws of bygone ages . . . we can say that they constitute the accumulated wisdom of generations of lawyers.' Koopmans: 'General principles of law in European and National systems of law: a comparative view' in Bernitz and Nergelius (eds) note 31 at 251. It is not unknown for the ECJ to look at the legal systems of the Member States to decide whether a given principle is common to them, see for example Case 155/79 *AM & S* [1982] ECR 1575.

[40] Herdegen (see note 38).

[41] Also Articles 34(2) 39; 42.

national legal systems.[42] It precludes comparable situations from being treated differently unless the difference in treatment is objectively justified.[43] Specific expressions of the principle of equality identify the criteria on which differentiation of treatment may not be based. By contrast, the general principle of equality leaves open the question of which grounds for differentiation are acceptable. It thus potentially implies a prohibition of discrimination on any ground that may be deemed unacceptable but a prohibition on any specific ground may be inferred from it. Such a prohibition has to be defined by the Community legislature and the Member States.

(2) The principle of proportionality

The principle of proportionality[44] requires that a measure must be appropriate **2.76** and necessary to achieve its objectives. Determining whether a provision of Community law or national law, which purports to implement Community law, is compatible with the principle of proportionality is a four-step process. It must first be established that the measure in issue is suitable to achieve a legitimate aim, secondly that it is necessary to achieve that aim, thirdly that there are no less restrictive means capable of producing the same result, and fourthly even if there are no less restrictive means available to achieve the desired objective, it must be established that the measure does not have an excessive effect on a person or person's interests.[45]

The principle of proportionality first articulated, and subsequently developed by **2.77** the ECJ, has now at least in respect of its application to the Community institutions, been enshrined in Article 5(3) EC, which states:

> Any action by the Community shall not go beyond what is necessary to achieve the objectives of the Treaty.

In social and employment law, the primary role of the principle of proportional- **2.78** ity is to safeguard against deprivation of Community law rights: restrictions, exceptions, and derogations must be kept to the minimum required to achieve a given legitimate objective. Examples of the application of the principle of proportionality can be found both in the case law of the ECJ and in the wording of secondary legislation itself which, in some cases, expressly requires conformity

---

[42] de Burca: 'The Role of Equality in European Community Law' in Dashwood and O'Leary *The Principle of Equal Treatment in EC Law* Sweet & Maxwell 1997 at 13–34.
[43] Joined Cases 117/78 and 16/79 *Ruckdeschel* [1977] ECR 1753 Judgment para 7.
[44] Emiliou: *The Principle of Proportionality in European Law* Kluwer 1996; de Burca: 'The Principle of Proportionality and its Application in EC Law' (1993) 13 YEL 105–150.
[45] Ibid at 113.

with the principle of proportionality. For example, the Race Directive[46] and the Framework Employment Directive[47] permit derogations to be made by the Member States to the principle of equal treatment subject to the principle of proportionality. The Race Directive provides:

> Notwithstanding Articles 2(1) and (2) Member States may provide that a difference in treatment which is based on a characteristic related to racial or ethnic origin shall not constitute discrimination where, by reason of the nature of the particular occupational activities concerned or the context in which they are carried out, such characteristics constitute a genuine and determining occupational requirement, provided that the objective is legitimate and the requirement proportionate.[48]

2.79 The Framework Employment Directive[49] provides in Article 6(1) that differences in treatment on grounds of age may not constitute discrimination if they are objectively and reasonably justified by a legitimate aim, which may include employment policy, the labour market, and vocational training objectives, and if the means of attaining that aim are appropriate and necessary. Article 5 of the same Directive provides that an employer shall take appropriate measures to enable a person with a disability to have access to or participate in, or to advance in employment or to undergo training unless such measures would place a disproportionate burden on that employer. This achieves a balance between the right of the disabled employee to be facilitated in the workplace, but, at the same time, places a limit on the extent of the obligations of the employer to make the necessary adjustments to the work environment.

2.80 The ECJ has upheld the full effect of Community law rights with the result that limitations, exceptions, and derogations from them must be interpreted strictly. *Johnston v RUC*[50] held:

> . . . in determining the scope of any derogation from an individual right such as the equal treatment of men and women provided for by the directive, the principle of proportionality, one of the general principles of law underlying the Community legal order must be observed. That principle requires that derogations remain within the limits of what is appropriate and necessary for achieving the aim in view and requires the principle of equal treatment to be reconciled as far as possible with the requirements of public safety which constitute the decisive factor as regards the context of the activity in question.[51]

---

[46] Directive 2000/43 [2000] OJ L180/22.
[47] Directive 2000/78 [2000] OJ L303/16. See Chapter 29.
[48] Art 4.
[49] Note 47. See Chapter 29.
[50] Case 222/84 [1986] ECR 1651.
[51] Ibid Judgment para 38.

Thus the decision of the Chief Constable of the Royal Ulster Constabulary that **2.81** men should carry firearms in the regular course of their duties in Northern Ireland, but that women would not be equipped with them, and would not receive training in the handling and use of firearms, could not justify a contract being denied to Mrs Johnston. The principle of proportionality required that it should be determined whether the necessity to refuse to grant such a contract in the interests of safety could be avoided by allocating to women duties which could be performed without firearms.

Indirect discrimination between men and women in the matter of pay can be **2.82** objectively justified only if the pay difference between men and women is necessary to attain a particular objective and provided that the alleged discriminatory measures are not more than is necessary to achieve that objective.[52]

In *Commission v United Kingdom*[53] the Court rejected the argument of the United **2.83** Kingdom to the effect that a number of the provisions of the Working Time Directive[54] were disproportionate as the level of health and safety of workers— which was their purported objective—could be achieved by less restrictive measures, such as by means of the risk assessment provided for in Directive 89/391,[55] which enables employers to carry out assessments to evaluate specific risks to the health and safety of workers, taking into account the nature of the activities of the undertaking:

> ... it is sufficient to note that Directive 89/391, as stated in Article 1 thereof, merely lays down, in order to encourage improvements in the health and safety of workers at work, general principles, as well as general guidelines for their implementation, concerning the prevention of occupational risks, the protection of health and safety, the elimination of risk and accident factors, and the provision of information to, consultation, participation and training of workers and their representatives. It is not therefore apt to achieve the objective of harmonizing minimum rest periods, rest breaks and a maximum limit to weekly working time, which form the subject-matter of the contested directive.

G. Soft Law [56]

Additionally and importantly, in the area of social and employment law, given the **2.84** paucity of legislative power, extensive use has been made of non-binding acts

---

[52] Case 170/84 *Bilka* [1986] ECR 1607.
[53] Case C-84/94 [1996] ECR I–5755.
[54] Directive 93/04 [1993] OJ L307/18.
[55] [1989] OJ L183/1.
[56] Senden: *Soft Law in European Community Law* Hart Publishing 2004.

such as resolutions, action programmes, and charters. Such instruments are generally of a programmatic nature, setting out objectives to be achieved. Given the political sensitivity arising from the tension between the Member States as to the extent to which they alone should remain responsible for such social and employment law and policy, soft law has often been the only means to mark a commitment, on a Community level, to social and employment objectives.

2.85 The Court has bolstered the status of a number of soft law instruments by decreeing them to be of interpretative value, thereby allocating to them a role within the Community legal order. Although not in themselves a source of justiciable rights, they influence the content and extent of those rights.[57]

2.86 Soft law serves a number of purposes. It can enunciate commonly held values which the Member States wish to be respected on a Community level; this is the case with the Community Charter of Fundamental Rights for Workers and the Charter of Fundamental Rights of the European Union. It can set guidelines and targets for Member States to achieve within their own legal and political systems, for example through the Open Method of Co-ordination. History has proved that soft law is not without effect; it can and does influence law and policy at Member State level. At Community level, it is often the predecessor to hard law measures. Many legislative instruments have their origins in soft law measures; some have even achieved the ultimate accolade and unimpeachable status which comes with enshrinement within the Treaty itself.

2.87 Soft law is said to fall into three categories, all of which are prominent in the areas under discussion:

  (i) preparatory and informative instruments;
  (ii) interpretative and decisional instruments; and
  (iii) formal and non-formal steering instruments.[58]

2.88 Preparatory instruments include Green Papers, White Papers, and Action Programmes. See paras 4.05–4.12.

Communications

2.89 Communications abound in the social and employment areas: their purpose is usually to indicate how legislation has been implemented or to voice thinking on any given issue, but they have also been used to evaluate and clarify the impact of ECJ case law.

---

[57] For example Case C-540/03 *Parliament v Council* [2006] ECR I–5769.
[58] Senden (see note 56) at 123.

H. International Conventions

International conventions inspire and inform social and employment rights on **2.90** many levels: the EC Treaty, legislation, the Charter for the Fundamental Social Rights of Workers and the case law of the ECJ.[59] The Conventions most commonly referred to as a source of social and employment rights are the European Social Charter and numerous Conventions of the International Labour Organization.

The Preamble to the Single European Act referred to respect for the **2.91**

> ... fundamental rights recognized in the constitutions and laws of the Member States, the Convention for the Protection of Human Rights and Fundamental Freedoms and the European Social Charter.

The Charter on the Fundamental Social Rights of Workers was modelled on the **2.92** European Social Charter. Its Preamble proclaims:

> Inspiration should be drawn from the Conventions of the International Labour Organization and from the European Social Charter of the Council of Europe.

Article 136 EC in laying down the objectives of social policy refers to '... the **2.93** fundamental social rights such as those set out in the European Social Charter signed in Turin on 16 October 1961 and the 1989 Community Charter of the Fundamental Social Rights of Workers'.

On the legislative front, Directive 94/33 on the protection of young people at **2.94** work,[60] and Directive 2003/38 on the organization of working time[61] both state in their preambles that account should be taken of the principles of the ILO regarding the protection of young people at work and the organization of working time.

Directive 99/63 on the working time of seafarers[62] reflects the provisions of ILO **2.95** Convention No 180 (1996) on Seafarers' Hours of Work and Directive 97/81 implementing the Framework Agreement on Part-time Work was influenced by

---

[59] O'Higgins: 'The interaction of the ILO, the Council of Europe and the European Union labour standards' in Hepple (ed) *Social and Labour Rights in a Global Context* Cambridge University Press 2002, 55–69; de Witte: 'The Trajectory of Fundamental Social Rights in the European Union' in de Burca and de Witte: *Social Rights in Europe* Oxford University Press 2005 Chapter 8; De Schutter: 'Anchoring the European Union to the European Social Charter' in de Burca and de Witte: ibid Chapter 7.

[60] [1994] OJ L216/12.

[61] [2003] OJ L299/9.

[62] [1999] OJ L167/35.

ILO Convention No 175 (1988) on Part-time Work.[63] The Council adopted a Resolution in December 1996[64] confirming its commitment to the United Nations Standard Rules on the Equality of Opportunity of Persons with Disabilities.[65] Both the Race Directive[66] and the Framework Equality Directive[67] refer in their respective preambles to a number of international conventions.

2.96 The European Court of Justice regularly uses international conventions as an interpretative tool in interpreting and applying Community law.[68] In *Defrenne v Sabena*[69] the Court referred to Article 2 of ILO Convention No 100 (1951) on equal pay in concluding that Article 119 should interpreted in the light of that provision to include the principle of equal pay for work of equal value. In *Commission v United Kingdom*[70] the Court interpreted the concepts of 'health' and 'safety' in Article 118a EC in the light of the meaning given to those concepts in the preamble to the Constitution of the World Health Organization whose members comprise all the Member States.

2.97 *Levy*[71] raised the issue of whether a national court is bound to refuse to apply a provision of national law which is intended to implement an agreement, such as an ILO Convention which was concluded by the Member State concerned with other Member States and third countries prior to the entry into force of the EEC Treaty. The Convention in issue was ILO Convention No 89 (1948) on night work for women in industry. The Court concluded that in such a situation the Member State in question is under an obligation to refrain from applying any conflicting provision of national legislation, unless the application of such a provision is necessary in order to ensure the performance by the Member State concerned of obligations arising under an agreement concluded with non-member countries prior the entry into force of the EEC Treaty. The Court looked to Article 307 EC which provides that the rights and obligations arising from treaties[72] concluded between one or more Member States on the one hand and one or more third countries on the other before 1 January 1958, or for acceding States, before their date of accession, are not affected by the provisions of

---

63 [1998] OJ L14/9.

64 [1997] OJ C12/1.

65 United Nations General Assembly Resolution 48/46 of 20 December 1993.

66 [2000] OJ L180/22.

67 [2000] OJ L303/16.

68 But it has no jurisdiction to interpret and apply those conventions themselves. Case C-361/07 Polier Order of the Court of 16 January 2008.

69 Case 43/75 [1976] ECR 455.

70 Case C-84/94 [1996] ECR I–5755.

71 Case C-158/91 [1993] ECR I–4287.

72 Art 307 applies to any international agreement regardless of its subject matter which is capable of affecting the application of the Treaty: Case 812/79 *Burgoa* [1980] ECR 2787.

the Treaty. Where such Treaties are not compatible with the Treaty, the Member States must take all appropriate steps to eliminate such incompatibilities. That obligation is not intended to affect the commitment of a Member State to respect the right of non-member countries with the result that the term 'rights' refers to the rights of third countries and 'obligations' to the obligations of Member States.[73] If the prohibition on night work for women as provided for in ILO Convention No 189 had been annulled by virtue of subsequent agreements binding the same parties, the national court could disapply any national provision implementing the Convention which was incompatible with Community law since the rights of third countries would not be prejudiced. But if this is not the case and third country rights are still extant, national provisions may be applied in so far as it is necessary to give effect to those rights. It is of interest to note that prior to the judgment in *Levy* on 2 August 1993 the French government had denounced ILO Convention No 189 with effect from 26 February 1993 but it maintained in force the national provisions giving effect to that Convention. In subsequent proceedings[74] the ECJ held that since the Convention had been denounced and the national provisions were incompatible with Community law, France was in breach of its Community obligations.

For the sake of completeness it should be mentioned that the EC Commission **2.98** has maintained a close working relationship with the ILO since 1958. The nature of this co-operation is periodically set out in an exchange of letters, the latest of which occurred in 2001.[75] Given the closeness of this co-operation, the influence of the ILO generally, and in particular, those Conventions to which the Member States are party, on the development and application of Community law, is inevitable. The EC Commission also has a framework for co-operation with the Organization for Economic Co-operation and Development. Meetings are held between the two organizations twice yearly.

Case law

Issues relating to employment and social law come before the Court mainly by **2.99** way of references for preliminary rulings from courts and tribunals throughout the Community, but there are a number of actions which have been brought by the EC Commission against the Member States for either failure to comply with their Treaty obligations or implement directives. The latter proceedings are brought directly before the Court by the Commission if, after issuing a reasoned opinion setting out the nature of the infringement, a Member State persists

---

[73] Case 10/61 *Commission v Italy* [1962] ECR 1.
[74] Case C-197/96 *Commission v France* [1997] ECR I–1489.
[75] [2001] OJ C165/23.

in failing to comply with its obligations.[76] In the case of preliminary rulings, proceedings are commenced in national courts by aggrieved individuals. Where the scope of their rights is unclear or where a national judge is uncertain as to the meaning of the particular provision of EC law upon which a litigant relies he, or the court, can (or indeed must in the case of a court of final instance) suspend proceedings and refer a question for interpretation to the ECJ.[77]

2.100 Once the ECJ has given judgment the case reverts back to the national court which then applies the law as interpreted to the particular facts of the case.

2.101 In the context of social and employment law the ECJ has adopted a broad and functional approach in exercising its interpretative role. It has looked at the objective of the rules in issue before it and has interpreted them according to what they were designed to achieve and the wider objectives of the Community. The specific objective of a particular rule has often been held to be subject to the broader objectives of the Community. For example, the right of citizens to seek cross-border health care services, and to be reimbursed for these under the social security system to which they are affiliated on the same basis as if the services had been provided in the recipient's home state, cannot be made subject to a prior discretionary authorization on the part of the competent social security authority.[78] Likewise in *Commission v United Kingdom*[79] the Court found that the requirement to inform and consult workers' representatives in the Transfer of Undertakings Directive[80] was an obligation which required the United Kingdom to put in place the structure necessary to achieve such a process. The fact that the Directive provided that such an obligation was to be regulated according to national law and practice did not mean that if there was no law or practice regarding the information and consultation of workers then none need be established. Similarly the Court has held that the information and consultation process had to be completed before any decision was taken as to the dismissal of employees since otherwise it would be without purpose.

2.102 In *Robins*[81] the Court found that the obligation in the Insolvency Directive[82] for Member States to safeguard employees' occupational pension rights in the case of the insolvency of their employer had to be meaningful. Although it found that, on the facts of the case, the protection available to the claimants was insufficient,

---

[76] Art 226 EC.
[77] Art 234 EC.
[78] Case C-120/95 *Decker* [1998] ECR I–1831; Case C-158/96 *Kohll* [1998] ECR I–1931.
[79] Case 165/82 [1983] ECR 3421.
[80] Directive 2001/83 [2001] OJ L82/16.
[81] Case C-278/05 [2007] ECR I–1053.
[82] Directive 80/987 [1980] OJ L283/2.

it was unable to say what precisely that protection should be, given the loose wording of the Directive.

The extent of the rights of Union citizens has been determined almost exclusively by the ECJ through preliminary rulings, no indication being given in the Treaty as to the extent of those rights or how they differed, if at all, from those of economically active persons and their families.[83] **2.103**

The influence of the Court on the development of the law on gender discrimination has been considerable. It is fair to say that the women of Europe owe a considerable debt to the ECJ, without which their position today might be considerably worse that it is. From the landmark *Defrenne* cases[84] in which the right to equal pay, and the parameters of that right, were established, to *Marshall II*[85] in which the Court held that even if national law governed the remedies to be made available to parties denied their Community law right to equal treatment, those remedies must be made effective with the result that they might have to go above and beyond what is provided for under national legal systems, the Court has not hesitated to give effect to the principle of equality between the sexes as expressed in the Treaty and legislation. Where Member States have failed to implement directives within the required time limit, the Court has found that the clear expression of the principle of equal treatment can give rise to directly effective rights with the result that women are entitled to the same treatment as men as from the date when the Directive ought to have been implemented. This was the case in *McDermott and Cotter*[86] where the Court found that women were entitled to receive the same unemployment benefit as men despite the fact that this could lead in some cases to families receiving double benefits for dependants where both parents were eligible for benefit. Since there had been no timely implementation of the Directive, the only valid point of reference, in determining the entitlement of women who had been the victims of discrimination, was the benefit level paid to men. **2.104**

The Court has been pivotal in developing social and employment rights, at times when the Community had either no competence to do so or was constrained by **2.105**

---

[83] Case C-85/96 *Martinez Sala* [1998] ECR I–2691; Case C-456/02 *Trojani* [2004] ECR I–7573; Case C-138/02 *Collins* [2004] ECR I–5547; Case C-200/02 *Chen* [2004] ECR I– 9925. Davies: 'Any Place I Can Hang my Hat? or Residence in the New Nationality' (2005) 11 European Law Journal 43–56 Mather: 'The Court of Justice and the Union Citizen European' (2005) 11 Law Journal 722–43.

[84] Case 80/70 *Defrenne 1* [1971] ECR 445; Case 43/75 *Defrenne 2* [1975] ECR 455; Case C-148/77 *Defrenne 3* [1978] ECR 1365.

[85] Case C-271/91 [1993] ECR I–4367.

[86] Case 286/85 [1987] ECR 1453.

the political sensitivities of the Member States.[87] In Chapter 12 we see how the Court had to define what constituted a transfer of an undertaking within the meaning of the Transfer of Undertakings Directive there being no definition in the Original Directive of that concept. Likewise the absence of any definition of 'disability' in the Employment Equality Directive placed the court in a position of having to draw the delicate line between what constitutes a disability and long-term—in the sense of 9 to 10 months—sickness.[88]

2.106 In its extensive interpretative case law the Court's approach has been to give a broad definition of rights and a correspondingly narrow view of exceptions and derogations to those rights. However, in defining the scope of rights the Court has been careful not to exceed the boundaries of either Treaty provisions or legislation. Thus it has interpreted 'pay' generously as including all remuneration in cash or in kind arising out of an employment relationship, but it has excluded from that concept statutory social security benefits and matters relating to equal treatment in the workplace. Discrimination on the basis of sex has been held to include unequal treatment on the grounds of gender re-assignment[89] but not sexual orientation.[90] The Transfer of Undertakings Directive[91] has been held to be applicable to both the public and private sectors[92] but not to administrative re-organization within a public administration.[93]

2.107 Likewise the Court has been sensitive to the impact of its judgments. Where rulings would have serious and adverse financial consequences, it has been persuaded to limit their temporal effect.[94] In areas where Community competence is of a complementary nature, in for example the area of disability discrimination and employment policy, the Court respects the limits of that competence by exercising restraint in the interpretation of key concepts[95] and so respecting the economic and financial considerations which govern the division of that competence between the Member States and the Community.[96]

---

[87] 'It is as much a series of rulings from the ECJ as the process of Commission and Council initiatives that has been the source of new social policy.' Leibfried and Pierson: 'Social Policy: left to Courts and Markets?' in Wallace and Wallace: *Policy-Making in the European Union* Fourth Edition Oxford University Press 2000 at 288 (Chapter 10).

[88] Case C-13/05 *Navas* note 11.

[89] Case C 423/04 *Richards* [2006] ECR I–3585.

[90] Case C-249/96 [1998] ECR I–621.

[91] Directive 2001/23 [2001] OJ L82/16.

[92] Case 29/91 *Dr Sophie Redmond* [1992] ECR I–3189.

[93] Case C-298/94 *Henke* [1996] ECR I–4987.

[94] Case 43/75 *Defrenne* 2 [1976] ECR 455; Case C-262/888 *Barber* [1999] ECR I–1889.

[95] Case C-13/05 *Navas* note 11.

[96] Ibid Opinion Advocate General Geelhoed paras 51–54.

The Court's efforts to render effective what at times have been rather sketchy and **2.108** opaque provisions have not been without criticism. Excessive judicial activism has been alleged. Accusations of poaching on the legislature's territory have been made.[97] But with what justification? What is the Court meant to do when faced with provisions which, by virtue of their very existence, it can be assumed were meant to be meaningful, but whose meaningfulness is not articulated? It can but look at the legal measure in issue and interpret it in a manner which fulfils its objectives.[98] If the Member States are concerned with the judicial activism of the Court they have but to be more specific as to the content and parameters of rights expressed either in the EC Treaty itself or legislation.[99]

---

[97] Hailbronner: 'Union Citizenship and access to social benefits' (2005) 42 CML Rev 1245–67; Hatzopoulos 'A "more" Social Europe; A Political Crossroads or a legal one way? Dialogues between Luxembourg and Lisbon' (2005) 42 CML Rev 1599–635; Simitis: 'Dismantling or Strengthening Labour law: The Case of the European Court of Justice' (1996) 2 European Law Journal 156–76.

[98] 'Once confronted with litigation the ECJ cannot escape making what are essentially policy decisions as a matter of routine': Leibfried and Pierson (see note 87 above) at 288.

[99] Similarly alleged overactivism by the Commission can be attributed to a dearth of specific provision in the Treaty circumscribing is competence: '. . . the Commission has been able to pursue an expansionist interpretation of treaty powers because of the absence of effective constraints on its behavior, the so-called "constitutional deficit"': Addison and Siebert: 'The Social Charter of the European Community: Evolution and Controversies' (1991) 44 Industrial and Labor Relations Review 597–625 at 615.

3

HISTORICAL DEVELOPMENT: MESSINO TO LISBON

A. Introduction

The evolution of social and employment law and policy in the European **3.01** Community has been a slow, and often confusing, process. Political commitment has been dependent upon the prevailing economic environment and has proved fragile at times of slow economic growth.[1] Ambition and rhetoric have so often given way to inertia if not regression. To understand what is social and employment law and policy today and where its future lies it is necessary to appreciate its ancestry.

Until some 15 years ago the Community institutions lacked any real competence **3.02** to regulate policy in these areas by way of measures which were either legally

---

[1] Kenner: *EU Employment Law: From Rome to Amsterdam and Beyond* Hart Publishing 2003; O'Keeffe: 'The Uneasy Progress of European Social Policy' (1996) 2 Columbia Journal of European Law 241–63; Shanks: 'The Social Policy of the European Communities' (1977) 14 CML Rev 375; Simitis and Lyon-Caen: 'Community Labour Law: A Critical Introduction to its History' in Davies, Lyon-Caen, Sciarra, and Simitis: *Principles and Perspectives* Clarendon Press 1996, Chapter 1.

binding on the Member State or at least politically compelling. A persistent division of opinion between the Member States as to the Community's role in these areas should be has resulted in policy evolving in a piecemeal and rather incoherent fashion dependent more on prevailing political will of the Member States rather than in pursuit of agreed Community objectives.

3.03 This rather chaotic state of affairs stems from the fact that that the role of the Community in employment and social matters has traditionally been, and arguably remains, unclear. Are they independent objectives, or subject to broader Community concerns? And if so to what extent? Should social and economic policy be regulated on a Community level or by the Member States or both? If the latter multi-level approach is to be the case, how should responsibility be divided? These are the issues which have dominated the development of social and employment policy since the beginning of the Community. At different periods they have been addressed but never satisfactorily.

3.04 This chapter attempts to describe the debate from the inception of the Community to the present day beginning half a century ago with the Ohlin Report which shaped the course of Community social and employment policy.

B. The Ohlin Report

3.05 In 1956 the Governing Body of the International Labour Organization appointed a group of independent experts chaired by Professor Ohlin to study and report on the social aspects of European Economic Co-operation.[2] This study was carried out in response to concerns about the social aspects of the liberalization of trade that would be brought about by the functioning of the common market. It was feared that the common market might bring about an imbalance in the economic development of Europe, with investment being concentrated in the industrially established areas of Europe, resulting in a move of capital and labour to those areas, to the detriment of the economically underdeveloped regions of Southern Europe, 'which would be in serious danger of remaining unindustrialized'.[3] Did this mean that there should be some degree of harmonization of social conditions

---

[2] *Social Aspects of European Economic Co-operation. Studies and Reports.* New Series No 46. ILO Geneva 1956. Summarized in 74 International Labour Review (1956) at 99–123. See Davies: 'The Emergence of European Labour Law' in McCarthy (ed) *Legal Intervention in Industrial Relations: Gains and Losses* London 1993 313–59.

[3] Ibid at 101. Interestingly the reverse argument has been advanced at the time of the latest adhesion to the European Union by many countries from Central and Eastern Europe.

and policies so as to bring about fair and effective competition within the Community?[4]

Whilst the Committee was of the view that if one set of producers pay wages or **3.06** have to bear social charges which were exceptionally low in comparison to those to which their competitors were subject, there could be a case for the harmonization of social conditions and policy, they concluded that this was not the position in Europe and therefore, to try to establish identical patterns of relative wage rates would be an unduly rigid approach.[5] The Ohlin Committee believed that workers' living standards would improve as productivity rose and trading barriers were dismantled following the establishment of the common market. Thus it concluded that differences in labour costs did not per se 'constitute an obstacle to the establishment of freer international markets'.[6]

However, there was one case where the Committee advocated intervention in **3.07** national pay policy and that was in the sphere of female labour which at the time, save in a few exceptional cases, notably France, was paid at a lower rate than that of male labour. This differential could, the Committee felt, lead to a distortion in production costs.

> A certain distortion of international competition arises from differences in the extent to which the principle of equal pay for men and women is applied in different countries. Countries in which there are large wage differentials by sex will pay relatively low wages in industries employing a large proportion of female labour and these industries will enjoy what might be considered special advantages over their competitors abroad where differentials are smaller or non-existent.[7]

As to social security costs the Committee concluded that harmonization was not **3.08** necessary for three reasons:

(i) The ultimate incidence of social charges can, in general, be shifted. They are not necessarily reflected in production costs.

---

[4] An argument advanced to support the introduction of international labour standards in the globalized economy. Arthurs: 'Reinventing Labor Law for the Global Economy: The Benjamin Aaron Lecture' (2001) 22 Berkeley Journal of Employment and Labor Law 272; Hepple: 'Enforcement: The Law and Politics of Cooperation and Compliance' in Hepple: *Social and Labour Rights in a Global Context* Cambridge University Press 2002 at 14–15.

[5] Ohlin Report paras 158–159.

[6] Ibid at 99.

[7] Ohlin Report 109. The French in particular were concerned that they would be at an economic disadvantage as their social and labour standards were higher than those of other countries. The Front Populaire government of Leon Blum had introduced the 40-hour week without any wage reductions, overtime pay, and paid holidays. The Mollet government argued that these social rights would disadvantage the French in the common market. In the event they secured in the final draft of the Treaty only a commitment to the principle of equal pay and paid holidays.

(ii) Social policy measures may have an impact on patterns of international trade, production, and employment but the overall effect of such measures is neutralized by changing patterns in trading.[8]

(iii) Taxes levied for the purpose of financing programmes of social security are only one element among a number of general measures of economic policy affecting conditions of employment and production.

3.09 It was therefore highly doubtful whether it would be desirable to undertake harmonization in one particular field of economic policy, such as the financing of social security schemes, without proceeding at the same time to the harmonization of other policies the economic effect of which might be similar. In any event the Committee concluded that it was not at all certain that even a measure of harmonization extending over a wide range of economic and social policies would in fact bring about a less distorted structure of production in trade. Harmonization should, therefore, only be attempted if there were substantial inequalities in the burdens imposed on industries, a situation which the Committee felt should become apparent in the transitional period.[9]

3.10 Aside from finding that the economic development of the Community would not be hindered by any lack of harmonization of social and labour conditions, the Ohlin Committee, influenced by the fact that should this not prove to be the case, and some alignment of national norms and practices might prove to be necessary, this could be done by the ILO and the Council of Europe. The ILO, at the time, was engaged in developing universal labour standards whilst the Council of Europe was drafting what became the European Social Charter. In all there seemed to be little point in the Community developing yet another set of norms.

3.11 The Ohlin Report was accepted by the inter-governmental committee, chaired by Paul-Henri Spaak, which foresaw a 'gradual coalescence' of standards but did not see harmonization of standards as necessary to the functioning of the common market but took the view that such harmonization would ensure from its operation.[10]

---

[8] 'A government taking a measure of general social policy certainly alters conditions of productivity in a country, The change may be considered favourable or unfavourable according to the criterion by which it is judged, but however this may be it remains true' Ohlin Report 108.

[9] To this general conclusion the Committee made one exception: if there were special industries such as coal mining, the production of which involved special dangers or hardships which would justify the payment of special compensation to workers, a system should be adopted under which such welfare schemes were financed by contributions payable by the industry itself.

[10] Rapport des Chefs de Delegations aux Ministères des Affaires Etrangères 21 April 1956. A position reflecting the agreement between Adenauer and Mollet reached at a meeting of 6 November

C. The Treaty of Rome 1957

The Treaty of Rome, therefore, made no reference either express or implied to the creation of a Community social policy and, accordingly, granted the Community institutions few specific powers to do so. The approach of the founder Member States was that of laissez faire coupled with a view that social policy was essentially a matter for national regulation. **3.12**

Social standards, and in particular social security provision, were matters for each Member State to determine according to the values of its citizens as expressed ultimately through the ballot box. Equal pay for equal work was an exception to this general thinking. Even then, competence was not ceded to the Community: equal pay for equal work would, it was believed, come about through the initiative of the Member States themselves. History proved this to be a rather naïve approach. **3.13**

The lack of commitment on the part of the Member States to the development of a Community social and employment law was reflected in the Treaty of Rome. Articles 117–122 were vague and repetitious, conferring no real powers upon the Community institutions, and little by way of direct rights upon the Community citizens.[11] **3.14**

Article 117 stated that Member States agreed upon the need to promote improved living and working conditions and an improved standard of living for workers. It did not confer any specific powers upon the Community institutions to bring about these objectives but assumed that such harmonization would result automatically from 'the functioning of the common market'.[12] Article 118 gave the Commission power 'to promote close co-operation between Member States in **3.15**

1956. Whilst the Treaty was to include a section on social policy, most of its provisions would not be binding. This enabled Mollet to gain support for the Treaty in France and at the same time assuaged German as to possible loss of control over welfare expenditure and policy. See Lynch: 'Restoring France' in Milward et al (eds) *The Frontier of National Sovereignty: History and Theory 1945–1992.* Routledge 1994 58–87 at 84; Manow, Schaefer, Zorn: *European Social Policy and Europe's Party-Political Centre of Gravity 1957–2003.* Discussion Paper 4/06 Max Planck Institute for the Study of Societies Cologne 2004.

[11] Hallstein: *Europe in the Making.* London 1972 at 119 et seq.

[12] 'Competition is the best stimulant of economic activity since it guarantees the widest possible freedom of action to all. An active competition policy pursued in accordance with the provisions of the Treaties . . . enables enterprises continuously to improve their efficiency, which is the sine qua non for a steady improvement in living standards and employment prospects within the countries of the Community. From this point of view competition policy is an essential means for satisfying to a great extent the individual and collective needs of our society' First Competition Report on Competition Policy Brussels 1971 at point 10.

the social field'. This provision thus excluded a transfer of powers from the Member States to the Community. It relied instead on 'soft co-ordination through information exchange, studies, opinions and consultations'.[13]

3.16 Article 117 was held by the ECJ to be 'more in the nature of a programme' for the development of social rights[14] rather than having any binding legal effects:

> Article 117. . . is essentially in the nature of a programme. It relates only to social objectives the attainment of which must be the result of Community action, close co-operation between Member States and the operation of the Common Market.[15]

3.17 Although Articles 117 and 118 did not endow the Community institutions with any legislative competence, they were not without legal effect since

> . . . they constitute an important aid, in particular for the interpretation of other provisions of the Treaty and of secondary Community legislation in the social field.[16]

3.18 The lack of specific law-making powers in the EEC Treaty, until the adoption of the Single European Act and, thereafter, the Agreement on Social Policy under the Maastricht Treaty, and its subsequent incorporation by virtue of the Treaty of Amsterdam into the EC Treaty, made the adoption of legally binding measures possible, up until 1987, only by reference to the general law-making powers contained in what was then Articles 100 and 235 EEC, now Articles 94 and 308 EC respectively.

3.19 These two provisions require, first, the existence of a Community objective, secondly, the necessity for Community measures to achieve that objective and, thirdly, a unanimous vote in the Council to secure the adoption of the appropriate measures. The requirement for complete agreement between the Member States, both on the necessity for Community legislation and its terms, made the

---

13 Manow, Schaefer and Zorn (see note 10 above) at 22.

14 Case 170/84 *Bilka Kaufhaus v Weber von Hartz* [1986] ECR 1607.

15 Joined Cases C-72–73/91 *Sloman Neptun* [1993] ECR I–887 Judgment para 25.

16 Joined Cases 281, 283, 285, and 287/85 *Germany and Others v Commission* [1987] ECR 3203; Case 126/86 *Zaera v Instituto Nacional de la Seguridad y Tesoreria General de la Seguridad Social* [1987] ECR 3697. It has been argued that Article 117 was more than a mere statement that improved social standards was agreed to be a desirable objective, it was a commitment to the upward harmonization of standards. In other words it was a standstill provision prohibiting any downward trend in the level of protection. See Kenner (note 1 above) at 8. Schnoor in Blanpain (ed) *International Encyclopedia of Labour Law and Industrial Relations* Kluwer 1980 at para 60, went further and read into Article 117 a contractual obligation. Article 117 '. . . contains an agreement between the Member States about the necessity to promote . . . progress. This means indeed a contractual obligation on all Member States to co-operate achieving the Community purpose of social progress.'

adoption of social policy measures a frequently difficult and lengthy process. The condition that any given proposal must be both necessary, and be adopted unanimously was a major obstacle to an effective legislative programme since unanimity proved difficult to attain in such a politically sensitive policy area, and even when reached, the demands of compromise resulted in less than optimal quality drafting. This particular legislative process, although tiresome, was indispensable to the development of social-economic rights, there being no other alternative.

Defective legislative instruments bred confusion, resulting in litigation before national courts which in turn led to a multiplicity of interpretative rulings from the ECJ, which proved, to the surprise of at least some Member States, to have a liberal approach to social and employment issues and it is to that liberal approach that progress on the development of a Community social policy was made. In many instances we see the ECJ taking the lead in enunciating social and employment rights, often subsequently enshrined in legislation and, in some cases, the EC Treaty itself.[17]   **3.20**

D. Three Schools of Thought

The difficulties in making legislative progress were exacerbated by differences of opinion between the Member States on what precisely the role of the Community should be in social policy and led to a division of opinion amongst them as to what powers the Community should have with respect to the formulation of social and employment policies and legally binding rights and obligations in those spheres.   **3.21**

The traditional division of opinion on what the Community's role in social policy ought to be falls roughly into three schools of thought.   **3.22**

The first school of thought advocates an active role for the Community in the social field. Its proponents regard the Community as having a duty to care for the social well-being of its citizens as much as the furtherance of their collective economic interests within the framework of a single integrated market. Consequently, they advocate the creation of a Social Europe in which improvements in living and working conditions would match economic progress.   **3.23**

---

[17] See paras 2.102–2.111: 'it is as much a series of rulings from the ECJ as the process of Commission and Council initiative that has been the source of new social policy' Liebfried and Pierson: 'Social Policy: Left to Courts and Markets' in Wallace and Wallace: *Policy Making in the European Union* Fourth Edition Oxford University Press 2000, Chapter 10 at 288.

3.24   The second school of thought views the Community as being primarily concerned with economic matters and, therefore, as being competent in the social field only in so far as is necessary to realize the economic objectives of the Community notably to prevent distortions of competition arising out of divergencies in production costs between Member States due to differences in national social standards, levels of health and safety protection, and other similar factors.[18] Some Community intervention was felt to be necessary to overcome regional disparities and distortions in competition within the Community which might given rise to social dumping whereby '. . . companies will invest where the wages and conditions are cheapest and therefore force the workers in other countries . . . to accept lower standards'.[19] In order to ensure the balanced geographical development of the Community's economy and to prevent a decline in social standards it was felt that there should be some harmonization of those standards.

3.25   The third school of thought claims, quite simply, that the Community has no competence whatsoever: social policy is a matter for national regulation. There is no firm evidence on the consequences of differing social standards or levels of health and safety protection on production costs and in the absence of such evidence, social policy remains a matter for national regulation in accordance with national traditions and desires.

3.26   These divergent viewpoints, set out above, have been described as reflecting the tension between welfare and competition.[20] This tension is longstanding, and it is not peculiar to the issue of whether the Community should be competent to deal with social and employment issues: the relationship between the competing objectives of welfare and competition has dominated the debate on the international regulation of labour standards for over a century and a half.[21]

3.27   Of these three schools of thought, the second has traditionally found the most favour within the Community. Welfare standards, reflective of societal values are generally acknowledged to be a matter for regulation for each Member State. Their supra-national regulation is seen as a means of ensuring equality of economic opportunity, a level playing field for all, and as a means of achieving the internal market and is tolerated only to the extent necessary to achieve these objectives.

---

[18] Watson: *Social Security Law of the European Communities* Mansell 1980 at 32–4.

[19] Blanpain: '1992 and Beyond: The Impact of the European Communities on Labour Law Systems of the Member States' (1990) 11 Comp Lab Law Journal 403.

[20] Wedderburn: 'The Social Charter in Britain: Labour Law and Labour Courts' (1991) 54 MLR 1–47 at 15.

[21] Hepple: *The Making of Labour Law in Europe* London 1986.

In spite of these deep divisions of opinion a Community social policy, albeit **3.28** dependent initially at least on political will and prevailing economic circumstances, has evolved in a number of phases which will be charted in the next section.

E. Beginnings

Community social policy developed in a number of phases. During the first **3.29** phase, ending around 1972, the Community's efforts were concerned with achieving the free movement of persons which, inter alia, required the co-ordination of national social security schemes to ensure that workers were not prejudiced in their welfare rights by the exercise of their right to free movement. Some efforts were made to harmonize social security and to introduce common health and safety standards but these did not result in any major achievement. Legislative efforts in the first years of the Community were, therefore, devoted to bringing about the free movement of persons, one of the fundamental pillars of the Community. Some efforts were made to harmonize social security but little came of them.[22] Attempts to introduce common health and safety standards likewise did not come to fruition. As a result, little happened.

F. The Paris Summit

In 1972, in a favourable economic environment and on the eve of the accession **3.30** of Denmark, Ireland and the United Kingdom to the Community, the heads of State and government meeting in Paris, noting the disparity between levels of economic growth within the Community and the quality of life of some of its citizens, resolved that the Community would assume 'a more human face' and stated that they attached as much importance 'to vigorous action in the social field as to the achievement of economic and monetary union'.[23] As a result of this initiative, the Social Action Programme was drawn up by the EC Commission in

---

[22] Watson: *Social Security Law of the European Communities* London 1980 at 41–4.

[23] EC Bull 10/1972, para 19. See Shanks: 'The Social Policy of the Community' (1977) 14 CML Rev 375 at 378: 'The Community had to be seen to be more than a device to enable capitalists to exploit the common market; otherwise it might not have been possible to persuade the peoples of the Community to accept the discipline of the market. The common market has to evolve into a genuine Community, a Community "with a human face" which would be able to command the loyalties of its citizens, strong enough to resist the centrifugal forces of nationalism and sectoral pressures.'

late 1973.[24] It was endorsed by the Council in January 1974[25] in a somewhat less favourable economic climate than prevailed when it was crafted. The Council's approval was therefore somewhat guarded. It cautioned that a standard solution to all social problems should not be attempted and that there should be no transfer to a Community level of responsibility assumed more effectively at other levels. The Council's view of the potential for the development of a Community social policy was considerably less ambitious that the Commission's vision.[26] It corresponded to the second school of thought discussed above at para 3.24. Social policy was to be developed to the extent necessary to achieve parity of competitive conditions within the Community.

3.31 This Social Action Programme had three main objectives: the attainment of full and better employment in the Community, the improvement of living and working conditions, and increased participation by both employers and workers in industry. In spite of being unaccompanied by any specific legislative powers to achieve its objective, a chilly economic environment, and following the accession of Ireland and the United Kingdom and Denmark, whose social policies differed both from each other and the original six Member States, the Social Action Programme marked the beginning of a period of relatively intense and unprecedented action in the social field resulting in the adoption of many measures, which had a profound and positive impact on the lives of Community citizens.

3.32 More importantly it indicated a political commitment on the part of the Community to an employment and social policy. This was a significant move forward. Here we see the beginning of a realization that an improvement and similarity in social and employment conditions might not necessarily follow as a matter of course from a betterment of economic conditions which the internal market might bring about.

G. Completing the Internal Market

3.33 Following the publication of the White Paper on the Completion of the Internal Market,[27] the Community acquired a new momentum and along with that a maturity. It seemed to aspire to its own social policy. Indeed it appeared to regard

---

[24] Bull EC Supp2/74 at 13–35.

[25] [1974] OJ C12.

[26] Addison and Siebert: 'The Social Charter of the European Community: Evolution and Controversies' (1991) 44 Industrial and Labor Relations Review 597–625 at 600.

[27] COM (85) 310 Final.

a social policy as an essential element in the creation of the single integrated market. Delors spoke of 'l'espace social européen' as an integral part of the internal market which he defined as a plinth or platform of guaranteed social rights, along the lines of the European Social Charter, backed up by an action programme to implement those rights:

> The creation of a vast economic area based on market and business co-operation, is inconceivable—I would say unattainable—without some harmonization of social legislation. Our ultimate aim must be the creation of a European social area.[28]

However, as the idea of the 'espace social européen' unravelled, its purpose was perceived to be essentially economic: the creation of a social dimension to the internal market was seen to be necessary to overcome potential regional disparities and distortions in competition which might give rise to social dumping. Social dumping occurs when companies invest where wages and other labour conditions are cheapest, thereby bringing about a lowering of standards in other countries thus forcing workers to accept inferior employment condition in order to safeguard their employment. **3.34**

In order to ensure the balanced geographic development of the Community's economy, in particular in view of the impending accession of the Iberian States, and to ensure fair competition, it was felt that there should be some harmonization of labour standards. **3.35**

H. The Single European Act

The Single European Act was signed in February 1986. It marked the first major Treaty reform since the founding of the Community. The political complexion of the Community had changed to one where the right or centre right dominated. Seven of ten prime ministers were either conservative or Christian Democrat. The Single European Act thus reflected a convergence within the Community of economic interests and a growing support for market integration. **3.36**

At the same time from a social policy, and in particular a social security, perspective, the Community had become more divergent. From the six founder Member States with their common Bismarckian tradition, there had been added two Anglo-Saxon and one Scandinavian welfare models. The imminent accession of Spain and Portugal would add to that of Greece in introducing a third form of social protection—the Mediterranean model. Thus the convergence in economic policy was not mirrored in social policy. **3.37**

---

[28] Bull EC Supp 1/86 at 9.

3.38 The Preamble to the Single European Act expressed the wish of the Member States to promote democracy on the basis of the rights set out, inter alia, in the European Social Charter of 1961. Article 158 was inserted into the EC Treaty committing the Community to strengthening social and economic cohesion so as to reduce regional disparities. The Social Dialogue was institutionalized in what is now Article 139 of the EC Treaty.

3.39 The most significant advance, however, was the extension of qualified majority voting to the field of health and safety by Article 118a, now subsumed into Article 137 of the EC Treaty. The concept of health and safety was interpreted broadly by the Commission which used it as a legal basis for the adoption of a number of measures, which would not have been regarded as coming within the ambit of health and safety in the traditional sense of that term: the Pregnant Workers' Directive,[29] the Working Time Directive,[30] and the Young Persons Directive.[31] The legality of the Working Time Directive was challenged albeit unsuccessfully by the United Kingdom.[32] These Directives laid down minimum standards for the protection of vulnerable groups of workers. Member States were free to set higher standards if they so wished and many key concepts and national laws and practices were retained. The Directives were therefore a floor of minimum rights with minimal change to national law and practice.

I. The Hannover Summit

3.40 At the Hannover Summit, held in June 1988, the European Council stressed the importance of the social aspects of the single integrated market and invited the Commission to draw up proposals on future social policy initiatives, but at the same time it recognized that the operation of the internal market was the best means of promoting employment and increasing the general prosperity of the Community.

3.41 In September 1988 the Commission produced a working paper, entitled 'The Social Dimension of the Internal Market',[33] which set out priorities and proposals for action. These divided into three main themes:

(a) the creation of a single labour market through the elimination of barriers to free movement;

---

[29] Directive 92/85 [1992] OJ L348/1.
[30] Directive 93/104 [1993] OJ L307/18.
[31] Directive 94/33 [1993] OJ L216/12.
[32] Case C-84/94 [1996] ECR I–5755. See paras 22.05–22.11.
[33] SEC (88) 1148 Final.

(b) the reduction of unemployment and regional disparities in unemployment; and

(c) the development of a social policy which ensures that economic measures do not affect standards of social protection in the Community. In particular, living and working conditions of workers, especially health and safety standards in the workplace, must be protected.

In November 1988, the Commission, wishing to canvass opinion on the best **3.42** possible means of attaining these objectives, asked the Economic and Social Committee to draw up possible components of a Community Charter of Basic Social Rights. The Committee was of the view that the best way forward was by means of a Charter along the same lines as the European Social Charter to which many Member States were signatories.[34] Accordingly the Commission drew up the Community Charter on the Fundamental Social Rights of Workers (the 'Social Charter'). It was adopted by the Council on 30 October 1989 and endorsed at the European Council meeting in Strasbourg on 9 December 1989. The United Kingdom did not give its approval to the Charter and so it remained applicable only between the other 11 Member States.

J. The Community Charter on the Fundamental Social Rights of Workers

The Charter guaranteed 12 fundamental rights which can be classified under **3.43** four broad headings: free movement of workers; rights of residence; frontier workers; and workers moving under a contract to provide services and social security.

The Charter was not legally binding; it could not be used as a source of rights **3.44** or obligations. It was no more than a solemn declaration of the social rights of Community citizens but many of its objectives were capable of being implemented by virtue of either specific or general legislative powers granted under the EC Treaty.[35] Many of the provisions of the Charter echoed initiatives taken previously which had failed to be adopted, prompting the observation:

> But it is also transparently the case that the Social Charter taken as a whole resurrects much of the Commission's past agenda and stalled directives. It is, then, less of a new departure than a reflection of the Commission's long held commitment to social justice.[36]

---

[34] [1989] OJ C126/4.

[35] Bercusson: 'The European Community's Charter of Fundamental Rights for Workers' 53 MLR 624–642; Watson: 'The Community Social Charter' (1991) 28 CML Rev 37–68.

[36] Addison and Siebert (see note 26 above) at 615.

3.45   Article 28 of the Social Charter invited the Commission to submit proposals for the implementation of the rights set out therein. The Commission responded with alacrity to this invitation and produced at the end of November 1989, some 10 days before the adoption of the Charter was an Action Programme which a detailed document of some 54 pages containing some 47 proposals for the adoption of various kinds of measures.[37] It was divided into 13 sections, 12 of which corresponded to each of the 12 fundamental rights set out in the Charter. A thirteenth section entitled 'The Labour Market' was concerned with employment.

3.46   By the end of 1991, the Commission had presented proposals to the Council on virtually all 47 initiatives announced in its Action Programme but few had been adopted by the Council of Ministers.[38] It began to be felt that the crux of the problem was the lack of legal powers, essential to realize the objectives of the Charter.

3.47   In a working document presented by the Commission to the Intergovernmental Conference on Political Union, the Commission attributed the lack of progress in attaining the objectives of the Charter to:

> . . . the wide gap between the powers available under the current legal bases and the ambition set out in the Charter and the new constraints arising out of the completion of the internal market.[39]

3.48   To overcome these difficulties the Commission proposed a revision of the social chapter of the EC Treaty to include the extension of '. . . qualified majority voting . . . to certain fields, notably some of those covered by the Charter'.[40]

3.49   The 11 Member States which had agreed to the Charter were happy to reiterate their commitment to its objectives and to broaden the Community's law-making powers to include increased qualified majority voting in many areas of social policy. The United Kingdom remained opposed to any extension of the Community's power in the social sphere. Accordingly, it was agreed among the 12 Member States that the amendments desired by the other 11 Member States should be contained in an agreement signed by those Member States which would form a Protocol annexed to the Maastricht Treaty binding those 11 Member States only. Thus, the Agreement on Social Policy came into being and so began an uneasy

---

[37] COM (89) 568 Final. See Hepple: 'The Implementation of the Community Charter of Fundamental Social Rights' 1994 53 MLR 643–55.

[38] First Report on the Application of the Charter COM (91) 511 Final.

[39] SEC (91) 500 Final at 84.

[40] Ibid at 86.

period in the history of Community social and economic policy. The Maastricht Treaty marked 'the institutionalization of differentiated integration'.[41]

K. The Agreement on Social Policy[42]

The Agreement on Social Policy resulted in two possible legal bases for legislative **3.50** measures, namely the provisions in Title VIII of the EC Treaty (now Title XI) and the Agreement on Social Policy. In the case of the latter, the United Kingdom could take no part in the legislative process and no measures adopted by the other Member States would bind the United Kingdom. In the case of the former, measures adopted under Title VIII, the United Kingdom could participate at all stages of the legislative process and any measures adopted would have force throughout the Community.

The legislative competence of the Community and the objectives for which leg- **3.51** islation could be adopted were considerably expanded under the Agreement. Additionally, and most importantly, the social partners were accorded a major role in the legislative process. From a hitherto largely consultative role they moved centre stage to share legislative competence with the Community institutions. The Agreement on Social Policy thus created an alternative legislative process unique to social policy.[43]

Three specific roles were envisaged for management and labour under the Agree- **3.52** ment. The first of these was the obligation on the part of the Commission to consult management and labour on the desirability and content of any proposed legislative action. Secondly, Article 2(4) of the Agreement specified that the Member States could entrust management and labour with the implementation of directives adopted under the Agreement. This was not new: Member States are free to implement directives in any way they please, including by means of legally binding collective agreements.[44] Thirdly, management and labour could undertake to draft by way of agreement between them a text giving effect to a proposal. Such agreements became legally binding and entered into the Community legal order by way of a Council Decision. A number of measures were adopted by this method.[45]

---

[41] Dinan: *Europe Recast: A History of the European Union* Lynne Rienner Publishers Boulder and London 2004 at 258.

[42] See generally Watson: 'Social Policy after Maastricht' (1993) 30 CML Rev 481–513.

[43] Ibid.

[44] Case 143/83 *Commission v Denmark* [1985] ECR 417 at para 8; Case 165/82 *Commission v United Kingdom* [1983] ECR 3431.

[45] Directive 96/34 on parental leave ([1996] OJ L145/4); Directive 97/81 on part time work ([1998] OJ L14/8); Directive 99/70 on fixed term work ([1999] OJ L174/43).

L. The Treaty of Amsterdam

3.53 It is with the Treaty of Amsterdam that social policy emerged from being periph-
eral and controversial and that Community employment policy came into being.
The latter institutionalized and clarified some of the Community's previous initiatives in the employment policy sphere, hitherto based on political initiatives
expressed at meetings of the European Council. Most importantly, the respective
roles of the Community and the Member States in the formulation of social
policy were clarified.[46]

3.54 Title XI, Chapter 1, Articles 136–145 merged the provisions on social policy
previously contained in Part III, Title III, Articles 117–122 of the EC Treaty
entitled 'Social Policy' and the Agreement on Social Policy, thereby bringing to
an end the two-speed social policy created by the Treaty of Maastricht. Article
137 gave the Community power to 'support and complement' actions of the
Member States. Whilst respecting the principle of subsidiarity, the legislative
competence of the Community was vastly extended, notably with respect to
employment rights. At the same time the Community's powers were expressly
limited and in certain sensitive areas such as social security they were prohibited
from undertaking any legislative initiatives. The result was that much of what the
Community had been obliged to try and achieve by way of soft law measures, and
with the occasional use of Article 94 and 308 EC, could now be the subject of
directives adopted on the basis of qualified majority voting.

M. The Lisbon Strategy

3.55 The challenges to Europe's economy and way of life from globalization and the
digital revolution prompted the Commission in early 2000[47] to propose four
strategic objectives to be pursued over the following five-year period: promoting
new forms of governance to give people a greater say in how Europe is run and to
ensure an active and distinctive European contribution to the development of
global governance; building a stable Europe by making a success of enlargement
and building relations with the Community's neighbours so as to enable Europe

---

[46] At the time of the adoption of the Treaty of Amsterdam on 17 June 1997 10 of the 15 prime
ministers of the Member States were socialists/social democrats. Only Germany, Ireland, and Spain
had centre right coalitions. Blair and Jospin were elected just weeks before the Amsterdam Summit.
Both their predecessor had opposed any expansion of Community competence. Source: Manow,
Schaefer, and Zorn note 10 at 29.
[47] COM (2000) 154 Final.

to take a lead in building the global economy; and pursuing a new economic and social agenda and creating a better way of life for Europe's citizens.

The European Council meeting in Lisbon on 23–24 March 2000, moving for- **3.56**
ward from this initiative, set out an ambitious strategy for growth and employment in Europe, building on its strength but attacking its weaknesses so as to harness the challenges posed to Europe by globalization and the knowledge society.[48]

Although the Union was experiencing its best macro-economic outlook for a **3.57**
generation, more than 15 million Europeans were unemployed. The labour market was characterized by insufficient participation by women and older workers and long-term structural unemployment. A marked regional imbalance remained 'endemic' in parts of the Union. The skills gap was widening and the services sector underdeveloped. The Union was challenged externally by the global economy and the digital revolution which was changing all aspects of life. At the same time both of these phenomena offered opportunities which Europe felt it must grasp.

In the face of these challenges and opportunities the Union set itself a strategic **3.58**
goal for the forthcoming decade: to become the most competitive and dynamic knowledge-based economy in the world, capable of sustainable economic growth with more and better jobs and greater social cohesion. Achieving this goal requires an overall strategy aimed at:

- preparing the transition to a knowledge-based economy and society by better policies for the information society and R&D, as well as stepping up the process of structural reform for competitiveness and innovation and completing the internal market;
- modernizing the European social model, investing in people and combating social exclusion;
- sustaining the healthy economic outlook and favourable growth prospects by applying an appropriate macro-economic policy mix.

This strategy was designed to bring about full employment 'more adapted to the **3.59**
personal choices of men and women' and strengthen regional cohesion. It was to be implemented by improving existing processes, the introduction of a new open method of co-ordination at all levels, coupled with a stronger guiding and co-ordinating role for the European Council. A meeting of the European Council every Spring would define relevant mandates and ensure that they were followed up.

---

[48] Presidency Conclusions, paras 3–5.

3.60 The Lisbon Strategy brought employment and social policy, into the heart of Community activity. Previously the Community's role had been largely complementary to that of the Member States.

3.61 A more active employment policy was to be encouraged by giving a new impetus to the National Employment Plans. Four key areas were to be addressed: improving employability and reducing the skill gap; giving higher priority to lifelong learning; increasing employment in the services sector; and furthering all aspects of equal opportunities. Realizing these objectives should, it was projected, raise the employment rate from the prevailing rate of 61 per cent to 'as close as possible to 70' by 2010 and increase the number of women in employment from the then average of 51 per cent to more than 60 per cent by 2010.

3.62 The Council's conclusions condemned prevailing poverty levels and social exclusion within the Union as 'unacceptable' and pledged the eradication of poverty by 2010. The new knowledge-based society would be creating economic conditions for greater prosperity through higher levels of growth and employment, social exclusion would be reduced. At the same time the Council warned of the 'risk of an ever-widening gap between those who have access to the new knowledge and those who are excluded'. Policies for combating social exclusion were to be based on the Open Method of Co-ordination.

3.63 With respect to social security systems, the European Council stated that these needed to be adapted to ensure that work paid and to ensure their long-term sustainability in the face of an ageing population.

3.64 From the Lisbon Strategy emerges a picture not too different from the traditional approach of the Community to social policy: focussed and centrally driven economic objectives will result in the eradication of poverty and an inclusive society. No effort is made to develop a social policy on a Community level. Employment is advocated as the solution to material deprivation and marginalization. The all-inclusive employment market is to be achieved through the furtherance of equal opportunities.

N. The Treaty of Nice

3.65 The Treaty of Nice concluded at the European Council meeting of 11 December 2000, slightly expanded Community competence in the social area to include the ability to take action to combat social exclusion and the modernization of social protection schemes. The adoption of legislative measures in these areas and any harmonizing measures were expressly excluded.[49] The High Level Working Party

---

[49] Art 137(2)(b).

on Social Protection, given a pivotal role in the eradication of poverty within the Union by the Lisbon European Council, was institutionalized in Article 144 EC becoming the Social Protection Committee, charged with four main tasks: to monitor the social situation and the development of social protection policies in the Member States and the Community; to promote exchanges of information, experience, and good practice between Member States and with the Commission; and to prepare reports and undertake other work either at the request of the Council or the Commission or on its own initiative. The Committee was to establish appropriate contacts with management and labour. Each Member State and the Commission appoints two members to the Committee.

O. Lisbon Revised

By the end of 2003 it became clear that the Community faced serious structural difficulties attributable to both internal and external factors. The targets set in the Lisbon Strategy looked increasingly unattainable. **3.66**

The European Council in March 2004 gave former Dutch Prime Minister Wim Kok a mandate to carry out an independent review, with a group of experts, of the Lisbon Strategy. The report of the Group entitled 'Facing the Challenge' was published in November 2004.[50] It was presented to the Commission on 3 November 2004 and considered by the European Council meeting in Brussels on 4 and 5 November 2004. The report was critical of the lack of progress made since 2000. At the same time it stated that 'Lisbon was not a picture of unrelieved gloom'.[51] There had been significant progress in employment between the mid 1990s and 2003 but the 2010 target of a 70 per cent employment rate would not be reached. R&D expenditure fell below the Lisbon targets. Progress in providing teachers with digital training was disappointing. At the same time Member States had progressed in the spread of ICT and Internet use. **3.67**

In the four years since the Lisbon strategy has been formulated the overall performance of the European economy had been disappointing. This was due in part to structural weaknesses and low demand. There were external challenges: the worldwide stock market bubble had imploded due to the collapse of the overvalued prices of US dot.com and telecoms shares amid evidence of financial and corporate malpractice. The terrorist attacks of September 11 2001 and subsequent events further darkened the international climate. The enlargement of the Community had made the achievement of the Lisbon goals harder. The new Member States had very much lower employment rates and productivity levels. **3.68**

---

[50] Facing the Challenge: The Lisbon Strategy for growth and employment. November 2004.
[51] Ibid at 10.

3.69 Despite the challenges posed by the above-mentioned factors, the Committee found that the European Union and its Member States had contributed to slow progress by failing to act on much of the Lisbon strategy with sufficient urgency:

> This disappointing delivery is due to an overloaded agenda, poor coordination and conflicting priorities. Still a key issue has been lack of political determination.[52]

3.70 In spite of this the Kok Committee did not advocate the abandonment of the strategy, stressing that it was 'even more urgent today as the growth gap with North America and Asia has widened while Europe must meet the combined challenges of low population growth and ageing'.[53] Better implementation was needed to make up for lost time. Determined action was need across five policy areas.[54] In terms of implementation of the strategy the Report found that the Open Method of Co-ordination had fallen short of expectations. At the same time the Community method had not delivered well in the sense that Member States were lagging behind in the implementation and transposition of directives.

3.71 On 2 February 2005 President Barrosa admitted that progress on the Lisbon strategy had been mixed.[55] The Commission appeared to accept most of the findings and recommendations of the Kok Report. It was admitted that economic conditions had been difficult in the years since the Lisbon Strategy had been designed. There were external and internal challenges. Competitors in other parts of the world had invested more in research and development and their production had grown at a more rapid pace. Europe needed to anticipate and manage change, particularly in the light of its demographic profile, both actual and future. There had been an ambitious enlargement of the Community to 27 Member States.

3.72 Aside from the constraints that the economic environment placed on achieving the Lisbon objectives, the process designed to attain those objectives had become overloaded and uncoordinated.

3.73 Governance issues needed to be resolved and objectives re-visited:

> The governance of the Lisbon Strategy needs radical improvement to make it more effective and more easily understood. Responsibilities have been muddled between the Union and the Member States. There are too many overlapping and bureaucratic reporting procedures and not enough political ownership.[56]

---

[52] Ibid at 6.
[53] Ibid at 6.
[54] The knowledge society, the internal market, the business climate, the labour market, and environmental sustainability.
[55] Working Together for Growth and Jobs: A New Start for the Lisbon Strategy COM (2005) 24.
[56] See note 56 at 10.

The Lisbon strategy should, the Commission stated, henceforth focus on growth **3.74** and jobs. Europe must make itself more attractive as a place in which to work and invest; policy should be orientated to creating more and better jobs and investment in research and development.

P. The Lisbon Treaty

The Lisbon Treaty—not as yet ratified at the time of writing—will, if ultimately **3.75** ratified, insert a new Article 136a into the EC Treaty which will further consolidate and clarify the role of the social partners in the making of social policy through the Social Dialogue and emphasizing their autonomy in doing so. Article 2c of the amended EC Treaty will provide for the shared competence between the Union and the Member States in 'social policy, for the aspects defined in this Treaty'. This is the first time that a reference has been made in the EC Treaty to shared competence. Shared competence is defined in Article 2a as empowering the Union and the Member States to legislate and adopt legally binding acts. Member States are to exercise their competence to the extent that the Union has not exercised its competence—that competence being of course circumscribed by the limits of their legislative powers as set out in the EC Treaty.

The Union itself, in defining and implementing its policies and activities, will be **3.76** required by Article 5a to take into account requirements linked to the promotion of a high level of employment, the guarantee of adequate social protection, the fight against social exclusion. Article 5b will require the Union, with regard to its policies and activities, to combat discrimination based on sex, race or ethnic origin, religion or belief, disability, age, or sexual orientation.

Q. Conclusion

The current position is that although employment and social policy have gradu- **3.77** ally emerged from the periphery of Community activity to take their place alongside other mainstream Community policies, the emphasis is on employment as the optimal solution to the Community's social ills. This has given rise to a number of legislative measures designed to combat discrimination in employment on the one hand and to bring about adjustments in the workplace to accommodate workers with specific needs such as the disabled. Furthermore, it has been acknowledged that employment and social policy are not to be viewed as ends in themselves but rather as an integral part of Community economic policy and essential to the attainment of the internal market. The Revised Lisbon Strategy advocates two principal objectives: delivering stronger, lasting growth and creating more and better jobs: the dual social policy objectives of the original Lisbon Strategy, modernizing social protection and promoting social inclusion appear to have been dropped, at least from the Lisbon agenda. Although the Commission's work in both areas will continue, they have lost their status as priority objectives.

3.78 As to the place of social and employment policy within the Community legal order, it is of interest to note the dicta of the ECJ in the recent cases of *Viking*[57] and *Laval*[58] on the relationship between the social policy objectives of the EC Treaty and the four freedoms—the foundation stones of the Community:

> Since the Community has thus not only an economic but also a social purpose, the rights under the provisions of the EC Treaty on the free movement of goods, persons, services and capital must be balanced against objectives pursued by social policy, which include, as is clear from the first paragraph of Article 136EC, inter alia, improved living and working conditions, so as to make possible their harmonization while improvement is being made maintained, proper social protection and dialogue between management and labour.[59]

3.79 These judgments appear to state that social policy objectives need to be balanced against the four fundamental economic objectives—the foundation stones of the Community—but it is unclear to what extent. Is the Court requiring the four freedoms to be subject to social policy considerations and vice versa? If this is in fact so this ruling is highly significant and appears to represent a milestone in the development of social policy.

---

[57] Case C-438/05 Judgment of 11 December 2007.
[58] Case C-341/05 Judgment of 11 December 2007.
[59] *Viking* note 57 Judgment para 79; *Laval* note 58 Judgment para 105.

4

POLICY-MAKING

A. Introduction

This chapter is concerned with the formulation of social policy pursuant to Title **4.01**
XI EC Treaty. The process by which the Common Employment Policy, Title VIII
EC Treaty is settled is discussed in Chapter 10.

The policy formation process, from inception to formation and implementa- **4.02**
tion, involves many entities and institutions. Policy initiatives can and do come
from multiple sources: business interests, non-governmental organizations,
the civil society, national governments, the Community institutions, and the
European Council. The judgments of the European Court of Justice can influence policy by clarifying the parameters of the competence of the Community
institutions, within what limits they can act and which policy and legislative
initiatives, both in terms of form and content, are lawful. The European Council
can set policy objectives to be developed by the EC Commission. Alternatively,
they can endorse and support proposals developed by the Commission. Objectives
can be set in Charters adopted by the Member States which can influence policy
on a Community level.

Responsibility for the development and policy, regardless of wherever and at what **4.03**
level the initiative for that comes, lies primarily with the European Commission.
That policy can result in the adoption of Community measures, either binding
or non-binding. Policy can also be made by means of the Social Dialogue or

through the Open Method of Co-ordination (OMC). Both of the latter processes are of relatively recent origin. They are discussed below.

4.04 The formation of policy has involved an increasing number of stakeholders. In the early years of the Community policy formulation was heavily centralized. The 1980s saw the increased and more direct involvement of the social partners through the medium of the Social Dialogue. More recently non-governmental organizations, both national and European, have been given a formal role and have actively participated in policy formation.

B. Policy Formation

4.05 The Commission has primary responsibility for the formulation and articulation of policy. It may go about this in a number of ways and may involve a wide range of interests in the process. In short, the Commission has a wide discretion in the formulation of policy. The sole instance in which consultation is required is where legislation based on Article 137(2) is contemplated, and that consultation is only to be with 'management and labour' by which is meant the European federations of the social partners organized with either at sectoral or cross-sectoral level.[1] Yet despite the dearth of any legal obligation to consult, there appears, in fact, to be consultations, both direct and indirect, of a wide range of interested parties.

4.06 The Commission can launch a general discussion, inviting debate and comment at large. This it can do by means of Green or White papers.

4.07 The concept of Green and White Papers derives from the United Kingdom. A Green paper discuss a particular policy objective launch a consultation process on both that objective and the means whereby it could best be achieved. A White Paper may follow which summarizes the results of the consultation process launched by the Green Paper, draw conclusions and invite further observations.

4.08 The Green Paper has been used by the EC Commission for over twenty-five years as a means of generating public debate and consultation on a given issue or a range of issues. The first Green Paper on Social Policy was published in 1993[2] when the Commission sought a wide-ranging debate on the future direction of social policy, to coincide with the ratification of the Maastricht Treaty.

---

[1] The Commission had listed 57 organizations to be consulted in Annex 1 COM (2002) 341 Final.

[2] Green Paper: European Social Policy. Options for the Union COM (93) 551.

Prior to the publication of the Green Paper it had invited, by way of announce-ment in the Official Journal and letters sent to governments, the social partners, the European Parliament, and the Economic and Social Committee, contribu-tions and comments on the direction of social policy. It was a result of this consultation—to which it received 150 responses—that the decision was taken to a launch a public debate. More recently, the Commission has published a Green Paper on Modernizing Labour to meet the challenges of the 21st century,[3] the stated objective of which is to launch a public debate on how labour law can evolve to support the Lisbon Strategy objectives of achieving sustainable growth with more and better jobs. Over 450 submissions have been received by the Commission to this consultation. Responses have been received from national authorities, trade unions and employers' organizations, as well as legal experts, non-governmental organizations, enterprises and the general public.

Typically a Green Paper will set out the prevailing state of law and policy and the issues it seeks to address. More recently there is a tendency for Green Paper to be more specific, setting out a list of issues which they would like to be addressed during the consultation process. **4.09**

Green Papers are sometimes, but neither often nor inevitably, followed by White Papers.[4] But White Papers may not necessarily be preceded by Green Papers. The first White Paper adopted by the Commission was the seminal White Paper on the Completion of the Internal Market.[5] White Papers set out in more precise terms the Commission's intended course of action on any given issue. They often put forward concrete proposals for legislative initiatives and, in any event, are a fairly precise indication of the Commission's orientation. As opposed to Green Papers they are addressed specifically to Member States and interest groups rather than to the community at large. **4.10**

Action Programmes drawn up by the EC Commission often follow Green and White papers, translating the ideas expressed therein and results of the consulta-tion process into concrete proposals. They go further than Green and White papers in that their objective is neither consultation nor debate. Action Programmes may be independent of any Green or White papers. They are simply a means whereby the Commission set out the steps it intends to take to achieve particular objectives and the time frame within which it will act. The Social **4.11**

---

[3] COM (2006) 798 Final.

[4] Green Paper on European Social Policy: Options for the Union COM (93) 551 was followed by White Paper on European Social Policy: A Way Forward for the Union COM (94) 333.

[5] COM (85) 410 Final.

Action Programme 1973 was one of the first Action Programmes to be adopted.[6] In the final stages of work leading to the adoption of the Community Charter on the Fundamental Social Rights of Workers, the Council invited the Commission to prepare an Action programme for its implementation[7] which was actually published 10 days before final adoption of the Charter.

4.12 Action Programmes are usually for a fixed period in time, the maximum usually being five years with a mid-term review inbuilt, thereby ensuring appropriate flexibility and adaptation of objectives to changing circumstances. Usually the Commission is responsible for the implementation of such programmes but they may involve others, notably the social partners.[8]

4.13 If the ultimate objective of the Commission is implement policy through legislation, it has an obligation to consult with the social partners, by virtue of Article 138 (2). The obligation is loosely worded, as applying to 'proposals in the social policy field'. The Commission has interpreted this restrictively, limiting the consultation process to proposals for legislation only, that is Directives and Regulations.[9] It does not, as a rule, consult on non-binding measures such as action programmes, recommendations or decisions. Moreover, the Commission, in spite of stating that a broad view should be taken of the concept of 'social policy measures',[10] appears to regard the obligation to consult as being confined to measures adopted on the basis of Article 137(2). Thus, for example, it does not appear to regard the obligation to consult as extending to measures whose legal basis lies in Article 141(4) or Article 13.[11] This is not, of course to say, that it will not consult with the social partners on policy issues. It may do so, but the social partners cannot oblige such a consultation.

4.14 The consultation process is discussed more fully in Chapter 5 at paras 5.04–5.09.

---

6 [1974] OJ C12.

7 COM (89) 568 Final.

8 Council Resolution of 21 May 1991 on the third medium term Community Action Programme on equal opportunities for men and women (1991–1995) [1991] OJ L142/1.

9 Commission Communication concerning the Development of the Social Dialogue at Community Level COM (96) 448 Final; Commission Communication 'Adapting and Promoting Social Dialogue at Community Level' COM (98) 322 Final.

10 COM (96) 448 Final Annex 1: the Commission 'signalled the possibility of formal consultations on envisaged proposals for legislation of a horizontal or specific sectoral nature which might have social implications' but it reserved to itself 'the right to decide whether and how such consultation should be conducted'.

11 For example the social partners were not consulted on the Framework Directive 2000/78 on equal treatment in employment and occupation [2000] OJ L78.

C. The Social Dialogue

The Social Dialogue[12] broadly signifies discussion and negotiation between **4.15** the social partners and, in some cases, between them and the Community institutions. It takes a number of forms, and operates on several levels, each of which will be discussed below. The Social Dialogue plays a pivotal role in the development of Community policy.

(1) Origins

The social partners have been involved in Community policy-making since the **4.16** 1960s and 1970s within Advisory Committees, the Standing Committee on Employment, and the Tripartite Conferences aimed at consultation between the Commission, the Council, and the social partners on broad macro-economic and social policy issues. This involvement did not bring about many constructive results as the respective mandates for such dialogue were unclear and there was persistent disagreement on the issue of representivity: which organizations should participate in the dialogue.[13]

The origins of the Social Dialogue, in its present form, can be traced back to **4.17** January 1985 when President Delors invited the chairs and general secretaries of all the national organizations affiliated to the European level organizations of employers and workers to a meeting at Val Duchesse, a castle outside Brussels. His aim was to bring the social partners to the core of European decision making. This was not the beginning of the Social Dialogue but rather an intensification and formalization of its place within the Community decision making process.

The Delors initiative aimed at establishing a bipartite dialogue between both **4.18** sides of industry, in particular on a cross-sectoral level. The Commission was to act as a facilitator in this process. This dialogue was institutionalized by the Single European Act which amended the EC Treaty to include Article 118B:

> ... the Commission shall endeavour to develop the dialogue between management and labour at European level which could, if the two sides consider it desirable, lead to relations based on agreement.

---

[12] See generally Smismans: *Law, Legitimacy and European Governance: functional participation in social regulation* Oxford University Press 2004.

[13] For example, for a period of five years between 1970 and 1975 the Standing Committee on Employment could not meet because of a dispute between management and labour as to its composition.

4.19 In the years immediately following the Single European Act the work of social partners consisted of agreeing upon, and adopting non-binding joint opinions, resolutions and declarations. Whilst these had no legal effect, and little political impact, they were not futile in the sense that they were an important factor in the process of fostering the partnership of employers and employees and harnessing their collective energies towards the realization of economic and social progress within the Community.

4.20 As from 1991 the Social Dialogue moved towards the centre of Community law and policy-making. In an agreement of 31 October 1991 the social partners set out what became the Agreement on Social Policy. This marked the beginning of a much enhanced role for the social partners both in the formulation of policy and in the legislative process. This role, first set out in the Agreement of Social Policy, is now enshrined in Articles 138 and 139 EC.

(2) Three levels

4.21 The Social Dialogue can be either bipartite or tripartite. The bipartite social dialogue consists of (i) the sectoral social dialogue; and (ii) the cross-sectoral social dialogue. The tripartite social dialogue takes place between the social partners and the Community institutions. The Social Dialogue has a twofold purpose: the making of Community policy and law and joint action and negotiation between the social partners leading to agreement between them.

The Sectoral Social Dialogue

4.22 The Social Dialogue, at sectoral level, has its origins in a myriad of joint Committees many of which dated back to the 1960s. They functioned mainly as consultative bodies for the Commission, adopting sectoral agreements and issuing joint opinions which were vague and of little practical impact.

4.23 In the mid-1990s the Commission decided to consult the social partners on the future development of the sectoral dialogue which had become an excessively costly exercise and suffered from problems relating to the identification of representative organizations within sectors.[14] Following this consultation, the Commission adopted a decision in 1998 abolishing the joint committees and informal working groups which had grown up in a rather ad hoc and chaotic manner, and instituting in their stead a general framework for Sectoral Dialogue Committees.[15] The maximum number of committee members was settled at 40,

---

[14] COM (96) 448 Final.
[15] Commission Decision 98/500 on the establishment of Sectoral Dialogue Committees [1998] OJ L225.

of whom only 30 can receive reimbursement for their expenses in participating in meeting. The Committee has to meet at least once a year.

The issues of representivity was resolved. Membership was to be drawn from **4.24** sectoral partners' organizations operating at European level as opposed to national level which was the case with the Joint Committees. The social partner organizations must apply to the EC Commission in order to participate in the dialogue on a European level. Organization must satisfy a number of criteria to be admitted to a committee:

  (i) they must relate to a specific sector or sectors organized at a European level;
 (ii) they must be recognized as part of a Member State's social partner structure, have the competence to negotiate agreements, and they must be representative of all the Member States as far as is possible;
(iii) they must have adequate structures to ensure their participation in the work of the committees.

Although the role of the Sectoral Dialogue Committees is mainly that of autono- **4.25** mous dialogue between management and labour, leading in some cases to agreement, many of the European social partners' organizations consulted under the two stage consultation procedure provided for under Article 138 EC are sectoral organizations

There are, at present, some thirty Sectoral Dialogue Committees established **4.26** in a multiplicity of areas ranging from agriculture to private security and telecommunications.[16]

The Commission is apparently of the view that the sectoral dialogue is the proper **4.27** level for discussions on many issues linked to employment, such as working conditions, vocational training and industrial change, the knowledge society demographic patterns and globalization.[17]

Independently of the role accorded to the social dialogue under Articles 138 EC, **4.28** the social partners can negotiate freely on any subject they chose and can negotiate European wide agreements on issues which are not within Community competence. Articles 138 simply accords them a particular role within the Community policy: it does not compromise any other function or duties that they may have. Article 139 provides that should management and labour so desire the dialogue with them at Community level may lead to contractual relations including agreements.

---

[16] A list is set out at Annex 2 of a Commission Communication: The European Social Dialogue: a force for innovative change. COM (2002) 321 Final.
[17] Ibid.

4.29　The Sectoral Dialogue has resulted in the adoption of approximately 300 texts which take a variety of forms ranging from joint opinions to guidelines, codes of conduct and agreements. In addition they undertake many transnational joint projects such as the organization of studies, conferences and the publication of information on diverse subjects such as vocational training, health and safety and public procurement practices.

4.30　This development marks a new phase in the evolution of the Social Dialogue. It is characterized by more autonomy on the part of the social partners leading to a broader range of agreements, both as regards type and subject matter and implementation. Mechanisms for autonomous implementation have been built into such agreements, with in some cases, the European Sectoral Dialogue Committee being entrusted with the task of evaluating at given intervals, the application of an agreement.

4.31　These agreements are not part of the Community legal order. Their effect, in terms of rights and obligations which they create, is determined by the signatories themselves and national law and practice.[18] But should the social partners decide, and provided the terms of the agreement in question come within the sphere of Community competence set out in Article 137 EC, the parties can request the at the agreement be adopted by a Council decision and so become part of Community law.[19]

4.32　Collective agreements, which are not the subject of a Council decision and therefore do not have Community law status, can be fairly said to be part of Community policy in the sense that the process by which they come into being is sanctioned by Article 139 EC Treaty and they are viewed as an appropriate and, in some cases a preferred method, of bringing about Community objectives. In that sense they are comparable to the National Action Plans which result from the OMC process discussed below, both being a devolution of policy formation from centralized institutions and processes to other levels.

4.33　Sectoral agreements may be a means of implementing the substance of Directives in sectors to which they are not applicable having been excluded as a result of their specific characteristics. For example, sectoral agreements implementing the principles of the Working Time Directive[20] to the sectors of sea transport,

---

[18] Note 12 at 322.

[19] This appears to be the position even if consultations were not initiated by the Commission COM (98) 322 Final.

[20] Directive 2003/88 [2003] OJ L299/9.

railways, and civil aviation were adopted in 1998.[21] The agreements in sector of civil aviation and sea transport have been implemented by Council directives.[22]

Cross-sector Social Dialogue

The cross-sector organizations participate in the consultation procedure and can, if they wish, enter to negotiations with a view to reaching an agreement, which may be become part of Community law. **4.34**

In 1993 the Commission carried out a study in order to understand how representivity within the Social Dialogue was achieved on national level and how that process could be transposed onto a Community level for the purpose of established which social partners should participate in the consultative process under Article 138 (2). It published the main findings of this study in a Communication.[23] **4.35**

The study found. that national practice was so diverse and varied that no single model could be replicated at European level. Accordingly the Commission concluded 'only the organizations themselves are in a position to develop their own dialogue and negotiating structure'. At the same time it indicated that formal consultation would be undertaken only with those social partners who met the following criteria: **4.36**

they must be cross industry or relate to specific sectors or categories and be organized at European Level;

- they must consist of organizations which are themselves an integral and recognized part of the Member States social partners structures and with the capacity to negotiate agreements and which are representative of all Member States as far as possible;
- they must have adequate structures to enable them to ensure effective participation in the consultative process.[24]

The Communication specified a list of 44 organizations which met these criteria. This list was subsequently updated to include 57 organizations.[25] **4.37**

---

[21] Directive 1999/63 [1999] OJ L167/37; Directive 1999/95 [2000] OJ L14/29; Directive 2000/79 [2000] OJ L302/57. See paras 22.100–22.102.
[22] Directive 2000/79 [2000] OJ L302/57; Directive 1999/63 [1999] OJ L167/37.
[23] COM (93) 600 Final.
[24] Ibid point 24.
[25] COM (2002) Final 341 Annex 1.

4.38 The cross-sectoral social dialogue has resulted in three framework agreements which have been incorporated into the Community legal order by Council Directive.[26]

4.39 As is the case with the sectoral dialogue, the cross-sectoral social partners are increasingly acting independently of the Commission. They are actively setting their own agenda and work programme rather than simply responding to Commission initiatives.

4.40 Recommendations made autonomously within the cross-sectoral dialogue have become known as 'new generation' texts which are:

> . . . characterized by the fact that the European social partners make recommendations to their members and the social partners undertake to follow them up on a national level.[27]

4.41 The first new generation text was the Framework of Actions on Lifelong Development of Competencies and Qualifications in March 2002. this was followed by the Framework Agreement on Teleworking in July 2002 and the Framework Agreement on Work Related Stress in October 2004.

4.42 The Commission has put forward the argument that autonomous agreements need to be divided into two categories:

(i) those which are initiated, negotiated, and implemented by the social partners themselves, entirely independently of the Commission; and

(ii) those which, although negotiated and implemented by the social partners were actually initiated by a consultation of the Commission under Article 138EC.[28]

In the case of the latter the Commission claims the right to assess the agreement to see if it fulfils the Community objective which was the basis for the consultation. It will therefore seek to assess the autonomous agreement on the basis of the same criteria which it uses when assessing agreements put forward by it for adoption by Council decision. Additionally it will monitor the implementation of the agreement.

---

[26] Directive 1999/70 on fixed term work [1999] OJ L175/43; Directive 97/81 on part-time work [1998] OJ L14/9; Directive 1999/63 on the organization of working time for seafarers [1999] OJ L167/33.

[27] Partnership for Change in an Enlarged Europe—Enhancing the Contribution of the European Social Dialogue COM (2004) Final at 13.

[28] Ibid 557 Final at 4.4.

In 2004 the Commission published a Communication[29] setting out how the **4.43** Social Dialogue could be made more effective. It was particularly critical of the new generation texts of the cross-sector social dialogue, discussed below. which they found to contain 'imprecise and vague follow-up provisions'[30] which hindered effective follow-up on a national level. The Commission urged the social partners to 'improve the clarity of their texts and to include detailed follow up provisions in their new generation texts'. It advised the establishment of a framework to help improve the consistency of the social dialogue process and improve transparency. Whilst the preferred approach would be for the social partners to negotiate their own framework, by way of assistance the Commission set out in Annex 2 to the Communication a typology in which it identified four categories of Social Dialogue instruments. It encouraged the social partners, for the sake of clarity and improvement of follow-up, to classify their texts according to this typology in the future. A further annex set out a drafting checklist of optimal features for new generation texts. Two further annexes set out the Sectoral Social Dialogue Committees by sector, composition, and date of creation and a list of the social partner organizations consulted under Article 138 EC.

The Tripartite Dialogue

The Tripartite Social Dialogue takes place within the Tripartite Social Summit **4.44** for Growth and Employment, established by a decision of the Council in March 2003,[31] thereby formalizing a practice instituted in 1997.

The Tripartite Social Summit consists of the Council Presidency, the two subse- **4.45** quent Presidencies, the Commission and the social partners. The social partners' representatives consist of two delegations comprising 10 workers' representatives and 10 employer's representatives. The task of the summit is to ensure the continuous consultation between the Council, the Commission, and the social partners.

D. Open Method of Co-ordination

The term 'Open Method of Co-ordination' was first used at the Lisbon European **4.46** Council meeting in March 2000. However, the process itself is somewhat older,

---

[29] Partnership for Change in an Enlarged Europe—Enhancing the Contribution of European Social Dialogue COM (2004) 557 Final.

[30] Ibid para 3.1.

[31] Council Decision establishing a Tripartite Social Summit for Growth and Employment [2003] OJ L70/13.

having been established by the Maastricht Treaty as an instrument to co-ordinate national macro-economic policies through the Broad Economic Guidelines (BEGS)[32] and to make recommendations to the European Council. It was extended, albeit in a different form, by the Treaty of Amsterdam to the common employment policy.

4.47 The OMC is characterized by respect for diversity and subsidiarity. The diversity and autonomy of national social and economic policies is respected whilst at the same time they are moulded towards agreed common objectives which are realized on a national level.

4.48 OMC is a fourfold process:

- ... fixing guidelines for the union combined with specific timetables for achieving goals in the short, medium and long term;
- establishing where appropriate, quantitative and qualitative indicators and benchmarks tailored to the needs of different member States and sectors as a means of establishing best practice;
- translating these European Guidelines into national and regional policies by setting specific targets;
- periodic monitoring, evaluation and peer review against a mutual learning process.[33]

4.49 This methodology departs from the traditional mutually exclusive alternatives of Community-level action or national action towards a combination of both. The OMC has been used in a growing number of policy areas[34] including social exclusion, pensions, education, health care, research and development, and immigration policy. These areas are typified by a lack of specific Community competence in the EC Treaty.

4.50 OMC[35] is thus seen as a means whereby the Community can harness national policy to Community objectives in spheres where it would otherwise have little

---

[32] Articles 98–104 EC Treaty.

[33] Presidency Conclusions point 37.

[34] Prompting the observation that it 'knows no bounds'. Kenner: *EU Employment Law: From Rome to Amsterdam and Beyond* Hart Publishing 2003 at 485.

[35] The OMC has generated a huge body of both academic and official literature, most of which is available at the website of the university of Wisconsin at Madison: <http://eucenter.wisc.edu/OMC>. See in particular Heidenreich and Bischoff: 'The open method of co-ordination' (2008) 46 Journal of Common Market Studies 497–532; de la Rosa: 'The Open Method of Co-ordination in the new Member States—The Perspectives for its use as a Tool of Soft Law' (2005) 11 European Law Journal 618–41; Hodson and Maher: 'The open method as a new mode of governance: The case of soft economic policy co-ordination' (2001) 39 Journal of Common Market Studies 719–46; Trubek and Trubek: 'Hard and Soft Law in the Construction of Social Europe: the Role of the Open Method of Co-ordination' (2004) 11 European Law Journal 343–64; Scott and Trubek: 'Mind the gap: law and new approaches to governance in the European Union' (2002) 8 European Law Journal 1–18.

or no influence. It entails the implementation of commonly agreed objectives by the Member States through domestic policy and legislation.

The Lisbon European Council emphasized the importance of the OMC process **4.51** in decentralizing policy-making to include local and regional government, the social partners, civil society bodies, and corporate and individual interests. It thus includes a wider range of actors and interests than the traditional Community law and policy-making processes.[36]

However, the level of involvement of these entities and interests is left to each **4.52** Member State with the result that the range and level of participation in policy formation has not been uniformly realized; participation is determined by national practice, the OMC being perceived as having no tangible influence on the issue.

The White Paper on European Governance,[37] published in July 2001, empha- **4.53** sized that the OMC should be a complement rather than a replacement for Community action. It should not be used when legislative action under the Community method was possible.[38] The European Parliament should not be excluded from the OMC process; a regular mechanism for reporting to Parliament should be established. The OMC should be used to achieve defined Treaty objectives and should not dilute the achievement of those objectives nor the responsibility of the Community institutions. The Commission should be involved in a co-ordinating capacity. The data and information generated from the process should be widely available and it should be used to determine whether legislative or programme based action is needed to overcome particular problems which have been highlighted.[39]

The OMC processes are not identical in the spheres in which they operate. There **4.54** is no single 'open method'. It is a process which broadly shares a number of characteristics including EU-wide objective, national actions plans, and peer

---

[36] de Burca: 'The Constitutional Challenge of New Governance in the European Union' (2003) 28 European Law Journal 814–39 at 835.

[37] COM (2001) 428 Final.

[38] Discussions within the European Convention which lead to the now-abandoned Constitution of Europe were divided on the merits of the OMC. There was opposition to the OMC by those who feared that it would pre-empt opportunities for hard legislation. 'In such a view, the OMC is like a virus that needs to be quarantined before it infects the whole community. If it were let loose in areas of existing legislative competence, it would sap the EU's will and capacity to do what really needs to be done, which is to pass uniform, binding and justiciable laws.' Trubek and Trubek: 'Hard and Soft Law in the Construction of Social Europe: the Role of the Open Method of Co-ordination' (2005) 11 European Law Journal 343–64 at 355.

[39] Ibid at 22.

review, but with 'variations and distinctive features according to the particular policy area'[40] in which it operates.[41] It provides no sanctions for Member States which do not follow the guidelines established and does not given rise to any justiciable rights. For example, the OMC in social inclusion does not have specific guidelines, reporting and plan revision is on a two-year, rather than a one-year cycle, and there is no provision for EU recommendations. The OMC on pensions is even more informal and open-ended.

4.55 Although it has become the dominant policy-making tool in the social policy area its effectiveness had not yet been proven.

4.56 The Kok report[42] on the Lisbon Strategy, published in November 2004, found that the Open Method of Co-ordination had 'fallen short of expectations' and proposed 'a radical improvement of the process'.[43] The revised Lisbon Strategy accordingly recommended a single reporting structure which it said would 'greatly simplify the myriad of existing reports under the Open Method of Co-ordination, which the Commission will review'.[44]

4.57 The OMC process is new to Community governance. Its dynamics are difficult to understand and it has inherent weaknesses. Its results are difficult to measure. There are no sanctions for non-compliance with the guidelines and standards it sets. Although it is not possible to say whether it is or may be successful in its aims,[45] it is clear that it engages debate on a number of issues common to the Member States, which would not otherwise take place. That in itself is beneficial. It is also a means of determining areas in which legislative initiative may be appropriate. Most importantly the OMC brings together a wide range of interests whose voice might not otherwise be heard.

E. The Social Agenda

4.58 The Commission sets out its agenda for social policy on a five-yearly basis. It is submitted to the European Parliament and endorsed by the European Council

---

[40] de Burca: note 36 at 828.

[41] Note 35 at 351.

[42] Facing the Challenge: The Lisbon Strategy for growth and employment. November 2004.

[43] Ibid at 43.

[44] COM (2005) 24 at 31.

[45] The Commission in a Communication of 2 July 2008 'A renewed commitment to social Europe: Reinforcing the Open Method of Coordination for Social Protection and Social Inclusion.' COM (2008) 418 Final whilst acknowledging the value and the inherent difficulties of the Social OMC process concluded at 2 that '. . . more can and should be done to make full use of the Social OMC'.

The agenda can be described as a mapping exercise: the Commission sets out what it hopes to achieve in the employment and social fields on multiples, levels ranging from putting forward legislative proposals to reflection and policy formulation.

Midway through the five-year period of the Social Agenda, the Commission car- **4.59** ries out a review, taking stock of what has been achieved and what remains to be done to attain the objectives it has set itself. The mid-term review enables the Commission to respond to and shape policy to meet new challenges which have risen since the beginning of the five-year term of the agenda. For example, the Social Agenda for the term 2000–2005 was the subject of a mid-term review at the beginning of June 2003[46] which took account of the changes in the economic and political environment which had occurred since 2000, resulting in an economic slowdown, geo-political instability, and a vulnerability to external circumstances.

The current Social Agenda, 2006–2010,[47] adopted by the Commission in **4.60** February 2005[48] and endorsed by the European Council in December 2006, differs from its predecessors, which were characterized by a commitment to a specific catalogue of initiatives. This Agenda is more loosely formulated, setting out policy objectives rather than making any commitment to concrete measures. It has two key priorities:

(i) employment; and
(ii) fighting poverty and promoting equal opportunities.

With respect to employment, the Agenda will focus on getting more, particularly women, into jobs, updating labour law to address new forms of work and managing restructuring through the Social Dialogue. On the poverty and equal opportunities front, the focus is to be on the ageing population, its impact both on the labour market and on welfare systems, and in supporting the Member States in reforming pensions and on tackling discrimination against ethnic minorities and fostering equal opportunities for men and women. Policy priorities are articulated but there little to indicate how and within what time scale they will be achieved.

---

[46] COM (2003) 312 Final.
[47] COM (2005) 12.
[48] COM (2005) 33 Final.

5

THE LEGISLATIVE PROCESS

A. Introduction

This chapter sketches how social and employment legislation is made. Article **5.01**
249 EC provides for three types of legislative measure: regulations, directives,
decisions. Such measures have binding legal force.

Legislative measures in the social and employment area usually take the form of **5.02**
directives, the exceptions being the European Company Statute,[1] the Statute
for a European Co-operative Society, both of which were adopted by means of
regulations,[2] and the regulations on the protection of the social security rights
of the employed and self-employed moving within the Community.[3]

B. Directives

A distinction needs to be drawn between directives adopted under Articles 13, **5.03**
141, 94, and 305 EC and those adopted under Article 137 EC. In the case of the
former, directives come into being through the classic Community legislative

---

[1] Regulation 2157/2001 on a Statute for a European Company ('SE') [2001] OJ L294/21.
[2] Regulation 1435/2003 on a Statute for a European Co-operative Society (SCE Statute).
[3] Regulation 1408/71 [1971] OJ Sp Ed (11) 46; as repealed and replaced by Regulation 883/2004 [2004] OJ L200/1; Regulation 574/72 [1972] OJ Sp Ed (1) 159. Proposals for the adoption of a regulation to replace Regulation 574/72 have been adopted by the EC Commission on 31 January 2006. COM (2006) 10 Final.

process set out in Article 251 EC, subject to any more specific provisions set out in the Treaty. In the case of Directives whose legal basis derives from Article 137, there is a choice of legislative method: either the classic legislative method can be used or a framework agreement made by the social partners which can be brought within the Community legal order by means of a measure adopted by the Council, which is usually, but not required to be, a directive.[4] There is thus a shared legislative competence which is unique to this area of Community law.

5.04 Both legislative avenues involve a consultation of the social partners. Before drawing up any legislative proposal the Commission must consult the legislative partners as to the desirability of the measure in question.[5] If, following this consultation, the Commission proceeds to draw up a proposal, a further consultation with the social partners must take place before the proposal is submitted to the Council. The consultations relate to 'proposals in the social policy field'.[6] The Commission has given a restrictive approach to the scope of this duty, by confining it to consultations on regulations or directives only. Proposals for decisions or other instruments are not subject to the consultation procedure. Although the Commission has stated that the concept of 'social policy field' should be interpreted broadly to include the possibility of formal consultations on legislative proposals of a horizontal or specific sectoral nature which have social implications, it would appear that it regards the duty to consult as specified in Article 138 as being confined to proposals whose legal basis is Article 137. For example, the Commission did not consult the social partners on the Framework Directive on Equal Treatment in Employment and Occupation,[7] which was based on Article 13 EC.

5.05 The first consultation can be in writing or by way of an ad hoc meeting. The consultation period should not exceed six weeks.[8] The second consultation requires the social partners to deliver an opinion in writing, in the form of a recommendation or an opinion, on the content of the proposal. This second consultation period should not normally exceed six weeks[9] The Commission is under no obligation to accept the views of the social partners.

---

[4] Art 139 (2).

[5] Art 138(2).

[6] Commission Communication concerning the development of the Social Dialogue at Community Level COM (96) 448 Final at point 56; Commission Communication: Adapting and Promoting the Social Dialogue at Community level COM (98) 322 Final at 3.3.

[7] Directive 2000/78 [2000] OJ L193/82.

[8] Commission Communication on the Application of the Social Agreement COM (93) 600 Final at point 9.

[9] Ibid at point 19.

C. The Legislative Role of the Social Partners

In the course of such consultations management and labour may inform the **5.06** Commission of their wish to implement the proposal in question by means of an agreement, concluded between them at Community level, in accordance with the procedure set out in Article 138. There is no obligation on the Commission to accede to such a request, but it would be unusual if it did not. In fact it is sometimes the Commission which takes the initiative in suggesting that a particular matter might be best dealt with by way of a collective agreement, but the social partners have on occasion been unable to agree to such a request.[10]

Up until 1998 it had been assumed that only agreements which were made fol- **5.07** lowing consultations with the Commission could be implemented by Council Decision. The Commission, in that year, made clear in a communication that agreements between the social partners which had not been the subject of any prior consultation could also be implemented by Council decision.[11]

If the social partners decide to proceed by way of a framework agreement, that **5.08** agreement should be made within nine months, unless management and labour on the one hand, and the Commission on the other, decide jointly to extend that period. Given the normal period for the adoption of legislation by the Community institutions under the classic legislative method, nine months appears to be an unjustifiably short period and might perhaps explain why such agreements are often of poorer quality than the classic directive.

If the social partners cannot reach an agreement within the nine-month period, **5.09** as extended as the case may be, the Commission can proceed by way of the classic legislative method set out in Article 251 EC, modified or supplemented by specific Treaty provisions.

D. Implementation of Collective Agreements

Agreements concluded by the social partners may be implemented either (i) in **5.10** accordance with the procedures and practices specific to management and labour and the Member States, or, (ii) where the matter is amongst those covered by

---

[10] For example on information and consultation within the European Works Councils COM (96) 448 (see note 6 above) at 24.

[11] COM (98) 322 Final.

Article 137, at the joint request of the signatory parties, by a Council decision on a proposal from the Commission.

5.11 Before presenting a proposal for the implementation of a collective agreement to the Council, the Commission will verify a number of factors inherent in the Community legislative process[12] namely:

(i) whether the agreement falls within Article 137 EC in the sense that it contributes to the realization of the social aims defined in that provision;

(ii) the legality of clauses in the agreement;

(iii) compliance with the provisions protecting SMEs;

(iv) compatibility with the principles of subsidiarity and proportionality.

5.12 The Commission will set out its assessment in an Explanatory Memorandum which is attached to the proposal for the implementation of the agreement. The Commission will also express its view of the agreement in the light of existing Community policies and needs and state whether it endorses its aims.

5.13 Agreements which are settled by means of collective bargaining carried out in accordance with the practices and procedures of the Member States, have no more force than is provided for under national law, with the result that such agreements have varying effects throughout the Community, and in some Member States may not be legally enforceable at all or only to a limited extent.[13] National social partners' organizations transpose such agreements within the industrial relations systems available to them at national level. There is no Community mechanism available for transposition. This was made clear in the Declaration to Article 139(2) EC attached to the Treaty of Amsterdam:

> . . . the High Contracting Parties declare that the first of the arrangements for application of agreements between management and labour at Community level— referred to in Article 139 (2)—will consist in developing, by collective bargaining, according to the rules of each Member State, the content of the agreements . . .

5.14 In the case of agreements implemented by way of Council decision, the European Parliament is not consulted. In general, the Council will act by qualified majority save when the agreement contains one or more provisions relating to one of the areas for which unanimity is required pursuant to Article 137(2), for example social security or employment termination protection.

---

[12] Smismans: 'The European social dialogue between constitutional and labour law' (2007) 32 EL Rev 341 at 351.

[13] COM (93) 600 Final point 37. Foden and Paris: 'Nature, Implementation and Control of Agreements' in *The European Dimension of Collective Bargaining after Maastricht* European Trade Union Institute 1992 at 100–1.

Agreements made between management and labour have, up to the present, been **5.15** adopted by means of directives only. Agreements adopted by the Council are part of the Community legal order.

Where management and labour wish to implement an agreement made between **5.16** them by means of a Council decision, they are in effect just using the Community's legislative machinery to endow those agreements with the legal standing which they might not otherwise have. This means that neither the Commission nor the Council are empowered to change the terms of such an agreement. The Council may decline to adopt the agreement in the terms presented to it. The Commission may even advise it to do so. But the Commission cannot refuse to forward the agreement to the Council when requested to do so—its role is simply that of a postbox.

If the Council decide not to implement an agreement concluded by the social **5.17** partners, the Commission will withdraw its proposal. It may then proceed to get the measure adopted by the classic legislative method.[14]

E. Implementation of Directives by Collective Agreements

Article 137(3) provides that a Member State may entrust management and **5.18** labour, at their joint request, with the implementation of directives adopted pursuant to that article. That in itself is not new, although the Treaty of Amsterdam institutionalized the process. Member States have always been free to implement directives in any way they please, including by means of legally binding collective agreement.

Since directives are addressed to the Member States, it is they who are ultimately **5.19** responsible for their execution.[15] Article 137(2) emphasizes this point, stating that where directives are to be implemented by means of collective agreements, these should be introduced no later than the date on which the directive must be transposed and the Member State concerned is 'required to take any necessary measures enabling it to be in a position to guarantee the results imposed by that directive'. The collective agreement must be legally binding and generally

---

[14] COM (93) 600 Final points 41 and 42.
[15] Case 143/83 *Commission v Denmark* [1985] ECR 417. Judgment para 8. See generally Wedderburn: 'Inderogability, Collective Agreements and Community Law' (1992) 21 ILJ 245–64 at 251–8.

applicable. Any collective agreement which does not have binding legal effects or which does not extend to all those sections of the population to which the directive is intended to apply will not be considered an adequate implementation of it and the Member State in question will be considered to have defaulted in its Community obligations.

PART II

SOCIAL POLICY

6

SOCIAL SECURITY

A. Introduction

Social security systems are traditionally viewed as being within the exclusive **6.01** competence of the particular state under whose laws and practices they are organized.[1] It is that state which determines the nature and content of its social security system: the range of benefits, the rate at which they are paid, the methods of financing those benefits, and conditions of eligibility.[2] Social security systems are thus essentially territorial: they relate to persons in, and events occurring within, the territory of a particular country. They do not, therefore, generally recognize social security rights acquired under the laws of other countries, nor do they make benefits available to those resident outside their particular national territory.

Member States jealously guard their sovereignty in the sphere of social security **6.02** and for understandable reasons. Welfare, its financing and organization are politically sensitive issues. Welfare provision reflects the values and mores of the society of which it is a product. Any welfare system is a prism of the society in which it

---

[1] 'Welfare States are National States' de Swaan: 'Perspectives for Transnational Social Policy'. (1992) 27(1) Government and Opposition 33–51 at 33.
[2] Case C-238/92 *Duphar* [1984] ECR 523; Case C-70/95 *Sodemare* [1997] ECR I–3395.

operates. Citizens are prepared to finance, through insurance contributions and taxes, the society in which they wish to live. They are simply not willing to fund welfare provision elsewhere. And the Member States realize that nothing is more unpopular than outward flows of welfare provision beyond national territory.

6.03 However, the essentially territorial nature of national social security systems can be an impediment to the realization of objectives which lie at the heart of the Community, and to the extent that they do, the sovereignty of Member States has been the subject of a degree of erosion. In other words social security is subject to requirements of the internal market such as the free movement of goods and services. The reconciliation of national sensitivity on welfare issues and wider Community objectives is difficult.

6.04 Not all of this tension was obvious in the early days of the Community and, for many years, the Member States remained secure in the belief that their welfare systems remained by and large outside the ambit of Community competence except to the extent that specific (and carefully circumscribed) competence had been granted under the EC Treaty.

6.05 This position has changed as from the mid-1990s, at which point in time the European Court of Justice made clear the obligation of Member States to ensure that national social security systems operated in compliance with, and further-ance of, the requirements of the internal market relating to the free movement of goods and services. The Court took the view that, apart from the limitations written into the EC Treaty itself, applied restrictively, and in accordance with the general principles of law, nothing should stand in the way of the achievement of the internal market. National social security systems are not inviolable: they must respect Treaty objectives and to that extent Member States' competence is limited. In general, this has meant a breaking down of the territorial scope of social security systems and a requirement to eliminate discrimination within those systems on the grounds of sex or race.

6.06 The emergence of the European citizen has further eroded national sovereignty, in that benefits traditionally reserved for the nationals or residents of a Member State or to the economically active non-nationals exercising their right to free movement, may be required to be made available in certain circumstances to the European citizen.[3] These circumstances, first elaborated by the ECJ, have now been set out in Directive 2004/38 on the rights of citizens of the Union and their

---

[3] Case C-85/96 *Martinez Sala* [1998] ECR I–2691; Case C-184/99 *Grezelczck* [2001] ECR I–6193; Case C-224/98 [2002] ECR I–6191; Case C-456/02 *Trojani* [2004] ECR I–7573; Case C-138/02 *Collins* [2004] ECR I–5547.

family members to move and reside freely within the territory of a Member State,[4] Article 24 of which provides that Member States are not obliged:

> . . . to confer entitlement to social assistance during the first three months of resi-
> dence . . . nor shall it be obliged, prior to acquisition of the right of permanent
> residence, to grant further aid for studies . . . consisting in student grants or student
> loans to persons other than workers, self-employed persons, persons who retain such
> status and members of their families.

Permanent residence is acquired by Union citizens after a continuous period of residence of five years in the host Member State.[5]   **6.07**

Monetary union further constrains the discretion of Member States in the organ-   **6.08** ization and financing of their social security systems. It may no longer be possible to pump funds at discretion into welfare at times of economic downturn given the necessary budgetary discipline required to meet the convergence criteria.

In the context of the social security rights of the migrant economically active,   **6.09** which will be outlined below, the case law of the ECJ has given rise to concern in that, in recent years its broad interpretation of social security rights both from the point of view of the persons entitled to benefits and the range of benefits for which they are eligible, appears to have extended this body of rights beyond previously perceived boundaries.[6] Potential classes of beneficiaries have been enlarged; territorial boundaries previously taken to be the outward limit of enti-tlement have been torn down.[7]

This gradual erosion of their sovereignty in the domain of welfare has caused the   **6.10** Member States considerable concern. A distortion between rights and obliga-tions between beneficiaries and social security institutions is leading to a mismatch between those entitled to benefits and those who fund those benefits.

---

[4] [2004] OJ L158/77.

[5] Art 16.

[6] Hailbronner: 'Union Citizenship and Access to Social Benefits' (2005) 42 CML Rev 1245–67; Hatzopoulous: 'A (More) Social Europe: A Political Crossroads or a Legal One way? Dialogue between Luxembourg and Lisbon' (2005) 42 CML Rev 1599; Watson: 'Recent Case law of the European Court of Justice on Social Security: a step too far?' in Maija Sakslin (ed) *Free Movement for All—a Challenge for Social Security* Kelan tutkimusosasto, Helsinki forthcom-ing 2009.

[7] The position is well summed up by Leibfried and Pierson: 'Social Policy: Left to Judges and Markets?' in Wallace and Pollack: *Policy Making in the European Union* Fifth Edition Oxford University Press 2005, Chapter 10 at 269–75; 'Territorial sovereignty in social policy so conven-tional wisdom holds, is alive and well. We disagree . . . national welfare states remain the primary institutions of European social policy, but they do so in the context of an increasingly constraining multi-tiered polity.'

This mismatch may, in the long term, result in financial and administrative disequilibrium which could threaten the foundations of some systems.[8]

6.11 This anxiety, on the part of the Member States, to ensure the financial equilibrium of their welfare systems has manifested itself in the proposal for the addition of the following paragraph to Article 42 EC:

> Where a member of the Council declares that a draft legislative act . . . would affect important aspects of the social security system, including its scope, cost or financial structure, or would affect the financial balance of that system, it may request the matter to be referred to the European Council. In that case, the ordinary legislative procedure shall be suspended. After discussion, the European Council shall, within four months of this suspension, either:
> (a) refer the draft back to the Council, which shall terminate the suspension of the ordinary legislative procedure;
> (b) take no action or request the Commission to submit a new proposal; in that case the act originally proposed shall be deemed not to have been adopted.

6.12 Quite what this provision, if adopted, will lead to, in practical terms, is difficult to envisage. Obviously it is designed to give the Member States some power of veto over legislative proposals but, given that such legislation is designed to give effect to the free movement of workers, a right derived from the EC Treaty itself, and, in many cases, implements, in practical terms, principles enunciated in the case law of the ECJ, its purpose is not apparent.[9] Where legislative proposals are designed to give effect to case law and are thus a mere codifying exercise, to abandon them will not have any substantive effect as their provisions are derived from case law and that case law will remain binding upon the Member States. The same reasoning applies to legislation which has as its objective the implementation of EC Treaty provisions. In fact, such a proposed amendment may be completely counter-productive in the sense that to restrain legislative initiative designed to implement, in a coherent practical manner, the case law of the ECJ or EC Treaty provisions is going to cause administrative difficulties and uncertainties and generate more requests for preliminary rulings from courts and tribunals unclear as to the meaning and application of particular judgments, within the context of their social welfare schemes.

6.13 This chapter will set out the provisions of Community law relating to social security, discuss the role of the Community in shaping national social security systems through the Open Method of Co-ordination (OMC) and other policy-making initiatives.

---

[8] Scarf MPIFG Working Paper 02/08 Max Planck Institute for the Study of Societies. Cologne. July 2002 at 11.

[9] Each year the Commission proposes what is commonly referred to as a 'sweeping regulation' which reflects and codifies case law of the ECJ and national developments.

B. Treaty Provisions

Social security is the subject of two provisions in the EC Treaty: Article 42 in Title   **6.14**
III 'Free Movement of Persons, Services and Capital' and Article 137 in Title XI
'Social Policy, Education, Vocational Training and Youth'.

Article 42 of the EC Treaty provides for the adoption by the Council, acting   **6.15**
unanimously, of '. . . such measures in the field of social security as are necessary
to provide for the freedom of movement for workers; to this end, it shall make
arrangements to secure for migrant workers and their dependants:

    (a) aggregation, for the purposes of acquiring and retaining the right to benefit and
         of calculating the amount of benefit, of all periods taken into account under the
         laws of the several countries;
    (b) payment of benefits to persons resident in the territories of Member States.

The wording of this provision has remained unchanged since the original EC   **6.16**
Treaty was adopted in 1957.

Article 137(1) provides that the Community   **6.17**

    . . . shall support and complement the activities of the Member States in the follow-
    ing fields . . .
    . . .
    (c) social security and social protection of workers
    . . .
    (k) the modernization of social protection schemes without prejudice to (c).

Article 137(2)(b) and (c) provide that directives may be adopted by unanimous   **6.18**
vote to implement the objective set out in Article 137(1)(c), but these must have
regarded to the 'conditions and technical rules obtaining in each of the Member
States'. Any directives are therefore subject to two limitations:

   (i) they must respect the principle of subsidiarity, and
  (ii) they can only concern social welfare schemes for workers.

This latter requirement is somewhat of an anomaly given that it is becoming less   **6.19**
common for social security schemes to be addressed to workers as opposed to
wider groups of the population or indeed the population at large.

In the case of Article 137(1)(k), the modernization of social security schemes,   **6.20**
'measures' without further definition, may be adopted to encourage co-operation
between the Member States but any harmonization of the laws and regulations of
the Member States are excluded. Presumably the term 'measures' does not include
directives since Article 137(2)(b) specifically excludes the possibility of directives
being adopted to modernize social protection schemes. Article 137(4) provides
that measures adopted under that provision.

... shall not affect the right of Member States to define the fundamental principles of their social security systems and must not significantly affect the financial equilibrium thereof.

C. Legislation

(1) Equal treatment: men and women

6.21   Directive 79/7 on the progressive implementation of the principle of equal treatment for men and women in matters of social security[10] was adopted on 23 November 1978 with an unusually lengthy implementation period of six years, the normal period at that time being two years. It has been the subject of a substantial body of case law.

6.22   The Directive establishes the principle of equal treatment in state social security systems with respect to benefits for risks specified therein. It applies to the working population only, a concept generously interpreted by the ECJ. The Directive has multiple exceptions, generally with respect to those benefits and situations where discrimination is most commonly found. It is discussed in detail below in Chapter 26.

(2) Equal treatment: race

6.23   Directive 2004/43 on the principle of equal treatment between persons irrespective of racial or ethnic origin[11] applies to 'social protection, including social security and healthcare'.[12] The legal basis for this Directive lies in Article 13 EC, which empowers the Council 'within the limits of the powers conferred by it upon the Community' to take appropriate action. In view of the paucity of legislative competence granted to the Council by the Treaty, in the areas of social protection, social security, and health care it is difficult to envisage the extent to which the right to equal treatment can be required in these areas.

(3) Free movement of persons

6.24   The European Union has a specific responsibility, under Article 42 EC, to ensure that people who move across borders, and hence come within the remit of different social security systems, are adequately protected in the sense that they are not prejudiced by the exercise of the right to move freely within the Community.

---

[10] [1979] OJ L6/24.
[11] [2000] OJ L180/22.
[12] Art 3(1)(e).

The social security regime envisaged by Article 42 EC was set up originally by **6.25** Regulations 3/58[13] and 4/58.[14] In the light of the case law of the ECJ and developments in national social security systems, these Regulations were revised and replaced by Regulations 1408/71[15] and 574/72 ('the Regulations').[16] These in turn have been the subject of multiple amendments and a vast body of case law from the ECJ running now to more than 500 judgments. Consolidating regulations have been published from time to time, the most recent in 1997[17] Regulation 883/2004,[18] adopted on 29 April 2004, modernizes and simplifies Regulation 1408/71. It is expected to enter into force in 2010.

The purpose of Article 42 of the EC Treaty, and the Regulations adopted there- **6.26** under, is to achieve the free movement of workers. Workers would be reluctant to move to a Member State to take up employment if they ran the risk of losing social security rights acquired or in the process of being acquired in their home Member States.[19] Likewise, neither they nor their employers would be willing to contribute to more than one social security system. The Regulations consist of a body of rules which coordinate the social security systems of the Member States (but leave their substance untouched) to ensure that nationals and non-nationals are treated alike under the social security system of the host Member State.

The social security systems of the Member States are linked together to provide **6.27** persons with constant coverage wherever they go throughout the Community. Co-ordination is to be contrasted with harmonization which would create a common social security system applicable throughout the Community. Co-ordination does not do this: it leaves national social security systems intact.

The Regulations extend national social systems beyond their territorial boun- **6.28** daries. The result is that contributions paid in one Member State may give rise to entitlement in another Member State. Benefits may be exportable if the beneficiary leaves the Member State in which he has gained title to such benefits. Benefits such as family allowances are required to be paid in respect of family members living in a Member State other than that in which title to such benefit arises.

---

[13] [1958] JO 581.
[14] [1958] JO 597.
[15] [1971] OJ L149/1.
[16] [1972] OJ L74/1.
[17] [1997] OJ L28/1.
[18] [2004] OJ L200/1.
[19] See: The Community Provisions on Social Security—Your rights when moving within the European Union. European Commission 2004; Pennings: *Introduction to European Social Security Law* Fourth Edition Intersentia 2004; Watson: in Toth (ed) *The Oxford Encyclopedia of European Community Law* Vol II Oxford University Press 2005, 656–92.

6.29   Apart from extending the territorial scope of social security systems, the Regulations have no impact upon those systems. Member States remain free to organize their social security systems as they wish. The can institute or abolish benefits, alter conditions of entitlement and the rate and burden of contributions. In the case of *Fahmi*[20] the ECJ held that a Member State was entitled to abolish an allowance for dependent children aged between 18 and 27 years who were pursuing higher education studies provided its abolition did not involve discrimination based on nationality. The position would have been otherwise if, for example, the allowance had been abolished only in respect of dependent children pursuing their studies in another Member State.

6.30   Co-ordination involves two processes: aggregation and proraterization. Aggregation enables a person to whom the Regulations apply to gain title to benefit in one Member State on the basis of contributions paid in another Member State. Contributions paid or periods of employment completed in several Member States can be added together to give title to benefit.

6.31   Proraterization is the process whereby the cost of providing benefits is divided out amongst the Member States in which the beneficiary has been insured. In this way each Member State bears the cost of providing the benefit in proportion to the contributions it has received from, or on behalf of, the beneficiary.

6.32   The fundamental principle underlying the co-ordination system envisaged by the EC Treaty and created by the Regulations is equality of treatment between nationals and non-nationals. This, in effect, means that the migrant employed and self-employed must be required to be affiliated, on a compulsory basis, to one social security system only, which, as a general rule, is that of their country of employment or self-employed activity. Migrant workers must be subject to the same conditions of affiliation as nationals[21] and be entitled to receive the same range and level of benefits, which in the case of the former may entail the export of benefits to another Member State.[22] The end result is parity, in social security terms, between the national and the non-national subject to the same social security system. Both contribute to, and receive, benefits on the same terms.

6.33   The personal scope of application of Regulation 1408/71 is defined in terms of national social security systems. The Regulation covers the employed, the self-employed, and students, and their families and survivors. Employed, self-employed persons, and students must be nationals of a Member State, as must their survivors. The nationality of family members is irrelevant. Their rights are

---

[20] Case C-33/99 *Hassan Fahmi v Bestuur van de Sociale Verzekeringsbank* [2001] ECR I–2415.
[21] Case 33/88 *Allue and Coonan* [1989] ECR 1591.
[22] Case 41/84 *Pinna* [1986] ECR 1.

deemed to derive from and are subject to the social security system to which the head of the family of which they are a member is affiliated. As long as he or she is a national of a Member State that is all that is required to claim rights under the Regulations.

Refugees and stateless persons resident in a Member State are also covered. In **6.34** terms of systems and risks, the Regulations cover state social security systems only and within them all the benefits designed to cover the classic major risks. Social assistance benefits and benefits for victims of war are excluded. Non-contributory benefits are covered but some such benefits may be enjoyed only on the territory of the Member State under whose social security system entitlement arises and in which the beneficiary is resident.

Article 42 EC and the Regulations apply within the territory of the European **6.35** Community. That territory is defined in Article 299 EC. The Regulations were extended to cover the French overseas departments in 1971.[23] Since the Regulations do not apply to third countries, social security contributions paid or periods of insurance completed under the legislation of those countries do not have to be taken into account, by virtue of the Regulations by Member States in establishing entitlement to benefits.[24] However, if contributions are paid to a social security system of a Member State it matters not that they were paid in respect of employment in a non-Member State: the essential criterion is whether they were paid under the legislation of a Member State: the place of employment is irrelevant.[25]

Limiting the requirement of compulsory affiliation to a single social security **6.36** system is essential to ensure equality of treatment: The purpose of this 'single system' rule is twofold:

(i) to minimize the administrative burden on employers and social welfare schemes; and
(ii) to avoid a situation where either an employer or an employee, or possibly both, could be subject to social security contributions in more than one Member State.

Title II, Articles 13–17 of that Regulation sets out the social security system **6.37** which is applicable to the employed and self-employed who move within

---

[23] Council Decision 71/238 [1971] OJ L149/1.
[24] Case 16/72 *Allgemeine Ortskrankenkasse Hamburg v Landesversicherungsanstalt Schleswig-Holstein* [1972] ECR 1141.
[25] Case 300/84 *Van Roosmalen* [1986] ECR 3097; Cases 82/86 etc *Giancarlo Laborero and Francesca Sabato v Office de sécurité sociale d'outre-mer (OSSOM)* [1987] ECR 3401.

the Community. The general rule is that a person should be compulsorily affiliated to the social security system of one Member State only.

6.38 As a general rule the law of the place of employment governs the social security
rights and obligations of the employed person. In the case of the self-employed
the relevant system is the law of the place where the person in question carries out
his economic activity. It is clear that this rule cannot apply to all situations. The
Regulations contain special provisions to deal with different combinations of
economic activity not all of which may take place within the same Member
State.

6.39 A common system for the claiming and calculation of benefits is set out in
the Regulations. Claims for benefits are made to the competent institution in
the competent Member State. The competent institution may be that with
which the claimant is insured or the institution in his place of residence or stay.
Article 1(o) of Regulation 1408/71 defines the possible competent institutions to
which a claim can be made:

   (i) the institution with which the person concerned is insured at the time of the
      application for the benefit;

  (ii) the institution with which the person concerned is entitled or would be
      entitled to benefits if he or the members of his family were resident in the
      territory of the Member State in which the institute is situate;

 (iii) the institution designated by the competent authority of the Member State
      concerned;

 (iv) where the liability of an employer or an insurer is in issue, the body or
      authority of the Member State concerned.

6.40 There is a uniform claim form designed by the Administrative Commission for
the Social Security of Migrant Workers. Claims may be made in any Community
language.

6.41 Periods of insurance, periods of employment, or residence completed in any
Member States in order to establish title to benefit. Such insurance contributions,
periods of employment, or periods of residence must be treated by the social
security institutions to which a claim is made (the competent institution) as
if they had been completed under its own legislation. It is for each Member
State to determine what is a period of insurance for the purpose of claiming entitlement to benefit under its social security scheme.[26] Periods of residence are
treated as such by the legislation under which they were completed.[27] Periods of

---

[26] Case 70/80 *Tamara Vigier v Bundesversicherungsanstalt für Angestellte* [1981] ECR 229.
[27] Art 1(s) Regulation 1408/71.

employment are those treated as such under the legislation in which they were completed.[28]

In addition to entitlement arising under Regulations 1408/71 and 572/72, **6.42** migrant workers and their families may be entitled to benefits under Article 7(2) of Regulation 1612/68 on the free movement of workers,[29] which provides that a migrant worker has the right to enjoy the same social and tax advantages as a national worker. Article 7(2) has been held to extend to workers' families.[30] The concept of 'social and tax advantages' has been interpreted broadly to include social security and social assistance benefits.[31]

Workers and their families are entitled to enjoy such benefits in the territory of **6.43** the Member State in which the worker is employed. It does not entail the right to have the benefits exported to another Member State nor does it require contributions or periods of insurance in another Member State to be taken into account when assessing entitlement to benefits.

D. General Measures

In the early 1990s, two recommendations were adopted by the Council on the **6.44** convergence of social security objectives and on the right to social assistance respectively. The origins of both of these initiatives can be traced back to the Community Charter on the Fundamental Social Rights of Workers.

(1) Convergence

The Commission, in its Action Programme on the implementation of the **6.45** Community Charter on the Fundamental Social Rights of Workers,[32] noted that differences in social security coverage might prejudice the free movement of workers and exacerbate regional differences. It was therefore decided to promote a strategy for the convergence of Member States' social security policies by establishing common objectives to be attained by all.

---

[28] Art 1(r) Regulation 1408/71 Case 126/77 *Maria Frangiamore v Office National de l'Emploi* [1978] ECR 725; Case 2/72 *Salvatore Murru v Caisse régionale d'assurance maladie de Paris* [1972] ECR 333.
[29] [1968] OJ Sp Ed (II) 475 as amended.
[30] Case 32/75 *Fiorini* [1975] 1085; Case 261/83 *Castelli* [1984] ECR 3199.
[31] Case 63/76 *Inzirillo* [1976] ECR 839; Case C-111/91 *Commission v Luxembourg* [1993] ECR I–817; Case 94/84 *Deak* [1985] ECR 1873 Case 157/84 *Frascogna* [1985] ECR I–1739 Case C-326/90 *Commission v Belgium* [1992] ECR I–5517; Case C-310/91 *Schmid* [1993] ECR I–3011.
[32] COM (89) 568 Final.

6.46 A Council Recommendation sets out the common objectives which should act as guiding principles in the development of national social security systems.[33] Emphasis is laid on the right of the Member States to determine how their systems should be financed and organized.

(2) Social assistance

6.47 Recommendation 92/44[34] on common criteria concerning sufficient resources and social assistance in social protection systems recommends that Member States recognize the basic right of a person to sufficient resources to live with dignity. It sets out a number of recommendations within which Member States are encouraged to organize their social assistance systems. Eligibility for social assistance benefit is to be on the basis of nationality or legal residence. The level of benefit is to be determined by the Member States, taking into account living standards and the cost of living on their respective territories. The Recommendation calls for administrative procedures to be simplified so as to facilitate access to benefits.

E. Policy Initiatives

(1) Modernizing social security systems

6.48 In 1995, the Commission launched a debate on the future of social protection.[35] The outcome of this debate was published in a Communication in 1997, entitled 'Modernising and Improving Social Protection in the EU',[36] in which the Commission concluded that there was an urgent need to adapt social security systems to the social and economic environment in which they were operating: the changing nature of work, demographic ageing, gender balancing, and increased movement of persons. It advocated the better use of available resources through more focused objectives. In 1999, the Commission issued a further Communication designed to open up a new phase in the process of reflection between the Member States and the Community institutions.[37] Four key points of discussion were identified:

(a) making work pay;

(b) safeguarding pensions and making pension systems sustainable;

---

[33] [1992] OJ L245/49.
[34] [1992] OJ L245/48.
[35] The Future of Social Protection: A Framework for European Debate, COM (95) 466 Final.
[36] COM (97) 102.
[37] COM (99) 347 Final.

(c) the promotion of social inclusion;

(d) ensuring high quality and sustainable health care systems.

The Council endorsed these four objectives[38] and supported the Commission's   **6.49**
suggestion to establish a high level permanent working party, composed of
representatives from the Member States, charged with the task of ongoing reflection. This working party, established by Council Decision in mid-2000[39] was
institutionalized by the Treaty of Nice, which inserted Article 144 into the EC
Treaty establishing the Social Protection Committee charged '. . . with advisory
status to promote co-operation on social protection policies between Member
States and the Commission'. This co-operation takes place mainly through the
Open Method of Co-ordination.[40]

F. Impact of the Internal Market: Goods and Services

In the field of health care, citizens, as recipients of services, are free to travel and   **6.50**
purchase goods and services where they wish. Should they wish to be reimbursed
by the social security system to which they are affiliated in their home country, for
the cost of such goods and services, their rights are more limited. *Decker*[41] held
that persons insured under the health care of a Member State have the right to be
reimbursed for those products at the rate prevailing in the Member State in which
they are insured. Prior authorization for the purchase of such products from the
relevant health insurance fund is not required. *Kohll*[42] ruled that national
rules that make reimbursement of the cost of dental treatment provided in a
Member State other than that in which the beneficiary is insured subject to the
prior authorization by the relevant social security institution is prohibited by
Articles 49 and 50 EC on the free provision of services.

Subsequent case law has refined the content of these rights. For example, where   **6.51**
reimbursement is sought for hospital treatment in a Member State other than
that in which the beneficiary is insured, the responsible social security institution
is entitled to require its prior authorization for treatment and that treatment
must be regarded as normal within the professional circles of that Member State.[43]

---

[38] [2000] OJ C8/7.

[39] Council Decision 2000/436 of 29 June 2000 [2000] OJ L172/26; repealed by Council
Decision 2004/689 [2004] OJ L314/8.

[40] See paras 4.47–4.58.

[41] Case C-120/95 [1998] ECR I–1831.

[42] Case C-158/96 [1998] ECR I–1931.

[43] Case C-157/99 *Geraerts-Smits and Peerboom* [2001] ECR I–5473; Case C-385/99 *Mueller-Faure and Van Riet* [2003] ECR I–4509.

Additionally the treatment must be necessary to the patient's condition and not capable of being provided without 'undue delay' within the health care system of the Member State in which the patient is insured.[44] The conditions attaching to authorization must conform to the principle of proportionality. The authorization system must be substantively and procedurally transparent so as to circumscribe the exercise of the national authority's discretion. It must be based on objective non-discriminatory criteria which are known in advance. The procedural system for obtaining such authorization must be easily accessible and capable of ensuring that such requests are dealt with objectively, impartially, and within a reasonable period of time. Refusals must be capable of being challenged in judicial or quasi-judicial proceedings.[45]

6.52 Where persons go to another Member State and receive non-hospital medical treatment without having obtained the prior authorization of their health insurance fund, reimbursement is only available within the limits of the social security system to which they are affiliated.[46]

---

[44] Ibid *Geraerts-Smit and Peerbooms* Judgment para 103.
[45] Case C-371/04 [2006] ECR I–4325.
[46] *Mueller-Faure* (see note 43) Judgment para 38.

7

DISABILITY

A. Introduction

Disability within the European Union is a serious issue.[1] For the disabled it often **7.01** signifies exclusion or less than full participation in professional or civilian life; for society as a whole it is costly as disability is a considerable burden on welfare systems. The less than optimal participation of the disabled in the workforce places a strain on those systems given the imbalance quantitatively (more beneficiaries than contributors) and qualitatively (poor status on the labour market leading to low-end contributions) between contributors and beneficiaries. This state of affairs could be alleviated if the disabled participated more fully in the economy. Not only would their dependency on social security benefits decline but they could become net contributors to the system, and more importantly their inclusion into mainstream economic and social life would be enhanced.

---

[1] The numbers of disabled persons excluded from the labour market are depressingly high: 'Disabled persons alone represent a population of 38 million in the EU; only 46% of those reporting a moderate disability and 24% of those reporting a severe disability are in work', The Future of the European Employment Strategy, COM (2003) 6 Final at para 2.1.3. See also data set out in Situation of disabled people in the enlarged European Union COM 2005 (604) Final para 2.1.

7.02 Community policy on the disabled has been developed in a fragmentary way as from around the 1980s. The original EC Treaty of 1957 made no reference to the disabled nor did any subsequent amendments to it, until the Treaty of Amsterdam in 1997, but in the intervening years there emerged a growing political commitment, albeit somewhat vague, to the betterment of the disabled in the Community and a disability policy began to be constructed.

7.03 The policy has developed in three phases, each reflecting a particular approach to disability. In the early years, the Community supported national disability policies in form of programmes designed to achieve the dissemination of information and knowledge about disability; then it progressed to facilitating the formation of non-governmental organizations representative of the interests of the disabled and the integration of the disabled into the employment market. Finally, within the last decade efforts have been made to formulate a coherent policy of integration of the disabled into employment and civilian life.

7.04 Throughout this process we see a shift away from treating the disabled as having specific needs which need to be the subject of compensation by way of special measures directed at them, to a policy of mainstreaming, that is, inclusion in any general policy-making process coupled with a rights-based approach to disability. This has been described as a shift from a 'medical' approach to disability to a 'social' approach signifying a re-balance of rights and obligations. From treating disability as a personal medical condition requiring special privileges and facilities, which in themselves constitute an isolating factor from society in general, there has been a shift towards making society responsible for the integration of the disabled into both economic and civic life. A policy of tolerance of disability coupled with adequate welfare provision for the disabled has moved to a rights-based approach.

7.05 The development of Community disability rights and policy is described below in chronological sequence.[2]

B. Phase I: 1970s and 1980s

7.06 The 1974 Social Action Programme[3] stated that '. . . the handicapped constitute a group which deserve immediate consideration by the Community as a whole'.[4]

---

[2] For a full account (upon which this chapter draws) see Waddington: *From Rome to Nice in a Wheelchair* Europa Publishing 2006.
[3] [1974] OJ C13/1; reproduced in Bull EC Supp 2/74.
[4] Bull EC Supp 2/74 at 16.

Seven proposals were made for various forms of action but little was achieved.[5] Initial efforts concentrated on getting the disabled into the employment market. A five-year Programme for the Vocational Rehabilitation of Handicapped Persons was adopted by a Council Resolution of 1974.[6]

A further recommendation was adopted by the Council in 1986 on the Employ- **7.07** ment of Disabled People in the Community.[7] The Member States were encouraged, in general terms, to provide fair opportunities for disabled people in the workplace. A Guideline annexed to the Recommendation set out in more detail what action Member States could take to achieve this objective. None of this was, of course, binding on the Member States.

There followed, in 1983, a five-year Community Action Programme on the **7.08** Social Integration of Handicapped People[8] which, although it represented a move away from the traditional approach of dealing exclusively with the employment-related aspects of disability, achieved little, save for the setting up of a multilingual information system on disability issues (Handynet) which ran until 1994 but which was apparently expensive and of dubious value.

C. Phase II: mid-1980s to mid-1990s

(1) Community Programmes: HELIOS, HORIZON, EQUAL

This period saw the setting up of the two HELIOS[9] Programmes which paved **7.09** the way for present-day policy: HELIOS I (1988–1993)[10] and HELIOS II (1993–1996).[11] The HELIOS Programmes succeeded in establishing the voice of the disabled in Europe by encouraging representation through Non-Governmental Organizations (NGOs). HELIOS I began a process of working with disability NGOs with a view to getting their input on disability policy. HELIOS II had four main objectives:

(i) the development of information gathering and dissemination within the Member States and NGOs;

---

[5] Ibid at 25.
[6] [1974] OJ C80/30.
[7] Council Recommendation 86/379 [1986] OJ L225/43.
[8] Pursuant to a Council Resolution [1981] OJ C347.
[9] An acronym for Handicapped People in the European Community Living Independently in an Open Society.
[10] [1988] OJ L104/38.
[11] [1993] OJ L56/30.

(ii) the co-ordination and improved effectiveness of existing disability programmes;

(iii) the promotion of policy co-operation and best practice between Member States; and

(iv) the encouragement of NGO activity on a European level. In this latter respect it was particularly successful.

The origins of the European Disability Forum can be traced back to Helios II. When that Programme ended, the Forum became an independent body with its own constitution. Today it represents the interests of more than 50 million disabled people in Europe. It works with Community Institutions, the Council of Europe, and the United Nations. Its objective is to promote equal opportunities for the disabled, to ensure their full access to fundamental and human rights, and foster their active involvement in policy development and implementation in the European Union. The Forum was successful in applying pressure at the Intergovernmental Conference, leading to the adoption of the Treaty of Amsterdam for the inclusion of Article 13 in the EC Treaty.

7.10 At the same time the European Social Fund, in 1989, allocated ECU 300 million to the HORIZON programme to improve the employment prospects of the disabled and other disadvantaged groups. A further ECU 730 million was allocated for the period 1994–1999. HORIZON's successor, EQUAL,[12] was set up in 2000 with the objective of funding projects in the Member States to combat all forms of discrimination within the labour market. Projects are co-financed by the Member States and the EU. The current financial contribution of the EU is in excess of €3 billion.

(2) The Charter on the Fundamental Social Rights of Workers

7.11 The Charter on the Fundamental Social Rights of Workers 1989 recognized the right of the disabled to full participation in social and economic life:

> All disabled persons, whatever their origins and nature of their disablement, must be entitled to additional concrete measures aimed at improving their social and professional integration. These measures must concern, in particular, according to the capacities of the beneficiaries, vocational training, ergonomics, accessibility, mobility, means of transport and housing.[13]

---

[12] Communication from the Commission to the Member States establishing the guidelines for the Community Initiative EQUAL concerning transnational co-operation to promote new means of combating all forms of discrimination and inequalities in connection with the labour market. [2000] OJ C127/2.

[13] Art 26.

The Action Programme[14] to implement the Charter advocated the adoption of a **7.12** third HELIOS programme and a directive on measures aimed at promoting an improvement in the travel conditions of workers with motor disabilities neither of which came to fruition.

(3) Education

In 1990 a Resolution was passed by the Council, calling for the integration into **7.13** normal schooling of children and young persons with disabilities.[15] This marked the beginning of a shift in strategy away from treating the disabled as a specific group for which special educational facilities had to be created to their integration into, in this case, the normal educational stream.

(4) The Single European Act

Following the Single European Act, Article 118a (now Article 137) of the EC **7.14** Treaty provided for the adoption of measures for health and safety at work. The Commission, interpreting the concept of health and safety broadly, proposed a number of employment measures including a Directive on Minimum Requirements to improve the Mobility and Safe Transport to Work of Workers with Reduced Mobility.[16] The purpose of this measure was to ensure accessibility to, and safety of, public transport, transport by employers, and special transport services for disabled people. Although it was possible to confine the latter two means of transport to workers, this was not the case with public transport which could be also used by the non-working disabled. Given that Article 118a was confined to health and safety measures related to work, ultimately the Member States felt that the Directive could not be based on this provision. Although this was understandable, it is regrettable, as the Directive would have brought real benefit to the disabled, lack of access to suitable transport being one of the main obstacles to both entry into and advancement in the labour market.

(5) The Agreement on Social Policy

The Maastricht Treaty did not refer to the disabled at all, but Article 1 of the **7.15** Agreement on Social Policy specified the combating of exclusion as one of the objectives of the Community and, with a view to achieving that objective, in Article 2 empowered the Community to 'support and complement the activities of the Member States' on the integration of persons excluded from the labour market. Presumably the disabled were amongst the sections of the population

---

[14] COM (89) 568 Final.
[15] [1990] OJ L162/2.
[16] COM (90) 588 Final.

regarded as suffering from exclusion but no specific measures were envisaged in their regard under the Agreement.

(6) The United Nations Standard Rules

7.16 On 20 December 1993 the General Assembly of the United Nations adopted the United Nations Standard Rules on the Equality of Opportunity for Persons with Disabilities (United Nations General Assembly Resolution 48/46 of 20 December 1993), the objective of which was to ensure that all persons with disabilities could exercise the same rights and be subject to the same obligations as others. This initiative influenced Community thinking.

(7) The 1996 Communication

7.17 In July 1996 the Commission committed itself to the United Nations Standard Rules, in a Communication entitled Equality of Opportunity for people with Disabilities: A New European Community Strategy,[17] (the 'Communication') in which it advocated the removal of barriers to the participation in society of the disabled, promoting employment opportunities for them and influencing public opinion on disablility. This Communication is significant in a number of respects: it was the first time the Commission had attempted to formulate a comprehensive strategy for the disabled in society, and that strategy encompassed all aspects of life, both economic and social; it signified a shift in the perception of disability from being a condition requiring adaptation on the part of the disabled person to participate in society to a position where society is regarded as having a responsibility to adapt to meet the needs of the disabled. At the same time, the Communication indicated a move towards a rights-based equal opportunities approach to disability and a move towards mainstreaming, a process that had been prevalent in the United States since the 1970s.

(8) Mainstreaming

7.18 Mainstreaming is defined, in the Communication, as a move away from disability policy formulation as a separate process to an integral element of general policy-making:

> . . . the formulation of policy to facilitate the full participation and involvement of people with disabilities in economic, social and other processes, while respecting personal choice. It also means that the relevant issues should no longer be considered separately from the mainstream policy-making apparatus, but should clearly be seen as an integral element.[18]

---

[17] COM (96) 406 Final.
[18] Ibid para 19.

Mainstreaming, in essence, represents a move away from the segregation of the **7.19**
disabled in education and employment, through measures and practices aimed at
creating educational facilities and employment opportunities suited to their
disabilities towards a policy of inclusion in mainstream education and employment by means of the necessary adaptation of the educational and employment
environment to their needs.[19]

The Communication referred to the need to identify and remove barriers to **7.20**
equal opportunities and full participation in all aspects of life. It put the case
for changes in the organization of society which could substantially reduce the
obstacles leading to the exclusion of the disabled from mainstream life, for
example, by making employment, goods, and services accessible to them on
an equal basis.

The Communication advocated dialogue with all stakeholders: NGOs, the **7.21**
Member States, the social partners. In the past there had been little such dialogue,
disability policy being superimposed by the Community and the Member States
on the disabled with little effort made to get information from them as to the
content of such policy.

In essence it proposed a broad-ranging strategy and the use of structural funds to **7.22**
implement that strategy. It drew up a draft resolution for adoption by the Council and a set of Guidelines for action by the Member States.

(9) The 1996 Council Resolution

The Resolution was adopted on 20 December 1996. In it, the Council confirmed **7.23**
its commitment to the UN Standard Rules adopted on the same day three years
earlier. Emphasizing that responsibility for disability lay with the Member States,
the Council nevertheless stated that the European Community could make a
contribution in fostering co-operation between Member States and in encouraging the exchange and development of best practice in the Community and within
the policies and activities of the Community institutions.[20] The Resolution urged
the Member States, within the framework of their national employment policies
and in co-operation with the social partners and the non-governmental organizations for people with disabilities, to place particular emphasis on the promotion
of employment opportunities. No funding or measures on a Community level

---

[19] See Quinn: 'The European Social Charter and EU Anti-discrimination Law in the Field of
Disability: Two Gravitational Fields with One Common Purpose' in de Burca and de Witte (eds)
Social Rights in Europe Oxford University Press 2005 at 299–303.
[20] Council Resolution on Equal Employment Opportunities for People with Disabilities
[1997] OJ C12/1.

were proposed for this initiative. It was all left to the discretion of the Member States.

D. Phase III: Amsterdam and Beyond

7.24 By virtue of the Treaty of Amsterdam, the EC Treaty was amended to include Article 13 which empowers the Commission to adopt measures to combat discrimination on the ground, inter alia, of disability. The disability lobby pressed for more specific rights and for a time during the IGC negotiations it looked as if they might have succeeded.[21] One of the measures sought was a reference to the disabled in the Article 95 EC which would require the needs of the disabled to be taken into account when formulating legislation laying down internal market industry norms.[22] The absence of such a requirement means that some products and services may be inaccessible or only partially accessible to the disabled.[23] Moreover it can actually worsen their position if such accessibility previously existed under national norms. Although no requirement was made in the Treaty to take the needs of the disabled into account in the formulation of industry norms, they were not entirely ignored. A Declaration was annexed to the Treaty of Amsterdam stating:

> The Conference agrees that, in drawing up measures under Article 95 of the Treaty establishing the European Community, the institutions of the Community shall take account of the needs of persons with a disability.

7.25 The disability lobby also pressed for a specific mention of the disability to be amongst the issues set out in Article 137 upon which the Community was endowed with competence to act. This was unsuccessful: the disabled remained within the collectivity of the socially excluded.

7.26 It is of interest to note that there was not much support initially for the inclusion of the disabled in Article 13. It was felt that their position might be made worse in that the adoption of non-discrimination laws might undermine the benefits they enjoyed under national welfare schemes, and other positive measures in their favour and that, accordingly, they might be better served by remaining a group apart. In the end this point of view did not prevail. It is difficult to see how

---

[21] Geyer: 'Can Mainstreaming save EU Social Policy: The Cases of Gender, Disability and Elderly Policy'. Chapter 4 in Columbus (ed) *European Economic and Political Issues* New York 2002 at 74–5.

[22] Waddington (see note 2 above) 9–10.

[23] Initial drafts of the Directive on telecommunications terminal equipment in 1994, did not include a requirement that such equipment be usable by those with sight difficulties. Equally draft legislation in the mid-1990s on buses and lifts failed to take account of accessibility for the disabled.

the disabled could be disadvantaged by the application of equal treatment in employment. Reasonable adaptations to the working environment might have to be made to meet their needs but this right to accommodation would enable them to enter mainstream employment and would therefore compensate for any advantage that, for example, sheltered employment might have hitherto given them. Their welfare entitlements might be reduced or lost as a result of income from employment, but the income from the latter would presumably be greater than the former so it is difficult to see any disadvantage there. All in all, the principle of equality ought to enable the disabled to enter and remain in normal employment but this does not mean that any advantages given to them unrelated to income replacement for inability to work (within their national welfare systems) to overcome the effects of their disability, such as help within the home, or assistance with transport to the place of work, would disappear. Such benefits are designed to provide facilities to overcome extra expenses or needs arising from disability and ought not to be affected by the taking up of employment.

Directive 2000/78 establishing a general framework for equal treatment in employment and occupation[24] (the Framework Equality Directive) prohibits discrimination, both direct and indirect, on a number of grounds including disability. Not only must employers refrain from discrimination, they must also take steps to accommodate people with disabilities in the workplace to ensure that they are all treated equally. The Directive is more fully considered below in Chapter 29. **7.27**

In 2003 the European Disability Forum proposed the adoption of a directive prohibiting discrimination against disabled people in housing, education, transport, welfare provision, social advantages, education, access to goods, facilities, and services. It envisaged conferring directly enforceable rights on the disabled.[25] The Commission has now published proposals for a Directive which will go a considerable way to meeting these concerns.[26] **7.28**

The Charter of Fundamental Rights 2000 of the European Union[27] prohibits discrimination on grounds of disability, which is a somewhat stronger statement than that of Article 13 EC which merely enables measures to be adopted to combat discrimination but gives the disabled no positive nor directly **7.29**

---

[24] [2002] OJ L303.

[25] <http://www.edf-feph.org> Press Release 12 March 2003.

[26] Proposal for a Council Directive on implementing the principle of equal treatment between person irrespective of religion or belief, disability, age, or sexual orientation COM (2008) 420 Final.

[27] [2000] OJ C364.

enforceable rights. Article 26 of the Charter provides for the integration into professional and civilian life of the disabled:

> The Union recognizes and respects the rights of persons with disabilities to benefit from measures designed to ensure their independence, social and economic integration and participation in the life of the community.

7.30 Following the inclusion of Title VIII in the EC Treaty by the Treaty of Amsterdam, the European Employment Strategy (EES) was developed. The three core objectives of the EES are all relevant to disability. The promotion of full employment requires the reduction of unemployment and inactivity. Improving quality and productivity at work aims to improve the attractiveness and quality of work; this implies meaningful and improved employment opportunities for the disabled. The third objective, improving social and territorial cohesion, is stated to require determined action to strengthen social inclusion and prevent exclusion from the labour market and support integration in the employment of people at a disadvantage.

7.31 The 2005–2008 Employment Guidelines[28] set, as a priority, the significant reduction of employment gaps for people at a disadvantage, including disabled people. Specific Guidelines set out how this is to be achieved in national employment policies.

7.32 In July 2005 the Commission published a working paper entitled 'Disability Mainstreaming in the European Employment Strategy'.[29] The purpose of the paper is twofold: to explore the concept of mainstreaming and to see how the Employment Guidelines can develop a mainstream approach for the integration of disabled people into national employment policy.

E. Social Integration

7.33 In July 2003, the Council adopted a Resolution on promoting employment and social integration of people with disabilities.[30] The Resolution calls on the Member States, the Commission, and the social partners to continue efforts to remove barriers to the integration and participation of people with disabilities in the labour market by enforcing equal treatment measures and improving integration and participation at all levels of the educational and training system.

---

[28] Council Decision 2005/600 [2005] OJ L205/21.
[29] EMPL/A/AK D 2005.
[30] [2003] OJ C175/1.

Other initiatives designed to further the full participation of the disabled in **7.34** society include Council Resolution of 6 February 2003 on eAccessibility— improving access of people with disabilities to the knowledge-based society[31] and Council Resolution of 6 February 2003 on accessibility of cultural infra- structure and cultural activities for people with disabilities.[32]

At the end of October 2003 the Commission published a Communication **7.35** setting out a ten-year action plan entitled 'Equal opportunities for people with disabilities' (the 'Disability Action Plan').[33] The purpose of the Disability Action Plan is to incorporate disability issues into relevant Community policies and to develop concrete action to achieve the social integration of the disabled.

The first phase of the Disability Action Plan, ran from the beginning of 2004 **7.36** until the end of 2005, and focused on creating the conditions necessary to pro- mote the employment of people with disabilities by making the labour market more accessible to them across the enlarged Community. Four employment- related priority actions were undertaken:

(a) access to, and retention in, employment including combating discrimination;
(b) lifelong learning to support and increase employability, adaptability, per- sonal development, and active citizenship;
(c) new technologies to empower people with disabilities and therefore to facilitate access to employment;
(d) accessibility to the public built environment to improve participation in the workplace and integration into the economy and society.

The Disability Action Plan endorsed the commitment of the European Union to **7.37** the approach to disability advocated first in its July 1996 Communication:

> The EU's long-standing commitment towards its disabled citizens goes hand in hand with a new approach to disability; from seeing people with disabilities as the passive recipients of compensation, society has come to recognize their legiti- mate demands for equal rights and to realise that participation relates directly to insertion.[34]

Phase two of the Disability Action Plan focuses on the active inclusion of people **7.38** with disabilities into society. The emphasis will be on encouraging independence by providing support from social services and facilitating access to goods and services.

---

31 [2003] OJ C39/03.
32 [2003] OJ C134/05.
33 COM (2003) 650 Final.
34 Ibid Action Plan at 4.

7.39 On 30 March 2007 the European Community signed the United Nations Convention on Disability Rights.[35] The Convention aims to ensure that people with disabilities enjoy human rights and fundamental freedoms on an equal basis with other citizens. It follows long-standing efforts by disability organizations— notably the European Disability Forum—and an increasing recognition that existing UN Human Rights treaties failed to fully protect people with disabilities who continue to suffer discrimination.

---

[35] Press Release IP/07446.

8

CORPORATE SOCIAL RESPONSIBILITY

A. Introduction

Over the past decade there has been increasing concern in a number of quarters **8.01** over the consequences of business activities, and the behaviour, in particular, of large corporations. Large corporations and their methods of operation are being subject to greater scrutiny by citizens, consumers, public authorities, and investors.

Success in business is no longer viewed as simply a question of maximizing **8.02** profits. It is seen intrinsically linked to sustainable development: business needs to integrate the economic, social, and environmental impact of their activities into the management of their concerns. This means taking cognizance of the wider economic, social, and environmental impact of their operations.

Globalization, although creating new economic opportunities, has also increased **8.03** the complexity of business operations. Moral and ethical issues arise in many centres of production geographically and culturally distant from company head-quarters. Transborder criminality, production conditions, and human rights issues in far-flung parts of the globe have become issues of immediate concern to the viability of European business. Consumers are increasingly sensitive to the conditions in which products and services are generated; this brings competitive advantages for firms seen to be socially, environmentally, and ethically responsible and proportionate disadvantages for those who perceived to be oblivious to such issues. Consumers' expectations are driving investors to demand more information on firms' policies in order to make informed decisions on investment choice.

8.04 Companies are being required—either legally or on a voluntary basis—to adopt standards recognizing values and minimum thresholds of behaviour to meet the concerns of the wider community—in other words to behave responsibly with respect to matters outside the immediate operation of their undertakings. This requirement is known as corporate social responsibility (CSR) and has been defined as '. . . the duty of an enterprise to consider in a general way the public interest'.[1]

8.05 CSR has a number of meanings[2] and takes a number of forms applicable both to inter-Community trade and on an external level[3] but, in the context of the Lisbon Strategy, the European Commission has signalled a commitment to the development of a European Framework for Corporate Social Responsibility. which it has defined as:

> . . . a concept whereby companies integrate social and environmental concerns in their business operations and in their interaction with their stakeholders on a voluntary basis.[4]

8.06 The development of this policy is traced below.[5]

B. The Green Paper

8.07 A Green Paper, published in 2001,[6] by the EC Commission, launched a debate on how to develop a European framework for CSR.

8.08 The Commission stated that CSR was voluntary. It was not to be viewed as a substitute to regulation or legislation concerning social rights or environmental rights or the development of appropriate legislation on these issues. Where, in countries where regulations governing CSR do not exist, efforts should be made to focus on putting the proper regulatory or legislative framework in place in order to establish a level playing field on the basis of which social responsible

---

[1] Roth and Fizt: 'Corporate Social Responsibility: European Models' (1978–1979) 30 Hastings Law Journal 1433.

[2] De Schutter: 'Corporate Social Responsibility European Style' (2008) 14 European Law Journal 203–36 at 203–4.

[3] MacLeod: 'Corporate Social Responsibility within the European Union Framework' (2005) 23 Wisconsin International Law Journal 541–52 at 541–2.

[4] Green Paper on Promoting a European Framework for Corporate Social Responsibility COM (2001) 366 Final at 8. CSR is capable of a number of definitions: De Schutter: 'Corporate Social Responsibility European Style' (2008) 14 European Law Journal 203–36 at 203–4.

[5] See Hermann: 'Corporate Social Responsibility and Sustainable Development: The European Union Initiative as a Case Study' (2004) 11 Indiana Journal of Global Legal Studies 205–32.

[6] Green Paper Promoting a European framework for Corporate Social Responsibility COM (2001) 366 Final.

practices could be developed. The Commission viewed its role on CSR to be voluntary, that is as going beyond compliance with legal obligations and investing more into 'human capital, the environment and relations with stakeholders'.[7]

Although CSR was practised mainly by large multinational companies, the **8.09** Commission stated that it was relevant to all types of companies and to all sectors of activity from small- and medium-sized undertakings to multinational enterprises.

Public authorities including international organizations, businesses of any **8.10** size, the social partners, NGOs, other stakeholders, and all interested individuals were invited to send in their views on developing a partnership approach to CSR.

More than 250 responses were received, half of which came from business,[8] the **8.11** remainder largely from other interest groups such as consumers, trade unions, and civic organizations.[9] The Community institutions themselves adopted positions in the debate as did a number of Member States. Almost all parties supported the idea of Community action, although there were differences in their respective positions:

(i) Business emphasized the voluntary nature of CSR thereby signalling its opposition to any fettering of their discretion in this area by the Community institutions. Whilst agreeing that it should be developed on a global level, attempts to regulate by the Community could, it believed, stifle creativity and innovation and lead to conflicting priorities for enterprises operating in different geographical areas around the globe.

(ii) Trade unions and civil society organizations argued for a Community regulatory framework establishing minimum standards, emphasizing that voluntary initiatives were in sufficient to protect workers' and citizens' rights.

(iii) Investors stressed the need to improve the disclosure and transparency of companies' practices and the investment management of socially responsible investments funds (SRI); consumer organizations underlined the importance of a full and frank disclosure of the ethical, social, and environmental conditions in which goods and services are traded to facilitate informed consumer choice.

(iv) The European Parliament advocated integrating CSR into all areas of Community competence.

---

[7] Ibid para 21.
[8] Half of the individual company responses came from United Kingdom-based companies.
[9] For an analysis of the Responses to the Green Paper see Macleod and Lewis: 'Transnational Corporations: Power, Influence and Responsibility' (2004) 4 Global Social Policy 77–98.

8.12 The Green Paper has been criticized on a number of grounds, in particular because it advocates a voluntary approach to CSR.[10] This runs the risk, as a number of NGOs pointed out in their response to the Green Paper, that CSR standards will either be completely ignored or selectively applied.[11] That the Commission advocated a voluntary approach to CSR is perhaps not an accurate assessment of its position as expressed in the Green Paper. What the Commission appears to be saying is that it did not envisage a Community regulatory or legislative approach to CSR but rather that it would complement and add value to various national and international initiatives such as the OECD Guidelines for Multinational Enterprises and ILO labour standards.[12]

C. The 2002 Communication

8.13 Drawing on these responses the Commission published a Communication in July 2002.[13] Whilst emphasizing that CSR was clearly a matter for business itself, thereby ruling out any policy of regulation of CSR on a Community level, the Commission concluded that:

> . . . there is a role for Community action to facilitate convergence in the instruments used in the light of the need to ensure a proper functioning of the internal market and the preservation of a level playing field.[14]

8.14 At the same time the Commission acknowledged that there was a role for public authorities in 'promoting transparency and convergence of CSR Practices and instruments'.[15] The Council in a subsequent resolution thus advocated incorporating CSR into Community policies and called upon the Member States 'to integrate, where appropriate, CSR policies into their own management'.[16]

8.15 The Commission's concern therefore is more economic than social: Community intervention is perceived to be necessary to ensure fair competition.

---

[10] Chanin: "'The Regulatory Grass is Greener": A Comparative Anlaysis of the Alien Tort Claims Act and the European Union's Green Paper on Corporate Social Responsibility' (2005) 12 Indiana Journal of Global Legal Studies 745–78 at 772–4.

[11] For example the Response of the Save the Children to the Green paper pointed out: 'An ILO study of voluntary labor codes adopted by multinational companies has concluded that there is a tendency to be selective in the inclusion of core ILO standards—less than 50% of the codes received included a clause on child labor—and a failure to develop standardized monitoring practice or to ensure transparency' <http://europa.eu.int/comm./employment_social/soc-dial/CSR/>.

[12] Green Paper para 17.

[13] Communication from the Commission concerning Corporate Social Responsibility: A business contribution to sustainable development COM (2002) 347 Final.

[14] Ibid at 8.

[15] Communication at note 13 at 5.

[16] Council Resolution of 6 February 2003 on corporate social responsibility [2003] OJ C39/3.

The Communication proposed a seven pronged strategy: **8.16**

  (i) raising awareness of the positive impact of CSR on business in European and third countries;

 (ii) developing an exchange of experience and good CSR practice within the business community;

(iii) promoting and developing CSR management skills;

(iv) encouraging CRS amongst SMEs whilst at the same time being aware of their needs and characteristics;

 (v) facilitating the convergence and transposition of CSR practice (eg information on investment of occupational pension schemes) and instruments (eg OECD Guidelines for Multinational Enterprises);

(vi) creating a forum representative of all interests (business, social partners, consumer organizations and public authorities) in CRS at a Community level;

(vii) integrating CSR into all Community policies.

To achieve these objectives the Commission has made a number of publications[17] **8.17** and fostered debate amongst interested parties.[18] The Commission is also aware of its ability to promote CRS through its agreements with third countries and regional groupings.[19]

The Communication proposed the setting up of the CSR Multi Stakeholder **8.18** Forum (the 'CSR EMU Forum') as a platform for discussion between various stakeholders on the promotion of innovation, transparency, and convergence of CSR practices and instruments. It was to be composed of representatives from states, non-governmental organizations, corporations, and the wider civil society and chaired by the European Commission. The Forum was formally established on 16 October 2002. It presented its final report in June 2004 but, in spite of having had 20 months of consultation and reflection its conclusion lacked substance. The report makes lengthy recommendations for 'increasing awareness' of CSR, encouragement of 'co-operation with stakeholders', support for research on CSR and the diffusion of information about CSR and co-operation between companies. Little is said about how these objectives were to be achieved and it was clear that there were differences between business and the other stakeholders, notably the NGOs and trade unions.

---

[17] ABC of the main instruments of Corporate Social Responsibility EC Commission April 2003; Mapping Instruments for Corporate Social Responsibility.

[18] European Multistakeholders Forum on CSR 29 June 2004 Final Report.

[19] See The Role of the EU in Promoting Human Rights and Democratisation in Third Countries COM (2001) 252 Final; Social governance in the context of globalization COM (2001) 416.

8.19   Although the Green Paper had, in the context of social and environmental label-ling, advocated the 'use of public procurement and fiscal incentives to promote labelled products',[20] by the time the Communication was published the Commission had issued its Interpretative Communications on the possibility of integrating social and environmental considerations into public procurement[21] and it was reluctant to go beyond what was said in those Communications.[22]

D. The 2006 Communication

8.20   On 22 March 2006, nearly two years after the final report of the CSR EMU Forum, the Commission published a Communication[23] in which it announced that CSR was essentially about voluntary business behaviour and the way for-ward was to work closely with business. It thus apparently abandoned all attempt to involve the wider society in the development of its strategy on CSR:

> Because CSR is fundamentally about voluntary business behaviour, an approach involving additional obligations and administrative requirements for business risks being counter-productive and would be contrary to the principles of better regula-tion. Acknowledging that enterprises are the primary actors in CSR, the Commission has decided that it can best achieve its objectives by working more closely with European business . . .[24]

8.21   The Communication announced the establishment of the European Alliance on CSR, described as 'the political umbrella for CSR for new or existing CSR initiatives by large companies, SMEs and their stakeholders'.[25]

8.22   CSR is primarily perceived as an issue for larger undertakings concerned with their image and reputation. Smaller undertakings are more concerned with sur-vival as a business and are largely unaware of CSR or at least its relevance to them. Yet it is arguable that CSR is not merely as 'external' issue but is also related to employment conditions and hence of relevance across the entire spectrum of

---

[20] Green Paper para 83.

[21] Interpretative communication of the Commission on the Community law applicable to public procurement and the possibilities for integrating social considerations into public procurement [2001] OJ C333/27; Commission interpretative communication on the Community law applica-ble to public procurement and the possibilities for integrating environmental considerations into public procurement [2001] OJ C333/12.

[22] McCrudden: *Buying Social Justice* Oxford University Press 2007 at 384.

[23] Communication of the Commission Implementing the Partnership for Growth and Jobs: Making Europe a Pole of Excellence on CSR COM (2006) 136 Final.

[24] Ibid at 1.

[25] Ibid at 2.

industry.[26] This has been recognized by a European Council in a Resolution of December 2003[27] which emphasized:

> ... undertakings should address not only the external aspects of CSR, but also the internal aspects such as health and safety at work and management of human resources.

At present responsibility for CSR is a matter for business self-regulation. Whilst **8.23** the Community is keen to mark a commitment to CSR within the Community economy and to develop a common CSR strategy, it does not at present envisage itself in any sort of regulatory role.

---

[26] Barnard, Deakin, Hobbs: 'Reflexive Law, Corporate Social Responsibility and the Evolution of Labour Standards: The Case of Working Time' in De Schutter and Deakin (eds) *Social Rights and Market Forces* Bruylant 2006.

[27] Resolution of the Employment and Social Policy Council on CSR [2003] OJ C39/3.

9

SOCIAL EXCLUSION

A. Introduction

Social exclusion signifies the marginalization of vulnerable sections of the population such as the long-term unemployed, the elderly, children, and single parents whose income, for the most part, derives from state welfare schemes and is often less than the resources required to participate in normal civic life.[1] Social exclusion distances groups in society from jobs, educational opportunities, social and community networks, and facilities.   **9.01**

Whilst poverty, and the income re-distribution and other policies required to overcome it, are the responsibility of the Member States, the Community has, since the early 1970s, assumed a supportive and complementary role towards its most deprived and marginalized citizens. This brief chapter will set out what this role has been and what it aspires to be.[2]   **9.02**

---

[1] 'Social exclusion is a process whereby certain individuals are pushed to the edge of society and prevented from participating fully by virtue of their poverty, or lack of basic competencies and lifelong learning opportunities, or as a result of discrimination. This distances them from jobs, income and education opportunities as well as social and community networks and activities. They have little access to power and decision-making bodies and thus often feeling powerless and unable to take control over the decisions that affect their day-to-day lives.' European Commission (2004) Joint Report on Social Inclusion.

[2] See generally: Marlier, Atkinson, Cantillon, and Nolan: *The EU and Social Inclusion: Facing the Challenges* The Policy Press 2007.

B. The EEC Treaty

9.03 When the European Economic Community was established in 1957 poverty and social exclusion were viewed as matters to be dealt with on a national level in accordance with national values, and within the limits of the national purse.

9.04 By 1972, on the eve of the of the first of six accessions which would bring the Community from six to 27 Member States, it was realized that, successful as it might have been as an economic trading area, and in maintaining peace in Europe, the Community had had little impact upon the lives of many citizens.

9.05 Accordingly the heads of State and government stated that they '. . . attached as much importance to vigorous action in the social fields as to the achievement of Economic and Monetary Union'. They asked the Community institutions, in consultation with management and labour, to draw up a programme of action providing for concrete measures in the social field.[3]

9.06 The Resolution of the Council in January 1974,[4] adopting the Social Action Programme put forward by the EC Commission at the end of 1973,[5] stated that Community social policy should define objectives of national social policies:

> . . . without however seeking a standard solution to all social problems or attempting to transfer to Community level any responsibilities which are assumed more effectively at other levels.[6]

9.07 In particular, the Council advocated the approximation of social protection policies and the gradual extension of national welfare systems to persons not covered or inadequately provided for by such systems.

9.08 As from 1975 until 1994 the Council established three programmes to combat poverty and social exclusion.[7] These were co-financed by the Community and national governments and were largely concerned with:

(i) the description, quantification, and understanding of poverty within the Community; and
(ii) the operation of a number of pilot projects designed to find solutions to the most acute forms of deprivation, both in urban and rural areas, within the Member States.

---

[3] Statement from the Paris Summit 19–21 October 1972 Point 6.
[4] [1974] OJ C13/1.
[5] Bull EC Supp 2/74 13-35.
[6] Recital 7.
[7] Poverty 1 1975–1980 Council Decision 75/458 [1975] OJ L199; Poverty 2 1985–1989 Council Decision 85/8 [1985] OJ L2; Poverty 3 1989–1994 Council Decision 89/457 [1989] OJ L224.

A Council Resolution of 1989 on Combating Social Exclusion[8] emphasized that **9.09** overcoming social exclusion was an important part of the social dimension of the internal market. It encouraged efforts in this respect with Community institutions and the Member States acting in common.

The Community Charter on the Fundamental Social Rights of Workers, adopted **9.10** at the end of 1989, was concerned with the protection of four population groups which it identified as having special needs: the young, the old, the disabled, and the unemployed. With respect to the elderly, the Charter confined itself to expressing the right to an adequate income. The Action Programme,[9] drawn up to implement the Charter's objectives, stated '. . . most action in the area falls within the direct responsibility of the Member States at national, regional or local level'. Consequently apart from two Recommendations on minimum income benefits[10] and converging social security objectives,[11] little was done to overcome social exclusion.

C. Social Exclusion Post-Amsterdam

Following the amendments introduced by the Treaty of Amsterdam, Article 2 of **9.11** the EC Treaty includes amongst its objectives '. . . a high level of employment and social protection and the raising of the standard of living and the quality of life'.

Article 136 provides that Community and the Member States have, as their **9.12** objective, the 'combating of exclusion'. To this end Article 137 empowers the Community to:

> . . . supplement and complement the activities of the Member States in the following fields:
> . . .
> (j) the combating of social exclusion

No specific legislative power is granted to the Commission to achieve this **9.13** objective. It is to be attained by means of:

> . . . the co-operation between Member States through initiatives aimed at improving knowledge, developing exchanges of information and best practice, promoting innovative approaches and evaluating experiences excluding any harmonization of the laws and regulations of the Member States.[12]

---

[8] [1989] OJ C 277/1.
[9] COM (89) 568 Final.
[10] [1992] OJ L245/43.
[11] [1992] OJ L245/49.
[12] Art 137(2)(a).

125

9.14 The Charter of Fundamental Rights of December 2000[13] provides in Article 34:

> In order to combat social exclusion and poverty, the Union recognizes and respects the right to social and housing assistance so as to ensure a decent existence for all those who lack sufficient resources, in accordance with the rules laid down by Community law and national laws and practices.

D. The Lisbon Strategy

9.15 At the launch of the Lisbon Strategy in March 2000, the European Council asked the European Commission and the Member States to take steps to make a decisive impact on the eradication of poverty by 2010,[14] and to work on the adequacy and sustainability of pension systems.[15] This work was to be carried out through the Open Method of Co-ordination (OMC) in two separate processes known respectively as the Social Inclusion Process and the OMC on Adequate and Sustainable Pensions. A further OMC process was established to deal with health care delivery and long-term care policy.

9.16 The OMC, as applied to social inclusion and pensions, has involved the following processes: agreeing common objectives, preparing National Action Plans (NAPS) in the case of social inclusion, and National Strategy Reports (NSRs) for pensions in which Member States set out how they will plan policies over an agreed period to meet common objectives; evaluation of these plans and strategies; Joint Commission/Council Reports analysing and assessing the National Reports on Strategies for Social Protection and Social Inclusion; joint work on indicators to facilitate mutual understanding; and measurement of progress and target setting. The OMC further provides a forum for exchanges of information. An evaluation of the OMC process in social inclusion and pensions was carried out in 2005. Seven questions were addressed to the Member States, to the European level social partners, and to the network of non-governmental organizations and social welfare institutions. A synthesis of the replies to this evaluation questionnaire was published in March 2006.[16]

A single process

9.17 As from 2006 the three OMC processes, dealing with social exclusion, pensions, and health care and long-term care were integrated into one.[17] Common

---

13 [2000] OJ C364/1.

14 Conclusions Lisbon European Council March 2000 para 32.

15 Ibid para 31.

16 Commission Staff Working Document: Evaluation of the Open method of Co-ordination for Social Protection and Social Inclusion SEC (2006) 345.

17 Working together, working better: A new framework for the open coordination of social protection and social inclusion of policies in the European Union COM (2005) 706 Final.

objectives were established and the process was structured as a three-year cycle with simplified reporting obligations. Member States were required to submit National Strategic Reports in the first year of this cycle which were then synthesized in a Joint Council and Commission Report on Social Protection and Social Inclusion. The Joint Report includes separate country profiles highlighting the priority themes and national challenges. The intervening years, which are free of reporting obligations, are dedicated to in-depth analysis and mutual learning on priority themes.

The first integrated National Reports on Strategies for Social Inclusion, pensions, **9.18** healthcare and long-term care were submitted to the European Council meeting of 8/9 March 2007.[18] An analysis of the reports reveals a number of key findings. Member States are taking initiatives to reduce child poverty. It is recognized that education plays a powerful role in achieving this objective but in order to broaden the educational opportunities of the poorer sections of society, emphasis needs to be placed on pre-schooling and tackling the problem of early school leavers. Moving people out of welfare into the labour market can be achieved by increased conditionality in accessing benefits and making work pay. At the same time attaching conditions to the receipt of benefits must not push those unable to work further into social exclusion. More rational use of resources is necessary to render health care systems sustainable and to maintain standards. Some Member States need to expand their financial and human resources to provide health care to the whole population. Demographic change requires new thinking on long-term care for the elderly. Care systems need to be reformed, properly resourced and put on a sound financial footing. There is consensus within the Member States that the elderly should be kept for as long as possible in their own homes. This requires coordinated support from social and health services. Sustainable pension systems require both an increase in the working population and longer working life. Additionally, predicted sharp increases in expenditure to provide the elderly with pensions, health care, and long-term care is putting, to varying degrees amongst the Member States, the long-term sustainability of public finances at risk. Public debt needs to reduced, employment levels must rise, and social protection systems must be reformed. The increased participation of a wide range of stakeholders in the governance of social policy, both at EU and national level, needs to be further reinforced and extended beyond policy formation to policy implementation.

On 2 July 2008, the Commission published a Communication addressed to the **9.19** European Parliament, the Council, the European Economic and Social Committee, and the Committee of the Regions entitled 'A Renewed Commitment

---

[18] <http://ec.europa.eu/employment_social/social_inclusion/naps_en.htm>.

to Social Europe: Reinforcing the Open Method of Co-ordination for Social Protection and Social Inclusion'.[19] The Communication whilst acknowledging that since its inception, the Social OMC 'had proved its worth' concluded that:

> ... delivery on common objectives—fighting poverty and social exclusion, pension adequacy and sustainability of pensions, ensuring equitable access to health and long-term care—remains a challenge.[20]

9.20 It was admitted that an open co-ordination process, based on voluntary co-operation between numerous and diverse Member States, cannot, by definition, produce large-scale results in a limited period of time. Yet the Commission concluded that there was evidence of a broad consensus both within the Social Protection Committee and amongst the relevant stakeholders that more can and should be done to make full use of the potential of the Social OMC. Emphasizing the 'positive results' of the OMC so far, the Commission concluded that change needed to come about in order to improve delivery on agreed common objectives. It was pointed out that in spite of the European Council's commitment in 2000 to make a decisive impact on the eradication of poverty rates in the EU, poverty persists;[21] the risk of inadequate pension provision for future generations,[22] and inequality in health persists, with disadvantaged groups being in relatively poorer health than other sections of the population and having a shorter life span.[23] In short, the Communication concludes that the Social OMC needs to move on from setting objectives to realizing them. To confine the process to the setting of objectives and a mutual learning exercise will not bring about tangible results.

9.21 The OMC process needs, the Communication states, to be reinforced by the introduction of selected indicators and quantitative targets. For example, in the case of poverty eradication, targets could be set for the reduction of poverty in general as well as specific forms of poverty. As to pension schemes, a target for reform could be related to the minimum level of income provided through pensions. The implementation of the objectives in health care and long-term care could be supported by targets related to access to, and the quality of, health care and long-term care, for example in the case of life expectancy and infant mortality.

---

[19] COM (2008) 418 Final.

[20] Ibid at 2.

[21] 16% of the Community's citizens (78 million) are at risk of poverty. Children are even at a greater risk with 19%—in some Member States one in four—either living in poverty or at risk of doing so. In work poverty which hits 8% of the working population is on the increase. Ibid at 5.

[22] Current pension levels are causing poverty amongst the over 65 age group. Ibid at 5.

[23] Life expectancy differs amongst the Member States by as much as 13 years in the case of men and 7 years in the case of women.

Whilst the Commission obviously feels that it is appropriate at this point in time to proceed to the realization of objectives by means of clearly quantifiable targets it is, nevertheless, aware of the differences between the Member States within the enlarged Union of 27 countries. It thus acknowledges that account must be taken of particular national contexts and differing points of departure. A process of 'differentiation along pathways' is thus proposed which would make it possible for groups of countries with similar situations and problems to work together. **9.22**

In addition to this reinforcement of the OMC process the Commission on 3 October 2008 adopted a Recommendation,[24] pursuant to Article 211 EC, setting out common principles to help guide the Member States in their strategies to tackle poverty. The Recommendation is based around three key aspects: adequate income support, inclusive labour markets, and access to quality services. National governments will be encouraged to refer to these common principles and define policies for 'active inclusion' on this basis so as to step up the fight against exclusion from society and from the labour market. **9.23**

E. The Social Agenda 2005–2010 [25]

The Social Agenda, published in 2005, setting out the EC Commission's strategy in the social field for the forthcoming five years noted that, encouraged by the OMC, Member States had sought to make their minimum income systems more effective but many people were still without either employment or minimum income support. Whilst most Member States have policies in place to bring excluded people back into the labour market, there remains a sizeable 'hard core' of persons with little prospect of finding a job who, for that reason, remain at high risk of falling into poverty and social exclusion. The main challenge facing the Community is to ensure that national social protection policies effectively contribute to mobilizing people who are capable of working whilst at the same time providing a decent standard of living to those who are and will remain outside the labour market. **9.24**

Consultations with the social partners on how to achieve these objectives were launched in early 2006.[26] The results of the consultation were published in autumn 2006. It was generally agreed that more needed to be done at EU level **9.25**

---

[24] Commisison Recommendation on the active inclusion of people excluded from the labour market. Com (2008) 639 Final.

[25] COM (2005) 33 Final.

[26] COM (2006) 44 Final 'Concerning a consultation action at EU level to promote the active inclusion of the people furthest from the labour market'.

to deal with the active inclusion of those furthest from the labour market; in particular the roles of the European Social Fund and the EQUAL Programme[27] were viewed as essential to promote employability and access to services needed for the integration of the excluded into the labour market. An impact assessment study is currently in progress to evaluate different policy options. The intermediate results of this exercise were presented at a conference on 15 June 2007.[28]

9.26 The Commission also proposed, in the Social Agenda, that 2010 be a European Year of combating poverty and social exclusion which will be a period both of review of the progress made since the start of the Lisbon strategy in combating poverty and exclusion and reflection on future policy directions to reduce the vulnerability of the most fragile population groups.

F. The PROGRESS Programme

9.27 The PROGRESS Programme was established on 24 October 2006[29] for a period of six years from 2007–2013. It replaces four previous programmes that ended in 2006 covering actions against discrimination, equality between men and women, employment measures, and the fight against social exclusion. The decision to opt for a single programme was prompted by a desire to rationalize and streamline EU funding and concentrate the impact of such funding. PROGRESS will support Member States to develop and deliver policy in five areas:

- employment;
- social inclusion and protection;
- working conditions;
- non-discrimination; and
- gender equality.

9.28 The global budget for this exercise is EUR 743.25 million. The largest proportion (30 per cent) is allocated to social inclusion and social protection.

G. Enlargement

9.29 As part of the process of preparing their membership of the Union all candidate countries are invited to draft, in co-operation with the European Commission,

---

[27] <http://ec.europa.eu/employment_social/equal/index_en.cfm>.
[28] <http://ec.europa.eu/employment_social/social_inclusion/active_inclusion_en.htm>.
[29] Decision 1672/2006EC establishing a Community Programme for Employment and Social Solidarity [2006] OJ L315/1.

a Joint Inclusion Memorandum (JIM). The JIM identifies and outlines the principal challenges which the candidate country faces in tackling poverty and social exclusion. It assesses the strengths and weaknesses of existing policies and identifies future challenges and policy priorities and paves the way for the candidate country to participate in the OMC. JIMs provide a detailed profile of the social situation in each Member State at the time of accession. They can be found at <http://ec.europa.eu/employment_social/social_inclusion/jmem_en.htm>.

Part III

EMPLOYMENT POLICY

10

COMMON EMPLOYMENT POLICY[1]

A. Introduction

10.01 Within the past decade employment policy has ceased to be a matter within the exclusive competence of the Member States. Up until around 1994 the Community's work in the field of employment was concerned almost exclusively with employment rights, that is the collective and individual rights of persons working under a contract of employment or in an employment relationship. The formulation of employment policy was regarded as a matter best left to the

---

[1] Ashiagbor: *The European Employment Strategy* Oxford University Press 2005; Biagi: 'The Implementation of the Amsterdam Treaty with regard to Employment: Coordination or Convergence' (1998) 14(4) IJCLLIR 325–36; Biagi: 'The Impact of European Employment Strategy on the Role of Labour Law and Industrial Relations' (2000) 16(2) IJCLLIR 155–73; Bruun: 'The European Employment Strategy and the "acquis communautaire" of Labour Law' (2001) 17(3) IJCLLIR 308–24; Goetschy: 'The European Employment Strategy from Stockholm to Amsterdam' (2001) 32 ILJ 401; Kenner: 'The EC Employment Title and the "Third Way": Making Soft Law Work' (1999) 15(1) IJCLLIR 33–66; Pavan-Woolfe: 'The European Strategy for Employment: What Lies Ahead' (2000) 16(3) IJCLLIR 299–303; Rhodes: 'Employment Policy' in Wallace, Wallace and Pollack (eds): *Policy Making in the European Union*. Fifth Edition Oxford University Press 2005, Chapter 11 at 279–304; Smismans: EU Employment Policy: Decentralisation or Centralisation through the Open method of Co-ordination EUI Working Paper LAW 2004/1; Szyszczak: 'The Evolving Employment Strategy' in Shaw (ed) *Social Law and Policy* Hart Publishing 2000, Chapter 10 at 197–223.

Member States.[2] This has now changed as the Community has assumed increasing responsibility for economic and monetary policy, of which employment policy is an integral part.

10.02 The current role of the Community is to promote active cooperation between the Member States' national employment policies by taking initiatives, reporting on employment trends and prospects, undertaking research and analytical work, and harnessing national employment policies to Community objectives. The diversity of Member States' employment policies are respected. But Member States are required to act within the constraints of Community parameters. Although the inclusion of employment policy within the objectives of the Community was a popular move and easy to 'sell' to European citizens, who were and continued to be concerned about levels of unemployment, the introduction of a single employment policy implemented by means of classic Community instruments would have been seen as too intrusive of the Member States' competence in this area.[3]

B. The Treaty of Amsterdam

10.03 The Amsterdam Treaty marks a commitment to achieving a high level of employment as one of the key objectives of the Community. Member States and the Community institutions are obliged to work together to develop a coordinated strategy for employment and in particular to promote a skilled, trained, and adaptable workforce and a labour market responsive to change.

10.04 Article 3(i) specifies one of the fundamental objectives of the EC to be:

> . . . the promotion of the co-ordination between employment policies of the Member States with a view of enhancing their effectiveness by developing a coordinated strategy for employment.

10.05 This new approach is indicative of the commitment of the Community towards employment policy. It is seen as a central policy objective, no longer a matter

---

[2] The Standing Employment Committee was established in 1970 (Council Decision 70/532 [1970] OJ L273) to deal with employment issues. It was a tripartite institution composed of ministers of labour, the social partners, and the EC Commission. The task of the Committee was to co-ordinate national employment polices to make them compatible with Community objectives. The Committee was the subject of a major reform in 1999 (Council Decision 1999/207 [1999] OJ L72/33) Throughout the 1980s the Community's efforts in the employment area were confined to structural fund support for vulnerable sections of the labour market (local employment initiatives, support for women and measures to facilitate the integration of young people, and the long-term unemployed into the labour market).

[3] Smismans (see note 1 above) at 2.

which should be left exclusively to the Member States nor to the informal efforts of the Community institutions to harness those policies to Community interests. Whilst the principle of subsidiarity requires that employment policy should remain a matter of national competence, it is accepted that the Community needs to play an active role in the co-ordination.

The importance attached to employment policy is signified by the place accorded to it in the EC Treaty by the Treaty of Amsterdam. It has a dedicated title, signifying its status as a major Community objective. **10.06**

Title VIII 'Employment' has six provisions—Articles 125–130. Article 127 makes employment policy an integral part of Community activity. The impact of all Community policies and activities on employment must be taken into account when they are being formulated and implemented. Article 128 empowers the Commission to develop general ideas about the optimal employment strategy for the Community. This policy is elaborated in co-operation with the Council, the Member States, and the social partners. **10.07**

Article 130 establishes, on a permanent basis, the Employment Committee which provides a continuous and transparent debate on employment and other structural policy.[4] The Employment Committee is composed of two representatives from each Member State and two from the Commission. Article 130 envisages the participation of the social partners through consultation by the Employment Committee. Article 129 creates a legal basis for analysis, research, exchange of best practice, and the promotion of incentive measures. This is the only provision in the Employment Title providing a specific legal basis for the adoption of binding measures. Such measures may not include the harmonization of the laws and regulations of the Member States. The European Parliament is involved through the co-decision procedure.[5] **10.08**

The Employment Title has a number of drawbacks. It does not provide '. . . a comprehensive framework for what might be a European employment policy in a multi-level context'.[6] The social partners do not participate directly in the policy formulation process[7] and there is no provision for the consultation of regional and local authorities who often have considerable responsibility in the organization and delivery of employment and social services. This was recognized by the **10.09**

---

[4] The Employment Committee was formally established by Council Decision 2000/98 [2000] OJ L29/21.

[5] Art 251 EC.

[6] Smismans note 1 at 10.

[7] There is no provision for the direct consultation of the management and labour on policy formation or execution similar to that provided for in Article 138 with respect to social policy measures.

Commission as far back as 2001[8] but no steps appear to have been taken to rectify the situation. In a Communication of 31 March 2005 the Commission again recognized the need for the participation of all stakeholders in the EES.[9]

C. Development

10.10 Employment policy has evolved in three phases beginning with the White Paper on Growth, Competitiveness and Employment: The Challenge and the Way Forward into the 21st Century, published at the end of 1993.[10] The White Paper acknowledged that economic growth following from the creation of the internal market was not sufficient to tackle the persistent high levels of employment within the Community not found in other competing economies. The level of unemployment at the time of the publication of the White Paper was described in it as of 'very serious proportions'.[11]

10.11 At the time the White Paper was published there was a widespread belief that economic integration was contributing to growing unemployment. At the same time there was increased criticism of the 'democratic deficit', a lack of representation of both civil and business interests at key levels of the Community decision making process. The White Paper sought to rally public opinion with an economy strategy for further European integration which would both increase employment levels and democratic accountability.

10.12 The White Paper set a target of job creation in the order of 15 million jobs by 2000. This was to be achieved by means of a the three-pronged strategy:

(a) the creation and maintenance of a macro-economic framework;
(b) structural change aimed at increasing European competitiveness and creating an adequate framework for developing new market opportunities;
(c) active policy and structural change in the labour market which would facilitate employment and increase the employment content of growth.[12]

10.13 These objectives could only be achieved by political co-operation amongst the Member States and this was not forthcoming. Although the Maastricht Treaty subscribed to promoting and sustaining a high level of employment[13] no specific

---

[8] Strengthening the local dimension of the European Employment Strategy COM (2001) 629 Final.
[9] COM (2005) 120 Final at 12.
[10] COM (93) 700 Final.
[11] Ibid para 1.2.
[12] Ibid para 1.4.
[13] Art 2.

means of attaining that objective were specified in the Treaty. There was thus little the Community institutions could do to achieve the ambitions of the White Paper.

Although the White Paper was widely discussed both within the Community **10.14** institutions and at multiple levels in the Member States, it brought about few concrete results. The Member States resisted the job creation measures set out in the White Paper as these would have entailed substantial financial transfers to fuel expenditure on a Community level of projects on which there was divided opinion amongst the Member States. The White Paper had advocated expenditure in the order of ECU 470 billion in infrastructure projects. It also recommended reducing employers' social security contributions on the lower paid to generate jobs at that end of the labour market which was particular susceptible to short-term employment and unemployment.

Despite the fact that it achieved few of its objectives the White Paper was not, **10.15** however, without impact. It provided a springboard and a reference point for further discussions during the 1990s.

Unemployment level grew rapidly between 1990 and 1994. Fifteen million jobs **10.16** were lost in the 15 Member States. The employment rate fell from 62 per cent in 1992 to less than 60.5 per cent in 1997, below the level of the turbulent 1970s. This position stood in stark contrast to the employment rate in Japan and the United States during the same period, which was around 74 per cent. Unemployment levels within the Community reached 11.1 per cent in 1994, up from 7.7 per cent in 1970. The position of the young and the long-term unemployed was particularly acute.[14]

By the end of 1994 it was clear that cohesive action on a Community level was **10.17** imperative. The Essen European Council, in December of that year, saw the beginning of the common employment policy.

D. The Essen European Council

The second phase in the development of the common employment policy began **10.18** in December 1994 at the Essen European Council.

---

[14] Goetschy: 'The European Employment Strategy: Genesis and Development' (1999) 5 European Journal of Industrial Relations 117–37. See also Symes: *Unemployment and Employment Policies in the EU* Kogan Page 1999, Chapter 1.

10.19 The strategy proposed by the Essen Council to tackle the problem of unemployment consisted of a combination of active employment policies and deregulation.

10.20 Five key objectives were to be pursued by the Member States:

(a) improving employment opportunities by promoting investment in vocational training;

(b) increasing the employment-intensiveness of growth through the more flexible organization of work and a wage policy which encourages job creation and the promotion of job creation initiatives, particularly in the regions;

(c) reducing non-wage labour costs;

(d) improving the effectiveness of labour market policy by avoiding practices which are a disincentive to work, particularly with respect to the formation of income support policies;

(e) imposing measures which help groups particularly vulnerable to unemployment, ie the young unqualified, the long-term unemployed, women, and the older unemployed.

10.21 The first objective raises skill levels and thus contributes to minimizing the negative consequences of structural and technological change. The second aims to create more jobs through increased labour market flexibility and investment in jobs in areas of common concern. The third is concerned with encouraging employers to create new jobs for low skilled/low paid workers. The fourth objective is to get people off welfare and into work; to make employment policies more inclusive[15] so as to enhance accessibility of, for example, the disabled to the labour market. This fourth objective can have twofold benefit in the sense that it can turn net welfare beneficiaries into net contributors, thus easing the day-to-day financial burden of welfare systems and at the same time boosting their resources so as to enable them to cope with sudden economic downturns which increase pressure on welfare expenditure. The fifth aim is to focus effort on the most vulnerable sections of the community—those least likely to even have an opportunity to access the labour market.[16]

10.22 The European Council urged the Member States to transpose these recommended priority actions into their national employment policies by means of multi-annual programmes. A pattern of co-operation between the Community institutions and the Member States was thus established.

---

[15] See Chapters 7 and 9.
[16] Symes (see note 14 above) 31–2.

The Essen Strategy, as it became known, was supported by successive European Councils and, in effect, was refined and institutionalized by the Treaty of Amsterdam. **10.23**

Whilst the Essen Strategy manifested a degree of political commitment to a co-ordinated employment policy, there were no specific Treaty provisions setting a framework within which this process should take place. Policy began to be developed on an ad hoc basis at various European Councils and was articulated in non-binding conclusions published at the end of each meeting. The Treaty of Amsterdam sought to put the process of policy formation on a more transparent and firmer footing and to clarify the respective roles of the Member States and the individual Community institutions. New tasks were allocated and the appropriate mechanisms by which they are to be fulfilled were articulated. **10.24**

E. European Employment Strategy

Once the employment provisions of the Treaty of Amsterdam had been settled but, before the Treaty had been ratified, the Member States set about implementing them. The European Council meeting in Luxembourg in November 1997 initiated the European Employment Strategy (EES).[17] **10.25**

The EES marked the beginning of a new working method at Community level known as the 'Open Method of Co-ordination'. It was based on five key principles: subsidiarity, convergence, management by objectives, country surveillance, and an integrated approach. This method of policy-making is discussed above in Chapter 4. **10.26**

The objective of the EES was to make decisive progress in the fight against unemployment within five years of its inception. This was to be achieved by setting common objectives and targets for employment, which were to be realized through the co-ordination of national employment policies. Employment Guidelines setting out common priorities were to be adopted annually by the Council, on a proposal by the Commission, following consultation of the European Parliament, the Economic and Social Committee, the Committee of the Regions, and the Employment Committee.[18] **10.27**

---

[17] 'The European Council noted with approval the agreement of the intergovernmental Conference to incorporate both the Social Agreement and a new title on Employment in the Treaty. The Council should seek to make the relevant provisions of this title immediately effective. This underlies the vitally important link between job creation, employability and social cohesion.' Presidency Conclusions. Amsterdam European Council 16/17 June 1997 <http://.www.europa.eu.int/european_council/conclusions>.

[18] Nine sets of guidelines have been published since 1997: [1998] OJ C30/1; [1999] OJ C69/2; [2000] OJ L72/15; [2001] OJ L22/18; [2002] OJ L60/60; [2003] OJ L197/13; [2004] OJ L326/45; [2005] OJ L205/21; [2008] OJ L198/47.

10.28   Each Member State would then draw up a National Action Plan putting the Guidelines into practice on a national level. The Commission and the Council would then proceed to examine jointly each National Action Plan and present a Joint Employment Report. Recommendations for the revision of the Employment Guidelines could be made by the Commission each year to the European Council. On the basis of the Commission's proposals country-specific recommendations would then be issued by the Council acting on a qualified majority.

F. The Lisbon Strategy

10.29   At a special meeting of the European Council held on 23–24 March 2000 (the 'Lisbon Summit'), the European Union, acknowledging the challenges to the European economy posed by globalization and the knowledge-based economy, set itself a strategic goal to be accomplished in the course of the following decade—to become the most competitive and dynamic knowledge-based economy in the world, capable of sustainable economic growth with more and better jobs and greater social cohesion. The Lisbon strategy was formulated as the Union experienced 'its best macro-economic outlook for a generation'.[19] Inflation and interest rates were low; public sector deficits had been reduced 'remarkably' and the EU's balance of payments was healthy. It was envisaged that the forthcoming enlargement would create new opportunities for growth and employment. The work force overall was well-educated and social protection systems were deemed to be strong enough to provide the framework for managing the structural changes inherent and the move towards a knowledge-based economy. Despite these strengths, unemployment ran at 15 million. There was long-term structural employment and regional disparities in employment levels. Women and older workers were underrepresented on the labour market. The services sector was seen as underdeveloped and increased skills were required in information technology to satisfy the demands of the market.

10.30   Achieving the strategic goal set by the Lisbon Summit required an overall strategy aimed at:

- preparing the transition to a knowledge-based economy and society by putting in place improved policies for the information society and R&D, stepping up the process for structural reform for competitiveness and innovation and by completing the internal market;
- modernizing the European social model, investing in people and combating social exclusion;

---

[19] Conclusions para 3.

- sustaining the healthy economic outlook and favourable growth prospects by applying an appropriate macro-economic policy mix.

Employment policy objectives moved from 'high employment' to 'full employment'. The target for the overall EU employment rate was rise to 70 per cent by 2010 from the then prevailing rate of 61 per cent. The number of women in employment, which stood at 51 per cent at the time of the Lisbon Summit, was to rise to 60 per cent. The Member States were required to set targets within their own employment environment to achieve these goals. **10.31**

A year later, in March 2001, the Stockholm Summit added two intermediate targets and one additional target: the employment rate should be raised to 67 per cent overall to be achieved by March 2003, 57 per cent for women by 2005, and over 50 per cent for older workers by 2010. **10.32**

These targets were to be achieved by improving employability and reducing skills gap, giving priority to lifelong learning, increasing employment in the services sector, and furthering equal opportunities. **10.33**

G. Assessment of the EES

The EES has been evaluated three times since it came into being. In 2000, a mid-term review was carried out in which three interrelated issues were addressed: the overall relevance of the EES at Community and Member State level; the implications of the Lisbon Strategy for future Employment Guidelines; and, finally, EES procedures were examined with a view to their simplification and increased effectiveness. Some strengths and weaknesses were identified. There had been an increased involvement by stakeholders in the development of employment policy; increased transparency of employment policies and enhanced political accountability for those policies. At the same time regional differences persisted and in some cases had actually been exacerbated. The skills gap also persisted. **10.34**

In July 2002 the Commission published a five-year review of the EES.[20] It found that 10 million new jobs had been created since the EES had been established, 6 million of which were taken up by women. Unemployment had dropped by 4 million. Overall the EES had succeeded in moving national employment policy away from managing unemployment to managing employment growth. Some Member States had adopted tax benefit schemes. Labour taxation had generally become more employment-friendly. Education and training systems **10.35**

---

[20] Taking Stock of Five Years of the European Employment Strategy, COM (2002) 416.

had increasingly adapted to market needs. Progress had been made in modernizing work organization, notably in terms of working time arrangements and more flexible work contracts. Gender mainstreaming had become more generalized and childcare facilities had improved. In spite of this tangible and positive progress, serious challenges remained in the form of regional differences, globalization, and enlargement of the EC and the impact of changing demographic patterns in the employment market.

10.36 The publication of the Communication stimulated an active debate on many levels.[21] The debate confirmed the importance of the EES in improving the employment situation in the Community and in achieving the convergence of national policies, but at the same time it was felt that the Guidelines needed to be revised to take account of the challenges posed by the '. . . acceleration of economic, social and demographic change, globalization and the demands of the modern economy and the forthcoming EU enlargement . . .'.[22] The EES needed to be revamped to align it more closely with the Lisbon strategy, which advocated an integrated approach to economic and employment policy. Whilst Guidelines should continue to be published annually, they should be 'fewer and simpler', more 'result orientated', and with 'appropriate targets'. Member States should be left to 'design the appropriate mix of action'.[23] The emphasis is on fewer and more coherent guidelines and a shift in focus from defining policy strategies towards implementing them.[24] The Guidelines would henceforth be substantially reviewed only on a three-year basis. A 10-year review of the EES was published in July 2007.[24a]

H. Reform of the Guidelines

10.37 In July 2003, the Council adopted the new format for its guidelines.[25] In addition to implementing the Employment Guidelines, Member States are encouraged to have regard to the Broad Economic Policy Guidelines and to ensure that the two instruments operate as a coherent whole on their national territory.

---

[21] A Strategy for Full Employment and Better Jobs for All, COM (2003) 6 Final.

[22] Proposals for a Council Decision on Guidelines for the Employment Policies of the Member States, COM (2003) 176 Final at 2.

[23] Ibid.

[24] '. . . the drafting and monitoring of the guidelines implies (both for the Commission and the Member States) a high bureaucratic workload not least because of the high numbers of guidelines. The energy spent on the formation, monitoring and (re-) drafting of guidelines may not be in proportion to the efforts done to implement the policy proposed in the guidelines.' Smismans (see note 1 above) at 9.

[24a] Ten years of the European Employment Strategy (ESS). Office of the Official Publications of the European Communities, Luxernbourg 2007.

[25] [2003] OJ L197/13.

The number of guidelines has been reduced, and the previous four pillar struc-   **10.38**
ture abandoned in favour of three overarching objectives: full employment,
quality and productivity at work, and social cohesion and inclusion.[26] As a general rule, the Member States are required to adopt a gender mainstreaming
approach across each of their policy initiatives.

The 10 specific actions required to implement the three objectives set out in the   **10.39**
Guidelines are:

(a)   active and preventative measures for the unemployed and inactive;
(b)   job creation and entrepreneurship;
(c)   the promotion of adaptability and mobility in the labour market to address
      change;
(d)   the development of human capital and lifelong training;
(e)   increasing labour supply and the promotion of active ageing;
(f)   gender equality;
(g)   the integration of people at a disadvantage in the labour market;
(h)   making work pay;
(i)   the transformation of undeclared work into regular employment;
(j)   addressing regional employment disparities.

In achieving these objectives, the Member States are urged to involve parliamen-   **10.40**
tary bodies, the social partners, and other relevant entities.

The specific guidelines set out in detail how the Council envisages the implemen-   **10.41**
tation of these objectives within national employment policy.

I. Streamlining Economic and Employment Policy

On 3 September 2002,[27] the Commission published a further Communi-   **10.42**
cation on the streamlining of the annual economic and employment policy
co-ordination exercises to facilitate coherence between them and set a new
schedule for the drawing up of the employment guidelines.

The new policy formulation cycle is to take the following pattern: the Commis-   **10.43**
sion is to present in January of each year its reviews of the Broad Economic Policy
Guidelines (BEPGs), the draft Joint Employment Report, the implementation
of the Internal Market Strategy, and a detailed assessment of the implementation
of various other policies. Following the conclusions of the Spring European

---

[26] Annex to the Employment Guidelines, [2003] OJ L197/13.
[27] COM (2002) 487 Final.

Council, the Commission will define and present its proposals for future action in a 'Guidelines Package' comprising Broad Economic Policy Guidelines, the Employment Guidelines, and Employment Recommendations. The June European Council will conclude on this, the guidelines will be drawn up, and National Action Plans settled accordingly.

J. The Revised Lisbon Strategy

10.44 The third phase in the evolution of Community employment policy began at the beginning of 2005 with the announcement of the revised Lisbon Strategy.

10.45 In a Communication to the Spring European Council[28] (the 'Barrosa Communication') President Barrosa admitted that progress on the Lisbon Strategy, five years after its adoption, had been 'mixed'. The Community faced serious structural difficulties. There were external and internal challenges. Economic conditions in the intervening years had been difficult. There had been a reversal of fortune for the global economy attributable to a number of factors: the down turn in world trade, accounting scandals, geopolitical uncertainty stemming from terrorist attacks and the war in Iraq. As a result average annual growth in some Member States remained below 1 per cent over the period 2001–2003. Research and development investment within the Community was close to stagnation; by contrast other parts of the world had invested more in research and development and their production had grown at a more rapid pace. Increasing globalization had exposed the European economy to increased competition. The ageing population in Europe posed challenges for the stability in the level of the working population, which, if not addressed, could lead to a dramatic decline in growth. In short, the favourable economic climate in which the Lisbon strategy had been conceived no longer existed. The issue was whether to abandon that strategy altogether or to revise it. The latter option was chosen.[29]

10.46 Aside from the constraints the changed economic environment placed on attaining the Lisbon objectives, the actual means of realizing those objectives was at fault. The Lisbon process had become overloaded and unco-ordinated, resulting in duplication and overlapping of efforts. Governance issues needed to be resolved and objectives re-visited. The Lisbon strategy needed to focus on growth and jobs. Europe needed to make itself more attractive as a place of work and investment. More and better jobs needed to be created and spending on research and

---

[28] Working together for Growth and Jobs: A new start for the Lisbon Strategy COM (2005) 24.
[29] Following the recommendation of the Kok Report—Facing the Challenge: The Lisbon Strategy for Growth and Employment November 2004.

development increased. To achieve these objectives the governance of the Lisbon strategy 'needs radical improvement to make it more effective and more easily understood'.[30]

Some two months after the Barroso Communication, the Commission set out its **10.47** thinking on restructuring and employment.[31] The objective of this paper was to set out how restructuring of the Community's labour market could be anticipated and managed and what role the European Union should play in this process. Expressing its firm belief that restructuring must not be seen as synonymous with social decline and a loss of economic substance, the Commission advocated a four-pronged strategy: consistency between the various Community policies; a long-term perspective of Community policies to enable economic and social stakeholders to act effectively; the participation of all stakeholders, notably the social partners; and the involvement of the local dimension in policy-making.

On the governance front, Employment Guidelines for the period 2005–2008 **10.48** and the Broad Economic Policy Guidelines were adopted as an integrated package in July 2005.[32] Both sets of guidelines are to be fully reviewed only at three-yearly intervals. Any updating in the intermediate years should be strictly limited.[33] In December 2005 the Commission published its thoughts on the streamlining of the three open-co-ordination processes operating in the social and employment field with the intent of strengthening the processes through collective engagement and further integrating social policy into the Broad Economic Policy Guidelines and the European Employment Strategy.[34]

---

[30] Ibid at 10.

[31] Restructuring and Employment: Anticipating and accompanying restructuring in order to develop employment: The Role of the European Union COM (2005) 120 Final.

[32] [2005] OJ L21.

[33] In January 2006 the Commission published a proposal for a decision maintaining in force the Guidelines agreed for the period 2005–2008. No revision was attempted. COM (2006) 32 Final. In July 2008 the Council adopted the Employment Guidelines for the period 2008–2010 [2008] OJ L198/47.

[34] Working together, working better: A new framework for the open co-ordination of social protection and inclusion policies in the European Union. Prior to making these proposals the Commission had carried out an evaluation of the OMC process for social inclusion and pensions. The results of this evaluation, in which the Member States, the European level social partner bodies and a sizeable number of European level NGOs participation, was published in March 2006; Evaluation of the Open Method of Co-ordination for Social Protection and Social Inclusion SEC (2006) 345.

PART IV

COLLECTIVE EMPLOYMENT RIGHTS

11

COLLECTIVE REDUNDANCIES

A. Introduction

Directive 75/129 laid down common procedures which had to be observed by all **11.01** undertakings carrying out collective redundancies.[1] It was amended by Directive 92/56,[2] which entered into force on 24 June 1994. Both Directives have been consolidated and replaced by Directive 98/59 (the 'Directive').[3] Directive 75/129 was the first in a series of directives adopted pursuant to the 1974 Social Action Programme[4] designed to reduce disparities between the laws and practices of the Member States relating to employment rights. It had both an economic and social purpose: to alleviate the consequences of redundancy for employees and to lay down common rules relating to the practical arrangements and procedures for collective redundancies throughout the Community.[5] Substantive and procedural redundancy rights under national law and practice are left intact save in so far as they are incompatible with the minimum standards laid down in the

---

[1] Directive 75/129 on the approximation of the laws of the Member States relating to collective redundancies. [1975] OJ L48/29.

[2] Directive 92/56 amending Directive 75/129 [1992] OJ L245/3.

[3] [1998] OJ L225/16.

[4] [1974] OJ C12/1.

[5] Case C-449/83 *Rockfon* [1995] ECR I–4291 Judgment at para 21.

Directive. Member States may apply or introduce provisions which are more favourable.[6]

11.02 The Directive provides for consultation with employee representatives and for notification of the competent authorities prior to multiple lay-offs.

11.03 The Directive does not affect the substantive right of employers to dismiss their employees[7] nor does it restrict their freedom to organize their undertakings in a manner best suited to their needs.[8] Thus the Directive does not preclude, for example, two or more interrelated undertakings in a group from establishing a joint recruitment and dismissal department, the approval of which is required for redundancies in any one of the undertakings.[9]

B. Scope of Application

11.04 The Directive applies to collective redundancies, which are defined as dismissals effected by an employer for one or more reasons, not related to the individual workers concerned.[10] The threshold at which the Directive becomes applicable—when redundancies fall to be defined as 'collective'—is prescribed. A twofold test determines the threshold:

(i) the size of the employing establishment's workforce;

(ii) the number of employees affected by the collective redundancies within a given time period.

11.05 The Directive applies where the number of redundancies is:

either, over a period of 30 days;
(a) at least 10 in establishments normally employing more than 20 but less than 100 workers;
(b) at least 10 per cent of the number of workers in establishments normally employing more than 100 but less than 300 employees;
(c) at least 30 in establishments normally employing 300 employees or more;
or, over a period of 90 days, at least 20 whatever the number of employees employed in the establishment in question.[11]

---

6 Case 91/81 *Commission v Italy* [1982] ECR 2133 Judgment para 11.

7 Case 284/83 *Dansk Metalarbejderforbund and Specialarbejderforbundet i Danmark v Nielsen & Son Maskin-Fabrik A/S* [1985] ECR 553; Case C-383/92 *Commission v United Kingdom* [1994] ECR I–2479.

8 See note 5 above.

9 Ibid Judgment para 32.

10 Art 1(a). For example as a result of reorganization within the undertaking making the redundancies.

11 Art 1(a)(ii).

The thresholds and the methods by which they are calculated are prescribed in **11.06**
clear terms by the Directive. They are absolute criteria of mandatory application.
If the position were otherwise, the Directive could be deprived of its full effect.
In *CGT and Others* [12] the ECJ held that a French rule which laid down the method
of calculation of workforce numbers had the effect of altering the scope of the
Directive. In issue was Article 1 of Order 2005-892, the objective of which
was to encourage youth employment, which amended the French Labour Code
to read:

> An employee engaged after 22 June 2005 who is under 26 years of age shall not be
> taken into account in calculating the size of the workforce of the undertaking by
> which he is employed until he reaches the age of 26, whatever the nature of his
> contract with the undertaking.

The Court held that the effect of this provision would be: **11.07**

> . . . liable to deprive, even temporarily, all workers employed in establishments
> employing more than 20 workers of the rights which they derive from Directive
> 98/59 and thus undermine its effectiveness. [13]

Such a rule of national law was thus precluded by virtue of Article I(1)(a) of the
Directive which prescribed the thresholds at which the Directive becomes applicable. National legislation cannot exclude, even for a limited period, a specific
category of workers from the calculation of staff numbers, where those numbers
are determinative of the applicability of the Directive to the workforce as a
whole.

The application of the Directive is not dependent upon the will of the employer. **11.08**
The termination of contracts of employment cannot escape the requirements
of the Directive simply because they result from circumstances external to the
employer undertaking and are not contingent upon its will. [14] Article 3(1) and the
ninth paragraph of the Preamble to the Directive make it clear that it applies, as
a rule, to collective redundancies caused by the termination of an establishment's
activities as a result of a judicial decision. [15] In that situation, the termination
of the contract of employment is the result of circumstances not generally willed
by the employer.

---

[12] Case C-385/05 [2007] ECR I–611.
[13] Ibid Judgment para 48.
[14] Ibid Judgment para 60.
[15] Case C-55/02 *Commission v Portugal* [2004] ECR I–9387.

C. Multiple Individual Dismissals

11.09   In calculating the number of redundancies, any termination of the employment contract of an individual worker is to be treated as falling within the scope of the Directive where at least five such terminations have occurred.[16] This provision is designed to prevent employers avoiding their obligations under the Directive by thinning out their workforce in a piecemeal manner and thus keeping redundancy levels below the thresholds at which the Directive becomes applicable. However, presumably even if there has been a series of five or more individual redundancies, if these have occurred for reasons connected with the individual dismissed workers themselves, the Directive will not apply.

D. Employer/Employee

11.10   The term 'employer' is to be interpreted broadly as including employers engaged in non-profit-making activities.[17] 'Employee' is defined according to national law and practice, there being no specific definition accorded in the Directive, but, following the Court's judgment in *CGT*[18] a Member State cannot adopt a definition of 'employee' which might result in the Directive being deprived of its full effect.

E. Establishment

11.11   The term 'establishment' has been held in *Rockfon*[19] to mean the unit to which the workers to be made redundant are assigned to carry out their duties.[20] That unit need not necessarily be endowed with the managerial capability to effect collective redundancies. This broad definition is designed to limit as far as possible cases of collective redundancies which are not subject to the Directive because of the legal definition of that term at a national level.[21]

---

[16] Art 1(1).

[17] Case C-32/02 *Commission v Italy* [2003] ECR I–12063 Judgment para 26.

[18] See note 12 above.

[19] Case C-449/93 [1995] ECR I–4291.

[20] Case 186/83 *Botzen* [1985] ECR 519; Case C-449/93 *Rockfon* [1995] ECR I–4291.Contrast with Article 2(b) of Directive 2002/14 establishing a general framework for informing and consulting employees ([2002] OJ L80/29) which defines establishment as 'a unit of business defined in accordance with national law and practice . . . where an economic activity is carried out on an ongoing basis with human and material resources'. See the reluctance of Advocate General Mengozzi in *CGT* (see note 12 above) to interpret the concept of 'establishment' in Directive 98/59 in the light of that provision.

[21] Joined Cases C-187/05 to C-190/05 *Agorastoudis* [2006] ECR I–7775 Judgment para 37.

F. Redundancy

The concept of 'redundancy' is not specifically defined in the Directive nor does **11.12** the Directive prescribe the determination of that term by reference to national law. The ECJ has held that it is a Community concept[22] which cannot be defined by reference to national law, but which must be given an autonomous and uniform interpretation[23] by reference to the purpose and the provisions of the Directive as expressed in all language versions thereof.[24]

The essential criterion is that the termination of the employment should be **11.13** against the will of the worker:[25]

> . . .the concept of 'redundancy' as mentioned in Article 1(1)(a) of the Directive, may not be defined by any reference to the laws of the Member States, but has instead meaning in Community law.

> The concept has to be interpreted as including any termination of contract of employment not sought by the worker, and therefore without his consent, It is not necessary that the underlying reasons should reflect the will of the employer.[26]

In Agorastoudis[27] the Court condemned the approach of the Greek courts which **11.14** took the view, expressed in settled case law, that if a decision to terminate an undertaking's activities definitively is made by an employer of his own volition, and in accordance with constitutionally guaranteed economic and financial freedoms, irrespective of a judicial decision, the Directive was not applicable. The application of the Directive, according to Greek case law was dependent on the undertaking's continued operation. The Court found this to be an incorrect application of the Directive:

> No basis can be found for that interpretation in the wording of Directive 75/129, in the objective or purpose pursued by it or in the Court's case-law relating to the directive.

> . . .

> . . . the answer to the question referred must be that Directive 75/129 must be interpreted as being applicable in the case of collective redundancies that result from the definitive termination of the operation of an undertaking or establishment which has been decided on by the employer of his own accord without a prior

---

[22] Case C-55/02 *Commission v Portugal* [2004] ECR I–9387 Judgment para 49.

[23] Case C-287/98 *Linster* [2000] ECR I–6917 Judgment para 43; Case C-40/01 *Ansul* [2003] ECR I–2439 Judgment para 26.

[24] Case C-188/03 *Junk* [2005] ECR I–885 Judgment para 33.

[25] Case C-55/02 (see note 22 above) Judgment at para 62.

[26] Ibid Judgment paras 49 and 50.

[27] See note 21 above.

judicial decision, and the exception laid down in Article 1(2)(d) of that directive cannot preclude its application.[28]

11.15 The Directive applies irrespective of the reason for the lay-offs. In *Commission v United Kingdom*[29] the ECJ held that the scope of the Directive was not confined to redundancies carried out as a result of the cessation of the business or a downturn in the volume of business of an undertaking but it must also extend to all cases where workers have been dismissed as a result of new working arrangements within an undertaking, unconnected with its volume of business. Similarly, the Court held in *Commission v Portugal*[30] that the Portuguese government, by restricting the concept of collective redundancy to dismissals for structural, technological, or cyclical reasons, thereby failing to extend that concept to dismissals for any reason not related to individual workers concerned, had failed to fulfil its obligations under Articles 1 and 6 of the Directive.

11.16 No indication is given in the Directive of what event triggers redundancy for the purpose of setting in motion the rights granted under the Directive, nor is there any provision referring the determination of this point in time to national law norms. In *Junk*[31] the ECJ was asked whether the event constituting the redundancy, for the purposes of the Directive, consisted of the expression by the employer of his intention to put an end to the contract of employment or an actual cessation of the employment relationship on the expiry of the period in the notices of redundancy. Analysing the words of the Directive the Court reasoned as follows: Article 2(1) of the Directive imposes an obligation on the employer to begin consultation with the workers' representatives in good time and in any case where he is 'contemplating collective redundancies'.

11.17 Article 3(1) requires the employer to notify the competent public authority of any projected collective redundancies. These requirements indicate a situation in which no decision has been taken, whereas the notification to a worker that his or her contract of employment has been terminated is an expression of a decision to sever the employment relationship and the actual cessation of that relationship on the expiry of the period of notice is no more than the effect of that decision. Articles 2(1) and 3(1) indicate the obligation to consult and notify arises prior to any decision by the employer to terminate the contract of employment. The purpose of the Directive, which is to avoid or at least reduce the termination of

---

[28] See note 21 above Judgment paras 25 and 45.
[29] Case C-383/92 [1994] ECR I-2479; Davies: 'A Challenge to a Single Channel' (1994) 23 ILJ 272-85 More: 'Community Labour Law and the Protection of Employees' Rights in the United Kingdom' (1994) 19 EL Rev 660-68; Skidmore: 'Enforcement of Rights to Worker Representation in Community Law' (1995) 58 MLR 744-51; Bercusson: Case C-382/92 *Commission v United Kingdom*; Case C-383/92 *Commission v United Kingdom* 33 CML Rev (1996) 589-610.
[30] See note 15 above.
[31] See note 24 above.

contracts of employment, would be jeopardized if the consultation of workers' representatives were to be subsequent to the employer's decision. Consequently the event constituting redundancy must consist in the declaration by the employer of his intention to terminate the contract of employment.[32]

There is no obligation, express or implied, under the Directive on employers to **11.18** foresee collective redundancies nor the circumstances or timeframe within which they will occur:

> ... there is no implied obligation under the directive to foresee collective redundancies. The Directive does not stipulate the circumstances in which the employer must contemplate collective redundancies and in no way affects his freedom to decide whether and when he must formulate plans for collective dismissals.[33]

G. Exceptions

The Directive does not apply to: **11.19**

(a) fixed-term contracts or contracts for the performance of specific tasks, except where the redundancies take place prior to the date of expiry or completion of the contracts;
(b) workers employed by public administrative bodies or in establishments governed by public law;
(c) crews of sea-going vessels.[34]

As exceptions to the general rules set out in the Directive, these types of employment must be construed narrowly.

Prior to the entry into force of Directive 92/56, redundancies which took place **11.20** following the closure of an establishment by a judicial decision were also excluded from the scope of application of the Directive.[35] They are now within the scope of the Directive but may be exempt from its application by the Member States at their discretion.[36] Where Member States do exercise their discretion and provide for a derogation in the case of termination of the activities of an establishment as a result of a judicial decision, that derogation does not apply to collective redundancies occurring on the same day as that on which the employer filed a winding

---

[32] Case C-188/03 *Junk* (see note 24 above).
[33] Case 284/83 *Nielsen* [1985] ECR 553 Judgment para 10.
[34] Art 1(2).
[35] By virtue of Article 1(2) of Directive 75/129. This provision was interpreted by the ECJ in *Agorastoudis* (see note 21 above) as meaning that the Directive was not to apply solely where the termination of an establishment's activities is the result of a judicial decision, for example, a decision ordering the compulsory liquidation or winding up of an undertaking.
[36] Art 4(4). Case C-55/02 *Commission v Portugal* note 15 Judgment para 54.

up petition and terminated the undertaking's activities. The fact that certain effects of the ultimate winding up order are retroactive from the date on which the winding up petition is filed is irrelevant.[37]

H. Information and Consultation Procedure

11.21 An employer who is contemplating collective redundancies has a twofold obligation:

(i) to inform the competent national authority; and
(ii) to consult with representatives of the workforce on the planned redundancy programme.

11.22 The employer is obliged to furnish the workers' representatives with all the relevant information relating to the proposed redundancies.[38] In particular, he must give the following information in writing: the reasons for the proposed redundancies; the number of categories of workers to be made redundant; the number of workers normally employed in the undertaking; the period of time over which the redundancies are to be effected; the criteria proposed for the selection of workers to be made redundant if national law empowers the employer to make this selection; the method of calculating redundancy payments other than those payable and calculable under national law. Article 2(4)(2) provides that it is not open to an employer to argue that the parent or controlling undertaking has not provided it with the necessary information.

11.23 Article 2 of the Directive provides that an employer who is contemplating making redundancies must begin consultations with workers' representatives in good time, with a view to reaching an agreement. Workers' representatives have to be consulted regardless of whether the decision regarding the dismissals is being taken by the immediate employer or a controlling undertaking.

11.24 The consultations must cover the ways and means of avoiding collective redundancies or reducing the number of workers affected, and of mitigating the consequences by social measures aimed at, inter alia, aid for redeploying or retraining workers whose redundancy is envisaged. The consultations must take place 'in good time'. This has been interpreted in *Junk*[39] as meaning 'prior to any decision to terminate contracts of employment'. The contract of employment

---

[37] Art 3(1).
[38] An employer cannot plead that the necessary information has not been supplied by the parent undertaking: it is his duty to ensure that all the relevant information is provided to both the workers' representatives and the competent public authorities (Art 2(4)).
[39] Note 24.

can only be terminated after the conclusion of the consultation procedure and the notification of the projected redundancies to the public authorities. It would be significantly more difficult for workers' representatives to achieve the withdrawal of a decision that had been taken than to secure the abandonment of a decision being contemplated.[40]

Junk[41] referred to Article 2 as imposing an obligation on the employer 'to negoti-   **11.25**
ate'. The use of the term 'negotiate' in this context is novel. The term appears nowhere in the Directive nor in any of the previous judgments of the Court interpreting and applying its provisions. It signifies, in ordinary parlance, a process leading to an agreement. Although the Directive does not specify that an agreement between the employer and the representatives of the employees must be reached, the Court had held in *Commission v United Kingdom*[42] that Article 2 required the consultation process to have as its objective the reaching of an agreement and to cover ways and means of avoiding the redundancies or reducing the numbers affected and of mitigating the consequences of the employer's decision where the redundancies were unavoidable. While the Court did not say that redundancies cannot take place in the absence of an agreement it is indicating that the consultation process must be meaningful: it cannot be a mere formality. This interpretation is borne out by its ruling in *Junk* to the effect that that termination of contracts can only occur after consultations have been completed. In *Commission v United Kingdom* the obligation on the employer to consult trade union representatives about the proposed dismissals, to 'consider' representations made and, in the case of rejection to give reasons, did not constitute a proper implementation of the Directive. Taken together the two cases signify that the consultation must be meaningful but it is doubtful as to whether such consultations can be equated to negotiation in the sense of requiring an agreement to be reached between the workforce or its representatives and the employer.

No time limit is laid down for the commencement or duration of consultations   **11.26**
but it is clear from the objective of the Directive that no redundancies should be made until the consultation procedure has been completed. What is in issue is not the period which has elapsed between the commencement of negotiations and the dismissal of the workers but the substance and effect of the consultations: the consultations must be meaningful and, if they are, notice of dismissal can be given after that process.

---

[40] *Junk* (see note 24 above) Judgment paras 43 and 44.
[41] Ibid.
[42] Case C-383/92 *Commission v United Kingdom* [1994] ECR I-2479.

I. Workers' Representatives

11.27 Workers' representatives are those provided for by the laws and practices of the Member States.[43] Where no workers' representatives are provided for under national law, Member States must take all steps necessary to ensure that representatives are designated so that the essential purpose of the Directive can be fulfilled. In *Commission v United Kingdom*[44] it was argued by the United Kingdom that representation of workers in undertakings had traditionally been based on voluntary recognition of trade unions by employers and for that reason an employer who does not recognize a trade union was not subject to the obligations laid down in the Directive. The Directive was not intended to amend national rules or practices concerning the designation of workers' representatives. Article 1(1)(b) provides that the term 'workers' representatives' is to be understood as meaning workers' representatives provided by the laws and practices of the Member States. Member States are not required to provide for specific representation of workers in order to comply with the obligations laid down by the Directive.

11.28 The ECJ rejected this argument:

> Article 1(1)(b) is not simply a renvoi to the rules in force in the Member States on the designation of workers' representatives. It leaves to the Member States only the task of determining the arrangements for designating the workers' representatives who, depending on the circumstances must or may intervene in the collective redundancy procedure . . .

11.29 The interpretation advocated by the United Kingdom would have allowed Member States to determine the cases in which workers' representatives may be informed and consulted and may intervene, since they can be informed and consulted and can intervene with public authorities only in undertakings where national law provides for the designation of workers' representatives. Such an interpretation would thus permit Member States to deprive Articles 2 and 3(2) of the Directive of their full effect.[45]

11.30 The combined effect of Articles 2, 3, and 6 of the Directive requires Member States to take all measures necessary to ensure that workers are informed, consulted, and in a position to intervene through their representatives in the event of collective redundancies.[46]

---

[43] Art 1(1)(b).
[44] See note 42 above.
[45] Ibid Judgment paras 19 and 20.
[46] *Commission v United Kingdom* (see note 42 above) Judgment para 23.

J. Notification

The competent public authority must be notified by the employer in writing **11.31** of any proposed collective redundancies. However Member States may provide that in the case of planned collective redundancies arising from the termination of the establishment's activities as a result of a judicial decision, the employer is obliged to notify the competent public authority in writing only if the latter so requires.[47] The notification must contain all relevant information concerning the planned redundancies and the proposed consultation of the workers' representatives. In particular, the same information as that required to be given to the workers' representatives concerning the reasons for the redundancies, the number of workers to be made redundant, the number of workers normally employed in the undertaking, and the period over which the redundancies are to be effected must be provided to the public authorities.

The employer must provide the workers' representatives with a copy of this **11.32** notification.[48] Workers' representatives may send comments to the public authorities.

There is no indication in the Directive as to the timing of the consultation and **11.33** notification procedures: simultaneous or consecutive? Advocate General Tizzano in *Junk* was of the view that notification can only come after the consultation stage given that it must contain information relating to the consultation of the workers' representatives.[49]

K. Suspension

As a general rule, collective redundancies may not take effect earlier than 30 days **11.34** after notification to the public authority. Member States may give the competent authority power to reduce this 30-day period but any such reduction must be 'without prejudice to any provisions governing individual rights with regard to notice of dismissal'.[50] This requirement is designed to prevent any diminution of rights as to notice periods provided for by national law which may be longer than the 30-day period specified under the Directive.[51]

---

[47] Art 3(1).
[48] Art 3(2).
[49] Note 25 Opinion at para 61.
[50] Article 4 (1).
[51] *Junk* (see note 24 above) Opinion Advocate General Tizzano para 66.

11.35 Where the initial period of notification is shorter than 60 days, Member States may grant the competent authority power to extend the initial consultation period to 60 days following the notification of the proposed redundancy plan where the problems created by that plan are unlikely to be solved within the initial period.

11.36 During the period of suspension, the competent public authority must try to seek solutions to the problems raised by the planned redundancies. In *Commission v Italy*[52] Italy argued that the provisions of Italian legislation and collective agreements on redundancies, taken as a whole, established procedures which attained the objectives of the Directive and in some instances exceeded it. But the Court found that there was no requirement for an employer envisaging collective redundancies to notify the public authorities nor was there any obligation on the part of the public authorities to intervene in order to seek solutions to alleviate the consequences of the planned redundancies. These lacunae meant that the provisions in force in Italy did 'not suffice to meet the totality of the requirements of the Directive'.[53]

L. Enforcement

11.37 The original Directive was silent on the question of enforcement. Following its amendment by Directive 92/56, Member States are required to ensure that administrative or judicial procedures for the enforcement of obligations under the Directive are available to workers' representatives and/or workers.[54] This provision was prompted by a number of high-profile redundancies where little, if any, regard was had to the provisions of the Directive. It is arguable that the amendment was superfluous, or at least it cannot be presumed that it introduced for the first time the possibility of enforcing rights under the Directive. In the *Commission v United Kingdom*[55] the sanctions provided under United Kingdom law in the case of a failure to consult and inform workers' representatives were largely deprived of any effect or deterrent value by concurrently applicable legislation relating to the calculation of redundancy payments, the result of which was to reduce the amounts paid by any amount received by the worker for breach of his rights under the Directive. The Court drew attention to Article 10 of the EC Treaty which required the Member States to take measures necessary to guarantee the applicability and effectiveness of Community law. Consequently,

---

[52] Case 91/81 *Commission v Italy* [1992] ECR 2133.
[53] Ibid Judgment para 10.
[54] Art 6. See Case C-12/08 *Mono Car Styling* SA [2008] OJ C 79/17 pending before the ECJ.
[55] See note 43 above.

where a Directive does not provide for a penalty in respect of an infringement of its provisions and there is no renvoi to national norms, Member States have a duty to provide a penalty. Whilst they have a certain discretion in this matter, they have an obligation to:

> ... ensure in particular that infringements of Community law are penalized under conditions, both procedural and substantive, which are analogous to those applicable to infringements of national law of a similar nature and importance and which, in any event make the penalty effective, proportionate and dissuasive ...[56]

---

[56] Ibid Judgment para 40.

12

TRANSFERS OF UNDERTAKINGS[1]

A. Introduction

Directive 77/187 on the approximation of the laws of the Member States relating to the safeguarding of employees' rights in the event of a transfer of an undertaking, business, or part of a business[2] was adopted pursuant to the Social Action **12.01**

---

[1] See Barnard: *EC Employment Law* Oxford University Press 2006 Third Edition Chapter 13; Barrett: 'Light acquired on acquired rights: Examining developments in employment rights on transfers of undertakings' (2005) 42 CML Rev 1053–105; Sciarra: *Labour Law in the Courts; National Judges and the European Court of Justice* Hart Publishing 2001 at 131–224.

[2] [1977] OJ L61/26.

Programme 1974[3] (the 'Original Directive'). It was required to be implemented by 5 March 1979.

12.02 The Original Directive was amended in 1998[4] (the 'Amended Directive') to reflect the impact of the internal market, changes in national law relating to the restructuring of undertakings in economic difficulties, and the case law of the European Court of Justice ('ECJ').

12.03 The Amended Directive took over six years to negotiate. When the Commission began its work of revising the Original Directive in the early 1990s, it envisaged a relatively simply exercise consisting of bringing the text into line with amendments made earlier to the Collective Redundancies Directive,[5] to reflect the increasing transnational dimension of corporate restructuring. Gradually it emerged that a number of further issues needed to be addressed in order to give the Directive its full effect, notably the application of its provisions to situations of insolvency, the joint liability of the transferor and the transferee with respect to obligations arising out of the transfer, and most controversially the applicability of the Directive to the contracting out of services.

12.04 Following discussions in early 1992 with the social partners, the Commission produced its first draft in September 1994,[6] a further draft followed intense discussions with the Economic and Social Committee, the Committee of Regions, and the European Parliament.[7] One of the particular points of disagreement concerned the definition of the concept of 'transfer of an undertaking' from which the Commission wished to exclude the contracting out of services by means of the insertion of the following provision:

> . . . the transfer of only an activity of an undertaking, business or part of a business, whether or not it was previously carried out directly, does not itself constitute a transfer within the meaning of the Directive.

12.05 This provision was ultimately dropped from the draft but in the meantime the ECJ had in a number of cases handed down rulings which gave effect to it.[8]

12.06 The upshot, therefore, was that the very provision which had caused so much heated debate and delay, in the course of the legislative process, resulting in

---

[3] [1974] OJ C6.

[4] Directive 98/50 ([1998] OJ L201/88) Hunt: 'Success at last? The Amendment of the Acquired rights Directive'. (1999) 24 EL Rev 215–30.

[5] [1977] OJ L48/20 as amended by Directive 92/56 [1992] OJ L245/3. See Chapter 11.

[6] [1994] OJ C274/10.

[7] [1997] OJ C33/81; [1995] OJ C133/13; [1996] OJ C100/25; COM (97) 60 Final.

[8] Case C-48/99 *Rygaard* [1995] ECR I–2745; Case C-298/94 *Henke* [1996] ECR I–4989; Case 13/95 *Suzen* [1997] ECR I–1259.

its eventual abandonment, became law as a result of a series of judgments of the ECJ.

Given the difficulties encountered during the legislative process, compromises had to be made, with the result that a number of matters were left to the discretion of the Member States. These included the possibility of imposing joint or several liability on transferors and transferees; a choice as to whether to adopt measures to ensure that full disclosure is made by the transferor of the rights and obligations under the contracts transferred; the option of making the Directive applicable to benefits which fall outside statutory social security systems and cases of insolvency. The result is that there is potentially a wide disparity within the Community, in the practical application of the Directive to transferors, transferees, and employees alike.

12.07

The amendments to the Directive were required to be implemented by the Member States by 17 July 2001. Both Directives have now been consolidated by Directive 2001/23 (the 'Directive').[9] The legal basis for all of these Directives is Article 94 EC, there being no other more specific competence designated in the Treaty. Two implementation reports have been published.[10]

12.08

All three Directives have generated—and continue to generate—a sizeable amount of case law, the majority of which has arisen out of requests for preliminary rulings. The result is a corpus of complex law which is difficult to navigate. Amendments to the Original Directive, and its ultimate repeal and replacement in 2001, have attempted to clarify matters but with questionable success.

12.09

With 30 years' hindsight it is easy to see that the Original Directive was framed in terms which were often too vague and general to permit of easy application. The consequential flow of requests for preliminary rulings placed the ECJ in the unenviable position of having to decide on how this loosely worded legislation, which failed to define even key concepts with any degree of clarity, should be applied to a myriad of situations which either the legislators did not anticipate or else chose not to address.[11] Many of the cases which have come before the Court raised fundamental issues, such as: what constitutes a transfer of an undertaking? What is an undertaking? What if a Member State does not have an institutionalized system of employee representation for the entire workforce?

12.10

---

[9] [2001] OJ L82/16.

[10] SEC (92) 857 Final on the state of implementation in the twelve member States which then comprised the EC and <http://ec.europa.eu/employment_social/labour_law/docs/08a_transfero-fundertakings_implreport_austria_finland_sweden_en.pdf> on the implementation of the Directive in Austria, Finland, and Sweden.

[11] For an in-depth discussion of this case law see O'Leary: *Employment Law at the European Court of Justice* Hart Publishing 2006, Chapter 6.

How should the information and consultation provisions apply to such a situation? Can an employer and an employee agree to waive the rights laid down in the Directive? These and other fundamental issues have been left to the Court to decide and in doing that:

> ... the Court has been forced to make difficult policy choices.[12]

12.11　These choices have been made difficult by the tension within the Directive between, on the one hand, employment protection objectives and, on the other, the demand for labour market flexibility in a changing competitive environment.

12.12　Although the poor drafting of the Original Directive has generated litigation in many Member States, that litigation has also arisen because legislation has failed to keep pace with changes in the business world. The ECJ has had to grapple with the application of the Directive to new and evolving methods of doing business in the globalized economy. Transfers of undertakings nowadays take place in a multiplicity of ways, either not known or not in common usage, when the original Directive or the 1998 amendment was adopted and the wording used in that legislation is often not such as to be readily applicable to the modern business world.

12.13　The law on the transfers of undertakings is thus essentially judge-made. This has meant that:

> (i) there is an abundance of case law dealing with particular situations which cannot be resolved on the basis of the wording of the Directive alone;
>
> (ii) attempts to distill these interpretative rulings into clearly defined legislation have been difficult and largely unsuccessful;
>
> (iii) from time to time the Court refines its thinking, leading sometimes to less than optimal legal certainty which breeds more case law; and
>
> (iv) key concepts have been, allegedly, interpreted more liberally than was envisaged when the Member States committed themselves to the Directive, and this has provoked accusations of excessive judicial activism.

12.14　In particular, it has been difficult for the Court to put flesh on the rather skeletal form of the Original Directive in the context of the preliminary ruling procedure which is based upon a clear division of responsibility between the ECJ and national courts, the latter being responsible for the application of Community law, as interpreted by the former, to the facts of the case before it.

12.15　The Court's approach has been to develop a set of principles, based on the objectives of the Directive for the guidance of national courts in the application of the

---

12 Ibid at 242.

Directive to particular circumstances. In doing this it has adopted a purposive approach in interpreting the Directive, avoiding involvement with the technicalities of employment and company law, which in any event are matters of national law and thus variable from Member State to Member State.

This chapter will attempt to set out this body of law, beginning with the objectives of the Directive, moving to its scope of application, in terms of persons and situations covered, addressing, in particular, how a transfer must be executed, the obligations of the transferor and the transferee, and what are the rights of employees when the responsibility for the undertaking employing them is transferred to another entity.

12.16

B. Objectives

The Directive has a dual purpose. First and foremost, it provides for the protection of employees in the event of a change of employer by safeguarding their rights which have been acquired or are in the process of being acquired in the course of an employment relationship and by transferring the employment relationship to the transferee; secondly, it provides for transparency in the case of any envisaged change of employer due to a transfer of the employing undertaking, by means of an information and consultation process prior to the transfer of the business, thus eliminating the possibility of the workforce and its representatives being unaware of an imminent change in the working environment.

12.17

The Directive grants employees collective and individual rights: the former provides for negotiation and consultation on the effects of the transfer and the reduction of its impact on the employment relationship;[13] the latter protects debts incurred towards the employee prior to the transfer and ensures the continuity of the employment contract or relationship after the transfer.[14]

12.18

More particularly the Directive provides:

12.19

(i) that the rights and obligations arising out of the contract of employment or employment relationship existing on the date of the contract are to be transferred to the transferee;[15]

---

[13] Articles 7(1) and (2).
[14] Case 324/86 *Daddy's Dance Hall* [1988] ECR 739 para 9; Case C-362/89 *D'Urso and Others* [1991] ECR I–4105 para 9; Case C-399/96 *Europieces* [1998] ECR I–6965 para 37; Case C 499/04 *Werhof v Freeway Traffic Systems* [2006] ECR I–2397 para 25.
[15] Art 3(1).

(ii) the transfer of the undertaking is not a justification for the dismissal of the employee by either the transferor or the transferee save in the limited circumstances set out in the Directive;[16] and

(iii) in the event of the undertaking which is being transferred preserving its autonomy, the preservation of the status and functions of the representative or representatives of the employees affected by the transfer.[17]

12.20 The Directive does not provide for any particular level of employment protection but simply ensures that employees' rights under existing employment relationships are not prejudiced by the transfer.[18]

12.21 Member States may provide that, after the date of transfer, the transferor and the transferee shall be jointly and severally liable in respect of obligations which arose before the date of transfer from a contract of employment or employment relationship.[19]

12.22 Member States may adopt measures to ensure that the transferor notifies the transferee of all the rights and obligations which will be transferred in so far as those rights and obligations are or ought to have been known to the transferor at the time of the transfer. Any failure to make such a notification does not affect the transfer of such rights and obligations.[20]

C. Partial Harmonization

12.23 Since the Directive only partially harmonizes national law,[21] it can be relied upon only to ensure that the employee is protected in his relations with the transferee to the same extent as he was in his relations with the transferor under the law of the Member State concerned.[22] It can go no further: the extent of an employee's protection is co-terminous with that accorded to him under national law.

---

[16] Art 4(1).

[17] Art 6(ii).

[18] Davies: 'Acquired Rights, Creditors' Rights, Freedom of Contract and Industrial Democracy' (1989) 9 Yearbook on European Law 21–53 at 21.

[19] Art 3(1).

[20] Art 3(2).

[21] Case 324/86 *Daddy's Dance Hall* note 14 Judgment para 16; Joined Cases C-132/91 etc *Katsikas* [1992] ECR I–6577 Judgment para 31.

[22] Case 105/84 *Danmols* [1985] ECR 2639; Case 324/86 *Daddy's Dance Hall* note 14; Case C-209/91 *Watson Rask* [1992] ECR I–5755; Case C-392/92 *Schmidt* [1994] ECR I–1311. See A Garde: 'Partial Harmonisation and European Social Policy: A Case Study on the Acquired Rights Directive' 5 Cambridge Yearbook of European Legal Studies Hart Publishing 2004 at 173–93.

Consequently, the Directive does not preclude changes in the employment rela- **12.24**
tionship following a transfer of an undertaking where national law allows an
employment relationship to be altered (even in a manner unfavourable to the
employee), in situations which arise independently of the transfer of the undertaking. The decisive factor is that the alterations in the employment relationship
should not be connected to the transfer:

> . . . an employee cannot waive the rights conferred on him by the mandatory provi-
> sions of the directive. Nevertheless the directive does not preclude an agreement
> with the new employer to alter the employment relationship, in so far as such an
> alteration is permitted by the applicable national law in situations other than the
> transfer of an undertaking.[23]

In *Watson Rask*[24] the issue between the parties in national proceedings was **12.25**
whether the transferee was bound to maintain the terms and conditions agreed
between the employees and the transferor with regard to the payment of salary, in
particular the date on which the salaries were paid and the items making up the
salary package, even if the total amount of the salary remained unchanged.
The ECJ held that if national law permits such aspects of the employment relationship, independent of any transfer, to be altered even if that be in a manner
unfavourable to the employee, then the transferee can make such alterations,
otherwise it cannot even if the total amount of the salary remains the same. Since
Article 3(1) of the Directive subrogates the transferor's rights and obligations to
the transferee, the employment relationship may be altered by the transferee in
the same way as it could by the transferor but the transfer itself may 'never constitute the reason for that amendment'.[25]

The latter conclusion is somewhat puzzling. What the Court appears to say is **12.26**
that no aspect of an employment relationship, even if it is merely of an administrative nature and has, therefore, no bearing on the substance of the employee's
rights, can be altered unless:

(i) such alteration is permitted under national law, and
(ii) is independent of the transfer itself.

But why should the Directive preclude alterations of an administrative nature
having no effect on the substance of the employees' rights, even if they are brought
about because of the transfer? The Directive has as its objective the protection of
the substance of the employment relationship between the transferred employees

---

[23] Case 324/86 *Daddy's Dance Hall* note 14, Judgment at para 18; Case C-4/01 *Martin* [2003]
ECR I– 12859 Judgment paras 42 and 43.
[24] Note 22.
[25] Ibid Judgment para 28, following *Daddy's Dance Hall* note 14 Judgment at para 17.

and the transferor. It is not necessary, nor indeed desirable, that it should go beyond what that requires of the transferee. Indeed, the imposition of excessive obligations on the transferee, which bring no substantial benefit to the employee, may infringe the principle of proportionality. If the transferee is obliged to maintain administrative arrangements pertaining to the employment relationship it has assumed by virtue of the transfer, this could be administratively burdensome and costly. In particular this could be the case where the acquired business is to be subsumed into an already existing business of the transferee, which has an administrative structure different to that under which the transferor operated. Is the transferee, in such circumstances, obliged to maintain a multiplicity of administrative structures and arrangements applicable to different groups of employees according to how and when they entered into his employment?

12.27 Although the Directive is one of partial harmonization and thus largely leaves national law and practice untouched, Member States are required to ensure that it is fully effective and to that end prevailing industrial relations practices may have to be altered.[26]

D. Mandatory Application

12.28 The provisions of the Directive are mandatory: they do not permit of any derogation.[27] The purpose of the Directive is to ensure that the rights of an employee arising from a contract of employment are safeguarded. This is a matter of public policy; it is independent of the will of the parties to the contract:

> . . . the rules of the directive, in particular those concerning protection against dismissal by reason of the transfer must be considered to be mandatory, so that it is not possible to derogate from them in a manner unfavourable to employees.[28]

12.29 The result is that employees are not entitled to waive the rights conferred on them by the Directive and these rights cannot be restricted even with their consent. This remains the case even where, viewed as a whole, the employee would not be disadvantaged by the waiver of his rights under the Directive.[29] Given the disequilibrium inherent in the employment relationship, the mandatory application of the Directive offers a guarantee that employment rights will be safeguarded.

---

[26] Case C-383/92 *Commission v United Kingdom* [1994] ECR I-2479.

[27] Case 324/86 *Daddy's Dance Hall* note 14; Case C-209/91 *Watson Rask* note 22.

[28] Case 324/86 *Daddy's Dance Hall* note 14 at 754; Joined Cases 144 and 145/87 *Berg* [1998] ECR 2559; Case C-4/01 *Martin* [2003] ECR I–12859.

[29] Joined Cases 144 and 145/87 *Berg* note 27.

Likewise, the intentions of the transferor and the transferee are irrelevant. The **12.30** transfer of rights and obligations is not dependent upon the intention of either or both, neither is it subject to the consent of the employees' representatives or the employees themselves.[30] In particular the transferee may not obstruct the transfer by refusing to fulfil his obligations.[31]

However, of course an employee may decide not to continue to work for his new **12.31** employer after the transfer.[32] In such a case the position of the employee depends on the legislation of the individual Member State.[33] *Danmols*[34] held that the protection which the Directive was intended to guarantee was redundant where a person decided of his own accord not to continue the employment relationship with the new employer after the transfer. Whilst an employee may remain in the employment of his new employer on the same conditions as were agreed with the transferor, the Directive cannot be interpreted as obliging him to continue his employment relationship with the transferee:

> Such an obligation would jeopardize the fundamental rights of the employee, who must be free to choose his employer and cannot be obliged to work for an employer he has not freely chosen.[35]

Where an employee decides not to maintain his contract of employment with the **12.32** transferee, the Directive neither requires nor precludes the maintenance of the relationship with the transferor. In such circumstances it is for national law and practice to determine what the fate of the contract or employment relationship should be.[36] A number of options are possible. The contract can be regarded as terminated either by the employee or the employer or the contract may be regarded as being maintained with the transferor.

Mr *Katsikas*[37] claimed various sums by way of remuneration which he claimed **12.33** were due in respect of a period prior to his dismissal. He had worked in a restaurant run by Mr Konstantinidis which was sublet to Mr Mitossis as from 2 April 1990. In the sublease Mr Mitossis had undertaken to discharge Mr Konstantinidis from any obligations arising out of the operation of the restaurant, in particular

---

[30] Case C-51/00 *Temco* [2002] ECR I–969 Judgment para 35.
[31] Joined Cases C-132, 138, and 139/91 *Katsikas* [1992] ECR I–6577, Judgment at para 36; Case C-51/00 *Temco*, note 30, Judgment at para 36.
[32] Case 105/84 *Danmols* [1985] ECR 2639; Case C-362/89 *D'Urso* [1991] note 14; Joined Cases C-132, 138, and 139/91 *Katsikas* note 32; Joined Cases C-171 and 172/94 *Merckx and Neuhuys* [1996] ECR I–1253; Case C-51/00 *Temco* note 30.
[33] Case C-139/91 *Katsikas* note 32 judgment paras 31–33.
[34] Note 28.
[35] *Katsikas* note 32 Judgment para 32.
[36] Ibid para 35.
[37] Note 32.

those relating to the payment of remuneration. Mr Katsikas refused to work for Mr Mitossis. He was dismissed by Mr Konstantinidis on 26 June 1990. Mr Konstantinidis argued that he had ceased to be Mr Katidis's employer on 2 April 1990, the date of the transfer of the lease on the restaurant to Mr Mitossis. He was therefore not responsible for the sums in question. The Court held:

> . . . in the event of the employee deciding of his own accord not to continue with the contract of employment or employment relationship with the transferee, the directive does not require the Member States to provide that the contract or relationship is to be maintained with the transferor. In such a case, it is for the Member States to determine what the fate of the contract of employment or employment relationship should be.
>
> The Member States may, in particular, provide that in such a case the contract of employment or employment relationship must be regarded as terminated either by the employee or by the employer. They may also provide that the contract or relationship should be maintained with the transferor.[38]

E. Date of the Transfer

12.34   The transfer of obligations from the transferor to the transferee takes place on the date of the transfer. There is no indication in the Directive as to what constitutes that point in time. There can be no postponement of any of the consequences of the transfer, even by agreement within the parties, to another date:[39]

> . . . Contracts of employment, or employment relationships existing on the date of the transfer referred to in Article 3(1) between the transferor and the worker assigned to the undertaking transferred are automatically transferred from the transferor to the transferee, by the mere fact of the transfer of the undertaking.[40]

12.35   *Celtec*[41] raised squarely, for the first time, the issue of the date on which a transfer takes place. The case involved the privatization of an activity previously carried on by a government department. For a period of three-years following the privatization, a number of civil servants were seconded to the new business. They retained their status as civil servants. At the end of the three-year period they were required to opt to remain in the newly privatized business or to return to the civil service. The question arose as to when their employment relationship

---

[38] Note 32 Judgment paras 34 and 35.
[39] Case C-362/89 *d'Urso* note 15; Case C-305/94 *Rotsart de Hertsaing* [1996] ECR I–5927.
[40] *d'Urso* note 15 Judgment para 20.
[41] Case C-478/03 [2005] ECR I–4389. For comment see Barrett: 'Celtec; Asking the Court of Justice for a date or the limits of consensual behaviours in privatization' 30 EL Rev (2005) 891–202.

was transferred. Could this be viewed as having taken place over a period of time or on a single date and if so what was that date?

The Court held that the use of the word 'date' in Article 3(1) of the Directive and reasons of legal certainty indicated that, in the mind of the Community legislature, workers entitled to benefit from the protection of the Directive must be identified at a particular point in the transfer process and not in relation to the length of time over which that process extends. As to what that point in time was the Court held: **12.36**

> . . . the date of a transfer . . . is the date on which responsibility as an employer for carrying on the business of the unit transferred moves from the transferor to the transferee. That date is a particular point in time which cannot be postponed to another date at the will of the transferor or the transferee.[42]

This ruling seems to deprive employees of the degree of flexibility in their employment arrangements which, in practice, appears to be customary in cases where businesses are transferred from the public sector into private ownership. In such privatization situations it is common (and this was the case in *Celtec*) for civil servants to be seconded to the business which has been transferred for a fixed period of time after which they are required to decide either to retain their civil service status and return to public sector employment or to resign from the civil service and enter into the employment of the newly privatized entity. Following *Celtec*, this may no longer be possible. It would appear that once responsibility for running the business passes to the transferee, civil servants cannot remain in the employment of their original employer, the transferor: **12.37**

> . . . contracts of employment or employment relationships existing on the date of the transfer . . . between the transferor and the workers assigned to the undertaking transferred are deemed to be handed over, on that date, from the transferor to the transferee, regardless of what has been agreed between the parties in that respect.[43]

This ruling potentially denies the possibility of a period of secondment from transferor to the transferee following the completion of the transfer. The transfer of the employment relationship to the entity to which the privatized activities are entrusted, will be both immediate and irrevocable, a situation possibly not to the liking of the employee in question as it means the immediate abandonment of civil service status. For a seasoned civil servant it may be difficult to choose between taking the risk of abandoning that status, which is normally attended by an enviable degree of security, both in terms of employment conditions and pension rights, and going into a fledgling business which may or many not ultimately **12.38**

---

[42] Note 39 Judgment para 44.
[43] Ibid.

prove to be successful. That choice is more easily made after the transferred business has been operating for some time. From the point of view of the transferee, it is frequently the continued availability of the expertise of personnel in the business after the transfer which ensures the immediate and successful functioning of the business by the transferee. In the absence of a guarantee on the part of the transferor to make available the necessary expertise by way of secondment of experienced civil servants, for a limited period of time, the acquisition may not be quite so attractive to the potential transferee, especially in those sectors which have traditionally been in public ownership and in which, therefore, there may be little know-how or expertise in the private sector.

12.39 In *Celtec*[44] Advocate General Poiares Madura had put forward a different approach which he felt to be suited to economic reality and the need '. . . to allow some flexibility in the practical arrangements for the transfer which reflects economic and political considerations':[45]

> In the context of a privatization the transfer of the contract of employment may take place after the transfer of assets, as long as that does not result in the diminution of the protection conferred by the Directive on the employees and as long as those employees have signalled their agreement.[46]

12.40 The Advocate General would thus have allowed the transferee and the employees to agree to a postponement of the transfer of rights and obligations to a mutually convenient date, provided that the rights under the Directive were preserved. This approach, rejected by the ECJ, would perhaps have resolved some of the issues raised above at paras 12.36–12.37 but, at the same time, might, in some cases, have created a situation of legal uncertainty, and, in any event, would have been difficult to reconcile with previous case law, which had consistently held that the transfer brought about an automatic transfer of the employment relationship and which the Advocate General had sought to distinguish by claiming that such cases did not involve 'complex transfers' such as the one in issue in *Celtec*.

12.41 The Advocate General's approach would have introduced a distinction between different types of transfers on the basis of their complexity, or otherwise, with one entailing the full transfer of all obligations on the date of the transfer and the other not. This could have been difficult to apply in practice. The requirement of the agreement of the employee might also have been problematic since it would have left open the possibility of duress being brought to bear on the part of either the transferor or the transferee, precisely the type of situation the mandatory application of the Directive was designed to avoid.

---

[44] Note 42.
[45] Opinion para 67.
[46] Opinion para 75.

F. Scope of Application

The Directive applies to any transfer of an undertaking, business, or part of a **12.42**
business to another employer as a result of a legal transfer or merger. It applies to
public and private undertakings engaged in economic activities whether or not
they are they are operating for gain. The Original Directive did not specify that
it applied to non-profit making entities. *Dr Sophie Redmond*[47] held that the
Directive was applicable to such entities. This ruling is now reflected in
Article 1c which provides that the Directive applies to:

> . . . public and private undertakings engaged in economic activities whether or not
> they are operating for gain.

A reorganization within public administration authorities, or the transfer of **12.43**
administrative functions between public administrative authorities, is not a
transfer within the meaning of the Directive (Article 1c).[48]

The Directive does not apply to seagoing vessels (Article 1(3)). In the first draft **12.44**
of its proposal for the Amended Directive, published in 1999, the Commission
proposed to extend the scope of the Directive to sea-going vessels but to allow
Member States the option of not applying the information and consultation
obligations to them. In the event this proposal was dropped with the result that
sea-going vessels remain entirely outside the scope of the Directive.

G. Territorial Application

The Directive applies where and in so far as the undertaking, business, or part of **12.45**
the business to be transferred is in the territorial area covered by the EC Treaty[49]
or a member country of the European Economic Area—Norway, Iceland, and
Lichenstein. The essential criterion is the location of the undertaking or business:
the whereabouts of the owners of the business is irrelevant.

H. Undertaking

The Directive does not offer any definition of what constitutes an undertaking or **12.46**
business. In *Schmidt*,[50] Advocate General van Gerven stated that a common

---

[47] Case C-29/91 [1992] ECR I–3189.
[48] Case C-298/94 *Henke* [1996] ECR I–4989.
[49] Art 1(2).
[50] Case C-392/92 *Schmidt* [1994] ECR I–1311.

denominator underlay the three concepts of 'undertaking', 'business', and 'part of business', namely that of an economic unit or a business, terms which refer to a unit with a minimum level of organizational experience which can either exist by itself or form part of a larger undertaking and which consists of persons and assets by means of which an economic activity is carried out.[51]

12.47 In the subsequent case of *Suzen*[52] the ECJ held that the transfer must relate to a stable economic entity and the concept of an 'undertaking' refers to an organized grouping of persons and assets facilitating the exercise of an economic activity which pursues a specific objective. Thus there is no transfer of an undertaking within the meaning of the Directive where the performance of one specific works contract is transferred: one contract does not constitute a stable economic entity, a concept signifying a period of presence on the marketplace beyond the performance of a single contract.

12.48 This principle emerges from *Rygaard*[53] in which the Court held that the taking over of a contract for building works (with the agreement of the awarder of the contract) by another undertaking, together with the material assigned to the works, an employee, and two apprentices did not constitute the transfer of an undertaking:

> That is not the case of an undertaking which transfers to another undertaking one of its building works with a view to completion of that work. Such a transfer could come within the terms of the directive only if it included the transfer of a body of assets enabling the activities or certain activities of the transferor of the undertaking to be carried on in a stable way.
>
> That is not so where, as in the case now referred, the transferor undertaking merely makes available to the new contractor certain workers and material for carrying out the work in question.[54]

I. Part of a Business

12.49 Advocate General Slynn in *Botzen*[55] stated that the question of what was a 'part of' a business was largely a question of fact although it would usually involve the transfer of a department or factory or facet of a business. It could also involve the sale of a fraction of a single business unit.

---

[51] Ibid at 1319.
[52] Case C-13/95 [1997] ECR I-1259.
[53] Case C-48/94 [1995] ECR I-2745.
[54] Ibid Judgment paras 21 and 22.
[55] Case 186/83 [1985] ECR 519.

In *Jouini*[56] it was held that the decisive criterion in determining whether a part of a business had been transferred was whether the assets transferred by the transferor constituted an operational grouping sufficient in itself to provide services characterizing the business's economic activity without recourse to other significant assets or other parts of the business.

12.50

(1) Ancillary activities

Even if the part of an undertaking transferred is concerned with activities which are ancillary and unconnected to the main business of the undertaking, such as catering and cleaning, the Directive applies. In *Watson Rask*[57] Philips entrusted the management of its four canteens to ISS. It was argued that this arrangement related to a facility which was ancillary to the transferor's main business and therefore fell outside the scope of the Directive. The Court did not accept this reasoning:

12.51

> . . . where one businessman entrusts, by means of an agreement, responsibility for running a facility of his undertaking, such as a canteen, to another businessman . . . the resulting transaction may fall within the scope of the Directive . . . The fact that in such a case the activity transferred is merely an ancillary activity for the transferor without a necessary connection with its company objects cannot have the effect of excluding the transaction from the scope of the Directive. Nor does the fact that the agreement between the transferor and the transferee relates to provision of services exclusively for the benefit of the transferor in return for a fee, details of which are laid down by the agreement, preclude the applicability of the Directive.[58]

(2) Employees of the part transferred

Where part of a business is transferred, the protection offered by the transfer relates only to employees wholly engaged in that part of the business. An employment relationship is essentially characterized by the link between the employee and the part of the business to which he was assigned to carry out his duties.[59]

12.52

The protection offered by the Directive relates only to the contracts of employees wholly engaged in that part of the business which is transferred to the new employer.

12.53

In order to determine whether a worker is wholly engaged in the part of the business transferred, it is necessary to consider whether the worker would have been employed by the owners of that part, or the owners of the remaining part

12.54

---

[56] Case C-458/05 [2007] ECR I-7301. The case of *Klarenberg* (Case C-466/07 [2008] OJ C8/5), pending at the time of writing, raises the issue of whether there is a transfer of a part of a business only if the new employer operates that part of an undertaking or business as an organizationally autonomous part of a business or undertaking.

[57] Note 22.

[58] Ibid Judgment para 17.

[59] Case C-392/92 *Schmidt* note 22.

(which was not the subject of the transfer), if the part of the business transferred had been owned separately before the transfer.

12.55 In *Botzen*[60] the Court of Justice held that the decisive criterion in determining whether an employee was employed in the part of the business transferred is whether or not a transfer concerns the department to which he/she was assigned and which formed the organizational framework within which the employment relationship took effect. An employment relationship is essentially characterized by the link existing between the employee and the part of the undertaking or business to which he is assigned to carry out his duties. Such a relationship is not established where an employee was not assigned to that part of the organization transferred but whose work involved the use of assets of that part of the undertaking or who, whilst working in the administrative part of the undertaking which has not itself been transferred, carried out certain duties for the benefit of the part transferred.

12.56 In practice, given the horizontal nature of some types of employment within an organization, it may be difficult to determine to which part of the undertaking an employee is assigned. This may be the case, for example, where an employee provides technical support throughout a large undertaking. In such a case if part of the undertaking is transferred, the question of which employment relationships are transferred may depend upon the proportion of working time the employee in question spent in the part transferred: where did he spend the greater part of his time? If his primary task was to work in a particular department then his employment relationship must be regarded as being with that department, even if he serviced other parts of the undertaking.

J. Transfers Within a Group

12.57 The Directive can apply to a transfer between two companies in the same group which have the same ownership, management, and premises and which are engaged in the same work.

12.58 *Allen*[61] concerned a case involving two companies, AMS and ACC, both of which were wholly owned subsidiaries of the AMLO Group. ACC and AMS, in addition to having the same ownership, had the same management, the same premises, and shared the same work. Before the ECJ, in support of the argument as to the non-applicability of the Directive, reliance was placed on *Viho*[62] in which the

---

[60] Case 186/83 *Botzen* [1985] ECR 519 at 528; Case C-392/92 *Schmidt* note 22.
[61] Case C-234/98 *Allen* [1999] ECR I–8643.
[62] Case C-73/95 [1996] ECR I–5457 Judgment para 6.

Court has held that that two companies which had the same ownership, management, and supervisory staff and which did not enjoy legal autonomy with respect to their actions on the market were considered to be a single undertaking for the purposes of Article 81(1) EC.

The Court, in rejecting this argument, held that *Viho* had to be confined to the **12.59** concept of an economic unit for the purposes of Article 81(1). If formal legal separation between two companies, which had distinct legal personalities (and thus an employment relationship with their respective workforces), were required for the application of the Directive, its purpose, which is to ensure as far as possible that the rights of employees are safeguarded in the event of a change of employer, would be defeated. Accordingly, it held that the Directive can apply to a transfer between two companies in the same corporate group which have the same ownership, management, and premises and which were engaged in the same work:

> . . . the Directive applies to a situation in which a company belonging to a group decides to subcontract to another company in the same group contracts for driveage work in mines in so far as the transaction involves the transfer of an economic entity between the two companies. The term 'economic entity' refers to an organized grouping of persons and assets facilitating the exercise of an activity which pursues a specific objective.[63]

K. Transferor

A transferor is defined in Article 2 of the Directive as any natural or legal person **12.60** who, by reason of the transfer, ceases to be an employer in respect of an undertaking, business, or part of an undertaking or business. A transferee is any natural or legal person who, by reason of a transfer, becomes an employer in respect of the undertaking, business, or part of the undertaking or business. This approach presupposes that the transfer of the employment relationship, which may not in fact occur, if the requirements of the Directive are not fulfilled. A better solution might have been to define transferor and transferee as those persons involved with the disposal/acquisition of the business.

L. Employee

An employee is a person who, in the Member State concerned, is protected as **12.61** such under national employment law.[64] Part-time and other atypical workers

---

[63] Allen note 61 Judgment para 39.

[64] Art 2(1)(d). The Original Directive adopted in 1977 did not define the term 'employee'. In *Danmols Inventar* Case 105/84 [1985] ECR 2639 the ECJ held 'The term "employee" must be

benefit from the same rights under the Directive as full-time workers regardless of what national law provides. Member States may not exclude from the scope of application of the Directive contracts of employment or employment relationships solely because:

(a) of the number of hours of work required to be performed;

(b) the employment relationship is governed by a fixed duration contract within the meaning of Directive 91/383;[65]

(c) the employment relationship is temporary within the meaning of Directive 91/383[66] and the undertaking, business, or part of the undertaking or business transferred is, or is part of, the temporary employment business which is the employer.

12.62 Employees must be designated as such under national employment law. This may imply the exclusion in some Member States of public sector employees and others, whose employment or occupation is governed by special regimes laid down by statute or terms of office as opposed to generally applicable employment legislation.

12.63 In *Collino*,[67] for example, the claimants were employed by ASST, the state body responsible for the operation of certain telecommunication services for public use in Italy. The Court held that the Directive applied only to employees protected as such under national employment law. The nature of the tasks performed in the course of employment was irrelevant.

> In the present case, the case-file suggests that, at the time of the transfer at issue in the main proceedings, ASST's employees were subject to a public-law status, not to employment law. That, however, is for the national court to verify.

> Consequently, the answer to be given to the first question must be that Article 1(1) of the Directive is to be interpreted as meaning that the Directive may apply to a situation in which an entity operating telecommunications services for public use and managed by a public body within the State administration is, following decisions of the public authorities, the subject of a transfer for value, in the form of an administrative concession, to a private-law company established by another public body which holds its entire capital. The persons concerned by such a transfer

---

interpreted as covering persons who, in the Member State concerned is protected as an employee under national employment law. It is for the national court to establish whether this is the case in the instance.' (Judgment para 28). Article 2(1)(d), introduced into the Directive by Directive 98/50, is based on this ruling.

65 [1991] OJ L206/19.

66 Ibid Art 2(2).

67 Case C-343/98 *Collino* [2000] ECR I–6659 Judgment paras 39–40; Case C-425/02 *Delahaye* [2004] ECR I–10823.

must, however, originally have been protected as employees under national employment law.[68]

The number of employees engaged in the business or part of business transferred **12.64** is irrelevant. The protection offered by the Directive is applicable to all staff employed by the transferor at the time of the transfer, and must thus be guaranteed even when only one employee is affected by it.[69]

(1) Employed at the transfer date

The Directive can only be relied upon by employees whose contract of employ- **12.65** ment or employment relationship is in force on the date of the transfer. The Directive does not protect employees engaged after the date of the transfer or who were otherwise not in the employment of the transferor at the time of the transfer. The existence or otherwise of a contract of employment or an employment relationship on the date of the transfer is a matter to be established by national law, subject to the requirement to observe the mandatory provisions of the Directive, and in particular Article 4(1) thereof concerning the protection of employees against dismissal by the transferor or the transferee by reason of the transfer.[70]

(2) Dismissal prior to transfer

Where an employee is dismissed contrary to Article 4(1) of the Directive imme- **12.66** diately prior to the transfer, his contract of employment will be treated as still being in existence at the date of the transfer with the result that his employer's obligations towards him are automatically transferred to the person to whom the business is being transferred.[71] Consequently it is not just those who were employed at the actual moment of the transfer, who must be considered employees for the purposes of the Directive, but also those who would have been employed had they not been dismissed immediately before the transfer by reason of the transfer.

> It is therefore consistent with the scheme of the directive to interpret it as meaning that unless otherwise expressly provided it may be relied on solely by workers whose contracts of employment or employment relationship is in existence at the time of the transfer subject, however, to compliance with the mandatory provisions of the directive concerning protection of employees from dismissal as a result of the transfer.[72]

---

[68] *Collino* note 67 Judgment paras 40 and 41.
[69] *Schmidt* note 23 Judgment para 15.
[70] Case 19/83 *Wendelboe* [1985] ECR 457 at 467.
[71] Case 101/87 *Bork* [1988] ECR 3057.
[72] Case C-287/86 *Ny Moelle Kro* [1987] ECR 5465 Judgment paras 25 and 26.

M. Insolvency

12.67 The earliest cases which came before the Court were concerned with the question of whether the transfer of an undertaking as a result of insolvency proceedings fell within the scope of application of the Directive.[73] The Court held that they did not. The rules on liquidation proceedings and analogous proceedings are different in the various Member States. Likewise, insolvency law is the subject of specific rules in the legal systems of the Member States and in the Community legal order. Had the Directive been intended to apply also to the transfer of undertakings in the context of such proceedings, an express provision would have been included for that purpose. Article 4a, inserted into the Directive by Directive 98/50, now Article 5(1), of the Directive makes this principle clear. It provides that employees' rights are not safeguarded (unless otherwise provided by the Member States) in the case of:

> . . . a transfer of an undertaking, business or part of a business where the transferor is the subject of bankruptcy proceedings or analogous insolvency proceedings which have been instituted with a view to liquidation of assets of the transferor and are under the supervision of a competent public authority.

12.68 Member States are required to take 'appropriate measures' to prevent the misuse of insolvency proceedings in such a way as to deprive employees of their rights under the Directive.[74]

12.69 If a Member State chooses to apply the Directive to a transfer which takes place in the course of insolvency proceedings it may provide that the transferor's debts arising from any employment contract or employment relationship and payable before the transfer or before the opening of the insolvency proceedings shall not be transferred to the transferee provided that the such proceedings give rise to a level of protection at least equivalent to that provided for by the Insolvency Directive.[75] Alternatively, the transferee, transferor, or person exercising the transferor's functions, on the one hand, and the representatives of the employees on the other, may agree alterations (in so far as national law permits), to the employees' terms and conditions of employment, designed to safeguard employment opportunities by ensuring the survival of the undertaking, business, or part of the undertaking or business.[76] A Member State may also permit such

---

[73] Case 19/83 *Wendelboe* [1985] ECR 457; Case 135/83 *Abels* [1985] ECR 469; Case 179/83 FNV [1985] ECR 511; *Botzen* note 60.

[74] Art 5(4).

[75] Directive 80/987 on the protection of employees in case of insolvency [1980] OJ L283/2. See Chapter 13.

[76] Art 5(2).

negotiations where the transferor is in a situation of serious economic crisis, as defined by national law. provided:

(i) the situation has been declared by a competent public authorities;

(ii) is open to judicial supervision; and

(iii) provisions for such an eventuality existed in national law on 17 July 1998.

N. What Constitutes a Transfer?

The issue of what constitutes a transfer of an undertaking has given rise to a sub- **12.70**
stantial body of case law emanating from the ECJ, the flow of which does not seem to abate as ways and means of doing business change. The Original Directive did not define what constituted a transfer of a business. It fell to the Court to do so subsequently in a series of preliminary rulings, relying for its conclusions on the objectives of the Directive as set out in its sparse wording.

That case law is reflected in the Amended Directive, and now Article 1b of the **12.71**
Directive:

> . . . there is a transfer within the meaning of this Directive where there is a transfer of an economic entity which retains its identity, meaning an organized grouping of resources which has the objective of pursuing an economic activity, whether that activity is central or ancillary.

Article 1b was intended to reflect the case law of the Court on the concept **12.72**
of a transfer, but the distillation of principles evolved over decades of case law into a single provision proved difficult. Reference back to case law is therefore necessary—and indeed required by the provisions of the Directive itself[77]—for a clear picture.

This case law is analysed below. From it the following two general principles can **12.73**
be extrapolated:

(i) The transfer must take place by means of a contractual arrangement between the transferor and the transferee. The nature of this contractual arrangement is irrelevant; it can take a number of forms.

(ii) The identity of the business must be preserved in the sense that the means essential to its operation must be transferred.

---

[77] Preamble Recital 8: 'Considerations of legal security and transparency require that the concept of a transfer be clarified in the light of the case-law of the Court of Justice. Such clarification has not altered the scope of Directive 77/187 as interpreted by the Court of Justice.'

(1) The transfer vehicle

12.74 The transfer of an undertaking[78] is required to take place by way of legal transfer or merger. Neither concept is defined in the Original Directive and it has thus fallen to the Court to define them. In doing so it has adopted a functional approach, taking a liberal view as to the means by which a transfer takes place, thereby avoiding what could have become an arid debate on technicalities. The focus is on the essential question of whether a business activity has actually been transferred or not.

12.75 As long as the transfer has resulted from a contractual arrangement such that the responsibility for the running of the business has passed from the transferor to the transferee, the Court is not particularly concerned as to how the transfer has been effected.

12.76 The concept of a legal transfer may cover a written or oral agreement between the transferor and the transferee relating to a change in the person responsible for the operation of the economic entity purportedly transferred and a tacit agreement between them resulting from aspects of practical co-operation which imply an intention to make such a change.[79] A legal transfer may also be found to have taken place in the absence of any agreement either written or oral: what is determinative is the intention of the parties to effect a transfer, not how it is brought about.[80]

12.77 A number of types of transactions which the Court has held to be a means of transferring a business are analysed below. Before doing so we will briefly consider what constitutes a merger for the purposes of the Directive.

Mergers

12.78 Initially, it was assumed[81] that the Directive referred to a merger within the meaning of Directive 78/855 on the mergers of public limited companies,[82] Article 12 of which states that the protection of employees of the companies involved in a merger operation are to be regulated in accordance with the Transfer of

---

[78] Art 1(a).
[79] Note 56 Judgment para 25.
[80] Ibid Judgment para 27.
[81] De Groot, 'The Council Directive on the Safeguarding of Employees' Rights in the Event of Transfers of Undertakings: An Overview of the Case Law' (1993) 30 CML Rev 31 at 334.
[82] [1978] OJ L295/36.

Undertakings Directive. That Directive covers both mergers by acquisition[83] and mergers by the formation of a new company.[84]

Advocate General van Gerven in *Dr Sophie Redmond Stichting*[85] took a different view. He argued that, since the preamble to the Directive[86] refers to 'changes in the structure of undertakings' brought about by economic trends, the word 'merger' as used in the Directive refers to the concept of 'concentration' in the broad sense as set out in Article 3(1) of Council Regulation 4064/89 on the control of concentrations between undertakings.[87]   **12.79**

According to that provision, a concentration arises where 'two or more previously independent undertakings merge' and where one or more undertakings 'acquire, whether by purchase of securities or assets, by contract or by any other means, direct or indirect control over the whole or parts of one or more other undertakings'. The decisive criterion in deciding whether the transfer of an undertaking is the result of a merger within the meaning of the Directive is whether the transaction in issue is part of a restructuring operation which gives rise to a concentration of previously independent undertakings irrespective of the legal technique by which this has come about. If this results in a change of employer, the Directive must apply.[88]   **12.80**

---

83 Article 3.
   1. For the purposes of this Directive, 'merger by acquisition' shall mean the operation whereby one or more companies are wound up without going into liquidation and transfer to another all their assets and liabilities in exchange for the issue to the shareholders of the company or companies being acquired of shares in the acquiring company and a cash payment, if any, not exceeding 10 % of the nominal value of the shares so issued or, where they have no nominal value, of their accounting par value.
   2. A Member State's laws may provide that merger by acquisition may also be effected where one or more of the companies being acquired is in liquidation, provided that this option is restricted to companies which have not yet begun to distribute their assets to their shareholders.

84 Article 4.
   1. For the purposes of this Directive, 'merger by the formation of a new company' shall mean the operation whereby several companies are wound up without going into liquidation and transfer to a company that they set up all their assets and liabilities in exchange for the issue to their shareholders of shares in the new company and a cash payment, if any, not exceeding 10 % of the nominal value of the shares so issued or, where they have no nominal value, of their accounting par value.
   2. A Member State's laws may provide that merger by the formation of a new company may also be effected where one or more of the companies which are ceasing to exist is in liquidation, provided that this option is restricted to.

85 Note 47 at 3196.
86 First Recital.
87 [1989] OJ L395/1; Repealed and replaced by Regulation 139/2004 [2004] OJ L24/1.
88 Opinion *Dr Sophie Redmond* note 47 at 3210.

12.81 Given that neither of the two above-mentioned Directives which set out definitions of mergers were in existence when the Original Directive was adopted and neither is specifically referred to in the amendments made to it, the question seems to remain open as to how a 'merger' should be defined in Community law or whether indeed it is a Community law concept at all. Since the Directive only partially harmonizes national law with the result that a number of key concepts are specifically required to be defined by reference to national law, it is arguable that what constitutes a merger should be a matter for national law also.

Legal transfer

12.82 Given the discrepancies in the various linguistic versions of Article 1(1) coupled with the divergences between the legal systems of the Member States with respect to the concept of a legal transfer the Court in *Abels*[89] held that the meaning of Article 1(1), and hence the scope of the Directive, could not be determined on the basis of a textual interpretation alone. Its meaning had to be derived from the scheme of the Directive and its place in the system of Community law.

12.83 The concept has been given a broad interpretation by the ECJ which has held the Directive to be applicable wherever, in the context of contractual relations, there is a change in the natural or legal person responsible for carrying on the business and assuming the obligations of an employer towards employees of an undertaking.[90] The Directive does not require that ownership of an undertaking pass from the transferor to the transferee. It includes arrangements such as leasing, the transfer or withdrawal of subsidies by a public authority from one organization and the granting of them to another, subcontracting, outsourcing, and insourcing. A transfer of an undertaking can also come about as a result of a judicial decision or legislation. A number of the cases dealing with these arrangements and the Court's assessment of the applicability of the Directive to them are set out below

12.84 (i) **Leasing arrangements.** Various types of leasing arrangements can constitute a transfer of a business within the meaning of the Directive.

12.85 *Ny Moelle Kro*[91] raised the question of whether there could be a transfer of an undertaking within the meaning of the Directive where the owner of a leased undertaking takes over its operation following a breach of the lease by the lessee. The Court held that it was irrelevant that there had been no change in the

---

[89] Case 135/83 [1985] ECR 469.
[90] Case 101/87 *Bork* [1988] ECR 3057 Judgment para 13; Case C-29/91 *Dr Sophie Redmond Stichting* [1992] ECR I–3189 Judgment para 11.
[91] Note 72.

ownership of an undertaking. Employees of an undertaking whose employer changes, without there being any change in the ownership of the undertaking, are in a situation comparable to that of employees of an undertaking which is sold. In both situations, the employees are at risk and so they require equivalent protection. Since the purpose of the Directive is to ensure, as far as possible, that the rights of the employees are safeguarded in the event of a change of employer by enabling them to remain in the employment of the new employer on the terms and conditions agreed with the transferor, issues relating to ownership are not relevant; it is the change in the natural or legal person responsible for carrying on the business which potentially triggers the application of the Directive.

The Court then went on to consider whether a transfer might actually have occurred in the circumstances of the case. It appeared, at the time of the alleged transfer of the undertaking, that it was closed. Being a seasonal business, it was not open all year and the transfer occurred during its normal period of closure. The Court held that the essential criterion in establishing whether a transfer had occurred was whether the undertaking had been transferred as a going concern, which could be indicated, in particular, by the fact that its operation was continued or resumed by the new employer, carrying on the same or similar activities. The fact that an undertaking was temporarily closed at the time of the transfer and had no employees did not, of itself, preclude the possibility that there had been a transfer of the undertaking. This was especially the case with a seasonal business when the transfer takes place during the season when it is normally closed. As a general rule, such closure did not mean that the undertaking ceased to be a going concern. **12.86**

In *Daddy's Dance Hall*,[92] it was held that where, upon the expiry of a lease, the lessee ceases to be the employer and a third party becomes the employer under a new lease concluded with the owner, the resulting operation can fall within the scope of the Directive. **12.87**

In *Berg*[93] the Court ruled that the Directive could be applied when an undertaking was transferred as a result of a lease purchase arrangement: **12.88**

Where an undertaking which has been the subject of a lease purchase agreement is restored to the former employer, following the termination of the lease purchase agreement, that transaction falls to be considered a transfer of an undertaking. It deprives the purchaser of the status of employer, a status which reverts to the vendor. This principle applies regardless of whether the termination of the **12.89**

---

[92] Note 14.
[93] Joined Cases 144 and 145/87 [1998] ECR 2559.

lease purchase agreement results from an agreement between contracting parties or a unilateral decision by one of them or a judicial decision. In all cases, the transfer takes place on the basis of a contract:

> ... in so far as the purchaser of an undertaking becomes, by virtue of a lease purchase agreement, the employer . . . the transfer must be regarded as the transfer of an undertaking as a result of a legal transfer within the meaning of Article 1(1) of the directive, notwithstanding the fact that such a purchaser acquires the ownership of the undertaking only when the totality of the purchase price has been paid.[94]

12.90   (ii) **Transfer of subsidies.**   *Dr Sophie Redmond Stichting*[95] concerned the transfer of subsidies from one foundation engaged in providing assistance to drug addicts to another performing a similar function. In considering where these circumstances constituted a transfer of an undertaking, the Court held that it was for the national court to make the necessary factual appraisal but went on to state that the following facts were 'essential if not decisive features of a transfer':

> ... the transfer of subsidies from the one foundation to the other has the following characteristics: the Redmond Foundation ceased its activities; the two foundations pursue the same or similar aim; the Sigma Foundation partially absorbed the Redmond Foundation; the two foundations cooperated in finalizing the transfer operations; it was agreed that the Redmond Foundation's knowledge and resources could be transferred to the Sigma Foundation; the premises rented by the Redmond Foundation were leased to the Sigma Foundation; and the latter offered new employment contracts to some of the Redmond Foundation's former employees.[96]

12.91   It is of interest to note that the Court held that the non-transfer of immovables did not in itself exclude the application of the Directive, but, at the same time, the national court should appraise their importance by incorporating them in the overall assessment which has to be made in deciding the applicability of the Directive. Presumably if the immovables are an essential part of the business of the undertaking, their transfer is pertinent to the question of whether or not the business activity continues under the new owner. This point is discussed below at paras 12.117–12.125.

12.92   The Court held, that the alleged legal transfer in *Dr Sophie Redmond*[97] was 'comparable in structure' to those considered in the previous cases discussed above in paras 12.83–12.88:

> The operation to which the Kantongerecht's questions relate, as described in the order for reference, is comparable in structure. The situation in question is where a municipality which finances, through subsidies, the activities of a foundation

---

[94] Judgment para 18.
[95] Note 47.
[96] Ibid Judgment para 26.
[97] Note 47.

engaged in providing assistance for drug addicts decides to discontinue the subsidies, and this causes the foundation to cease its activities and transfer them to another foundation carrying on the same activities.[98]

The fact that the transfer decision was taken unilaterally by the public authority **12.93** was of no importance: the change in the recipient of the subsidy was carried out in the context of contractual relations within the meaning of the Directive and the relevant case law thereon. The decision to terminate the subsidy paid to one legal person, as a result of which the activities of that person were fully and definitively terminated, and to transfer it to another legal person with a similar aim, constituted a legal transfer for the purposes of the Directive.

(iii) Subcontracting. The Directive does not specifically deal with the issue **12.94** of subcontracting. If a contractor to whom a contract for services has been awarded (Undertaking A), subcontracts the performance of those services to another undertaking (Undertaking B), what is the position when the contract terminates with Undertaking A and is awarded to another undertaking, Undertaking C? Can there be a transfer of an undertaking from Undertaking B to Undertaking C?

The ECJ considered the issue in *Temco Service Industries SA*.[99] It ruled that the **12.95** Directive applies to a situation in which a contractor has entrusted a contract for cleaning its premises to a first undertaking which has those services performed by a subcontractor, terminates that contract, and enters into a new contract for the performance of the same work with a second undertaking, where the transfer does not involve any transfer of tangible or intangible assets between the first undertaking or the subcontractor and the second undertaking, but the second undertaking has taken on part of the staff of the subcontractor provided that the staff taken on are an essential part, in terms of their number and skills, of the staff assigned by the subcontractor, to the performance of the subcontract.

(iv) Outsourcing and Insourcing. The outsourcing of certain functions by an **12.96** undertaking which has previously carried on those functions in-house, to another undertaking has become increasingly common both in the public and private sectors.

Assuming that the business to which the provision of services or the supply of **12.97** goods is entrusted retains the identity of the business, the transfer will come within the scope of the Directive and the employment relationship of those working in the part of the business outsourced may be transferred to the service provider or supplier of goods to which the outsourcing contract has been awarded.

---

[98] Note 47 Judgment para 14.
[99] Note 30.

Some of the most controversial judgments of the Court have concerned outsourcing issues.

12.98 *Hernandez Vidal*[100] and *Sanchez Hidalgo and Ziemann*[101] concerned the contracting out and, for the first time, the contracting in, of services. Both involved situations in which contracts of services awarded by public authorities were terminated which one service provider and awarded to another service provider.

12.99 *Hernandez Vidal* arose out of a claim by two ladies for unfair dismissal. The ladies were employed by the cleaning company Contratas y Limpiezas for several years. They were charged with cleaning the premises of Hernandez Vidal, a company manufacturing sweets and chewing gum pursuant to a cleaning contract concluded between that undertaking and Contratas y Limpiezas.

12.100 Hernandez Vidal terminated the contract and assumed responsibility for cleaning its own premises. Neither Hernandez Vidal nor Contratas y Limpiezas wished to continue employing the two ladies who had previously cleaned the premises. The ladies brought an action against both companies for unfair dismissal. The national judge upheld their claim with respect to Hernandez Vidal which appealed against that finding arguing that there had been no transfer of a business or part of a business. The issue before the ECJ was whether the Directive applied to a situation where an undertaking decided to terminate a contract for services, the provision of which it had contracted out to another undertaking, in order to perform those services itself. The Court held that such a situation could, in principle, give rise to the application of the Directive:

> Thus the Court has held that a situation in which an undertaking entrusts to another undertaking by contract the responsibility for performing cleaning operations which it previously carried out directly ... and a situation in which a contractor who had entrusted the cleaning of its premises to a first undertaking terminates the contract binding it to that undertaking and concludes, for the purposes of similar operations, a new contract with a second undertaking ... may come within the scope of Directive 77/187.

> Similarly Directive 77/187 must be capable of applying where, as in these cases before the national courts, an undertaking which used to have recourse to another undertaking for the cleaning of its premises or part of them decides to terminate its contract with that undertaking and in future to carry out the work itself.[102]

12.101 *Sanchez Hidalgo and Ziemann*[103] raised a number of issues some of which had been the subject of previous judgments of the Court.

---

[100] Joined Cases C-127/96, C-229/96, and C-74/97 [1998] ECR I–8179.
[101] Joined Cases C-173/96 and C-247/96 [1998] ECR I–8237.
[102] Judgment paras 24 and 25.
[103] Joined Cases C-173/96 and C-247/96 [1998] ECR I–8237.

The Municipality of Guadalajara had contracted out its home help services for persons in need to Minerva which, for the purpose of this contract, had employed Mrs Sanchez Hildalgo and four other employees as home helps for several years. When the contract with Minerva expired, the Municipality awarded a fresh contract to Aser who engaged Mrs Sanchez Hildalgo and her four colleagues on a part-time basis but refused to recognize their previous periods of service with Minerva.

12.102

Mr Ziemann had been employed from 1979 to 1995 as a guard in a medical supplies depot of the Bundeswehr—the Federal Armed Forces. During that time he was employed by five companies in turn, which each successively obtained a contract for maintaining the surveillance of the depot. From 1990–1995 he was employed by Ziemann GmbH. In September 1995 the Bundeswehr terminated the contract with Ziemann GmbH and awarded it to Horst Bohn. Horst Bohn did not take on Mr Ziemann although it did take on other watchmen of Ziemann GmbH who had been employed at the depot. Ziemann GmbH terminated Mr Ziemann's contract. Mr Ziemann alleged that there had been a transfer of part of Ziemann GmbH's business to Horst and consequently he had been unfairly dismissed.

12.103

Both cases concerned the question of whether the absence of a contractual relationship between the transferor and the transferee precluded the application of the Directive. The Court held that, of itself, it did not:

12.104

> Whilst the absence of any contractual link between the transferor and the transferee, as in these cases, between two undertakings successively entrusted with the task of providing a home help service or the task of maintaining surveillance at a medical supplies depot, may be evidence that no transfer within the meaning of the directive has occurred, it is certainly not conclusive.[104]

In *Ziemann* the Court was asked whether there could be a transfer of a business where essentially the same employees continue to perform the same surveillance duties on the same terms, which were largely predetermined by the body awarding the contract. The Court replied that, in principle, the fact that the undertaking which had been awarded a contract was obliged to observe precise obligations imposed on it by the contract awarding body would not affect the issue:

12.105

> Although the influence which the contract-awarding body has on the service provided by the undertaking concerned may be extensive, the service-providing undertaking nevertheless normally retains a certain degree of freedom, albeit reduced, in organizing and performing the service in question, without its task being capable

---

[104] Ibid Judgment para 22.

of being interpreted as simply making personnel available to the contract-awarding body.[105]

12.106 Presumably if the undertaking awarded the contract was simply providing personnel, the situation would be comparable to *Rygaard*[106] with the result that when the contract with it terminated, there could be no issue of a transfer to the new contractor.

12.107 **(v) Transfer of administrative functions with a public administration.** The reorganization of structures of the public administration or the transfer of administrative functions between public administrative authorities does not constitute a transfer of an undertaking within the meaning of the Directive.[107] The issue is whether it is part of a restructuring operation which gives rise to a concentration of previously independent undertakings irrespective of the legal technique (contractual or otherwise) by which this came about. If this results in a change of employer, the Directive must apply.[108]

(2) Preservation of the identity of the business

12.108 The essential criterion in determining whether there has been a transfer of a business or not is whether that business has retained its identity—this will be the case where the same business is carried on by the new owner and the means by which the business is operated has been transferred. Thus the nature of the business must remain for the most part unchanged, and the assets or manpower necessary to carry on that business must pass from the transferor to the transferee. In the case of a business which is heavily dependent upon the availability and use of certain assets, the necessary assets will have to have been taken over by the transferee; where a business is labour-intensive the taking on by the transferee of a sizeable part, in terms both of number and skills, of the workforce will be indicative of a transfer of an undertaking within the meaning of the Directive.[109]

12.109 Although the case law of the Court is rich with examples of what does and what does not constitute a transfer for the purposes of triggering the application of the Directive, essentially it is a question of fact in each case.

12.110 The Court made this clear in *Spijkers*[110] and at the same time set out a number of factors, by way of illustration, which were indicative of a transfer.

---

[105] Note 97 Judgment para 27.
[106] Note 8.
[107] Case C-298/84 *Henke* note 8; Art 1(c).
[108] Ibid Opinion of Advocate General van Gerven at 3210.
[109] Shrubshell: 'Competitive tendering, outsourcing and the Acquired Rights Directive' (1998) 61 MLR 85 at 91.
[110] Case 24/85 [1986] ECR 1119.

The Spijkers *case*

Mr Spijkers was employed by Colaris, a slaughterhouse in The Netherlands, as an **12.111** assistant manager. By 27 December 1982, Colaris ceased its business activities. The entire slaughterhouse with various rooms and offices, the land, and certain specified goods were bought by Benedik Abattoir. All the employees of Colaris were taken over by Benedik apart from Mr Spijkers and one other employee. It appeared that the business activity of Benedik Abattoir was the same as that previously carried on by Colaris and the transfer of the business assets enabled Benedik Abattoir to continue the activities of Colaris, although Benedik did not take over Colaris's customers. Mr Spijkers claimed that there had been a transfer of an undertaking.

The ECJ held that the decisive criterion in determining whether there had been **12.112** a transfer of an undertaking was whether a business retains its identity: was the business disposed of as a going concern? This would be the case where, for example, the same or similar business was resumed or continued by the new employer. This was essentially a question of fact in which a consideration of the following factors was relevant:

(a) the nature of the undertaking or business;
(b) whether or not the business's tangible assets, such as buildings and moveable property, were transferred;
(c) the value of the intangible assets of the business at the time of the transfer;
(d) whether or not the majority of its employees were taken over by the new employer;
(e) whether or not its customers were transferred;
(f) the degree of similarity between the activities carried on before and after the transfer;
(g) the period, if any, for which those activities were suspended.

It was for the national court to make the necessary factual appraisal of the situa- **12.113** tion claimed to be a transfer of an undertaking in the light of these factors which, the Court emphasized, could not be considered in isolation. The entirety of the circumstances surrounding a transfer were to be taken into account in determining the applicability of the Directive. The circumstances of the alleged transfer needed to be looked at in the round.

Case law subsequent to *Spijkers* divides businesses into two categories: those **12.114** which operate on the basis of assets and those which are dependent for their operation on manpower. In the case of the former it is essential that the assets necessary to the carrying on of the business be transferred to the transferee, or at the least be made available to him in the same way as they were made available to the transferor; in the case of the latter, a major part of the transferor's manpower, not simply in terms of numbers but also taking account of skills, must be transferred to the transferee.

12.115   In sum, the means of doing business has to be transferred. The transfer of a business activity per se is not sufficient to invoke the application of the Directive.

12.116   Determining what precisely is the essence of a business venture—assets, manpower, or both and in which proportion—can be problematic. Even in sectors heavily reliant on manpower, the non-transfer of assets necessary for that manpower to carry out its functions may render the Directive inapplicable.

12.117   In *Jouini*[111] the ECJ had to consider the transfer of a temporary employment business to another temporary employment business. The nature of such business is characterized, in general by a '. . . lack of suitable business structure from which it is possible to identify, within such a business, various economic entities which can be detached on the basis of the transferor's organizational arrangements'.[112] However, the nature of such a business consists of the temporary assignment of employees to user undertakings in order that they may carry out a range of tasks according to the needs and instructions of those undertakings. The pursuit of such an activity requires, inter alia, expertise, an administrative infrastructure capable of organizing the assignment of employees, and a grouping of temporary workers who are capable of integrating into the user undertaking and of carrying out the tasks required of them but other significant assets are not indispensable for the pursuit of the business. In determining whether a transfer had taken place it was therefore necessary to focus on the facilities and skills essential to the operation of that business. Applying that criterion the ECJ held that the transfer of part of the administrative personnel and part of the corpus of temporary workers from one temporary employment business to another in order to carry out the same business for the same client is a situation capable of constituting the transfer of an undertaking or part of an undertaking within the meaning of the Directive.

Asset-based businesses

12.118   Whether a business functions essentially on the basis of assets or manpower is a question of fact. For example, in *Oyliikenne Ab*,[113] the Court found, on the facts of the case, that there had not been a transfer of an undertaking. The undertaking whose activity had been transferred was engaged in the business of bus transport.

---

[111] Note 56.
[112] Ibid Judgment para 33.
[113] Case C-172/99 [2001] ECR I–745.

Although the transferee re-engaged 33 of the 45 drivers previously employed by the transferor, none of the 26 buses in the fleet were transferred. The transferee leased two buses for a short period whilst waiting for the delivery of 22 new buses. The ECJ found that the business transferred could not be regarded as a business based essentially on manpower as it required substantial plant and equipment. Basically a bus company cannot operate without buses. It held, therefore, that the absence of a transfer of such assets meant that the entity did not retain its identity and, accordingly, that the Directive was not applicable:

> If an award procedure such as the one in issue in the main proceedings provides for the new contractor to take over the existing contracts with customers, or if the majority of customers may be regarded as captive, then it should nevertheless be considered that there is a transfer of customers.

> However, in a sector such as scheduled public transport by bus where the tangible assets contribute significantly to the performance of the activity, the absence of a transfer to a significant extent from the old to the new contractor of such assets, which are necessary for the proper functioning of the entity, must lead to the conclusion that the entity does not retain its identity.[114]

12.119 Thus it would appear that a transfer of assets in all but situations where an economic entity's activities are essentially based on manpower without the use of any significant assets is essential to the application of the Directive.

12.120 The ownership of the assets need not pass to the transferee. It is enough that they are put at his disposal. It is irrelevant by whom or what means the assets are made available.

12.121 In *Allen*[115] it was customary within the industry in issue, mining, for the essential assets for the service provision to be provided by the mine owner to the service provider. The Court found that the fact that ownership of the assets was necessary to operate the undertaking did not preclude a transfer within the meaning of the Directive. The lack of a transfer of assets between the alleged transferor and transferee was 'not of decisive importance'.[116]

12.122 *Abler*[117] worked for Sanrest, an undertaking catering meals to a hospital both for staff and patients. Meals were prepared on the hospital premises. The premises, water, energy, and equipment were provided to Sanrest. Sanrest bore the cost of the wear and tear to the equipment. In April 1999 Sanrest was given notice that the contract would be terminated in six months. Sodexho was subsequently

---

[114] Ibid Judgment paras 41 and 42.
[115] Note 61.
[116] Case C-234/98 [1999] ECR I–8643 Judgment para 30.
[117] Case C-340/01 [2003] ECR I– 4023.

awarded the catering contract. Sodexho refused to take over Sanrest's materials, stock, and employees. Sodexho therefore received no 'know-how' in the form of accounting data, menu plans, diet plans, recipe collections, or general record from Sanrest. Sanrest terminated its contract with its employees. Mr Alber and others brought proceedings alleging that their contracts of employment had been transferred to Sodexho. Sodexho raised three main arguments in support of its contention that there had not been a transfer of Sanrest's business or part of business to it: (i) it did not take on any of Sanrest's staff; (ii) it had no contractual relationship with Sanrest; (iii) the management authority remained the owner of the premises and equipment necessary for the performance of the activity.

12.123 The Court held that all the features of the business alleged to have been transferred had to be taken into account. On the basis of such an analysis it concluded that a transfer had taken place:

> Catering cannot be regarded as an activity based essentially on manpower since it requires a significant amount of equipment. In the main proceedings, as the Commission points out, the tangible assets needed for the activity in question—namely the premises, water and energy and small and large equipment (inter alia the appliances needed for preparing meals and the dishwashers)—were taken over by Sodexho. Moreover a defining feature of the situation at issue in the main proceedings is the express and fundamental obligation to prepare the meals in the hospital kitchen and thus to take over those tangible assets. The transfer of the premises and the equipment provided by the hospital which is indispensable for the preparation and distribution of meals to the hospital patients and staff is sufficient, in the circumstances, to make this a transfer of an economic entity. It is moreover clear that, given their captive status, the new contractor necessarily took on most of the customers of its predecessor.[118]

12.124 *Guney Gorres and Demir*[119] the first case which has come before the Court on Directive 2001/23, raised the novel issue of whether the assets which are the subject of a transfer must be available for independent commercial use by the transferee. Ms Gunney Gorres and Mrs Demir were employed by Securior as security attendants. In April 2000 Securior was awarded a contract by the German state represented by the Federal Minister of the Interior (BMI) to carry out checks on passengers and their baggage at Dusseldorf airport. BMI made available to Securior the aviation security equipment necessary to provide these services. The equipment consisted of walk through metal detectors and explosive detectors. BMI notified Securior in June 2003 that the contract would not be extended beyond its original term. In September 2003 BMI informed Securior that the contract had been awarded to Kotter. Kotter notified Securior that it

---

[118] Ibid Judgment para 36.
[119] Joined Cases C-232/04 and C-233/04 [2005] ECR I–11237.

proposed to take over only a small proportion of its employees. On 1 January 2004 Kotter's contract commenced. It was essentially the same as that of Securior. Kotter also used the aviation security equipment owned by BMI. It took on 167 of Securior's employees. Ms Guney Gorres and Ms Demir were not amongst these. They sought a declaration before the Employment Tribunal in Dusseldorf that their employment had continued with Kotter since Securior had been transferred to Kotter. It was argued that there had been no transfer of assets to Kotter since Kotter did not have any independent use of the assets used to perform the services. They were owned by BMI and could only be used for the purpose of providing services under the contract. The Court found that this factor did not preclude the transfer falling within the scope of the Directive.

Following *Alber*[120] the Court reasoned: **12.125**

> ... it must be noted that it is clear from the wording of Article 1 of Directive 2001/23 that it is applicable whenever, in the context of contractual relations, there is a change in the legal or natural person who is responsible for carrying on a business and who by virtue of that fact incurs the obligations of an employer vis a vis the employees of the undertaking or business regardless of whether or not the ownership of tangible assets is transferred

> ... the fact that the tangible assets taken over by the new contractor did not belong to its predecessor but were provided by the contracting authority cannot preclude the existence of a transfer of an undertaking ...

> It does not appear that the fact that independent commercial use was made of assets taken over by the contractor is decisive in establishing whether or not there has been a transfer of assets.[121]

Merckx and Neuhuys,[122] an undertaking holding a motor vehicle dealership for a   **12.126**
particular territory, discontinued its activities and the dealership was then transferred to another undertaking which took on part of its staff. The Court held that it was irrelevant that there had been no transfer of assets nor any preservation of the undertaking's structure and assets. The fact that the transferor had ceased trading definitively, had been put into liquidation, and had dismissed its employees were factors that the Court did not consider to be such as to render the Directive inapplicable:

> ... having regard to the nature of the activity pursued, the transfer of tangible assets is not conclusive of whether the entity in question retains its economic identity ... The purpose of the exclusive dealership for the sale of motor vehicles of a particular make in a certain sector remains the same even if it is carried on under a different

---

[120] Note 117.
[121] Ibid Judgment paras 37, 38, 39.
[122] Joined Cases C-171/94 and C-172/94 [1996] ECR I-1253.

name, from different premises and with different facilities. It is also irrelevant that the principal place of business is situated in a different area of the same conurbation, provided that the contract territory remains the same.

> . . . if the Directive's aim of protecting workers is not to be undermined, its application cannot be excluded merely because the transferor discontinues its activities when the transfer is made and is then put into liquidation. If the business of that undertaking is carried on by another undertaking, those facts tend to confirm, rather, that there has been a transfer for the purposes of the Directive.[123]

Labour-intensive businesses

12.127 In labour-intensive sectors, a group of workers engaged in a joint activity on a permanent basis may constitute an economic entity and such an entity may be considered to have been transferred where the transferee takes over a major part, in terms of their numbers and skills, of the employees previously engaged in that activity. In those circumstances the transferor has the means enabling him to carry on the activities or certain activities of the transferor undertaking on a regular basis.

12.128 *Schmidt*[124] held that, where the cleaning activities of a branch of an undertaking which had been performed by a single employee were transferred to an outside firm, that transaction could be a transfer of an undertaking. The similarity of the cleaning work performed before and after the transfer, coupled with the offer to re-engage the employee in question, was typical of an operation which fell within the scope of the Directive with the result that the sole employee whose activity had been transferred was entitled to the protection of that Directive. Both the German government and the United Kingdom government argued that absence of a transfer of tangible assets precluded a finding that a transfer had occurred. The Court rejected this reasoning holding that the absence of a transfer of tangible assets was not decisive in determining whether a transfer had occurred:

> The fact that in its case-law the Court includes the transfer of such assets among the various factors to be taken into account by a national court to enable it, when assessing a complex transaction as a whole, to decide whether an undertaking has in fact been transferred does not support the conclusion that the absence of these factors precludes the existence of a transfer . . . the decisive criterion for establishing whether there is a transfer for the purposes of the directive is whether the business in question retains its identity.

12.129 *Suzen*[125] concerned the transfer of a cleaning contract from one undertaking to another without any concomitant transfer of tangible or intangible assets or any

---

[123] Judgment paras 21 and 23.
[124] Note 22.
[125] Case C-13/95 [1997] ECR I–1259.

transfer of part of the workforce. Mrs Suzen was employed by Zehnacker which assigned her (along with seven others) to clean the premises of Aloisiuskolleg, a secondary school, under a cleaning contract concluded between the school and Zehnacker.

The school terminated the contract for cleaning services with Zehnacker which **12.130** then dismissed Mrs Suzen and the seven other employees who had performed the cleaning work at the school. The school subsequently awarded a cleaning contract to another entity, Lefarth. Lefarth had no dealings with Zehnacker The Court began by stating that the mere fact that the service provided by the old and the new contractors is similar is not enough to support the conclusion that an economic entity has been transferred. An entity cannot be reduced to the activity entrusted to it. There must be other factors present before a transfer can be found to have occurred, and those factors must entail either a transfer of manpower or a transfer of assets or both:

> . . . the concomitant transfer from one undertaking to the other of significant tangible or intangible assets or taking over by the new employer of a major part of the workforce in terms of their number and skills, assigned by his predecessor to the performance of the contract.[126]

The Court further held in *Suzen* that the mere loss of a service contract to a competitor cannot by itself indicate the existence of a transfer within the meaning of the Directive. The service undertaking previously entrusted with the contract does not, on losing a customer, thereby cease fully to exist and a business or part of a business cannot be considered to have been transferred to the person to whom the new contract has been awarded.

Suzen[127] differed from *Schmidt*[128] in that no members of the workforce were **12.132** taken over by Lefarth and possibly even if only Mrs Suzen had been taken on there would still not have been a transfer as the 'major part of the workforce' would not have been taken on as was the case in Schmidt—where Mrs Schmidt, although the only worker, constituted the entire workforce.

O. Consequences of a Transfer

(1) The employment relationship

The Directive provides for the safeguarding of the rights and obligations of the **12.133** transferor which arise under a contract of employment or from an employment

---

[126] Ibid Judgment para 23.
[127] Note 125.
[128] Note 22.

relationship existing on the date of the transfer. Such rights are automatically transferred to the transferee on the date of the transfer:[129]

> ... the scheme and purpose of the Directive ... is intended to ensure, as far as possible, that the employment relationship continues unchanged with the transferee and by protecting workers against dismissal solely motivated by the fact of the transfer.[130]

12.134 The entire bundle of rights to which the employment relationship gives rise must be conserved and transferred. This includes acquired rights and rights in the process of being acquired. Thus in *Collino*[131] the Court held that the transferee had to take account of the entire length of periods of service of the employees transferred in calculating rights such as termination of payments or salary increases.[132]

12.135 The transfer relieves the transferor of all his obligations towards his employees and results in the immediate transfer of these to the transferee, irrespective of the wishes or contrary intentions of any of the parties.[133]

12.136 *Martin*[134] held that a transferee is precluded from offering the employees of a transferred undertaking terms less favourable than those offered to them by the transferor in respect of early retirement. Employees may not accept such less favourable terms. If employees are offered early retirement following the transfer, but on terms less favourable than those to which they were entitled under their employment relationship with the transferor, and if the employees accept such offers of early retirement, the transferee must ensure that that retirement is granted upon the same terms and conditions as it would have been under the employment relationship with the transferor.

12.137 Whether an employment contract exists or not at the time of the transfer is a question of national law.[135] Rights contingent upon dismissal or the grant of early retirement by agreement between the employee and the employer are rights and obligations within the meaning of Article 3(1) of the Directive.[136]

---

[129] Art 3(1); Case C-362/89 *d'Urso* note 14; Case C-305/94 *Rotsart de Hertaing* [1996] ECR I–5927.
[130] Case 19/83 [1985] ECR 457 Judgment para 15.
[131] Note 67.
[132] Ibid Judgment para 50.
[133] Case C-305/94 *Rotsart* note 129.
[134] Case C-4/01 [2003] ECR I–12859.
[135] Art 3(1). Although Member States are free to determine who is or who is not covered by a contract of employment or an employment relationship at the time of the transfer, they may not exclude from the scope of the Directive contracts of employment or employment relationships solely because of the number of hours worked or because they are temporary or of fixed duration: Case 18/93 *Wendelboe* [1985] ECR 457.
[136] Note 22.

It is irrelevant that the obligations in question arise under legislation as opposed **12.138**
to under a contract of employment.[137]

Member States may provide that the transferor and the transferee shall be jointly **12.139**
and severally liable in respect of obligations towards employees which arose before
the date of the transfer from the contract of employment or an employment
relationship which existed at the date of the transfer.[138]

Member States may (but are not obliged to) adopt measures to ensure that the **12.140**
transferor notifies the transferee of all the rights and obligations which are or
ought to have been known to the transferor at the time of the transfer. Any failure
on the part of the transferor to notify the transferee of such rights and obligations
does not affect the transfer of those rights and obligations nor the rights of any
employees against the transferor or transferee in respect of them. In the context
of a transfer which takes place as a result of the contracting out or the contracting
in of services it may be important, if the contract is subject to the requirements of
Directive 92/50 relating to the co-ordination of the procedures for the award
of public service contracts,[139] for the transferee to know what the transferor's
obligations are, since without that knowledge he may find it difficult to formulate
his tender.

Collective agreements

The transferee is placed under an obligation to observe the terms and conditions **12.141**
agreed in any collective agreement on the same terms applicable to the transferor
under that agreement, until its date of expiry or termination or the entry into
force of another agreement.[140]

Member States may limit the period for observing such terms and conditions but **12.142**
any such limitation must not be for less than one year.

Where a contract of employment refers to a collective agreement binding on the **12.143**
transferor of an undertaking, the Directive does not require the transferee, who is
not a member of the employer's federation which negotiates such agreements, to
apply agreements which have replaced the collective agreements in force at the
time of the change in ownership of the undertaking.

The transferee in such circumstances is only bound by an agreement existing at **12.144**
the time of the transfer. He cannot be required to be bound by future agreements
in which he did not participate in the negotiation procedure nor can he be

---

[137] Case C-164/00 *Beckmann* [2002] ECR I–4893.
[138] Article 3(1).
[139] [1992] OJ L209/1.
[140] Art 3(3).

required to join the employer's federation in order to engage in such negotiation.[141] Freedom of association, which also includes the right not to join an association, is one of the fundamental rights which, in accordance with the Court's settled case law, are protected in the Community legal order.[142] If future collective agreements were to apply to a transferee who was not party to a collective agreement, his fundamental right not to join an association could be affected.

Pension entitlement

12.145 Unless Member States provide otherwise, employees' rights to old age, invalidity, or survivors' benefits under occupational social security schemes are not covered by the Directive,[143] with the effect that the transferor's obligations with respect to those benefits are not transferred to the transferee.[144]

12.146 Member States are charged with the duty of adopting measures necessary to protect the interests of employees and of persons no longer employed in the transferor's business at the time of the transfer in respect of rights conferring on them immediate or prospective entitlement to old age benefits and survivors' benefits under occupational social security schemes.[145] The nature and level of such protection is not specified. But the level of protection offered must be such as to be meaningless.[146]

12.147 Early retirement benefits, and associated benefits intended to enhance the enjoyment of such retirement, paid in the event of retirement before normal retirement age, by virtue of an agreement between the employer and his employees, to employees who have reached a certain age are not old age, invalidity, or survivors' benefits under occupational pension schemes within the meaning of the Directive. Consequently:

> . . . Article 3 of the directive is to be interpreted as meaning that obligations arising upon the grant of such early retirement, arising from a contract of employment, an employment relationship or a collective agreement binding the transferor as regards the employees concerned, are transferred to the transferee subject to the conditions and limitations laid down by that article, regardless of the fact that those obligations

---

[141] Case C-499/04 *Werhof* [2006] ECR I–2397 Judgment para 33.

[142] Case C-415/93 *Bosman* [1995] ECR I–4921 Judgment para 79, as is restated in Art 6(2) EU see Case C-274/99P *Connolly* [2001] ECR I–1611.

[143] Art 3(4)(a).

[144] Ibid.

[145] Art 3(4)(b).

[146] By analogy with Art 8 of Directive 80/987 on the protection of employees in the event of the insolvency of their employer [1980] OJ L283/23 see Case C-278/05 *Robins* [2007] ECR I–1053.

derive from statutory instruments or are implemented by such instruments and regardless of the practical arrangements adopted for such implementation.[147]

Early retirement benefits paid in the event of the dismissal of employees who have reached a certain age are protected by the Directive. Such benefits are not to be considered old age, invalidity, or survivors' benefits within the meaning of Article 3(3).[148]   **12.148**

Protection against dismissal

Article 4(1) of the Directive provides that the transfer of an undertaking shall not of itself constitute grounds for dismissal of any of the employees by the transferor or the transferee.[149] Whether a dismissal has taken place by reason of a transfer is a question for the national court to decide. If the national court decides that the dismissal occurred because of the transfer then the employees in question must be considered as being still employed by the transferor on the date of the transfer, with the result that the transferor's obligations towards those employees are transferred to the transferee in accordance with Article 3 of the Directive.[150]   **12.149**

If national legislation lays down provisions in favour of the transferor enabling the burden of surplus employees to be alleviated or removed, the Directive does not prevent those provisions being applied to the transferee's advantage after the transfer.[151]   **12.150**

Member States may exclude certain specific categories of employees who are not covered by national laws or practices on dismissal from the protection conferred by Article 4(1)[152] but this right may not be used to deprive workers of rights under the Directive where they have some, albeit limited, protection against dismissal under national law.[153]   **12.151**

Dismissals for economic, technical, or organizational reasons

Article 4(1) of the Directive does not prohibit dismissals for economic, technical, or organizational reasons. Where employees are dismissed prior to a transfer taking place and immediately taken on by the transferee following the transfer, there is a presumption that the dismissals did not take place for economic,   **12.152**

---

[147] Case C-4/01 *Martin* note 23.
[148] Case C-164/00 *Beckmann* [2002] ECR I–4893.
[149] Note 122.
[150] Case 101/87 *Bork* [1988] ECR 3057.
[151] Note 114.
[152] Art 4(1), para 2.
[153] Case 237/84 *Commission v Belgium* [1986] ECR 1247.

technical, or organizational reasons.[154] *Dethier*[155] raised the issue of whether the right to dismiss for economic, technical, or organizational reasons applied to dismissals by the transferor before the transfer as well as to dismissals effected by the transferee after the transfer. Relying on *Bork*,[156] the Court found that the right to dismiss was conferred on both the transferor and the transferee but if such dismissals were ultimately proved to be unlawful, the transferee was liable:

> ... employees unlawfully dismissed shortly before the undertaking is transferred and not taken on by the transferee may claim as against the transferee, that the dismissal was unlawful.[157]

12.153 The remedies available to employees in these circumstances are determined by national law subject to the principles of equivalence and effectiveness whereby remedies must be of a similar nature to those available for infringements of comparable rights under national law and in any event be effective, proportionate, and dissuasive.[158]

Substantial change in working conditions

12.154 If the contract of employment or employment relationship is terminated because the transfer of the undertaking involves a substantial change in working conditions to the detriment of the employee, the employer is to be regarded as being responsible for the termination.[159] In *Merckx and Neuhuys*[160] the Court held that a change in the level of remuneration given to an employee is a substantial change in working conditions even where the remuneration depends, in particular, on the turnover achieved. Likewise in *Delahaye*[161] it was found that a transfer of a private undertaking to the State which entailed a transfer of employees from contracts of employment governed by private law to public sector employment, and which resulted in a considerable reduction in remuneration (in that case 37 per cent) constituted a substantial change in the conditions of employment to the detriment of the employee.

---

[154] *Bork* note 150. See Opinion of Advocate General van Gerven in *D'Urso* at 4137 where he states that the Directive prohibits dismissals where they occur as a result of the transfer of the undertaking. It is only where dismissals have already been decided upon before the transfer of the undertaking that they come within the scope of Art 4(1).

[155] Case C-319/94 [1998] ECR I–1061.

[156] Note 154.

[157] Ibid Judgment para.

[158] Case C-382/92 *Commission v United Kingdom* [1994] ECR I–2435.

[159] Art 4(2).

[160] Joined Cases C-171 and 172/94 [1996] ECR I–1253.

[161] Case C-425/02 [2004] ECR I–10823.

Information and consultation

The transferor and the transferee are required to inform the representatives of **12.155** their respective employees affected by the transfer of:

(a) the date or the proposed date of the transfer;
(b) the reasons for the transfer;
(c) the legal, economic, and social implications of the transfer for the employees;
(d) any measures envisaged in relation to the employees.[162]

Where there are no representatives of the employees in an undertaking or busi- **12.156** ness, the employees must be informed directly of the four matters set out above.

Such information by the transferor to his employees must be given in 'good time' **12.157** before the transfer is carried out. The transferee must give the required informa- tion to the representatives of his employees in good time, and in any event before his employees are directly affected by the transfer as regards their conditions of work and employment.[163] Where either the transferor or the transferee envisages measures in relation to his respective employees, he must consult the representa- tives of the employees in good time with a view to reaching agreement.

The information and consultation obligations apply regardless of whether the **12.158** decision resulting in the transfer is taken by the employer or an undertaking controlling the employer.

P. Implementation and Enforcement

Article 8 of the original Directive required Member States to bring into force **12.159** laws, regulations, and administrative provisions to comply with the Directive by 16 February 1979. In *Commission v Italy*[164] the Court of Justice held that Italy had not properly implemented the Directive in that the collective agreement which purported to do so only covered specific sectors of the economy.

Article 2 of the Amended Directive required that Member States transpose its **12.160** provisions into national law by 17 July 2001 at the latest. The Directive, adopted on 12 March 2001, being a consolidating measure, did not lay down any dead- line for implementation, the two previous implementations being applicable *mutatis mutandis*.

---

[162] Art 7(1).
[163] Art 7(2).
[164] Case C-235/84 [1986] ECR 2291.

12.161 Article 9 of the Directive, reproducing Article 7a of the Amended Directive, obliges Member States to introduce into their national legal systems such measures as are necessary to enable all employees and representatives of employees who are alleging non-compliance with the requirements of the Directive to pursue their claims by judicial process after possible recourse to other competent authorities.

13

INSOLVENCY

A. Introduction

Directive 80/987 on the protection of employees in the case of insolvency[1] (the **13.01** 'Directive') was the third in a series of directives adopted pursuant to the 1974 Social Action Programme[2] designed to improve the protection of employees and to introduce common minimum standards for such protection throughout the Community. It was amended in 1987,[3] and thereafter by the various Accession Treaties. Directive 2002/74 introduced a number of new provisions designed to reflect changes in the insolvency laws of the Member States and the development of the internal market.[4]

Member States were required to ensure compliance with the provisions of **13.02** Directive 2002/74 by 8 October 2005.[5] The second subparagraph of Article 2(1)

---

[1] Directive 80/987 on the protection of employees in the event of the insolvency of their employer ([1980] OJ L283/2; [1987] OJ L60/11).

[2] [1974] OJ C12/1.

[3] Directive 87/164 ([1987] OJ L60/11).

[4] [2002] OJ L270/10.

[5] Art 2(1).

provides that Member States are to apply national provisions adopted prior to the deadline for the adoption of implementing measure (8 October 2005) to any state of insolvency occurring after the date of entry into force of the Directive (8 October 2002). An employer's state of insolvency and its consequences fall within the scope of Directive 80/987, as amended by Directive 2002/74, from the date of entry into force of the latter (8 October 2002) as opposed to the expiry of the transposition period (8 October 2005).[6] Where no national implementing measures have been adopted the Directive applies to insolvencies occurring after 8 October 2005.[7]

13.03   Any insolvency proceedings initiated prior to 8 October 2002 are subject to the provisions of Directive 80/987 as it stood before the adoption of Directive 2002/74. This rule extends to the interpretation of Directive 80/987 which cannot be required to be read or applied in the light of Directive 2002/74 to circumstances or to events and facts which arose before 8 October 2002. In *Robins*[8] Advocate General Kokott held:

> . . . the amending directive did not enter into force until after the insolvency proceedings had been initiated against ASW and its pension schemes terminated. That directive cannot therefore have a direct effect on the legal appraisal of the case in hand.[9]

B. Objective of the Directive

13.04   The objective of the Directive is twofold:

(a) to protect employees in the case of the insolvency of their employers so as to ensure that their rights under their contracts of employment or arising out of their employment relationships are safeguarded; and

(b) to approximate the laws of the Member States so as to reduce disparities between them in the provision of employee protection in the case of the insolvency of employers. The Directive guarantees a minimum level of protection and applies without prejudice to more favourable national provisions.[10]

---

6 Case C-81/05 *Alonso* [2006] ECR I-7569.
7 Case C-246/06 *Navarro* Judgment of 17 January 2008.
8 Case C-278/05 *Robins* [2007] ECR I-1053.
9 Ibid Opinion at para 68.
10 Case 125/97 *Regeling* [1998] ECR I-4493.

C. Scope of Application

(1) Employee

The term 'employee' is not defined save to say that the Directive is 'without **13.05** prejudice to any national law as regards the definition of the term employee'.[11] Directive 2002/74 provides that part-time workers, workers with fixed-term contracts, and temporary workers may not be excluded from the scope of the Directive.[12] Member States are prohibited from setting down a minimum period of employment as a requirement to qualifying for claims under the Directive.[13]

(2) Employment relationship

'Employment relationship' has been held to be a term of Community law which **13.06** requires a uniform interpretation in all Member States.[14] It must be interpreted and applied in the light of the purpose of the Directive which is to ensure a minimum level of protection for all workers. It cannot be interpreted in such a way as to allow the minimum guarantees laid down by the Directive to be reduced to nothing. Consequently, in *Mau*,[15] the ECJ held that it must exclude periods of time:

> ...which by their very nature cannot give rise to outstanding claims. Periods during which the employment relationship is suspended on account of child raising are therefore excluded by reason of the fact that no remuneration is due during those periods.[16]

(3) Excluded categories of employee

The original Directive permitted Member States to exclude from the scope of **13.07** its application certain categories of employees, either because of the special nature of their contracts of employment or employment relationship or by reason of the existence of other forms of guarantees equivalent to those envisaged by the Directive.

The categories of employee which could be so exempt from the original Directive, **13.08** were set out in Annex 1. Since the aim of the Directive was to ensure the

---

[11] Directive 80/987 Art 1(2).
[12] Directive 2002/74 Art 2(2).
[13] Ibid Art 2(3).
[14] Case C-125/97 *Regeling* (see note 10 above).
[15] Case C-160/01 [2003] ECR I–4791.
[16] Ibid at para 44.

minimum degree of protection for all employees, the exclusions specified in the Annex were required to be interpreted strictly.[17] Only categories of employees listed in the Annex could be excluded from the scope of the Directive.[18] For example, the United Kingdom excluded share fishermen and spouses of employers, whilst Ireland additionally excluded persons working for 18 hours or less per week for one or more employers who did not derive their basic means of subsistence from pay for this work, close relatives of the employer working at a private dwelling or farm in, or on which, the employer resides, and piece workers working in their own homes without a written contract of employment.

13.09 The Annex has been removed by Directive 2002/74. Article 1(3) of Directive 2002/74 specifies that Member States may only exempt domestic servants employed by natural persons and share fishermen if they have a degree of protection under national law equivalent to that laid down by the Directive.

D. Exceptions

13.10 The Directive does not apply where the contract of employment or the employment relationship is with an employer who cannot, under the provisions of national law, be subject to proceedings involving assets in order to satisfy collectively the claims of contractors. Such an employer cannot be said to be in a 'state of insolvency' within the meaning of the Directive.[19] It may therefore be the case that the protection afforded by the Directive may vary from one Member State to another depending on the provisions of national insolvency regimes.

13.11 Such differences in treatment of employees from Member State to Member State have been held by the ECJ not to be contrary to the principle of equal treatment: the distinction drawn between employees according to whether or not their employer is or is not subject to proceedings to satisfy the claims of creditors derives from a concept of insolvency based on a criterion which is in itself objective and is justified by reason of the difficulties of harmonizing the rules relating to employee protection in the event of insolvency.[20]

---

[17] Case 22/87 *Commission v Italy* [1989] ECR 143; Case C-441/99 *Rijsskatteverkey v Gharehveran* [2001] ECR I–7687.
[18] Case C-334/92 *Wagner-Miret v Fondo de Garantia Salarial* [1993] ECR I–6911.
[19] Case C-479/93 *Francovich v Italy* [1995] ECR I–3843.
[20] Ibid.

E. Insolvency

The original Directive applied where an employer was in a state of insolvency, **13.12** that is:

(a) where a request had been made for the opening of proceedings involving the employer's assets as provided for under national law in order to satisfy collectively the claims of creditors; and

(b) where the competent authority in the Member State had either decided to open proceedings or had established that the employer's business had been definitively closed down and there were insufficient assets to warrant the opening of proceedings.[21]

Following the amendments introduced by Directive 2002/74, an employer is **13.13** deemed to be in a state of insolvency where a request has been made for the opening of collective proceedings based on insolvency of the employer, as provided under the laws, regulations, and administrative provisions of a Member State, and involving the partial or total divestment of the employer's assets and the appointment of a liquidator or a person performing a similar task, and the authority which is competent pursuant to the said provisions has:

(a) either decided to open the proceedings; or

(b) established that the employer's undertaking or business has been definitively closed down and that the available assets are insufficient to warrant the opening of the proceedings.[22]

F. Guarantee Institutions

The Directive obliges Member States to set up 'guarantee institutions'. The **13.14** Member States are responsible for the organization, financing, and operation of the guarantee institutions. The guarantee institutions are responsible for the payment of sums due to employees at the time of the insolvency, within the limits laid down by the Directive and permitted derogations therefrom by Member States.

The assets of the guarantee institutions must be independent of the employ- **13.15** er's operating capital and be inaccessible in proceedings for insolvency.[23]

---

[21] Art 2.
[22] Art 2(1).
[23] Art 3.

Employers must contribute to the financing of the guarantee institutions unless such financing is fully covered by the public authorities.

13.16   The liability of guarantee institutions must not depend on whether the obligation to contribute to its financing has been fulfilled.[24]

13.17   Where an employer is established in a Member State other than that of the employee's place of residence or employment, the responsible guarantee institution is that of the State in which

   (a) it has been decided to open proceedings for the collective satisfaction of the creditors' claims; or

   (b) it has been established that the employer's undertaking or business has definitively closed down.[25]

13.18   In *Mosbaek*,[26] an employee of a United Kingdom insolvent company acted as an agent for that company in Denmark. The company itself was not established in Denmark nor was it registered in Denmark. In particular, it was not registered with the tax or customs authorities. Mrs Mosbaek's remuneration was paid to her by her employer with no deduction for tax, pension, or other social security contributions under Danish law. When the company became insolvent, Mrs Mosbaek, along with its other employees, was dismissed. She made a claim to the Danish guarantee institution for a sum representing her salary, commission, and expenses. That guarantee institution refused to settle the claim on the ground that the responsibility lay with the guarantee institution of the State in which the employer was established, in this case the United Kingdom National Insurance Fund.

13.19   In reply to a request for a preliminary ruling, the Court of Justice held that the United Kingdom guarantee institution was liable for the employee's claim. Since Article 5(b) of the Directive provided that the guarantee system is to be financed by employers (unless it is fully covered by the public authorities) it followed, in the absence of any indication to the contrary, that the guarantee institution responsible for employees' outstanding claims should be the one which levied or should have levied the employer's contributions. That cannot be the case of the institution of a Member State with which the employer had no establishment or commercial presence even if the employee resided and worked there. Given that there was no system of set-off or reimbursement of payments between the guarantee institutions of the Member States, this confirmed that the Community

---

[24] Art 5.
[25] Arts 3(2) and 4(2).
[26] Case C-17/96 [1997] ECR I–5017.

legislature intended, in the event of an employer's insolvency, that the guarantee institution of only one Member State should be involved.

In *Everson and Barrass*[27] the position was different. Bell Lines Ltd ('Bell'), a company incorporated under Irish law, with a registered office in Dublin, carried on business as a shipping agent from various addresses in the United Kingdom. It employed some 209 persons in the United Kingdom. The employer's and employees' social security contributions were paid into the National Insurance Fund. The High Court of Ireland made an order that Bell be wound up on the grounds of insolvency, and appointed a liquidator. The English High Court recognized the appointment of the liquidator and appointed joint special managers to assist in the winding up of Bell's affairs in the United Kingdom. Bell's employees were dismissed. Most of them applied to the Secretary of State under Part XII of the Employment Rights Act 1996 (the 'Act') for compensation for arrears of pay, outstanding holiday pay, and compensatory payments in lieu of notice. These claims were rejected on the ground that there was no obligation to make such payments under the Act, by virtue of *Mosbaek*. **13.20**

The Court distinguished *Mosbaek* from *Bell*. In *Mosbaek*, the insolvent company did not have any establishment in the territory of the Member State in which the employee was working. *Bell* was different in that it was established in the United Kingdom and employed more than 200 persons there. The Court concluded: **13.21**

> In such a case, the institution which must settle any outstanding claims is that of the Member State within whose territory the branch is established.[28]

The guarantee institution in the Member State of employment in this case, the United Kingdom, was held liable for the outstanding claims of those employees. **13.22**

Directive 2002/74 inserted Article 8a into the original Directive, providing that, where an undertaking with activities in at least two Member States is in a state of insolvency, the institution responsible for meeting employees' claims is that of the Member State in whose territory they work or habitually work. This reflects the judgment of the ECJ in *Everson and Barrass*.[29] The extent of employees' rights is determined by the law governing the competent guarantee institution. **13.23**

---

[27] Case C-198/98 [1999] ECR I–8903.
[28] Ibid Judgment para 23.
[29] See note 27 above, note 183.

13.24 The case of *Holmqvist*[30] raises the issue of what constitutes 'activities in at least two Member States' within the meaning of Article 8a. What level of economic activity or presence in a Member State by an undertaking potentially creates a liability for the guarantee institution of that Member State in the event of the insolvency of that undertaking? Andres Holmqvist was employed by a Swedish transport company to transport goods from Italy to Sweden and to load and unload the goods at their point of departure and point of arrival. In the course of his work he travelled through Austria and Germany. The transport company had no branch or representative office outside Sweden. When it was declared insolvent the issue arose as to which guarantee institution was responsible for settling the salary claim of Mr Holmqvist. The Court held, in view of how forms of cross-border work may vary, and given the recent changes in terms and conditions of employment and progress of the telecommunications sector, that to require an undertaking necessarily to have a physical infrastructure in order for it to be deemed to have a stable economic presence in a Member State other than that in which it has its seat, was untenable. The various aspects of an employment relationship, internal communication of instructions to the employee and his reporting back to the employer, and the payment of remuneration, can now be performed remotely. Therefore an undertaking may employ a large number of workers in a Member State, other than that in which it has its seat and be able to carry out significant economic activities there without having a physical infrastructure or an office in the territory of that other Member State. Nevertheless, in order for an undertaking established in a Member State to be regarded as having activities in the territory of another Member State, that undertaking must have a stable economic presence in the latter State, featuring human resources which enable it to perform activities there. In the case of a transport undertaking established in a Member State the mere fact that a worker employed by it, in that State, delivered goods between that State and another Member State cannot demonstrate that the undertaking has a stable economic presence in that other Member State.

G. Outstanding Claims

13.25 The guarantee institutions must ensure the payment of employees' outstanding claims arising from the contracts of employment or the employment relationship for a period prior to a given date. The responsibilities of the bankrupt

---

[30] Case C-310/07 Judgment of 16 October 2008.

employer are assumed by the guarantee institutions. These responsibilities may be subject to temporal limitations set by the Member States.[31]

The Directive covers claims made by workers that arise from a contract of employ- **13.26** ment or employment relationship where those claims relate to pay within the meaning of Article 3(1).[32] It falls to the national court to define the concept of 'pay' within the meaning of national law.[33] The principle of equality and non-discrimination, whereby comparable situations should not be treated differently unless such difference in treatment is objectively justified,[34] requires that where compensation for unfair dismissal awarded by judgment or administrative decision falls within the concept of 'pay' under national law identical awards established in the context of a judicial conciliation procedure must be regarded as claims arising under a contract of employment or an employment relationship.[35] By contrast the right to compensation for unfair dismissal made in the context of an extra-judicial settlement may be excluded from the payment guarantee payable by the guarantee institutions on the ground that an extra-judicial conciliation procedure differs from a judicial conciliation procedure in that it does not offer the same safeguards against abusive claims as a judicial conciliation procedure and thus falls within the category of measures envisaged by Article 10(a) of the Directive as being objectively justified in the interest of avoidance of abuse.[36]

The position pre-2002 Amendment

Article 3(1) of the Directive, prior to its amendment by Directive 2002/74, **13.27** defines 'outstanding claims' as relating to pay for a guaranteed period prior to a given date. Member States can choose that date and the period for which pay is guaranteed subject to certain minimum requirements laid down by the Directive. Article 3(2) of the Directive requires that the date be one of the following three:

(a) that of the onset of the employer's insolvency;
(b) that of the notice of dismissal issued to the employee concerned on account of the employer's insolvency; or

---

[31] Art 4(2).
[32] Case C-442/00 *Rodriguez Cabellero* [2002] ECR I–11915 Judgment para 26.
[33] Case C-520/03 *Valero* [2004] ECR I–2065.
[34] *Rodriguez Cabellero* note 32 Judgment paras 29–32; Case C-177/05 *Guerrero Pecino* [2005] ECR I–10887 Judgment paras 25 and 26; Case C-81/05 *Alonso* (see note 6 above) Judgment para 37.
[35] *Valero* (see note 32 above) Judgment para 38.
[36] Case C-498/06 *Nunez* Judgment of 21 February 2008.

(c) that of the onset of the employer's insolvency or that on which the contract of employment or employment relationship with the employer concerned was discontinued on account of the employer's insolvency.

13.28 By way of derogation from Article 3(1), the Member States have, by virtue of Article 4(1), the option to limit the liability for pay claims to a given period fixed in accordance with a number of rules set out in Article 4(2). These are as follows:

(a) Where the date chosen by a Member State under Article 3(2) is that of the onset of the employer's insolvency, the Member State must ensure the payment of all outstanding claims relating to pay for the last three months of the contract of employment occurring within a period of six months preceding the date of the onset of the insolvency.

(b) If the chosen date under Article 3(2) is that of the notice of dismissal issued to the employee on account of the employer's insolvency, the Member State must ensure the payment of outstanding claims relating to pay for the last three months of the contract of employment preceding the date of the notice of dismissal issued to the employee on account of the employer's insolvency.

(c) If the date chosen by the Member State under Article 3(2) is that of the onset of the employer's insolvency or that on which the contract of employment was discontinued on account of the employer's insolvency, the Member State must ensure the payment of outstanding claims relating to pay for the last 18 months of the contract of employment preceding the date of the onset of the employer's insolvency or the date on which the contract of employment with the employee was discontinued on account on the employer's insolvency. Where this is the case, Member States may limit the liability to make payment to a period of a total of eight weeks.

13.29 Article 4(3) states that in order to avoid the payment of sums going beyond the 'social objectives' of the Directive, Member States could set a ceiling to the liability of employees' outstanding claims. The Commission must be informed of the methods used to set the ceiling.

The position post the 2002 Amendment

13.30 Directive 2002/74 replaced the rules set out in Articles 3 and 4 of the Original Directive, set out in the preceding paragraphs. Article 3 now provides that, subject to Article 4, Member States shall take measures necessary to ensure that guarantee institutions honour payment of employees' outstanding claims resulting from contracts of employment or employment relationships, including, where provided for by national law, severance pay, on termination of an employment relationship. The claims taken over by the guarantee institution are to relate to a period prior to and/or after a given date determined by the Member States.

Article 3, despite its apparent direct effect, cannot be relied upon in relation to a state of insolvency which occurred before the transposition of the Directive into national law. Ms *Navarro*[37] brought a claim against the Spanish guarantee fund (Fogasa) for payment of compensation agreed under a judicial conciliation settlement between herself and her former employer, Camisa Leica. Her claim was refused. Camisa Leica was declared insolvent on 5 March 2003. Directive 2002/74 entered into force on 8 October 2002. It was required to be transposed into national law by 8 October 2005. Spain took no steps to implement the Directive because it believed that Spanish domestic legislation in force since 21 December 1997 fully complied with the provisions of the Directive.[38] The Court held that Ms Navarro could not rely on Article 3 in her claim against Fogasa: **13.31**

> The reply to the questions referred must therefore be that, where Directive 2002/74 has not been transposed into national law by 8 October 2005, the possible direct effect of the first paragraph of Article 3 of Directive 80/987 cannot, in any event, be relied upon in relation to a state of insolvency which occurred before that date.

Article 4 gives the Member States the option to limit the liability of the guarantee institution. Member States may specify the length of the period for which outstanding claims are to be met by the guarantee institution. This period may not be shorter than a period covering the remuneration of the last three months of the employment relationship prior to/after the date settled by the Member State in pursuance of Article 3(1). Member States may include this minimum period of three months in a reference period with a duration of not less than six months. **13.32**

Member States having a reference period of not less than 18 months may limit the period for which outstanding claims are met by the guarantee institution to eight weeks. In this case, those periods which are most favourable to the employee must be used for the calculation of the minimum period. **13.33**

The right of the Member States to set a ceiling on the payments made by the guarantee institution is preserved: such limits must not fall below a level with is **13.34**

---

[37] See note 7 above.
[38] This proved not to be the case and infringement proceedings were brought: Case C-6/07 *Commission v Spain* Judgment of 29 November 2007.

'socially compatible with the social objective of this Directive'.[39] The Commission must be informed of the methods used to set this ceiling.

Principles derived from case law

13.35　The case law to date has been concerned with the interpretation of Articles 3 and 4 of the Directive prior to the 2002 amendment, but the rulings given in that context appear to be equally applicable to Articles 3 and 4 of the Directive following its amendment in 2002.

13.36　Article 4(2) has been held to preclude a rule whereby an employee with a significant shareholding in a private limited company which employs him, but over which he does not exercise a dominant influence, loses his entitlement to the guarantee in respect of a claim for outstanding pay which results from the employer's insolvency but Article 4(2) applies if, in the 60 days from the time he first could have become aware that the company was no longer creditworthy, he fails to make any genuine demand for payment of salary owed to him.[40]

13.37　Where a worker has simultaneous claims against his employer in respect of periods of employment before the reference period laid down in Article 4(2), as described in the preceding paragraph, and claims relating to the reference period itself, any payments made by the employer during the reference period must be set against earlier claims.[41]

13.38　Article 4(3) permits the Member States to set a ceiling on the liability for employers' outstanding claims. The purpose of this limitation is to confine the application of the Directive to those sums which achieve its social objective. The social objective of the Directive is to guarantee employees a minimum level of Community protection in the event of their employer's insolvency, through payment of outstanding claims resulting from contracts of employment or employment relationships and relating to pay for a specific period.[42] If Member States exercise the option of setting a ceiling, they are obliged to inform the Commission of the methods used to set the ceiling they impose. Since the purpose of this obligation is merely to keep the Commission informed as to which Member States have set such ceilings and the methods they have employed in

---

[39] Art 4(3).
[40] Case C-125/97 *Regeling* (see note 10 above).
[41] Case C-201/01 *Walcher* [2003] ECR I–8827.
[42] *Regeling* (see note 10 above) Judgment para 20; *Gharehveran* (see note 17 above) Judgment para 26.

fixing them, a failure on the part of a Member State to comply with this obligation does not affect its substantive right to set such a ceiling.[43]

Whilst the Member States are entitled to set a ceiling to the liability for outstanding claims, they are bound to ensure, within the limits of that ceiling, the payment of all outstanding claims in question. Any part payment received on account by the employee in respect of the guarantee period must be deducted in order to determine what payments from the employer are genuinely outstanding. In *Barsotti and Castelliani*[44] the ECJ held that a rule of national law according to which remuneration paid to employees during the guarantee period must be deducted from the ceiling set by the Member States in respect of liability for outstanding claims directly undermines the minimum protection guaranteed by the Directive and is not permitted. Such a rule would mean that employees whose remuneration was greater than the ceiling guaranteed by the guarantee fund would receive only a partial payment or possibly in some cases nothing at all, whereas employees whose remuneration was less than the ceiling could obtain payment of their entire claim.

13.39

Time limits may be laid down by national law for the lodging of claims by an employee provided they are not less favourable than those governing similar domestic claims and in any event are not such as to render impossible the exercise of rights conferred by the Directive.[45]

13.40

H. Social Security Contributions

The Member States may stipulate that the obligations of the guarantee institution shall not apply to contributions due under national social security systems or under supplementary company or inter-company pension schemes.[46]

13.41

Even though the guarantee institutions may be relieved of the obligation to pay social security contributions, there is a general obligation imposed on Member States to ensure that employees' entitlement to social security contributions will not be adversely affected even if the employer did not pay compulsory contributions due before the date of insolvency, where those contributions were deducted by the employer from the remuneration paid to the employee.[47]

13.42

---

[43] Case C-235/95 *Assedic* [1998] ECR I–4531.
[44] Joined Cases C-19/01, 50/01, and C-84/01 [2004] ECR I–2005.
[45] Case C-125/01 *Peter Pfluecke* [2003] ECR I–9375.
[46] Art 6; Case 22/87 *Commission v Italy* [1989] ECR 143.
[47] Art 7.

I. Occupational Pension Schemes

13.43 The loss of occupational pension rights may, for many employees, be the most serious consequence of an employer's insolvency. Article 8 requires Member States to ensure that necessary measures are taken to protect the interests of employees and former employees with respect to their old age benefits under occupational pension schemes. With respect to rights acquired, or in the process of being acquired, Article 8 of the Directive provides that Member States are required to ensure 'that the necessary measures are taken to protect the interests of employees . . . in respect of rights conferring on them immediate or prospective entitlement to old age benefits'. Up until the *Robins*[48] case, judgment in which was handed down on 25 January 2007, there had been little guidance as to what constituted 'necessary measures' within the meaning of Article 8 and arguably, even after that judgment this remains the position. *Robins* is authority for the proposition that Article 8 is not meaningless and is intended to impose obligations with respect to the safeguarding of occupational pension rights in the case of insolvency but as to precisely what those obligations are, and the rights deriving therefrom, remains uncertain.

13.44 The claimants in the main proceedings were former employees of an insolvent company. By reason of the company's insolvency two occupational pension schemes were closed down. During the winding up of the scheme it transpired that their assets would be inadequate to meet all the claims of its members. The result was that the claimants faced a significant reduction in the level of their contractually agreed pension rates. In the case of Ms Robins her actual entitlement was 20 per cent of what her full entitlement would have been had the insolvency not occurred. Her colleague Mr Burnett was entitled to 49 per cent of what would have been his due had the company not become insolvent.

13.45 The claimants brought proceedings for damages against the United Kingdom government, in which they sought payment of the difference between the pension payments contractually promised to them and those which they could expect following the insolvency. They based their claim on Article 8 of the Directive 80/987.

13.46 It was argued that the structure of the Directive and the wording of Article 8 imposed on the Member States an obligation of result. If need be, accrued rights must therefore be fully funded by the Member States. The ECJ did not accept this reasoning. It held that wording of Article 8 to the effect that the Member

---

[48] See note 8 above.

States 'shall ensure that the necessary measures are taken' did not oblige the Member States themselves to fund the benefits which were required to be protected by the Directive.

Article 8 left a degree of latitude to the Member States as to the means by which **13.47** the protection granted by that provision could be achieved. Funding need not necessarily be provided by the public authorities. For example, a Member State could impose an obligation on employers to insure against the risk of loss of pension entitlement by reason of insolvency or provide for the setting up of a guarantee institution in respect of which it could lay down detailed rules.

Looking at the Directive as a whole, the Court noted that by virtue of the first **13.48** recital to the Preamble, the measures taken to protect employees in the event of their employer's insolvency must take account 'of the need for balanced economic and social development in the Community'.[49] The Directive is thus designed to reconcile the interests of employees with the need for balanced social and economic development. Even though Article 8, unlike Articles 3 and 4 of the Directive on outstanding claims relating to pay, did not provide any express option for Member States to limit the degree of protection for which they were liable to their employees, it could not be interpreted as meaning that where, on the insolvency of the employer the amount of funding of a company or intra-company pension scheme is insufficient to meet the pension rights of its members, accrued pension rights need not be funded by the Member States 'or be funded in full'.

As to whether the system of protection in issue in the case of Ms Robins and her **13.49** fellow claimants was compatible with Article 8, the Court had little difficulty in concluding that it was not:

> . . . it must be held that provisions of domestic law that may, in certain cases, lead to a guarantee of benefits limited to 20% or 49% of the benefit to which an employee was entitled, that is to say of less than half of that entitlement, cannot be considered to fall within the definition of the word 'protect' used in Article 8.[50]

It found therefore that the measure in issue did not constitute a proper imple- **13.50** mentation of Article 8. The Court offered no guidance as to what would be an appropriate level of protection for the purposes of Article 8.

The position following *Robins* appears to be: **13.51**

(i) Article 8 does not require that pension schemes need not be funded by the Member States themselves or be funded in full;

---

[49] Ibid Judgment para 38.
[50] Ibid Judgment para 57.

(ii) a scheme whereby an employee loses half or more than half of his pension entitlement due to the insolvency of his employer is not compatible with Article 8.

13.52   Since the Court was not able to suggest what would be an appropriate level of protection under Article 8, Mrs Robins and her fellow claimants potentially faced a not inconsiderable battle in their claim for damages. Not only was quantum an issue, but the Court's remarks on burden of proof could have created difficulties. The Court found that the standard of proof was a finding of 'manifest or serious disregard' by the Member State in question for the limits set on its discretion. In determining that question the national court had to take account of all the factors which characterize the situation. The Court proceeded to draw attention to two matters which the national court could have regard to in determining whether the Member State had acted in manifest or serious disregard of its obligations under the Directive. First the national court would have to take into account the fact that 'neither Article 8 of the Directive nor any other provision therein contains anything that makes it possible to establish with any precision the minimum level required in order to protect entitlement to benefits'.[51] Secondly the Court added that the national court 'may' take into consideration the Commission's report on the transposition of the Directive by the Member States, published in 1995[52] in which it concluded that the United Kingdom provisions appeared to meet the requirement of Article 8 and which may have 'reinforced the view of the Member State concerned with regard to the transposition of the Directive into domestic law'.[53]

13.53   It is difficult to accept that an administrative report drawn up on the basis of information provided by the Member States themselves can be used to mitigate the liability of a Member State in a situation such as this. The EC Commission itself realizes the limitations of those reports which it does not accept as constituting evidence of compliance with the obligations imposed by a Member State by a directive.[54] Moreover, some of the national legislation in issue in the *Robins* case appears to have been adopted after 1995 and would not, therefore, have been taken into consideration by the EC Commission in drawing up its report. The relevance of the report in any damages claim was not therefore obvious. In the event Mrs Robins and her colleagues did not pursue their claim for damages. So many questions as to the liability of Member State governments under Article 8 remain unanswered.

---

[51] See note 43 above, Judgment para 80.
[52] COM (95) 164 Final.
[53] See note 43 above, Judgment para 81.
[54] Equality and Non-Discrimination Annual Report 2006 European Commission at 9.

J. Abuse

Article 10(a) and (b) of the Directive grant the Member States an option to take measures to avoid abuses and to refuse or reduce the liability referred to in Article 3 or the guarantee obligation referred to in Article 7 if it appears that 'the fulfilment of the obligation is unjustifiable because of the existence of special links between the employee and the employer and of common interests resulting in collusion between them'. **13.54**

The case of *Nunez*[55] is illustrative of the type of measure which, although it reduces or eliminates the rights of a claimant under Article 3, can be regarded as justifiable under Article 10. Ms Nunez was employed by Linya Fish. In January 2003 she was dismissed. Following an extra-judicial conciliation procedure before the Algericas Centre for Mediation, Arbitration and Conciliation an agreement was reached whereby Linya Fish recognized the unfairness of her dismissal and that it should pay her compensation. Linya Fish never in fact paid the compensation. In May 2004 a provisional insolvency order was made. On the basis of that Ms Nunez claimed from Fogasa, the Spanish guarantee fund, the compensation which, although agreed by Linya Fish, it had never actually paid her. Fogasa dismissed the application on the ground that it had not been awarded by a judicial or administrative action. When the case came before the ECJ the Spanish government argued that it was entitled to exclude from the payment guarantee provided for in Article 3(1) of the Directive compensation agreed as a result of an extra-judicial settlement. It will be recalled that in *Guerrero Pecino*[56] compensation for unfair dismissal awarded in a judicial conciliation procedure fell within the scope of Article 3(1). The ECJ found that compensation for unfair dismissal awarded as a result of an extra-judicial conciliation procedure differed from that awarded in the course of a judicial conciliation procedure in a number of respects: **13.55**

(i) an agreement on compensation for dismissal concluded during extra-judicial conciliation proceedings occurs without the intervention of a judicial body; the drawing up of the agreement is not supervised by, nor subject to, the approval of a judge;

(ii) in contrast to a judicial conciliation procedure there was no provision for the intervention of Fogasa in an extra-judicial conciliation procedure. Fogasa is not therefore in a position to verify whether there are any abusive or fraudulent circumstances surrounding the award;

---

[55] See note 36 above.
[56] See note 34 above.

(iii) Fogasa has no means during the insolvency proceedings to challenge a claim relating to compensation for dismissal which it suspects was established fraudulently;

(iv) Fogasa can refuse to pay compensation for unfair dismissal if it is able to adduce evidence of abuse but since it does not participate in extra-judicial conciliation proceedings it is difficult to envisage how it could have proof of abusive circumstances.

13.56 The ECJ accordingly concluded that compensation for unfair dismissal recognized by an extra-judicial conciliation settlement does not offer sufficient guarantee of the avoidance of abuse. Accordingly that exclusion of compensation for unfair dismissal from the payment guarantee of the guarantee institution where it has been recognized in an extra-judicial conciliation settlement is objectively justified since it constitutes a measure necessary to avoid abuses within the meaning of Article 10(a) of the Directive.

14

INFORMATION AND CONSULTATION

A. Introduction

Community initiatives in the field of information and consultation have **14.01** intensified in the course of the last decade. This is, in part, due to the realization of the internal market which has given rise to situations where decisions relating to employment and working conditions are, in many cases, taken at a level in the employing undertaking or group of undertakings, which may be far removed from the actual place where the employee affected by the decisions actually works. There is, therefore, a risk in that the employee may be unaware of matters which are important to his employment and, likewise, the ultimate employer may not be fully informed, when formulating policy having an effect on

227

employees' terms and conditions of employment, of the overall economic situation of the immediate employing undertaking.

14.02 From the limited rights set out in the Collective Redundancies Directive[1] and the Transfer of Undertakings Directive[2] there has been a shift to more general information and consultation rights at first within large Community-wide undertakings,[3] and more recently, in smaller national undertakings.[4] Information and consultation rights and the right to participate in management have been established within the European Company (SE)[5] and the European Co-operative Society (SCE).[6] The right of information and consultation has been recognized in the Charter of Fundamental Rights of Workers 1989[7] and the Charter of Fundamental Rights of the European Union 2000.[8]

14.03 This chapter will set out the various information and consultation rights currently prevailing within the Community. As a general rule, more specific information and consultation rights, such as those provided for in the case of collective redundancies and the transfer of undertakings, take precedence over more general information and consultation rights such as those set out in the European Works Council Directive (EWC Directive), or the more general Information and Consultation Directive. In the case of the SE and the SCE, provisions are laid down regarding the applicability of the EWC Directive with a view to avoiding duplication of consultation obligations.

B. Collective Redundancies

14.04 The Collective Redundancies Directive,[9] requires an employer who is contemplating redundancies of a given scale, to inform his workforce and the competent national authorities of his intention and to consult his workforce. The provisions of this Directive have been discussed above in Chapter 11. The consultation procedure is required to cover ways and means of avoiding collective redundancies

---

1 Directive 98/59 ([1998] OJ L225/16).
2 Directive 2001/23 ([2001] OJ L82/16).
3 Directive 94/45 ([1994] OJ L254/64).
4 [2002] OJ L80/29.
5 Directive 2001/86 supplementing a Statute for a European Company with regard to the involvement of employees ([2001] OJ L294/22).
6 Directive 2003/72 supplementing the Statute for a European Co-operative Society with regard to the involvement of employees ([2003] OJ L207/25).
7 Articles 17 and 18.
8 Articles 27 and 28.
9 Directive 98/59 ([1998] OJ L225/16).

or reducing the number of workers affected and mitigating the adverse consequences of the redundancy plan.

C. Transfer of Undertakings

The Transfer of Undertakings Directive,[10] which has been discussed above in **14.05** Chapter 12, requires, in the case of a transfer of an undertaking, the transferor and the transferee to inform representatives of their respective employees affected by the transfer of:

(a) the date or the proposed date of the transfer;
(b) the reason for the transfer;
(c) the legal, economic, and social implications of the transfer for employees;
(d) any measures envisaged in relation to the employees.

Where there are no representatives of employees, the employees themselves must be informed directly of the four matters set out above.[11]

D. The European Works Council

The origins of the European Works Council Directive (the EWC 'Directive')[12] **14.06** can be traced back to the Vredling proposals of the 1980s.[13] Its immediate background lay in the Commission proposal for a directive based on Article 100 (now Article 94), and published in early 1991, the adoption of which was blocked, notably by the United Kingdom.[14]

The EWC Directive was adopted on 22 September 1994 and was required to **14.07** be transposed into national law no later than 22 September 1996. Originally applicable to all Member States save the United Kingdom, the application of the EWC Directive was extended to the United Kingdom in 1997.[15]

---

[10] Directive 2001/23 ([2001] OJ L82/16).

[11] Art 7(6).

[12] Council Directive 94/45 on the establishment of a European Works Council ([1994] OJ L254/64). Extended to the United Kingdom by Directive 97/74 ([1998] OJ L10/22). Report from the Commission to the European Parliament and the Council on the application of the Directive on the establishment of a European Works Council on a procedure in Community scale undertakings and groups of undertakings for the purpose of informing and consulting employees, COM (2000) 188 Final.

[13] [1980] OJ C297/3. See Docksey, 'Information and Consultation of Employees: The United Kingdom and the Vredling Directive' (1986) 49 MLR 281.

[14] [1991] OJ C39/10; [1991] OJ C336/1; [1994] OJ C135/8.

[15] Directive 97/74 ([1998] OJ L10/22).

14.08 The EWC Directive recognizes, and provides for, the right of information and consultation of employees in large-scale multinationals operating within the Community. Whilst national information and consultation rules in some Member States prior to the adoption of the EWC Directive, were capable of ensuring a degree of information and consultation within entities operating on a national scale, in the case of multinational entities this was not always necessarily so. Employees in one Member State might be unaware of matters which were of direct concern to them being decided in another Member State.[16] The EWC Directive is designed to move away from the territorial limitations of national measures by establishing a mechanism for information and consultation at a level which spans the entirety of an undertaking's operations within the Community.

(1) Community-scale undertakings

14.09 The EWC Directive applies to Community-scale undertakings or groups of undertakings. A Community-scale undertaking is one employing at least 1,000 persons within the Community and at least 150 in each of at least two Member States.[17] A Community-scale group of undertakings means a controlling undertaking and its controlled undertakings which have the following characteristics:

- at least 1,000 employees within the Member States;
- at least two group undertakings in different Member States;
- at least one group undertaking with at least 150 employees in one Member State and at least one other group undertaking with at least 150 employees in another Member State.[18]

14.10 The Directive is applicable regardless of the location of the headquarters of the Community-scale undertaking or controlling undertaking. The Directive does not apply to merchant navy crews.[19]

(2) Controlling undertaking

14.11 A controlling undertaking means any undertaking which can exercise a dominant influence over another undertaking by virtue, for example, of ownership, financial participation, or the rules which govern it.[20] The ability to exercise a

---

[16] 'Whereas procedures for informing and consulting employees as embodied in legislation or practice in the Member States are often not geared to the transnational structure of an entity which takes decisions affecting those employees; Whereas this may lead to the unequal treatment of employees affected by decisions within one and the same group of undertakings', Preamble to the Directive, Recital 10.

[17] Art 1(a).

[18] Art 2(1)(c).

[19] Art 1(5).

[20] Art 3(1).

dominant influence shall be presumed when, in relation to another undertaking directly or indirectly:

- holds a majority of that undertaking's subscribed capital; or
- controls a majority of the votes attached to that undertaking's issued share capital; or
- can appoint more than half of the members of that undertaking's administrative, management, or supervisory body.

The law applicable in order to determine whether an undertaking is a 'controlling **14.12** undertaking' is the law of the Member State which governs that undertaking. If this is a the legal system of a non-Member State, the applicable law is that of the Member State within whose territory the representative of the undertaking, or in the absence of such representative, the central management of the group undertaking which employs the greatest number of employees is situated.[21]

(3) Residual application

The Directive applies without prejudice to other specific information and con- **14.13** sultation rights imposed, for example, by the Collective Redundancies Directive and the Transfer of Undertakings Directive and to employees' rights of information and consultation under national law.[22]

(4) Information and consultation processes

The Directive prescribes three means whereby employees may be informed and **14.14** consulted. The preferred course is for the employer and its employees to establish a European Works Council ('EWC') through which the information and consultation process can take place. Alternatively, an information and consultation procedure in accordance with the terms of the Annex to the Directive may be established. Failing that, the subsidiary requirements apply.

(5) Establishment of an EWC

An employer is obliged to initiate negotiations for the purpose of establishing an **14.15** EWC at the written request of at least 100 employees or their representatives,[23] working in at least two undertakings or establishments in two Member States. An employer may, of course, take the initiative in setting up such negotiations.

---

[21] Art 3(6).
[22] Art 12.
[23] Art 5(1). Employees' representatives means the employees' representatives provided for by national law and practice (Art 1(d)).

14.16 Central management is responsible for creating the conditions and means necessary for the setting up of the EWC or information and consultation procedure.[24] Central management is defined as meaning the central management of the controlling undertaking, that is the undertaking which can exercise a dominant influence over all the other controlled undertakings of the group.[25] Where central management is not situated within a Member State, this task can be fulfilled by a representative agent designated by central management or, if there is no representative agent, the management of the establishment or group undertaking employing the greatest number of employees in any one Member State ('deemed central management').[26]

(6) Right to information

14.17 Article 11(2) provides that information on the number of employees in a Community-scale undertaking or a Community-scale group of undertakings is made available by undertakings 'at the request of the parties concerned'.

14.18 Three cases before the ECJ have raised the issue of the extent to which information must be provided to workers' representatives in order that they may ascertain, first, whether they have a right to seek negotiations with a view to establishing an EWC and, secondly, with whom such negotiations should take place. All three cases came to the Court through references for preliminary rulings from German labour courts. The ECJ gave a broad functional interpretation to the obligations imposed on management to facilitate the establishment of EWCs—essentially management is constrained from withholding information necessary to enable the process of establishing an EWC to take place.

Bofrost

14.19 The dispute in *Bofrost*[27] arose out of request by the Works Council of one of the companies in the Bofrost Group for information on the number of employees and the structure of undertakings in the Bofrost Group. The undertaking in question refused to supply the information. The Bofrost group consisted of several companies, some established in Germany, some in other Member States. In April 1997 the undertakings comprising the group concluded an agreement intended to establish parity between the various undertakings within the group, in order that none should be dominant and that there should be no hierarchical relations between them.

---

[24] Art 4(1).
[25] Case C-349/01 *Anker* [2004] ECR I 6803 Judgment para 52.
[26] Art 4(2).
[27] Case C-62/99 [2001] ECR I–2579.

Before the ECJ, the undertaking from which the information had been requested, **14.20** argued that an undertaking is obliged under the EWC Directive, to supply information only if it has already been established that it is a controlling undertaking within the group of undertakings. This was not the case with any of the undertakings in the Bofrost group: all had equal status.

The position of the Works Council was that workers must have access to infor- **14.21** mation about the undertaking in order to enable them to ascertain whether they are entitled to require negotiations to be opened with a view to establishing an EWC. Without that information the workforce would not be in a position to exercise rights under the Directive.

The Court accepted this argument: **14.22**

> . . . if the Directive is to serve a useful purpose, it is essential that the workers concerned be guaranteed access to information enabling them to determine whether they have the right to demand an opening of negotiations with central management once its existence is established and the workers' representatives.[28]

Consequently, an undertaking, which is part of a group of undertakings is **14.23** required to supply information to internal workers' representative bodies, even where it has not yet been established that the management of the undertaking to which the worker's request is addressed is the management of the controlling undertaking within the group of undertakings. All of the undertakings within the group are required to supply the information which they possess or are able to obtain.

As to the information which must be supplied, this may include documents clari- **14.24** fying and explaining the information which are indispensable for the determination of the question, whether or not they are entitled to request the opening of negotiations. The essential criterion is that the information supplied must be adequate enough to enable the workers' representatives to ascertain whether a request for negotiations with a view to setting up an EWC is in order.

Kuhne and Nagel

Kuhne and Nagel[29] raised the issue of how information is to be obtained when **14.25** central management of an undertaking, which is not situate within the Community, fails to make available to the management regarded as the deemed central management under the rules set out in Article 4(2) of the EWC Directive information for the purposes of setting up an EWC. Are other undertakings within the group obliged to provide such information, what by way of information

---

[28] Ibid Judgment para 32.
[29] Case C-440/00 [2004] ECR I–1.

can legitimately be requested, and how may such requests be enforced in the face of refusals?

14.26 Following *Bofrost*[30] the Court held that all undertakings within a group are required to supply the information which they possess or are able to obtain.

14.27 Central management of the controlling undertaking is in a position to obtain such information since it exercises a dominant influence but deemed central management may not be similarly placed. It may not have the necessary authority to require the information in question to be provided to it by other undertakings within the group or may be constrained by central management from seeking such information. In such a situation, the Court held that deemed central management may require—and has a right to—information from undertakings within the group located in the Member States. The corollary of that right is an obligation on the part of each undertaking belonging to the group situate within the Community, which is in possession of the information or in a position to obtain it, to supply deemed central management with the information. Since the Member States have an obligation under Article 14(1) of the Directive to take all necessary steps to bring about the results required by the Directive, they must provide for appropriate measures in the event of a failure to comply with the Directive and, in particular, they must ensure that adequate administrative or judicial proceedings are available to enable obligations arising from the Directive to be enforced.

14.28 As to the nature of the information which must be provided to workers' representatives, the Court held in *Kuhne and Nagel* that this was a question of fact in each case, but it indicated that the following information could be requested provided it was 'essential' to ascertaining the right to open negotiations for the establishing the EWC:

(i) average total number of employees and their distribution across the Member States;

(ii) the establishments of the undertaking and the group undertaking;

(iii) the structure of the undertaking and of undertakings in the group;

(iv) the names and addresses of the employee representatives which might participate in the setting up of a special negotiating body.

Anker

14.29 *Anker*[31] raised the question of whether the central management, or deemed central management, is obliged to supply information which is essential in order

---

[30] Note 27.
[31] Note 25.

to open negotiations to set up an EWC, to a controlled undertaking within the group, the request for information having been presented to the controlled undertaking and whether that undertaking is entitled to require that the information should be supplied to it. The Court replied to this in the affirmative: central management or deemed central management was under an obligation to supply information necessary for opening negotiations to set up an EWC either directly to employees' representatives or, through the group undertaking to which an application for information had been made. As to the elements of information to be supplied the Court followed the position that it had adopted in *Kuhne and Nagel*.

Member States must be mindful of the interest of the undertakings in question in protecting their confidential information. The right to confidentiality must be adequately protected. An administrative or judicial procedure must be made available to undertakings wishing to assert their rights in this respect. **14.30**

Deemed central management is limited in the use to which it may put any information obtained from other undertakings within the group: such information may only be used for the purpose of ascertaining if the conditions and means necessary for the setting up of an EWC have been satisfied. **14.31**

(7) The Special Negotiating Body

Negotiations leading to the setting up of an EWC are required to take place within a Special Negotiating Body ('SNB').[32] The appointment of members to the SNB is to be determined by the law and practice of the Member States.[33] This sets the Directive within the structure of the industrial relations systems of the different Member States. **14.32**

An SNB must be composed of at least three and no more than 17 worker members including at least one representative from each Member State where the company does business and supplementary members in proportion to the number of employees working in the establishment, the controlling undertaking, or the controlled undertaking.[34] **14.33**

The task of the SNB is to establish, with central management, the scope, composition, functions, and term of office of the EWC or the arrangements for **14.34**

---

[32] Art 5(1).
[33] Art 5(2).
[34] Art 5(b) and (c).

implementing a procedure for the information and consultation of employees and in particular:

(a) the functions and the procedure for information and consultation of the EWC;

(b) the venue, frequency, and duration of meeting of the EWC;

(c) the financial and other resources to be allocated to the EWC;

(d) the duration of the agreement and the procedure for its renegotiation.[35]

The SNB may decide, by at least a two-thirds majority, not to open negotiations or to terminate negotiations already opened.[36]

(8) Alternative information and consultation procedures

14.35 Where no EWC is established because central management and the SNB have so decided, or where central management refuses to commence negotiations within six months of being requested to do so by the requisite number of employees, or where no agreement has been concluded within three years of the request for negotiations, the subsidiary requirements are applicable. The subsidiary requirements must reflect the provisions set out in the Annex to the Directive.[37] The majority of EWCs have been set up after successful negotiation; not much resort seems to have been had to either the alternative information or consultation procedure provided for under Article 5(3) or to the subsidiary requirements.

(9) Confidential information

14.36 The Member States are required to ensure that members of the SNB, and any experts who may assist them, do not disclose any information which may have been provided to them in confidence.[38] A similar requirement is to be imposed on employee representatives in the framework of an information and consultation procedure. This obligation must remain in force even after the expiry of the term of office of such persons.

14.37 Each Member State is required to lay down the conditions and cases in which central management situated in its territory may be permitted not to transmit information when its nature is such that, according to objective criteria, it would seriously harm the functioning of the undertakings concerned or would be

---

[35] Art 6(2).
[36] Art 5(5).
[37] Art 7(2).
[38] Art 8(1).

prejudicial to them.[39] Such a dispensation may be made subject to prior administrative or judicial authorization.[40]

(10) Preservation of existing agreements

Agreements in force on the date laid down for the implementation of the Directive **14.38**
or the date of its transposition into national law are preserved: they are not
required to comply with the requirements of the Directive. They may be renewed
by agreement between the parties on their expiry; otherwise the provisions of the
Directive apply.[41] The majority of EWCs have been established by this means.
Some 400 agreements were adopted Community-wide before the date of
adoption of the Directive, 22 September 2006. Some 40 to 50 have since been
adopted annually. It was estimated that in February 2008 approximately
820 companies or groups of companies had an EWC agreement covering an
estimated 14.5 million employees with the direct involvement of 10,000
employee representatives. This represents less than 36 per cent of approximately
1,800 companies or groups of companies which fall within the scope of the
Directive.[42]

In April 2004 the Commission, pursuant to Article 138 EC, launched the first **14.39**
phase of consultation of the social partners on how the EWC Directive could
best respond to the challenges of a changing economic and social environment.
In particular they were asked to consider the impact of enlargement of the
Community to 27 Member States. This consultation revealed that employee
organizations wanted a revision of the Directive whilst employers' organizations
were content to leave it as it is. Whilst all the social partners agreed on the useful-
ness of the EWCs, they noted that it was difficult to organize useful information
and consultation without delays and uncertainties and that getting workers to
accept an EWC was a challenge. The second stage of consultation was launched
on 20 February 2008, giving the social partners the opportunity to start negotiations on updating and improving the way EWCs operate, with a view to revising
the Directive. In response to the latter consultation, the employers' organizations
BusinessEurope, CEEP, and UEAPME declared that they were ready to open
negotiations within the European Social Dialogue. The European Trade Union
Confederation felt that such negotiations were unrealistic. Following a further

---

[39] Art 8(2).
[40] Ibid.
[41] Art 13. Between the date of adoption of the Directive (22 September 1994) and the date of
its required transposition into national law (22 September 1996) 450 agreements were concluded.
The Directive was thus largely implemented voluntarily before the required implementation date.
[42] COM (2008) 419 Final at 2.

appeal to European management and labour, the Commission concluded that it was up to it to come up with proposals. These proposals have been agreed and were published on 2 July 2008.[43]

14.40 The proposed directive will make substantive changes to the provisions of the current Directive and repeal and replace it. The main substantive changes will be:

- the introduction of general principles regarding the arrangement for transnational information and consultation of employees, the introduction of a definition of information, and making the definition of consultation more precise;

- the limitation of the competence of European Works Councils to issues of a transnational nature and the introduction of a link, defined as a priority by agreement within the undertaking, between the national and transnational levels of information and consultation of employees;

- clarification of the role of employees' representatives and of the opportunity to benefit from training, as well as recognition of the role of trade union organizations in relation to employees' representatives;

- clarification of the responsibilities regarding the provision of information enabling the commencement of negotiations and rules on negotiating agreements to set up new European Works Councils;

- adaptation of the subsidiary requirements applicable in the absence of an agreement to developing needs;

- introduction of an adaptation clause applicable to agreements governing European Works Councils if the structure of the undertaking or group of undertakings changes and, unless the adaptation clause is applied, continuation of the agreements in force.

E. The Information and Consultation Directive

14.41 Directive 2002/14 establishing a general framework for informing and consulting employees in the European Community (the 'Directive')[44] lays down minimum requirements for informing and consulting employees, whilst at the same time permitting Member States to grant more favourable rights.

14.42 A large measure of discretion is left to the Member States and to management and labour in implementing the Directive. Compliance can be assured by 'national

---

[43] Proposal for a European Parliament and Council Directive on the establishment of a European Works Council or a procedure in Community-scale undertakings and Community-scale groups of undertakings for the purposes of informing and consulting employees (Recast) COM (2008) 419 Final.

[44] [2002] OJ L80/29.

law and industrial relations practice in individual Member States';[45] at the same time arrangements for the informing and consulting of employees can be settled by management and labour according to their needs and wishes.

The Directive is expressed not to affect more specific rights of information and **14.43** consultation under Community law, in the Collective Redundancies Directive, the Transfer of Undertakings Directive and the European Works Council Directive.[46] The Directive is to apply without prejudice to any other rights of information, consultation and participation under national law and it must not lead to any regression in existing rights.

(1) Implementation

The Directive was required to be transposed into national law by 23 March **14.44** 2005.[47]

In one specific case Member States may limit the application of national imple- **14.45** menting measures for a further two or three years.

(i) where on the date of entry into force of the Directive, that is 23 March 2002, neither a general, permanent, and statutory system of information and consultation of employees nor a general, permanent, and statutory system of employee representation in the workplace exists, the requirement date for the application of national implementing measures, in the case of undertakings employing at least 150 employees or establishments employing at least 100 employees may be put forward to 23 March 2007;

(ii) in the case of undertakings employing 100 employees or establishments employing 50, the relevant date is 23 March 2008.

(2) Scope of application

The Member States have a choice in determining the scope of application of the **14.46** Directive. It can apply either to undertakings employing at least 50 employees in any one Member State or to establishments having at least 20 employees in any one Member State.[48] Article 1 entrusts the determination of the method of calculating the thresholds of employees employed in an undertaking to the Member States but this methodology may not be of such a nature as to defeat

---

[45] Art 1(2).
[46] Art 9.
[47] Greece did not implement the Directive within this time frame and was accordingly found to be in breach of its obligations under Community law: Case C-381/06 *Commission v Greece* [2007], Rec. p 1–112, Summ.pub.
[48] Art 3(1).

the objective of the Directive.[49] The Directive is intended to apply to all employees protected as such under national employment law, apart from those
specifically exempted by the Directive itself.

14.47   Consequently national legislation such as that in issue in *CGT*[50] which seeks
to remove certain categories of workers from being accorded the status of
members of the workforce, and hence from being included in the calculation of
the threshold at which the Directive become applicable is unlawful. All workers
must be taken into account in the calculation of thresholds since otherwise both
the rights of excluded category and potentially the entire workforce would be
meaningless and ineffective.

(3) Undertaking/Establishment

14.48   An undertaking is defined as a public or private entity carrying on an economic
activity, whether or not operating for gain, which is located in the territory of a
Member State.[51] An establishment is a unit of business defined in accordance
with national law and practice which carries on an economic activity on an
ongoing basis with human and material resources within the territory of a
Member State.[52]

(4) Exceptions/Derogations

14.49   Member States can derogate from the Directive in the case of crews of vessels ply-
ing the high seas.[53] Specific provisions, prevailing within a Member State at the
date of entry into force of the Directive, with respect to employee information
and consultation rights within undertakings and establishments which pursue
political, professional, organization, religious, charitable, educational, scientific,
or artistic aims, as well as aims involving the information and expression of
opinions, may be maintained.[54]

(5) Information and consultation rights

14.50   Article 4 of the Directive sets out the issues on which employees are to be
informed and consulted:

(a) information on the recent and probable development and economic situation of the establishment or undertaking;

---

[49] Case C-151/02 *Jaegar* [2003] ECR I–8380 Judgment para 29.
[50] Case C-385/05 [2007] ECR I-611 at para 34.
[51] Art 2(a).
[52] Art 2(b).
[53] Art 3(3).
[54] Art 3(2).

(b) information and consultation on the situation, structure, and probable development of employment within the undertaking or establishment and, in particular, whether there is a threat to employment;

(c) information and consultation on decisions likely to lead to substantial changes in work organization or contractual relations.

Information is defined in Article 2(f) as 'the transmission by the employer to the employees' representatives of data in order to enable them to acquaint themselves with the subject matter to be examined'. **14.51**

Information must be given in such a way as to enable employees' representatives, if necessary, to prepare for consultation.[55] Consultation must take place at the relevant level of management and representation and on the basis of information supplied by the employer. **14.52**

(6) Confidential information

Member States may lay down provisions which prevent the disclosure of confidential or sensitive information to employees or third parties.[56] A confidentiality obligation may continue to apply to employee representatives and experts who assist them, after the expiry of their term of office.[57] Member States may provide in specific cases that information need not be communicated nor a consultation procedure undertaken where it would seriously harm the functioning of the undertaking or establishment or would be prejudicial to it. **14.53**

(7) Protection of employee representatives

Member States must ensure that employee representatives enjoy adequate protection and guarantees to enable them to perform their duties properly. **14.54**

(8) Enforcement

Adequate administrative and judicial remedies must be available to enable the obligations under the Directive to be enforced. Effective proportionate and dissuasive sanctions must be applied in the case of non-compliance with the Directive by the employer or employee representatives. **14.55**

---

[55] Art 4(3).
[56] Art 6(1).
[57] Art 6(2).

F. The European Company

14.56 Regulation 2157/2001 on a Statute for a European Company ('SE'),[58] which entered into force on 8 October 2004, creates a public limited liability company which can be set up in territory of the Community. Employee involvement in such a company is governed by the provisions of Directive 2001/86 (the 'SE Directive').[59] The Preamble to the SE Statute states that involvement of employees '. . . forms an indissociable complement to this Regulation and must be applied concomitantly'.[60]

(1) Information and consultation rights

14.57 The SE Directive provides for the information and consultation of employees of SEs. Employees have the right through their representative bodies, to be informed on questions which concern the SE itself and any of its subsidiaries or establishments situated in another Member State. This information in terms of its content, manner, and timing of delivery is to be such as to allow employees' representatives to undertake an in-depth assessment of the possible impact and, where appropriate, prepare consultations with the competent organs of the SE.[61]

14.58 Consultation is defined as the establishment of a dialogue and exchange of views between the body set up by the employees and the competent organ of the SE for the purpose of enabling the former to express a view on measures envisaged by the latter so that that opinion may be taken into account in the decision-making process within the SE.[62]

14.59 The information and consultation structure provided for in the SE Directive mirrors that of the EWC Directive. Information and consultation rights arise as soon as the SE is formed. The Directive provides for the establishment of a Special Negotiating Body ('SNB'). Information as to the identity of the participants in the SE, other concerned entities (eg subsidiaries), and the number of employees involved must be provided.

14.60 The social partners, through the SNB, may negotiate with management to establish within the SE consultation arrangements in conformity with the requirements of Article 4 of the Directive. Alternatively, the social partners may

---

[58] [2001] OJ L294/21.
[59] Directive 2001/86 supplementing the Statute for a European Company with regard to the involvement of employees ([2001] OJ L294/22).
[60] Recital 19.
[61] Art 2(i).
[62] Art 2(j).

agree to use the Standard Rules set out in the Annex to the Directive. If no agreement is reached on the information and consultation procedure to be followed, the Standard Rules apply.[63] Article 13(1) excludes the application of the provision of the EWC Directive where the SE is a Community-wide undertaking or a controlling undertaking of a Community-scale group of undertakings where either the consultation procedure provided for by Article 4 of the Directive or the Standard Rules apply.

Where the SNB decides not to open negotiations or to terminate negotiations **14.61** which have already begun, the rules on information and consultation applicable in the Member State where the SE has employees may apply.[64] In this event, the provisions of the EWC Directive also apply.[65] This ensures the applicability of transnational information and consultation rights which might otherwise be absent if only national information and consultation rules prevailed.

(2) Participation

The SE Statute provides for the participation of employees in the management of **14.62** the SE.

An SE may not be registered unless one of three conditions relating to employee **14.63** involvement is satisfied:

(a) management and employee representatives have reached an agreement on employee involvement; or

(b) the employee representatives have decided that they do not want to negotiate information and consultation rights for the SE; and

(c) the Standard Rules are applicable (either by agreement with the employee representatives or in default of such agreement following the opening of negotiations).

The SE Statute provides for the participation of employees on the board of man- **14.64** agement. Participation is defined in Article 2(k) as:

> . . . the influence of the body representative of the employees and/or employees' representatives on the affairs of the company by way of:
>
> (a) the right to elect or appoint some of the members of the legal entity's supervisory or administrative organ, or
>
> (b) the right to recommend and/or oppose the appointment of some or all of the members of the legal entity's supervisory or administrative organ.

---

[63] Art 7(1)(b).
[64] Art 3(6).
[65] Art 13(1).

14.65　In contrast to information and consultation rights, the right of employee participation is not mandatory. Management and the employees may agree to opt out of employee rights to participate.[66] In any event, participation of employees at board level arises only where such a requirement exists under the national law governing a substantial part of the workforce to be employed by the SE after its formation.

G. The European Co-operative Society (SCE)

14.66　Regulation 1435/2003 on a Statute for a European Co-operative Society ('SCE Statute')[67] enables an SCE to be established in five different ways:

(a) by five or more natural persons resident in at least two Member States;

(b) by five or more natural companies or firms formed under the law of a Member State, resident in, or governed by the law of at least two different Member States;

(c) by a merger between co-operatives formed under the law of a Member State with registered offices within the Community, provided that at least two of them are governed by the law of different Member States;

(d) by conversion of a co-operative formed under the law of a Member State which has its registered office and head office within the Community if for at least two years it has had an establishment or subsidiary governed by the law of another Member State;

(e) by companies or firms and other legal entities governed by public or private law formed under the law of a Member State which are governed by the law of at least two Member States.

14.67　The rules on the involvement of employees in the SCE are laid down in Directive 2003/723 (the 'SCE Directive'). Those provisions 'form an indissoluble complement' to the SCE Regulation and are to be applied concomitantly with that Regulation.[68]

14.68　The information and consultation procedures set out in the SCE Directive mirror those of the SE Directive and will not be reiterated here.

---

[66] SE Directive, Preamble, Recitals 3 and 18; Standard Rules, Part 3(a) and (b).
[67] [2003] OJ L207/1.
[68] Preamble to SCE Statute, para 17.

PART V

INDIVIDUAL EMPLOYMENT RIGHTS

15

TERMS OF EMPLOYMENT

A. Introduction

The Community Charter on the Fundamental Social Rights of Workers,[1] whilst **15.01** respecting the principle of subsidiarity, laid down that all the conditions of employment of every worker should be known to him either by being laid down in laws, collective agreements, or in his contract of employment according to arrangements applying in each country.[2] It inspired the adoption of Directive 91/553 on the employer's obligation to inform employees of the conditions applicable to the contract of employment or the employment relationship (the 'Directive').[3] Its legal basis is Article 94 of the EC Treaty.

The Directive implements the right of employees to information about their **15.02** employment conditions by imposing an obligation on employers to provide each employee with the essential elements of his contract of employment or his employment relationship.

The Directive has two objectives: **15.03**

(i) to improve the living and working conditions of the labour force as required by the Treaty, by providing employees with a degree (albeit minimal) of certainty and security as to their terms of employment relationship; and

---

[1] [1989] OJ C 248/1.
[2] Ibid, point 9.
[3] [1991] OJ L288/32.

(ii) to achieve a degree of convergence in the employment legislation of the Member States, whose employment regimes, at the time of the adoption of the Directive, were widely divergent on the issue of the required level of awareness of the employee on the precise details of his employment relationship. This divergence was believed to be potentially prejudicial to the achievement of the internal market.[4]

15.04 The Directive lays down common requirements as to the information to be provided to employees on the main terms of their contract of employment or employment relationship. Not every term need be specified nor need the information be given before the commencement of employment. The Directive was required to be implemented into national law no later than 30 June 1993.[5]

B. Scope of Application

15.05 The Directive applies to all employees who work for remuneration and who have a contract of employment or a relationship which is regarded as employment under the laws of a Member State.[6] No indication is given as to which Member State this may be. There are several possibilities: the Member State in which the employment is to be carried out, the Member State where the employer is established, or the Member State where the employee was recruited. Presumably it is the law of the Member State which governs the employment contract or employment relationship which is applicable.

15.06 The essential criterion for the applicability of the Directive is the existence of a contract of employment or an employment relationship. This embraces all types of employment (save those expressly excluded by the Directive itself) and must include part-time and temporary employment, employment both of indefinite duration as well as fixed-term, and any other form of relationship that can be viewed as employment for remuneration.[7]

---

4 Recitals 3 and 4.
5 A Report on the Implementation of the Directive was published in 1996 See <http://ec.europa.eu/employment_social/labour_law/docs/05_emplconditions_implreport_en.pdf>.
6 Art I(I).
7 The Commission in its Explanatory Memorandum to the proposal for Directive 91/533 (COM (90) 563 Final at para 11) stated: 'The Directive concerns any working relationship emanating from a contract of employment or any other legal form of recruitment (eg, teleworking, training, employment-training, etc) which links a worker to an employer and which is subject to the legislation in force in a Member State. The concepts of employee and employer are based on Member States' national laws.'

Member States are permitted to exclude certain types of employment from the **15.07** scope of application of the Directive. Short-term employment, that is employment not exceeding a duration of one month, and some part-time work, provided that the average working week is less than eight hours, may be exempt. Casual employment and employment of a specific nature may also be exempt,[8] but in such cases exemption must be objectively justified.[9] The burden of proving such objective justification lies on the employer.

C. Employer's Obligations

The employee must be informed by his employer of the following matters: **15.08**

    (i) the identity of the parties to the contract;

    (ii) his place of work;

    (iii) a brief specification or description of the work to be carried out or the title, grade, or category attaching to it;

    (iv) the date of commencement of the contract or the employment relationship;

    (v) in the case of a temporary contract or employment relationship, the expected duration thereof;

    (vi) entitlement to paid leave or the procedures for determining such leave;

    (vii) the length of the period of notice (or the method whereby such a period is determined) to be observed by the employer and the employee in case of the termination of the employment;

    (viii) the basic level of remuneration and other elements of remuneration and the frequency of payment of such remuneration;

    (ix) the length of the employee's normal working day or week.[10]

The information referred to in points (vi), (vii), (viii), and (ix) above may also **15.09** be given to the employee by way of reference to relevant laws, regulations, or collective agreements,[11] no later than two months after the commencement of the employment. If the employment relationship comes to an end within two months of commencement, the required information must be made available to the employee at the date of termination at the latest.[12]

---

[8] Art 1(2)(a).
[9] Art 1(2)(b).
[10] Art 2.
[11] Art 2(2).
[12] Art 3(2).

15.10 Where appropriate, collective agreements which govern the employee's conditions of work must be indicated to him.[13] In the case of agreements concluded by special joint bodies or institutions, the name of the competent body or institution within which the agreements were concluded must be provided.

15.11 The information required to be furnished must be provided to the employee in writing. This may take the form of a written contract of employment, and/or a letter of engagement or any other written document.[14]

15.12 Changes in any of the employment conditions which are required to be given to the employee must equally be furnished in writing to the employee no later than one month after the modified conditions of employment come into effect.

15.13 Any variation in employment conditions brought about by statute, administrative regulation, or collective agreement need not be notified to the employee.

(1) *Kampelmann*[15]

15.14 The *Kampelmann* case raised the important issue of the status of the information given to the employee as to his terms and conditions of employment. What was the position if that information subsequently turned out to be factually inaccurate? Each of the claimants in *Kampelmann* was notified in writing by his employer of his grade and category of activity. Some years later they applied for promotion to a higher grade. Their applications were refused on the ground that the information notified to them as to their grade and category of work was inaccurate. Their work in fact corresponded to a lower category which did not qualify them for promotion to the higher grade they sought. Their applications before a German labour court for a declaration of their entitlement to the higher grade were dismissed because they had not provided proof of the necessary length of service in the grade and category of service required for the advancement they sought.

15.15 In preliminary ruling proceedings before the ECJ, the Court found that the notification of terms and conditions of employment provided for in Article 2(1) must be given such evidential weight as to allow it to serve as factual proof of the essential aspects of the employment relationship. If an employee were unable, in any way, to use the information contained in the notification provided for in Article 2(1) as evidence before national courts, particularly in disputes concerning essential aspects of the contract or employment relationship, the

---

[13] Art 2(3).
[14] Art 3(1).
[15] Cases C-253 to 256/96 [1997] ECR I–6907.

objective of Article 2(1) would not be achieved. It would simply serve no purpose at all.

Therefore the information provided to the employee must enjoy the same **15.16** presumption of correctness as would attach, in domestic law, to any similar document drawn up by the employer and communicated to the employee. The employer must nevertheless be allowed to bring evidence to the contrary by showing that the information given was either inherently incorrect or has been shown to be so in fact.

D. Expatriate Employees

Employees who are sent to work abroad for a period of more than one month **15.17** must receive the following further information:

(a) the duration of their employment abroad;
(b) where appropriate, the conditions governing their repatriation;
(c) the currency in which their remuneration will be paid;
(d) any benefits in kind specifically related to their employment abroad.[16]

Where any of the above matters are regulated by laws, administrative provisions **15.18** or collective agreements, the information obligation will be fulfilled if reference is simply made to those sources.

E. National Law

The Directive lays down minimum information requirements. It applies without **15.19** prejudice to national rules governing the form or terms of the contract of employment or employment relationship and proof of these terms. Member States remain free to adopt provisions more favourable to the employee.[17]

F. Enforcement

Article 8(1) provides that Member States are obliged to introduce measures to **15.20** enable all employees who consider themselves wronged by failure on the part of their employers to comply with the provisions of the Directive to pursue their claims by judicial process after possible recourse to other competent authorities.

---

[16] Art 6.
[17] Art 7.

Member States may provide that access to means of redress is subject to the notification of the employer by the employee and the failure by the employer to reply within 15 days of notification. However, Article 8(2) states that the formality of prior notification may in no case be required in the cases of expatriate workers or workers with a temporary contract or employment relationship, nor for employees not covered by a collective agreement or by collective agreements relating to the employment relationship.[18] In a preliminary ruling referred to the ECJ by the Danish Supreme Court, *Ruben Andersen*[19] on the issue of what constitutes a 'temporary contract' and whether a collective agreement which is intended to implement Article 8(1) is to be interpreted as meaning that a collective agreement which is intended to implement the provision of the Directive cannot be applied to an employee who is not a member of an organization which is party to that agreement.

15.21 The Advocate General, in an opinion of 19 June 2008, ruled that a Member State can extend the provisions of such a collective agreement to employees who are not members of any of the trade unions which negotiated it.

15.22 As to the meaning of 'temporary contract' and 'temporary employment relationship' in Article 8(2) the Advocate General was of the view that these terms do not refer to all fixed-term contracts but only those which are of a short duration. The ECJ held that the Community legislation, when it referred to workers with a 'temporary contract or employment relationship', intended to refer to workers whose contract is of such short duration that the obligation to notify the employer before taking legal proceedings could compromise effective access to judical means of redress. The question of what constitutes a short-term employment contract is one which, in the absence of any national rules fixing the duration of short-term contracts, must be dealt with on a case-by-case basis, taking into account the characteristics of the contract in question and the normal duration of employment in the sector in question.

15.23 Article 6 of the Directive provides that it applies without prejudice to national law and practice concerning:

- the form of the contract or employment relationship;
- proof as regards the existence and content of a contract or employment relationship; and
- the relevant procedural rules.

---

18 Art 8(2).
19 Case C-306/07 Judgement of 18 December 2008.

G. Burden of Proof

Kampelmann[20] found that although national rules on burden of proof were not **15.24** affected by the Directive, they must be applied and interpreted in the light of the purpose of the Directive. Since the Directive did not lay down any specific rules of evidence, proof of the essential aspects of the contract or employment relationship cannot depend solely on the employer's notification under Article 2(1). That information must be capable of challenge. But the burden of proving that the information in the notification is inaccurate or incorrect lies on the employer. The employer must be allowed to bring any evidence to show that the information is inherently incorrect or has been shown to be so in fact. To place that burden on the employee could potentially give rise to a situation where information was given without any regard for its accuracy to the employee thus misleading him, albeit possibly inadvertently, as to his employment conditions, or worse still employers faced with requests for promotion or other benefits which come with seniority or change in quality of work, could simply avoid their obligations by claiming that the information in the notification upon which the employee relied to enforce his right to advancement was incorrect—a position which the employee could find it difficult to refute. Consequently there is a presumption of correctness but this is challengeable, the evidential burden falling on the employer.

H. Direct Effect

Kampelmann held the Directive to be of direct effect. The fact that it allowed the **15.25** Member States to choose between the categories of information to be notified and the means by which they were notified to the employee did not render it impossible to determine with sufficient precision on the basis of the Directive alone, the content of the right conferred upon an individual, the scope of which is not in the discretion of the Member State:

> The provisions in question here are unconditional and sufficiently precise to enable individuals to rely on them directly before the national courts either where the Member State has failed to transpose the Directive into national law within the prescribed period or where it has not done so correctly.[21]

---

[20] Note 15.
[21] Note 15 Judgment para 40.

16

PARENTAL LEAVE

A. Introduction

The EC Commission proposed a directive on parental leave in 1983.[1] This **16.01** proposal was never adopted. More than ten years later, following the entry into force of the Agreement on Social Policy, the Commission consulted the social partners on the question of possible Community action to facilitate the reconciliation of working and family life. Following this initial consultation, the social partners were invited to give their opinion on the substance of a proposal on parental leave. At this point, they informed the Commission of their desire to initiate the procedure provided for in Article 4 Agreement on Social Policy (now Article 138(4) of the EC Treaty).

Within six months, a framework agreement had been made (the 'Agreement'). **16.02** Directive 96/34 implements this Agreement.[2] Initially the Agreement did not apply to the United Kingdom. It was extended thereto at the end of 1997 with a required implementation period of two years.[3]

The Member States were obliged to ensure that the provisions of the Agreement **16.03** were implemented by 3 June 1998 at the latest. If a Member State had special difficulties, or if it wished to implement the Directive by means of a collective agreement, it could have had a further implementation period of one year.

---

[1] [1983] OJ C333/6, as amended by [1984] OJ C316/7.

[2] Directive 96/34 on the framework agreement on parental leave ([1996] OJ L145/4).

[3] A report on the state of implementation of the Directive was published by the Commission in 1993: COM (1993) 358.

The EC Commission was required to be informed of the circumstances which allegedly warranted such an extension.

16.04 The Agreement lays down minimum requirements on parental leave for the purpose of bringing up children and time off work for parents on the grounds of *force majeure*. The Preamble to the Agreement laid down a number of objectives it wished to achieve. These refer, inter alia, to Point 16 of the Community Charter of Fundamental Social Rights of Workers, which specifies that measures should be developed to enable men and women to reconcile their work and family life. Flexibility in the organization of work is seen as necessary in the light of demographic change. The ageing of the population and declining birth rate requires both the participation of women in the workplace to satisfy manpower needs and at the same time the care of the old and the young needs a degree of flexibility in working conditions.

16.05 Parental leave is expressed to be distinct from maternity leave; the two are thus mutually exclusive. A parent or family is entitled to both.

B. Scope

16.06 The Agreement applies to all workers who have an employment contract or employment relationship as defined by the national law, collective agreement, or practices.

16.07 Employees are given the right to a period of time to be defined by the Member States, but which the Directive requires to be at least three months, to look after a child until a given age (to be laid down by each Member State) of up to eight years. The right should be granted on a non-transferable basis.

16.08 The employment relationship is maintained during the period of parental leave.[4]

C. Access to Leave

16.09 The conditions for access to parental leave are a matter for national law or regulation, for example by way of generally applicable collective agreement.

16.10 The Agreement, in Clause 2(3), sets out some of the issues which may be addressed in the implementation process:

(a) whether parental leave can be granted on a full-time or part-time basis, in a piecemeal way, or in the form of a time credit system;

---

[4] Case C-116/06 *Sari Kiiski* [2007] ECR I-7643.

(b) making entitlement to parental leave subject to a minimum period of employment or service not exceeding one year;

(c) the adjustment of the rules of parental leave to the special circumstances of adoption;

(d) the notice periods to be given to an employer by an employee exercising his right to parental leave;

(e) the circumstances in which parental leave may be postponed by an employer;

(f) special arrangements to meet the operational and organizational needs of small undertakings.

Sari Kiiski[5] raised the issue of whether and in what circumstances an employee   **16.11** could change the dates of a period of parental leave which had been granted to her to care for a child as a result of a new pregnancy of which the employee was aware before that period of leave commenced. Ms Kiiski was a teacher. She gave birth to a child in 2003 and applied for leave to care for that child from 11 August 2004 until 4 June 2005. She became pregnant again and applied on 1 July 2004 for an alteration of the decision granting the child care leave so that her leave period would run from 11 August 2004 until 22 December 2004. Her request was refused on the grounds that under Finnish law a new pregnancy did not justify altering the duration of child care leave already applied for and granted. Such a refusal in effect deprived Ms Kiiski of her right to maternity leave as provided for by the Pregnancy Directive.[6] The ECJ held that a period of leave guaranteed by Community law cannot affect the right to another period of leave guaranteed by that law.[7]

> Community law therefore precludes a decision by an employer such as that taken in this case, the consequence of which is that a pregnant worker is not permitted to obtain, at her request, an alteration of the period of her child care leave at the time when she requests her maternity leave and which thus deprives her of the rights inherent in that maternity leave which result form Articles 1 and 8 of Directive 92/85.[8]

Although a worker may thus obtain a change to parental leave arrangements the ECJ acknowledged that 'strict conditions' could attach to the circumstances in which such an alteration is available. The grant of leave affects the organization of the business in which the worker is employed and may necessitate the recruitment of a replacement and must therefore be subject to regulation. Thus although

---

[5] Ibid.

[6] Directive 92/85 [1992] OJ L348/1.

[7] Case C-519/03 *Commission v Luxembourg* [2005] ECR I–3067 Judgment para 333; Case C-124/05 *FNV* [2006] ECR I–3423.

[8] See note 4 above, Judgment para 57.

a worker cannot be deprived of maternity leave, in other circumstances any alteration to the grant of parental leave may be subject to conditions justified in the interests of the proper functioning of the employing undertaking. Such conditions would be subject to the principles of equality and proportionality. Parental leave must be granted under the same conditions to all beneficiaries and any restriction on the alteration of periods of leave in the interests of the proper functioning of the business or service with which the beneficiary has an employment relationship must be necessary and proportionate.

D. Preservation of Employment-linked Rights

16.12 Implementing measures must ensure that workers are not dismissed because they choose to exercise their right to parental leave.[9] At the end of the period of leave, workers must have the right to return to their jobs or similar jobs.[10] Rights acquired or in the process of being acquired at the start of a period of parental leave must be maintained subject to the application of any changes in national law or collective agreements.[11]

E. Social Security

16.13 All matters relating to social security during parental leave are left to the discretion of each Member State.[12] The Agreement makes reference to 'the importance of the continuity of the entitlements to social security cover . . . in particular health care'.[13]

16.14 In Part 1 of the Agreement, entitled 'General Considerations', the signatory parties emphasize the importance of the preservation of social security rights:

> 10. Whereas Member States should provide for the maintenance of entitlements to benefits in kind under sickness insurance during the minimum period of parental leave;
> 11. Whereas Member States should also, where appropriate under national conditions and taking into account the budgetary situation, consider the maintenance of entitlements to relevant social security benefits as they stand during the minimum period of parental leave.

---

[9] Cl 2(4).
[10] Cl 2(3).
[11] Cl 2(4).
[12] Cl 2(8).
[13] Cl 2(8).

Although these provisions urge the maintenance of social security benefits, in **16.15** particular medical care, the reality is that they impose no obligations on the Member States. The lack of any requirement to ensure at least the continuity of medical care provision, and family benefits, could operate as a disincentive to the exercise to the right to parental leave. Moreover it could result in the rights offered by the Directive being denied to single parent families—possibly amongst the most in need of its benefits—since they may have no other possibility of support during their chosen period of parental leave other than the state social security system.

17

PREGNANT WORKERS

A. Introduction

Directive 92/85 on the introduction of measures to encourage improvements in the safety and health in the workplace of pregnant women, and women who have recently given birth or are breastfeeding, lays down a number of standards which are designed to promote the welfare of pregnant workers and those who have recently given birth (the 'Directive').[1] It was required to be implemented by 19 October 1994. A report on the state of implementation of the Directive was published in 1999.[2] **17.01**

The Directive relates to the health and safety aspects of pregnancy and its immediate aftermath. For a full account of how pregnant women are protected in the workplace reference must also be had to Part VI, which analyses the application of the principle of equal treatment in pay and employment to pregnancy and related conditions. **17.02**

The objective of the Directive is to protect the health and safety of pregnant women and women who have recently given birth or who are breastfeeding. Such women are viewed as a particularly sensitive group of workers, given the potential risk to their health and that of their child in certain work environments. **17.03**

---

[1] [1992] OJ L348/1.
[2] COM (1999) 100 Final.

Although the health and safety of both mother and child must be safeguarded, at the same time, disadvantages both to the employee and employer which such protection may bring about must be minimized.

17.04 Accordingly, the Preamble to the Directive specifies that the protection of the health and safety of workers, within its scope of application, should not 'treat women on the labour market unfavourably nor to the detriment of directives concerning equal treatment for men and women'.[3] Presumably this means that health and safety measures must be proportionate, in the sense of being confined to what is necessary to achieve their objective, without more, since in many instances such measures may constrain the worker's employment opportunities. These 'equal treatment directives' referred to in the Preamble are discussed in Part VI. They relate to equality of treatment in all aspects of pay and employment, including social security and occupational welfare schemes, notably pensions.[4]

17.05 The Directive is based on Article 118a EC Treaty, now Article 137, and is the tenth individual directive to be adopted pursuant to Directive 89/391, the Framework Directive on health and safety of workers at work.[5]

B. Scope of Application

17.06 The Directive applies to pregnant workers who have informed their employer of their pregnancy in accordance with national rules and practice.[6] 'Pregnant worker' is a Community law concept, even if one element of that definition namely that relating to the method of communicating the condition of pregnancy to the employer refers back to national law and practice.[7] Workers who have given birth or who are breastfeeding within the meaning of national law and practice are also covered by the Directive. Although the Directive makes it incumbent upon women in these circumstances to inform their employer

---

[3] Recital 9.
[4] Directive 75/117 on equal pay for men and women [1975] OJ L45/19; Directive 76/207 on the implementation of the principle of equal treatment for men and women as regards access to employment, vocational training and promotion and working conditions [1976] OJ L39/40; Directive 79/7 on the progressive implementation of the principle of equal treatment for men and women in matters of social security [1979] OJ L6/24; Directive 86/378 on the implementation of the principle of equal treatment for men and women in occupational social security schemes [1986] OJ L225/40.
[5] [1989] OJ L183/1.
[6] Art 2(a).
[7] Case C-116/06 *Sari Kiiski* [2007] ECR I-7643.

of their pregnancy in order to be afforded the protection of the Directive, it does not specify when or how this should be done.

While the requirement to inform ensures that employers are not liable for risks to employees' health because of situations of which they were unaware, it does mean that placing the burden on women to declare pregnancy or recent birth or the fact that they are breastfeeding may give rise to a situation where some women may not provide this information out of concern that they will lose their jobs or be otherwise unfairly disadvantaged, thereby exposing themselves and their child (albeit voluntarily) to the very risks the Directive is designed to avoid. **17.07**

There is no requirement to actually provide evidence, of a medical or other nature, of pregnancy, or a recent birth. **17.08**

The case of *Sari Kiiski*[8] raised the issue of whether a woman who was not in employment at the time she became pregnant because she was on child care leave could claim the right to maternity leave under the Directive. The ECJ found that she could. The Directive was applicable to such a woman. Whilst the Community legislature intended to protect pregnant workers from the risks which they could face in their employment by giving them the right to maternity leave, it did not make the right to leave subject to the condition that the pregnant woman who claims enjoyment of that leave must herself be in a situation in which she is exposed such risks. The fact that the Directive aims to improve the protection of pregnant women at work cannot justify the assumption that the Community legislature intended to exclude a worker from the enjoyment of that leave if, at the time when she wishes to take up such leave, she has already left her job for a temporary period because she is enjoying another form of leave. **17.09**

C. Night Work

Workers may not be obliged to perform night work during pregnancy for a given period of time (to be determined by the Member States) after giving birth except where a medical certificate states that this is necessary for the safety and health of the woman in question.[9] Workers who cannot perform night work must be offered the possibility of transferring to daytime work or, if this is not possible, must be given leave from work.[10] **17.10**

---

[8] Ibid.
[9] Art 7(1).
[10] Art 7(2).

D. Maternity Leave

17.11 Workers are entitled to a continuous period of maternity leave of at least 14 weeks before or after confinement. Leave of a period of two weeks is compulsory.[11] During maternity leave, all rights connected with employment must be preserved.[12] This requirement applies only to employment completed more than 12 months prior to the presumed date of confinement. Workers must be given a maternity allowance of a sufficient level to guarantee an income equivalent to sickness pay, subject to any ceiling laid down by national legislation. Eligibility for a maternity allowance may be made conditional upon fulfilling the conditions prescribed under national law governing the entitlement to such benefit, such as attendance for ante-natal care.[13] These conditions may not provide for periods of previous employment in excess of 12 months immediately prior to the presumed date of confinement.

E. Ante-natal Care

17.12 Workers are entitled to take time off without loss of pay to attend ante-natal examinations.[14]

F. Health and Safety in the Workplace

17.13 Employers are obliged to assess the risk to pregnant workers of exposure to chemical, physical, or biological agents and industrial processes considered to be hazardous.[15] A non-exhaustive list of such agents and processes is set out in Annex 1 to the Directive. This list is indicative only.

17.14 If as a result of such an assessment it appears that there is a risk to the health and safety of pregnant workers, the working conditions of such workers must be adjusted to avoid such a risk. If necessary, the worker should be removed from the risk altogether and placed in another job or granted leave from work.[16]

17.15 No exposure whatsoever to any of the agents or working conditions specified in Annex II Section A to the Directive is permitted in the case of pregnant women;

---

[11] Art 8.
[12] Art 11(2).
[13] Art 11(4).
[14] Art 9.
[15] Art 4(1).
[16] Art 5.

in the case of women who are breastfeeding, there must be no exposure to any of the agents or working conditions specified in Annex II Section B If a pregnant or breastfeeding worker is at risk of exposure to such agents or working conditions, she must be removed from that risk.[17]

Annexes I and II may be amended. Article 13 of the Directive sets out the procedure to be followed in such an event.   **17.16**

G. Remedies

Member States must establish procedures to enable workers to enforce their rights under the Directive.[18]   **17.17**

H. Dismissal

Article 10 provides that workers may not be dismissed during the period commencing with the beginning of the pregnancy until the end of maternity leave save in exceptional cases not connected with their pregnancy.[19] This provision has direct effect and may be relied upon before national courts and tribunals in actions against State authorities.[20]   **17.18**

> It must therefore be concluded that the provisions of Article 10 of Directive 92/85 impose on Member States, in particular in their capacity as employers, precise obligations which offer them no margin of discretion in their performance.[21]

The protection established by Article 10 cannot be extended to a worker who is undergoing in vitro fertilization treatment when, on the date she was given notice of her dismissal, the in vitro fertilized ova had not yet been transferred into her uterus.[22] The prohibition of dismissal in such circumstances would run counter to the principle of legal certainty. In certain Member States fertilized ova may be kept for an indeterminate period. In others they may be kept for a fixed but lengthy period of time such as ten years. If Article 10 were to be interpreted as requiring protection against dismissal before the transfer of the fertilized ova, a woman, in the event of the postponement for whatever reason of the transfer   **17.19**

---

[17] Art 6(1).
[18] Art 12.
[19] Art 10.
[20] Case C-438/99 *Melgar* [2001] ECR I–6915.
[21] Ibid Judgment para 33.
[22] Case C-506/06 *Sabine Mayr* Judgment of 26 February 2008.

of the ova into her uterus, could have the benefit of that protection for a number of years or even indefinitely if the transfer is definitively abandoned.

17.20 The prohibition against dismissal applies in the case of fixed-term workers even where they have been unable to work for a substantial part of their contract term. This principle was established in the *Tele Danmark* case.[23]

17.21 Mrs Brandt Nielsen was recruited by Tele Danmark for a period of six months from 1 July 1995 to work in its customer services department for mobile phones. In August 1995 she informed Tele Danmark that she was pregnant and expected to give birth in early November. She was dismissed with effect from 30 September 1995 on the ground that she had not informed Tele Danmark that she was pregnant when she was recruited, the implication being that had she done so she would not have been engaged.

17.22 The Court found that Article 10 did not provide for any exception or derogation from the prohibition against dismissal of pregnant workers, save in exceptional cases not connected with their condition. Specific protection against dismissal was laid down by the Community legislature:

> . . . in view of the risk that a possible dismissal may pose for the physical and mental state of pregnant workers, workers who have recently given birth or those who are breast feeding, including the particularly serious risk that they may be encouraged to have an abortion . . .[24]

17.23 Protection against dismissal is not prejudiced by the fact that the worker did not inform the employee that she was pregnant when the contract of employment was concluded. The non-renewal of a fixed-term contract cannot in itself be regarded as equivalent to dismissal within the meaning of the Directive,[25] but where such non-renewal is due to the pregnancy of the worker it constitutes discrimination contrary to Articles 2(1) and 3(1) of Directive 76/207 on equal treatment for men and women.[26]

17.24 The case of *Nadine Paquay*[27] raised the question of whether Article 10 of the Directive must be interpreted as being confined to the prohibition of a notification of dismissal to the employee in question during the period running from the onset of pregnancy to the end of maternity leave or could it also be read as prohibiting any attempt to find a permanent replacement for an employee before

---

[23] Case C-109/00 *Tele Danmark* A/S [2001] ECR I–6693.
[24] Ibid Judgment para 26.
[25] Case C-438/99 *Melgar* [2001] ECR I–6915 at para 45.
[26] Ibid at para 46, following Case C-177/88 *Dekker* [1990] ECR I–3941 and Case C-207/68 *Mahlburg* [2000] ECR I–5549.
[27] Case C-460/06 Judgment of 11 October 2007.

the end of that period? The ECJ found that the protection granted to workers by Article 10 of the Directive excludes both the taking of a decision to dismiss as well as the steps taken to prepare for the dismissal such as searching for and finding a permanent replacement for the employee in question:

> . . . an employer . . . who decides to replace a pregnant worker or a worker who has recently given birth or is breast feeding, on the grounds of her condition and who, from the moment when he first had knowledge of the pregnancy, takes concrete steps with a view to finding a replacement, is pursuing the objective which is specifically prohibited by Directive 92/85, that is, to dismiss a worker on the grounds of her pregnancy and/or the birth of a child.[28]

---

[28] Ibid Judgment para 34.

18

YOUNG WORKERS

A. Introduction

Directive 94/33 on the protection of young people at work (the 'Directive')[1] aims to protect the health and safety of children and adolescents at work.[2] It is based on Article 137 of the EC Treaty and was adopted pursuant to Article 15 of the Framework Directive on the Health and Safety of Workers at Work.[3] **18.01**

The Directive has its origins in the Community Charter of the Fundamental Social Rights of Workers, which in Point 20 stated that the minimum employment age should not be lower than the minimum school leaving age, and in any case, not lower than 15 years. Point 21 of the Charter states that measures should be taken '... to adjust labour regulations applicable to young workers so that their specific development and vocational training and access to employment needs are met'. **18.02**

---

[1] [1994] OJ L216/2.
[2] '... children and adolescents must be considered specific risk groups, and measures must be taken with respect to their safety and health', Preamble, para 5.
[3] Directive 89/391 [1989] OJ L183/1.

(1) Implementation

18.03 The Directive was required to be implemented by 22 June 1996.[4] Article 17(1)(b) granted a further transitional period of four years to the United Kingdom in respect of the implementation of certain provisions. A further extension of this period was possible by way of Council decision.

18.04 A report published in 2000[5] concluded that the six-year implementation period was sufficient to allow the United Kingdom to adapt its legislation but in the case of any further problems, the Directive contained sufficient possibilities for derogations to cater for the United Kingdom's concerns, making any further delay in implementation unnecessary.[6]

B. Objective

18.05 The objective of the Directive is to protect young persons against economic exploitation and against work likely to harm their safety, health, or physical, mental, moral, or social development. It also aims to ensure that their education is not be prejudiced by employment whilst still in full-time schooling.

C. Minimum Requirements

18.06 The Directive lays down minimum requirements; it does not aim at aligning the Member States' legislation. Its objective is to support and complement national standards, while setting a floor under those standards.

18.07 The implementation of the Directive may not justify a reduction in the general level of protection under national law prevailing at the time of adoption. Thus the minimum standard of protection is either that set by the Directive or where this is lower than the standards in force in any particular Member State at the time of adoption, the latter must be regarded as the minimum standard.

18.08 As a general rule, employment of young persons below the minimum compulsory school leaving age and in any event below the age of 15 years is prohibited.

---

[4] An implementation report has been published by the Commission. It is available at <http://ec.europa.eu/employment_social/labour_law/docs/10_youngpeople_implreport_en.pdf>.

[5] COM (2000) 457 Final.

[6] Infringement proceedings were taken against Italy, France and Luxembourg in respect of failure to implement the Directive. Italy had failed to fulfil its obligations within the required implementation period but subsequently did so and proceedings were withdraw. The Court found that France and Luxembourg had failed to fulfil their obligations Case C-45/99 *Commission v France* [2000] ECR I–365; Case C-47/99 *Commission v Luxembourg* [1999] ECR I–8999.

Work by adolescents must be strictly regulated and employers must ensure that young people work in conditions suitable to their age and development. In particular they must be protected against economic exploitation and any situations which are prejudicial to their general well-being and education.[7]

D. Scope of Application

The Directive applies to young persons, that is those under the age of 18 years, **18.09** who have an employment contract or employment relationship defined by the law of a Member State.[8] Children are defined as young persons of less than 15 years of age or who are still required to be in compulsory full-time schooling under national law.[9] Adolescents are persons of at least 15 years of age but less than 18 years who are no longer subject to a compulsory full-time schooling requirement.[10]

Member States may, at their discretion, make provision for the Directive not to **18.10** apply to occasional work or short-term work involving:

(a) domestic service in a private household;
(b) work regarded as not being harmful, damaging, or dangerous to young people in a family undertaking.[11]

E. Prohibited Work

Work by children is prohibited.[12] **18.11**

The employment of young persons is also prohibited in the case of five types of **18.12** occupation:

(a) work which is objectively beyond their physical or psychological capacity;
(b) work involving harmful exposure to agents which are toxic, carcinogenic, cause heritable genetic damage or harm to the unborn child, or which in any way chronically affect human health;
(c) work involving harmful exposure to radiation;

---

[7] Art 1.
[8] Art 2(2).
[9] Art 3(b).
[10] Art 3(c).
[11] Art 2(2).
[12] Art 4(1).

(d) work involving the risk of accidents which it may be assumed cannot be recognized or avoided by young persons owing to their insufficient attention to safety or lack of experience or training; or

(e) work in which there is a risk of health from extremes of temperature or from noise or vibration.[13]

18.13 In the case of these five categories of employment, Member States can permit derogations from the normal rule of prohibition which are indispensable for vocational training, but the health and safety of young persons must at all times be ensured.[14]

F. Night Work

18.14 Member States may authorize night work to be performed by adolescents but there is a prohibition on adolescents working between the hours of midnight and 4 am.[15]

18.15 Night work may be authorized in the case of certain types of employment such as shipping or in the fishing sector or in the case of cultural, artistic, or advertising activities.[16]

G. Health and Safety Protection

18.16 A number of obligations relating to the safeguarding of the health and safety of young persons are imposed on employers. In the case of work which is not specifically prohibited by the Directive, Member States must ensure that it is performed in conditions in which young persons are protected from risks to their health and development, in particular exposure to the physical, biological, or chemical agents referred to in Point I of the Annex to the Directive and the processes and work referred to in Point II of the Annex.[17]

18.17 Prior to the commencement of employment, and where there is any major change in working conditions, the employer must assess the hazards to young people. If the assessment shows that there is a risk to the safety or physical or mental health of young people, their health must be monitored at regular intervals to

---

[13] Art 7(2).
[14] Art 7(3).
[15] Art 9(2).
[16] Art 10(2).
[17] Art 7(2).

reduce the possibility of the materialization of such risks.[18] A non-exhaustive list of potential hazardous processes, agents, and work is set out in the Annex to the Directive.[19]

H. Cultural, Artistic, Sports, and Advertising Activities

Children may be permitted to undertake work which involves performing in **18.18** cultural, artistic, sporting, or advertising activities, but permission or authorization must be given in each case by a competent authority appointed by each Member State.[20] The child's health, safety, and development must not be prejudiced by such activities nor must their attendance at school. In the case of children over the age of 13 years, Member States can dispense with the requirement to obtain prior authorization for each performance, if there is in place a legislative or regulatory provision setting out the conditions under which such children may perform.[21]

I. Light Work and Training

Children over 14 years are permitted to work in a work/training scheme and to **18.19** engage in light work.[22] Light work is defined as all work which is not harmful to the health, safety, or development of children and which does not prejudice their attendance at school. In the case of these two permissible types of employment, the working hours of children are limited to:

(a) eight hours a day and 40 hours a week for work performed under a combined work/training scheme or an in-plant work experience scheme;

(b) two hours on a school day and 12 hours a week for work performed in term time outside the hours fixed for school attendance, provided this is not prohibited by national law or practice. In no circumstances may the daily working time exceed seven hours or eight hours in the case of children who have reached the age of 15 years;

(c) seven hours a day and 35 hours a week in the case of work performed by children during a period of at least a week when school is not operating.

---

[18] Art 6(1).
[19] Art 6(2).
[20] Art 5.
[21] Art 5(3) The rules relating to children engaged in cultural or artistic performances are set out in Annex 1 to the Implementation Report on the Directive at <http://ec.europa.eu/employment_social/labour_law/docs/10_youngpeople_implreport_en.pdf> at 93.
[22] Art 4(2)(b) and (c).

In the case of children who have reached the age of 15 years, the relevant permitted hours of work are eight hours a day and 40 hours a week respectively;

(d) seven hours a day and 35 hours a week for light work performed by children no longer subject to compulsory full-time schooling.[23]

18.20 Work by children is prohibited between the hours of 8pm and 6am.[24]

18.21 During school holidays, children can work seven hours a day and 35 hours a week. These limits can be raised to eight hours a day and 40 hours a week in the case of children who have reached the age of 15 years.

J. Rest Periods

18.22 Where children are permitted to work, Member States must adopt measures to ensure that for each 24-hour period they are entitled to a minimum rest period of 14 consecutive hours. The period in respect of adolescents is 12 hours.[25]

18.23 For each seven-day period, children and adolescents are entitled to a minimum rest period of two days, preferably consecutive.[26] The rest period must in principle include Sunday.

18.24 Member States may provide for derogations from these required rest periods in the case of certain types of employment performed by adolescents and activities split up over the day, eg shipping or fishing, the armed forces, the police, hospital or similar employment, agriculture, and tourism.[27] Such employment must be objectively justified. Compensatory rest time must be given and in no circumstances must adolescents' education be compromised by such employment.

K. Breaks

18.25 Where daily working time is more than four-and-a-half hours, young persons are entitled to a break of 30 minutes.[28] Children are entitled to a rest period of 14 consecutive hours in each 24-hour period.[29] The relevant rest period for adolescents is 12 hours.[30]

---

[23] Art 8(1).
[24] Art 9(1).
[25] Art 10(1)(a) and (b).
[26] Art 10(2).
[27] Art 10(4).
[28] Art 12.
[29] Art 10(1)(a).
[30] Art 10(1)(b).

L. Annual Rest

Member States must ensure that children have a period away from any work   **18.26** during school holidays.[31]

M. Information Requirements

Young persons and the legal representatives of children must be informed of   **18.27** possible risk and all measures adopted concerning children's health and safety.

---

[31] Art 11.

19

PART-TIME WORK[1]

A. Introduction

The social partners reached agreement on the rights of part-time workers on **19.01** 6 June 1997 following a year of discussions. That Framework Agreement was implemented by Directive 97/81,[2] adopted on 15 December 1997 (the Directive). The Directive was required to be implemented by 20 January 2000.[3] Member States had an additional year in which to implement the Directive in the case of special difficulties or implementation by collective agreement.[4] The Directive was extended to the United Kingdom in 1998, with a two-year implementation period.[5] A report on the state of implementation of the Directive was published by the Commission in January 2003.[6]

---

[1] See generally Sciarra, Davies, and Freedland (eds): *Employment Policy and the Regulation of Part-time Work in the EU: a Comparative Analysis.* Cambridge University Press 2004; Jeffrey: 'Not really going to work? Of the directive on part-time work "atypical work" and attempts to regulate it' (1998) 27 Industrial Law Journal 193.

[2] [1998] OJ L14/8.

[3] The Commission published a report on the implementation of the Directive on 21 January 2003. <http://ec.europa.eu/employment_social/labour_law/docs/06_parttime_implre port_en.pdf>.

[4] Art 2.

[5] Directive 98/23 on the extension of Directive 91/81 on the Framework Agreement on part-time work concluded by UNICE,CEEP and the ETUC to the United Kingdom[1998] OJ L131/10.

[6] See <http://ec.europa.eu/employment_social/labour_law/docs/06_parttime_implreport_en. pdf>.

B. Objectives

19.02 The Framework Agreement has four main objectives:

(a) to remove discrimination against part-time workers;
(b) to improve the quality of part-time work;
(c) to facilitate the development of part-time work on a voluntary basis;
(d) to contribute to the flexible organization of working time in a manner which takes account of the needs of the employers and workers.

19.03 The Framework Agreement thus fulfils the dual objectives of introducing flexibility into the employment relationships, thereby facilitating job creation, and at the same time providing an element of the traditional security associated with full-time employment contracts of indefinite duration. The Directive thus '. . . captures this double necessity to "contribute" to the European strategy on employment and to combat discrimination against part-time workers'.[7]

19.04 The Framework Agreement lays down minimum rights. Member States may introduce more favourable provisions if they so wish.[8] Its application is without prejudice to more specific Community provisions concerning equal treatment or opportunities for men and women.

C. Scope of Application

19.05 The Framework Agreement applies to part-time workers who have an employment contract or employment relationship as defined by the laws, collective agreements, or practices of the Member States.[9]

19.06 A part-time worker is defined as an employee whose normal hours of work calculated on a weekly basis, and over a period of employment of one year, are less than the normal working hours of full-time workers employed in the same establishment engaged in the same or similar types of employment.[10] A part-time employment relationship to which the Directive is applicable may be one in which the length of weekly working time and the organization of working time are not fixed but dependent on quantitative needs in terms of the work to be

---

[7] Sciarra: 'New Discourses in Labour Law: Part-time Work and the Paradigm of Flexibility' in Davies, Sciarra, and Freedland (eds) (see note 1 above) at 22.
[8] Cl 6(1).
[9] Cl 2(1).
[10] Cl 3(1).

performed determined on a case-by-case basis with workers being entitled to accept or refuse that work.

Ms *Wipple*[11] was employed under a framework contract based on the principle **19.07** of 'work on demand'. Her contract stipulated neither the weekly hours of work nor the manner in which working time was to be organized and left her the choice whether to accept to refuse the work offered. Remuneration was at an hourly rate for hours actually worked. The issue was whether workers employed under such arrangements came within the scope of the Directive. The Court held that they did if the following conditions were satisfied:

- they have a contract or employment relationship as defined by the law, collective agreements, or practices in force in the Member State;
- they are employees whose normal working hours, calculated on a weekly basis or on average over an employment period which may be up to a year, are less than those of a comparable full-time worker within the meaning of Clause 3(2) of that Framework Agreement; and
- in regard to part-time workers working on a casual basis, the Member State has not, pursuant to Clause 2(2) of the Framework Agreement, excluded them, wholly or partly, from the benefit of the terms of that agreement.

D. Casual Workers

Part-time workers working on a casual basis may be excluded from the scope of **19.08** application of the Framework Agreement[12] after consultation with the social partners. Any exclusion of such workers from the principle of equal treatment must be objectively justified. No definition is given of what constitutes work on a 'casual basis'. Recital 16 of the Directive provides that where terms are not specifically defined in the Framework Directive, Member States are free to define those terms in accordance with national law and practice, provided 'the said definitions respect the content of the Framework Agreement'.

E. Principle of Non-discrimination

The Agreement provides that part-time workers must not be treated less favour- **19.09** ably than comparable full-time workers solely because they work part-time unless the treatment is justified on objective grounds.[13] A comparable full-time worker

---

[11] Case C-313/02 *Wippel* [2004] ECR I– 9483.
[12] Cl 2(2).
[13] Cl 4.

means a full-time worker in the same establishment having the same type of employment contract or relationship, who is engaged in the same type of work. If there is no comparable full-time worker in the same establishment, reference must be made to the applicable collective agreement or national law, collective agreements, or practices.[14]

19.10 *Wipple*[15] found that there was no full-time worker in the employing undertaking which had the same type of contract of employment or employment relationship as Ms Wipple. Full-time workers were employed under a contract which fixed the working week at 38.5 hours, for a fixed salary, and which required them to work for the whole working time specified in the contract without the possibility of refusing that work. Ms Wipple, on the other hand, worked under a contract which did not specify her weekly working hours nor the manner in which they were to be organized but left it up to her whether to accept work offered or not. Her salary was not fixed—she was paid for the hours she chose to work. Her situation could not therefore be compared to that of the full-time worker and consequently no claim of discrimination could be upheld.

19.11 The Framework Agreement provides that, where applicable, the principle *pro rata temporis* applies.[16] Where access to particular conditions of employment is subject to a period of service, time worked, or an earnings qualification, this must be objectively justified and the right of access by part-time workers must be reviewed periodically.[17]

F. Opportunities for Part-time Work

19.12 Member States and the social partners are required by the Framework Agreement to identify and review obstacles of a legal or administrative nature and provisions in collective agreements which may limit opportunities for part-time work and, where appropriate, eliminate them.[18] It is doubtful if this provision creates any justiciable right to part-time work. By contrast the right of equal treatment, as set out in Clause 4 of the Framework Agreement, appears to create a directly effective right.

19.13 *Michaeler, Subito, and Volgger*[19] condemned a provision of Italian law which, at the relevant time, required undertakings to send to the competent authority a

---

[14] Cl 3(2).
[15] See note 11 above.
[16] Cl 4(2).
[17] Cl 4(4).
[18] Cl 5(1).
[19] Joined Cases C-55/07 and C-56/07 Judgment of 24 April 2008.

copy of every part-time employment contract within 30 days of the signature of that contract. The penalty for failure to comply with this obligation was an administrative fine of EUR 15 for each worker concerned and for each day of delay. There was no ceiling on the amount of the level of the fine. The ECJ found the notification obligation set an administrative obstacle likely to limit the opportunities for part-time work within the meaning of Clause 5(1)(a) of the Framework Agreement. Aside from the financial burden which the administrative formality of notification imposed on undertakings, the system of penalties prescribed for failure to notify was such as to discourage employers from making use of part-time work. The obligation to notify affected, in particular, small and medium-sized undertakings which, not having the same resources as large undertakings, might be inclined to avoid the use of part-time work which the Framework Agreement aimed to promote.

The Framework Agreement envisages more mobility between part-time work and full-time work and states that employers should encourage part-time work by giving consideration to requests by workers for transfers from full-time work to part-time work or by part-time workers to increase their working time by providing information on part-time work opportunities and facilitating access to part-time work.[20] **19.14**

G. Protection against Dismissal

A refusal to transfer from part-time work to full-time work may not in itself constitute a valid reason for dismissal.[21] **19.15**

H. Vocational Training

Employers should consider facilitating access by part-time workers to vocational training to enhance their career opportunities and career mobility.[22] **19.16**

No specific obligation is placed on employers to provide access to vocational training by part-time workers. It is arguable that the principle of equal treatment requires that such access should be facilitated. Thus if full-time workers are remunerated during periods of vocational training, part-time workers must also be remunerated on a pro rata basis or otherwise compensated even if vocational training takes place outside of their normal working hours. **19.17**

---

[20] Cl 5(3).
[21] Cl 5(2).
[22] Cl 5(3).

20

FIXED-TERM EMPLOYMENT[1]

A. Introduction

The Framework Agreement on Fixed-Term Work concluded by ETUC, UNICE, **20.01**
and CEEP (the 'Framework Agreement'), acting on the basis of Article 139(2)
EC Treaty has been fully incorporated into Community law by virtue of Directive
99/70.[2] The Agreement was required to be implemented by 10 July 1999 but
Member States which had special difficulties or who wished to implement the
Directive by way of collective agreement were allowed a further year to complete
transposition (until 10 July 2000). An implementation report on the state of
transposition of the Directive within the Community prior to the accession of
ten Member States on 1 May 2004 was published in August 2006.[3] A further
report on implementation in the ten Member States which acceded to the

---

[1] See generally: Kenner: *EU Employment Law from Rome to Amsterdam and Beyond* Hart
Publishing 2003 at 285–91; Murray: 'Normalising Temporary Work' (1999) 28 ILJ 269; Sciarra:
'Fundamental Labour Rights after the Lisbon Agenda' in de Burca and de Witte: *Social Rights in
Europe* Oxford 2005 201–7; Survey of National Law on Fixed Term Employment (1999) 15(2)
IJCLLIR 81–209.
[2] [1999] OJ L175/43. For background see Explanatory Memorandum COM (99) 203.
[3] SEC (2006) 1074.

Community on 1 May 2004 will be published in due course. The Agreement may be reviewed at the request of one of the parties five years after the date of the adoption of Directive 99/70.[4] At the time of writing no such request appears to have been made.

20.02 The purpose of the Framework Agreement is to offer protection to workers on fixed-term contracts. This objective is to be achieved in two ways:

(a) by eliminating discrimination between fixed-term contracts and comparable permanent work; and
(b) through the prevention of abuse of fixed-term workers by the use of continuous fixed-term employment contracts or employment relationships.

20.03 The Framework Agreement is stated to be without prejudice to more specific Community law provisions, particularly those concerning equal treatment or equal opportunities for men and women.[5]

B. Scope of Application

20.04 Clause 2 defines the scope of application of the Framework Agreement. It applies to fixed-term workers who have an employment contract or an employment relationship as defined in law, collective agreements, or practices in each Member State.

20.05 Member States have a discretion to exclude from the application of the Agreement:

(a) initial vocational training relationships and apprenticeship schemes;
(b) employment contracts and relationships which have been concluded within the framework of a specific public or publicly supported training, integration, and vocational retraining programme.

20.06 A Member State is, therefore, able to exempt itself and its contractors from the scope of application of the Directive where projects are linked with the employability and adaptability objectives which are part of the European Employment Strategy.[6] Given the breadth of these objectives, this exemption is capable of being quite extensive.

---

[4] Cl 8(6).
[5] Cl 8.
[6] Kenner (see note 1 above) at 287 and also paras 10.25–10.48.

The Framework Agreement extends to employment in both the public and the **20.07** private sectors. This was made clear by the ECJ in *Adenelar*[7] which found:

(i) that Article 2(1) of the Agreement was drafted in broad terms covering generally 'fixed-term workers who have an employment contract or an employment relationship';

(ii) Clause 3(1) defined the concept of fixed-term workers without drawing any distinction as to whether their employment is in the public or private sector; and

(iii) Clause 2(2) permitted Member States and the social partners to make the Agreement inapplicable to two types of employment only. Consequently the Court held that it was not, therefore, possible to conclude that the Agreement did not apply to fixed-term contracts concluded with the public authorities and other public sector bodies.

C. Fixed-term Worker

A fixed-term worker is defined in clause 3(1) of the Agreement as: **20.08**

> . . . a person having an employment contract or relationship entered into directly between an employer and a worker where the end of the employment contract is determined by objective conditions such as the reaching of a specific date, completing a specific task or the occurrence of a specific event.

D. Comparable Permanent Worker

A comparable permanent worker means a worker with an employment contract **20.09** or an employment relationship of indefinite duration, in the same establishment, engaged in the same or similar work or occupation, due regard being given to qualifications and skills.[8] Where there is no comparable permanent worker in the same establishment, the comparison is to be made by reference to national law, collective agreement, or practice.[9]

E. The Principle of Non-discrimination

Clause 4.1 of the Agreement provides for equal treatment between fixed-term **20.10** and permanent workers with respect to employment conditions. Fixed-term

---

[7] Case C-212/04 *Adenelar* [2006] ECR I– 6057.
[8] Cl 3(2).
[9] Cl 3 92).

workers are not to be treated in a less favourable manner than comparable permanent workers unless such treatment can be objectively justified. Where appropriate, the principle of *pro rata temporis* is to be applied. What constitutes equal treatment is a question of fact in each case. Responsibility for the application of the principle of equal treatment is entrusted to the Member States acting in consultation with the social partners. Any implementation exercise must be carried out with regard to Community law, national law, collective agreements, and practices.

20.11 Clause 4.1 has direct effect. It prohibits in a general manner, and in unequivocal terms, any difference in the treatment of fixed-term workers in respect of employment conditions, which is not objectively justified. Its subject matter is therefore sufficiently precise to be relied upon by an individual and to be applied by a national court.[10]

20.12 Employment conditions in Clause 4(1) have been held in *Impact*[11] to include conditions in an employment contract relating to remuneration and pensions. To exclude remuneration and pensions from the concept of 'employment conditions' would effectively reduce the scope of protection against discrimination for the workers concerned by introducing a distinction based on the nature of the employment conditions, which the ECJ found the wording of Clause 4.1 did not suggest.

F. Minimum Periods of Service

20.13 Where particular conditions or benefits of employment require a given period of service, these periods of service must be the same for fixed and permanent workers, unless there is some objective justification for differentiating between the two groups.[12]

G. Training

20.14 Employers must facilitate access by fixed-term workers to appropriate training opportunities to enhance their skills, career development, and occupational mobility.[13]

---

[10] Case C-268/06 *Impact* Judgment of 15 April 2008.
[11] Ibid.
[12] Cl 4(4).
[13] Cl 6(2).

H. Access to Permanent Positions

Fixed-term workers must be informed by their employers of available vacancies **20.15** within the employing undertaking or establishment in order to ensure that they have an opportunity to secure permanent positions. This information requirement may be satisfied by a general announcement at a suitable place in the employing undertaking: fixed-term employees need not be informed individually of vacancies for permanent positions.[14]

I. Prevention of Abuse

Clause 5 deals with the prevention of abuse arising out of the use of successive **20.16** fixed-term contracts. Paragraph 1 imposes an obligation on Member States to have, within their legal systems, certain measures to prevent abuse. Paragraph 2 enables Member States, after consultation with the social partners, to categorize contracts of employment as 'successive' or contractual relationships as of 'indefinite duration'.

Clause 5 (1) provides that where there are no legal measures in place in a Member **20.17** State to prevent abuse arising out of the use of successive fixed-term contracts, Member States must, after consulting with the social partners, introduce one or more of the following measures:

(a) objective reasons justifying the renewal of fixed-term contracts or employment relationships;
(b) the maximum total duration of such successive fixed-term contracts or employment relationships;
(c) the permitted number of renewals of such contracts or relationships.[15]

It is for the Member States, after consulting with the social partners, or the social **20.18** partners themselves, to determine what is meant by the concept of successive fixed-term contracts and which contracts or employment relationships must be deemed to be contracts or relationships of indefinite duration.[16]

Clause 5(1) has been held not to have direct effect. Its provisions do not contain **20.19** any unconditional and sufficiently precise obligations capable of being relied upon by an individual before a national court. Clause 5(1) effectively leaves it to

---

[14] Cl 6(1).
[15] Cl 5(1).
[16] Cl 5(2).

the discretion of Member States, in order to prevent the abusive use of successive fixed-term contracts, to rely on one or more of the measures listed in that clause, or even on existing equivalent legal measures while taking account of the needs of specific sectors or categories of workers.[17]

Clause 5 has been the subject of a number of references for preliminary rulings to the ECJ. The first case is *Adenelar*[18] which established the following principles:

(i) the fact that the conclusion of a fixed-term employment relationship is prescribed by national law is not an 'objective reason' justifying the renewal of such a relationship. An objective reason within the meaning of Clause 5(1)(a) must be understood as referring to precise and concrete circumstances characterizing a particular activity which are, therefore, capable in that particular context, of justifying the use of successive fixed-term employment contracts. These circumstances may result from the specific nature of the tasks for which the contracts have been concluded, from the inherent characteristics of those tasks or, as the case may be, from the pursuit of the legitimate social policy objectives of a Member State;

(ii) Clause 5(1), in conjunction with Clause 5(2)(a), precludes a provision of national law, under which one of the conditions governing the existence of successive employment contracts or relationships, is that there must be no more than 20 working days between the contracts concerned. If only those fixed-term employment relationships which were separated by intervals not exceeding 20 working days were deemed 'successive' it would be easy to circumvent the protection afforded to workers against abusive use of fixed-term contracts which constitutes the primary aim of the Agreement;

(iii) the Framework Agreement neither lays down a general obligation on the Member State to provide for the conversion of fixed-term employment contracts into contracts of indefinite duration, nor prescribes the precise conditions under which fixed-term contracts may be used. Where the domestic law of a Member State does not include, in the sector under consideration, any effective measure to prevent, and where relevant, punish the misuse of successive fixed-term contracts, the Framework Agreement precludes the application of national legislation, which in the public sector alone, prohibits absolutely the conversion into employment contracts of indefinite duration of a succession of fixed-term contracts, that, in fact have

---

[17] Note 11.
[18] Case C-212/04 (see note 7 above).

been intended to cover the 'fixed and permanent needs' of the employer therefore must be considered as abusive.

(iv) Clause 5(1) in conjunction with Clause 5(2)(b) does not preclude a prohibition in the public sector against converting fixed-term employment contracts into contracts of indefinite duration, even in cases where the statutory requirements governing the use of such fixed-term employment relationships might have been circumvented in an abusive manner. There were special considerations applying to employment in the public sector in the Member State in question in this case—Greece. Access to public service employment was regulated by specific legal procedures and there were strict limits imposed by law on recourse to employment relationships governed by private law for fixed-terms and the conversion of those relationships into public sector employment of indefinite duration was prohibited.

In *Marrosu*[19] and *Vassello*,[20] two references for preliminary rulings from Italy, the **20.20** Court was asked to rule on the question of whether an Italian law which prevents fixed-term contracts in public sector employment from being converted into indefinite contracts or working relationships, was precluded by the Agreement, in view of the fact that contracts and working relationships in the Italian private sector were subject to such a conversion requirement. The Court held that, since the Agreement did not lay down a general obligation on the Member States to provide for the conversion of fixed-term employment contracts into contracts of indefinite duration, Member States had a discretion in the matter. This discretion enabled it to treat the misuse of successive fixed-term employment contracts or relationships differently according to whether those contracts or relationships were made within the private sector or the public sector. Where national legislation precluded successive fixed-term employment contracts in the public sector from being converted into contracts of indeterminate duration, but such conversion was possible in private sector employment, this did not mean that abuse of fixed-term contracts could occur in the public sector. In the absence of any possibility, within the terms of the Directive, to impose an obligation to convert successive fixed-term contracts into contracts for an indefinite term, alternative effective means had to be found to prevent the abusive use of fixed-term contracts.

The most recent judgment on abusive use of fixed-term contracts is that of **20.21** *Impact*.[21] Impact is an Irish trade union which represents civil servants. It brought

[19] Case C-53/04 [2006] ECR I–7213.
[20] Case C-18O/04 [2006] ECR I–7251.
[21] See note 10 above.

an action on behalf of 91 of its members (the 'complainants') against a number of government departments. The complainants were all unestablished civil servants. Some had less than three years' continuous service as fixed-term employees, others had more than three years of continuous service. The purpose of the fixed-term contracts was to meet the temporary needs of the government departments in question and to cover situations in which the permanent funding for the posts involved could not be guaranteed. The general practice was to renew those contracts for periods of between one and two years. However, in the period immediately between the entry into force of the legislation transposing Directive 99/70 into Irish law, one of the respondent government departments renewed the contracts of a number of the complainants for a fixed period of up to eight years. The issue before the ECJ was whether a Member State, in its capacity as an employer, was precluded from renewing a fixed-term employment contract for up to eight years in the period between the deadline for transposing the Directive and the date on which the legislation transposing the Directive entered into force. The ECJ held that Article 10 EC and Article 249(3) as well as Directive 99/70 itself required Member States to take any appropriate measure, whether general or particular, to achieve the objective of that Directive and the Framework Agreement of preventing the abusive use of fixed-term contracts. That obligation would be rendered ineffective if an authority of a Member State, acting in its capacity as a public employer, were authorized to renew contracts for an unduly long term in the period between the deadline for transposing the Directive and the date on which the transposing legislation entered into force, thereby depriving the persons concerned of the benefit of the measures adopted by the national legislature for the purpose of transposing Clause 5 of the Framework Agreement.

J. Information and Consultation

20.22 Fixed-term workers must be taken into consideration in calculating the threshold above which worker representation may be required both under national or Community law.[22]

K. Implementation

20.23 Member States or the social partners can maintain or introduce more favourable measures concerning fixed-term workers than those provided for under

---

[22] Cl 7(1).

the Agreement.[23] Implementation of the Agreement must not result in any reduction in the prevailing level of protection afforded to workers.[24]

These provisions were considered by the ECJ in *Mangold*,[25] in which it was held **20.24** that the term 'implementation' refers not only to the transposition of the Agreement into national law but also to all domestic measures intended to ensure that the objectives pursued by the Agreement were attained, including those which add to or amend domestic rules previously adopted. Reduction of the levels of protection which workers are guaranteed in the sphere of fixed-term contracts is not prohibited where it is not connected with the implementation of the Agreement. Consequently, a change in German law which reduced the age (from 60 years to 58 years) above which fixed-term contracts, without the necessity of proving objective justification, could be concluded, was held not to be incompatible with Clause 8(3) of the Agreement as it was not concerned with the implementation of the Agreement but rather had as its objective the encouragement of the employment of older persons.[26]

Mangold is not particularly satisfactory. Essentially it appears to state that a **20.25** Member State is free to pursue an objective which will have the practical effect of reducing rights under the Agreement, provided its actions are 'not connected with the implementation of the Agreement'. What precisely does this mean and what are the consequences of this approach for many Framework Agreements and Directives which set out clearly permitted exceptions and derogations subject in many cases to the requirement of objective justification? Can further erosions be made in the bundle of rights granted under a measure in the interest of attaining a national social or employment objective?

Mangold[27] appears to condone a situation whereby Member States can justify **20.26** their failure to implement a Community measure by stating that their impugned measures have nothing to do with the implementation of a Community measure but have been adopted in pursuit of other legitimate national objectives, the result of which, even if true, may be to reduce the general effectiveness of the body of rights granted under the Directive.

---

[23] Cl 8(1). See Case C-378/07 *Angelidaki and Others* [2007] OJ C268/24; Case C-380/07 *Karabousanos and Mikhopoulos* [2007] OJ C269/27—pending before the ECJ at the time of writing.
[24] Cl 8 (3).
[25] Case C-144/04 [2005] ECR I–9981.
[26] Ibid Judgment para 53.
[27] See note 26 above.

21

TEMPORARY EMPLOYMENT

A. Introduction

Temporary employment has not so far been the subject of much regulation on a **21.01** Community level. At present temporary employment relationships are, by and large, governed by national law and practice. Apart from a number of broadly drafted health and safety provisions, any general legislative measure on temporary employment has been resisted by the Member States. A proposal for a directive adopted by the Commission in 2002 remains unadopted[1] but on 10 June 2008 the Member States agreed in principle to proceed to adopt most of its provisions. Final adoption is expected during the course of 2009, with full implementation being required by the Member States within three years.

B. Health and Safety

Directive 91/383, supplementing the measures to encourage improvements **21.02** in the safety and health at work of workers with a fixed duration employment

---

[1] The proposal was discussed at the Employment. Social Policy, Health and Consumer Affairs Council of 5–6 December 2007 but no agreement on its provisions was reached. It was agreed that discussions on the proposed directive should be linked to proposals for changes in Directive 93/104 on the Organization of Working Time [2003] OJ L299/9. Political agreement within the Council was reached on both sets of proposals on 10 June 2008.

relationship or a temporary employment relationship,[2] was adopted pursuant to Article 137 EC Treaty, and within the Framework Directive on Health and Safety.[3] It lays down the principle of equal treatment in health and safety. Its relevance to fixed-term workers has been superseded by the Fixed-Term Employment Directive[4] discussed in Chapter 20.

21.03   The Directive prescribes equality of treatment in health and safety matters: temporary workers must be afforded the same level of health and safety protection as other workers in the undertakings in which they work.[5] In particular they must be provided with the same protective equipment.

21.04   The Directive is expressed to apply to:

> . . . temporary employment relationships between a temporary employment business which is the employer and the worker, where the latter is assigned to work for and under the control of an undertaking or establishment making use of his services.[6]

21.05   Temporary workers must be informed of the risks they face in the course of their work[7] and receive sufficient training appropriate to the nature of their work.[8]

21.06   The user undertaking or establishment is obliged to inform the temporary employment business supplying the worker of the occupational qualifications required and the specific features of the work to be performed. This information must be brought to the attention of the worker by the temporary employment business. The objective of this provision is to ensure that both the temporary employment agency and the worker himself are fully aware of the risks inherent in any particular employment.

21.07   If the work requires special medical surveillance, Member States have the option of prohibiting temporary workers from being used for such work. If they choose not to exercise this option, workers must be provided with the appropriate medical surveillance. It is open to the Member States to provide that such surveillance may continue after the job for which the worker has been hired has been completed.

---

2 [1991] OJ L206/19.
3 Directive 89/391 [1989] OJ L183/1.
4 Directive 99/70 [1999] OJ L175/43.
5 Art 2(1).
6 Art 1(2).
7 Art 3.
8 Art 4.

C. The Proposed Directive on Working Conditions for Temporary Workers

The main objective of the Commission's proposal for a directive on working **21.08** conditions for temporary workers[9] is to reduce disparities between the Member States with respect to the legal status of temporary workers and at the same time to introduce common minimum standards with respect both to the agency which engages them in the first place and the user undertaking in which they are placed. A further objective is to minimize the prohibition on the use of temporary workers in certain types of employment. Over 3 million workers within the EU are temporary agency workers and the numbers are increasing.[10] The greatest proportion of temporary agency workers are low-skilled, but temporary agencies also supply highly skilled technical and professional workers. The working conditions of agency workers are typically inferior in terms of pay, holiday entitlement, training, and career development opportunities to those of non-agency workers. The proposed directive will bring to an end the discriminatory treatment of temporary agency workers within the labour market and ensure that they have equal treatment with permanent workers from day one in terms of pay, maternity leave, and leave entitlement.

D. Scope

The proposed directive applies to workers with a contract of employment or **21.09** an employment relationship with a temporary agency, who are posted to user undertakings to work there on a temporary basis.[11] It envisages being applied to public and private undertakings engaged in economic activities, whether or not they are operating for gain, which are temporary agencies or user undertakings.[12] The directive would permit Member States, after consultation with the social partners, to provide that it is not to apply to employment contracts or relationships concluded with specific or publicly funded vocational training, integration, or retaining programmes.[13] This mirrors the derogations permitted by the Fixed-Term Employment Directive discussed in Chapter 20.

---

[9] COM (2002) 701 Final, as amended by COM (2002) 149 Final.
[10] EC Commission Memo/08/646 of 22 October 2008.
[11] Art 1(1).
[12] Art 1(2).
[13] Art 1(3).

21.10 A temporary worker is defined as a person with a contract of employment or an employment relationship with a temporary agency with a view to being posted to user undertakings to work temporarily under their supervision.[14]

21.11 A temporary agency is one which concludes contracts of employment or employment relationships with temporary workers in order to post them to user undertakings to work there temporarily under their supervision.[15]

21.12 User undertaking means a natural or legal person for whom and under whose supervision a temporary worker works temporarily.[16]

E. Non-discrimination

21.13 The proposed directive put forward by the Commission in 2002 required that the basic working and employment conditions of temporary workers shall be '. . . at least those that would apply if they had been recruited directly by that enterprise to occupy the same job'.[17] These include rules relating to the protection of pregnant women, nursing mothers, and the protection of young people and children; equal treatment between men and women; and any measures to combat discrimination on grounds of sex, race or ethnic origin, religion, beliefs, disabilities, age, or sexual orientation. The Member States have now agreed that equal treatment should be available as from day one for temporary agency workers in terms of pay and maternity leave. It will be possible to derogate from this requirement through collective agreements and agreements made between the social partners at national level.

21.14 Equal treatment with respect to pay need not apply where temporary workers are paid by their agency in between postings.[18] Member States can derogate from the requirement of equal treatment with respect to pay where the assignment with the user undertaking can be accomplished in less than six weeks.[19] Member States would have liked to have discretion to suspend the right to equal treatment for assignments of longer than six weeks. This has not been agreed to.

21.15 Temporary workers must be given access to facilities in the user undertaking such as canteens, child care, and transport under the same conditions as workers

---

[14] Art 3(1)(b).
[15] Art 3(1)(d).
[16] Art 3(1)(e).
[17] Art 5.
[18] Art 5(1).
[19] Art 5(2).

employed directly by the undertaking.[20] Member States have to improve temporary agency workers' access to training and child care facilities in periods between their assignments so as to increase their employability.

F. Access to Permanent Employment

Temporary workers must be informed of vacant posts at the user undertaking. **21.16** Clauses in the contract between the temporary undertaking and the workers prohibiting them from concluding contracts of employment or employment relationships with the user undertakings are prohibited.[21] Temporary agencies cannot charge fees to workers for arranging for them to be recruited by the user undertaking or for concluding a contract of employment or an employment relationship with a user undertaking after carrying out a posting in that undertaking.[22]

---

[20] Art 6(4).
[21] Art 6(2).
[22] Art 6(3).

22

WORKING TIME

A. Introduction

Directive 2003/88 concerning certain aspects of the organization of working **22.01** time[1] lays down detailed rules in relation to almost every aspect of working time, in particular:

(a) minimum periods of annual leave, weekly rest, and daily rest;
(b) breaks during working time;
(c) maximum weekly working time;
(d) certain aspects of night work, shift work, and work patterns.[2]

---

[1] [2003] OJ L299/9.
[2] Art 1(2).

22.02 The origins of the Directive can be traced back to the Community Charter on the Fundamental Social Rights of Workers, which provides that workers should enjoy satisfactory health and safety conditions in their working environment and must have the right, inter alia, to a weekly rest period.[3]

22.03 The original Directive 93/104,[4] as amended by Directive 2000/34,[5] was repealed and replaced by Directive 2003/88[6] (the 'Directive'). The latter is primarily a consolidation measure. Further amendments to Directive 2003/88 have been proposed,[7] following a review of aspects of Directive 93/104 as prescribed by that Directive,[8] and in the light of the case law of the ECJ on 'on-call' periods of employment which is discussed below. Political agreement was reached on these proposals on 10 June 2008.

22.04 The legal basis for the Directive is Article 137(2) of the EC Treaty, which empowers the Community to support and complement the activities of the Member States with a view to improving the working environment to promote workers' health and safety. It was adopted within the framework of Directive 89/391 on the health and safety of workers at work (the 'Framework Health and Safety Directive').[9] The Preamble to the Directive emphasizes that its essential objective is the protection of the health and safety of workers.[10]

22.05 In *United Kingdom v Council*[11] the United Kingdom sought annulment of Directive 93/114 on the ground, inter alia, that it should have been adopted on the basis of Article 100 (now Article 94) or Article 235 (now Article 308), both of which require a unanimous vote within the Council, as opposed to Article 118a (now Article 137), under which measures can be adopted by a qualified majority vote.[12] Essentially it argued that the Directive was not concerned

---

[3] Points 8 and 19.

[4] Council Directive 93/104 concerning certain aspects of the organization of working time ([1993] OJ L307/18).

[5] Directive 2000/34 of the European Parliament and Council amending Council Directive 93/104 ([2000] OJ L195/41).

[6] [2003] OJ L299/9.

[7] COM (2005) 246 Final of 31 May 2005.

[8] Communication concerning the re-examination of Directive 93/104 concerning certain aspects of the organization of working time COM (2003) Final.

[9] Directive 89/391 on the introduction of measures to encourage improvements in the health and safety of workers at work ([1989] OJ L183/1).

[10] Preamble, Recitals 3 and 4.

[11] Case C-84/94 [1996] ECR I–5755.

[12] If this were the case the Directive would probably not have been adopted since the United Kingdom in all likelihood would have voted against it, at least in the form in which it was finally adopted.

with health and safety, with the result that Article 137(2) was an inappropriate legal basis.

Three main arguments were advanced before the Court, none of which was **22.06** accepted. The first argument contended that Article 137 only permitted the adoption of directives which have a genuine and objective link to the 'health and safety' of workers:

> That does not apply to measures concerning, in particular, weekly working time, paid annual leave and rest periods, whose connection with the health and safety of workers is too tenuous, That interpretation is borne out by the expression 'working environment' used in Article 118a which implies that directives based on that provision must be concerned only with the physical conditions and risks at the workplace.[13]

In refuting this argument the Court held that Article 137 should be interpreted **22.07** broadly as embracing all aspects of the health and safety of workers in the working environment, including certain aspects of the organization of working time. The Court derived support for this conclusion in the Preamble to the Constitution of the World Health Organization whose membership included all the Member States:

> Health is there defined as a state of complete physical, mental and social well-being that does not consist only in the absence of illness or infirmity.[14]

The second argument advanced by the United Kingdom was to the effect that the **22.08** Article 137(2) provided for the adoption of 'minimum requirements' for gradual implementation. Harmonization measures should therefore be at a level acceptable to all Member States and constitute a 'minimum benchmark'.[15] The Court disagreed, ruling that the term 'minimum requirements' was not determinative of the extent of action required to achieve a particular objective but simply an indication that the Member States were authorized to adopt more stringent measures than those laid down in the Directive.

The third argument went to the Court's powers of review of the legality of **22.09** Community measures and had implications wider than the resolution of the particular case in hand. The United Kingdom maintained that Article 137 did not authorize the adoption of directives on health and safety in a generalized, unspecific, and unscientific manner. It pointed to the requirement of a risk

---

[13] Note 11 Judgment para 13.
[14] Note 11 Judgment para 15.
[15] Note 11 Judgment para 16.

assessment in Directive 89/391[16] on the safety and health of workers. The Court paid little attention to this point, dismissing it somewhat brusquely:

> ... it is not the function of the Court to review the expediency of measures adopted by the legislature. The review exercised under Article 173 must be limited to the legality of the disputed measure.[17]

22.10 This statement is somewhat questionable. The control of the legality of a measure may, and indeed often does, necessitate the verification of the facts and scientific evidence alleged to satisfy the legal basis for its adoption. It may be difficult on the face of a piece of legislation to judge whether it actually is of the nature that it professes to be. The United Kingdom's argument did not simply go the expediency of any measure but to its lawfulness as a measure concerned with the concept of 'health and safety'. Given that it was adopted under the aegis of the Framework Health and Safety Directive, which requires a risk assessment, this should have been carried out. The Court chose to ignore this apparently valid point, preferring instead to accept at face value that the measure was concerned with health and safety simply because it was stated to be so in its preamble.

22.11 In sum the Court rejected the application holding that Article 137 was the proper legal basis for the Directive:

> where the principal aim of the measure in question is the protection of the health and safety of workers, Article 118a must be used ...[18]
>
> Since ... in terms of its aim and content the directive has as its principal objective the protection of the health and safety of workers ... neither Article 100 nor 100a could have constituted the appropriate legal basis for its adoption.[19]

B. Working Time

22.12 The concept of working time is defined as any period during which the worker is at the employer's disposal and carrying out his activity or duties in accordance with national law and practice.[20] A rest period is any period which is not working time.[21] The concept of 'rest' must be expressed in units of time, ie in

---

[16] [1989] OJ L183/1.
[17] Note 11 Judgment para 23.
[18] Note 11 Judgment para 23.
[19] Note 11 Judgment para 45.
[20] Art 2(1).
[21] Art 2(2).

days, hours, and/or fractions thereof.[22] The concepts of 'working time' and 'rest time' are mutually exclusive; time falls into either one category or another.

'Working time' and 'rest periods' are concepts of Community law which must be **22.13** defined in accordance with objective characteristics by reference to the scheme and purpose of the Directive. They may not be interpreted in accordance with national law since otherwise the full effectiveness of the Directive and the uniform application of its core concepts in the Member States would be prejudiced:[23]

> ... the concepts of 'working time' and 'rest period' within the meaning of Directive 93/104 may not be interpreted in accordance with the requirements of the various legislations of the Member States but constitute concepts of Community law which must be defined in accordance with objective characteristics by reference to the scheme and purpose of the directive, intended to improve workers' living and working conditions. Only such an interpretation is capable of securing full effectiveness for that directive and uniform application of those concepts in all the Member States . . .[24]

C. Scope of Application

As a general rule the Directive is applicable to all sectors of activity both public **22.14** and private, within the meaning of Article 2 of the Framework Health and Safety Directive. Article 2 is drafted in broad terms, and the Directive must be interpreted accordingly.

It reads: **22.15**

1. This Directive shall apply to all sectors of activity, both public and private (industrial, agricultural, commercial, administrative, service, educational, cultural, leisure, etc)
2. This Directive shall not be applicable where characteristics peculiar to certain specific public service activities, such as the armed forces or the police or to certain activities in the civil protection services inevitably conflict with it.

The Directive applies to all employees, whether their term of employment is of **22.16** indefinite duration or for a fixed term in the public and private sectors.[25]

There are a number of exceptions laid down in the Directive itself and Member **22.17** States are further allowed, at their discretion, to derogate from certain specified

---

[22] Directive 2003/88 Preamble Recital 5.
[23] Case C-151/02 *Jaeger* [2002] ECR I–8389; Case C-14/04 *Dellas* [2005] ECR I–10253; Case C-437/05 *Vorel* [2007] ECR I–331.
[24] *Dellas* note 23 Judgment para 44.
[25] Art 2(3).

provisions of the Directive. The exceptions and permissible derogations all relate to sectors of activity or particular types of employment to which the application of the hard and fast rules of the Directive would be inappropriate or simply unworkable, notably those referred to in Article 2(1) of the Framework Health and Safety Directive set out above. Such exceptions and derogations must be interpreted in accordance with the principle of proportionality: their scope must be limited to what is strictly necessary to safeguard the interests which those exclusions are intended to protect.[26]

22.18 The Directive applies without prejudice to national provisions which are more favourable to the worker.[27] Where there are provisions in national law which give more generous treatment to the worker than that required by the Directive, compliance with the Directive must be ascertained solely by reference to the standards prescribed by the Directive.[28]

D. Exceptions

(1) Seafarers

22.19 One group of workers is specifically excluded from the Directive—seafarers.[29] Seafarers are defined by reference to Directive 1999/63 on the Agreement on the organization of working time of seafarers.[30] A seafarer is described in that Agreement as:

> . . . any person who is employed or engaged in any capacity on board a seagoing ship to which the Agreement applies.[31]

22.20 The Agreement applies to all sea-going ships, whether publicly or privately owned, which are registered in the territory of a Member State and which are ordinarily engaged in commercial maritime operations.[32]

22.21 Workers on board sea-going fishing vessels are the subject of a number of specific provisions in the Directive designed to give them a degree of protection compatible with their working conditions.

---

[26] Case C-151/02 *Jaeger* note 23 Judgment para 89; Joined Cases C-397/01 to C-403/01 *Pfeiffer* [2004] ECR I–8835 Judgment para 67.
[27] Art 15.
[28] Case C-14/04 *Dellas* note 23 Judgment at para 44.
[29] Art 3.
[30] [1999] OJ L167/33.
[31] Agreement Cl 2(c).
[32] Agreement Cl 1(i).

(2) Workers on board sea-going vessels

Workers on board sea-going fishing vessels flying the flag of a Member State are **22.22** removed from the application of many of the general provisions of the Directive, but are made subject to a number of specific provisions deemed to be compatible with the demands of their trade and at the same time providing them with adequate protection.

The provisions relating to daily rest periods (Article 3), breaks during the work- **22.23** ing day (Article 4), weekly rest periods (Article 5), maximum weekly working time (Article 6), and length of night work (Article 8) are not applicable to such workers.[33] However, Member States must take steps to ensure that any worker on board a sea-going fishing vessel flying the flag of a Member State is entitled to adequate rest and to limit the number of working hours to 48 a week on average calculated over a reference period not exceeding 12 months.[34] The limits of hours of work and rest are either:

- maximum hours or work which shall not exceed: (i) 14 hours in any 24-hour period, and (ii) 72 hours in any seven-day period;
- minimum hours of rest shall not be less than (i) 10 hours in any 24-hour period; and (ii) 77 hours in any seven-day period.[35]

Hours of rest may be divided into no more than two periods, one of which must **22.24** be at least six hours in length, and the interval between consecutive periods of rest shall not exceed 14 hours.[36]

The master of a sea-going fishing vessel has the right to require workers on **22.25** board it to perform any hours of work necessary for the immediate safety of the vessel, person on board, or cargo, or for the purpose of giving assistance to other vessels or persons in distress at sea.[37]

Workers on board sea-going fishing vessels for which national legislation or **22.26** practice forbids those vessels from operating in a specific period of the calendar year exceeding one month, may be required to take annual leave during that month.[38]

---

[33] Art 21(1).
[34] Art 21(1).
[35] Art 21(3).
[36] Art 21(4).
[37] Art 21(6).
[38] Art 21(7).

(3) Specific Community measures

22.27 The Directive is not applicable where there are more specific provisions in EC law relating to the organization of working time for certain occupations or occupational activities.[39] Such directives have been adopted in the case of seafarers, mobile transport workers, and air transport workers. They are discussed below at Section J.

(4) Mobile workers/offshore workers

22.28 Two further groups are exempt from the application of specific provisions of the Directive. The provisions relating to daily rest periods (Article 3), breaks during the working day (Article 4), weekly rest periods (Article 5), length of night work (Article 8) are not applicable to mobile workers and those doing offshore work.

22.29 A mobile worker is any worker employed as a member of travelling or flying personnel by an undertaking which operates transport services for passengers for passengers or goods by road, rail, or inland waterway.[40]

22.30 Offshore work means work performed mainly on or from offshore installations (including drilling rigs) directly or indirectly in connection with the exploration, extraction, or exploitation of mineral resources, including hydrocarbons and diving in connection with such activities, whether performed from an offshore installation or vessels.[41]

(5) Transport workers

22.31 Transport workers are excluded from the Directive.[42]

22.32 In *Bowden and Others,*[43] the Court held that the transport sector was excluded from the Directive on the grounds that a Community regulatory framework already existed in that sector which laid down specific rules for the organization of working time taking into account the characteristics of the sector. The wording of the Directive made it clear that all workers employed in the road transport sector, including office workers were excluded from the scope of the Directive:

> Pursuant to Article 1(3) the Directive shall apply to all sectors of activity . . . with the exception of air, rail, road, sea, inland waterway and lake transport, sea fishing, other work at sea and activities of doctors in training . . .

---

[39] Art 1(3); Art 14.
[40] Art 2(7).
[41] Art 2(8).
[42] Art 1(3).
[43] Case C-133/00 [2001] ECR I–7031.

It is clear that, by referring to 'air, rail, road, sea, inland waterway and lake transport', the Community legislature indicated that it was taking account of those sectors of activity as a whole, whereas in the case of 'other work at sea' and the 'activities of doctors in training' it chose to refer precisely to those specific activities as such. Thus, the exclusion of the road transport sector in particular extends to all workers in that sector.[44]

The issue of the applicability of the Directive to emergency medical services arose in *Pfeiffer*.[45] The activity in that case consisted in using a vehicle to reach the patient, administering emergency help, and attending him on the journey to hospital. The ECJ held that the Directive was applicable to such an activity for three reasons: (i) although the transport sector was excluded from the scope of the Directive on the grounds that a Community regulatory framework already existed in that sector, that legislation did not apply to transport for emergencies or assistance; (ii) ambulance services, by virtue of Article 17(2), can be the subject of a derogation from certain specific provisions of the Directive; this provision would be otiose if such services were excluded from the scope of application of the entirety of the Directive and (iii) the main purpose of the emergency medical services was to provide initial medical treatment to persons who were ill or injured. Whilst that activity included the use of an emergency vehicle for the transport of the patient to hospital, it was not an 'operation relating to the road transport sector'.[46] Since the Directive does not apply to transport for emergencies or assistance the concept of 'road transport' in the Directive does not extend to emergency medical services the main purpose of which is to provide initial treatment to a person who is ill or injured. **22.33**

E. Derogations

Two types of derogation are permitted. Member States can derogate from the provisions relating to daily rest periods (Article 3), breaks during the working day (Article 4), weekly rest periods (Article 5), maximum weekly working time (Article 6), length of night work (Article 8), reference periods to be used in calculating rest time (Article 16), or in respect of specific activities where the duration of work is not measured or can be determined by workers themselves.[47] Such activities include those of managing executives or other persons with **22.34**

---

[44] Ibid Judgment paras 38 and 39.
[45] Joined Cases C-397/01 to C-403/01 *Pfeiffer* note 26 Judgment paras 68–70.
[46] Ibid Judgment para 70.
[47] Art 17.

autonomous decision-making powers, family workers, or workers officiating at religious ceremonies in churches and religious communities.[48]

22.35 In *Commission v United Kingdom*[49] the Count condemned the United Kingdom for extending the derogation to workers whose working time was only partially measured, predetermined, or determined by the worker. The derogation provided for in Article 17(1) applied only to workers whose working time, as a whole, is not measured or pre-determined but can only be determined by the worker himself. The interpretation placed on that provision by the United Kingdom was too broad, encompassing groups of workers who should have been regarded as subject to the full rigours of the Directive.

22.36 Further derogations can be made by means of laws, regulations, or administrative provisions or by collective agreements in respect of seven particular types of employment:[50]

    (a) activities where the worker's place of work and his place of residence are distant from one another, including offshore workers or where a worker has a number of places of work all distant from one another;

    (b) security and surveillance activities requiring a permanent presence in order to protect property or persons;

    (c) activities involving the need for continuity of service or production such as services relating to care provided by hospitals or other similar establishments; dock or airport workers; press, radio, television, cinematographic production, postal or telecommunications services, ambulance, fire and civil protection services; gas, water, and electricity production, transmission and distribution of household refuse collective and incineration plants; industries where work cannot be interrupted on technical grounds; research and development activities; agriculture; workers concerned with the carriage of passengers on regular urban transport services;

    (d) where there is a foreseeable surge in activity particularly in agriculture, tourism, or the postal services;

    (e) in the case of a person working in railway transport whose activities are intermittent, who spends time working on board trains or whose activities are linked to transport timetables and to ensuring the continuity and regularity of traffic;

---

[48] Art 17(1).
[49] Case C-484/04 [2006] ECR I-7471.
[50] Art 17(3).

(f) in case of accident or imminent risk of accident;

(g) in the circumstances set out in Article 5(4) of Directive 89/391.[51]

Derogations in respect of the above-mentioned types of employment are sub- **22.37**
ject to the obligation to grant the workers concerned equivalent periods of
compensatory rest periods or, in exceptional cases, where this is not possible,
workers must be afforded appropriate protection.[52]

F. Doctors

The Directive applies to doctors, but its application can be modified in the light **22.38**
of their particular working conditions. As mentioned above, Article 17(3)(c)
allows Member States to derogate from certain provisions of the Directive in the
case of activities involving the need for continuity of service in the reception,
treatment, and/or care provided by hospitals and similar institutions.

The ECJ confirmed the application of the Directive with respect to doctors' **22.39**
employment in *Simap v Conselleria de Sanidad y Consumo de la Generalidad
Valenciana*.[53] The case arose out of proceedings brought in Spain by the Union
of Doctors in the Public Health Service, acting on behalf of staff providing
primary care at health centres in the Valencia region. They sought a declaration
on a number of aspects of the working time of doctors in such centres. The case
was referred by the national tribunal to the ECJ which was asked to rule on two
issues:

(i) whether the activities of doctors working in primary health care centres was
within the scope of the Framework Directive on Health and Safety and the
Directive;

(ii) the status of on-call duty.

On the first question, the Court held that staff in primary health care centres were **22.40**
within the scope of the Framework Health and Safety Directive, which is the
point of reference for the scope of the Directive. Article 1 of that Directive
states that it applies to all sectors of activity both public and private. However
Article 2(2) provides that the Directive may not apply where characteristics

---

[51] Article 5(4) provides: 'This Directive does not restrict the option of the Member States
to provide for the exclusion or the limitation of employer's responsibility where occurrences are
due to unusual and unforeseeable circumstances, beyond the employer's control or exceptional
events, the consequences of which could not have been avoided despite the exercise of due care.'

[52] Art 17(2).

[53] Case C-303/98 [2000] ECR I–7963.

peculiar to specific public service activities, such as the armed forces or the police, or to certain activities in the civil protection services, which inevitably conflict with it. These public service activities are intended to uphold public order and security, which are essential for the proper functioning of society. It was clear that, under normal circumstances, the work of the primary care team could not be assimilated to such activities. It therefore fell within the scope of the Directive.

G. Doctors in Training

22.41 Doctors in training were excluded from the application of the original Directive. They were brought within the scope of its application by Directive 2000/34.[54] However, with respect to maximum weekly working time, there is a transitional period which will terminate on 1 August 2009, but which may be further extended by up to two years where Member States have difficulties in meeting their responsibilities with respect to the organization and delivery of medical care services. A further period of one year may be allowed where Member States have 'special difficulties' in meeting their responsibilities to organize and deliver medical care and health services.

22.42 The extension of the transitional period is subject to a number of procedural requirements. Any extension must be notified to the Commission which will give an opinion on it. If the Member State does not accept the Commission's opinion it must give the reasons why it does not. The request for the extension, the Commission's opinion on it, and any reasons for refusing to accept it are required to be published in the Official Journal and notified to the European Parliament.[55]

22.43 The employer must consult with representatives of the employees with a view to reaching an agreement on the arrangements to operate during the transitional period. Whilst the parties are free as to the matters they address in that agreement the Directive indicates (but does not appear to require) that it may cover (i) the average number of weekly hours of work during the transitional period; (ii) the measures to be adopted to reduce weekly working hours to an average of 48 hours by the end of the transitional period.

22.44 The discretion of Member States with respect to the required number of weekly working hours of doctors in training may be required to perform is limited

---

[54] [2000] OJ L195/41.
[55] Art 17(5).

during the transitional period. In no case can the number of weekly working hours exceed 58 during the first three years of the transitional period or an average of 56 for the following two years and an average of 52 hours for the remainder of the transitional period.[56]

H. On-call Duty

(1) *Simap*

The second issue on which the Court was asked to rule in *Simap*[57] was the status, under the Directive on on-call duty, that is periods of time when employees are required to be present at their workplace (in *Simap* this was the health centre) but not necessarily required to work or to be contactable, if not physically present at the workplace. How was such duty to be classified: working time or rest time or did it embrace both?   **22.45**

The Court began its analysis by looking at the definition of working time in the Directive and contrasted that with rest periods, ruling that the two are mutually exclusive: time is either working time or rest time. An employee's time is to be classified as working time when he is at his employer's disposal and carrying out his activity or duties. Doctors on call are obliged to be present and available at the workplace with a view to providing their professional services. They are therefore to be regarded as 'working' and such on-call periods are 'working time'. By contrast, where doctors have to be contactable without being required to be present at the workplace they 'may manage their time with few constraints and pursue their own interests'.[58] In those circumstances only time linked to the provision of primary health care services must be regarded as working time, and that work is 'shift work' within the meaning of Article 2(5) of the Directive. Doctors in primary health care teams who are regularly on call at night are not night workers by virtue of Article 2(4)(b) of the Directive but would be regarded as such if an agreement under Article 2(4)(b) chose to treat them as such.   **22.46**

(2) *Jaeger*

Jaeger[59] raised the issue of whether on-call duty should be considered in its entirety as working time, even if the person concerned does not in fact perform professional duties but is authorized to sleep during the on-call period.   **22.47**

---

[56] Art 17(5).
[57] Note 53.
[58] SIMAP Judgment para 50.
[59] Case C-151/02, note 23.

22.48 The Court held that whether doctors performing on call duty could rest or sleep was immaterial. Periods of professional inactivity of that kind were an inherent aspect of on-call duty:

> ... Directive 93/104 must be interpreted as meaning that a period of duty spent by a doctor on call ... where presence in the hospital is required must be regarded as constituting in its entirety as working time for the purposes of the Directive, even though the person concerned is permitted to rest at his place of work during the period when his services are not required, with the result that the Directive precludes a Member State's legislation which classifies as a rest period an employee's period of inactivity in the context of such on-call duty.[60]

22.49 The Court went on to hold that the decisive factor in considering whether the characteristic features of the concept of 'working time' were present in the case of time spent on on-call duty by doctors in the hospital itself, is that they are required to be present at the place determined by their employer in order to be able to provide services immediately in case of need. Those obligations make it impossible for the doctors concerned to choose the place where they stay during on-call periods and therefore these periods must be regarded as coming within the ambit of the performance of their duty.

(3) *Dellas*

22.50 *Dellas*[61] concerned the lawfulness of a system of calculating hours of work during on-call periods in France. The system governed the calculation of working hours by employers in the case of night duty during which staff were not continually called upon to work, or had periods of inactivity intercepted by periods of work. The legislation in question was intended to create a special method of calculating actual work time for the purposes, inter alia, of assessing the rules on remuneration and overtime, taking into account the intermittent nature of the activity which included periods of non-activity during the hours in question. The upshot of all this was that not all hours spent on on-call duty were considered as time worked. The system of equivalence established a 3 to 1 ratio for the first nine hours followed by a 2 to 1 ratio for subsequent hours between the hours of presence and working hours actually counted. The Court found this system to be incompatible with the Directive:

> ... Directive 93/104 does not provide for an intermediate category between working time and rest periods, and second, that the intensity of the work done by the employee and his actual output are not among the characteristic elements of the concept of 'working time' within the meaning of that directive.[62]

---

[60] Ibid Judgment para 61.
[61] Note 23.
[62] Note 23 Judgment para 43.

Confirming *Simap*[63] and *Jaeger*[64] the Court held that on-call duty performed by **22.51** a worker required to be physically present on the employer's premises must be regarded in its entirety as working time within the meaning of the Directive, regardless of the work actually done by the person concerned during on-call duty. The fact that on-call includes some periods of inactivity is thus completely irrelevant.

(4) *Vorel*

The practical effect of the above case law which requires periods of on-call duty **22.52** to be regarded as working time has been thrown into question by the case of *Vorel*,[65] judgment in which was handed down on 11 January 2007. Dr Vorel was employed on the basis of a permanent contract in a hospital in the Czech Republic. The Employment Code of the Czech Republic drew a distinction between working time, rest periods, and on-call duty. Working time was defined as 'the period during which the employee is required to perform work for the employer', rest periods were periods which are not working time and on-call duty was specified to be 'the period during which the employee is available to work pursuant to a contract of employment which has to be performed, in an emergency, outside normal working hours'.

Where work was performed during on-call duty it was considered to be working **22.53** time and paid accordingly. Where no work was actually performed it was remunerated according to a fixed tariff the rates of which were lower than normal pay. Dr Vorel brought a claim against his employer for a supplement to his salary, representing the difference between the remuneration which was due to him for on-call duty under the Czech Employment Code and the salary which would have been paid if those services had been recognized as working time payable at the agreed rate of remuneration, for work done. He relied on *Jaegar*,[66] from which he concluded that his periods of on-call duty should be classified as working time and remunerated in the same way as if work had really been performed. His employer argued that on-call duty where no work is performed is not regarded as working time under Czech law but did give rise to some financial compensation.

On a reference for a preliminary ruling, the Court held that the Directive **22.54** did not provide for any intermediate category between working time and rest periods, nor were the intensity of work done by the employee or his output

---

[63] Note 53.
[64] Note 23.
[65] Note 23.
[66] Note 23.

among the defining characteristics of 'working time'. Given that the concepts of 'working time' and 'rest periods' were concepts of Community law, it followed that on-call duty was to be regarded as 'working time' regardless of the work actually done during that time. The Court went on to hold that the Directive was limited to regulating aspects of the organization of working time, such as length of working hours and rest periods, but it excluded the remuneration of working time.

22.55   It held that *Jaegar*,[67] upon which Dr Vorel placed reliance:

> . . . concerned only aspects of labour law in connection with on-call periods and not the conditions for remunerating those periods.[68]

22.56   The Court therefore concluded:

> Directive 93/104 and 2003/88 do not prevent a Member State applying legislation on the remuneration of workers and concerning on call duties performed by them at the workplace which makes a distinction between the treatment of periods in the course of which work is actually done and those during which no actual work is done, provided that such a system wholly guarantees the practical effect of the rights conferred on workers by the said directives in order to ensure the effective protection of their health and safety.[69]

22.57   From *Vorel* we may conclude that on-call duty falls within the scope of the Directive for the purposes of all aspects of employment relative to the scope of application of the Directive, such as hours of work, rest periods, and breaks, but the level of remuneration for such duty is left to the discretion of the Member States.

22.58   Whilst it true that the Directive is not concerned with remuneration, nor indeed could it be, given that Article 137(5) expressly excludes 'pay' from its scope, at the same time the principle of effectiveness requires that any regulation of remuneration for on-call duty should not render rights granted by the Directive completely devoid of practical effect. This would appear to imply that whilst periods of on-call duty in which no work was required to be performed can be remunerated at a rate different from periods of on-call duty where work is required to be performed, that rate must not be such as to render the provisions of the Directive nugatory which would be the case, for example if no remuneration or a derisory sum were paid for such on-call periods.

[67] Note 23.
[68] Note 23 Judgment para 33.
[69] Vorel note 23 Judgment para 35.

I. Organization of Working Time

The Directive lays down detailed rules on daily and weekly rest periods, maxi-   **22.59**
mum weekly working hours, annual leave, night work, and shift work.

(1) Daily rest

Workers are entitled to a minimum rest period of 11 consecutive hours in respect   **22.60**
of every 24-hour period.[70]

(2) Weekly rest periods

Every worker is entitled to a minimum uninterrupted rest period of 24 hours   **22.61**
in every seven-day period, in addition to the prescribed 11 hours' daily rest
period. However, the total rest period may be confined to 24 hours where objective technical or work organization conditions so require.[71]

A rest period is defined as any period which is not working time.[72] Working time   **22.62**
is any period during which the worker is working, at his employer's disposal,
and carrying out his activity or duties.[73]

In *Commission v United Kingdom*[74] the Court held that workers must be in a   **22.63**
position to take the rest periods due to them and are not, for example, deterred
from doing so by constraints within the workplace:

> . . . in the present case by restricting the obligations on employers as regards the
> workers' right to actually benefit from the minimum rest periods . . . and letting it be
> understood that, while they cannot prevent those rest periods from being taken
> by the workers, they are under no obligation to ensure that the latter are actually able
> to exercise such a right, the guidelines are clearly liable to render the rights enshrined
> in Articles 3 and 5 of that directive meaningless and incompatible with the objective
> of the directive, in which minimum rest periods are considered essential for the
> protection of worker's health and safety.[75]

---

[70] Art 3.
[71] Art 5.
[72] Art 2(2).
[73] Art 2(1).
[74] Case C-484/04 [2006] ECR I–7471.
[75] Ibid Judgment para 44 Advocate General Kokott in para 69 of her Opinion gave some examples of how workers could be deterred from taking rest periods.
   '. . . it is for the employer actively to see to it that an atmosphere is created in a firm in which the
minimum rest periods prescribed by Community law are . . . effectively observed. There is no doubt
that this first presupposes that within the organization of the firm appropriate work and rest periods
are actually scheduled. In addition it must, however, be a matter of course within a business, in
practice as well, that workers' rights to rest periods not only exist on paper but can effectively be

22.64   At the same time, the Court held, compliance with the provisions of the Directive should not, as a general rule, extend to requiring an employer to force his workers to claim the rest periods due to them.[76]

22.65   The employer's obligation is to make possible, in practical terms, the taking of rest periods from the point of view both of the organization of working time and the culture of the work environment.

(3)   Breaks

22.66   Where a working day is longer than six hours, workers are entitled to rest breaks, the details of which must be prescribed by collective agreement, agreement between the two sides of industry, or national legislation.[77] It is not clear whether the duration of these rest breaks is included in the calculation of working time.

(4)   Maximum weekly working time

22.67   Periods of weekly working time must be limited by law, collective agreement, or agreement between the two sides of industry and must not, in the event, exceed 48 hours.[78] This includes overtime.

22.68   In order to calculate the average working week, Member States may apply a reference period not exceeding four months. Periods of paid leave or sick leave may not be included in the calculation.[79]

22.69   Member States have the option (the 'opt out') not to apply the rules on maximum weekly working time, provided:

- no employer requires a worker to work more than 48 hours over a seven-day period, calculated as an average of a reference period not exceeding four months, unless he has first obtained the worker's agreement to perform such work;
- no worker is subject to any detriment by his employer because he is not willing to give his agreement to perform such working hours;
- the employer keeps up-to-date records of all workers who carry out such work;

---

observed. In particular, no de facto pressure should arise which may deter workers from actually taking their rest periods. In that regard it is irrelevant whether such pressure derives from the employer—for example through performance targets set by him—or from the fact that some of the employees do not use up their rest periods due to them, and therefore a kind of group pressure arises for other workers to do the same.'

[76] Note 74 Judgment para 43.
[77] Art 4.
[78] Art 6.
[79] Art 16(1).

- the records are placed at the disposal of the competent authorities which may prohibit or restrict the possibility of exceeding the maximum weekly working hours in the interests of the health and safety of the workers;
- the employer must provide the competent authorities, at their request, with information on cases in which agreement has been given to workers to perform work exceeding 48 hours over a period of seven days calculated as an average of a reference period not exceeding four months.[80]

The decision not to be covered by the maximum weekly working time must be taken by the worker himself. In *Simap*[81] the Court held consent given by trade union representatives in the context of a collective or other agreement is not equivalent to that given by the worker himself. **22.70**

The worker's agreement must be free and informed. Pressure may not be put on him to sign the agreement and he must not be prejudiced if he does not sign. The conditions set out in the Directive for the use of the opt out are designed to achieve this objective.[82] **22.71**

The Commission was required to appraise the working of this opt out within seven years of the adoption of the Directive, ie 23 November 2000. It published its review on 1 December 2000.[83] At that time only the United Kingdom had made general use of the possibility of the opt out. **22.72**

Other Member States either did not avail themselves at all of the opt out or did so only in the case of specific sectors, notably the health care services and hotel and catering. There was a noticeable increase in the use of the opt out in the health care sector after the judgment of the ECJ in *Simap*[84] prompting the observation that 'this may undermine the very health and safety objective the Court is seeking to uphold'.[85] **22.73**

---

[80] Art 22.

[81] Note 53.

[82] Joined Cases C-397/01 and C-403/01 *Pfeiffer* note 26 Advocate General Colomer: 'It should not be forgotten that the prime objective of the Directive is to ensure the health and safety of workers who constitute the most vulnerable part of the employment relationship. In order specifically to prevent the employer from achieving, by subterfuge or through intimidation, a situation whereby the employee renounces the right of his weekly working time not to exceed the maximum laid down this express manifestation of consent is surrounded by a series of guarantees to ensure that the interested party suffers no harm if he refuses to work more than 48 hours per week under the terms mentioned, that the employer keeps up to date records of employees carrying out such work where hours exceed the weekly maximum that the records in question are made available to the competent authorities, and that the entrepreneur provides to the competent authorities, at their request, information relating to agreements given by the workers.'

[83] COM (2000) 786 Final.

[84] Note 53.

[85] Kenner: 'Re-evaluating the concept of Working Time: An analysis of recent case law' (2004) 35 ILJ 588 at 599.

22.74 Prior to the amendment of the original Directive by Directive 2000/34, the weekly rest period was obliged, in principle, to include Sunday.[86] This requirement was not binding as the Preamble to the Directive indicated.[87] Nevertheless, the ECJ held it to be invalid in *United Kingdom v Council*:[88]

> ... the Council has failed to explain why Sunday, a weekly rest day, is more closely connected with the health and safety of workers than any other day of the week. In those circumstances ... the second sentence of Article 5, which is severable, from the other provision of the Directive must be annulled.[89]

(5) Annual leave

22.75 The Directive provides for a minimum of four weeks' annual paid leave.[90] It is unclear whether this period is inclusive or exclusive of public holidays.

22.76 The Court has noted that this right to four weeks' annual paid leave is a 'particularly important principle of Community law'.[91] It is enshrined in both the Community Charter of Fundamental Social Rights of Workers[92] and the Charter of Fundamental Rights of the European Union.[93]

22.77 Given that the purpose of Article 7 is to ensure that annual leave is actually taken in the interests of the health and safety of the worker, it cannot be replaced by the payment of an allowance in lieu, except where the employment relationship has terminated.[94] Since no derogation is allowed from this provision it is, therefore, immaterial whether financial compensation for annual leave is or is not based upon a contractual arrangement between the parties; the parties are not at liberty to contract out of the mandatory annual leave provisions. *FNV v Staat der Nederlanden*[95] raised the issue of whether Article 7 precluded a national provision, which permits days of annual leave which are not taken in the course of a given year of employment, to be replaced by an allowance in lieu, in the course

---

[86] Directive 93/104, Art 5.
[87] Recital 10.
[88] Note 11.
[89] Ibid Judgment para 37.
[90] Art 7.
[91] Case C-342/01 *Merino Gomez v Continental Industria de Caucho SA* [2004] ECR I–2605; Joined Cases C-350/06 and C-520/06 *Schultz-Hof and Stringer* Judgement of 20 January 2009 at paras 22 and 54.
[92] Point 8.
[93] Art 31(2).
[94] Case C-173/99 *ex parte BECTU* [2001] ECR I–4881 Judgment para 43; *Schultz-Hof and Stringer* (see note 91 Judgment at paras 56–92).
[95] Case C-124/05 *FNV v Staat der Nederlanden* [2006] ECR I–3423.

of the following year. The ECJ held that such a provision was incompatible with the Directive.

> ... the positive effect which leave has for the safety and health of workers is deployed fully if it is taken in the year prescribed for that purpose, namely the current year, however the significance of that period ... remains if it taken at a later period.[96]

Thus the Court accepted that the taking of annual leave could be postponed but **22.78** it drew the line at the granting of financial compensation in lieu of leave, holding that the possibility of such compensation in respect of the minimum period of annual leave carried over would create an incentive incompatible with the objective of the Directive for employees not to take leave and for employers not to encourage them to do so.[97]

The conclusion to be drawn from *FNV* is that annual leave not taken in the year **22.79** in which it falls due can be carried over, and this process is compatible with the requirements of the Directive but the possibility of financial compensation in lieu of such leave is not. It is to be noted that Advocate General Kokott in her Opinion[98] stated that leave should be taken within the relevant year or as soon as possible thereafter. The Court did not prescribe any particular timeframe as to when days of leave carried over from one year to the next should be taken. It is arguable that they should not be allowed to be carried over indefinitely, since otherwise the effective protection of the health and safety of the worker and indeed, the workforce in general would be prejudiced. It also leaves open the possibility of leave being accumulated until the termination of employment where it could give rise to financial compensation.

The Directive grants the right to pay during leave only. Other aspects of leave **22.80** such as when leave may be taken are left to the discretion of the Member States, subject to the requirement that the right to paid annual leave must be effective. Any rule or practice which eliminates or substantially reduces that right is incompatible with the Directive. *BECTU*[99] was a trade union with about 30,000 members working in the broadcasting, film, theatre, cinema, and related sectors. BECTU brought proceedings challenging the validity of the United Kingdom Regulations which implemented the Directive under which entitlement to annual leave did not arise until a worker had been continuously employed for 13 weeks. *BECTU* claimed that most of its members were engaged on short-term contracts of frequently less than 13 weeks' duration with the same employer.

---

96 Ibid Judgment para 30.
97 Ibid Judgment para 32.
98 Note 94 Opinion at para 32.
99 Case 173/99 [2001] ECR I-4881.

Many were therefore deprived of any entitlement to annual paid leave or any right to an allowance in lieu thereof. Although they worked on a regular basis they did so for successive employers. The Court found that Article 7(i) did not allow the adoption of national rules under which a worker does not begin to accrue rights to paid annual leave until he has completed a minimum of 13 weeks' uninterrupted employment with the same employer. Although Member States may regulate the conditions for the exercise of the right to annual leave, they are precluded from limiting the entitlement to paid annual leave by applying a precondition for such entitlement which has the effect of preventing certain workers from benefiting from it.[100]

22.81 When the dates of a worker's maternity leave coincide with those of the entire workforce's obligatory annual leave period, with the result that the workers in question could not take annual leave, the requirement of Article 7(1) laying down a minimum period of paid annual leave could not be met. This principle was laid down in *Merino Gomez*.[101]

22.82 Under the terms of a collective agreement governing her terms and conditions of employment, Mrs Merino Gomez could only take annual leave between 16 July and 12 August or 6 August and 2 September. She was on maternity leave at that time. The Court held that this should not deprive her of her right to annual leave which she should be able to take at a time other than that laid down by the collective agreement.[102]

22.83 The Directive gives no indication of what arrangements are to be made for remuneration during periods of leave. On the wording of the Directive it is therefore an open question as to whether remuneration should be paid during the leave period or whether it can be paid before or after this period.

22.84 *Robinson Steele*[103] concerned the validity of a system of 'rolled up' holiday pay. Payment for annual leave was made in the form of payments staggered over the annual period of work. It was paid together with remuneration for work done, rather than in the form of payment in respect of a specific period during which the worker took leave, there being no separate indication of the element of that pay representing payment for annual leave.

---

[100] ibid Judgment paras 52 and 53; *Schultz-Hof and Stringer* (see note 91 Judgement paras 28 and 29).

[101] Note 91; *Schultz-Hof and Stringer* (see note 91 Judgement paras 29–31).

[102] See also C-519/03 *Commission v Luxembourg* [2005] ECR I–3067 in which the Court re-affirmed the principle that a period of leave guaranteed by Community law cannot affect the right to take another period of leave guaranteed by Community law such maternity leave or paternal leave. All period of leave must be regarded as individual rights.

[103] Joined Cases C-131/04 and C-257/04 [2006] ECR I–2531.

The Court found that such an arrangement might lead to situations in which the **22.85**
minimum period of leave is, in effect, replaced by an allowance. The point at
which payment for annual leave is made must be fixed in such a way that during
the period of leave, the worker is, as regards remuneration, put in a position comparable to periods of work. In other words his income during the holiday period
must be the same as that when he is working. Accordingly payment for leave
could not be staggered throughout the working year and paid along with remuneration for work done, but had to take the form of a payment in respect of a
specific period during which the worker actually takes leave.

The judgment in *Robinson Steele* is rather terse. It requires that holiday pay be **22.86**
paid contemporaneously with the taking of leave to which it relates. The Advocate
General adopted a more flexible approach being of the opinion that rolled up pay
could be justified on 'serious grounds of practicability'.[104] Ultimately she felt the
issue of the compatibility of rolled up pay with Article 7 was a matter for the
national court to decide. Her guiding principle in assessing agreements on rolled
up holiday pay was whether workers had an effective possibility of actually taking
the minimum annual leave to which they were entitled. This possibility she felt
would be excluded if the agreement was confined to providing for payment of
minimum annual leave to be made together with basic pay without regulating the
taking of leave itself. These were issues for the national court to examine.

The Advocate General further stated that where holiday pay is included in remu- **22.87**
neration paid, this should be made clear to the employee. Lack of transparency
on the components of pay received would deter the taking of minimum annual
leave.

(6) Night work

Normal hours of work for night workers may not exceed on average eight hours **22.88**
in any 24-hour period. An eight-hour maximum limit on work in any period of
24 hours is applicable where the work in question involves special hazards or
heavy physical and mental strain.[105]

A night worker is one who, during the night time, normally works at least three **22.89**
hours of his daily working time and any worker who is likely during the night to
work a certain proportion of his annual working time.[106]

---

[104] Note 103 Opinion para 84.
[105] Art 8.
[106] Art 2(4).

22.90 Night time means any period of not less than seven hours which must include the period between midnight and 5 am.[107]

22.91 Night workers are entitled to a health check, free of charge, before commencing night work and at regular intervals thereafter.[108] The results of this check must be kept confidential.

22.92 Where a night worker suffers health problems, which are connected with the performance by him of night work, he must be transferred, wherever possible, to day work to which he is suited.[109]

22.93 National law may provide protection for workers who are vulnerable to safety and health risks linked to night work. But it is prohibited to exclude women from night work on the grounds of their gender alone.[110]

22.94 *Stoeckel*[111] was prosecuted for employing 77 women to work at night on 28 October 1988 contrary to Article 213-1 of the French Labour Code which prohibits the employment of women for any nightwork. He argued that this provision was incompatible with Article 5 of Directive 76/207 on the principle of equal treatment for men and women as regards access to employment, vocational training, and promotion and working conditions[112] which required that men and women be offered the same conditions of employment.

22.95 The ECJ found that there was no objective reason for prohibiting women for doing nightwork, where there is no similar prohibition on the carrying out of night work by men:

> . . . the concern to provide protection, by which the general prohibition of night-work by women was originally inspired, no longer appears to be well-founded and the maintenance of that provision, by reason of risks that are not peculiar to women or pre-occupations unconnected with the purpose of Directive 76/207 cannot be justified.[113]

---

[107] Art 2(3).
[108] Art 9(1).
[109] Art 9(1).
[110] Art 10. Case C-312/86 *Commission v France* [1988] ECR I–3559; Case C-345/89 *Stoeckel* [1991] ECR I–4097; Case C-158/91 *Levy* [1993] ECR I–4287; Case C-197/96; *Commission v France* [1997] ECR I–1489; Case C-207/96 *Commission v Italy* [1997] ECR I–6869.
[111] Ibid.
[112] [1976] OJ L39/40.
[113] Stoeckel note 110 Judgment para 18.

In the subsequent case of *Levy*,[114] a prosecution for violation of the same provi- **22.96** sion as was in issue in *Stoeckel*, it was argued that since Article L-213-1 was adopted in order to implement Convention No 89 of 9 July 1948 of the International Labour Organization on night work for women in industry, it could not be discriminatory within the meaning of Directive 76/207.[115]

The ECJ held that it was for the national court to ensure that Article 5 of Direc- **22.97** tive 76/207 was fully complied with, by refraining from applying any conflicting provision of national legislation, unless the applicability of that provision was necessary in order to ensure the performance by the Member States concerned of obligations arising under an agreement concluded with non-member countries prior to the entry into force of the EC Treaty or its predecessors.

(7) Shift work

Shift work is defined in Article 2(5) of the Directive as a method of organizing **22.98** work in shifts whereby workers succeed each other at the same work stations according to a certain pattern, including a rotating pattern and which may be continuous or discontinuous entailing the need for workers to work at different times over a given period of days or weeks.

No specific provision is made in respect of shift workers save that they, like night **22.99** workers, must have the health and safety protection appropriate to the nature of their work.[116] Work performed by doctors in primary health care teams whilst on call constitutes shift work.

J. Specific Sectors

(1) Shipping

A number of initiatives have been taken at Community level with respect to the **22.100** working time rights of workers employed in specific sectors, notably seafarers and mobile workers. Two Directives implement ILO Convention No 180 concerning seafarers' hours of work and the manning of ships. Directive 1999/63[117] applies to seafarers on board every sea-going ship, whether publicly or privately owned, which is registered on the territory of any Member State and is ordinarily engaged in commercial maritime operations. Directive 1999/95[118] applies to all

---

[114] Note 110.
[115] Note 112.
[116] Art 12.
[117] [1999] OJ L167/33. See 22.19–22.21.
[118] [2000] OJ L14/29.

such vessels calling at a Community port irrespective of the flag they fly. Neither Directive applies to fishing vessels.

(2) Mobile road transport

22.101 Directive 2002/15[119] governs the working time of a person performing mobile road transport activities. A mobile worker is defined as:

> ... any worker forming part of the travelling staff, including trainees and apprentices, who is in the service of an undertaking which operates transport services for passengers or goods by road or hire and reward on his own account.[120]

(3) Mobile air transport workers

22.102 Directive 2000/79 implements the European Agreement on the Organization of Working Time in Civil Aviation.[121] Such workers are described as crew members on board a civil aircraft employed by an undertaking established in a Member State.

K. Proposed Amendments

22.103 The Directive prescribes a review of two aspects of its provisions: the derogation to the reference period for the application of Article 6 (maximum weekly working time) and the possibility not to apply Article 6 if the worker gives his agreement to work more than the maximum weekly working period specified in the Directive (the 'opt out'). To these two issues, a third was added to the review process: the treatment of on-call duty following the judgments of the Court in *SIMAP*[122] and *Jaegar*.[123]

22.104 Following the completion of the review[124] the Commission, pursuant to Article 138, consulted the social partners first, on the issue of whether Community action was necessary and if so, what that action was to be. Secondly, when it was agreed that the Directive should be amended, the Commission invited the social partners to negotiate an Agreement on those amendments.[125] Given the deep divisions between the social partners on what those amendments should be,

---

[119] [2002] OJ L80/35.
[120] Art 3(2)(d).
[121] [2000] OJ L302/57.
[122] Note 53.
[123] Note 23.
[124] COM (2003) 843 Final.
[125] COM (2003) 843 Final; SEC (2004) 610.

they declined to enter into negotiations. The Commission thus formulated proposals[126] which were then subsequently amended.[127] They have not, at the time of writing been adopted but political agreement was reached on a slightly amended version of the Commission's proposals on 10 June 2008.

With respect to the 'opt out' the United Kingdom was originally the only Member **22.105** State to allow for it, following the adoption of the original Directive in 1993. Following the accession of ten Member States in May 2004, Cyprus and Malta introduced a generalized opt out. Spain, France, and Germany have put in place measures to allow an opt out in specific sectors (for example health and the hospitality trade).

Although the Commission admits that the opt out in the United Kingdom is **22.106** not as widespread as was generally perceived,[128] it is dissatisfied with the way in which it operates for two reasons:

(i) Employees are often asked to sign an opt out agreement at the same time as they enter into a contract of employment. This practice may undermine the second indent of Article 18(1)(b)(i), which aims to guarantee the worker's free consent by ensuring that no worker may suffer harm due to the fact that he is not prepared to give his agreement. The Commission believes that it is legitimate to suppose that if the opt out agreement must be signed at the same time as the employment contract, freedom of choice is compromised by the worker's situation at that moment. This may put them under pressure to sign the opt out.

(ii) The United Kingdom implementing regulations only provide for the recording of the opt out agreement itself to be kept, contrary to Article 18(1)(b)(i) of the Directive, which obliges employers to keep a record 'of all workers who carry out such work' (ie who work more than 48 hours during the reference period applicable) and not of workers who have signed a declaration. In order to know which workers 'carry out such work', it is necessary to keep records of the number of hours actually worked.

The proposed amendments would limit the period during which Member States **22.107** can allow an opt out from the maximum weekly working time to three years from the date of the adoption of the amending directive.[129] No employer may

---

[126] COM (2004) 607 Final.
[127] COM (2005) 246 Final.
[128] Although 33% of the workforce sign an opt out agreement in fact only 16% actually work more than forty-eight hours a week.
[129] Note 127 at 9.

require an employee to work more than 48 hours a week unless he has first obtained his consent. Any agreement to work more than 48 hours a week given at the start of employment or during a probation period is null and void. Employers must keep a record of the working hours of the employees who have opted out of the 48-hour maximum working week. The victimization of employees who refuse to agree to the opt out or who withdraw from it is prohibited. An agreement to opt out would be valid for a period not exceeding one year, renewable. No employee could work more than 55 hours in one week, unless a collective agreement or agreement concluded between the social partners provides otherwise.[130]

22.108   Article 2 which presently defines 'working time' and 'rest time' is to be expanded to include a third category, 'on-call time'. On-call time is defined as any period during which the worker has an obligation to be available at the workplace, in order to intervene, at the employer's request, to carry out his activity or duties.[131] On-call time is to be split into active and non-active call time. Active call time is to be counted as working time.

22.109   The 'inactive part of on-call time' is defined as being the period during which the worker is on call but is not required by his employer to carry out his activity or duties.[132] The inactive part of on-call time is not to be regarded as working time unless national law or a collective agreement provides otherwise. Where inactive call time is counted as working time, the maximum working week is to be 65 hours. This cap applies to all workers who have worked for longer than 10 weeks for one employer.

22.110   The inactive part of on-call time may not be taken into account in calculating daily or weekly rest periods. This amendment would mean less rights with respect to on-call time which, after *Vorel*,[133] was to be taken into account in calculating such rest periods, and also apparently to be remunerated albeit not at the same rate as time actually worked.

22.111   A new provision, Article 2B, is added to foster compatibility between working and family life. The Member States are required to take measures to ensure that:

• employers inform workers in good time of any change in the pattern or organization of working time;

---

[130] Note 127 at 10.
[131] Note 127 at 6.
[132] Note 127 at 7.
[133] Note 64.

- workers may request changes to their working hours and patterns that employers are obliged to examine taking into account employer's and worker's needs for flexibility.

The social partners are to be encouraged to conclude agreements aimed at improving compatibility between working and family life.[134]   **22.112**

---

[134] Note 126 at 7.

23

POSTING OF WORKERS[1]

A. Introduction

The EC Treaty provides for the right of free movement of the employed[2] and the **23.01** self-employed.[3] The rights of such persons to enter, accompanied by their families, a Member State, take up residence therein, and engage in economic activity on the same basis as nationals of that State are set out in some considerable detail in various regulations and directives.[4]

---

[1] See generally: Ojeda-Aviles: 'European Collective Bargaining and Posted Workers' [1997] 13 IJCLLIR 127–30; Giesen: 'Posting: Social Protection of Workers vs Fundamental Freedoms' (2003) 40 CML Rev 143–58.

[2] Arts 39–42 EC.

[3] Arts 43–48 EC and Arts 49–55 EC.

[4] Regulation 1612/68 on freedom of movement of workers within the Community [1968] OJ Sp Ed (II) 475; Regulation 1251/70 on the right of workers to remain in the territory of a Member State after having been employed in that State [1970] OJ Sp Ed (II) 402; Directive 2004/38 on the

23.02   Further directives provided for the free movement of students[5] and the non-economically active.[6] These directives have all been repealed and replaced as from 30 April 2004 by Directive 2004/38.[7] The rights of these groups to settle on the territory of a Member State other than that of their nationality are subject to a number of restrictions, designed to ensure that they do not become a burden on the public funds and services of the host Member State.

23.03   Although restrictions on the provision of services are prohibited by Article 49 EC, the Treaty is silent on all other matters relevant to the provision of cross-border services. The right to provide services implies the right to move within the Community for that purpose.[8] The prohibition on restrictions on the provision of services equally implies that service providers and recipients of services have the right to provide and receive services on the same terms as nationals of the host Member State.[9]

23.04   The growth of a Community-wide services market—and particular the opening up of the public procurement markets for works, supplies, and services[10]—has bred a class of person who has become known by the rather inelegant term of the 'posted worker'. Such a person is not a provider of services himself. He is in the employment of the provider of services and in the course of that employment he is sent by the service provider to perform whatever services that provider has contracted to perform within the host Member State.

23.05   Posted workers, in contrast to the traditional migrant economically active, do not move into and take up residence with their families in the host Member State but enter and work in that State on a temporary basis, within the context of a contract to provide services. Posted workers are not themselves party to that contract nor do they enter the labour market of the country to which they are posted by their employer. They remain part of the labour force of their home Member State.

---

right of citizens of the Union and their family members to move and reside freely within the territory of the Member States [2004] OJ L158/77.

   [5] Directive 93/96 [1993] OJ L199/1.

   [6] Directive 90/364 on the right of residence [1990] OJ L180/26; Directive 90/365 on the right of residence for employees and self-employed persons who have ceased their occupational activity [1990] OJ L180/28.

   [7] Note 4.

   [8] Directive 73/148 [1973] OJ L172/14; Case 286/82 *Luisi and Carbone* [1984] ECR 377.

   [9] Case 33/74 *Van Binsbergen* [1974] ECR 1299; Case 110/78 *Van Wesemael* [1979] ECR 35; Case 251/83 *Haug-Adrion* [1984] ECR 4277.

   [10] Directive 2004/18 on the co-ordination of procedures for the award of public works contracts, public supply contracts and public services contracts [2004] OJ L134/114; Directive 2004/17 co-ordinating the procurement procedures of entities operating in the water, energy, transport and postal services sectors [2004] OJ L134/1.

In short, posted workers are, to all intents and purposes, part of the equipment **23.06**
and facilities which the service provider moves to the host Member State to exe-
cute the contract. Throughout the term of the service contract, the posted worker
remains in the employment of the service provider and at the end of the term of
posting he returns home. As a general rule, he remains affiliated to the social
security system of his home Member State; the power to terminate his contract
of employment remains exclusively with the posting undertaking; the posting
undertaking remains responsible for determining the nature of the work and its
performance in the sense of determining the end product of that work or the basis
on which it is to be provided. Responsibility for the worker's remuneration rests
with the undertaking which concluded the contract of employment, regardless of
who actually makes the payment to the worker.

Posting has become the most common form of movement for economic purposes **23.07**
within the Community. Its incidence has risen sharply in the past decade or so[11]
as the expansion of the European Community to include many Member States
with low wage economies challenges traditional patterns of service provision.

The implications of this phenomenon are manifold. For the sender Member **23.08**
State large-scale posting may result in a skills and labour shortage; for the
recipient Member State there is the advantage of the availability of services at
competitive prices but this may challenge the market position of the traditional
home service provider. At the place where the services are provided, there are
social and industrial relations implications.

Posted workers may be paid less, or have less favourable employment conditions, **23.09**
than the host state workers with whom they work alongside, frequently doing the
same work or work of equal value. If such divergence takes place on a large
scale this might undermine the organization and functioning of local labour
markets. At the same time, restrictions on labour market access by non-nationals
may encourage resort to undeclared work which will lead to undesirable social
consequences both for the undeclared workers and the regular labour force.[12]

From an industrial relations point of view neither the posted worker nor his **23.10**
employer may be represented, nor can they be required to become either members of a trade union or an association of employers. To that extent they may be

---

[11] In 2005 the overall estimated number of posted workers was 1 million. They represent significant numbers in some Member States, for example Germany, France, Luxembourg, and Belgium
but the phenomenon is increasingly widespread and now affects all Member States as sending or
receiving countries. Source: Communication from the Commission: Posting of Workers in the
framework of the provision of services COM (2007) 304 at 3.
[12] Commission report on the functioning of the transitional arrangements set out in the 2003
Accession Treaty COM (2006) 48 Final at para 20.

excluded from participation in processes and decisions which may affect them directly. Moreover these factors may be prejudicial to the overall harmony of the workplace.

23.11 Apart from the social security position of the posted worker, no other aspects of his employment in the Member States to which he was posted were regulated in a systematic fashion until the adoption of Directive 96/71 on the posting of workers in the framework of the provision of services[13] (the 'Directive'). The result was that workers deployed on a temporary basis to another Member State could legitimately be subject to different conditions of employment, possibly, and indeed most probably, less favourable than nationals of that Member State performing the same type of work.

23.12 Issues surrounding posting began to arise in the early 1980s with the case of *Seco, Desquenne & Giral,*[14] and the subsequent landmark judgment of 1990 in *Rush Portugesa.*[15] It was these cases that prompted the adoption of legislation to regulate the pay and working conditions of the posted worker in the Member State to which he is posted.

B. *Seco, Desquenne & Giral*

23.13 The first case, *Seco, Desquenne & Giral,* arose out of a dispute between two French undertakings carrying out work of various kinds in the Grand Duchy of Luxembourg, and the Luxembourg social security authorities. The two undertakings had sent workers, who were non-EC nationals, from France to Luxembourg for the purpose of carrying out work there pursuant to certain construction contracts. The workers remained at all times compulsorily insured under the French social security system.

23.14 The Luxembourg Social Insurance Code (the 'Code') required workers employed in Luxembourg to be insured, on a compulsory basis, under its old age and invalidity insurance scheme. Half of the contributions were payable by the employer, the other half by the insured employees. However, by virtue of Article 174(2) of that Code, the Luxembourg government could exempt from this insurance obligation foreigners who were only temporarily resident in Luxembourg. In such a case Article 174(3) provided that the employer neverthe-less remains liable for the share of contributions for which he was responsible

---

[13] [1997] OJ L18/1.
[14] Joined Cases 62 and 63/81 [1982] ECR 223.
[15] Case C-113/89 [1990] ECR I–1417.

although those contributions did not entitle the workers concerned to any social security benefits.

Pursuant to these provisions, the Luxembourg social security authorities req- **23.15** uired the two plaintiff undertakings to pay employers' contributions to their old age and invalidity insurance systems. They appealed against this decision, arguing that the legislation in question was discriminatory and likely to impede the freedom to provide services within the Community.

The ECJ found that the relevant provisions of the Code were contrary to **23.16** Articles 49 and 50 EC which prohibit not only overt discrimination but also covert discrimination, that is treatment which, although based on criteria which appear to be neutral, in practice disadvantages one group of persons more than another comparable group. Such was the case with the Luxembourg legislation in issue. Although equally applicable to undertakings established in Luxembourg and those established elsewhere but carrying out work in Luxembourg, it imposed more onerous economic obligations on the latter since they were already liable for contributions in respect of the same risks for the same workers in their Member State of establishment. Since the contributions levied on the employers did not result in any additional benefits for the workers in question they could not be considered justified as providing the workers with social security.[16]

The Luxembourg government advanced two arguments in justification of **23.17** Article 174 of the Code:

(i) Since Member States may refuse entry to third country nationals, they may, *a fortiori*, attach to any work permit which they may chose to grant, conditions or restrictions such as the compulsory payment of the employers' share of social security contributions, and

(ii) the application of national legislation such as Article 174 of the Code to undertakings providing services was justified in order to offset the economic advantages which such persons may have gained by not complying with the legislation of the State in which their services are provided in particular legislation on minimum wages.

The Court dismissed both of these arguments, ruling in respect of (i) that a **23.18** Member State could not use its power to control the employment of third country nationals by imposing a discriminatory burden on undertakings established

---

[16] Ibid Judgment para 10.

in another Member State providing cross-border services under Article 49 EC. As to (ii) the Court held:

> It is well established that Community law does not preclude a Member State from applying their legislation or collective agreements . . . relating to minimum wages to any person who is employed, even temporarily within their territory, no matter in which country the employer is established, just as Community law does not prohibit Member States from enforcing those rules by appropriate means.

23.19 However the Court found that it was not possible to describe as 'appropriate means' a rule or practice which imposes a general requirement to pay social security contributions or other such charges affecting the freedom to provide services on all persons established in another Member State who employ non-nationals in the performance of a services contract in Luxembourg since such a measure was unlikely to make employers comply with minimum wage legislation or be of any benefit to the workers whatsoever.

C. *Rush Portugesa*

23.20 *Rush Portugesa*[17] followed and clarified the principles set out in *Seco and Desquenne.*[18]

23.21 Rush Portuguesa was a Portuguese undertaking specializing in construction and public works. It entered into a subcontract with a French undertaking to carry out works for the construction of a railway line in the west of France. For that purpose it brought its Portuguese employees from Portugal.

23.22 By virtue of Article L 341 of the French Labour Code the Office National d'Immigration had the exclusive right to recruit third country nationals in France. Since Rush Portuguesa had not complied with that provision but had brought the workers into France itself, it was required to pay a special contribution, which was levied on all those who did not comply with Article L341 of the French Labour Code.

23.23 Rush Portuguesa brought proceedings for the annulment of this decision before the Tribunal Administratif of Versailles which referred a series of questions to the ECJ.

23.24 The Court ruled that Articles 49 and 50 EC precluded a Member State from prohibiting a person providing services established in another Member State from moving freely on its territory with all its staff and equally precluded that

---

[17] See note 15.
[18] See note 14.

Member State from making the movement of staff in question subject to restrictions, such as a condition as to engagement in situ or an obligation to obtain a work permit. To impose such conditions on the person providing services established in another Member State, discriminated against that person in relation to his competitors established in the host country who were able to use their own staff without restrictions and, moreover, affected his ability to provide the services in question. The temporary movement of workers to another Member State to carry out construction work as part of a provision of services by their employer does not pertain to the free movement of persons. The movement of workers in pursuance of a contract for services entered into by their employer did not mean that they entered onto the labour market of the host Member State. Their personal status was not affected. Their country of employment remained that of their home Member State. The rules relating to the free movement of workers are thus irrelevant, since such workers return to their country of origin after the completion of their work without at any time gaining access to the labour market of the host Member State.

As to the conditions of employment which may be imposed on workers tempo- **23.25** rarily working in the context of their employer's contract to provide services, citing *Seco, Desquenne & Giral*[19] the Court held that Community law did not preclude Member States from extending their legislation, or collective labour agreements, entered into by both sides of industry, to any person who is employed, even temporarily, within their country no matter in which country the employer is established. Moreover Community law did not prohibit Member States from enforcing those rules by appropriate means.

The Court's judgment in *Rush Portuguesa* is broader than that of *Seco, Desquenne* **23.26** *& Giral* in that the latter only referred to legislation and collective agreements to minimum wages whereas *Rush Portuguesa* refers to legislation and collective agreement in general terms thereby implying compliance with a much wider (and undefined) range of employment conditions on the part of service providers with respect to the personnel they move onto the territory of another Member State.

D. The Posted Workers Directive

Following *Rush Portugesa*[20] the European Commission, under pressure from a **23.27** number of host Member States, and the construction industry in particular,

---

[19] See note 14.
[20] Case C-113/89 [1990] ECR I–1417.

began drafting a framework of rules designed to provide minimum protection to workers performing work temporarily on the territory of a Member State other than that of their habitual employment.[21] A proposal was submitted to the Council on 28 June 1991 which, following the opinions of the Economic and Social Committee[22] and the European Parliament[23] resulted in an amended proposal.[24] Following further debate Directive 96/71 concerning the posting of workers in the framework of the provision of services was adopted on 16 December 1996 (the 'Directive').[25] A report on its implementation in the Member States was published on 25 July 2003.[26]

23.28 The stated purpose of the Directive is to co-ordinate the laws of the Member States in order to lay down a 'nucleus' of mandatory rules on the minimum protection of workers performing work on a temporary basis on the territory of another Member State[27] so as to create 'a climate of fair competition and measures guaranteeing respect for the rights of workers'.[28] Additionally, the Directive aims to eliminate any problems regarding the legislation applicable to the employment by setting out the terms and conditions governing the employment relationship.[29]

23.29 The mandatory rules do not affect the substance of the employment legislation of the host Member State nor must they prevent the application of terms and conditions of employment prescribed by that legislation which are more favourable to the posted worker. The result is a floor of rights bringing the posted worker on to a level of social protection similar to that enjoyed by the worker in the host Member State.

23.30 The burden of complying with these rules lies with the service provider. The ECJ has held that where a building contractor subcontracts the execution of building works to another undertaking, the former remains liable in respect of obligations under the Directive, as guarantor for the subcontractor's obligations towards its workforce.[30]

---

[21] COM (91) 230 Final.
[22] [1992] OJ C49/41.
[23] [1993] OJ C72/78.
[24] [1993] OJ C187/5.
[25] [1997] OJ L18/1.
[26] COM (2003) 458 Final.
[27] Preamble Recital 13. The rules laid down by Directive 96/71 have been described as designating at a Community level mandatory rules within the meaning of Article 7 of the Rome Convention in transnational posting situations (Report para 2.3.11). The position is therefore that the choice of law rules laid down by the Rome Convention remain largely unaffected but the mandatory rules laid down by the Directive must be observed during the period of posting in the host Member State.
[28] Preamble Recital 5.
[29] Preamble Recital 6.
[30] Case C-60/03 *Wolff and Muller* [2004] ECR I–9553.

(1) Scope of application

The Directive applies to undertakings established in a Member State which in the framework of the provision of transnational services post workers to the territory of a Member State[31] in one of three sets of circumstances: **23.31**

(i) the workers are posted by the undertaking to the territory of a Member State on their own account and under their direction, under a contract concluded between the undertaking making the posting and the party for whom the services are intended operating in that Member State provided that there is an employment relationship between the undertaking making the posting and the worker during the period of posting; or

(ii) the workers are posted to an establishment or to an undertaking owned by the group in the territory of a Member State, provided there is an employment relationship between the undertaking making the posting and the worker during the period of posting; or

(iii) the undertaking, being a temporary or placement agency, hires out a worker to a user undertaking established or operating in the territory of a Member State, provided there is an employment relationship between the temporary employment undertaking or placement agency and the worker during the period of posting.

A posted worker is defined in Article 2(1) of the Directive as a worker who, for a limited period, carries out his work in the territory of a Member State in which he normally works. The law of the Member State to which the worker is posted determines his status. Thus although a person may not be regarded as a 'worker' in his home state he may be classified as such in the host Member State.[32] **23.32**

Although the period of posting must be 'limited' in the sense that it cannot be indefinite, no indication is given in the Directive of what this means. Rules are laid down for the calculation of a period of posting, but these appear to have a practical application only in so far as an exemption from the provisions of the Directive may be accorded by a Member State. The rules relating to these exemptions are discussed below. In order to determine what period may be deemed to be the maximum within which a worker may retain his status as a posted worker, reference may be made by analogy to the rules on the social security status of a posted worker, discussed below, by virtue of which a worker remains affiliated to his home social security system during a period of posting not exceeding an initial 12 months but which may be extended for a **23.33**

---

[31] Art 1(1).
[32] Art 2(2).

further 12 months. Applying those rules by way of analogy, a period of posting may be taken as not to exceed 24 months unless the Member States agree otherwise. It can thus be concluded that in principle, a posted worker retains his status, as such, for a period of 24 months.

(2) Equality of treatment

The posted worker

23.34 Posted workers, regardless of the law governing their employment relationship, are guaranteed the terms and conditions as nationals of the host with respect to the following terms and conditions of employment:

   (i) maximum work periods and minimum rest periods;

  (ii) minimum paid annual holidays;

 (iii) minimum rates of pay[33] including overtime rates. Minimum rates of pay are defined by the law or practice of the host Member State. Allowances specific to the posting are to be considered part of the minimum wage, unless they are paid in reimbursement of expenditure actually occurred on account of the posting, such as expenditure on travel, board, and lodging;

 (iv) the conditions of hiring out of workers in particular the supply of workers by temporary employment agencies;

  (v) health and safety at work;

 (vi) measures concerning the terms and conditions of employment of pregnant women or women who have recently given birth, of children, and of young persons;

(vii) equality of treatment between men and women in pay and conditions of employment and other provisions of the host state on non-discrimination.

23.35 These terms and conditions must be laid down by the law, regulation, or administrative provision of the host Member State[34] or by way of a collective agreement which is universally applicable or which has been declared universally applicable pursuant to Article 3(8). A legislative measure which seeks to make a collective agreement providing for a given rate of pay binding on particular undertakings cannot be regarded as having been fixed in accordance with the procedures laid down in Article 3(1) or Article 3(8).[35]

23.36 Many of these employment conditions are regulated on a Community level, as we have seen in previous chapters of this Part, so there may in fact be little

---

[33] Supplementary or occupational retirement pension schemes are outwith the concept of pay for the purposes of the Directive.

[34] Art 3(1).

[35] Case C-346/06 *Rueffert* Judgment of 3 April 2008.

difference between the employment regime of the sending Member State and that of the host Member State. The exception is pay.

Construction industry

Workers in the construction industry have broader rights if posted to another **23.37** Member State to perform any of the activities specified in the Annex to the Directive. In addition to being guaranteed parity of treatment, with respect to the terms and conditions of employment set out above in 23.34–23.35, which are laid down by law, regulation, or administrative provisions of the host Member State, they are also guaranteed the same treatment as nationals of the host state where those terms and conditions are set out in collective agreements or arbitration awards which have been declared universally applicable.

Universally applicable collective agreements

Collective agreements or arbitration awards which have been declared universally **23.38** applicable are, according to the Directive, those collective agreement or arbitration awards which must be observed by all undertakings in the geographic area and in the profession or industry concerned.

Where there is no system for declaring collective agreements to be of universal **23.39** application, which is the case for example in Sweden, a Member State may, by virtue of Article 3(8) of the Directive, extend collective agreements to foreign service providers, which are generally applicable to similar undertakings and/or are concluded by the most representative organizations of both sides of industry and are applied throughout the national territory provided that it ensures equality of treatment between national and non-national service providers. This latter requirement avoids a situation whereby collective agreements, which are not legally binding in the host Member State, could be extended to foreign service providers whilst a great majority of domestic employers might not be covered by it at all.[36]

Member States may apply to national undertakings and undertakings of other **23.40** States, on the basis of equality of treatment:

(i) Terms and conditions of employment other than those specified in the Directive which relate to public policy. Examples of public policy objectives which may justify the imposition of obligations on posting undertakings include those pertaining to the 'protection of the worker'[37] and minimum wages.

---

[36] Case C-341/05 *Laval* Judgment of 18 December 2007 Advocate General Mengozzi at para 175.
[37] Case C-164/99 *Portugaia Construcoes* [2002] ECR I– 787 Judgment para 20.

    (ii) terms and conditions of employment laid down in collective agreements or arbitration awards of universal application other than those referred to in the Annex.[38]

The service provider

23.41 Equality of treatment implies that non-national service providers should not be treated differently to national service providers. Thus in *Portugaia Construcoes*[39] the Court found that the possibility accorded to employers established in the host Member State, but unavailable to a service provider established in another Member State, to avoid paying the minimum wage laid down by a generally applicable collective agreement by negotiating a collective agreement specific to a particular undertaking, violated the principle of equality of treatment:

> . . . the fact that, in concluding a collective agreement specific to one undertaking, a domestic employer can pay wages lower than the minimum wage laid down in a collective agreement declared to be generally applicable, whilst an employer established in another Member State cannot do so, constitutes an unjustified restriction on the freedom to provide services.[40]

23.42 In *Laval*[41] Advocate General Mengozzi pointed out that Sweden 'precisely in order to ensure equal treatment with domestic undertakings considered that it could not require foreign service providers to observe automatically the terms and conditions of employment laid down or governed by collective agreements, since domestic employers were not subject to any such automatic procedure. Furthermore, since Swedish employers could be compelled by collective action taken by trade unions to conclude a collective agreement, foreign service providers could likewise be so compelled.'

23.43 A number of exceptions are possible to the general principle of equality of treatment applicable to all posted workers.

(3) Exceptions

23.44 Member States, may, at their discretion, and after consultation with management and labour, relieve the service provider of the obligation to pay the minimum

---

[38] Art 3(10).
[39] Note 37.
[40] Ibid Judgment para 35.
[41] Note 36.

rate of pay and/or the minimum annual paid holiday period prevailing in the host Member State in the following two situations:

(i) in the case of the deployment of workers to another Member State (other than by a temporary employment agency) for a period of less than one month; and

(ii) where the work to be performed is 'not significant'[42] the criteria for this are to be laid down by the Member State. In this case a Member State may also provide for an exemption from the requirement to observe rules or practices relating to annual paid holidays in the host Member State;

The posting of skilled or specialist workers of undertakings supplying goods who carry out the first installation of such goods where this service is an integral part of the contract for the supply of the goods and necessary for putting them into use is not subject to the requirement to pay the minimum wage or the minimum annual paid holidays of the host Member State, if the period of posting does not exceed eight days (Article 3(2)).

23.45 The reference period for calculating the length of a posting, for such purposes, is one year from the beginning of the posting. Account must be taken of any previous periods in which the post has been filled by the worker.

23.46 Apart from these exceptions which are specifically written into the Directive, it must be remembered that measures restricting the freedom to provide services must be proportionate and this may, in a given set of circumstances, require that the rules set out in the Directive be departed from.

23.47 Although the application by the host Member State of minimum wage legislation to providers of services on its territory pursues an objective of public interest namely the protection of workers,[43] *Mazzoleni*[44] held that the application of such rules on minimum wages, to service providers in a frontier region of a neighbouring Member State might result in a disproportionate administrative burden being placed on employers. It could entail the calculation, hour by hour, of the appropriate remuneration of each employee according to whether he has crossed the frontier of another Member State and the payment of different levels of wages to employees who are all attached to the same operational base and carrying out identical work. In these circumstances the host Member State has an obligation to determine whether the imposition of minimum wage rules are necessary and appropriate.

---

[42] Art 3(5).
[43] Laval see note 36.
[44] Case C-165/98 [2001] ECR I-2189.

(4) Temporary workers supplied by agencies

23.48 Member States may provide that workers hired out by temporary employment agencies are guaranteed the terms and conditions applicable to temporary work in the Member State in which the work is carried out.[45]

E. Social Security

23.49 The Posted Workers Directive exempts from its scope of application state social security systems[46] and supplementary occupational retirement schemes.[47]

23.50 The social security position of posted workers and their employers is set out in Regulation 1408/71 on the application of social security schemes to employed person to self-employed persons and to members of their families moving within the Community.[48]

23.51 Title II, Articles 13–17 of that Regulation sets out the social security system which is applicable to the employed and self-employed who move within the Community. The general rule is that a person should be compulsorily affiliated to the social security system of one Member State only. The purpose of this 'single system' rule is twofold:

(i) to minimize the administrative burden, and

(ii) to avoid a situation where either an employer or an employee, or possibly both, could be subject to social security contributions in more than one Member State.

23.52 Employed persons, as a general rule, are required to be affiliated to the social security system of their place of employment. Article 14(1) of Regulation 1408/71 sets out the position governing the social security affiliation of posted workers. It is as follows.

23.53 A person employed in the territory of a Member State by an undertaking to which he is normally attached, who is posted to the territory of another Member State by that undertaking to perform work there for and on behalf of it, continues to be subject to the legislation of the first Member State. In other words he remains affiliated to his home social security system. This rule both reduces the administrative burden on employers which would ensue from multiple

---

[45] Art 3(9).

[46] Art 3(c).

[47] Preamble Recital 21.

[48] [1971] OJ Sp Ed (II) 416; Consolidated by Regulation 118/97 [1997] OJ L28/1. Regulation 1408/71 has been repealed and replaced by Regulation 883/2004 [2004] OJ L166/1 which is expected to enter into force in 2010.

short-term affiliations, and minimizes the risk to the employee of low or nil benefit entitlement as a result of a series of short-term affiliations to multiple social security systems.

The availability of this home country rule is subject to the fulfilment of two **23.54** conditions:

(i) the anticipated duration of the work in question, at the start of the posting, is not expected to exceed 12 months, and

(ii) the worker must not be sent to replace another person who has completed his term of posting.[49]

If the duration of the work to be done extends beyond the period originally **23.55** anticipated, owing to unforeseeable circumstances, and the posting is expected to exceed 12 months, the legislation of the first Member State may continue to apply, after that period, provided that the competent authority of the Member State to which the worker has been posted gives its consent to such an arrangement. Such consent cannot be given for a period exceeding 12 months.[50] Thus, in effect a posting cannot, in principle, exceed 24 months. Article 17 of Regulation 1408/71 provides that two or more Member States may by common agreement provides for exceptions to this rule. Thus, for example, there could be an agreement extending the permitted period of posting for the purposes of retaining home country social security affiliation, beyond the period of 24 months allowed for in Article 14(1).

Undertakings providing temporary personnel

Workers provided by an undertaking established in one Member State to a user **23.56** undertaking in another Member State may remain affiliated to the social security system of the first Member State if two conditions are satisfied:

(i) the worker must maintain a direct relationship with the undertaking in question throughout the period of the posting;

(ii) the undertaking engaged in providing personnel to undertakings based in another Member State must normally carry on its activities in the Member State in which it is established.

An undertaking is deemed to carry on its activities normally in the Member **23.57** State in which it is established if it habitually carries on significant activities in that state.[51] In other words it must have a genuine business base in that country

---

[49] Art 14(1)(a) and (b).

[50] Art 14(1)(b).

[51] Case C-202/97 *Fitzwilliam Executive Search* [2000] ECR I–883; Administrative Commission Decision No 181 [2001] OJ L329/73.

and have performed business activities in that state for a period of over four months. Whether a business has significant activities in the posting state is an objective test involving a consideration of the business as a whole but the following factors are of particular importance:[52]

- the place where the posting undertaking has its registered office and its administration;
- the number of administrative staff of the posting undertaking in the posting state and in the state of employment (the presence of only administrative staff in the posting state rules out per se the applicability to the undertaking of the provisions governing posting;
- the place of recruitment of the posted worker;
- the place where the majority of contracts with clients are concluded;
- the law applicable to the contracts signed by the posting undertaking with its clients and workers;
- the turnover achieved by the posting undertaking in the posting state and in the state of employment during an appropriately typical period.[53]

23.58 The requirement to satisfy these criteria avoids a situation where an undertaking could affiliate workers to the social security system of a Member State with which neither it nor the workers had any real connection. As a consequence of lower social security contributions and tax rates this might give the undertaking and its client user undertakings a competitive advantage, but equally could result in a diminution in the level of social protection which should normally be available to the worker.

Evidence of home country affiliation

23.59 The continued affiliation of the posted worker to his home social security system is evidenced by a special form,[54] issued by the competent authorities of his home state. This form is valid until withdrawn by the issuing state and neither its validity nor the status of the posted worker to which it relates can be questioned by the host country.[55] This form can be issued with retroactive effect—that is it can be issued in respect of workers who have already been posted to another Member State.[56]

---

[52] Practical Guide for the Posting of Workers EC Commission <http://ec.europa.eu/employment_social/social_security_schemes/docs/posting_en.pdf>.

[53] Ibid at 4 Turnover of approximately 25% of the total turnover in the posting state could be a sufficient indicator but less would require closer scrutiny.

[54] Form 101—a form designed by the EC Commission for use throughout the Member States.

[55] Case C-2/05 *Rijksdienst voor Sociale Zekerheid v Herbosch Kiere NV* [2006] ECR I–1071.

[56] Case C-178/97 *Barry Banks* [2000] ECR I–2005.

Extra benefits

Although the general rule is thus that a posted worker remains affiliated to the **23.60** social security system of his home country, he may be required to be affiliated to the host Member State's social security system where that affiliation gives him benefits over and above those available under his home country affiliation.

In *Guiot*[57] the Court held that the social protection of workers in the construc- **23.61** tion industry might '. . . because of conditions specific to that sector, constitute an overriding requirement justifying such a restriction on freedom to provide services'.[58] However, this would not be the case 'where the worker in question enjoys the same protection or essentially similar protection by virtue of the employer's contributions already paid by the employer in the State of establishment'.[59] It is for the national court to determine whether this is in fact the case. This ruling establishes the principle that service providers may be required to pay social security contributions in the host Member State if such contributions give the staff in question entitlement to benefits not provided under the social security system of their home state, that is the country in which their employer is established and in which they normally work and are insured. Thus in *Finalarte*[60] the Court held:

> Since the Federal Republic of Germany has determined that a period of paid leave equal to 30 days worked per year is necessary for the social protection of construction workers Articles 59 and 60 of the Treaty do not, in principle, prevent that Member State from extending the level of protection to workers posted by providers of services established in other Member States during the period of posting.[61]

Since a genuine benefit was conferred on workers their employer undertakings **23.62** could be required to pay the necessary contributions towards the funding of the scheme.

F. Third Country Undertakings

Recital 20 of the Preamble to the Directive emphasized that national law contin- **23.63** ues to govern the entry, residence, and access to employment of third country workers and any agreement concluded by the Community with third countries or national legislation governing access by third country service providers to Community or national territory remains unaffected.

---

[57] Case C-272/94 [1996] ECR I–1905.
[58] Ibid Judgment at para 16.
[59] Ibid Judgment at para 17.
[60] Case C-49/98 [2001] ECR I–7831.
[61] Judgment para 59.

23.64 However as regards the terms and conditions of employment which third country service providers must grant to their posted workers, the Directive provides that undertakings established in a non-Member State must not be given more favourable treatment than undertakings established in a Member State.[62] In effect this means that third country undertakings are subject to the Directive, at least as regards the minimum package of terms and conditions they can offer their employees.

23.65 The validity of this provision is open to question on two fronts. First the scope of application of the Directive is set out in Article (1)(1) as being confined to undertakings established in a Member State and secondly the legal basis of the Directive is expressed to be Articles 57(2) and 66, now Articles 52(1) and 55, both of which concern measures that are applicable to the Member States only.

G. Administrative Co-operation between Member States

23.66 Article 4(1) and (2) of the Directive impose both an obligation of administrative co-operation on the Member States and the creation of the necessary conditions for such co-operation. This obligation includes the designation of a monitoring authority organized and equipped to deal promptly with requests regarding the terms and conditions of employment covered by the Directive.

23.67 Article 4(3) obliges Member States to make available information on the terms and conditions of employment applicable to foreign service providers and posted workers.

H. Enforcement

23.68 Member States are entitled to take steps to ensure the protection of the posted worker and this may entail the imposition of restrictions on the service provider.

23.69 Member States also have the right to take preventative action and to impose appropriate sanctions aimed at countering illegal employment and undeclared work, including in the form of disguised self-employment, as well as combating unlawful activities by fictitious foreign temporary employment agencies. But whatever measures are adopted to pursue these objectives must be proportionate: those objectives must not be capable of being achieved in a less restrictive, but equally effective, manner.

---

[62] Art 1(4).

Member States may not proceed, in their treatment of service providers, and **23.70**
workers employed and posted by those service providers onto their territory,
on the general assumption that fraud and abuse are widespread to justify a
restriction on a fundamental freedom guaranteed by the Treaty, in this case the
freedom to provide services.[63]

In its case law, the Court of Justice has confirmed that the Member States may **23.71**
verify that there has been no abuse of the freedom to provide services by a non-
national service provider.[64] The competent authorities of the host Member State
can therefore carry out inspections to verify compliance with national and
Community provisions in respect of the provision of services. Inspection
measures may be justified to monitor the observance of obligations justified by
imperative reasons of general interest,[65] and they must always be appropriate to
the objective they seek to achieve and in accordance with the principle of proportionality. In other words the inspection measures and procedures must not be
such as to impose unjustified or disproportionate restrictions on the provision
of services.[66] In *Commission v Italy* the requirement to have a subsidiary on the
national territory was held to constitute 'the very negation of the free provision
of services'.[67] Equally, national rules which stipulate that the provision of services
on national territory by a company established in another Member State
was subject to the obtaining of an administrative authorization constituted an
unacceptable restriction on the provision of services.[68]

Records may be required to be kept for inspection but any record keeping **23.72**
requirements must be reasonable.

Arblade[69] held that a service provider may not be required by the host Member **23.73**
State to draw up records such as a special staff register or particulars for each
worker where the social protection of the workers in question is already satisfied
by compliance with the administrative requirements of the Member State of
establishment. Nevertheless the Court admitted:

> The items of information respectively required by the rules of the Member States of
> establishment and by those of the host Member State . . . may differ to such an extent

---

[63] Case C-255/04 *Commission v France* [2006] ECR I–5251 Judgment para 52; Case C-433/04
Commission v Belgium [2006] ECC I–10653 Judgment para 35.
[64] *Rush Portugesa* (see note 15 above) Judgment at para 17; Joined Cases C-369/96 and 376/96
Arblade [1999] ECR I–8453 Judgment para 62.
[65] *Rush Portugesa* (see note 15 above) Judgment para 18; Joined Cases C-369/96 and 376/96
Arblade (see note 64 above) Judgment paras 60–63 and 74.
[66] Case C-445/03 *Commission v Luxembourg* [2004] ECR I–10191 Judgment para 40.
[67] Case C-279/00 [2002] ECR I–1425 Judgment para 18.
[68] Case C-43/93 *Vander Elst* [1994] ECR I–3803.
[69] Ibid.

that the monitoring required under the rules of the host Member State cannot be carried out on the basis of documents kept in accordance with the rules of the Member State of establishment.[70]

23.74 Articles 49 and 50 EC do not preclude the imposition of an obligation to keep records accessible, and in a clearly identified place within the territory of the host Member State, to enable the effective protection of workers, particularly as regards health and safety matters and working hours.

23.75 But an obligation to retain such documents on the territory of the host Member State at an address of a natural person who acts as an agent or servant of the service provider for a period of five years after the service provider has ceased to have staff on the territory of the host Member State has been held to be incompatible with Articles 49 and 50 of the Treaty. In short whilst administrative requirements can be imposed on service providers these must be proportionate and necessary to the objective they seek to pursue.

23.76 In *Finalarte*[71] the Court held that although the requirements imposed on businesses established outside Germany with respect to the information to be supplied to the German competent authorities were more onerous than those imposed on undertakings established in Germany and this was a restriction on the freedom to supply services, such information requirements could be justified if they were necessary to safeguard effectively, and by appropriate means, the overriding public interest of the social protection of workers. But, following *Arblade*, the Court held that it was necessary to check whether the information provided in the documents required under the Member State of establishment were sufficient as a whole to enable the checks needed in the host Member State to be carried out before making supplementary demands on service providers.

23.77 Of particular sensitivity is the issue of posted workers who are third country nationals. The earlier cases of *Vander Elst*[72] and the *Commission v Luxembourg*[73] held that workers who were regularly and habitually employed by a service provider established in a Member State could be posted to another Member State without being subject in the latter state to administrative formalities such as the obligation to obtain a work permit.

23.78 Furthermore in *Commission v Luxembourg* it was held that legislation requiring posted workers to have been employed for at least six months before being

---

70 *Arblade* (see note 64 above) Judgment para 63.
71 Joined Cases C-49/98 etc [2001] ECR I-7831.
72 See note 68 above.
73 Case 244/04 [2006] ECR I-885.

posted went beyond what was required for the social welfare protection of workers who were nationals of third countries and was therefore not justified.

In *Commission v Germany*[74] the Court found that German legislation requiring **23.79** nationals of third countries posted to Germany by a service provider established in another Member State to have been employed in that Member State for at least a year in order to be eligible for a residence visa was incompatible with Article 49.

The EC Commission has expressed the view that although the host Member **23.80** State could not impose administrative formalities or additional conditions on posted workers who are third country nationals when they were lawfully employed by the service provider in the Member State of establishment, they could check compliance with this requirement.[75]

I. The Commission Communications

In April 2006 the Commission published, in the form of a Communication,[76] **23.81** guidance (the 'Guidance') on the posting of workers. The aim of this Communication was to assist Member States to comply with their obligations under Article 49 EC as regards administrative requirements and control measures imposed on non-national service providers. The Guidance identified unacceptable practices and suggested alternative methods and procedures which could be considered to be compatible with Article 49 EC.

For example, whilst a service provider could be not be required to obtain a prior **23.82** authorization to post workers onto the territory of the host Member State, the requirement to submit a declaration at the time of the start of the work containing information on the workers who have been posted, the type of services they will provide and where and how long the work will take would be in accordance with the principle of proportionality.[77] The formalities for making such a declaration may not be so costly or difficult as to hamper unnecessarily the provision of services.

---

[74] Case C-244/04 [2006] ECR I–885.

[75] Guidance on the posting of workers in the framework of the provision of services COM (2006) 439 at para 2.2.

[76] Guidance on the posting of workers in the framework of the provision of services COM (2006) 159 Final.

[77] Although the ECJ had not given any guidance on the admissibility of an obligation to make a declaration concerning the posting of workers, it had indicated in Case C-244/04 *Commission v Luxembourg* (see n74) that such an obligation would be an acceptable means of ensuring compliance with Luxembourg social welfare legislation.

23.83 A year after the Guidance was published the Commission published another Communication[78] (the '2007 Communication') in which it sought to assess the progress achieved since April 2006 in the control measures used by the Member States. It concluded, from the information supplied to it[79] by the Member States, that a number of control measures applied by the Member States did not seem to be in conformity with Article 49. In particular, it pointed to the fact that six Member States[80] explicitly required the posting undertaking to have a representative in the host country. In three further Member States this requirement was implicit.[81] A specific authorization/registration regime for the posting of workers existed in Malta and Luxembourg but, in the case of the latter, this requirement was confined to cases where third country nationals were to be posted onto its territory.

23.84 The requirement to make a declaration prior to the commencement of work by the service provider existed in 16 Member States.[82] The Czech Republic imposed such an obligation on the recipient of services. No indication is given as to the nature of these declarations or whether the substantive or procedural rules or practices relating to them are such as to be disproportionate to the purpose they seek to achieve and hence contrary to Article 49 EC.

23.85 The obligation to keep and maintain certain documents on the territory of the host country were imposed by 14 Member States in varying ways and with respect to different types of documents.[83]

23.86 The information received by the Commission from the Member States showed that 15 of them require a work permit or impose access-to-the-labour-market related visa requirements for posted third country workers who are legally staying and legally employed in another Member State.

23.87 Additional conditions are still applied with regard to residence permits and/or visa requirements which the Commission felt might hamper the effective exercise of a fundamental freedom by the service provider. Among such conditions were minimum employment periods or particular types of employment contracts in

---

[78] Posting of workers in the framework of the provision of services—maximizing its benefits and potential whilst guaranteeing the protection of workers COM (2007) 304 Final.

[79] Set out in Staff Working Document accompanying the Communication SEC (2007) 747.

[80] Germany, Greece, Luxembourg, Austria, Finland, and Sweden.

[81] Estonia, France, and Latvia.

[82] Belgium, Germany, Greece, Spain, France Cyprus, Latvia, Lithuania, Luxembourg, Hungary, Malta, Austria, Portugal, Slovenia, Slovakia, and Finland.

[83] Austria Belgium, Estonia, Germany, Greece, Finland, France Italy, Luxembourg, Malta, Portugal, Spain, Slovakia, and Sweden.

the Member State of origin (eg of indefinite duration), or a minimum duration of the residence permit in the country of establishment of the employer.

Such measures, the Commission states, are not in conformity with the Treaty **23.88** rules on the freedom to provide services as interpreted by the ECJ.

From the information gathered during this monitoring exercise the Com- **23.89** mission concluded that many Member States exercised control over service providers established in other Member States which were not compatible with either Article 49 EC nor the Posted Workers Directive. This situation was related to, if not caused by, the virtual absence of administrative co-operation between Member States. The Commission therefore proposed measures to reinforce such co-operation and to assist Member States in identifying and exchanging good practices. Whilst the Commission was prepared to support and assist the Member States to fulfil their Treaty obligations, it did state that infringement proceedings would be brought where Member States persisted in following practices which had been declared by the ECJ to be incompatible with Article 49 and the Posted Workers Directive.

J. Jurisdiction and Applicable Law in Employment Disputes

Regulation 44/2001 on jurisdiction and the recognition and enforcement of **23.90** judgments in civil and commercial matters[84] establishes Community rules on jurisdiction and recognition of judgment in civil and commercial matters. Article 19 provides that an employer domiciled in a Member State may be sued in the courts of the Member State where he is domiciled or in the courts of the place where the employee habitually carried out his work.[85] Article 6 of Directive 96/71 modifies this rule in that it introduces a new specific jurisdiction clause which permits, in respect of claims under the Directive, judicial proceedings to be instituted in a Member State in which the worker was posted.

As to the law applicable in employment disputes, the Convention of Rome of **23.91** 19 June 1980 on the Law Applicable to Contractual Relationships[86] provides, as a general rule, for freedom of choice by the parties as regards the law applicable to the employment contract. Consequently in the absence of any express provision in the contract, employment contracts were, pursuant to Article 6(2), governed by the law of the country in which the employee habitually performs his work,

---

[84] [2001] OJ L12/1.
[85] [1980] OJ L266/1.
[86] [1980] OJ L266/1.

even if he is in temporary employment outside that country. Where work is habitually carried out in more than one country, the applicable law is that in which the place of business through which he was engaged is situate unless on the whole the contract is more closely connected with another country in which case the law of that country governs the employment.

23.92 An employee cannot be deprived of the protection available to him by the legal system applicable under Article 6(2) (which as a general rule will be the law of the country of his habitual employment) in the absence of the choice of another legal system. Thus, the employee's standard of protection under the law governing his habitual contract of employment cannot be eroded. This is important given the disequilibrium in the bargaining power of the parties to the employment contract. Article 7 moreover envisages the concurrent application of the mandatory rules of the law of the country of temporary employment—which remains more or less the position following the adoption of the Directive. These mandatory rules are not defined by the Convention.

K. The *Laval* Case

23.93 The *Laval*[87] case raised a number of complex issues relating to the posting of workers.

(1) Facts

23.94 Vaxholm is a town north of Stockholm. Laval un Partneri Ltd (Laval) is a Latvian construction company. L&P Baltic Bygg (Baltic), a Swedish company, was awarded a contract to renovate and build an annex onto an old school in Vaxholm. Laval and Baltic were in common ownership. Laval hired out Latvian construction workers to Baltic to carry out work on the school. Laval was approached in June 2004 by the local section of the Swedish Building Workers Union (Byggnards) and asked to sign a collective agreement in respect of the work being carried out at Vaxholm by the Latvian posted workers. Despite protracted negotiations over a number of months, no collective agreement was signed. Instead Laval informed Byggnards that it had signed a collective agreement with the Latvian Building Workers' Trade Union. Byggnards gave notice of industrial action, banning all building and installation work at the Vaxholm site as from

---

[87] Case C-341/05 Judgment of 18 December 2007. For a discussion of the issues see: Ahlberg, Bruun, and Malmberg: 'The Vaxholm case from a Swedish and a European Perspective' 12(2) Transfer (2006) 155; Woolfson and Somers: 'Labour Mobility in Construction: European Implications of the Laval un Partneri Dispute with Swedish labour' (2006) 12 EJIR 49–68.

2 November 2004 Some six week later the Electricians Union took secondary action in support of Byggnards.

(2) Swedish labour practices

The *Laval* dispute has to be seen in the context of Swedish labour law and **23.95** Swedish industrial relations practices. Sweden, in contrast to most other Member States, does not have any statutory minimum wage. Minimum wages are not fixed by statute nor by any collective agreement applicable erga omnes. Trade unions have the exclusive competence to settle wage and employment conditions. Consequently Swedish legislation implementing the Posted Workers Directive does not contain any provision regarding the application of the minimum wage to posted workers: this is simply not a matter regulated at governmental level nor is it a matter over which the government has any control. Minimum wages are settled by collective agreement between Swedish employers' organizations and trade unions.

Non-Swedish undertakings which do not belong to a Swedish employers' organi- **23.96** zation are asked to sign a non-application agreement under which the employer undertakes to apply the collective agreement to the activity in which they are engaged on Swedish territory. It was such an agreement that Byggnards asked Baltic to sign. In case of a refusal to sign such an agreement the relevant trade union normally organizes a boycott against the employer by virtue of which the members of the trade union refuse to work for him. However this may have little impact as in the case of a contract to provides services as the employer may have imported most of his workforce from the Member State where he is established and accordingly may have few Swedish unionized members working for him. If this is so the trade union can organize secondary action which will isolate the employer, for example, by cutting off essential supplies and services on which he is dependent.

(3) National proceedings

Laval brought proceedings in Sweden to have the industrial action declared **23.97** unlawful and an injunction to halt with immediate effect the industrial action taking place at the Vaxholm site. This was refused, but in the proceedings in the main case the Swedish Court referred two questions to the ECJ for a preliminary ruling, which sought to establish the validity, under EC Law, of the industrial action. The proceedings gave rise to the greatest number of interventions from Member States—twenty in all—an indication of the interest in the outcome of the case on the part of both Member States who are typically recipients of cross-border services and those which are the providers of such services.

23.98 The first question referred by the Swedish court in essence concerned the extent to which collective industrial action could be used within a Member State to force a provider of services established in another Member State to enter into negotiations with it on rates of pay for posted workers and to enter into a collective agreement on terms and conditions of employment, some of which were more favourable than those specified in national law and some of which related to matters other than those specified in Article 3 of the Posted Workers Directive. In the second question the national court asked whether there was a prohibition in a Member State against trades unions undertaking collective action with a view to having a collective agreement set aside or amended, Articles 49 EC and 50 EC precluded that prohibition from being subject to the conditions that such action must relate to terms and conditions of employment to which national law applies directly with the result that it is impossible for an undertaking which posts workers to that Member State to enforce such a prohibition vis-à-vis that trade union.

23.99 The judgment of the Court addresses two separate and distinct issues: (i) the right under Community law to take collective industrial action, and (ii) the extent of the obligations of a service provider vis-à-vis his posted workforce under both the Posted Workers Directive and Article 49 EC. Issue (ii) is addressed below. The question of the extent of the right to take collective action has been discussed above in paras 2.35–2.48 and 3.43–3.49.

23.100 The Court began by noting that Sweden had not provided for minimum rates of pay by legislation nor were such minimum rates of pay laid down by collective agreement which had been declared universally applicable pursuant to Article 3(8). It had entrusted to management and labour the task of settling, by way of collective negotiations, the wage rates which national undertakings are to pay their workers and that as regards undertakings in the construction sector, such a system requires negotiation on a case-by-case basis, at the place of work, having regard to the qualifications and tasks of the employees concerned. Article 3(1) of the Posted Workers Directive relates only to minimum rates of pay. It therefore cannot be relied upon to justify an obligation on service providers to comply with rates of pay which do not constitute minimum wages and which are not laid down in accordance with the means specified in Article 3(1) and Article 3(8) of the Directive. Moreover service providers cannot be required under the terms of the Directive to enter into negotiations on a case-by-case basis so that they may ascertain the wages which they are asked to pay their posted workers. Although the Court came to this conclusion on the basis of the Posted Workers Directive, it is clear that undertakings must be able to ascertain their obligations towards their workers in order to avail themselves of the right to tender for, and be awarded, public procurement contracts. If they do not know the cost of their labour how can they respond to an invitation to tender?

Turning to conditions of employment other than pay, the Court noted that in respect of some of the matters referred to in Article 3(1) first subparagraph (a)–(g) of the the Posted Workers Directive, the terms of the collective agreement in issue were more favourable than those provided for by Swedish law and exceed the minimum requirements provided for in the Directive. For example, signing the collective agreement entailed an acceptance by undertakings of certain pecuniary obligations such as a requirement to pay the union a sum equal to 1.5 per cent of total gross wages for the purpose of a pay review which that trade union carries out and a number of insurance premiums consisting of contributions for welfare benefits such as sickness benefits, supplementary retirement insurance (which was explicitly excluded under Article 3(1) of the Directive), and survivors' benefits for which the workers were already covered under the Latvian social security scheme or benefits which did not concern them such as unemployment benefit (since the workers would not become unemployed at the end of the contract but would remain in the employment of their employer). Moreover some of the payments made under the terms of the collective agreement funded vocational training in the building sector and thus had 'no connection with the protection of workers or any real advantage significantly contributing to the social protection of the worker'.[88] **23.101**

Although Article 3(7) of the Directive provides that paragraphs 1 to 6 may not prevent the application of terms and conditions of employment which are more favourable to workers and in addition Recital 17 states that the mandatory rules for minimum protection in force in the host country must not prevent the application of such terms and conditions, this cannot be taken to mean that the host Member State may make the provision of services in its territory conditional on the observance of terms and conditions of employment which go beyond the mandatory rules for minimum protection. The Directive expressly lays down the degree of protection which must be afforded to posted workers and that is the sum of the obligations of the service provider towards his workforce. Nothing more can be required of him, unless pursuant to the law or collective agreements in the Member State of origin those workers already enjoy more favourable terms and conditions of employment as regards the matters referred to in Article 3.[89] It is difficult to see why this should be so: the Directive specified the obligations **23.102**

---

[88] Opinion of the Advocate General at para 295.
[89] *Laval* (see note 36) Judgment para 81; *Rueffert* (see note 35) Judgment para 34.

to be imposed on the service provider. To require him to respect terms and conditions prevailing in the Member State of establishment when providing service in another Member States where terms and conditions of employment are less favourable will in effect deprive him of providing service in those States since his labour costs will put him at an competitive disadvantage vis-à-vis national service providers.

23.103 Article 3(10) also gives the Member States the possibility of applying terms and conditions of employment on matters other than those specified in Article 3, first subparagraph (a) to (g) in compliance with the Treaty and on the basis of equality of treatment, to national undertakings and undertakings of other Member States.

L. Conclusion

23.104 The posting of workers is one of the most sensitive issues of the day. All Member States are affected either as providers or recipients of services. The service provider States tend, by and large, to be the newer Member States; the recipients of such services, by contrast, are the older Member States. This tension between the provider State and recipient State is caused, on the one hand, by the resentment of competition in the service sector of the recipient Member States, as they see markets lost to more cost effective foreign workforces and, on the other, by service providers who wish to exercise their right, not to be unreasonably constrained to provide cross-border services.

23.105 The tension in the area can be traced back to the enlargement of the European Community in 1986 to include Spain and Portugal. Public debates about the feared mass influx of workers from the Iberian peninsula, following confirmation by the Court in *Rush Portugesa*[90] of the right of service providers to bring their workforce from their home Member State, to perform services under a contract of services in another Member State, fuelled anxiety about job losses among the general public, and resentment within the service sectors in recipient Member States, in particular within the construction industry which saw the real possibility of loss of large-scale lucrative contracts to foreign service providers. Added to this was the drive, following the publication of the White Paper on the Internal Market,[91] to open up public procurement markets to cross-border competition. Such markets were traditionally national, often being used to further domestic policy objectives and were serviced by national providers. The fall of the

---

[90] Note 15.
[91] COM (85) 310.

Berlin Wall and the opening up of the hitherto closed economies of Eastern European led politicians, under pressure from business and the general population alike, to espouse a 'something has to be done' attitude.[92]

Whilst *Rush Portugesa* left the requirement of service providers and posted work- **23.106** ers to adhere to local employment conditions to the discretion of each Member State, European building unions advocated a 'social clause' in Community public procurement legislation on works guaranteeing compliance with working conditions and the collective agreements of the host Member State. This reflected the ILO Convention 94 Labour Clauses (Public Contracts) Convention 1949.[93]

Early drafts of the Community Charter of the Fundamental Rights of Workers[94] **23.107** advocated such a labour clause in all public contracts. This provision was dropped from the final version of the Charter, but the Action Programme[95] proposed the adoption of an instrument requiring a labour or social clause in all public contracts guaranteeing equal treatment to workers employed by those tendering for public contracts so as to prevent 'social dumping'.

What was ultimately proposed became the Posted Workers Directive, a much **23.108** broader instrument extending beyond the public sector to all service providers and their employees. It took five years to negotiate. The Directive is based on what were Articles 57(2) and 66 EC on the free provision of services. Recital 5 states that the promotion of the transnational provision of services 'requires a climate of fair competition and measures guaranteeing respect for workers rights'.

---

[92] Cremers: Free movement of services and equal treatment of workers: the case of construction. Transfer 2/06 167–81 at 170.

[93] <http://www.ilo.org/ilolex/cgi-lex/convde.pl?C094>. Article 2 of the Convention reads:
  1. Contracts to which this Convention applies shall include clauses ensuring to the workers concerned wages (including allowances), hours of work and other conditions of labour which are not less favourable than those established for work of the same character in the trade or industry concerned in the district where the work is carried on—
     (a) by collective agreement or other recognized machinery of negotiation between organizations of employers and workers representative respectively of substantial proportions of the employers and workers in the trade or industry concerned; or
     (b) by arbitration award; or
     (c) by national laws or regulations.
  Other examples of Labour clauses include the Davis Bacon Act of the United States passed in 1931 requiring the payment of prevailing wages on public works projects. All federal government construction contracts, and most contracts for federally assisted construction over $2,000, must include provisions for paying workers on-site no less than the locally prevailing wages and benefits paid on similar projects. The British Fair Wages Resolution required firms undertaking government contracts to observe fair labour standards including those set down in collective agreements.

[94] See paras 2.60–2.62 and 3.43–3.49.

[95] COM (89) 568 Final.

The implication here is that the Directive will achieve these objectives. This may not necessarily be so. The Directive, in imposing local labour conditions on service providers, restricts their freedom to negotiate. Far from ensuring fair competition, the Directive may in fact be restricting competition in that it takes away the right of the service provider to fix the terms and conditions upon which he will provide services. Moreover in many cases, the non-national service provider will be at a competitive disadvantage vis-à-vis national service providers in that he will have to bear the cost of the transport, board, and lodging of his employees in addition to their remuneration, costs which the national service provider does not incur. The onerous controls and administrative conditions imposed on the non-national service provider by many Member States as discussed above in paras 23.81–23.89 also place him at a disadvantage. A reading of the case law of the ECJ and the Commission's findings as set out in the Communications discussed above in Section G indicates that the 'fair competition' allegedly pursued by the Posted Workers Directive is protecting indigenous service providers from unwelcome and unwanted competition.

23.109 Apart from the questionability of the legality of the substance of the Posted Workers Directive, it has had the unfortunate consequence of creating a breeding ground for procedural requirements, purportedly designed to ensure compliance with Article 49 EC and the Directive, which potentially operate as a stranglehold on the provision of services. There is thus a situation where, even if genuine efforts are made to comply with the substance of the rules on service provision, the additional procedural burdens operate in a discriminatory and restrictive manner.

23.110 The Posted Workers Directive sits uneasily beside the Public Procurement Directives[96] the objective of which is to open up public procurement markets to Community-wide competition. How can this occur if, for example, prospective tenderers for public works contracts, which are labour-intensive, have no discretion as to a core set of costs when formulating their tenders and which is the principal competitive advantage they have to offer? Does the inability of the tenderer to fix his contract costs penalize both him and the contracting authority which is awarding the contract? The former may lose an economic opportunity and the latter the right to get value for the public purse.

---

[96] Directive 2004/17 co-ordinating the procedures of entities operating in the water, energy, transport, and postal services sectors [2004] OJ L134/1; Directive 2004/18 co-ordinating the procedures of the award of public works contracts, public supply contracts an public service contracts [2004] OJ L134/14.

As to the workers themselves, it is questionable whether the Posted Workers **23.111** Directive offers them any more protection over and above that inherent in Article 49 EC itself and in the Community legislation governing employment conditions. Take for example, workers in a low wage economy with a relatively high unemployment rate. If they are posted to another country by their employer they are usually paid at a rate which is higher than what they are normally paid by their employer when working in their home country. This was certainly the case in *Laval*. Additionally, in most cases, they are provided, either in cash or in kind, fully or partially, with board and lodging. They are therefore financially better off than if they were working in their home state even if they are not paid the same rate as that prevailing in the host Member State. Moreover they do not have the same financial demands on their salary as a worker from the host Member States as, being from a low wage economy, their living costs will be proportionally lower. Is it so wrong to deprive the posted worker (and his employer) of the opportunity to sell his labour at a price which is advantageous to him? Is it not better to leave the matter of pay and employment to the employer and the employee to settle between themselves than potentially depriving him altogether of an economic opportunity of which he and his family would like to avail?

Part VI

EQUALITY OF TREATMENT: MEN AND WOMEN

24

EQUAL PAY[1]

A. Introduction

The principle of equal pay for men and women is enshrined in Article 141 EC, **24.01**
formerly Article 119. It provides as follows:

> 1. Each Member State shall ensure that the principle of equal pay for male and
> female workers for equal work or work of equal value is applied.

---

[1] Ellis: *EU Anti-Discrimination Law* Oxford University Press 2005, Chapter 4; Toth:
The Oxford Enclopedia of European Community Law Oxford University Press 2005, 131–64.

2. For the purpose of this article 'pay' means the ordinary basic or minimum wage or salary and any other consideration, whether in cash or in kind, which the worker receives directly or indirectly in respect of his employment from his employer.

Equal pay without discrimination based on sex means:

(a) that pay for the same work at piece rates shall be calculated on the basis of the same unit of measurement;

(b) that pay for work at time rates shall be the same for the same job.

. . .

(1) Equal Pay Directive

24.02 Directive 75/117 on equal pay for men and women[2] (the 'Equal Pay Directive') was adopted to implement Article 119, the belief being, at the time of its adoption, that Article 119 did not have direct effect and, absent the goodwill of the Member States to implement the principle of equal pay voluntarily, legislation was imperative. The legal basis for the Directive was what is now Article 94 EC,[3] there being no specific legal basis in the social policy chapter of the EC Treaty, as it stood at that time.

24.03 Following the Treaty of Amsterdam, the equal pay provisions of the EC Treaty were enhanced to include specific legislative competence. Article 141(3) provides that the Council, after consulting the Economic and Social Committee, may adopt measures, by a qualified majority vote, to ensure the application of the principle of equal opportunities and equal treatment of men and women in matters of employment and occupation, including the principle of equal pay for equal work or work of equal value.

24.04 Article 141(4) permits a degree of positive action. The principle of equal treatment may not prevent a Member State from maintaining or adopting measures providing for specific advantages in order to make it easier for the underrepresented sex to pursue a vocational activity or to prevent or compensate for disadvantages in professional careers.

(2) The Recast Directive

24.05 The Equal Pay Directive has been repealed with effect from 15 August 2009. It will be replaced by Directive 2006/54 on the implementation of the principle of equal opportunities and equal treatment of men and women in matters of employment and occupation (recast)[4] (the 'Recast Directive').

---

2 [1975] OJ L45/19.
3 See Chapter 2.
4 [2006] OJ L204/23.

This chapter will set out the development of the principle of equal pay for men **24.06** and women beginning with Article 119 of the original EC Treaty and the *Defrenne* litigation which charted the way forward.

B. Article 119

Article 119 was informed by, and its wording largely reflected, International **24.07** Labour Organization (ILO) Convention No 100, 1951[5] which provided in Article 2(1) that each signatory State:

> . . . shall by means appropriate to the methods in question for determining rates of remuneration, promote and in so far as is consistent with such methods, ensure the application to all workers of the principle of equal remuneration for men and women workers for work of equal value.

Article 119 did not refer to 'work of equal value' but used instead the phrase **24.08** 'equal work'. Article 141 refers to 'equal work or work of equal value' thereby bringing EC law into line with ILO Convention No 100.

Article 119 did not grant the Community institutions power to enforce the **24.09** principle of equal pay for equal work either by way of legislative measures or otherwise. It was left to the Member States themselves to bring about equal pay for equal work within their respective legal systems before the end of the first transitional period, ie by 31 December 1961.[6] Although in some Member States implementation had occurred before that date by means of constitutional or legislative provisions or collective agreements, in many other Member States little progress had been made. On 31 December 1961, the Member States adopted a Resolution granting themselves a further period of three years (until 31 December 1964) in which to eliminate all discrimination both direct and indirect in matters of pay. This deadline was not respected and so the Commission proceeded to draw up proposals for a directive on equal pay which was eventually adopted in 1975. Meanwhile there began a series of actions which shaped the development of equal rights for men and women in pay and employment within the European Community.

C. The *Defrenne* Cases

In 1970 a Miss Gabrielle Defrenne began a series of actions against her emp- **24.10** loyer, the now defunct Belgian airline company, SABENA. She brought three

---

[5] UNTS Vol 165, 303.
[6] In the case of Denmark, Ireland, and the United Kingdom, the relevant date for implementation of Article 119 was 1 January 1973, the date of their accession to the Community.

separate actions and all three cases eventually came before the ECJ by way of references for preliminary rulings from the Cour de Travail, Brussels.[7] In her second case, *Defrenne 2*, Miss Defrenne invoked Article 119 to claim the right to parity of pay with her male colleagues.

(1) *Defrenne 2*[8]

24.11 Gabrielle Defrenne was employed as a air hostess by SABENA. She claimed that she was paid less than her male colleagues who were employed as 'Cabin Stewards'. It was agreed that the work of an air hostess and a cabin steward was identical. In those circumstances the existence of discrimination in pay to the detriment of Miss Defrenne was not disputed. The first of two questions referred to the ECJ asked whether Article 119 introduced directly into national law the principle that men and women should receive equal pay for equal work, with the result that, independently of national provisions, workers were entitled to institute proceedings before national courts to ensure its observance? If the answer to this question was in the affirmative, the Cour de Travail, Brussels wished to know from what date the principle of equal pay had to be recognized.

(2) The judgment

24.12 The Court began its analysis by stating that Article 119 had a double aim. It addressed both economic concerns and social objectives.[9] Its aim was to avoid a situation whereby undertakings in Member States where the principle of equal pay had been implemented, suffered a competitive disadvantage vis-à-vis undertakings established in other Member States which had not yet eliminated pay discrimination. Article 119 was also part of a chapter in the Treaty devoted to social policy, the aim of which was to improve working conditions and living standards. The principle of equal pay the Court said 'formed part of the foundations of the Community'.

24.13 The Court went on to find that Article 119 was 'directly applicable and may therefore give rise to individual rights which the Courts must protect'.[10] Article 119, it held, imposed on States a duty to bring about a specific result within a fixed period. It was not a 'vague declaration'; the fact that it was addressed to Member States did not preclude the conferring of rights on individuals which may be enforced by courts. It was mandatory by nature and applied to both

---

[7] Case 80/70 [1971] ECR 445; Case 43/75 [1976] ECR 455; Case 149/77 [1978] ECR 1365.
[8] Case 43/75 [1976] ECR 455.
[9] Ibid Judgment paras 8–12.
[10] Ibid Judgment para 24.

public authorities, contracts of employment concluded by individuals, and collective agreements.

(3) Direct or overt discrimination

The Court was careful to limit the scope of Article 119 to cases of direct or overt **24.14** discrimination which may be identified solely with the aid of criteria based on equal work and equal pay. Among the forms of direct discrimination which could be so identified were those which had their origins in legislative provisions or collective labour agreements or which could be detected on the basis of a purely legal analysis of the situation to which they pertained. In such cases a court is in a position to establish all the facts which may enable it to decide whether a female worker is receiving lower pay than a male worker performing similar tasks. This was Miss Defrenne's position: she was performing the same tasks as a male cabin steward, for which she was receiving less pay.[11] The comparison between her work and that of her male colleagues was easy for a court to make and, in any event, was not even in dispute in those proceedings, all concerned having agreed that there was indeed a difference in rates of pay between the two groups of employees doing the same work.

(4) Indirect or covert discrimination

By contrast, indirect or disguised discrimination could, in certain circumstances, **24.15** involve the elaboration of criteria whose implementation necessitated the taking of appropriate measures at Community and national level. Such discrimination could not be readily discerned by a court of law and so could not form the basis of a claim based on Article 119 alone.

(5) Temporal effect

The second question put to the Court in *Defrenne 2* concerned the date from **24.16** which Article 119 was to be regarded as having direct effect. The Court held that the express terms of Article 119 required that the principle of equal pay was to be 'fully secured and irreversible' by the end of the first stage of the transitional period.[12] The Resolution of the Member States of 31 December 1961 could not modify that time limit. But even though Article 119 had direct effect as from 1 January 1962, or in the case of Denmark, Ireland, and the United Kingdom, 1 January 1973, the Court ruled that it could not be relied on in order to support claims concerning pay periods prior to the date of the judgment, ie 8 April 1976,

---

[11] Case 129/79 *McCarthys* [1980] ECR 1275; Case 69/80 *Worringham and Humphreys* [1981] ECR 767.

[12] Judgment para 56.

save as regards those workers who had already brought legal proceedings or made an equivalent claim. In reaching this conclusion the Court was persuaded by two factors:

(i) the arguments of the governments of Ireland and the United Kingdom on the possible economic consequences of claims dating back to 1 January 1973, which undertakings could not have foreseen and which might therefore seriously affect the financial situation of such undertakings possibly to the extent of driving some into bankruptcy; and

(ii) the failure of the Commission to start infringement proceedings against Member States for failure to fulfil their obligations which was '. . . likely to consolidate the incorrect impression as to the effect of Article 119'.[13] This inertia led to the belief that practices such as those complained of by Miss Defrenne, which were not contrary to national law, were also legitimate under Community law.

24.17 In the light of these factors, the Court therefore concluded that considerations of legal certainty justified a temporal limitation on the effect of the judgment. This was the first time the Court had ruled that that a judgment, rendered in the context of proceedings for a preliminary rulings, had prospective effect only.[14]

D. The Equal Pay Directive

24.18 The Equal Pay Directive came into force some eight weeks before the judgment in *Defrenne 2* was pronounced. That judgment did not make it in any way redundant and required no amendment to its provisions. From being perceived as the sole source of enforceable equal pay rights, the Directive became complementary and subject to Article 141, in the sense that it could not detract from its provisions and main role was to provide a source of rights for those cases of indirect discrimination which could not be dealt with under Article 141:

> Directive 75/117 was intended to encourage the proper implementation of Article 119. . .in order, in particular, to eliminate indirect forms of discrimination,

---

[13] Judgment para 73.

[14] In Case C-262/88 *Barber v Guardian Royal Exchange* [1990] ECR I–1889 which found occupational pensions to be 'pay' within the meaning of Article 119, the Court similarly limited the temporal effect of its judgment ruling that reliance could not be placed upon Article 119 in order to claim entitlement to a pension with effect from a date prior to that of the judgment, 17 May 1990, except in the case of workers who had before that date instituted legal proceedings or made an equivalent claim under applicable national law. The Court was swayed by the same considerations as it had been some 14 years before in *Defrenne*: 'In those circumstances, overriding considerations of legal certainty preclude legal situations which have exhausted all their effects in the past from being called into question where that might upset retroactively the financial balance of many contracted-out schemes' (Judgment para 44).

but was unable to reduce the effectiveness of that Article or modify its temporal effects.[15]

The Equal Pay Directive is relatively short and simple consisting of ten articles. **24.19** Article 1 provides that where a job classification system is used to determine rates of pay, that scheme must be based on the same criteria for men and women. Any discrimination on grounds of sex must be excluded. Article 3 obliges the Member States to abolish all discrimination between men and women in laws, regulations, and administrative provisions which is contrary to the principle of equal pay. Employees must be informed of the provisions adopted in pursuance of the Directive. Article 4 obliges Member States to ensure that collective agreements, wage scales, wage agreements, or individual contracts of employment which are contrary to the principle of equal pay, may be declared null and void or be amended. Articles 2 and 5 concern the remedies to be made available to aggrieved employees. They should have the right to pursue their claims by judicial process after possible recourse to other competent authorities. Member States are obliged to take measures to ensure that employees are protected against dismissal if they complain of unequal treatment or begin legal proceedings aimed at enforcing compliance with the principle of equal pay.

E. The Recast Directive

The purpose of the Recast Directive, according to the Explanatory Memoran- **24.20** dum[16] which accompanied the Commission's proposal, is to simplify and modernize Community law by putting together in one single text the provisions of a number of directives dealing with equality between men and women in the matter of pay, pensions, and work opportunities. In particular, the Recast Directive transposes into legislation some of the Court's extensive case law on equal pay and articulates the remedies to be made available for breach of the principle of equal treatment, in particular the right to compensation.

The Recast Directive sets out the principle of equal pay in Article 4. Definitions **24.21** of direct and indirect discrimination are provided in Article 2. Positive action is permitted within the limits of Article 141(4) at Member State level. Article 17 provides for access to judicial remedies even if the employment relationship in which the discrimination is alleged to have occurred has ended. Legal entities

---

[15] Ibid Judgment para 60. Whilst this seemed to rule out any interpretation of the Directive which could limit the effectiveness of Article 119 but did not detract from the possibility that it might have a broader approach than Article 119, in *Jenkins* (Case 96/80 [1981] ECR 911) and *Helmig* (Joined Cases C-399/92 etc [1994] ECR I–5727) the Court indicated that the scope of both instruments was co-terminous.

[16] COM (2003) 279 Final at 2.

which have a legitimate interest in ensuring that the provisions of the Directive relating to equal pay are complied with may engage either on behalf of or in support of any complainant in proceedings to enforce it. National law governs time limits in any proceedings. Article 18, discussed below, sets out the right to compensation or reparation.

F. Workers

24.22 Article 141 and the Equal Pay Directive guarantee equal pay for equal work to male and female workers. Article 141(1) does not define workers and there is no single definition of that concept within the Community legal order.[17] It varies according to the context to which it relates and the objectives of the Treaty. Neither the Equal Pay Directive nor the Recast Directive offer any definition of who is a worker.

24.23 The criterion on which Article 141(1) is based is the comparability of the work done by workers of each sex.[18] For the purpose of making that comparison the women and men in question must be workers working under a contract of employment or within an employment relationship as opposed to the self-employed working on their own account under multiple contracts for services.

24.24 Both Article 141 and its predecessor Article 119, refer to pay which a worker '. . .receives directly or indirectly from his employer'. Article 4(1) of the Recast Directive and Article 1 of the Equal Pay Directive both make reference to a 'job classification system' and Article 6 of the same Directive provides a specific definition of the personal scope of Chapter 2 of the Directive which is concerned with equal treatment in occupational pension schemes. It refers to members of the working population which includes self-employed persons. This stands in contrast to Chapter 1 on equal pay and is indicative that Chapter 2 is to have a broader scope of application.

(1) Community concept

24.25 The issue of who is a worker for the purposes of Article 141 arose only relatively recently in the *Allonby* case;[19] it does not appear to have been raised previously before the ECJ.

---

[17] Case C-85/96 *Martinez Sala* [1998] ECR I–2691 Judgment para 31.
[18] Case 149/77 *Defrenne (No 3)* [1978] ECR 1365 Judgment para 22.
[19] Case C-256/01 [2004] ECR I–873.

The Court in *Allonby* began its analysis of what is a worker for the purposes of   **24.26**
Article 141(1) by stating that the term was a Community concept which could
not be defined by reference to national law. Moreover it could not be interpreted
restrictively. Although the ECJ emphasized that the term 'worker' varies according to the area of law in which the concept is relevant, it did proceed to look
at its case law on the free movement of workers for guidance. Citing *Lawrie-
Blum*[20] and *Martinez Sala*[21] it held that:

> . . . there must be considered as a worker a person who for a certain period of time
> performs services for and under the direction of another person in return for which
> he receives remuneration.[22]

It was clear, the ECJ held, from the definition of pay in Article 141(2) that the   **24.27**
authors of the Treaty did not intend the term worker to include independent
providers of services who are not in a relationship of subordination with the
person who received those services.[23]

(2) Question of fact

The question of whether an employment relationship exists is one of fact to be   **24.28**
determined in each particular case, having regard to all the circumstances by
which the relationship between the parties is characterized. It is not dependent
upon formal classification of the claimant's economic activity under national law
or any subjective classification thereof by an employer but rather on an objective
assessment of the characteristics of the performance of economic activity.

The formal classification of a person under national law as self-employed does   **24.29**
not exclude the possibility that a person could be classified as a worker under
Article 141(1) if his independence was merely notional. A worker thus might
be treated as self-employed under national law but as employed for the purposes
of Article 141 or the Equal Pay Directive.

By making the concept of 'worker' a matter of objective determination the Court   **24.30**
excluded the possibility of circumventing the principle of equal treatment through
the formal categorization of economic activity. Thus in *Allonby*[24] a case involving
teachers who were, vis-à-vis an intermediary undertaking, made available to
undertake assignments at a college of further education, the Court held that it was
necessary in order to determine whether they were workers or not to consider

---

[20] Case 66/85 [1986] ECR 2121.
[21] Case C-85/96 [1998] ECR I–2691.
[22] *Allonby* (see note 19 above) Judgment para 67.
[23] Judgment para 68. The Court relied upon Case C-337/97 *Meeusen* [1999] ECR I–3289 in
support of this conclusion.
[24] Case C-256/01 [2004] ECR I–873.

factors such as the extent of any limitation their right to choose their timetable, the place and the content of their work. The fact that there was no obligation on them to accept an assignment was, the Court ruled, of no consequence.

(3) Public and private sector employment

24.31 The term 'worker' encompasses those in both private sector employment and public service. In *Commission v Germany*[25] the Court held that Article 141 and the Equal Pay Directive were '. . .of general application, a factor which is inherent in the very nature of the principle which they lay down'[26] and accordingly applied to public sector employment:

> New cases of discrimination may not be created by exempting certain groups from the provision intended to guarantee equal treatment of men and women in working life as a whole.

24.32 Some 12 years later *Gester*[27] confirmed *Commission v Germany*:

> To exclude the public sector from the scope of Article 119 would run counter to that provision's objective. Moreover the Court stated in Case 248/83 *Commission v Germany*. . . that both Directive 76/207 and Directive 75/117 apply to employment in the public service. It further stated that those directives—like Article 119—are of general application, a factor inherent in the very nature of the principle which they lay down.[28]

(4) Principle of the single source

24.33 Nothing in the wording of Article 141(1) suggests that the applicability of the provision is limited to situations in which men and women work for the same employer and indeed where pay rates are fixed horizontally on a cross-industry basis, for example by collective agreement, they may well not be working for the same employer. However it must be possible to compare the rates of pay in issue and some person or entity must be responsible for implementing the principle of equal pay. Where differences in pay between workers performing equal work or work of equal value cannot be attributed to a single source there is no entity responsible for the inequality and therefore no entity which can be held responsible for ensuring equal treatment. Such a situation does not come within Article 141(1) since no comparison can be carried out between the work of the two groups. This principle was established in the *Lawrence*[29] and *Allonby*[30] cases.

---

25 Case 248/83 [1985] ECR 1459.
26 Ibid Judgment para 16.
27 Case C-1/95 [1997] ECR I–5353.
28 Ibid Judgment para 18.
29 Case C-320/00 [2002] ECR I–7325.
30 See note 24 above.

The Lawrence *case*

The applicants in this case were a Mr Lawrence and 446 other workers, almost **24.34**
all of whom were women. The respondents were three private undertakings
who were or had been the employers of the applicants at the time of the dispute.
The background to the case lay in the outsourcing of certain services by North
Yorkshire County Council to the respondent undertakings.

Until 1990 the Council had assumed responsibility for the cleaning and catering **24.35**
services in schools and educational establishments under its control. When the
Council contracted out catering and cleaning services to the respondent undertakings, the latter re-employed a number of female staff originally employed by
the Council and also recruited new female employees who had never been
employed by the Council. Most of the applicants had been originally employed
by the Council. The central issue was whether the applicants were entitled, for
the purpose of establishing a claim to equal pay, on the basis of Article 141(1)EC,
to compare themselves to men employed by the Council performing work of
equal value.

The Court held that Article 141 EC was not applicable in the circumstances **24.36**
of the case:

> . . .where, as in the main proceedings here, the differences identified in the pay con-
> ditions of workers performing equal work or work of equal value cannot be attrib-
> uted to a single source, there is no body which is responsible for the inequality
> and which could restore equal treatment. Such a situation does not come within the
> scope of Article 141(1) EC. The work and pay of those workers cannot therefore be
> compared on the basis of that provision.[31]

The Allonby *case*[32]

The position in *Allonby* was similar to Lawrence. It was sought to compare the **24.37**
pay received by a person providing services through an agency to a college of
higher education with that of full-time employees of the college working directly
for it under a contract of employment. The Court, following *Lawrence*, held
that it could not be done: in effect no single source could be held responsible for
the discrepancies in the level of remuneration and consequently no entity was
responsible for the inequality (each having independent responsibility for setting
remuneration levels).

---

[31] Ibid Judgment para 18.
[32] See note 19 above.

Admittedly there is nothing in the wording of Article 141(1) to suggest the applicability of that provision is limited to situations where men and women work for the same employer.

. . .

However, where the differences identified in the pay conditions of workers performing equal work or work of equal value cannot be attributed to a single source, there is no body which is responsible for the inequality and which could restore equal treatment . . .[33]

G. Pay

24.38 'Pay' is defined in Article 141 in broad terms. It has been interpreted accordingly by the ECJ. Any consideration which is derived from employment, in whatever form, be it cash or in kind, is 'pay' for the purposes of Article 141 and the Equal Pay Directive. The test is whether the recipient of the benefit which is alleged to be paid, would have been entitled to, or received, that benefit if it were not for his or her employment. If he or she would have been so entitled the benefit in question, whatever form it takes, is pay: it derived from and is dependent upon the employment.

24.39 'Pay' has been held to include the following: piece work schemes in which pay depends on the individual output of each worker;[34] sick leave payments;[35] pay received during maternity leave either by virtue of the employment contract, a collective agreement, or under legislation;[36] family and marriage allowances;[37] compensation for unfair dismissal following judicial proceedings the amount of which was fixed by legislation;[38] travel concessions paid to employees and to their spouses or long-term partners of the opposite sex or to their dependants;[39]

---

[33] Ibid Judgment paras 45 and 46 The Commission's original draft of the Recast Directive published in 2004 proposed integrating the 'single source principle' into Article 4 which would have read: 'For the same work or work to which equal value is attributed, discrimination on the grounds of sex with regard to all aspects and conditions of remuneration attributable to a single source shall be eliminated.' In the event, this proposal was not adopted. There is no reference in Article 4 to the requirement that remuneration which is to be compared must derive from a single source.

[34] Case C-400/93 *Royal Copenhagen* [1995] ECR I–1275.

[35] Case 171/88 *Rinner-Kuhn* [1989] ECR 2743; Case C-66/96 *Hoj Pedersen* [1998] ECR I–7327.

[36] Case C-343/93 *Gillespie* [1996] ECR I–475; Case C-411/96 *Boyle* [1998] ECR I–6401; Case C-218/98 *Aboulaye* [1999] ECR I–5723.

[37] Case C-187/98 *Commission v Greece* [1999] ECR I–7713.

[38] Case C-167/97 *Seymour-Smith and Perez* [1999] ECR I–623.

[39] Case 12/81 *Garland* [1982] ECR 359; Case C-249/96 *Grant* [1998] ECR I–621.

an end of year Christmas bonus;[40] supplements paid for specific duties or inconvenient working hours;[41] paid leave;[42] pay in respect of loss of earnings due to attendance at training courses for staff council members;[43] occupational pensions paid under contractual arrangements with an employer;[44] redundancy payments[45] and severance grants.[46]

Pay includes allowances paid to an employee by an employer during maternity **24.40** leave. This means that a woman whose contract of employment or employment relationship continues to subsist during a period of maternity leave must receive pay rises which are awarded during that period to her fellow employees doing work similar to her usual employment.[47]

Compensation for time spent on a training course necessary for the perfor- **24.41** mance of staff functions is pay even if it does not derive from the contract of employment: it is paid by the employer by reason of the existence of the employment relationship.[48] Although the staff functions may be honorary in themselves, in the sense that they are not the subject of specific remuneration, the only compensation paid being in respect of loss of earnings, where represen- tative functions or related training courses take place during working hours such payments arise out of the employment relationship and are not inde- pendent of it.

(1) Sources of pay

The source of remuneration is irrelevant: it can derive from a contract of employ- **24.42** ment, a collective agreement, an ex gratia payment from an employer, under a statutory provision or by virtue of a judicial decision. It matters not from where pay comes provided it is linked to employment in the sense that it is the emp- loyment relationship which gives rise to the right or the opportunity to be paid. For example, compensation for time spent on a training course is pay.[49]

---

[40] Case C-281/97 *Kruger* [1999] ECR I–5127; Case C-333/97 *Lewen* [1999] ECR I–7243.
[41] Case C-381/99 *Brunnhofer* [2001] ECR I–4961; Case C-236/93 *JamO* [2000] ECR I–2189.
[42] Case C-360/90 *Botel* [1992] ECR I–3589.
[43] Case C-278/93 *Freers and Speckmann* [1996] ECR I–1165.
[44] Case 262/88 *Barber* [1990] ECR I–1889.
[45] Case C-33/99 *Kowlaska* [1990] ECR I–2591.
[46] Case C-249/97 *Gruber* [1999] ECR I–5295.
[47] Case *Gillespie* [1996] ECR I–475; Case C-218/98 *Abdoulaye* [1999] ECR I–5709.
[48] Case C-360/90 *Boetel* [1992] ECR I–3589; Case C-457/93 *Lewark* [1996] ECR I–243; Case C-278/93 *Freers and Speckmann* [1996] ECR 1165.
[49] Ibid.

Collective agreements

24.43   Article 141 does not specifically mention collective agreements as a source of pay but *Defrenne 2*[50] held that the principle of equal pay in Article 141 extended to pay levels regulated by collective agreement:

> . . . since Article 119 is mandatory in nature, the prohibition on discrimination between men and women . . . extends to all agreements which are intended to regulate paid labour collectively, as well as to contracts between individuals.[51]

24.44   The Equal Pay Directive expressly states that it is applicable to collective agreements,[52] as does the Recast Directive.[53]

24.45   In *Kowalska*[54] the Court found a clause in a collective wage agreement applying to the national public service excluding part-time employees, who were largely female, from the benefit of a severance grant on termination of their employment to be contrary to Article 141. In *Krieza*[55] an end of year bonus paid under a collective agreement applicable to public sector employees was held to be pay and so the exclusion of a large groups of female employees from entitlement to it was found to be contrary to Article 141.

24.46   *Nimz*[56] raised the interesting issue of how discrimination in a collective agreement should be rectified. It held that where a provision in a collective agreement is discriminatory, the national court is required to set aside that provision without requesting or awaiting its practical removal by the collective bargaining process or any other procedure. In such a case the groups disadvantaged by the discriminatory provision must be treated in the same way as other employees to which their situation compared unfavourably since that is the only other valid point of reference. This is the same approach as the ECJ adopted with respect to inequality in social security entitlements contrary to the Equal Treatment in Social Security Directive:[57] where national legislation infringed the principle of equal treatment by denying women entitlement to benefits in circumstances where men would have had a right to benefits, the Court held that women were to be granted the same benefits as men since there was no other point of reference.[58] The Court

---

[50]   See note 8 above.

[51]   Judgment para 39; Case C-281/97 *Krieza*; Joined Cases C-399/92 etc *Helmig* [1994] ECR I–5727.

[52]   Article 4.

[53]   Article 23.

[54]   Case C-33/89 [1990] ECR 2591.

[55]   See note 51 above.

[56]   Case C-184/89 [1991] ECR I–297.

[57]   Directive 79/7 [1979] OJ L6/24.

[58]   Case 286/85 *McDermott and Cotter* [1987] ECR 1453.

thus requires that the perpetuation of the inequality, pending amendment to its source, be avoided.

Enderby[59] raised a different issue concerning collective agreements: to what **24.47** extent can separately negotiated collective agreements be compared for the purpose of determining whether there is gender discrimination in the pay levels fixed by the two collective agreements for two jobs of equal value? Enderby was a speech therapist. She complained that as a member of a health care profession which was largely female, she was paid less than a pharmacist which she claimed was doing the same work or work of equal value. The rate of pay for both professions was settled by collective bargaining processes. Within each collective agreement there was no difference in the treatment of men and women but when both were compared there were differences in the pay of both professions. Could the two agreements be compared for the purposes of determining whether the alleged discrimination between the two professions existed or not? The Court held that they could:

> The fact that the rates of pay at issue are decided by collective bargaining processes conducted separately for each of the two professional groups concerned without any discriminatory effect within each group, does not preclude a finding of prima facie discrimination where the results of these processes show that two groups with the same employer and the same trade union are treated differently. If the employer could rely on the absence of discrimination within each of the collective bargaining processes taken separately as sufficient justification for the difference in pay, he could easily circumvent the principle of equal pay by using separate bargaining processes.[60]

Ex gratia payments

The employer may not necessarily be contractually or otherwise legally bound **24.48** to furnish the payment or benefit in question. Ex gratia payments paid over voluntarily are pay if linked to employment. *Garland*[61] concerned the right to travel facilities by spouses and children of retired employees. Such facilities were granted to the spouses and children of male employees but not to female employees. The employer, British Rail, was not contractually bound to grant such facilities but generally did so with the result that male employees had a legitimate expectation that they would be so granted after their retirement.

The Court found that the facilities in question were pay for the purposes of **24.49** Article 141; provided they were granted in respect of employment, their precise legal nature was not relevant. As long as they were made available to employees or

---

[59] Case C-127/92 [1993] ECR I–5535.
[60] Judgment para 22.
[61] Case 12/81 [1982] ECR 359.

retired employees they were subject to the principle of equal treatment set out in Article 141.

24.50 Similarly in *Lewen*[62] a Christmas bonus, equal to one month's salary, which was a voluntary benefit revocable at any time payable as an incentive for future work and loyalty, was held to be pay for the purposes of Article 119.

Statutory payments

24.51 The concept of 'pay' can also cover payments which an employer is obliged to make to an employee under statute irrespective of any agreement between them. An example of such a payment arose in *Rinner-Kuhn*[63] which concerned a German legislative provision entitling employees who worked more than 10 hours a week or 45 hours a month to the continued payment of their salary by their employee in the event of illness. Redundancy payments or severance payments prescribed by statute, but payable by the employer, are also pay.

Judicial decision

24.52 *Seymour-Smith*[64] held that a judicial award of compensation for breach of the right not to be unfairly dismissed constitutes pay:

> . . . the compensation granted by an employer to an employee on termination of his employment . . . is a form of deferred pay to which the worker is entitled by reason of his employment but which is paid to him on termination of his employment with a view to enabling him to adjust to the new circumstances arising from such termination . . .
>
> The fact that the compensation at issue in the main proceedings is a judicial award made on the basis of applicable legislation cannot invalidate that conclusion. As the Court has already stated in this connection, it is irrelevant that the right o compensation, rather than deriving from the contract of employment is, for instance, a statutory right.[65]

(2) Access to pay

24.53 The right of access to elements of consideration is also pay, for example the right to join an occupational pension scheme has been held to be within the scope of Article 141[66] as has the automatic reclassification to a higher point in the salary scale on the basis of length of service[67] and a system for classifying workers

---

62 Case C-333/97 [1999] ECR I–7266; Case C-281/97 *Kruegar* [1999] ECR I–5127 (special annual bonus).
63 Case C-173/91 [1993] ECR I–673; C-166/99 [2000] ECR I–6155.
64 Case C-167/97 *ex parte Seymour-Smith* [1999] ECR I–666.
65 Ibid Judgment paras 25 and 29.
66 Case 170/84 *Bilka Kaufhaus* [1986] ECR 1607.
67 *Nimz* (see note 56 above).

converting from job sharing to full-time employment which determines their pay level.[68] However, the possibility of a promotion leading to a higher salary is not 'pay':[69]

> ... where, in the present case, a civil servant is placed on a list of candidates eligible for promotion, his progression to a higher grade and accordingly a higher level of remuneration, is not a right but a mere possibility. Actual promotion depends on various factors such as first, the availability of a post in the higher grade and, secondly the maintenance of his position on the list of person eligible for promotion . . .[70]

(3) Methods of payment

The consideration may be paid directly by the employer to the employee or indi- **24.54** rectly through another entity, for example in the case of an occupational pension by a trust set up to manage and administer the pension scheme from which pension entitlements are claimed[71] or a sum payable as result of a judicial award to an employee following proceedings against his employer for employment-related benefits.[72]

(4) Social security benefits

Social security benefits payable under statutory schemes are not pay. In **24.55** *Defrenne I*[73] it was held that retirement pensions, which are governed by statute without any element of negotiation within the employer undertaking or sector in question, and which apply on a compulsory basis to general categories of workers are not 'pay'. Such schemes provide workers with benefits under a statutory scheme which is financed by workers, employers, and in some cases public authorities and is governed more by considerations of social policy than the employment relationship. Although 'pure' social security benefits do not therefore constitute 'pay', any supplements paid by an employer to the beneficiary of a social security benefit such as unemployment benefit may constitute 'pay' if they are contractual in the sense of arising out of negotiations between an employer and his employees:

> ... the additional payment, although linked to unemployment benefit as regards the manner in which it is made, is independent of the general social security system as

---

[68] Case C-243/95 *Hill and Stapleton* [1998] ECR I–3739.
[69] Case C-1/95 *Gerster* [1997] ECR I–5253.
[70] Ibid Judgment para 23.
[71] Case C-262/88 *Barber* [1990] ECR I–1889.
[72] Case C-167/99 *Seymour-Smith and Perez* [1999] ECR I–623.
[73] Case 80/70 [1971] ECR 445.

regards both its structure and financing, the latter being the responsibility of the employer alone.[74]

H. Equal Pay for Equal Work

24.56 Article 119 referred to 'equal pay for equal work'. The Equal Pay Directive in Article 2(1) refers to equal pay for work of equal value, reflecting the terms of ILO Convention No 100 on equal pay.

24.57 In *Defrenne 2*[75] the ECJ stated that the Directive had extended the narrow criterion of 'equal work' in Article 119 thereby implying that 'equal work' and 'work of equal value' were somehow different concepts the latter being broader in meaning than the former.[76]

24.58 *Jenkins v Kingsgate Clothing*[77] held that Article 1 of the Equal Pay Directive was designed to facilitate the practical application of the principle of equal pay as outlined in Article 119 and consequently it in no way altered the scope or content of that provision: it could neither be given a broader nor a narrower interpretation than Article 119. This conclusion can be queried: the Equal Pay Directive has as its sole legal basis Article 94. It is therefore arguable that since it was not based on Article 119 it could have a broader (but not narrower) scope than that provision.

24.59 In *Worringham and Humphreys*[78] the Court clarified the position ruling that the concept of 'same work' in Article 119 included cases of 'work to which equal value is to be attributed'.

24.60 Article 141 now provides for 'equal pay for male and female workers for equal work or work of equal value'. Article 4 of the Recast Directive reproduces the working of Article 1 of the Equal Pay Directive.

24.61 Whatever the wording in the various instruments which have governed the right to equal pay over the years, the Court has consistently adopted a broad approach focusing on the essential objective of the principle of equal pay which is to ensure that men and women who do the same work receive the same remuneration.

---

[74] Case C-173/91 *Commission v Belgium* [1993] ECR I–673 Judgment para 21; Case C-166/99 *Defreyn v Sabena* [2000] ECR I–6174.

[75] See note 8 above.

[76] This was the view taken by the Court in Case 143/83 *Commission v Denmark* [1985] ECR 427 in which it found Denmark to have failed to implement the Equal Pay Directive by providing only for equal pay for the same work and failing to provide for equal pay for work of equal value.

[77] Case 96/80 [1981] ECR 911.

[78] Case 69/80 [1981] ECR 767.

It has accordingly laid down principles to ensure that job classification schemes do not contain features that would result in the discriminatory treatment of one sex or the other. It has allowed comparisons to be made between jobs held at different points of time and between jobs having a higher value to the jobs with which a comparison is sought to be made.

(1) Job classification schemes

In the case of different types of work, it may not be easy to determine whether **24.62** they are comparable in value, and in order to facilitate comparisons for the determination of pay rates. Employers may choose set up a job classification scheme in order to evaluate the different components in any given job but that job classification scheme may in itself have discriminatory consequences.

The Equal Pay Directive, in Article 1, and the Recast Directive, in Article 4, **24.63** provide that where a job classification system is used for determining pay, it must be based on the same criteria for both men and women and so exclude any discrimination on grounds of sex. More precise indications of how this may be achieved are set out in case law.

Rummler v Dato Druck[79] laid down a number of principles by which job classifi- **24.64** cation schemes should be governed:

(i) The criteria governing the pay rate classification must ensure that work which is objectively the same attracts the same rate of pay whether it is performed by a man or a woman.

(ii) The use of values reflecting the average performance of workers of one sex as a basis for determining the extent to which work makes demands or requires effort or whether it is heavy physical work constitutes a form of discrimination on the ground of sex which is contrary to the Equal Pay Directive.

(iii) In order for a job classification system not to be discriminatory as a whole it must, in so far as the nature of the tasks carried out in the undertaking permits, take into account criteria for which workers of each sex may show particular aptitude.

Brunnhofer[80] further clarified the principles on job classification and work of **24.65** equal value setting out the following principles:

(i) The fact that a female employee who claims to be the victim of discrimination on grounds of sex and the male comparator are classified in the same job

---

[79] Case 237/83 [1986] ECR 2101.
[80] Case C-381/99 [2001] ECR I–4961.

category under the collective agreement governing their employment is not in itself sufficient for concluding that the two employees concerned are performing the same work or work to which equal value is attributed since this is only one indication amongst others that this criterion is met.

(ii) A difference in pay may be justified by circumstances not taken into consideration under the collective agreement applicable to the employees concerned, provided that they constitute objective reasons unrelated to any discrimination based on sex and respect the principle of proportionality.

(iii) In the case of work paid at time rates, a difference in pay awarded at the time of their appointment, to two employees of different sexes for the same job or work of equal value, cannot be justified by factors which have become known only after the employees concerned take up their duties and which can be assessed only once the employment contract is being performed, such as a difference in individual work capacity of the persons concerned or in the effectiveness of the work of a specific employee compared with that of a colleague.

(2) Contemporaneity

24.66 *Macarthys*[81] raised the issue of the point in time when job comparisons could be made.[82] Mrs Smith was employed as a manager of a warehouse at a salary of £50 per week. Her predecessor, who had left that job some four months earlier, had been paid £60 per week. Could Mrs Smith compare herself to him in spite of the fact that they were not both in the employment of Macarthys at the same time? Could her employer offer her a lower rate of pay where there was no change in the work required to be performed but she had been hired some four months after her predecessor had left the post? The ECJ held in principle that it could not. The scope of the concept of 'equal work' could not be restricted by the introduction of a requirement of contemporaneity. Where the work was of equal value a female employee had to receive the same pay as her male predecessor even if he had vacated the job some time before she was appointed. If the situation were otherwise, it would be all too easy to avoid the principle of equal pay.

24.67 However, the position might be otherwise if the difference in pay between workers occupying the same post but at different periods in time is based on the operation of factors unconnected with sex. *Macarthys* does not give any indication of the periods of time over which comparisons can be made. It is possible

---

[81] Case 129/79 [1980] 1275.
[82] Case C-400/93 *Royal Copenhagen* [1995] ECR I–1275 Judgment paras 32 and 33; Case C-309/97 *Angestelltenbetriebstrat* [1999] ECR I–2865 Judgment para 17; Case C-381/99 *Brunnhofer* (see note 80 above).

that in the case of a lengthy period between the employment of two employees the nature of a job, which although formally the same, in terms of title and grade, may change. It is also possible that the market rate for that job may change. These would be factors which could justify offering a different rate of pay to an employee's successor.

(3) Equal work

Macarthys held that the scope of the concept of 'equal work' is entirely qualitative **24.68** in character in that it is exclusively concerned with the nature of the services in question. The point of focus in determining whether jobs are of equal value is the nature of the work performed not its formal classification within the employer organization.

Absolute parity is not necessary. Work may be of lesser value than that with **24.69** which it is sought to be compared. This stands to reason. If work of equal value is required to be remunerated on the same basis why should work of lesser value not be so required?

In *Murphy*[83] a group of women who were employed as factory workers claimed **24.70** the right to be paid the same as male workers employed as store labourers. It was established that the women's work was, on the whole, of a higher value than the men with whom they sought to be compared. The ECJ held that Article 141 could be relied upon where a worker was engaged in work of higher value than that of the person with whom the comparison was sought to be made. If the position were otherwise Article 141 could be rendered nugatory as an employer could circumvent it by assigning additional or more onerous duties to workers of a particular sex who could then be paid at a lower rate.

Whether work is of equal value or not, is, therefore, a subjective matter to be **24.71** determined on the basis of the facts of each case. There is no hard and fast rule. It is for the national court to determine whether in the light of the actual nature of the activities carried out by those concerned. Rates of pay fixed by two distinct collective bargaining processes for each profession are not conclusive evidence that the two jobs in question are not of equal value.[84] Neither is the fact that the employees concerned are classified in the same job category under the collective agreement applicable to their employment sufficient to conclude that they perform the same work or work of equal value.

---

[83] Case 157/86 [1988] ECR 673.
[84] *Enderby* (see note 59 above).

24.72 Similarity or differences in professional qualifications are not in themselves decisive. The essential criterion is what the workers actually do or can be required to do, not what qualifications they have. Comparisons based on qualifications alone could be misleading. They must be made in the context of the employment environment.

24.73 In *Angestelltenbetriebsrat der Wiener Gebietskrankenkasse*[85] the issue was whether different groups of persons who carried out seemingly identical tasks but who did not have the same training or professional qualifications performed the same work. In that case there were three types of psychotherapists employed by the Vienna Health Fund: doctors who had completed their general practitioners' or specialists' training; graduate psychologists qualified to practise in the health sector or on a self-employed basis; and lastly those who are neither doctors nor psychologists but who had a general education and had undergone specialized training in psychotherapy. Were these three categories comparable? The order for reference to the ECJ stated that although psychologists and doctors employed as psychotherapists by the Health Fund performed identical activities, in treating their patients they drew upon knowledge and skills acquired in very different disciplines, the expertise of psychologists being grounded in the study of psychology, that of doctors in the study of medicine. Even though doctors and psychologists both in fact perform work of psychotherapy the former were also qualified to perform other tasks in a field which is not open to the latter, who could only perform psychotherapy:

> In those circumstances two groups of persons who have received different professional training and who, because of the different scope of the qualifications resulting from that training, on the basis of which they were recruited, are called upon to perform difference tasks or duties, cannot be regarded as being in a comparable situation.[86]

24.74 The Court was not influenced in its findings by the fact that a single tariff was charged for psychotherapeutic treatment since that may 'be the result of social policy'.

24.75 If it is the case that two groups of persons with different professional training do perform different tasks, then they are not in comparable situations. But if in fact those with different professional qualifications are also doing the same tasks they may be doing the same work or work of equal value. Whether this is the case or not must be ascertained by looking at the tasks assigned to each group and the training requirements for the performance of those tasks. If the tasks are

---

[85] Case C-309/97 [1999] ECR I–2865.
[86] Judgment para 21.

performed by persons having different qualifications but whose training is suitable for the execution of those tasks, it would appear difficult to argue that they are not doing 'equal work'. This may be the case of the 'overqualified' worker whose skills exceed those required for the job in question. Conversely if persons having the same qualifications are in fact doing different tasks they may not be doing equal work.

I. Discrimination

Both direct and indirect discrimination are prohibited. The concept of indirect **24.76** discrimination was developed by the ECJ[87] and subsequently incorporated into the Burden of Proof Directive.[88]

Article 2 of the Recast Directive[89] defines what is meant by direct and indirect **24.77** discrimination:

(a) 'direct discrimination': where one person is treated less favourably on grounds of sex than another is, has been or would be treated in a comparable situation;

(b) 'indirect discrimination': where an apparently neutral provision or practice would put persons of one sex at a particular disadvantage compared with persons of the other sex, unless that provision, criterion or practice is objectively justified by a legitimate aim, and the means of achieving that aim are appropriate and necessary.

(1) Direct discrimination

Direct discrimination is easier to discern than indirect discrimination in that **24.78** it concerns a difference in the rate of pay for male and female employees doing the same work or work of equal value and therefore is, or ought to be, obvious.

Direct discrimination has been found to exist in the following circumstances: **24.79**

(i) Where a woman receives less pay than a man who previously carried out the same work in the same undertaking;[90]

---

[87] See Section J below.
[88] Directive 97/80 on the Burden of proof in cases of discrimination based on sex [1998] OJ L14/6.
[89] See note 4 above.
[90] Case 129/79 *Macarthys v Wendy Smith* note 81.

(ii)   where a male and female employee performing the same work receive the same basic salary but the male employee is paid a higher salary supplement than the female employee;[91]

(iii) where retired male transport employees enjoy travel facilities denied to retired female employees;[92]

(iv)   where retirement pensions under an occupational pensions scheme are paid out at different pensionable ages for men and women;[93]

(v)   where the conditions attaching to the receipt of survivors' pensions differ for widows and widowers;[94]

(vi)   where redundancy payments awarded by virtue of a collective agreement are granted to male workers aged between 60 and 65 years but are denied to female workers within the same age group;[95]

(vii) denial of pay increases to women during periods of maternity leave.[96]

(2) Indirect discrimination

24.80   Indirect discrimination is more difficult to detect (and prove) than direct discrimination, given that pay rates will, in principle, appear to be the same for workers in doing the same work under comparable conditions. The classic case, and one of the first to come before the ECJ, is that of the part-time worker who tends to be female and may be paid proportionately less or receive less favourable terms of employment than the full-time worker. Equality of treatment for part-time workers has now been ensured in the Part-time Workers Directive[97] but some 25 years ago the position was not quite so clear in the then prevailing state of Community law.

24.81   Mrs Jenkins[98] worked part-time in the Kingsgate Clothing company. She claimed that she was receiving an hourly rate of pay which was less than that of her male colleagues employed full-time doing the same work. The part-time work force of Kingsgate Clothing was predominantly female. The Court held that a difference in pay between full-time and part-time workers does not amount to discrimination prohibited by Article 141 of the Treaty unless it is in reality merely an indirect way of reducing the level of pay of part-time workers on the ground that that group of workers is composed exclusively or predominantly of women.

---

91 Case C-381/99 *Brunnhoffe* note 80.
92 Case C-12/81 *Garland* note 61.
93 Case C-262/88 *Barber* note 14.
94 Case C-147/75 *Evenopoulous* [1997] ECR I-2057; Case C-50/99 *Podesta* [2000] ECR I-4039.
95 Case C-173/91 *Commission v Belgium* [1993] ECR I-673.
96 Case C-342/83 *Gillespie* [1996] ECR I-475; Case C-147/02 *Alabastor* [2004] ECR I-3101.
97 Directive 97/81 [1998] OJ L14/8. See Chapter 19.
98 Case 96/80 [1981] ECR 911.

If the difference in pay between the two groups of workers is attributable to factors which are objectively justified there is no unlawful discrimination. This might be the case if the employer was endeavouring to encourage full-time work irrespective of the sex of the worker.

Further examples of findings of indirect discrimination in preliminary rulings **24.82** proceedings before the ECJ in which part-time workers have been denied benefits or advantages given to full-time employees include:

(i) the exclusion of part-time workers from membership of occupational pension schemes;[99]

(ii) the exclusion of part-time workers from the payment of a severance grant on termination of employment;[100]

(iii) non-payment of salary to part-time workers during periods of illness;[101]

(iv) the exclusion of workers in minor employment (less than fifteen hours a week) from a special Christmas bonus equivalent to one month's salary;[102]

(v) the placement of job sharers who worked part-time to a pay level less than that for full-time job sharing staff upon their conversion to full-time employment;[103]

(vi) the non-payment of compensation to part-time workers for attendance at staff training courses outside their normal working hours, where full-time staff receive compensation for loss of earnings due to attendance at such courses during their normal working hours;[104]

(vii) there is prima facie case of discrimination where the pay level of one group of workers (predominantly women) is less than another group of workers (predominantly men) working for the same employer in jobs which are of equal value;[105]

(viii) a requirement for access to membership of an occupational pension scheme which is more difficult for women to fulfil than men.[106]

(3) Time rates/piece work

Where work is paid at time rates the employer may take the employee's level of **24.83** productivity into account[107] with the result that different rates may be applicable,

---

99 Case C-170/84 *Bilka* [1986] ECR 1607.
100 Case 33/89 *Kowalska* note 54.
101 Case C-171/88 *Rinner-Kuhn* [1989] ECR 2743.
102 Case C-281/97 *Kruger* note 62.
103 Case C-243/95 *Hill and Stapleton* note 68.
104 Case C-360/90 *Botel*; Case C-457/93 *Lewark*; Case C-278/93 *Freers and Speckmann* [1996] ECR I–1165, all in note 48.
105 Case C-127/92 *Enderby* [1993] ECR I–5535.
106 Case C-256/ 01 *Allonby* note 19.
107 Case C-381/99 *Brunnhofer* [2001] ECR I– 4961 Judgment para 72.

but since the pay differentials will not be attributable to sex but to objective differences in the value of the work to the employer, the principle of equal pay will not be violated. Likewise where the unit of measurement is the same for two groups of workers carrying out the same work at piece rates, the principle of equal pay does not prohibit those workers from receiving different pay if that is due to levels of individual output.[108] Therefore, in a piece work scheme the mere finding that there is a difference in the average pay of two groups of workers, calculated on the basis of the total individual pay of all workers belonging to one or other group, is not sufficient to establish that there is discrimination with regard to pay.[109]

(4) Computation of pay

24.84 The basic methodology by which an employment package is calculated may affect aspects of an employee's remuneration and must therefore be the same for men and women. It is necessary to look at each aspect of the remuneration package and the relationship between those elements.

24.85 In *Worringham and Humphreys*[110] Lloyds bank had two retirement schemes, one for men and one for women established under collective agreements made between Lloyds and the trade union representative of Lloyds' employees. Under the retirement schemes, men under the age of 25 years were required to contribute 5 per cent of their salary to these schemes whereas women under 35 years were not. In order to cover the compulsory contributions of the young men, Lloyds added the amount of the contribution—5 per cent—to their gross salary. This amount was then deducted and paid directly into the pension scheme. The men in question therefore never actually received the 5 per cent extra pay. But the basis on which other employment related benefits such as redundancy payments, unemployment benefits, family benefits, mortgage, and credit allowances were calculated included that 5 per cent figure. The Court found that in the circumstances of the case the pension contributions paid by Lloyds on behalf of the men constituted 'pay' since they directly determined the calculation of other advantages linked to salary with the result that the men received benefits from which women engaged in the same work or work of equal value were excluded, or received on that account greater benefits or social advantages than those to which women were entitled.

---

[108] *Brunnhofer* Judgment para 73.
[109] Case C-400/93 *Royal Copenhagen* [1995] ECR I–1275.
[110] Case 69/80 [1981] ECR 767.

The *Worringham and Humphreys* case was followed some three years later in **24.86**
Liefting[111] in the context of a pension scheme for civil servants where, in the case
of married civil servants, contributions to the scheme were calculated on the basis
of their combined salaries subject to an upper limit. The result of this was that in
certain cases the contributions chargeable to the wife's employing authority
might be lower than would be the case is she were not married to a civil servant.
The ensuing impact on the amount of gross salary meant that related benefits
which were based on that salary such as severance pay, unemployment benefit,
family allowances, and loan facilities, would be calculated on a less favourable
basis that that of a male civil servant performing the same work.

Liefting, like *Worringham and Humphreys*, was concerned with the impact of dif- **24.87**
ferent methods of calculating gross salary on salary related benefits. *Newstead*[112]
differed in the sense that men and women received the same gross salary but a
sum of 1.5 per cent of that was deducted in the case of men as a contribution to a
widow's pension fund. The result was that the net pay of men and women was less
than that of women doing the same job. The Court, in contrast to the approach
it had adopted in *Worringham and Humphreys*, ignored the patent disparities in
net pay finding that there was no discrimination since gross pay for men and
women was the same:

> The deduction in question results in a reduction in net pay because a contribution is
> paid to a social security scheme and in no way affects gross pay, on the basis of which
> other salary-related benefits . . . are normally calculated.[113]

Although the Court referred to the widow's pension scheme as 'social security' **24.88**
this was not in fact the case: the scheme in question was an occupational pension
scheme. Had it been a statutory social security scheme, there would have been no
issue under Article 141 as such schemes are not 'pay'.

A factor which, although not alluded to by the Court, may have influenced its **24.89**
thinking was that a civil servant who, like Mr Newstead, was a 'confirmed
bachelor', who had never married, would have been entitled upon retirement to
have his contributions to the widow's pension scheme returned to him with com-
pound interest at a rate of 4 per cent per annum when he left the civil service or
paid to his estate should he die before that time.

Although Mr Newstead would have thus got his contributions back, it seems dif- **24.90**
ficult to see that that factor alone would justify the disparity in net salary between

---

[111] Case 23/83 [1984] ECR 3225.
[112] Case 192/85 [1987] ECR 4753.
[113] Judgment para 18.

a male married civil servant and female civil servant who was not obliged to join the scheme.

24.91 In *Nimz*[114] a collective agreement, providing for the period of service of employees working at least three-quarters of normal working time to be fully taken into account for reclassification in a higher salary grade but only one-half of such period of service to be taken into account in the case of employees whose working hours were between one-half and three-quarters of those normal working hours, and the latter group of employees comprised a considerably smaller percentage of men than women, was found, in the absence of objective justification on the part of the employer, to be precluded by Article 141 where those working three-quarters time or less were predominantly women.

24.92 *Gerster*[115] distinguished *Nimz* and held that, in the circumstances of the case periods of employment during which the hours worked were between one half and two thirds of normal working hours were counted only as two thirds of normal working hours did not fall within the scope of Article 141, such a provision being primarily designed to lay down promotion conditions, in terms of length of service. A civil servant's access to a higher grade, only affected indirectly the level of pay to which he would be entitled upon completion of the promotion procedure. The basis for calculating the periods of service was therefore only one of a number of factors determining promotions and an accompanying raise in salary.

24.93 The difference between *Nimz* and *Gester* thus lay in the fact that the calculation of periods of service in *Nimz* directly affected salary levels whereas in *Gester* the impact of the calculation of periods of service only contributed towards a possible promotion which would bring about a salary raise. The Court went to on to find that Mrs Gester's complaint more properly lay under the Equal Opportunities Directive[116] which precluded the method of calculating the period or salary in issue. In the subsequent case of *Hill and Stapleton*[117] the Court condemned a system whereby job sharers (who were predominantly female) who converted to full-time employment were given a point on the pay scale applicable to full-time staff which was lower than the point they previously occupied when job sharing because their periods of job sharing were calculated by actual length of service in that particular post.

---

114 Case C-184/89 [1991] ECR I–297.
115 Case 1/95 [1997] ECR I–5253.
116 Directive 76/207 [1976] OJ L39/40.
117 Case C-243/95 [1998] ECR I–3739.

J. Grounds of Discrimination: Limited to Sex

Discrimination with respect to pay under Article 141 and the Equal Pay Directive **24.94** is prohibited on the grounds of sex only.[118] Where persons or groups of persons are the subject of comparison for the purposes of ascertaining whether there are inequalities in their remuneration are not of different sexes, that comparison cannot be made and no claim to equal pay will lie—at least on the basis of the above-mentioned provisions.

An employer is entitled to restrict employment benefits to married couples **24.95** thereby excluding couples who are not married. Equally an employer may restrict benefits to spouses or persons of the opposite sex who are in a relationship with the employee from whose remuneration the entitlement to those benefits derives. Neither of these situations comes about because of any unlawful discriminatory conduct. Each employee is subject to the same conditions of entitlement. But what if an employee is prevented from getting a benefit related to his employment either for himself or for his partner or family member because under national law he cannot put himself in a position to fulfil the requirements of entitlement? This was the situation in *K.B.*

In *K.B.*[119] the Court held that it was in principle contrary to Article 141 for **24.96** national legislation to prevent a couple from fulfilling the marriage requirement which must be met for one of them to be able to benefit from the salary benefits of the other. The Court in reaching this conclusion was influenced by the fact that the national provision in issue had been held to be contrary to the European Convention of Human Rights. Somewhat surprisingly it left it to the national court to determine whether, on the facts of the case, Article 141 could be relied upon to achieve recognition of the right of an employee to nominate her partner as a beneficiary of a survivor's pension payable by her employer to survivors of married employees.

In *Grant*,[120] Lisa Grant claimed the right to travel concessions from her employer, **24.97** South West Trains, in respect of her female partner. Travel concessions were granted to employees, their spouses, and/or partners of the opposite sex with whom the employee has been in a meaningful relationship for two years. Ms Grant's application for these concessions for her partner was rejected on

---

[118] Case 96/80 *Jenkins* [1981] ECR 911 Judgment para 10; *Brunnhofer* note 107 Judgment para 40.
[119] Case C-117/01[2004] ECR I–241.
[120] Case C-249/96 [1998] ECR I–621.

the ground that in the case of unmarried employees travel concessions would only be granted for partners of the opposite sex. Ms Grant claimed that such a restriction constituted discrimination on two counts:

(i) the male worker who had previously occupied her post had obtained travel concessions for his female partner and consequently any refusal to give the same concessions to Ms Grant's partners amounted to direct discrimination based on sex;

(ii) the denial of the concessions constituted discrimination on the ground of sexual orientation which was included within the concept of 'discrimination based on sex' in Article 141.

24.98 The Court rejected both of these arguments. It held that Ms Grant was refused the concession because she did not live with a spouse or person of the opposite sex, which was a condition for entitlement. That condition applied to all employees regardless of their sex. Travel concessions were not made available to a male worker if he was living with a person of the same sex just as they were unavailable to a female worker if she were living with a person of the same sex. Article 141 did not cover discrimination based on sexual orientation. The Court came to this conclusion having had regard to the wording of the provision of Article 141, its place in the Treaty, and its legal context. In reaching this conclusion the Court was influenced by the fact that the Treaty of Amsterdam, which had been signed some four months previously, empowered the Council to take action to eliminate discrimination based on sexual orientation, from which it could be deduced that Article 141 was not concerned with sexual orientation.

K. Burden of Proof

24.99 It is clear that in a claim for equal pay, adducing evidence of discriminatory behaviour on the part of an employer may be difficult. An aggrieved employee may simply not be in a position to produce a clear picture of levels of remuneration. In particular, the methods by which pay levels are computed may not transparent and establishing that different jobs require comparable skills, and so are of equal value, may also be problematic. The ECJ has recognized these difficulties and has developed principles to ensure 'equality of arms' in equal pay and other disputes involving discriminatory practices in the workplace.

24.100 *Danfoss*[121] was the first of these cases. It concerned a system of supplements to basic pay, the criteria for which were unclear. Comparisons between the various components of pay for different groups of workers was therefore not realistic.

---

[121] Case 109/88 [1989] ECR 3199.

... a situation where a system of individual pay supplements is completely lacking in transparency is at issue, female employees can establish differences only in so far as average pay is concerned. They would be deprived of any effective means of enforcing the principle of equal pay before the national courts, if the effect of adducing such evidence was not to impose upon the employer the burden of proving that his practice in the matter of wages is not in fact discriminatory.[122]

24.101 *Enderby*,[123] which we have considered above, followed and reinforced *Danfoss*. The case concerned a group of speech therapists who were all female. They complained of being paid less than other predominantly male groups of health care professionals such as pharmacists and psychologists, whose jobs they considered to be of equal value.

24.102 The Court in a terse judgment ruled:

Where there is a prima facie case of discrimination, it is for the employer to show that there are objective reasons for the difference in pay. Workers would be unable to enforce the principle of equal pay before national courts, if evidence of a prima facie case of discrimination did not shift to the employer the onus of showing that the pay differential is not in fact discriminatory.[124]

24.103 Subsequent case law confirmed these principles:[125] if a claimant made out a prima facie case, the burden of proof shifted to the employer. The principles developed by the ECJ were codified in the Burden of Proof Directive[126] adopted in 1997. This Directive has been repealed and replaced by the Recast Directive, Article 19 of which provides that persons who consider themselves wronged because the principle of equal treatment has not been applied to them must establish facts from which it may be presumed there has no direct or indirect discrimination and it is for the respondent to prove that there is no breach of the principle of equal treatment. Member States may introduce rules of evidence which are more favourable to plaintiffs. Member States need not apply the burden of proof rule set out in Article 19 to proceedings in which it is for the court or competent body to investigate the facts of the case. Unless otherwise provided by the Member States, Article 19 does not apply to criminal proceedings.

L. Defences

24.104 Claims for breach of the principle of equal pay can be defended on the grounds of objective justification, the essence of which is that the alleged discrimination

---

[122] Ibid Judgment para 13.
[123] See note 23.
[124] Ibid Judgment para 18.
[125] See note 59.
[126] Directive 97/80 on the Burden of proof in cases of discrimination based on sex [1998] OJ L14/6.

in pay rates is due to considerations other than the sex of the worker concerned. The justification in question must be based on a legitimate objective and the means to achieve that objective must be appropriate and necessary.[127]

24.105 *Enderby*[128] ruled that proportionality was a question of fact in each case. The Court found that the state of the employment market might lead an employer to increase the rate of pay of a particular job in order to attract candidates. That would be a legitimate objective in itself. But the role of market forces in determining the rate of pay had to be sufficiently significant to justify the difference in rates of pay between two groups of workers doing equal work.

24.106 Length of service may also justify pay differentials. Mrs *Cadman*[129] complained that she received less pay than four of her male colleagues doing the same work. They had been in service for longer than she had. Citing *Danfoss*[130] the Court held that, as a general rule, recourse to the criterion of length of service was a legitimate objective of pay policy. Length of service went hand in hand with experience and experience helped the worker to perform duties better. An employer can reward length of service without having to establish the impact it has on the performance by its employee of specific tasks unless there is evidence capable of raising doubts as to this. In those circumstances the burden was on the employer to prove that length of service gives the experience which enables the employee to do his/her job better. If a job classification system is used in which length of service is a factor there is no need for the employer to prove that the individual worker has acquired experience during the relevant period which has enabled him to perform his duties better.

24.107 Any legitimate aim of social policy may constitute an objective justification:

> . . . if the Member State can show that the means chosen meet a necessary aim of its social policy and that they are suitable and requisite for attaining that aim, the mere fact that the provision affects a much greater number of female workers than male workers cannot be regarded as constituting an infringement of Article 119.[131]

24.108 That said, the implementation of national social policy objectives cannot have the effect of frustrating the implementation of a fundamental principle of Community law such as equal pay.[132]

---

[127] *Bilka* (see note 99) Judgment para 37.
[128] Note 59.
[129] Case C-17/05 [2006] ECR I–9583.
[130] *Danfoss* (see note 121).
[131] *Rinner Kuhn* (see note 101) Judgment para 14; See Case C-317/93 *Nolte* [1995] ECR I–4625 and Case C-444/93 *Megner* [1995] ECR I–4741.
[132] *Seymour Smith* (see note 72).

The Court has refused to accept broad generalizations as justifying unequal treat- **24.109**
ment.[133] The objective justification must relate to the particular circumstances
in issue. For example mere generalizations as to the capacity of a specific measure
to encourage recruitment are not acceptable as objective justification for a
discriminatory practice. Nor is established practice a sufficient justification.[134]

Cost is not acceptable as a justification for pay differentials: **24.110**

> So far as the justification based on economic grounds is concerned, it should be
> noted that an employer cannot justify discrimination arising from a job-sharing
> scheme solely on the ground that avoidance of such discrimination would involve
> increased costs.[135]

M. Remedies

Article 141 of the EC Treaty has direct effect with the result that it can be invoked **24.111**
by individuals as a source of rights in legal proceedings before national courts.
Although it grants rights, Article 141 is silent on the remedies which should be
given for breach of those rights. Whilst it is, therefore, for national law systems
to determine what remedies should be available, their discretion in this matter is
not entirely unfettered. The ECJ has established a number of principles which
must be respected by national legal systems. The essence of these principles is to
ensure that that Community law rights are not rendered nugatory. Accordingly:

(i) Community law rights must not be treated less favourably than similar
national law rights; in equal pay terms this would mean, in the first place,
that a claim based on Article 141 EC or the Equal Pay Directive would have
to give rise to the same range of remedies as a claim based on national equal
pay legislation and practice;[136]

(ii) remedies must be such as to ensure the effective protection of Community
law rights.[137]

In general the remedy to be given in the case of claimant unlawfully denied equal **24.112**
pay is quantifiable: what is the difference between the rate of pay actually granted
to the claimant within the employment relationship and what is the rate of pay
enjoyed by male workers doing the same work or work of equal value? The latter
rate of pay is that due to the claimant.

---

[133] *Nimz* note 56.
[134] Case C-243/95 *Hill and Stapleton* [1998] ECR I–3739.
[135] Ibid Judgment para 40.
[136] Case 106/77 *Simmenthal* [1978] ECR 629 Judgment paras 14–17.
[137] Case C-26/95 *Palmisani* [1997] ECR I– 4025 at 4045.

Accordingly, for the purposes of Article 119, there is a very simple and effective method of moving against a discrimination: it is enough for the national courts to declare null and void any clause in an individual or collective contract which conflicts with the aforesaid provisions. On the question of pay nullity means that the rate of pay provided for by the clause which is void is automatically replaced by the higher rate of pay granted to the male worker.[138]

24.113 In *Kowalska*[139] the Court found that the provisions of a collective agreement which provided for the payment of a severance grant on termination of the employment relationship to full-time workers only was discriminatory where a considerably lower percentage of men than women worked part-time, unless such exclusion could be objectively justified.

24.114 If no objective justification existed the termination provision of the collective agreement had to be applied proportionately to the part-time work force.

24.115 The Recast Directive contains specific provisions on remedies. Article 18 entitled 'Compensation or Reparation' obliges the Member States to introduce into their national legal systems such measures as are necessary to ensure real and effective compensation or reparation for loss or damage sustained by a person as a result of discrimination on grounds of sex 'in a way which is dissuasive and proportionate to the damage suffered'. Such compensation or reparation may not be restricted by the fixing of a prior upper limit. Article 25 provides for the adoption by Member States of penalties, which may comprise the payment of compensation to victims of discrimination. The penalties must be effective, dissuasive, and proportionate.

---

[138] Advocate General Trabucchi in *Defrenne 2* (see note 8) at 489–90.
[139] Case 33/89 [1990] ECR 2591.

25

EQUALITY OF OPPORTUNITY

A. Introduction

The principle of equal opportunities for men and women in employment is laid down in Directive 76/207 on the implementation of the principle of equal treatment for men and women as regards access to employment, vocational training and promotion and working conditions (the 'Equal Opportunities Directive').[1] **25.01**

The Equal Opportunities Directive shares its origins with the Equal Pay Directive.[2] Both derive from in the Social Action Programme of 1974[3] which included amongst its priorities 'action for the purpose of achieving equality **25.02**

---

[1] [1976] OJ L39/40.
[2] Directive 75/117 [1975] OJ 145/19.
[3] [1974] OJ C13.

between men and women as regards access to employment and vocational training and promotion and as regards working conditions including pay'.[4]

25.03 Many of the provisions of the Equal Opportunities Directive reflect those of the Equal Pay Directive; both are designed to be complementary and much of the case law on each Directive can be transposed to the other. However, whereas exceptions to the principle of equal opportunities are permitted, the Equal Pay Directive provides for no exceptions: parity in pay for equal work is at all times required unless differential treatment is objectively justified that is unrelated to sex and therefore not prohibited.

25.04 Since there was no specific legislative competence granted in the original EC Treaty, the Equal Opportunities Directive was adopted on the basis of the Community's general law-making powers enshrined in Article 308.

25.05 This position has now changed as a result of amendments introduced by the Treaty of Amsterdam. Article 141(3) provides that the Council, after consulting the Economic and Social Committee, may adopt measures, by a qualified majority vote, to ensure the application of the principle of equal opportunities and equal treatment of men and women in matters of employment and occupation, including the principle of equal pay for equal work or work of equal value.

25.06 It is on the basis of this provision that the Equal Opportunities Directives was amended in 2002 by Directive 2002/73[5] (the 2002 Amendment), which was required to be transposed into national law by 5 October 2005. The purpose of this amendment[6] was to take account of the sizeable body of case law which had emanated from the ECJ during the previous 25 years, to define sexual harassment as discrimination based on sex; to reinforce the protection afforded to employees who allege discriminatory conduct; to acknowledge that special protection be granted to women because of their biological condition and their right to return to the same work place after maternity leave; to clarify the rights of Member States to provide for derogations from the principle of equal access to employment and the right to adopt positive action measures to promote equality for men and women and to define the concepts of direct and indirect discrimination in line with the provisions of the Framework Employment Directive[7] and the Race Directive.[8]

---

4 Preamble, recital 1.
5 [2002] OJ L269/15.
6 Proposal for a Directive amending Directive 76/207 COM (2000) 334 Final Explanatory Memorandum para 4.
7 Directive 2000/78 [2000] OJ L303/16. See Chapter 29.
8 Directive 2000/43 [2000] OJ L180/22. See Chapter 28.

The Equal Opportunities Directive, along with The Equal Pay Directive, has **25.07** been repealed with effect from 15 August 2009. It will be replaced by Directive 2006/54 on the implementation of the principle of equal opportunities and equal treatment of men and women in matters of employment and occupation (recast)[9] (the 'Recast Directive').

B. Relationship with Other Provisions on Equal Treatment

Article 141(1) EC laid down the principle of equal pay for equal work. It has **25.08** no application to equal opportunities[10] nor statutory social security schemes.[11] The right to equality of treatment in those spheres derives from the Equal Opportunities Directive, the Equal Treatment in Social Security Directive,[12] and the more recent Framework Employment Directive.[13]

Below we examine the relationship between these Directives. **25.09**

(1) Equal Pay Directive

The Equal Pay and Equal Opportunities Directives have been found to be mutu- **25.10** ally exclusive: a claim in equal pay cannot be grounded in the Equal Treatment Directive:

> In that regard, it should be borne in mind that the benefit paid during maternity leave constitutes pay and therefore falls within the scope of Article 119 of the Treaty and Directive 75/117. It cannot therefore be covered by Directive 76/207 as well. That directive, as is clear from its second recital in the preamble, does not apply to pay within the meaning of the abovementioned provisions.[14]

A certain degree of confusion has arisen since the adoption of the 2002 amend- **25.11** ment to the Directive, Article 3(1) of which refers to 'employment and working conditions including dismissals as well as pay provided for in Directive 75/117'. Does this mean 'pay' is now within the scope of the Directive or, since Directive 75/117 is specifically referred to, does it mean that 'pay' is within the scope of that Directive to the exclusion of the Equal Opportunities Directive? There is no evidence in the Explanatory Memorandum to the proposal for the 2002 amendment[15] as to what the provision is supposed to mean, which one might

---

9 [2006] OJ L204/23.
10 Case 149/77 *Defrenne 3* [1978] ECR 1365 Judgement para 21.
11 Case 80/70 *Defrenne I* [1971] ECR 445.
12 Directive 79/7 [1979] OJ L6.
13 Directive 2000/78 [2000] OJ L303/16.
14 Case C-342/93 *Gillespie* [1996] ECR I–475.
15 See note 6 above.

expect if it were to change previous perceptions. It appears to have been inserted rather late in the legislative process, which might mean that it is not significant.[16]

(2) The Equality of Treatment in Social Security Directive

25.12 The Equal Opportunities Directive provides for the adoption of a further directive on equality of treatment in social security, thereby indicating that it does not to apply to statutory social security systems.[17]

25.13 However, not all matters relating to social security are outside the ambit of the Equal Treatment Directive. Any social security matter which relates to access to employment, vocational training, or working conditions will be covered by the Directive. For further discussion see paras 26.02–26.05.

25.14 Linking the age at which employees are to be dismissed from employment to the date on which they become eligible for a state social security pension has also been held to be within the scope of the Equal Treatment Directive since linking the two determines the age of dismissal.[18]

(3) The Framework Employment Directive

25.15 The Framework Employment Directive prohibits discrimination on a number of grounds, including sexual orientation. The Equal Opportunities Directive has been held to apply only to differences of treatment based on sex only. Consequently it has no application in situations where the alleged discrimination is based on sexual orientation.[19] Such discrimination falls within the scope of the Framework Equality Directive.

C. Scope of Application

25.16 The scope of the Directive is expressed broadly; it lays down the principle of equal treatment for men and women with respect to the following matters:

(i) conditions for access to employment, to self-employment, or occupation including selection criteria and recruitment conditions for access to all jobs, and to all levels of the occupational hierarchy;

---

[16] Ellis: *EU Anti-Discrimination Law* Oxford University Press 2005 at 216–18.
[17] Art 1(2).
[18] Case 152/84 *Marshall v Southampton and South West Area Health Authority* [1986] ECR 723.
[19] Case C-249/96 *Grant v South West Trains* [1998] ECR I–621.

(ii) access to all types, and all levels, of vocational guidance, vocational training, and advanced vocational training and retraining including practical work experience;

(iii) working conditions, including conditions governing dismissal;

(iv) membership of, and involvement in, an organization of workers or employers, or any organization whose members carry on a particular profession, including the benefits provided for by such organizations.

The prohibition is general, extending to both the public and private sectors of the labour market, including public bodies, whatever the sector or branch of activity.[20] No sector of the labour market is given a blanket immunity from the application of the principle of equal treatment. The Directive itself permits a number of exceptions in certain defined circumstances. These are discussed below in paras 25.59–25.81. **25.17**

The objective of the Directive to bring about equality of treatment in substance rather than form.[21] Member States may introduce or maintain provisions which are more favourable to the protection of the principle of equality than the provisions of the Directive.[22] The implementation of the Directive cannot justify a reduction in the level of protection on a national level. **25.18**

Sirdar[23] raised the question of whether decisions taken by the Member States with regard to access to employment, vocational training, and working conditions in the armed forces fell within the scope of Community law. **25.19**

The ECJ held that it is for the Member States which have to adopt measures to ensure their internal and external security to take decisions on the organization of their armed forces but such decisions might not necessarily fall outside the scope of Community law. **25.20**

The principle of equal treatment of men and women was not subject to any general reservation as regards measures for the organization of the armed forces taken on the grounds of the protection of public security, apart from the application of Article 297 EC,[24] which concerned a wholly exceptional situation. **25.21**

---

[20] Case 1/95 Gerster [1997] ECR I–5253; Case C–79/99 *Schnorbus* [2002] ECR I–10997; Article 3(1).

[21] Case C–342/01 *Merino Gomez* [2004] ECR I–2605 Judgment para 37.

[22] Article 8e.

[23] Case C–273/97 [1999] ECR I–7403.

[24] Article 297 provides that Member States shall consult each other with a view to taking together the steps needed to prevent the functioning of the common market being affected by measures which a Member State may be called upon to take in the event of serious internal disturbances affecting the maintenance of law and order, in the event of war, serious international tension constituting a threat of war, or in order to carry out obligations which it has accepted for the purpose of maintaining peace and international security, interests of its security.

Although certain provisions in the EC Treaty provide for derogations applicable in situations which may affect public security it was not possible to infer from those articles that there was inherent in the Treaty a general exception covering all measures taken for reasons of public security. To do so 'might impair the binding nature of Community law and its uniform application'.[25]

25.22 In *Kreil*[26] the Court, following *Sirdar*, refused to allow a general derogation from the principle of equal treatment. It held that the Equal Opportunities Directive precluded the application of certain provisions of German law, which generally excluded women from military posts involving the use of arms, allowing them access only to medical and military music services. The fact that persons serving in the armed forces may be called upon to use arms cannot in itself justify the exclusion of women from access to military posts.

25.23 *Dory*[27] came to the ECJ by way of reference from a German court. The issue was simple: Was the fact that, in Germany, military service was compulsory only for men contrary to Community law? Dory's argument essentially was that compulsory military service prevented him from exercising an occupation during that period of service and delayed his access to employment, putting him at a disadvantage with women who were in a position to start on the career path much earlier in life.

25.24 The Court accepted that this was the case but held that the delay in the careers of persons called up for military service is an inevitable consequence of the choice made by Germany regarding the organization of its armed services. It was up to the Member States to adopt appropriate measures to ensure their internal and external security. The existence of adverse consequences for access to employment, cannot, without encroaching on the competence of the Member States, have the effect of compelling the Member State in question, in this case Germany, either to extend the obligation of military service to women, thus imposing on them the same disadvantage with regard to access to employment or to abolish compulsory military service.[28] The Commission and the Advocate General approached the issue from a different perspective; they were of the view that compulsory military service does not place the persons subject to it in an

---

25 Ibid Judgment para 16.
26 Case C-285/98 [2000] ECR I-69.
27 Case C-186/01 [2003] ECR I-2479.
28 Judgment para 41.

employment relationship, thus the Equal Opportunities Directive was not applicable.[29]

The *Dory* judgment accepts that Member States have the right to organize their **25.25** internal and external security as they wish, but it is clear from *Sirdar* and *Kreil* that within that organization, the principle of equal treatment prevails.

(1) Access to employment

Article 3 of the Directive covers access to employment. This provision has direct **25.26** effect[30] and has a wide meaning, encompassing not only conditions obtaining before an employment relationship comes into being but also to any matter which affects the decision to seek or accept employment. For example, a social security benefit designed to keep low income workers in employment or to encourage them into employment is within the scope of the Directive, being directly related to access to employment:[31]

> ... the prospect of receiving family credit if he accepts low paid work encourages an
> unemployed worker to accept such work with the result that the benefit is related to
> considerations governing access to employment.[32]

In considering whether the principle of equal treatment has been violated the **25.27** essential issue is whether employment has been refused on the ground of sex which will not be the case if it was on grounds equally applicable to both sexes. The refusal of employment or the termination of employment on the grounds of pregnancy constitutes discrimination on the grounds of sex since pregnancy is a condition unique to the female sex. The issue of pregnancy and discrimination is considered below in Section F.

(2) Vocational training

Article 3(1)(b) provides for the application of the principle of equal treatment **25.28** with regard to access to all types of and all levels of vocational training, advanced vocational training, and retraining. This provision has been found to have direct effect.[33]

In *Schnorbus*[34] the ECJ found that giving preferential treatment in the matter of **25.29** admission to practical legal training to male applicants who have completed

---

[29] Koutrakos: 'How far is Far Enough? EC Law and the Organisation of the Armed Forces after *Dory*' (2003) 66 MLR 759; Trybus (2003) 40 CML Rev 1269.
[30] Case 222/84 *Johnston v Chief Constable of RUC* [1986] ECR 1651.
[31] Case C-116/94 *Meyer v Chief Adjudication Officer* [1995] ECR I–2131.
[32] Ibid Judgment para 22.
[33] See note 30 above.
[34] Case C-79/99 [2000] ECR I–10997.

compulsory military or civil service indirectly discriminates against women since they are not required to do military or civilian service and hence cannot benefit from such preferential treatment. However, the Court went on to find that such differential treatment was objectively justified:

> ... it is clear that the provision at issue, which takes account of the delay experienced in the progress of their education by applicants who have been required to do military or civilian service, is objective in nature and prompted solely by the desire to counterbalance to some extent the effects of that delay.[35]

(3) Employment conditions including dismissal

25.30 The application of the principle of equal treatment to working conditions has direct effect[36] and the Directive may be invoked against any state body, whatever its legal form.[37]

25.31 The concept of 'working conditions' has been given a broad interpretation: it is not confined to conditions prevailing in the workplace or in the contract of employment. It concerns all aspects of the conditions in which the worker performs his job. For example in *Meyer*[38] the right to family credit was held to part of a person's working conditions. To that extent, working conditions may be subjective in the sense of varying from one employee to another.

25.32 A prohibition on night work by women where there was no equivalent provision applicable to men has been held to be discriminatory and therefore prohibited.[39]

(4) Dismissal

25.33 In *Burton v British Railways Board*[40] it was held that the concept of dismissal must be construed broadly so as to include the termination of an employment relationship between a worker and his employer even as part of a voluntary redundancy scheme.

25.34 *Roberts v Tate and Lyle Ltd*[41] held that the age limit for compulsory redundancy of workers as part of a mass redundancy falls within the concept of 'dismissal' in

---

[35] Ibid Judgment para 44.
[36] Case C-152/84 *Marshall I* [1986] ECR 723.
[37] Case 188/89 *Foster* [1990] ECR I–3313.
[38] See note 31.
[39] Case C-197/96 *Commission v France* [1997] ECR I–1489; Case C-345/89 *Stoeckel* [1991] ECR I –4097; Case C-13/93 *Minne* [1994] ECR I–371.
[40] Case 19/81 [1982] ECR 535.
[41] Case 151/84 [1986] ECR 703.

the Directive. Joan Roberts worked for Tate and Lyle for 28 years. At the age of 53 years she was made redundant along with the other employees at the depot at which she worked in Liverpool, which was closed by Tate and Lyle. Employees were offered either a cash payment or a early pension. All employees both male and female over the age of 55 were offered an early pension. The normal retirement age for men was 65 and women 60. Ms Roberts contended that the early pension entitlement under the severance package was discriminatory since men were entitlement to an immediate pension 10 years before retirement age whereas women were not so entitled until 5 years before their normal retirement age. The Court ruled that there was no discrimination:

> . . . the grant of a pension to persons of the same age who are made redundant amounts merely to a collective measure adopted irrespective of the sex of those persons in order to guarantee them all the same rights.[42]

Judgment in *Marshall I*[43] was handed down on the same day as *Roberts*. **25.35** Miss Marshall was employed as a dietician by an area health authority. She was dismissed at the age of 62 years solely because she had reached retirement age. The health authority had a policy which fixed retirement age at the age at which the statutory pension becomes payable, which was 60 years in the case of women and 65 years in the case of men. The health authority had exercised its discretion to allow Miss Roberts to continue working until the age of 62 years but she wished to work until the age of 65 years.

On a reference for a preliminary ruling from the Court of Appeal, the ECJ held: **25.36**

> . . . a general policy concerning dismissal involving the dismissal of a woman solely because she has attained the qualifying age for a state pension, which age is different under national law for men and women, constitutes discrimination on the grounds of sex.[44]

Article 5(1) prohibits the dismissal of a woman who is (i) pregnant: (ii) on mater- **25.37** nity leave; (iii) for reasons of absence due to illness during maternity leave attributable to pregnancy or the birth of a child.

Issues relating to discrimination against pregnant women are dealt with in **25.38** Section F below.

---

[42] Ibid para 36.
[43] Case 152/84 [1986] ECR 723.
[44] Ibid Judgment para 38.

D. Equality of Treatment

25.39 Article 2(1) of the Directive provides that the principle of equal treatment means that there shall be no discrimination whatsoever '. . . on grounds of sex either directly or indirectly by reference in particular to marital or family status'.

25.40 The Directive extends to differences in treatment related to sex only. If there is no difference in the treatment of men and women, there is no violation of the principle of equal treatment. Consequently, differences based, for example, on marital status or sexual orientation are not prohibited by the Directive.

25.41 In *Grant v South West Trains*[45] the ECJ held that the refusal of an employer to allow travel concessions to a person of the same sex with whom a worker had a stable relationship outside marriage did not constitute discriminatory conduct within the meaning of the Directive:

> . . . In the present state of law within the Community, stable relationships between two persons of the same sex are not regarded as equivalent to marriages or stable relationships outside marriage between persons of the opposite sex. Consequently, an employer is not required by Community law to treat the situation of a person who has a stable relationship with a partner of the same sex as equivalent to that of a person who is married or has a stable relationship outside marriage with a partner of the opposite sex.[46]

25.42 By contrast, in *P and S v Cornwall County Council*[47] the ECJ held that the Directive applied to transsexuals with the result that it prohibited the dismissal of a transsexual for reasons relating to gender reassignment. The dismissal was therefore gender related:

> . . . the scope of the directive cannot be confined simply to discrimination based on the fact that a person is of one or the other sex. In view of the purpose and the nature of the rights which it seeks to safeguard, the scope of the directive is such as to apply to discrimination arising, in this case, from the gender reassignment of the person concerned.[48]

25.43 Harassment and sexual harassment are deemed to be discrimination within the meaning of the Directive and therefore prohibited.[49] A person's rejection of, or submission to, such conduct may not be used as a basis for a decision affecting that person.

---

[45] Case C-249/96 [1998] ECR I–621.
[46] Ibid Judgment para 35.
[47] Case C-13/94 [1996] ECR I–2143.
[48] Ibid Judgment para 20.
[49] Art 2(3).

An instruction to discriminate against persons on the grounds of sex is deemed **25.44** to be discrimination.[50]

Both direct and indirect discrimination are prohibited.[51] **25.45**

(1) Direct discrimination

Direct discrimination is defined as the treatment of one person less favourably on **25.46** the grounds of sex than another is, has been, or would be treated in a comparable situation.[52] For example, a scheme under which nursery places are made available only to female staff constitutes unlawful discrimination.[53] On the other hand where, as in the case of *Nikoloudi*,[54] only women were employed as part-time cleaners there could be no issue of discrimination. Any differential treatment must be by reason of the sex of the person concerned. Thus for example, a rule whereby general medical training must includes periods of full-time training has been held not to constitute direct discrimination since it applies to both men and women equally.[55] In *P etc and D and Sweden v Council*[56] the restriction of a household allowance to married EC officials under the Staff Regulations was held not to discriminate against those who were in married partnerships. Refusal of access to the allowance was not because of sex (or sexual orientation) but by reason of the nature of the relationship between the official in question and the partner:

> . . . as regards infringement of the principle of equal treatment of officials irrespective of their sexual orientation, it is clear that it is not the sex of the partner which determines whether the household allowance is granted, but the legal nature of the ties between the official and the partner.[57]

(2) Indirect discrimination

Indirect discrimination[58] arises where an apparently neutral provision, criterion, **25.47** or practice would put persons of one sex at a particular disadvantage compared with persons of another sex, unless that provision, criterion, or practice is objectively justified by a legitimate aim, and the means of achieving that aim are appropriate and necessary.[59] This is the case, for example, where access to

---

[50] Art 2(4).
[51] Art 2(1).
[52] Art 2(2).
[53] Case 496/99 *Lommers* [2002] ECR I-2891 Judgment para 30.
[54] Case C-196/02 [2005] ECR I–1789.
[55] Case C-25/02 *Rinke* [2003] ECR I–8349.
[56] Joined Cases C-122/99 [2001] ECR I–4319.
[57] Ibid Judgment para 47.
[58] Case C-444/93 *Megner and Scheffel* [1995] ECR I–4741; Case C-343/92 *De Weerd (nee Roks) and Others* [1994] ECR I–571; Case C-100/95 *Kording* [1997] ECR I–5289.
[59] Ibid.

vocational training, promotion, or other employment conditions is made more difficult for part-time workers since, although particular employment conditions may apply to the part-time workforce as a whole, in general, women predominate in that kind of employment and so any difference in treatment between part-time workers and full-time workers will affect women more than men.

25.48 In *Rinke*,[60] the Court found that a requirement that general medical training must include periods of full-time training worked to the disadvantage of a much higher percentage of women than men since a '. . . much higher percentage of women than men wishing to train in general medicine have difficulties working full time during part of their training'.[61] Likewise in *Kording*[62] part-time employees, more than 90 per cent of whom were women, suffered discrimination because they had to work for a number of years longer than full-time employees in order to be exempt from the compulsory qualifying examination for tax advisers. But in *Kirsammer-Hack*[63] the exclusion of the employment force of small businesses from protection against unfair dismissal was held not to be discriminatory since it applied to all employees of such businesses whether they work full-time, part-time, or half time. However, the Court pointed out that if it were established that small businesses employed a considerably higher percentage of women than men, that would constitute indirect discrimination.

(3) Harassment

25.49 Harassment is where unwanted conduct relating to the sex of a person occurs with the purpose or effect of violating the dignity of a person, and of creating an intimidating, hostile, degrading, humiliating, or offensive environment. Sexual harassment is defined as any form of unwanted verbal, non-verbal, or physical conduct of a sexual nature that occurs, with the purpose or effect of violating the dignity of a person in particular when creating an intimidating, hostile, degrading, humiliating, or offensive environment.[64]

E. Objective Justification

25.50 Any rule or practice which indirectly discriminates against women will not be unlawful if it is objectively justified, ie if the motive behind it is unrelated to the sex of the person in question. For example, under Article 141(4) EC Member

---

[60] See note 55 above.
[61] Ibid Judgment para 35.
[62] Note 58.
[63] Case C-189/91 [1993] ECR I–6185.
[64] Ibid.

States can, with a view to ensuring full equality in practice between men and women in working life, use the principle of equal treatment to maintain or adopt measures providing for specific advantages in order to make it easier for the under-represented sex to pursue a vocational activity or to prevent or compensate for disadvantages in professional careers.

F. Pregnancy

The issue of pregnancy and the consequences for a woman's employment **25.51** conditions have been the subject of a number of cases before the ECJ. Before setting out this case law, it is useful to indicate the basic principles which emerge from it:

(a) A pregnant woman or a woman on maternity leave cannot be compared to a man or non-pregnant woman at work:

'The present case is concerned with women taking maternity leave provided for by national legislation. They are in a special position which requires them to be afforded special protection but which is not comparable to either that of a man or that of a woman actually at work.'[65]

(b) From the onset of pregnancy to the end of maternity leave, a woman employed under a contract or a relationship of indefinite duration cannot be dismissed even in circumstances in which a man would have been dismissed (eg, prolonged illness).

(c) When maternity leave terminates, the woman reverts back to the position where she is entitled only to be treated in the same way as her male colleagues; she has no special 'protected' status.

(d) A woman cannot be prejudiced either through a reduction in pay or in the matter of promotion during pregnancy and maternity leave.

In *Dekker*[66] the ECJ held that the refusal to employ a woman because she was **25.52** pregnant constituted direct discrimination:

. . . only women can be refused employment on the ground of pregnancy and such a refusal therefore constitutes direct discrimination on grounds of sex.[67]

Mrs Dekker was refused an appointment at a training centre for young adults. **25.53** She was pregnant and had informed her potential employer of this fact. She was told that she could not be employed as there was no possibility of employing a

---

[65] Case C-342/93 *Gillespie v Northern Health and Social Services Board* [1996] ECR I–475, Judgment para 17.
[66] Case 177/88 [1990] ECR I–3941.
[67] Ibid Judgment para 12.

replacement during her maternity leave. The insurance fund would not reimburse the daily benefit which would be due to her during this period and so the hiring of a replacement was not a financially viable proposition for the training centre.

25.54 The Court found that such discrimination could not be justified on the ground of financial loss to the training centre:

> The reason given by the employer for refusing to appoint Mrs Dekker is basically that it could not have obtained reimbursement from the Risicofonds of the daily benefits which it would have had to pay her for the duration of her absence due to pregnancy, and yet at the same time it would have been obliged to employ a replacement...
>
> In that regard it should be observed that only women can be refused employment on grounds of pregnancy and such a refusal therefore constitutes direct discrimination on grounds of sex. A refusal of employment on account of the financial consequences of absence due to pregnancy must be regarded as based, essentially, on the fact of pregnancy. Such discrimination cannot be justified on grounds relating to the financial loss which an employer who appointed a pregnant woman would suffer for the duration of her maternity leave.[68]

25.55 *Mahlberg*[69] differed from *Dekker*[70] in that there was a statutory prohibition on the employment of pregnant women in particular posts but the Court held that this could not justify a refusal to appoint such persons:

> ... the principle of equal treatment for men and women as regards access to employment, vocational training and promotion, and working conditions precludes a refusal to appoint a pregnant woman to a post for an indefinite period on the ground that a statutory prohibition on employment attaching to the condition of pregnancy prevents her from being employed in that post from the outset and for the duration of the pregnancy.

25.56 *Webb*[71] refined the ruling in *Dekker* somewhat. The ECJ held that the dismissal of a pregnant woman recruited for an indefinite period to replace an employee who was on maternity leave could not be justified. The Court's ruling appear to apply only to women recruited for an indefinite period of time. This leaves open the possibility of dismissing lawfully a woman recruited for a fixed term to replace another on maternity leave.

25.57 Termination of a contract of employment of a pregnant employee could not be justified on the ground that a statutory prohibition on night work by pregnant employees affected the performance by the employee of her duties as a night

---

[68] Note 66 Judgment paras 11 and 12.
[69] Case C-207/98 [2000] ECR I-549.
[70] Note 66.
[71] Case C-321/93 [1994] ECR I-3567.

attendant in an old persons' home.[72] The Court emphasized that the contract was not for a fixed term. The relevant criterion in assessing the lawfulness of a dismissal of a pregnant woman seems therefore to be the nature of her contract: fixed-term or of indefinite duration?

Maternity leave should not have prejudicial consequences for an employee. **25.58** Accordingly, national rules which deprive a woman of her right to an assessment of her performance at work, and consequently affect her promotion prospects because of absence on maternity leave, are discriminatory and therefore unlawful.[73]

Illness during pregnancy cannot justify dismissal but periods of illness after the **25.59** end of a period of maternity leave, even if linked to pregnancy, are not a bar to dismissal. Outside the period of pregnancy and maternity leave, a woman can be dismissed in the same circumstances as a man even if the reason for dismissal is linked to pregnancy.

In *Hertz and Aldi*[74] the ECJ refused to distinguish between illness attributable to **25.60** pregnancy and confinement from any other illness. If a period of sick leave would lead to the dismissal of a male worker in the same circumstances, there is no direct discrimination on grounds of sex:

> Male and female workers are equally exposed to illness. Although certain disorders are, it is true, specific to one or other sex, the only question is whether a woman is dismissed on account of absence due to illness in the same circumstances as a man; if that is the case there is no direct discrimination on grounds of sex.[75]

Mary Brown v Rentokil[76] differed from *Hertz and Aldi* in that the illness which **25.61** provoked the dismissal arose during pregnancy and was caused by pregnancy. Rentokil's contract of employment included a clause stipulating that, if an employee was absent from work because of illness for more than 26 weeks continuously, he or she would be dismissed. The Court found that, although the term applied to men and women, it was discriminatory since the situation for a pregnant worker who was unfit to work as a result of disorders associated with her pregnancy could not be considered to be the same as that of a male worker who was ill and absent from work for the same period of time:

> . . . the dismissal of a woman during pregnancy cannot be based on her inability, as a result of her condition, to perform the duties which she is contractually bound to carry out. If such an interpretation were adopted, the protection afforded by '

---

[72] Case C-421/92 *Haberman-Beltermann* [1994] ECR I–1657.
[73] Case C-136/95 *Thibault* [1998] ECR I–2027.
[74] Case C-179/88 [1990] ECR I–3979.
[75] Ibid Judgment para 17.
[76] Case C-394/96 [1998] ECR I–4185.

Community law to a woman during pregnancy would be available only to pregnant women who were able to comply with the conditions of their employment contract with the result that the provisions of Directive 76/207 would be rendered ineffective.[77]

25.62 Thus, periods of absence due to illness from the start of pregnancy to the start of maternity leave cannot be taken into account in computing the period justifying dismissal under national law.

25.63 The 2002 Amendment codified the Court's case law and set out more clearly than in the original Directive the rights of pregnant women in the workplace. Article 2(7) provides that a woman on maternity leave is entitled, after the end of the period of such leave, to return to her job or an equivalent post on terms and conditions which are no less favourable to her and to benefit from any improvement in working conditions to which she would have been entitled during her absence.

25.64 Member States have a right to recognize distinct rights to paternity and/or adoption leave. Those Member States which recognize such rights shall take the necessary measures to protect those who chose to exercise them from dismissal and to accord them the right to return to their jobs or to equivalent posts on terms and conditions which are no less favourable to them, and to benefit from any improvement in working conditions to which they would have been entitled during their absence.

G. Exceptions

25.65 There are a number of exceptions to the principle of equal treatment set out in the Directive. In addition the Court has held that the principle of equal treatment can be departed from in the interest of public safety. These exceptions must be interpreted restrictively.

25.66 The Directive specifies that principle can be departed from in the following three situations:

(a) where the sex of a worker is a determining factor in the performance of a particular job (Article 2(6));
(b) in the interests of the protection of women, particularly as regards pregnancy and maternity (Article 2(7));

---

[77] Ibid Judgment para 21.

(c) in the case of measures to promote equal opportunities for men and women, in particular by removing existing inequalities which affect women's opportunities (Article 2(8)).

(1) Sex as determining factor

The original Directive, as adopted in 1976, recognized that certain types of **25.67** occupation or activity might be reserved to workers of one sex only 'by reason of their nature or the context in which they are carried out'.[78] Member States were therefore given the right to exclude those activities from the scope of application of the Directive.

The Court has recognized that sex may be a determining factor for posts such **25.68** as those of prison warders and head prison warders[79] or for certain activities such as policing where there are serious internal disturbances.[80] In *Commission v United Kingdom*[81] when the ECJ found the United Kingdom was not in breach of its obligation in keeping in place legislation which limited access by men to the profession of midwife—a profession which at the time was not traditionally engaged in by men because at the time of the case 'personal sensitivities' played an important role in the relationship between midwife and patient. At the same time, the Court refused to accept that the exclusion of employment in private households and small businesses (where the number of employees did not exceed five) could be the subject of a broad inclusive exemption from the principle of equal treatment although it did accept that for certain kinds of employment in private households sex could be a determining factor.

In the course of proceedings the United Kingdom stated that it intended to keep **25.69** the position under review and to open up progressively the midwifery profession to men. The importance of re-assessment to permit the adaptation of national legislation to social developments was emphasized in the subsequent case of *Commission v France*[82] which concerned separate recruitment procedures according to sex for certain civil service corps.

The Directive, as amended in 2002, provides that any derogation is subject to the **25.70** principle of proportionality and requires that the objective be 'legitimate'. This reflects the case law discussed above:

> Member States may provide, as regards access to employment including the training leading thereto that a difference in treatment which is based on a characteristic

---

[78] Article 2(2) Note 1.
[79] Case 318/86 *Commission v France* [1988] ECR 3559.
[80] Case 222/84 *Johnston* [1986] ECR 1651 Judgment para 37.
[81] Case 165/82 [1983] ECR 3431.
[82] Case 318/86 [1988] ECR.

related to sex shall not constitute discrimination where, by reason of the nature of the particular occupational activities concerned or the context in which they are carried out, such a characteristic constitutes a genuine and determining occupational requirement, provided that the objective is legitimate and the requirement is proportionate.[83]

25.71   In *Johnston v Chief Constable of the RUC*[84] the Chief Constable's refusal to renew Mrs Johnston's contract as a member of the RUC full-time reserve and to allow her to be given training in the handling and use of firearms was held to be discriminatory. The ECJ held that the difference in treatment between men and women allowed by Article 2(2), now Article 2(6), does not include risks and dangers such as those to which any armed police officer is exposed in the performance of his duties in any given situation that does not specifically affect women as such. However, Member States can take into consideration requirements of public safety in order to restrict general policing duties, in an internal situation characterized by frequent assassinations, to men equipped with firearms.

25.72   In *Sirdar*[85] a woman was refused employment with the UK Royal Marines as a chef. Women were excluded from such posts on the ground that their presence was incompatible with the requirement of 'interoperability', ie the need for every marine, irrespective of his specialization, to be capable of fighting in a commando unit. The ECJ held that the exception fell within Article 2(2) on the basis that the Marines were an exceptional and small force intended to be in the front line of attack. The Court found that:

> In such circumstances the competent authorities were entitled, in the exercise of their discretion as to whether to maintain the exclusion in question in the light of social developments, and without abusing the principle of proportionality, to come to the view that the specific conditions for deployment of the assault units of which the Royal Marines are composed, and in particular the rules of interoperability to which they are subject, justified their composition remaining exclusively male.[86]

25.73   In *Kreil*,[87] a general prohibition under German law barred all women from access to all military posts involving the use of firearms. Women could only have posts in the military music services or the medical services. The ECJ found that Article 2(2) was designed to apply only to specific activities and could not be applied to the general prohibition in issue in the case.

---

[83] Art 2(6).
[84] Case 222/84 [1986] ECR 1651.
[85] Case C-273/97 *Sirdar* [1999] ECR I–7403.
[86] Ibid Judgment para 31.
[87] Case C-285/98 [2000] ECR I–69.

(2) Protection of women

The question of whether and to what extent occupations that are dangerous can **25.74**
be denied to women but not to men on the grounds that women need protection
has arisen in a number of cases, the first being *Johnston*.[88]

Johnston held that the express reference in Article 2(3) to pregnancy and mater- **25.75**
nity meant that the Directive was intended to protect a woman's biological
conditon and the special relationship which exists between a woman and her
child. That provision of the Directive could not therefore allow women to be
excluded from certain types of employment on the ground that public opinion
demands that women be given more protection than men against risks which
affect men and women in the same way and which are distinct from women's
specific needs of protection.

The subsequent case of *Kreil*[89] raised issues similar to *Johnston*. The Court follow- **25.76**
ing *Johnston* held that the Directive permitted a woman to be protected in so far
as her biological condition or the relationship between her and her child required
protection, but not in the face of risks which were the same for men and
women.

(3) Positive measures

The third exception to the principle of equal treatment relates to positive dis- **25.77**
crimination. The ECJ has considered this matter in three cases and its position
has shifted from one in which it viewed positive measures as unlawful per se to a
more moderate approach conceding that positive discrimination with respect to
access to employment can be justified provided both male and female candidates
are 'equally qualified'. In other words, a policy of positive discrimination cannot
entail an absolute right for a woman candidate to be given preference over a man
regardless of their respective qualifications and merits.

Kalanke[90] concerned a German law which provided that, where male and female **25.78**
applicants for a job were equally qualified, the female was to be appointed in
preference to the male where women represented less than half the employees in
the relevant undertaking. The ECJ found the system was not justified under
Article 2(4) of the Directive:

> National rules which guarantee women absolute and unconditional priority for
> appointment or promotion go beyond promoting equal opportunities and overstep
> the limit of the exception in Article 2(4). . .

---

[88] See note 30.
[89] See note 26.
[90] Case C-450/93 [1995] ECR I–3051. See Commission Communication, COM (96) 88 Final.

Furthermore, in so far as it seeks to achieve equal representation of men and women in all grades and levels within a department, such a system substitutes for equality of opportunity as envisaged in Article 2(4) the result which is only to be arrived at by providing such equality of opportunity.[91]

25.79 In *Marschall*[92] the Court moved away from the strict stance it had adopted in *Kalanke*. A male teacher had been denied promotion because of a law providing for preference to be given to an equally qualified female candidate where there were fewer women than men in the job grade in question but women were only to be preferred to men where 'reasons specific to another candidate' did not predominate. Distinguishing *Kalanke*, the Court held:

> . . . a national rule which, in a case where there are fewer women than men at the level of the relevant post and equally qualified in terms of their suitability, competence and professional competence and professional performance requires that priority be given to the promotion of female candidates unless reasons specific to an individual male candidate tilt the balance in his favour is not precluded by Article 2(10) and (4). . . provided that:
>
> (a) in each individual case the rule provides for male candidates who are equally as qualified as female candidates a guarantee that candidatures will be the subject of an objective assessment which will take account of all criteria specific to the candidates and will override the priority accorded to female candidates where one or more of the criteria tilts the balance in favour of the male candidate; and
>
> (b) such criteria are not such as to discriminate against female candidates.[93]

25.80 *Marschall* has been followed in the subsequent cases of *Badeck*[94] and *Abrahamsson and Anderson*.[95]

25.81 This case law was reflected in the 2002 amendment to the Directive. Article 8(2) permits Member States to maintain or adopt measures within the meaning of Article 141(4) of the Treaty with a view to ensuring full equality between men and women. Article 141(4) provides that with a view to ensuring full equality in practice between men and women in working life the principle of equal treatment shall not prevent any Member State from maintaining or adopting measures in order to make it easier for the underrepresented sex to pursue a vocational activity or to prevent or compensate for disadvantages in professional careers.

---

91 Ibid Judgment paras 22 and 23.
92 Case C-409/95 [1997] ECR I–6363.
93 Ibid Judgment para 54.
94 Case C-158/97 [2000] ECR I–1875.
95 Case C-407/98 [2000] ECR I–5539.

H. Implementation and Enforcement of the Principle of Equal Treatment

(1) Implementation

Member States are obliged to take the necessary measures to ensure that: **25.82**

(i) any laws, regulations, or administrative practices contrary to the principle of equal treatment are abolished; and

(ii) any provisions contrary to the principle of equal treatment which are included in contracts or collective agreements, individual contracts of employment, internal rules of undertakings, or rules governing the independent occupations and professions and worker's and employer's organizations shall be, or may be, declared null and void or may be amended.[96]

(2) Enforcement

The 2002 amendment inserted Articles 6, 7, and 8 into the original Directive, **25.83** reinforcing the means by which the principle of equal treatment can be enforced. These provisions are extensive, requiring the principle of equal treatment to be enforced on multiple levels.

Article 6 provides that Member States must ensure that judicial and/or admin- **25.84** istrative procedures, including, where they deem it appropriate, conciliation procedures are available to all persons who consider themselves wronged by failure to apply the principle of equal treatment even after the relationship in which the alleged discrimination occurred has terminated.

Real and effective compensation or reparation must be made available for loss or **25.85** damage sustained by a person as a result of a breach of the principle of equal treatment. The compensation or reparation must be dissuasive and proportionate to the damage suffered and may not be restricted by the fixing of an upper limit except in cases where the employer can prove that the only damage suffered was the refusal to take a job application into consideration.

Additionally, Member States must lay down rules for sanctions applicable to **25.86** infringements of national provisions. The sanctions must be effective, proportionate, and dissuasive and 'may comprise the payment of compensation to the victim'.[97]

---

[96] Art 3(2).
[97] Art 8d.

25.87   Associations or organizations which have a legitimate interest in ensuring that the provisions of the Directive are complied with may engage either on behalf of or in support of complainants, with their approval, in any judicial or administrative procedure provided for the enforcement of obligations under the Directive.[98]

25.88   National time limits for the bringing of procedures prevail.

25.89   Article 7 provides that Member States must protect employees and employees' representatives against dismissal or other adverse treatment by the employer as a reaction to a complaint within the undertaking or to any legal proceedings aimed at enforcing compliance with the Directive.

25.90   Article 8a requires the Member States to designate and make the necessary arrangements for a body or bodies for the promotion, analysis, monitoring, and support of equal treatment of all persons without discrimination on the grounds of sex. These entities must be capable of providing independent assistance to victims of discrimination in pursuing their complaints, conducting independent surveys concerning discrimination and publishing independent reports, and making recommendations.

25.91   Articles 8b and 8c require Member States to promote dialogue and the conclusion of agreements between the social partners to promote equal treatment between men and women, and with non-governmental organizations which have a legitimate interest in furthering equal treatment.

25.92   Employers should be encouraged to provide appropriate information, for example statistics on the proportions of men and women at different levels within their undertakings.

---

[98] Art 6(3).

26

EQUALITY OF TREATMENT IN SOCIAL SECURITY[1]

A. Introduction

(1) *Defrenne 1*

The ECJ in *Defrenne 1*[2] held that statutory social security systems could not be **26.01**
considered to be 'pay' within the meaning of Article 141 (ex 119) of the EC
Treaty. Miss Gabrielle Defrenne claimed that the exclusion of air hostesses from
the retirement pension scheme of civil aviation crews was contrary to the principle of equal pay laid down by Article 119 since the pension in question was 'pay'
within the meaning of that provision. The Court rejected this argument on the

---

[1] Cousins: 'Equal Treatment and Social Security' (1994) 19 EL Rev 123; Ellis: *EU Anti-
Discrimination Law*. Oxford University Press 2005, Chapter 8; Hoskyns and Luckhaus: 'The
European Community Directive on Equal Treatment in Social Security' (1989) 17 Policy
and Politics 321 et seq; Pennings: *Introduction to European Social Security Law* Fourth Edition
Intersentia 2004, Chapter 25.

[2] Case 80/70 [1971] ECR 445.

ground that social security benefits, although not entirely unconnected with employment,[3] do not solely derive from employment nor are they financed exclusively by employers and employees:

> Although consideration in the nature of social security benefits is not therefore in principle alien to the concept of pay, there cannot be brought within this concept, as defined in Article 119, social security schemes or benefits, in particular retirement pensions directly governed by legislation without any element of agreement with the undertaking or the occupational branch concerned, which are obligatorily applicable to general categories of workers.

> These schemes assure for workers the benefit of a legal scheme, the financing of which workers, employers and possibly the public authorities contribute in a measure determined less by the employment relationship between the employer and the worker than by considerations of social policy.[4]

(2) The Equal Opportunities Directive

26.02   The Equal Opportunities Directive,[5] in draft form, envisaged including social security amongst the working conditions subject to the principle of equal treatment. This proposal was ultimately dropped. The complexity and diversity of national social security systems, plus the general hesitancy on the part of the Member States to commit to a general principle of equal treatment within those systems, led instead to a commitment, expressed in Article 1(2), that the Council would adopt separate provisions defining the substance, the scope, and the arrangements for the application of the principle of equal treatment in social security.

26.03   Whilst to all intents and purposes the Equal Opportunities Directive is not therefore relevant to social security,[6] it may still be applicable in a number of circumstances. If the subject matter of a particular benefit or benefit regime in a national social security system is related to access to employment including vocational training and promotion or working conditions, the Equal Opportunities Directive applies. This would be the case, for example, if a benefit was granted to facilitate training for entry or re-entry into the labour market, or an allowance was paid to cover childcare whilst a parent undertook such training. For the

---

[3] Employment will give rise to contributions and hence eligibility to benefits, in particular contributory social security benefits.

[4] *Defrenne 1* (see note 2 above) Judgment paras 7 and 8.

[5] Directive 76/207 on the implementation of the principle of equal treatment for men and women as regards access to employment, vocational training and promotion, and working conditions [1976] OJ L39/40.

[6] Case 192/85 *Newstead* [1987] ECR 4753 Judgment para 24.

Equal Opportunities Directive to be applicable in such a situation, there must be a clear and strong link between the benefit in question and access to employment or working conditions.

In *Jackson and Cresswell*[7] the Court found that the method of calculating a mini-   **26.04**
mum income benefit, which might affect the recipient's ability to avail of vocational training opportunities or part-time employment, was not sufficient to bring that benefit within the scope of the Equal Opportunities Directive.[8]

By contrast, *Marshall*[9] held that Article 1(2) of the Equal Opportunities Direc-   **26.05**
tive must be interpreted strictly. Consequently the exception to the prohibition of discrimination on grounds of sex provided for in Article 7(1) in the Equality of Treatment in Social Security Directive applies only to the determination of pensionable age and the possible consequences thereof for other benefits and the age at which a person can be dismissed is a matter falling within Article 5 of the Equal Opportunities Directive, with the result the linking of dismissal to the qualifying age for a state pension, which age was different for men and women, constituted discrimination on the grounds of sex contrary to that provision. The Court refused to accept argument to the effect that the provision of a state pension constitutes an aspect of social security; social security does not fall within the Equal Opportunities Directive; therefore the fixing by the contract of employment of different retirement ages linked to the different minimum pensionable ages for men and women under national legislation did not constitute unlawful discrimination.

(3) The Framework Equality Directive

The Framework Equality Directive,[10] considered below in Chapter 29, contains   **26.06**
a broad exclusion of social security schemes from its scope of application:

> This Directive does not apply to payments of any kind made by state schemes or similar, including state social security or social protection schemes.[11]

---

[7] Case C-63/91 [1992] ECR I–4737.

[8] See n 5 above.

[9] Case 152/84 *Marshall* [1986] ECR 723.

[10] Directive 2000/78 establishing a general framework for equal treatment in employment and occupation [2000] OJ L303/16.

[11] Art 3(3). Recital 13 is worded more broadly: 'This Directive does not apply to social security and social protection schemes whose benefits are not treated as income within the meaning given to that term for the purpose of applying Article 141 of the EC Treaty not to any kind of payment by the State aimed at providing access to employment or maintaining employment.'

B. The Equal Treatment in Social Security Directive

26.07 Shortly after the adoption of the Equal Opportunities Directive,[12] work began on what became Directive 79/7 on the progressive implementation of the principle of equal treatment for men and women in matters of social security (the Equal Treatment in Social Security Directive).[13]

26.08 Based on the general law-making powers set out in Article 308 of the EC Treaty, there being no specific legal basis in the Treaty, it was adopted on 23 December 1978 with an unusually lengthy implementation period of six years, the normal period of implementation at that time being two years.

C. Direct Effect

26.09 Article 4(1), which lays down the principle of equal treatment, was found by the ECJ in its early case law on the Directive to have direct effect and it is by virtue of this quality that equal treatment has largely been achieved, given the fact that even after a six-year implementation period many Member States had not taken steps to transpose the Directive into their national legal systems.

26.10 Shortly after the implementation date had passed, women began to invoke the Directive to claim equal treatment before their national social security authorities and courts. Uncertain of whether and, if so, how in practical terms, equality of treatment could derive directly from the Directive, national courts made a number of references for preliminary rulings to the ECJ which took a robust view of the effects of the Directive.

26.11 *FNV*[14] was the first case to come before the Court on the issue of direct effect. It concerned a provision of the Dutch law on unemployment benefit (WWV) which excluded from entitlement to benefit workers who were married women who did not live apart from their husbands, on the ground that they were not main breadwinners. This provision remained in force after 23 December 1984. FNV, the Dutch Trades Union Federation, brought an action alleging that the Dutch government had acted unlawfully in maintaining this provision in force after that date.

---

[12] See note 5 above.
[13] [1979] OJ L6/24.
[14] Case 71/85 [1986] ECR 3855.

McDermott and Cotter [15] concerned a claim by two Irish women alleging breach   **26.12**
of the principle of equal treatment in the Irish unemployment benefit scheme.
Both the duration for which benefit was paid and the rate of benefit were less
that than awarded to men in the same circumstances. The Directive had not been
implemented in Ireland and the preliminary issue was therefore whether the
women could rely on the Directive in support of their claim.

Both cases raised the issue of direct effect of the Directive and in both the ECJ   **26.13**
ruled that it had:

> . . . standing by itself, and in the light of the objective and contents of the Directive,
> Article 4(1) is sufficiently precise to be relied upon in legal proceedings and applied
> by a Court. Moreover, that Article in no way permits Member States to restrict or
> place conditions on the application of the principle of equal treatment in its particu-
> lar area of application. [16]
>
> . . .
>
> It follows from the foregoing that Article 4(1) is sufficiently precise and uncondi-
> tional to allow individuals, in the absence of implementing measures to rely on it
> before national courts as from 23 December 1984 in order to preclude the applica-
> tion of any national provision inconsistent with that article. [17]

In *FNV* the Court found that the direct effect of Article 4(1) was not compro-   **26.14**
mised by Article 7, which reserved to Member States the right to exclude from the
scope of the Directive certain matters. Likewise Article 5, in prescribing that
Member States should take measures to implement the principle of equal treatment, did not lay down conditions to which the principle of discrimination is
subject. It left to Member States a discretion with regard to methods of implementation whereby the principle of equality of treatment is to be achieved.

As to how the principle of equal treatment was to be applied in the absence of   **26.15**
any measures implementing Article 4(1) of the Directive, the Court's approach
was quite straightforward: women were entitled to have the '. . . same rules
applied to them as men who are in the same situation since where the directive
has not been implemented, those rules remain the only valid point of reference'. [18]
Thus the conditions of entitlement to benefits must be the same for men and
women and in the absence of rules setting out the conditions of entitlement
applicable to both, the conditions applicable to the most favoured sex, in this
case men, must apply to women. Thus in the *FNV* case this would mean that
married women could no longer be automatically excluded from unemployment

---

[15] Case 286/85 [1987] ECR 1453.
[16] Ibid Judgment para 14, following Case 71/85 *FNV* [1986] ECR 3855.
[17] *Jackson and Cresswell* (see note 7 above) Judgment para 16.
[18] Ibid Judgment para 9.

benefits and Mrs McDermott and Mrs Cotter were entitled to unemployment benefit at the same rate and for the same duration as men.

D. Scope of Application

(1) Persons covered

26.16 The Directive applies to the working population which includes:

(a) the employed and the self-employed;
(b) those whose economic activity has been interrupted by one of the risks enumerated in Article 3(1) of the Directive; and
(c) those seeking employment.[19]

26.17 The ECJ has interpreted the concept of 'working population' broadly as including people who are working, those who are seeking employment, and those whose work or efforts to find work have been interrupted by the materialization of one of the risks set out in Article 3.[20] In *Drake*[21] the Court further held that a person is still a member of the working population even if the interruption of work is due to the invalidity of a parent,[22] ie the suffering of a risk by a third party, or where a risk materializes when the claimant has been seeking employment after a period without occupational activity,[23] or in the case of minor employment of less than 15 hours a week remunerated at less than one-seventh the average monthly salary.[24]

26.18 The essential criterion appears to be that the person in question must normally be on the labour market or seeking to enter it. The Court has been generous with regard to the length of time a person can be absent from the labour market before losing his or her status as a member of the working population, Mrs *Nolte*[25] had a small job as a cleaner, in the sense that she worked less than 18 hours a week. She stopped work in March 1987. In June 1988 she fell seriously ill and was incapable of working. The Court held that she fell within the scope of the Directive. Although, at the time of the materialization of her disability, she had been absent from the labour market for 15 months she was a person who

---

[19] Art 2.
[20] Case C-77/85 *Zuechner* [1996] ECR I–5089.
[21] Case 150/85 [1986] ECR 1995.
[22] Case 150/86 *Drake* [1986] ECR 1995.
[23] Case C-31/90 [1991] ECR I–3723.
[24] Case C-317/93 *Nolte* [1995] ECR I–4925; Case C-444/93 *Megner* [1995] ECR I–4741.
[25] Ibid.

normally worked for remuneration and thus was a member of the working population.

Those who have never exercised an economic activity, in the sense of an activity in return for remuneration, are not within the scope of the Directive, neither are those persons whose absence from the labour market is not attributable to one of the risks set out in the Directive. **26.19**

Mrs *Johnson*[26] had given up work in 1970 to look after her six-year-old daughter. **26.20** Ten years later she wished to re-enter the labour market but was unable to do so because of a back condition. The Court found that a person who has given up work to bring up a child is not within the scope of the Directive, since bringing up children is not one of the risks listed in Article 3(1)(a) of the Directive. As to whether a person in Mrs Johnson's position could be regarded as a person seeking employment and, by virtue of that fact, bring herself within the Directive, was a matter to be determined by the national court taking into account whether he or she was actually seeking employment at the time of becoming afflicted with one of the risks enumerated in the Directive. This could be evidenced, for example, by registration with the appropriate employment agencies, by completed job applications or attendance at job interviews.

Mrs *Zuechner's*[27] position differed from that of Mrs Johnson. Her husband had **26.21** an accident, following which he became a paraplegic and hence unable to work. Mrs Zuechner cared for him. She claimed to be a member of the working population since she provided care for which she had to undergo training and which, by virtue of its nature and scope, could be assimilated to an occupational activity. If she had not provided care for her husband, this would have to be provided by someone else against payment or in a hospital. The Court refused to accept this argument stating that to do so would have

> . . . the effect of infinitely extending the scope of the directive, whereas the purpose of Article 2 of the directive is precisely to delimit that scope.[28]

Consequently, 'activity' in relation to the expression 'working population' in **26.22** Article 2 can be construed as only referring to an economic activity, that is an activity undertaken for remuneration.

The level of earnings from that economic activity is irrelevant. *Megner and* **26.23** *Scheffer*[29] concerned a provision of German legislation by virtue of which persons

---

[26] Case C-410/92 [1994] ECR I–5483.
[27] Case C-77/95 [1996] ECR I–5689.
[28] Judgment para 15.
[29] Case 444/93 [1995] ECR I–4741.

425

working less than 18 hours a week were not insured for unemployment. Two female cleaners whose normal working time was a maximum of 10 hours a week applied for admission to the unemployment insurance scheme but their applications were refused due to their low level of working hours. Before the ECJ, the German government argued that persons in minor employment are not members of the working population within the meaning of Article 2 of the Directive, in particular because the small earnings they receive from employment are not sufficient to satisfy their needs. The Court rejected this argument:

> That argument cannot be upheld. The fact that a worker's earnings do not cover all his needs cannot prevent him from being a member of the working population. It appears from the Court's case law that the fact that his employment yields an income lower than the minimum required for subsistence . . . does not prevent the person in such employment from being regarded as a worker within the meaning of Article 48 (the Levin and Kempf cases) . . .[30]

26.24 The claimant must, at the time of the claim, be available on the labour market or have ceased to be so due to the materialization of one of the risks enumerated in the Directive.

26.25 In the case of a person seeking employment, the reasons for leaving a previous employment or even the fact that a person has not previously carried on an occupational activity are irrelevant. The mere seeking of employment suffices to bring a person within the scope of the Directive. The Directive does not apply to persons who have not had an occupation and who are not seeking work or to persons who have had an occupation which was not interrupted by one of the risks referred to in Article 3(1) and who are not seeking work.[31]

26.26 *Verholen*[32] raised two interesting points:

   (i) Could someone who was not a person covered by the Directive but who was insured under one of the social security schemes to which the Directive was applicable claim the right to equal treatment on the basis of the Directive?

   (ii) Could the spouse of a person who had suffered discrimination claim rights under the Directive?

26.27 The Court replied to (i) in the negative, holding that where a provision of a directive determines precisely the persons to whom that directive is to apply, a national court could not extend the personal scope of the Directive by reference

---

[30] Ibid Judgment para 18. Art 48 EC is now Art 39 EC. See Case 53/81 *Levin* [1982] ECR 1035; Case 139/85 *Kempf* [1986] ECR 1741.
[31] Case 48/88 *Acterberg-te-Riele* [1989] ECR 1963.
[32] Joined Cases 87/90 etc [1991] ECR 3757.

to its material scope, that is the benefits covered by the Directive. With respect to (ii) the Court held that the right to rely on provisions of the Directive is not confined to individuals coming within the scope *ratione personae* of the Directive but can extend to other persons who may have 'a direct interest in ensuring the principle of non-discrimination is respected as regards persons who are protected'.[33] Nevertheless an individual who bears the effects of a discriminatory national provision may be allowed to rely on the Directive only if his wife, the victim of the discrimination, herself comes within the scope of the Directive. Thus, for example, a man who is prejudiced because of the way in which his wife is treated under a national social security system cannot rely on the Directive if his wife has never been a member of the working population.

(2) Schemes and benefits covered

The Directive applies to: **26.28**

(a) statutory schemes which provide protection against the following risks:
    (i) sickness;
    (ii) invalidity;
    (iii) old age;
    (iv) accidents at work and occupational diseases;
    (v) unemployment;
(b) social assistance in so far as it is intended to supplement or replace the schemes referred to in (a).[34]

These benefits are designed to replace income from employment or to provide **26.29** income to those who cannot take up employment due for example to ill health or disability.

The essential criterion in establishing whether any particular benefit is subject **26.30** to the principle of equal treatment is whether it is part of a statutory scheme providing protection against one of the risks specified in the Directive. The statutory scheme governing the benefit may not necessarily be part of the national social security regime.

In *Richardson*[35] the benefit in question was governed by the National Health **26.31** Service Act 1977 as opposed to the legislative corpus governing the social security system. The Court found that it covered one of the risks enumerated in the Directive and was thus amongst the benefits to which the principle of equal treatment applied.

---

[33] Ibid Judgment para 23.
[34] Art 3(1).
[35] Case C-137/94 [1995] ECR I–3407.

26.32 *Atkins*[36] followed this broad approach as to what is to be regarded as a 'statutory scheme'. It found that a benefit granted by statute but implemented and operated by a local authority, which has a discretion with respect to benefit entitlement, is still considered to be a benefit for the purposes of Article 3(1) of the Equality of Treatment in Social Security Directive:

> Similarly the fact that the scheme in question is not formally part of national social security rules and is not the responsibility of the Department of Social Security . . . cannot exclude it from the scope of Directive 79/7.[37]

26.33 The Directive must be given a purposive interpretation in view of the diversity of social security provision in the different Member States. The focal point in deciding whether a benefit is within the scope of the Directive is the nature of the risk it was designed to cover, not the means whereby that risk was covered, nor its formal designation within any given benefit scheme.[38]

26.34 *Taylor*[39] concerned winter fuel payments payable to those who had reached retirement age—60 years in the case of women, 65 years in the case of men. The United Kingdom and Austrian governments argued before the Court that the benefit was aimed at helping people in need to pay their heating expenses during the winter months. It was not, therefore, payable in respect of a risk enumerated in Article 3(1). The Court rejected this argument pointing out that the benefit was only aimed at those who had reached the statutory retirement age. It was consequently aimed at protecting against the risk of old age which was specified in Article 3(1).

26.35 By contrast, the Court held that the benefit in question in *Atkins* was not within the scope of the Directive

> The purpose of such a benefit is to facilitate access to public transport for certain classes of persons who, for various reasons, are recognized as having a particular need for public transport and who are . . . less well off financially and materially.[40]

26.36 Benefits of a general nature, entitlement to which is enjoyed by a wide class of beneficiary, some of which may be suffering from one or more of the risks set out in the Directive, are not within the scope of the Directive.

---

[36] Case C-228/94 [1996] ECR I–3633.
[37] Ibid Judgment para 15.
[38] Case 150/85 *Drake* [1986] ECR 1995.
[39] Case C-382/98 [1999] ECR I–8955.
[40] Ibid Judgment para 17.

Smithson[41] concerned a dispute between Florence Smithson and the United **26.37** Kingdom social security authorities. The issue was whether the Directive applied to a scheme for housing benefit, the amount of which was calculated on the basis of a relationship between a notional income to which the beneficiary was entitled and his or her actual income, if criteria based on protection against certain risks covered by the Directive, such as sickness and invalidity are applied in order to determine the amount of that notional income. The Court found the Directive not to be applicable. The benefit in question was intended to compensate for the fact that the beneficiary's income was insufficient to meet housing costs, and could not be characterized as an autonomous scheme intended to provide protection against one of the risks listed in Article 3(1) of the Directive. In order to come within the Directive the benefit had to be effectively linked to the protection provided against one of the risks specified in Article 3(1) of the Directive.[42]

Some months after *Smithson* the Court adopted the same reasoning in *Jackson* **26.38** *and Cresswell*,[43] finding that a statutory scheme which on fulfilment of certain conditions provides persons whose income falls below a legally defined limit with a special allowance designed to enable them to meet their needs, was not within the scope of the Directive, not having as its objective protection against one of the specified risks or being a social assistance benefit having the same objective. The fact that the claimant is actually suffering from one of those risks is irrelevant. The relevant point of focus is the benefit itself: the circumstances of the claimant, in the sense of why the claimant needs the special allowance are irrelevant.

Stanley *Atkins*[44] was refused a public transport concession under a scheme **26.39** operated by a local council. He was 63 years old; a woman of that age would have been entitled to the concession; men were not entitled to it until they reached the age of 65 years. The Court found that the concession fare could have been granted to a number of persons having particular need for public transport and who were relatively less well off financially and materially. These persons might have included a person who had reached statutory retirement age or be a young or disabled person but this was not sufficient to endow the concession scheme with the necessary direct and effective protection against one of the risks listed in Article 3(1).

---

[41] Case C-243/90 [1992] ECR I–467.
[42] Ibid Judgment para 14.
[43] Joined Cases C-63 and 64/91 *Jackson and Cresswell* [1992] ECR I–4737.
[44] Case C-228/94 [1996] ECR I–3633.

E. The Principle of Equal Treatment

26.40 The principle of equal treatment is defined in Article 4 of the Directive as meaning that there must be no discrimination, either direct or indirect, on the grounds of sex in the following matters:

(a) the scope of social security schemes to which the Directive relates;

(b) the obligation to pay contributions and the calculation of the amount of such contributions;

(c) the calculation of benefits including increases payable in respect of a spouse and for dependants and the conditions governing the duration and retention of benefits.

26.41 The equal treatment principle is expressed to apply without prejudice to the provisions relating to the protection of women on the grounds of maternity.

26.42 The Directive is not confined to discrimination based on the fact that a person is of one or the other sex. In *Richards*[45] the Court held that it also applies to discrimination arising out of gender re-assignment. Sarah Richards' birth certificate registered her gender as male. In 2001 she underwent gender re-assignment. The following year, when she was 60 years of age, she applied for a retirement pension, 60 years being the age at which women became eligible for such a pension; in the case of men the relevant age was 65 years. Her claim was refused on the ground that she had applied for a pension more than four months before she reached 65 years, the implication being that she would get a pension only when she attained 65 years, the pensionable age for men.

26.43 The Court held that the unequal treatment of which she complained was discriminatory within the meaning of Article 4(1) of the Directive. Following *K.B.*[46] it held:

> . . . national legislation which precludes a transsexual, in the absence of recognition of his new gender, from fulfilling a requirement which must be met in order to be entitled to a right protected by Community law must be regarded as being, in principle, incompatible with the requirements of Community law.[47]

26.44 Discriminatory treatment within a single sex benefit scheme is not a matter which can be dealt with under the Directive, which defines equal treatment in terms of the comparative rights of men and women.[48] Thus unless both groups of

---

[45] Case C-423/04 [2006] ECR I-3585.
[46] Case C-117/01 [2004] ECR I-541.
[47] Ibid Judgment para 31.
[48] Case C-200/91 *Coloroll* [1994] ECR I-4389 Judgement paras 100-104.

claimants are envisaged by the benefit scheme no comparison of their rights or obligations can be made.

(1) Mandatory application

The principle of equal treatment is mandatory. It applies subject to the excep- **26.45** tions set out in Article 7 of the Directive considered below. In *Thomas*[49] the court refused to accept the position of the United Kingdom government to the effect that the discrimination in issue in that case—the denial of the severe disablement allowance and the invalid care allowance to women who had attained the retirement age of 60 years—would affect only an exceptional number of women since the vast majority of the female population received an old age pension (which replaced the allowances in issue) at the age of 60 years. The Court held that persons could not be denied rights granted under the Directive even if they were exceptional cases. Social security systems had to be organized in such a way that their rights were respected:

> . . . suffice it to say that the grant of benefits such as severe disablement allowance or invalid care allowance constitutes for women who are not yet in receipt of old-age pension despite their having attained the normal retirement age, an individual right which cannot be denied to them on the ground that, statistically, their situation is exceptional by comparison with other women.[50]

There is thus no *de minimis* rule with respect to the principle of equality of **26.46** treatment.

Cotter and McDermott[51] claimed the right to increases for dependants in social **26.47** welfare benefits on the same terms and conditions as men. By virtue of the Irish Social Welfare (Consolidation) Act 1981 a married man was automatically entitled to increases in his social security benefits in respect of his spouse and children without having to prove that they were actually dependent on him, whereas married women were required to prove dependency. On a reference for a preliminary ruling from the Irish Supreme Court, the Irish government argued before the ECJ that Article 4(1) of the Directive applied only to circumstances in which the person in respect of whom an increase is granted is actually financially dependant on the claimant. The Court rejected this argument. It held that the principle of equality of treatment set out in Article 4(1) of the Directive must be interpreted as including any increases due in respect of spouses and children who are not dependants. While Member States may stipulate whatever conditions they wish for entitlement to increases in social security benefits, they were required

---

[49] Case C-328/91 [1993] ECR I–1247.
[50] Ibid Judgment para 19.
[51] Case C-377/89 *Cotter and McDermott* [1991] ECR I–1155.

to comply fully with the principle of equal treatment. This meant that if married men automatically received increases in benefits in respect of persons deemed to be dependants without having to prove that those persons were actually dependent on them, a married woman was also entitled to those increases without having to prove dependency. The Irish government argued that to grant such a right to married women could result in double payment of the same increases to the same families, if both the husband and wife were receiving social welfare benefits. Such payments would be '. . . manifestly absurd and would infringe the principle of unjust enrichment laid down by national law'.[52]

26.48 The Court dismissed this argument saying that to permit reliance on the principle of unjust enrichment would enable the national authorities to use their own unlawful conduct as a ground for depriving Article 4(1) of the Directive of its full effect.

(2) Direct discrimination

26.49 Both the rate of benefit payable, the duration for which it is payable, and the conditions of entitlement to benefit must be the same for men and women. This means, for example, that in the case of contributory benefit rates of contributions and contributions, conditions must be the same.

26.50 We have seen above in *McDermott and Cotter*,[53] the ECJ found that different rates of unemployment benefit payable to men and women offended against the principle of equal treatment as did the difference in the duration of benefit entitlement. In *Cotter and McDermott*[54] differential entitlement conditions were held to be contrary to the principle of equal treatment.

26.51 Mrs Jacqueline *Drake*[55] was married. She lived with her husband. Until the middle of 1984 she held a variety of full-time and part-time jobs. In June 1984 her mother, who was severely disabled, came to live with her. Mrs Drake thereupon gave up work to look after her mother. She applied for an invalid care allowance which was a benefit payable to any person who was regularly and substantially engaged in caring for a disabled person and who was not in gainful employment. The allowance was not paid to specified groups of persons including a married woman who lives with her husband or to whose maintenance her husband contributes a weekly sum not less than the weekly rate of the allowance.

---

52 Ibid Judgment para 20.
53 Case 286/85 [1987] ECR 1453.
54 Note 21.
55 Case 150/85 [1986] ECR 1995.

Mrs Drake was refused the allowance because she was a married woman living **26.52** with her husband. She contested this refusal, and on a preliminary ruling to the ECJ from the United Kingdom Social Security Commissioner, the ECJ held that the United Kingdom legislation on entitlement to invalid care allowances was discriminatory because the allowance was not payable to a married woman living with her husband and maintained by him but was paid to a married man in similar circumstances:

> It should be noted that Article 4(1) of Directive 79/7 provides that the implementation of the principle of equal treatment means that there should be no discrimination whatsoever on the grounds of sex.
>
> . . .
>
> The answer to Question 2 must therefore be that discrimination on grounds of sex contrary to Article 4(1) of Directive 79/7 arises where legislation provides that a benefit which forms part of one of the statutory schemes referred to in Article 3(1) of that Directive is not payable to a married woman who lives with or is maintained by her husband, although it is paid in corresponding circumstances to a married man.[56]

(3) Indirect discrimination

It may be that access to benefits is granted on equal terms but in reality it is more **26.53** difficult for one sex to satisfy conditions of eligibility. It is necessary, therefore, to look beyond strict legal provisions to their practical application and if the result of that exercise is that access to benefits is more difficult, or in extreme cases, impossible for one sex then there is possibly—but not necessarily—an issue of discrimination.

Teuling Worms[57] came before the ECJ by way of preliminary ruling from the **26.54** Raad van Beroep of Amsterdam. It raised the issue of discrimination on the basis of marital status. The question put to the Court was whether a system of entitlement to supplements to benefits for incapacity to work whereby the amount of benefit is determined by three factors namely (i) marital status, (ii) the income earned by the spouse of the claimant, and (iii) the presence of a dependent child within the family, was compatible with the principle of equality given that a considerably smaller proportion of married women have a dependent spouse with the result that their benefits are generally less than those of men in the same circumstances.

---

[56] Ibid Judgment paras 31 and 34.
[57] Case 30/85 [1987] ECR 2497.

26.55 The Court found held that such a system of calculation of benefit amounts, was contrary to Article 4(1) unless it could be objectively justified:

> ... it should be pointed out that a system of benefits in which, as in this case supplements are provided for which are not directly based on the sex of the beneficiaries but take account of their marital status or family situation and in respect of which it emerges that a considerably smaller proportion of women than of men are entitled to such supplements is contrary to Article 4(1) of the directive

> ... according to statistics ... a significantly greater number of married men than married women receive a supplement linked to family responsibilities ... this results from the fact that in The Netherlands there are at present considerably more married men than married women who carry on occupational activities and therefore considerably fewer women who have a dependant spouse.

> In such circumstances a supplement linked to family responsibilities is contrary to Article 4(1) of the directive if the grant thereof cannot be justified by reasons which exclude discrimination on the grounds of sex.[58]

F. Exceptions and Derogations

26.56 The Directive contains numerous exceptions to the principle of equal treatment.

26.57 It does not apply to occupational social security schemes.[59] Such schemes, however, may fall within the scope of Article 141 as they are deemed to be constitute 'pay'[60] and, in any event, they are the subject of a separate directive on equal treatment.[61] Occupational social security schemes are considered in Chapter 27. As to the dividing line between those welfare schemes which fall within the concept of pay and those which do not, suffice it to say at least in the context of occupational pension schemes, the following factors have been deemed to be relevant in determining whether a particular pension scheme is to be classified as being 'pay' and therefore not social security:

(i) the existence of a link between the employment relationship and the retirement benefit in the sense that title to the retirement benefits arises as a result of the employment relationship negotiated and agreed between the

---

[58] Ibid Judgment paras 13–15 See also Case C-229/89 *Commission v Belgium* [1991] ECR I–2205 held that a provision in Belgian law under which the benefit rate for unemployed persons who were financially responsible for a partner was higher than for person who were not responsible for a partner was in principle discriminatory.

[59] Art 3(1)(a) and (2).

[60] Case C-262/88 *Barber* [1990] ECR I–1889.

[61] Directive 86/378 on equal treatment in occupational schemes of social security [1986] OJ L225/40, as amended by Directive 96/97 [1997] OJ L46/20.

employee and the employer, as opposed to being laid down without any
involvement of the employee, by legislation of general application;
(ii) the applicability of the scheme to a particular category of worker as opposed
to the general working population;
(iii) benefits are related to periods of service completed;
(iv) the level of benefit is calculated by reference to salary.[62]

26.58 Article 3(2) exempts from the principle of equal treatment family and survivors'
benefits. It provides that the Directive shall not apply to the provisions of national
social security schemes concerning survivors' benefits nor to those concerning
family benefits except in the case of family benefits granted by way of increases to
benefits payable for one of the risks specified in Article 3(1). This provision must
be interpreted strictly.

26.59 *Steenhorst-Neerings*[63] concerned a rule of Dutch law which provided that women
lost entitlement to incapacity benefit when they became eligible for a widow's
pension but no similar rule applied to men. The Court held that it was irrelevant
that withdrawal of incapacity benefit was linked to the award of a survivor's
|benefit which was not within the scope of the Directive. What was in issue was
not title to the survivor's benefit—a matter which would have been outwith the
Directive—but the conditions of continued entitlement to incapacity benefit
which were different for men and women.

26.60 Article 7(1)(a) permits a number of derogations. It allows Member States to
exclude the following matters from the principle of equal treatment:

(a) the determination of pensionable age for the purpose of granting old-age
and retirement pensions and the possible consequences thereof for the
beneficiary;
(b) benefits and privileges granted in respect of old age pension schemes to persons who have brought up children;
(c) old age and invalidity benefits to which married women may be entitled on
the basis of their husband's insurance record;
(d) increases in pensions awarded to a man in respect of a dependent wife.

26.61 These derogations from the principle of non-discrimination, in general, concern
advantages given to women but denied to men in the same circumstances. The
Preamble to the Directive does not reveal the reasoning underlying the exceptions set out in Article 7(1) but the Court has held that, from the nature of the
exceptions contained in Article 7(1), the Community legislature intended to

---

[62] Case C-351/00 *Pirkko Niemi* [2002] ECR I–7007 Judgment para 45.
[63] Case C-338/91 [1993] ECR I–5475.

allow Member States to maintain temporarily the advantages accorded to men with respect to retirement in order to enable them progressively to adapt their pension systems in this respect without disrupting the complex financial equilibrium of those systems.[64] They are intended to enable Member States to maintain the advantages accorded to women in retirement and old age in national social security schemes without disrupting the financial equilibrium of those schemes.[65] Important also is the necessity to preserve coherence in retirement benefit schemes. Incoherence could arise, for example, through the unjust enrichment of beneficiaries of one sex or another or the elimination of one form of discriminatory treatment could give rise to other types of differential, and possibly worse, consequences.

26.62 The method of calculation of pension rates is consequential upon the presence or absence of differences in pensionable age. The result is that Member States are not authorized to maintain a difference according to sex in the method of calculating the pension when it has abolished differences in pensionable age. By contrast, where national legislation has maintained a different pensionable age for male and female workers, the Member State concerned is entitled to calculate the amount of pension differently depending on the worker's sex.[66] These principles were established in a number of cases arising out of changes in the Belgian pension scheme in the 1990s.

26.63 Mr *Van Cant*[67] challenged the legality of the method used for the calculation of his pension, which he claimed yielded a lesser amount than would have been the case had he been a woman. Belgian Royal Decree No 50 of 24 October 1967 fixed the normal pensionable age at 65 years for men and 60 years for women. Entitlement was calculated on the basis of the most advantageous 45 and 40 years of employment respectively. A law of 20 July 1990 entitled all employees, both male and female, to retire at the age of 60 years but pension entitlement was to continue to be calculated according to the rules set out in Royal Decree No 50.

26.64 Mr Van Cant retired at the age of 65 years. His pension was calculated on the basis of the best 45 years of his employment. He challenged this, arguing that

---

[64] Case C-9/01 *ex parte Equal Opportunities Commission* [1992] ECR I–4297 Judgment para 15. *Richards* (see note 45 above) Judgment para 35.

[65] These permitted derogations must be construed strictly: Case C-328/91 *Thomas* [1993] ECR I–1247 Judgment para 8; Joined Cases C-377 to 384/96 *de Vriendt and Others* [1998] ECR I–2105.

[66] Joined Cases C-377 to 384/96 *De Vriendt* [1998] ECR I–2105; Case C-154/96 *Wolfs* [1998] ECR I–6173.

[67] Case C-154/92 [1993] ECR I–3811.

the correct basis for calculation should have been the best 40 years of his employment—which would have been the case had he been a woman.

The ECJ found that a method of calculation of retirement pensions, which **26.65** differed according to the sex of the beneficiary, was discriminatory and could only be justified under Article 7(1)(a). But if there were no difference in pensionable age, that having been abolished by national law, a Member State could not rely on Article 7(1)(a) to maintain differential methods of calculating pensions.

In the subsequent case of *De Vriendt* [68] the Court confirmed that where differ- **26.66** ences in pensionable age for men and women had been maintained, the method of calculating pension entitlement could differ according to the sex of the beneficiary. It elaborated the rationale behind the *Van Cant* judgment. The age at which a pension is awarded effectively determines the length of the period during which a person can contribute to a pension scheme. Any discrimination in the method of calculating pension would be thus necessarily and objectively linked to differences in pensionable age. [69]

Balestra [70] concerned a dispute between Mrs Balestra and her employer about **26.67** the calculation of credit for supplemental retirement contributions towards a statutory scheme for early retirement.

The scheme in question provided that male and female employees were entitled **26.68** to retire at 60 and 65 years respectively on condition that they had paid the minimum specified number of contributions. In the case of undertakings declared to be in critical difficulties (which was the case here), the scheme allowed men and women to take early retirement at the ages of 55 and 50 years respectively. The applicable pension was calculated on the basis of the actual contribution period completed increased by a period equal to that between the date of the 60th birthday in the case of men and the 55th birthday in the case of women ('credit for supplemental contributions').

Mrs Balestra resigned at the age of 54 years and seven months. She was credited **26.69** with five months', contributions. She alleged that the statutory scheme governing the calculation of credit for supplemental contributions was discriminatory and claimed credit for five years of supplemental contributions. A woman who retired at the age of 55 years was not entitled to be credited with any

---

[68] Joined Cases C-377/96 and C-384/96 [1998] ECR I–2105.
[69] *Van Cant* and *De Vriendt* were followed in Case C-154/96 *Wolfs* [1998] ECR I–6173.
[70] Case C-139/95 [1997] ECR I–549.

contributions with the result that a man and a woman, both aged 55 years, who have paid the same contributions would receive different levels of benefit, with men receiving a higher rate of benefit than women. Put otherwise, if the contributions actually paid had been the same the woman would have to work some five extra years (until the age of 60 years) in order to be entitled to a pension of the same amount as a man taking early retirement at the age of 55 years. Although it was for the national court to assess whether that discrimination was objectively and necessarily linked to the setting of pensionable ages which differ according to sex, the ECJ indicated that it believed this to be the case.

26.70   The discrimination in question was objectively linked to the setting of different retirement ages in that the scheme enabled men and women to take early retirement no more than five years before the date on which they became entitled to a retirement pension and to obtain credit for the intervening period. The purpose of the early retirement pension was thus to guarantee an income to a person leaving the employment market before reaching the age entitling him or her to a retirement pension. There was, therefore, a link between the retirement pension scheme and the early retirement scheme in question.

26.71   The next issue to be decided was whether denying women, who are entitled to work until the age of 60, the right to be credited with contributions for the period after the date on which they reach 55 years, was necessary in order to preserve this link.

26.72   If a woman taking early retirement between the ages of 50 and 55 was credited with five years of contributions without taking into account the ordinary pensionable age, she would receive a pension higher than that of the woman who had paid contributions until she had reached the age of 55 years and then retired without being able to claim a credit for contributions.

26.73   Moreover such a scheme was liable to give rise to discrimination against men in the sense that a man taking early retirement at an age between 55 years and 60 years is only entitled to a credit for contributions covering the period from the date on which he takes early retirement until he reaches ordinary pensionable age; a woman who takes early retirement during the five years prior to the date on which she qualifies for a retirement pension would, as a matter of course, be entitled to a credit of five years' contributions.

26.74   Consequently, even though women are entitled to work until they reach the age of 60 years, denying them a credit of contributions in respect of the period after the date on which they reach the age of 55 years, the age at which they are entitled to a pension, was necessary to preserve the coherence between the retirement pension scheme and the early retirement scheme in question.

In *Rose Graham*[71] the ECJ found also that although men and women were treated **26.75** in a discriminatory manner, with respect to certain invalidity benefits, this was justified. The United Kingdom invalidity pension and invalidity allowance were contributory benefits. Invalidity pensions were paid to men and women under pensionable age (65 years in the case of men and 60 years in the case of women) and to men and women not more than five years over that age who had deferred their state pension or elected not to receive it. For those under pension age, the rate of invalidity pension was the same rate as the basic rate of retirement pension. For those over pensionable age but not more than five years over pensionable age who continued to receive an invalidity pension, the amount of that benefit was limited to the amount of the state pension which they would have received (by reason of their contributions) but for the deferral or the election. Invalidity allowance was paid only to those who were more than five years below pensionable age (that is 60 if male and 55 if female) when their invalidity began.

The Court of Appeal found that such legislation was discriminatory in two **26.76** respects. First, the rate of invalidity pension for women was limited to the rate of retirement pension to which they would have been entitled had they not opted to defer payment of that pension from the age of 60 years whereas that was not the position for men until they reached the age of 65 years. Secondly, women were not entitled to an invalidity allowance in addition to invalidity pension if their incapacity commenced after the age of 55 years whereas, in the case of men, that is the position only if their incapacity commenced after they reached the age of 60 years.

The ECJ found that these forms of discrimination were objectively linked to the **26.77** setting of different pensionable ages for women and men. To prohibit a Member State which has set different pensionable ages, from limiting, in the case of persons becoming incapacitated for work before reaching pensionable age, the rate of invalidity benefit payable to them from that age to the actual rate of the retirement pension to which they are entitled under the retirement pension scheme would undermine the coherence between the retirement pension scheme and the invalidity pension scheme in at least two respects.

First the Member State would be prevented from granting to men who became **26.78** incapacitated for work before reaching pensionable age invalidity benefits greater than the retirement benefits that would have been payable to them if they had continued to work until pensionable age unless it granted to women over pensionable age retirement pensions.

---

[71] Case C-92/94 [1995] ECR I–2521.

26.79 Secondly, if women did not have their invalidity pension reduced to the level of their retirement pension until they reached the age of 65 years, as in the case of men, women aged between 60 and 65 and thus over pensionable age would receive an invalidity pension at the rate of a full retirement pension if their incapacity for work commenced before they reached pensionable age and a retirement pension corresponding to the rate actually payable if not.

26.80 As to whether differential pensionable ages have 'possible consequences' for other benefits, and are therefore within the exception set out in Article 7(1)(a), the essential criterion is whether the allegedly discriminatory rule or practice is necessary in order to avoid disrupting the complex financial equilibrium of the social security system or to ensure consistency between retirement pension schemes and other benefit schemes.

26.81 If the benefit in question is not in any way linked financially to the state pension scheme, even if some of its conditions of entitlement—such as the age at which eligibility arises—reflect those of that scheme, it will not come within the exception set out in Article 7(1)(a). Therefore, as a general rule, non-contributory benefits are unlikely to come within the scope of the exception in Article 7(1)(a), which is essentially designed to ensure that the class of beneficiaries is reflective of those who have and are paying the contributions which provide the benefits in question. The sudden expansion of the number of actual or potential beneficiaries of a contributory benefit scheme would almost certainly affect its financial equilibrium since there would be an excess of unforeseen and unprovided-for demand. This would not necessarily be the case with non-contributory schemes although it cannot be ruled out that financial disequilibrium would not arise if there were an unforeseen heavy increase in demand for a particular benefit.

26.82 In *Taylor*[72] it was conceded by all parties to the proceedings that any argument concerning the financial equilibrium of the social security scheme in question could not apply to non-contributory benefits such as the winter fuel payment in issue in that case. Eliminating discrimination within non-contributory benefit schemes had no impact on the financial equilibrium of the social security system as a whole and there was therefore no justification in maintaining differential treatment.

26.83 In *ex parte Equal Opportunities Commission*[73] the ECJ was asked to consider whether the United Kingdom rules on pension contributions which provided that, in order to get a full pension, men were required to pay contributions for

---

[72] See note 39 above.
[73] See note 64 above.

44 years whilst women were only required to pay contributions for 39 years to get the same level of benefit, were justifiable on the basis of Article 7(1). The ECJ held that they were. In a pension scheme such as that of the United Kingdom, whose financial equilibrium is based on men contributing for a longer period than women, a different pensionable age cannot be maintained without altering that financial equilibrium unless inequality concerning the length of the contribution periods is also maintained. To restrict the scope of the derogations in Article 7(1)(a) to the time of granting of the pension only and not to the contribution periods would lead to financial disequilibrium. Accordingly, the Court ruled that Article 7(1)(a) allowed the maintenance of different pension ages and also forms of discrimination such as different contributions periods 'which are necessarily linked to that difference'.

By contrast, in *Thomas*[74] and *Taylor*[75] the Court held that discriminatory **26.84** practices and rules within non-contributory benefits which had no bearing on the financial equilibrium of pension schemes could not be said to be necessary to ensure the financial equilibrium of pension schemes.

Mrs *Thomas* and four other ladies challenged the lawfulness of a denial of title **26.85** to a benefit to women over the age of 60 years. Men could receive benefits up until the age of 65 years. This age differential reflected that applicable to the state pension scheme.

The claimants were refused either a severe disablement allowance or an invalid **26.86** care allowance. The severe disablement allowance is granted to persons who are incapable of work and an invalid care allowance is granted to person engaged in caring for a severely disabled person. Persons who have attained retirement age, that is 65 years in the case of men and 60 years in the case of women, are not entitled to these benefits. In reply to a series of question put to it by the House of Lords, the ECJ found that the benefits in question were granted to persons in respect of whom certain risks have materialized, regardless of any title they may have to a contributory old age pension. They were therefore discrete benefits not linked to the pension scheme. They had thus no direct influence on the financial equilibrium of the contributory pension scheme. Consequently, the denial of benefits to women in circumstances in which they would not be denied to men was discriminatory.

Mr *Taylor*[76] had worked in the post office all his life. He received a post office **26.87** pension. At the age of 62 years he applied for a winter fuel payment. He was

---

[74] See note 49 above.
[75] See note 39 above.
[76] See note 39 above.

refused this payment on the ground that he had not attained the statutory retirement age for men, that is 65 years. Had he been a woman he would have received the payment as the statutory retirement age for women was 60 years. The United Kingdom government argued that if the benefit were regarded as designed to meet the risk of old age (which in fact was what the Court ultimately found), it would not be consistent to choose an age other than that applicable to the payment of state retirement benefits. The Court rejected this proposition, holding that even if the benefit was designed to be paid to those over a certain age it did not follow that the age must necessarily coincide with the statutory age of retirement. This being so, the discriminatory treatment complained of by Mr Taylor was not linked to the statutory age of retirement and was not, therefore, covered by the derogation in Article 7(1).

26.88 *Richardson*[77] concerned the exemption from prescription charges, eligibility for which arose at 60 years in the case of women and 65 years in the case of men. There was thus direct discrimination between men and women. These age limits corresponded to the statutory pensionable age for men and women but the Court found that they were not linked to those ages and therefore the derogation provided for in Article 7(1)(a) could not be invoked. The exemption from prescription charges for the elderly could be justified in view of the fact that they were likely to have increased prescription charges at a time when their disposable income had shrunk but the exemption need not necessarily be linked to the statutory retirement age—it could operate at any age level. The Court accepted that extending the entitlement to exemption for prescription charges in the case of men to 60 years would increase the financial burden borne by the State in funding the national health service but this could not justify maintaining in force a discriminatory provision. Member States were at liberty to adopt measures to control their social security expenditure, including withdrawing benefits from certain categories of persons, provided that the measures were compatible with the principle of equal treatment. Important also is the necessity of keeping coherence in the retirement pension scheme.

G. Objective Justification

26.89 Differences in treatment may be objectively justified and therefore not unlawful under the Directive.[78] *Ruzius Wilbrink*[79] concerned the calculation of an

---

[77] Case C-137/94 [1995] ECR I–3407.
[78] Case C-343/92 *De Weerd (nee Roks)* [1994] ECR I–571.
[79] Case 102/88 [1989] ECR 4311.

allowance in respect of incapacity for work. The Dutch legislation in issue granted an allowance to all insured persons, with the exception of part-time workers. The level of the allowance, which corresponds to a minimum subsistence income, was not dependent upon previous earnings. The allowances granted to part-time workers were calculated by reference to their income. There were, in the Netherlands, considerably fewer male part-time workers than female part-time workers. In principle, therefore, female workers were the subject of discrimination and that discrimination was unlawful under the Directive unless it could be objectively justified.

It was argued by the Dutch authorities that the system of calculating the allowances was designed to prevent part-time workers from receiving benefits which were worth more than their previous salary. The Court did not accept this argument. It pointed out that in a substantial number of other cases, the amount of the allowance was higher than previous income. **26.90**

In *Commission v Belgium*,[80] the Court accepted the argument of the Belgian government seeking to justify different rates of unemployment and sickness benefit for different categories of beneficiary according to their family circumstances. The method of calculation of these benefits resulted in women being treated less favourably than men but the Court found that the objective of the Belgian legislation was to take into account differing levels of need: **26.91**

> With regard to a guaranteed minimum subsistence level, the Court has already held that Community law does not preclude a Member State, in controlling its social expenditure, from taking into account the relatively greater needs of beneficiaries who have a dependant spouse or a dependant child or receiving a very small income in relation to the needs of a single person . . .[81]

Nolte[82] and *Megner*[83] concerned access to sickness and old age insurance by those in minor employment (less than 15 hours a week remunerated at less than one-seventh the average monthly salary). Such persons were excluded from compulsory insurance under the statutory sickness and old age insurance schemes. There was no direct discrimination since the exclusion applied to all those in minor employment regardless of their sex, but there were many more women than men in minor employment with the result that there was indirect discrimination of a kind prohibited by Article 4(1) of the Directive unless the differential treatment of those in minor employment could be objectively justified. By way of justification the German government pleaded that the exclusion of persons in minor **26.92**

---

[80] Case C-229/89 [1991] ECR I–2205.
[81] Ibid Judgment para 24.
[82] Case C-317/93 [1995] ECR I–4623.
[83] Case C-444/93 [1995] ECR I–4741.

employment from compulsory insurance corresponds to a structural principle of the German social security system. There was a demand for minor employment, and the only means of ensuring the existence and supply of such employment within the structural framework of the German social security system was to exclude minor employment from compulsory insurance. If this could not be done the demand for minor employment would be satisfied by unlawful employment practices.

26.93 The Court emphasized that social policy was a matter for the Member States. It is for them to chose the measures capable of achieving the objectives of their social and employment policy and in exercising that competence they had a broad margin of discretion.

H. The Self-employed

26.94 Directive 813/86 on the application of the principle of equal treatment between men and women engaged in an activity, including agriculture, in a self-employed capacity and on the protection of self-employed women during pregnancy and motherhood,[84] provides in Article 6 that where a contributory social security system for the self-employed exists in a Member State, that Member State shall take the necessary measures to enable spouses of the self-employed, not being employees or partners, who habitually work with them but are not protected under the self-employed worker's social security scheme, to join a contributory scheme voluntarily.

I. The 1987 Proposal

26.95 For the sake of completeness it should be mentioned that the Commission proposed the adoption of a directive in 1987[85] which would have removed many of the exceptions and permitted derogations in both statutory and occupational social security schemes.

26.96 The proposal had three main objectives:

(i) the extension of the principle of equal treatment in statutory social security schemes to survivors' benefits and family benefits;

---

[84] [1986] OJ L359/56.
[85] [1987] OJ C309/11.

(ii)   the extension of the principle of equal treatment to corresponding provisions of occupational social security schemes;

(iii) the extension of the principle of equal treatment to benefits and schemes excluded under Article 7(1) of the Directive[86] and Article 9(a) of the Equality Treatment in Occupational Social Security Directive.[87]

This proposal has never been adopted.   **26.97**

---

[86] See paras 26.60–26.88.
[87] Directive 86/378 [1986] OJ L225/40.

27

OCCUPATIONAL SOCIAL SECURITY BENEFITS

A. Introduction

The previous chapter has discussed the application of the principle of equality **27.01**
of treatment to statutory social security schemes. This is achieved by means of
the Equal Treatment in Social Security Directive.[1] Such schemes are not 'pay'
within the meaning of Article 141.[2] By contrast, occupational social security
benefits may be pay if they fulfil certain conditions.

Equality of treatment in occupational welfare has been largely achieved through **27.02**
the case law of the European Court of Justice (ECJ) which stretches back over
a period of more than 30 years. As is usual when an area of law falls to be developed through legal proceedings, the case law is complex and substantial. This
chapter will analyse it and the provisions of the Equal Treatment in Occupational

---

[1] Directive 79/7 [1979] OJ L6/24. See Chapter 26.
[2] Case 80/70 *Defrenne 3* [1971] ECR 445.

Social Security Directive,[3] first adopted in 1986 as a sister directive to the Equal Treatment in Social Security Directive, extensively amended in 1997 to bring it into line with ECJ case law, and now repealed and replaced by Directive 2006/54 on the implementation of the principle of equal opportunities and equal treatment of men and women in matters of employment and occupation (the 'Recast Directive').[4]

B. The Position pre-*Barber*

27.03 Until the judgment of the ECJ in *Barber*[5] it was generally assumed that occupational social security benefits were outwith the scope of Article 141 EC. The basis for this assumption is uncertain; perhaps it was by reason of false analogy with benefits paid under statutory social security schemes which were held not to constitute 'pay' in *Defrenne (No 1)*,[6] an understanding which appeared to be confirmed by the provisions of the Equality of Treatment in Social Security Directive. In any event, it was certainly a misapprehension as the ECJ had strongly indicated many years before *Barber* that occupational pensions were within the scope of Article 141.

27.04 In *Burton v British Railways Board*[7] the Court stated:

> . . . the question of interpretation which has been referred to the Court concerns not the benefit itself, but whether the conditions of access to the voluntary redundancy scheme are discriminatory. This is a matter covered by Council Directive 76/207 and not Article 119.[8]

27.05 The implication here is that the benefit itself fell within Article 119, now Article 141, but that conditions of access to that benefit would be governed by the Equal Opportunities Directive.[9]

27.06 Some two years later in *Razzouk and Beydoun v Commission*,[10] a case concerning the European Communities Staff Pension Scheme, Advocate General Slynn stated:

> The judgment of the Court in Case 80/70 *Defrenne v Belgium* excluded from the scope of Article 119 'social security schemes or benefits, in particular retirement

---

3 Directive 86/378 on the implementation of the principle of equal treatment for men and women in occupational social security schemes [1986] OJ L225/40.
4 [2006] OJ L204/23.
5 Case C-262/88 [1990] ECR I–1889.
6 Case 80/70 [1971] ECR 445.
7 Case 19/81 [1982] 55. See comment Bradley (1982) 19 CML Rev 625.
8 Judgment para 8.
9 Directive 76/207 [1976] OJ L39/40. See Chapter 25.
10 Joined Cases 75 and 117/82 [1984] ECR 1509.

benefits, directly governed by legislation without any element of agreement with the undertaking or the occupational branch concerned which are obligatorily applicable to general categories of workers'. That description cannot, in my view, be applied to benefits and pension schemes entered into by employers outside a national system of social security. Nor does it in my view fit the benefits provided under the Staff Regulations . . . In substance the official's entitlement to, for example, a retirement pension is part of the consideration (albeit deferred) that he receives in respect of his employment.[11]

In 1986 *Bilka Kaufhaus*[12] the Court made much clearer the relationship between Article 141 and occupational pensions. Although the issue in *Bilka* was that of the unequal treatment of a largely female part of the workforce with respect to membership of an occupational pension scheme, the Court did not follow its previous reasoning in *Burton*, and treat the issue as falling within the Equality of Opportunities Directive, but chose instead to view the case as falling within the scope of Article 141.   **27.07**

This marked a departure from the 'split' approach in *Burton*, which would have treated access to membership as being within the scope of the Equality of Opportunities Directive, but the benefit itself as being within Article 141, an approach which might have proved somewhat problematic in its practical application. The Court held that two criteria need to be satisfied if a particular occupational scheme is to be deemed 'pay' within the meaning of Article 141 and hence subject to the principle of equality of treatment: **27.08**

(i) the scheme must be financed, at least in part by the employer. In that way the pension forms part of the consideration for work performed;

(ii) the scheme must be contractual, that is, formed out of an agreement between an employer and his employees, rather than a creature of statute.

The requirement in *Bilka* that occupational pension schemes must be of a contractual nature in order to be considered 'pay' as opposed to a creature of statute, raised the further question of what was the position if an occupational pension scheme complemented a state pension scheme or was a substitute therefor? In such a case the occupational scheme was closely intertwined with the state social security pension scheme and could be said, in some cases, to fulfil all or part of its function. How then was it to be classified? What was the dividing line between an occupational pension which had to be considered as 'pay' and hence within the scope of Article 141 and one which was to be considered social security and therefore outside Article 141? The outcome of this analysis   **27.09**

---

[11] Ibid at 1540.

[12] Case 170/84 [1986] ECR 1607. See comment Arnull: 'Sex Discrimination in Occupational Pension Schemes' (1986) 11 EL Rev 363.

has serious consequences in the sense that if an occupational benefit is to be considered a social security benefit, a claimant must rely on the Equal Treatment in Social Security Directive,[13] which permits many exceptions and derogations to the principle of equal treatment. There is thus a sharp difference in the extent of the rights which can be claimed on the basis of Article 141 and the Directive, the former being much broader than the latter.

27.10 Advocate General Warner in *Worringham and Humphreys*,[14] a case in which judgment was pronounced some five years before *Bilka*, had addressed this matter. He found that where privately established pension schemes supplemented state social security schemes they could be regarded as 'pay' but not where they were a substitute for all or part of such a scheme. His opinion was given in the context of the United Kingdom's 'contracted out' scheme. The Advocate General's view was that to require a Member State to ensure that the contracted out scheme afforded equal rights for men and women, whilst it was under no equivalent obligation as regards the state scheme, would be an 'unbalanced result to reach as well as one designed to deter contracting out'. The Court in *Bilka* did not address the issue.

27.11 A little over two months after the judgment in *Bilka*, Directive 86/373 on the implementation of the principle of equal treatment for men and women in occupational social security schemes[15] (Equal of Treatment in Occupational Social Security Schemes Directive) was adopted in the belief that occupational social security schemes were not 'pay'. It was based on Articles 94 and 308 EC and came into force on 1 January 1993 and reflected many of the provisions of the Equal Treatment in Social Security Directive.[16]

27.12 Thus was the state of the law at the time the *Barber* proceedings.

C. The *Barber* Case

27.13 Mr Barber was a member of a pension scheme established by his employer, the Guardian Royal Exchange Assurance Group (the 'Guardian'). The scheme was wholly financed by his employer. It was a 'contracted out' scheme in that it was a substitute for the earnings related part of the United Kingdom state pension scheme. Members of contracted out schemes paid reduced social security contributions but were not entitled to the earnings related part of the state

---

13 Note 1.
14 Case 69/80 [1981] ECR 767.
15 [1986] OJ L225/40.
16 Note 1.

pension scheme: they received only the flat rate benefit to which all workers were entitled regardless of their earnings. The normal pensionable age fixed by the Guardian scheme was 62 years for men and 57 years for women. The five-year difference in pensionable age between men and women corresponded to that in the state pension scheme.

Mr Barber's contract of employment provided that in the event of redundancy **27.14** members of the pension fund were entitled to an immediate pension subject to their having attained the age of 55 years in the case of men, and 50 in the case of women. Staff who did not fulfil these conditions received certain cash benefits calculated on the basis of their years of service and a deferred pension payable at normal pensionable age.

Mr Barber was made redundant when he was 52 years. He was not therefore **27.15** entitled to an immediate pension. A woman in the same position as Mr Barber would have received an immediate pension as well as the statutory redundancy payment and the total of these amounts would have been greater than the cash benefits received by Mr Barber. Mr Barber commenced proceedings alleging unlawful discrimination based on sex. Five questions were referred to the ECJ by the Court of Appeal. Collectively they raised three issues:

(i) whether redundancy payments and occupational pensions fell to be considered as 'pay' within the meaning of Article 141; if so
(ii) whether in the circumstances of the case, Article 141 had direct effect;
(iii) whether on the facts of the case the principle of equal treatment had been violated.

The first question concerned which were the relevant provisions in the **27.16** Community legal order governing Mr Barber's rights: Article 141 EC, the Equal Pay Directive,[17] or the Equal Opportunities Directive?[18] The Court found that the benefits in issue were pay within the meaning of Article 141. Compensation for compulsory redundancy constituted a form of pay to which a worker was entitled in respect of his employment. It was paid to an employee on termination of employment to facilitate his adjustment to the loss of his employment and provide him with a source of income during the period in which he was seeking new employment. The fact that redundancy payments were statutory in nature did not mean that they fell to be classified as social security as opposed to pay. The worker was entitled to receive such a payment from his employer by reason of the existence of his employment relationship.

---

[17] Directive 75/117 [1975] OJ L45/19.
[18] Note 9.

27.17 On the issue of whether a retirement pension paid under a private contracted out scheme fell within the scope of Article 141, the Court found that, in contrast to statutory social security schemes, the pension scheme in question was the result of an agreement between workers and employers or of a unilateral decision, taken by the employer. Accordingly such schemes form part of the consideration offered to workers by the employer. Moreover, affiliation to those pension schemes derives of necessity from the employment relationship with a given employer and this is so even if the schemes are established in conformity with national legislation and satisfy the conditions to be recognized as contracted out schemes. Further, even if the contributions to those schemes and the benefits which they provide are a substitute for those of the general statutory schemes, a pension paid out under a contracted out scheme constitutes consideration paid by an employer to a worker in respect of his employment and is therefore 'pay' within the meaning of Article 141.

D. Temporal Effects of *Barber*

27.18 In the course of the proceedings before the ECJ, the United Kingdom government raised the issue of the temporal effects of the *Barber* judgment, arguing that for reasons of financial and legal stability it should have prospective effect only.

27.19 The Court accepted this position. Following the approach first adopted in *Defrenne 2* it limited the temporal effects of its judgment. Its reasons for doing so were set out in paragraph 40 *et seq* of its judgment. They were twofold:

(i) The financial consequences: the effect of a judgment not limited in time could be serious, a point argued strenuously by the United Kingdom government. This would be the case in particular in the United Kingdom, where large numbers of workers were affiliated to contracted out insurance schemes which frequently derogated from the principle of equality between men and women, notably by providing for different pensionable ages.

(ii) The Member States and all the parties concerned were reasonably entitled to believe that Article 141 did not apply to pensions paid out under contracted out schemes. Derogations from the principle of equality between men and women still appeared to be permitted in that sphere in that the Equal Treatment in Social Security Directive[19] authorized Member States to defer the compulsory implementation of the principle of equal treatment

---

[19] See note 1 above.

with regard to the determination of pensionable age for the purposes of granting old age pensions and the possible consequences thereof for other benefits. Those exceptions were incorporated into the Equal Treatment in Occupational Social Security Schemes Directive which was viewed as being applicable to contracted out schemes such as the one in issue in *Barber*.

In the light of these circumstances the Court was persuaded that both the **27.20** Member States and the parties concerned were reasonably entitled to consider that Article 141 did not apply to pensions paid out under such schemes and that derogations from the principle of equality between men and women were permitted in that sphere:[20]

> ... Article 7(1) of Council Directive 79/7/EEC ... authorized the Member States to defer the compulsory implementation of the principle of equal treatment with regard to the determination of pensionable age for the purposes of granting old-age pensions and the possible consequences thereof for other benefits. That exception has been incorporated in Article 9(a) of Directive 86/378/EEC ...
>
> In the light of those provisions, the Member States and the parties concerned were reasonably entitled to consider that Article 119 did not apply to pensions paid under contracted-out schemes and that derogations from the principle of equality between men and women were still permitted in that sphere.
>
> In those circumstances overriding considerations of legal certainty preclude legal situations which have exhausted all their effects in the past from being called into question where that might upset retroactively the financial balance of many contracted out pension schemes.[21]

Accordingly the Court ruled that the direct effect of Article 141 could not be **27.21** relied upon in order to claim entitlement to a pension with effect from a date prior to that of the judgment, that is, 17 May 1990. Exceptionally, and in accordance with the Court's usual treatment of temporal limitations on the effects on its judgments, that general rule did not apply to persons or those claiming under them who had initiated legal proceedings or raised equivalent claims under applicable national law, before 17 May 1990.[22]

The Court emphasized that as from 17 May 1990 there could be no restriction **27.22** on the grounds of gender as regards the acquisition or entitlement to a pension. Thus equality of treatment with respect to access and membership of an

---

[20] Case C-262/88 *Barber* [1990] ECR I–1889 Judgment para 43.

[21] Ibid Judgment para 44.

[22] This difference in treatment by the Court between those who had brought claims or instituted proceedings before 17 May 1990 has been criticized, as creating in itself 'gross inequalities' since Mr Barber and those similarly placed have the benefit of their entitlement backdated whereas others do not. See Honeyball and Shaw: 'Sex, law and the retiring man' (1991) 16 EL Rev 47 at 57–8.

occupational pension scheme could be claimed as from the date of the judgment in *Defrenne 2*, that is 8 April 1976.

27.23 Following this ruling tremendous confusion ensued. It failed in its very objective, which was to provide legal certainty to both providers and recipients of pensions. It was aptly described as '. . . a recipe for divergent results in different Member States'.[23] There could be no legal certainty until three key concepts capable of multiple interpretations were clarified. What were 'legal situations which have exhausted all their effects in the past'? What did 'acquisition of entitlement to a pension' mean? What was to be understood by 'entitlement to a pension with effect from a date prior to this judgment'?

27.24 Numerous interpretations were advanced of the relevant paragraphs in the Court's judgment: Advocate General Van Gerven set out four of the most common in his opinion in *Ten Oever, Moroni, Neath,* and *Coloroll*.[24] Academic writings suggested further permutations and combinations.[25]

27.25 More confusion was engendered by the fact that *Barber* concerned a contracted out scheme pension scheme. Was it thus limited to schemes of that nature? Did it extend to supplements to state pension schemes? What about allied benefits within an occupational pension scheme that might be paid to a third party? What was the determining factor in classifying a welfare benefit as 'pay' as opposed to a social security benefit? Was it sufficient that entitlement arose because of employment? And did the scheme have to be contractual in nature or could it be based in statute or otherwise organized? And how and by whom was equality to be achieved?

27.26 These issues occupied the Court for many years after *Barber*.

E. The *Barber* Protocol

27.27 In an effort to clarify the extent of the temporal effect of the judgment, a Protocol to the Maastricht Treaty was adopted,[26] laying down how the *Barber* judgment was to be interpreted:

> For the purposes of Article 119 of this Treaty, benefits under occupational social security schemes shall not be considered as remuneration if and insofar as they are attributable to periods of employment prior to 17 May 1990, except in the case of

---

[23] Ibid at 57.

[24] [1993] ECR I–4893 at 4901.

[25] Honeyball and Shaw (see note 22 above) at 56–7; Curtin: 'The Constitutional Structure of the Union: A Europe of Bits and Pieces' (1993) 30 CML Rev 50–1.

[26] Protocol No 2; now Protocol No 17 of the EC Treaty.

workers or those claiming under them who have before that date initiated legal proceedings or introduced an equivalent claim under applicable national law.

The adoption of a Protocol interpreting a judgment of the ECJ was unprece- **27.28** dented. It was in response to huge pressure from the pensions industry and a general conviction that were the temporal effects of *Barber* to be interpreted and applied in a manner other than that set out in the Protocol, the financial disequilibrium in occupational pension provision would be such as to lead to the collapse of such schemes. Whilst the Protocol would avert this, it occupied an uneasy place within the Community legal order. Was the ECJ bound by it? Could it be bound by it? On the one hand the Protocol enjoyed Treaty status and so was binding *erga omnes*, on the other hand it purported to set out what the Court meant in *Barber*. It is arguable that it is for the Court alone and not the Member States, by way of protocols to treaties or otherwise, to articulate what its rulings mean. If the position were otherwise the Member States could overrule the judgments of the Court by 'interpretative' instruments. Such a development or even the possibility of it would strike at the institutional framework of the Community, which has been constituted to achieve a balance of power both between its various branches and the Member States.

Fortunately, some months before the Maastricht Treaty entered into force, the **27.29** ECJ in *Ten Oever*[27] clarified its ruling in *Barber* in terms identical to those of the Protocol, thereby rendering it largely otiose. At the same time the Court took the opportunity of further justifying its ruling in *Barber*:

> The Court's ruling took account of the fact that it is a characteristic of this form of pay that there is a time-lag between accrual of entitlement to the pension, which occurs gradually throughout the employee's working life, and its actual payment, which is deferred until a particular age.

> The Court also took into consideration the way in which occupational pensions are funded and financed and thus of accounting links existing in each individual case between the periodic contributions and the future amounts to be paid.[28]

F. Membership

Bilka Kaufhaus[29] held that membership of occupational pension schemes was a **27.30** matter governed by the principle of equal treatment set out in Article 141 EC. No temporal limitation was placed the effect of the Court's judgment in that case.

---

[27] Case C-109/91 [1993] ECR I–4879.
[28] Ibid Judgment paras 17 and 18.
[29] Case 170/84 [1986] ECR 1607.

27.31 No temporal limitation can be read into the right to join an occupational pension scheme as a result of the *Barber* judgment or the *Barber* Protocol interpreting that judgment. Indeed the Court made it plain in *Barber* that the temporal limitations did not extend to the right to membership.[30]

27.32 The temporal effects of the *Barber* judgment are thus confined to those kinds of discrimination which employers and pension schemes could reasonably have considered as being permissible owing to derogations for which Community law had provided notably under the Equal Treatment in Social Security Directive.

27.33 *Bilka* had made it clear that any discrimination based on sex with respect to the right to join an occupational pension scheme was contrary to Article 141, therefore, in contrast to the situation in *Barber* there could be no reason why those concerned could have been mistaken as to the applicability of Article 141 to the right to membership of an occupational pension scheme and therefore no reason to limit in point of time the right to equality with respect to membership access and conditions:

> . . . since the judgement in *Bilka* included no limitation of its effects in time, the direct effect of Article 119 could be relied upon in order retroactively to claim equal treatment in relation to the right to join an occupational pension scheme and that could be done as from 8 April 1976, the date of the *Defrenne* judgment in which the Court held for the first time that Article 119 had direct effect . . .[31]

27.34 *Fisscher*[32] and *Vroege*[33] confirmed the right of equality of membership of occupational pension schemes, as from 8 April 1976.[34]

27.35 Membership in itself is of no value to the employee unless it brings entitlement to benefits. Entitlement is dependent upon the payment of contributions with the result that any claim to retroactive membership of an occupational scheme requires that employers and employees alike must pay contributions for the membership period concerned:

> . . . equal treatment is to be achieved by placing the worker discriminated against in the same situation as that of the worker of the other sex. It follows that the worker cannot claim more favourable treatment, particularly in financial terms, than he would have had had he been duly accepted as a member.[35]

---

[30] See note 5 above.
[31] Case C-435/93 *Dietz* [1996] ECR I–5223 Judgment para 21; Case C-270/97 and Case C-271/97 *Sievers and Schroeder* 2000 ECR I–929.
[32] Case C-128/93 [1994] ECR I–4583.
[33] Case C-57/93 [1994] ECR I–4541.
[34] Followed in *Dietz* (see note 31 above) and Case C-246/96 *Magorrian and Cunningham* [1997] ECR I–7135.
[35] Fisscher (see note 32 above) Judgment paras 35 and 36.

Subsequent references for preliminary rulings from the United Kingdom courts **27.36** raised the issue of the extent to which the right to retroactive membership could be limited in time and conditions of access to membership.

(1) The *Preston* case

The background to *Preston*[36] lay in the practice of not allowing part-time **27.37** workers to become members of certain contracted out pension schemes.

Following the *Vroege*[37] and *Fisscher*[38] judgments, some 60,000 part-time work- **27.38** ers, in both the public and private sectors in the United Kingdom, commenced proceedings before industrial tribunals claiming unlawful exclusion from membership of various occupational pension schemes.

The Occupational Pension Schemes (Equal Access to Membership) (Amend- **27.39** ment) Regulations 1995 prohibited, as from 31 May 1995, all direct and indirect discrimination on grounds of sex regarding membership of any occupational pension scheme. The claimants sought recognition of their entitlement to retroactive membership to various pension schemes for periods of part-time employment completed prior to the passage of the Amendment Regulations.

Twenty-two claims were selected as 'test cases'. In the first series of cases, the pen- **27.40** sion scheme in issue had been amended more than two years prior to the issuance of proceedings by the claimant. By virtue of Regulation 12 of the Occupational Pension Regulations the claimants could not claim pension rights based on periods of service completed more than two years prior to the institutions of proceedings. In the second series of cases the claimants had ceased their employment with their employer more than six months before bringing proceedings and by virtue of Section 2(4) of the Equal Pay Act 1970 they were deprived of the right to secure recognition of earlier part-time service for the purpose of calculating their pension rights.

In the third series of cases, the claimants had worked for the same employer **27.41** under successive legally separate contracts. They could secure recognition of periods of part-time employment for pension entitlement purposes only if proceedings were commenced within six months following the end of each contract governing the relevant employment.

These proceedings resulted in the reference of three questions to the European **27.42** Court of Justice, the first of which was whether Community law precluded a

---

[36] Case C-78/98 [2000] ECR I–3201.
[37] See note 33 above.
[38] See note 32 above.

national procedural rule under which a claim to membership of an occupational pension scheme must, if it is not to be time barred, be lodged within six months following the end of the period of employment to which it relates. The Court replied to this question in the negative. Such a time limit was not incompatible with Community law provided that the limitation period in issue was not less favourable for actions based on Community law than for those based on domestic law.

27.43   The second question sought to ascertain whether Community law precluded a national procedural rule which required claimant's pensionable service to be calculated only by reference to service after a date falling no earlier than the year prior to the date of the claim.

27.44   The Court, following *Magorrian and Cunningham*,[39] held that even though the procedural rule in issue did not totally deprive the claimants of access to membership, it did prevent the entire record of service completed before the two years preceding the date of commencement of proceedings from being taken into account for the purpose of calculating the benefit that would be payable even after the date of the claim. The objective of such proceedings is not to obtain, with retroactive effect, arrears of benefits but to secure recognition of the right to retroactive membership of a pension scheme in order to obtain benefits in the future.

27.45   A further issue in the case concerned the criteria to be used to determine whether the procedural rules in issue were less favourable than other domestic rules applicable to cases of a similar nature. The Court held that this was a matter for the national court, which must be guided by the purpose and essential characteristics of allegedly similar types of actions. The rules in question must be viewed objectively, that is, not by reference solely to the case at hand, to see if they were similar, taking into account the role played by those rules in the proceedings as a whole, as well as the operation of that procedure and any special feature of the rules. An example of an infringement of the principle of equivalence would be where a person relying on a right conferred by Community law was forced to incur additional costs and delay in comparison with a claimant whose action was based solely on domestic law.

---

[39] See note 34 above. The Court held that a national rule whereby entitlement to join an occupational pension scheme, in the event of a successful claim for equal treatment, was limited to a period which started to run from a point of time two years prior to the commencement of proceedings, was precluded.

In reply to the third question, the Court ruled that the requirement that a claim **27.46** for membership of an occupational pension scheme be submitted within six months following the end of each contract of employment to which the claim related could not be justified on the grounds of legal certainty. That was not to say that there should be no limitation period:

> Where, however, there is a stable relationship resulting from a succession of short-term contracts concluded at regular intervals in respect of the same employment to which the same pension scheme applies, it is possible to fix a precise starting point for the limitation period.
>
> There is no reason why that starting point should not be fixed as the date on which the sequence of such contracts has been interrupted through the absence of one or more of the features that characterize a stable employment relationship of that kind, either because the periodicity of such contracts has been broken or because the new contract does not relate to the same employment as that to which the same pension scheme applies.[40]

G. Relationship with Statutory Pension Schemes

Advocate General Warner's view in *Worringham and Humphreys*[41] on the effect of **27.47** a link between a statutory pension scheme and an occupational pension scheme has been set out above in para 27.10.

The position was clarified by the ECJ in *Moroni v Collo*.[42] The Court found that **27.48** an occupational pension scheme which was designed to supplement a state social security scheme was 'pay' even if it was closely linked to the state scheme in that there was a statutory obligation to pay the occupational scheme at the same time as the statutory pension:

> . . . an obligation imposed by a national provision to pay an occupational pension at the same time as the statutory pension cannot have the effect of excluding the occupational scheme from the scope of Article 119 of the Treaty.[43]

H. Organization of Pension Schemes

A number of aspects of the organization of pension schemes have been the subject **27.49** of references from national courts to the ECJ.

---

[40] See note 34 above, Judgment paras 69 and 70.
[41] See note 14 above.
[42] Case C-110/91 [1993] ECR I–6591.
[43] Ibid Judgment para 19.

27.50 First there is the means by which a pension scheme is established: if it is a creature of statute does this mean that it is outwith Article 141? Are all statutory welfare schemes to be classified as 'social security' as opposed to pay?

(1) Creatures of statute

27.51 This issue arose in *Beune*[44] and *Evrenopoulos*.[45]

27.52 *Beune* raised the question of whether a Dutch civil servant's pension scheme (ABPW) fell within the scope of the Equal Treatment in Social Security Directive or Article 141 EC.

27.53 The Court began by summarizing the criteria to be applied in determining the nature of the pension schemes in question:

> On the basis of the situations before it the Court has developed inter alia, the following criteria: the statutory nature of the pension scheme, negotiation between employers and employees' representatives, the fact that employee benefits supplement social security benefits, the manner in which the pension scheme is financed, its applicability to general categories of employees and finally the relationship between the benefit and the employee's employment.[46]

27.54 Applying these criteria the Court reasoned as follows. If a pension scheme is governed directly by statute, there is a strong indication that the benefits provided under the schemes are social security benefits of the kind which are not pay on the basis of the reasoning in *Defrenne 1*.[47] However, the fact that a scheme like the ABPW is directly governed by statute is not sufficient of itself to exclude it from the scope of Article 141. Thus a pension scheme which has been agreed between employers and employees concerning only a particular category of workers, which is directly related to periods of service and the amount of which is calculated by reference to final salary, is 'pay' even if it is established by statute. Such a pension scheme has been negotiated between employers and employees and is a product of such negotiation with the result that even if it is endorsed or given effect by statute it is not a creature of statute and may therefore be pay.

27.55 The scheme was created by an agreement between employers and employees and was therefore 'contractual' in nature, even if the contract in question is given effect by statute.

---

[44] Case C-7/93 [1994] ECR I–4471.
[45] Case C-147/95 [1997] ECR I–2057.
[46] *Beune* (see note 44 above) Judgment para 23.
[47] Case 80/70 [1971] ECR 445.

In the subsequent case of *Evrenopoulos*,[48] the Court, following *Beune*, held that a   **27.56**
pension scheme set up by the Greek electricity company under statute, to which
all persons connected to the company by an employment relationship, together
with the members of their families, were compulsorily affiliated, fell within the
scope of Article 141. The level of retirement pension granted was calculated on
the basis of the beneficiary's pay during his final years of service and was directly
related to the number of years of service and the scheme covered a defined
groups of persons.

Likewise in *Griesmar*[49] the Court found that the French retirement scheme for   **27.57**
civil servants was to be considered as 'pay' within the meaning of Article 141.
The pensions paid out under it were directly determined by length of service and
the amount calculated on the basis of the salary which the person concerned
received during his or her final six months at work. It was irrelevant that the pensions were financed directly from the annual law on finances, without the need
for management or capitalization of any fund. The arrangements for the funding
and management of a pension scheme were not conclusive in the determination
of whether that scheme fell within the scope of Article 141 or not.

From these cases it can be seen that the dividing line between pension schemes   **27.58**
which are to be classified as social security schemes or as occupational welfare
schemes seems to hinge upon three factors:

(i) the existence of a defined and limited class of beneficiary;
(ii) a relationship between length of service and benefit levels;
(iii) an employment relationship which gives the right to membership of the
scheme.

If a pension scheme is statutory by nature, open to all who satisfy objectively   **27.59**
defined criteria which are independent of any particular employment relationship, and benefits are neither related to length of service in a particular employment nor linked to final salary, the scheme is unlikely to qualify as 'pay'.

Unlike remuneration, the existence of an employment relationship is therefore   **27.60**
not the sole criterion in determining the status of a pension or other welfare
scheme. Employment is likely to be a common factor in both occupational and
state social security schemes.[50] The consideration of other factors which may
serve to distinguish a benefit which is part of the social policy of a state and a
benefit which arises out of employment, is therefore necessary.

---

[48] Case C-147/95 [1997] ECR I–2057.
[49] Case C-366/99 [2001] ECR I–9383.
[50] *Beune* (see note 24 above) Judgment para 45.

461

(2) Pension schemes administered by trusts

27.61 Pensions paid out under an occupational pension scheme, set up in the form of a trust administered by trustees who were technically independent of the employer, may be 'pay'.[51]

27.62 *Fisscher*[52] and *Coloroll*[53] confirmed that administrators of a pension scheme are obliged to comply with Article 141 'by doing all their powers to ensure that the principle of equal treatment is observed' and the members of such a pension scheme can rely on Article 141 as against the administrators of that scheme:

> The effectiveness of Article 119 would be considerably diminished and the legal protection required to achieve that equality would be impaired if an employee could rely on that provision only as against the employer and not against the administrators of the scheme who are expressly charged with performing the employer's obligations.[54]

27.63 *Coloroll* raised the issue of how trustees were to comply with Article 141 if certain rules or schemes were incompatible with that provision. Should the trustees administer the scheme with regard to Article 141 or was there an obligation on the employer and the trustees to amend those rules so as to make them compatible with Article 141? Further, what were the respective liabilities of the employer and the trustees in view of the direct effect of Article 141 which could be relied upon against the employer and the trustees?

27.64 On the first issue the Court began by emphasizing that the employer and the trustees cannot rely on the rules of their pension scheme or those contained in the trust deed to evade their obligations to ensure equal treatment in the matter of pay. If they were in a position under the terms of the trust deed to rectify the inequalities in the pension scheme, they must do so. But if the rules of national law prohibited them from acting beyond the scope of their powers or in disregard of the provision of the trust deed, employers and trustees were obliged to use 'all the means available under domestic law, such as recourse to national courts . . . to amend the provisions of the pension scheme or the trust deed'.[55]

27.65 As to the division of liability between the employer and trustees, the Court ruled that this was a question for national courts to settle in accordance with national law. The Court gave some guidance as to how liabilities might be discharged:

> . . . it [the national court] may order the employer to pay additional sums into the scheme, order that any sum payable by virtue of Article 119 must first be paid out of

---

[51] *Barber* (see note 20 above) Judgment para 29.
[52] Note 32.
[53] Case C-200/91 [1994] ECR I-4389.
[54] *Fisscher* (see note 32 above) Judgment para 31; *Coloroll* see note 53 above Judgment paras 20–22.
[55] *Coloroll* (see note 53 above) Judgment para 28.

any surplus funds of the scheme or order that the sums to which members are entitled must be paid by the trustees out of the scheme's assets, even if no claim has been made against the employer or the employer has not reacted to such a claim.

I. Equal Treatment

The principle of equal treatment requires that men and women should be subject to the same obligations as regards access to occupational welfare schemes and receive the same benefits from such schemes. The obligation to comply with the principle of equality of treatment as set out in Article 141 is mandatory.[56]   **27.66**

In the case of direct discrimination this is relatively easy to establish, or is at least a lighter task than is the case with indirect discrimination. For example, in *Barber*[57] the difference in treatment in issue was that of the age at which entitlement to a pension arose – different pensionable ages prevailed for men and women – the inequality was thus plain: **27.67**

> . . . it is contrary to Article 119 to impose an age condition which differs according to sex in respect of pensions paid under a contracted out scheme, even if the difference between pensionable age for men and for women is based on the one provided for by the national statutory scheme.

(1) Methods of compliance

Where different pensionable ages exist within a scheme these must be eliminated. There is a discretion in how this is to be achieved: where the pensionable age for men is higher than that for women (which is generally the case) the age at which women become entitled to a pension can be raised to match that of the date of the men's entitlement. Alternatively the men's pensionable age can be lowered to that of the women, which is traditionally 60 years. A further option could be to choose a common age at which entitlement arises. That said, the ECJ in *Smith and Others v Avdel*[58] found that the employer's discretion in implementing the principle of equal treatment is limited.   **27.68**

The Avdel *case*

The issue was whether it was consistent with Article 141 of the Treaty for an employer who sought, in the light of *Barber*,[59] to eliminate discrimination in an occupational pension scheme which had different pensionable ages for men and women (in this case 65 and 60 years of age respectively) by adopting a   **27.69**

---

[56] Case C-28/93 *van den Akker* [1994] ECR I–4527 Judgment para 24.
[57] Case C-262/88 [1990] ECR I–1889.
[58] Case C-408/92 [1994] ECR I–445.
[59] See note 57 above.

common age of 65 years. The result of such a change in pensionable age would be to take away the advantage enjoyed by women. The Court found that given the temporal limitation placed in the effect of the *Barber* judgment which made it prospective except as regards those who had made claims before 17 May 1990, a distinction had to be drawn between what was permissible, before that date and what could only be done after that date.

27.70 As regards the period between 17 May 1990 (the date of the *Barber* judgment) and 1 July 1991 (the date on which Advel adopted measures to ensure equality) the pension rights of men must be calculated on the basis of the same retirement age for men and for women. With respect to periods prior to 17 May 1990 employers were not required to ensure equal treatment, with the result that Community law imposed no obligation which would justify the retroactive reductions of the advantages which women enjoyed.

27.71 With respect to periods of service completed after the entry into force of measures designed to eliminate discrimination, Article 141 did not preclude measures which reduced advantages of persons previously favoured (ie women). Article 141 merely requires that men and women should receive the same pay for the same work without imposing any specific level of pay.

The Van den Akker *case*

27.72 Mrs *Van den Akker*[60] was employed by the Royal Shell Group and, by virtue of that employment, was a member of the Stichting Shell *Pensioenfonds*, the Shell Group occupational pension scheme. Until 31 December 1984, the retirement age was set at 65 years for men and 55 for women. The distinction was abolished as from 1 January 1985, when the retirement age was set uniformly for all employees at 60 years but with the following transitional arrangements: female employees who were already members of the scheme on 1 January 1985 had the option, to be exercised before the 31 December 1986 at the latest, of either accepting the raising of pensionable age from 55 to 60 years or maintaining their pensionable age at 55 years. In the absence of an express election, a female employee was deemed to have opted to maintain her pensionable age at 55 years.

27.73 Following the *Barber*[61] judgment, Shell further amended the rules of its pension scheme by abolishing, with effect from 1 June 1991, the possibility for women to maintain a pensionable age of 55 years. Shell claimed that such an

---

[60] Case C-28/93 [1994] ECR I–4527.
[61] See note 57 above.

amendment was necessary to comply with the *Barber* judgment. Mrs Van den Akker and a number of her colleagues contested this decision.

When the matter came before the ECJ the Court adopted the same reasoning as **27.74** it had in the *Smith* judgment and held:

(i) In the absence of any measures to achieve equal treatment the disadvantaged class should enjoy the same advantages as the favoured class, with the result that as regards the period between 17 May 1990 (the date of the *Barber* judgment) and 1 June 1991 (the date on which the scheme in question compulsorily set the retirement age for all workers at 60 years) pension rights of men must be calculated on the basis of the same retirement age as that for women (ie 55 years).

(ii) With respect to periods of service completed after 1991, measures which achieve equal treatment by reducing the advantages of the person previously favoured (ie female employees) are not precluded since Article 141 merely requires than men and women should receive the same pay for the same work, without, however imposing any specific levels of pay.

With respect to women who had not asked for their retirement age to be raised to **27.75** 60 years at the time of the amendments to the pension scheme introduced by Shell on 1 January 1985, with the result that they were deemed to have opted to maintain their retirement age at 55 years, the Court found that:

> . . . since the obligation laid down in Article 119 to comply with the principle of equal treatment in the matter of pay is mandatory, an occupational scheme cannot evade the obligation simply because a discriminatory situation has arisen from an election made, expressly or by implication, by employees to whom such an option had been granted.[62]

(2) Actuarial factors

The use of different actuarial values for men and women can lead to a difference **27.76** in actual benefit received but they have been held not to be within Article 141 with the result that gender-based differences in those factors are permissible. This principle was laid down by the ECJ in *Neath*.[63]

Mr Neath complained of inequality of treatment with respect to the transfer **27.77** value of his acquired pension rights. His employer's contributions to the occupational pension fund were higher for female employees than for male employees on the grounds of the longer life expectancy of the former. This had an

---

[62] Judgment para 24.
[63] Case C-152/91 [1993] ECR I–6953; See Hervey: (1994) 31 CML Rev 1387–97.

impact upon the transfer value of acquired pension rights. Likewise if Mr Neath were to opt for a defined pension and ask for part of it to be converted into a capital sum, he would receive less than that of his fellow female colleagues. Mr Neath alleged inequality of treatment was contrary to Article 141, but the ECJ dismissed his argument finding that, whilst the employer's commitment to his employees concerning the payment of a periodic pension constituted 'pay' within the meaning of Article 141, funding arrangements used to secure the pension did not constitute 'pay' and were not therefore within the scope of Article 141. The Court drew a distinction between employees' contributions and employers' contributions, finding that Article 141 required equality with respect to the former but not the latter:

> In contributory schemes funding is provided through the contributions made by the employees and those made by the employers. The contributions made by the employees are an element of their pay since they are deducted directly from their salary . . . The amount of those contributions must therefore be the same for all employees, male and female, which is indeed so in the present case. This is not so in the case of contributions which ensure the adequacy of funds necessary to cover the cost of pensions promised so securing their payment in the future, that being the substance of the employer's commitment.[64]

27.78 The subsequent case of *Coloroll*[65] followed the principle established in *Neath*. *Coloroll* concerned a money-purchase scheme in which the sum of fixed annual employer's contributions, plus interest, is used on retirement to purchase an annuity on the insurance market. Approving its judgment in *Neath* that actuarial values for men and women differing according to sex are 'not struck by Article 119' the two situations in issue in *Coloroll* where a reversionary pension was payable to a dependant in return for surrendering part of the annual pension, and where a reduced pension is paid when the employee opts for early retirement:

> Since those arrangements are not covered by Article 119, any inequality of the amount of those benefits, arising from the use of actuarial factors in the funding of those schemes is not struck at by that article.

27.79 The position with respect to the application of the principle of equal treatment to actuarial factors has changed with the adoption of Directive 2004/113 implementing the principle of equal treatment between men and women in

---

[64] Judgment para 31.
[65] See note 53 above.

the access to and supply of goods and services.[66] Article 5 of that Directive provides:

> Member States shall ensure that in all new contracts concluded after 21 December 2007 at the latest, the use of sex as a factor in the calculation of premiums and benefits for the purposes of insurance and financial related services shall not result in differences in individual's premiums and benefits.

However, Member States are permitted to derogate from this general principle.[67] **27.80** Before 21 December 2007 they had the possibility to permit proportionate differences in individuals' premiums and benefits where the use of sex is a determining factor in the assessment of risk based on relevant and accurate actuarial and statistical data. Member States wishing to avail themselves of this derogation were required to inform the Commission and were obliged to ensure that accurate data relevant to the use of sex as an actuarial factor are compiled, published, and regularly updated.

(3) Single sex schemes

Article 141 is not applicable to schemes whose membership consists of persons **27.81** of one sex only.[68] The essential criterion for the application of the principle of equal pay is the performance of the same work for the same pay and this requires a comparison to be made between workers of different sex performing the same work.[69] Where this is not possible, the principle of equality is not in issue.

J. Survivors' Pensions

Survivors' pensions are thought to be considered pay even though the pension is **27.82** not paid to the employee but to his survivor.

In *Ten Oever*[70] the ECJ held that if entitlement to benefits is conferred as part of **27.83** the employment relationship, the fact that they are provided after the employment has ended does not change their character nor bring into question their status as 'pay'.[71]

---

[66] [2004] OJ L373/37.
[67] Art 5(2).
[68] *Coloroll* (see note 53 above).
[69] Case 129/79 *Macarthys Ltd v Smith* [1980] ECR 1275.
[70] Case C-109/91 [1993] ECR I–4939.
[71] This follows the reasoning adopted in Case 12/81 *Garland* [1982] ECR 359. See para 24.48.

27.84   Survivors' pensions are to be considered pay even though the pension as such is not paid to the employee but to his survivor:

> Entitlement to such a benefit is a consideration deriving from the survivor's spouse's membership of the scheme, the pension being vested in the survivor by reason of the employment relationship between the employer and the survivor's spouse and being paid by him or her by reason of the spouse's employment.[72]

K. The Equal Treatment in Occupational Social Security Systems Directive

27.85   The Equal Treatment in Occupational Social Security Systems Directive was adopted almost four years before the judgment of the ECJ in *Barber*,[73] at a time when it was believed that such welfare schemes were not to be considered pay. After the *Barber* judgment it was amended extensively to reflect both the judgment in that case and subsequent judgments.

27.86   Following *Barber* the position is that the right to equal treatment derives from Article 141. The Directive is indicative of the extent of that right but it cannot detract from its substance as provided for in Article 141.

27.87   *Barber* changed both the status and the relevance of many of the provisions of the Equal Treatment in Occupational Social Security Systems Directive. No longer was the latter Directive the sole source of the right to equal treatment. That right post *Barber* had a two-fold source: Article 141 and Directive 86/376. These two sets of provisions were not mutually exclusive as is the position with Directive 79/7 and Article 141. As in the case of equal pay, Article 141 prohibits discrimination between men and women in occupational social welfare schemes, but only in so far as the discrimination in issue:

> . . . could be identified solely with the aid of the criteria of equal work and equal pay referred to by that article without national or Community measures being required to identify them with greater precision in order to permit their application.[74]

27.88   Thus where discrimination can be directly identified the Directive is irrelevant: rights and obligations derive directly from Article 141. On this basis the Court held in *Beune*[75] that even though the Directive was to be implemented in The Netherlands by 1 January 1993, a provision in a Dutch pension scheme which was directly discriminatory, which was due to be kept in force until that date,

---

[72] *Ten Oever* (see note 70 above) Judgment para 13. Followed in *Coloroll* (see note 53 above).
[73] See note 57 above.
[74] Case C-110/91 *Moroni* 1993 ECR I–6591 Judgment para 23.
[75] See note 44 above.

could not prevent Article 141 from being relied on directly and immediately before national courts.

By contrast, where the discrimination is indirect, reliance must be placed on Directive 86/378 as implemented into national law. **27.89**

Barber thus clarified the status of Directive 86/378. It also made a number of its provisions unlawful, thereby requiring it to be extensively amended. This was done by Directive 96/97.[76] It may be queried why Directive 86/378 was not repealed and replaced in its entirety by Directive 96/97, given the fundamental nature of the amendments made to it in its original form. **27.90**

(1) Scope of application

The Directive applies to occupational social security schemes which are defined as 'schemes not covered by Directive 79/7 whose purpose is to provide the economically active, whether employees or the self-employed, in an undertaking, group of undertakings, area of economic activity, occupational sector or group of sectors with benefits intended to supplement the benefits provided by statutory social benefits or to replace them whether membership of such schemes is compulsory or optional'.[77] The fact that legislation extends the applicability of occupational schemes to various categories of employees is not pertinent to their status as pay.[78] **27.91**

An occupational scheme which provides protection against the risk of unemployment by providing workers with benefits intended to supplement unemployment benefit provided under a statutory social security scheme is an occupational social security benefit within the meaning of the Directive.[79] **27.92**

The Directive does not apply to: **27.93**

(i) individual contracts for self-employed workers;
(ii) schemes for self-employed workers having only one member;
(iii) schemes to which an employer is not a party in the case of the self-employed, in other words purely private insurance arrangements made between insurers and the self-employed;
(iv) optional provisions of occupational schemes offered to individuals to guarantee them either benefits supplementary to those offered under their

---

[76] [1997] OJ L46/20.
[77] ibid.
[78] Case C-50/99 *Podesta* [2000] ECR I–4039.
[79] Case C-166/99 *Defreyn* [2000] ECR I–6153.

state social security schemes or a choice of dates on which benefits will start or a choice of benefits;

(v) occupational schemes in so far as benefits are financed by voluntary contributions paid by workers.[80]

27.94   The Directive applies to members of the working population, including self-employed persons, whose activity is interrupted by illness, maternity, accident, or involuntary unemployment and persons seeking employment, to retired and disabled workers and to those claiming under them, in accordance with national law and practice.

27.95   Article 6 of the Directive gives examples of provisions contrary to the principle of equal treatment including those based on sex, either directly or indirectly, in particular by reference to marital or family status, for:

(i) determining the persons who may participate in the occupational scheme;

(ii) fixing the compulsory or optional nature or participation in an occupational scheme;

(iii) laying down different rules as regards the age of entry into the scheme or the minimum period of employment or membership of the scheme required to obtain the benefits thereof;

(iv) laying down different rules, except as provided for by points (viii) and (ix) below, for the reimbursement of contributions when a worker leaves a scheme without having fulfilled the conditions guaranteeing a deferred right to long-term benefits;

(v) setting different conditions for the granting of benefits or restricting such benefits to workers of one or the other sex;

(vi) fixing different retirement ages;

(vii) suspending the retention or acquisition of rights during periods of maternity leave or leave for family reasons which are granted by law or agreement and are paid by the employer;

(viii) setting different levels of benefit, except in so far as may be necessary to take account of actuarial calculation factors which differ according to sex in the case of defined-contribution schemes;

(ix) setting different levels for worker's contributions; setting levels for employer's contributions except:

- in the case of defined-contribution schemes, if the aim is to equalize the amount of the final benefits, to make them more nearly equal for both sexes,

---

[80] Art 2(2).

- in the case of funded defined benefit schemes where the employer's contributions are intended to ensure the adequacy of the funds necessary to cover the cost of the benefits defined;

(x) laying down different standards or standards applicable only to workers of a specified sex, except as provided for in points (viii) and (ix) as regards the guarantee or retention of entitlement to deferred benefits when a worker leaves a scheme.

PART VII

EQUALITY OF TREATMENT: RACE

28

THE RACE DIRECTIVE[1]

A. Introduction

The European Community has been committed to the elimination of discrimi-   **28.01**
nation between Community nationals since its inception. Its commitment to
eliminating racial discrimination is somewhat more recent.

---

[1] See generally: Barbera: 'Not the Same? The Judicial Role in the New Community Anti-Discrimination Law Context' (2002) 31 ILJ 82–91; Bell: 'A Patchwork of Protection: The New Anti-Discrimination Law Framework' (2002) 67 MLR 465–77; Bell: 'Beyond European Labour Law? Reflections on the EU Equality Directive' (2002) 8 ELJ 384 Brennan: 'The Race Directive, Institutional Racism and Third Country Nationals' in Tridimas and Nebbia (eds) *European Union Law for the Twenty-first Century Vol 2* Hart Publishing 2004, Chapter 21, 371–87; Bell: *Anti-Discrimination Law and the European Union* Oxford University Press 2002; Brennan: 'The Race Directive: Recycling Racial Inequality' [2004] Cambridge Yearbook of European Legal Studies; Brown: 'The Race Directive: Towards equality for all the people of Europe' (2003) 22 YEL; Chalmers, Hadjiemmanuil, Monti, and Tomkins: *European Union Law; Text and Materials* Cambridge University Press 2006, Chapter 20, 195; Ellis: *EU Anti-Discrimination Law* Oxford 2005; Guild: 'The EC Directive on Race Discrimination: Surprises, Possibilities and Limitations' (2000) 29 ILJ 9; Hepple: 'Race and Law in Fortress Europe' (2004) 67 MLR 1–15; Waddington and Hendriks: 'The Expanding Concept of Employment Discrimination in Europe: From Direct and Indirect Discrimination to Reasonable Accommodation' (2002) IJCLLIR 403–27.

28.02 For many years the issue of racial discrimination was left to regulation on an international and national level. This, however, did not provide an adequate guarantee of racial equality. Although the right to non-discrimination is recognized in a number of instruments of both the United Nations[2] and the Council of Europe[3] ratified by the European Community institutions and the Member States, those instruments are limited in their effectiveness in that they mark a commitment on the part of the signatory states to guarantee respect for the right to non-discrimination within their jurisdictions but they do not give a legally enforceable right either to individuals or to groups of individuals.

28.03 On a national level, there is considerable diversity in the constitutional and ordinary laws of the Member States on equality and the prohibition of discrimination. The constitutions of the Member States outlaw various forms of discrimination, including discrimination on the grounds of race, but their wording varies. Some Member States set out a specific list of grounds on which discrimination is prohibited; in others a commitment to equal treatment is phrased in more general terms. In the case of most constitutions anti-discrimination provisions may be legally enforceable by individuals but in others they serve to impose public policy obligations and only in limited cases can they be used to challenge the constitutionality of allegedly anti-discriminatory legislation.

28.04 On the legislative level, although the laws of Member States provide for equal treatment and non-discrimination in many aspects of employment, the substance and effectiveness of this legislation is variable. There is thus overall, within the Community, a lack of comprehensive legislation to combat discrimination on grounds of racial or ethnic origin.

B. Community Initiatives pre-Amsterdam

28.05 The Community institutions expressed a commitment to combating racial discrimination as far back as the 1980s.[4]

28.06 In the decade preceding the adoption of the Treaty of Amsterdam there were a number of initiatives, which sought both to heighten awareness of the issue of racial discrimination and to seek means by which it could be at least attenuated,

---

[2] See for example The International Convention on Economic, Social and Cultural Rights and The Convention on the Elimination of all Forms of Racial Discrimination.

[3] The Convention for the Protection of Human Rights and Fundamental Freedoms (ETS No 5); The European Social Charter (ECTS No 35); Framework Convention for the Protection of National Minorities (ETS 157).

[4] Joint Declaration of the Institutions against Racism and Xenophobia [1986] OJ C158/1.

if not altogether eliminated. A rise in immigration highlighted racist attitudes within the Member States during the 1990s. Increased lobbying, particularly by the Starting Line Group, an organization representing some 200 non-governmental organizations, established in 1991,[5] focused on the adoption of legislation on a Community level to outlaw discrimination on the grounds of race and ethnic origin.[6]

Starting Line drafted a proposal for a Directive in 1992, which was somewhat **28.07** premature since there was no specific legal basis whereby it could be adopted, but it was well-supported and ultimately influenced the Commission in its preparation of what became the Race Directive.[7]

The Commission's Communication on Racism, Xenophobia and Antisemitism **28.08** of 13 December 1995[8] proposed the insertion, where appropriate, of anti-discrimination clauses in new Community instruments and in instruments revising and updating Community legislation. This resulted in a number of general anti-discriminatory clauses in legislative and other proposals, notably the amendments to Regulation 1612/68 on the free movement of workers.[9]

Momentum for legislation grew during 1997, designated the European Year **28.09** against Racism, which had as its objective the raising of awareness of racism. That year also saw the establishment of the European Monitoring Centre on Racism and Xenophobia,[10] entrusted with the broad mandate of gathering of information on racism and assisting in the formulation of policy on a Community level.

These efforts culminated in the inclusion, by virtue of the Treaty of Amsterdam, **28.10** of Article 13 within the EC Treaty. Article 13 singles out specific grounds of discrimination which it treats as suspect grounds or suspect classifications. The aim of Article 13 is 'to protect the dignity and autonomy of persons belonging to those suspect classifications'.[11]

---

[5] At the initiative of the British Commission for Racial Equality, the Dutch National Bureau against Racism and the Churches Commission for Migrants in Europe. Other pan–European organizations soon joined the Groups including the European Jewish Information Centre, the European Anti-Poverty Network, the Belgian Centre for Equal Opportunities, and the Commissioner for Foreigners of the Berlin Senate.

[6] Chopin: 'The Starting Line Group: A Harmonised Approach to Fight Racism and to Promote Equal Treatment' (1999) 1 European Journal of Migration and Law 111–29.

[7] Tyson: 'The Negotiation of the European Community Directive on Racial Discrimination or Ethnic Origin' (2001) 3 European Journal of Migration and Law 199.

[8] COM (95) 653 Final.

[9] [1968] JO L257.

[10] Regulation 1035/97 [1997] OJ L151.

[11] Case C-303/06 *Coleman* Judgment of 17 July 2008 Opinion of the Advocate General at 15.

28.11 Article 13 provides a legal basis for the adoption of measures but it does not impose any specific obligations on the Member States. In contrast, therefore, to Article 12 which is concerned with the elimination of discrimination on the grounds of nationality, it has no direct effect.

28.12 An Action Programme against Racism was drawn up by the EC Commission in early 1998.[12] It promised the introduction of legislative proposals to combat racial discrimination before the end of 1999. Working to this deadline it published its proposal for a directive on 25 November 1999.

C. The Race Directive

28.13 Directive 2000/43 implementing the principle of equal treatment between persons irrespective of racial or ethnic origin lays down the framework for combating discrimination on the grounds of racial or ethnic origin (the 'Directive').[13] It was adopted on 6 June 2000, a little over a year after the entry into force of the Treaty of Amsterdam. As with the common employment policy, efforts to implement Article 13 began before the ratification of the Treaty.[14] It was fast tracked through the legislative process achieving final adoption in a record six-month period. The speed with which the proposal was adopted can be attributed to three factors:

  (i) the lengthy period of preparation prior to the introduction of the proposal which dated back to, and gathered momentum through, a number of soft law measures and other initiatives adopted throughout the 1990s;
  (ii) the growing concern amongst the Member States about increased and perceptible levels of overt racial discrimination within their national territories and in particular the entry into government in Austria of the far right Freedom Party;[15]
  (iii) the adoption of the Directive ahead of the forthcoming enlargement of the Community would indicate to the candidate Member States the Community's commitment to equality of treatment.[16]

---

[12] An Action Plan against Racism COM (1998) 183 Final.

[13] [2000] OJ L180/22.

[14] COM (1999) 566.

[15] De Burca: 'The Drafting of the European Charter of Fundamental Rights' (2001) 26 EL Rev 126 at 136.

[16] Brown: 'The Race Directive: Towards Equality for All Peoples of Europe?' (2002) 3 YEL 195 at 196–204.

(1) Purpose

The purpose of the Directive, as expressed in Article 1, is to lay down a frame-   **28.14**
work for combating discrimination on the grounds of racial or ethnic origin
with a view to putting into effect in the Member States the principle of equal
treatment. It lays down minimum provisions: Member States can adopt more
favourable provisions but the Directive should not serve to justify any regression
in standards prevailing at the time of its adoption.[17] It is thus a measure of upward
harmonization. In *Firma Feryn*[18] the Advocate General[19] held that the Directive
must be interpreted in the light of the values of Article 13 EC, on the basis of
which it was adopted. Even though the Directive lays down minimum measures
there is no reason to construe its scope more narrowly than a reading of those
values would warrant.

(2) Implementation

Laws, regulations, or administrative provisions which are contrary to the prin-   **28.15**
ciple of equal treatment are required to be abolished.[20] Member States are required to take the necessary measures to ensure that any provisions contrary to the
principle of equal treatment which are in individual contracts, collective agreements, internal rules of undertakings, rules governing profit-making or non-
profit-making organizations, and rules governing the independent professions
and workers' and employers' organizations are or may be declared null and void
or are amended. Thus the Race Directive, like the Framework Employment Directive discussed in the next chapter, imposes on the Member States the duty to
render its provisions effective right across the entire spectrum of those aspects of
economic and social life with which it is concerned.

The Directive was required to be implemented by 19 July 2003.[21] A number of   **28.16**
Member States, namely Austria, Finland, Germany, and Luxembourg, had
not implemented the Directive by this date and accordingly the Commission
commenced infringement proceedings which resulted in these countries being

---

[17] Art 6.
[18] Case C-54/07 Judgment of 10 July 2008.
[19] Opinion of 12 March 2008 para 14.
[20] Art 14(c).
[21] Art 16. Member States were required to communicate to the EC Commission by 19 July 2005
all the information necessary to enable the Commission to draw up a report to the European
Parliament and the Council on the application of the Directive. A report on the state of transposition of the Directive was published in 2006.

condemned by the ECJ for failure to fulfil their obligations.[22] The vigilance with which the Commission prosecuted these proceedings is indicative of the importance which it attaches to the accurate and immediate implementation of the Directive.[23]

28.17 In September 2006 the Commission, in its annual report on equality and non-discrimination,[24] reported that all Member States had taken steps to implement the Directive, although it declined to state whether the measures taken in its view transposed the Directive fully into national law.[25]

28.18 On 27 June 2007 the Commission announced[26] that it had sent a reasoned opinion to 14 Member States[27] requiring them to implement the Directive fully. The problem areas include:

(a) national legislation which is limited in scope to the workplace whereas the Directive also prohibits discrimination in social protection, education, and access to goods and services, including housing;

(b) definitions of discrimination which are narrower than those set out in the Directive;

(c) inconsistencies in the provisions designed to help victims of discrimination such as protection against victimization;

(d) the onus of the burden of proof and the right of associations to assist individuals with their cases.

28.19 The Member States in question were given two months in which to respond to the case against them. If, after that period the Commission was not satisfied that they had fully implemented the Directive, it had the intention of commencing infringement proceedings pursuant to Article 226 EC.

---

[22] Case 327/04 *Commission v Finland* Judgment 24 February 2005; Case C-329/04 *Commission v Germany* Judgment of 28 April 2005; Case 320/04 *Commission v Luxembourg*; Case C-335/04 *Commission v Austria* Judgment of 4 May 2005.

[23] Nevertheless it can be queried whether the Commission was somewhat too brisk in launching proceedings. For example, Germany in its defence argued that it was in the process of drawing up a general law on the abolition of discrimination which included the implementation of the Directive, the Framework Employment Directive, and the amendments to the Equal Opportunities Directive. Such an overhaul of national legislation in a sensitive area required timely and careful management.

[24] Office for the Official Publications of the European Communities 2006.

[25] Ibid; see Table of Legislation implementing the Directive at 9–13.

[26] IP/07/928.

[27] Spain, Sweden Czech Republic, Estonia, France, Ireland, United Kingdom, Greece. Italy, Latvia, Poland, Portugal, Slovenia, and Slovakia.

Scope of application

The Directive applies, within the limits of the powers conferred upon the **28.20**
Community, to all persons and to the public and private sectors, including public
bodies,[28] with respect to the following matters:

(a) conditions for access to employment, to self-employment, and to occupa-
     tion including selection criteria and recruitment conditions, whatever the
     branch of activity and at all levels of the professional hierarchy, including
     promotion;
(b) access to all types and all levels of vocational training, vocational guid-
     ance, advanced vocational training and retraining, including practical work
     experience;
(c) employment and working conditions, including dismissal and pay;
(d) membership of, and involvement in, an organization of workers or employ-
     ers or any organization whose members carry on a particular profession,
     including the benefits provided to such an organization;
(e) social protection including social security and healthcare;
(f) social advantages;[29]
(g) education;
(h) access to and supply of goods and services, which are available to the public,
     including housing.[30]

The Directive thus marks a departure from the approach to gender discrimina- **28.21**
tion which is limited in scope to differences in treatment in employment and
social security matters. Discrimination on grounds of race or ethnic origin is
recognized as not being confined to the workplace but extends beyond that into
many aspects of life in the community. The Preamble to the Directive explains
that the broad scope of the Directive is necessary to achieve its objectives:

> To ensure the development of democratic and tolerant societies which allow the
> participation of all persons irrespective of racial or ethnic origin, specific action in
> the field of discrimination based on race or ethnic origin should go beyond access
> to employed and self-employed activities and cover areas such as education, social

---

[28] The specific reference to public bodies here may impose upon them a duty with respect to
institutional racism in relation to matters such as housing and education. See Brennan in Tridimas
and Nebbia (note 1 above) at 379.
[29] See Ellis: 'Social Advantages: A New Lease of Life' (2003) 40 CMLR 639–59. The Commission
has stated that the concept of social advantages in the Race Directive should be interpreted in the
same way as that figuring on Art 7 of Regulation 1612/68 [1968] OJ L257. It covers benefits of an
economic or cultural nature granted either by public authorities or private organizations, such as
concessions on public transport services, reduced prices for cultural or sports events, subsidized
meals for school children from low income families. COM (1999) 566 Final at 5–7.
[30] Art 3(2).

protection, including social security and health care, social advantages and access to and supply of services.[31]

28.22 The Directive extends to discrimination in matters such as educational fees, restrictions on the production and sale of foodstuffs such as halal meat or kosher products, the allocation of housing (an area in which discrimination is traditionally rife), and bans on the wearing of clothing with religious significance such as certain types of headwear.[32] The extent of the right to equal treatment with regard to matters unconnected with employment may in reality be limited given that such a right is co-terminous with the extent of the Community's competence.[33] Thus its scope of application with respect to, for example, housing and health care may be limited. It is also uncertain to what extent the Directive applies to the provision of services by the private sector in, for example, banks, shops, and hotels.[34] The lack of any general provision imposing an obligation to eliminate discrimination in general public services, such as policing, is also a matter of concern.[35]

28.23 The Directive applies to all persons regardless of their nationality.

Discrimination

28.24 Both direct and indirect discrimination are prohibited.

28.25 Race and ethnic origin are Community concepts but their meaning is not set out in the Directive and there does not appear to be any uniform practice which can be drawn upon.[36] Recital 6 of the Preamble states that the European Union 'rejects theories which attempt to determine the existence of separate human races'.

28.26 Whilst the Directive refers only to discrimination on grounds of racial or ethnic origin, it has been argued that it also encompasses discrimination on the grounds of skin colour even if this is not expressly articulated.[37]

28.27 Harassment and instructions to discriminate on racial and ethical grounds are deemed to be discrimination for the purposes of the Directive.

---

[31] Preamble to the Directive at para 12.

[32] Chalmers: 'The Mistakes of the Good European' in Fredman (ed) *Discrimination and Human rights: the Case of Racism* Oxford University Press 2001 at 215.

[33] Waddington: 'Testing the limits of the EC Treaty Article on Non-Discrimination' (1999) 28 ILJ 133.

[34] Chalmers, Hadjiemmanuil, Monti, and Tomkins (see note 1 above) at 913.

[35] Brown: 'The Race Directive: Towards Equality for All the Peoples of Europe' (2002) 3 YEL 195 at 215.

[36] Guild: 'The EC Directive on Race Discrimination: Surprises, Possibilities and Limitations' (2002) 24 ILJ 416.

[37] See Bell (n 1 above) at 467.

Harassment is defined as unwanted conduct related to racial or ethnic origins, the **28.28** purpose or effect of which is to violate the dignity of a person and to create an intimidating, hostile, degrading, humiliating, or offensive environment.[38] Interest or motive seems to be irrelevant: the effect of the conduct in question is the essential and sole criterion.

In *Firma Feryn*[39] the ECJ has given a broad interpretation to the types of acts **28.29** which may be deemed to be discriminatory within the meaning of the Directive. Prohibited discriminatory acts must not be confined to those in which there is an identifiable complainant. To ignore a public statement by an employer that certain persons because of their racial or ethnic origins stand no chance of being recruited is an act of discrimination. To limit the scope of the Directive to cases where there is an identifiable victim would undermine its effectiveness:

> The objective of fostering conditions for a socially inclusive labour market would be hard to achieve if the scope of Directive 2000/43 were to be limited to only those cases in which an unsuccessful candidate for a post, considering himself to be the victim of direct discrimination, brought legal proceedings against an employer.[40]

Direct discrimination

Direct discrimination is deemed to have occurred where one person is treated less **28.30** favourably than another is or would be treated in a comparable situation on grounds of racial or ethnic origin.[41] No guidance is given on the meaning of 'comparable situations'. In the area of sex discrimination law this has, at times, provided problematic. Hypothetical comparators, save in cases relating to discrimination on the grounds of pregnancy, have not been accepted.[42] However, the wording in the Race Directive appears to admit the possibility of a hypothetical comparator.[43]

In the case of *Firma Feryn*,[44] the ECJ held that a public statement by an employer **28.31** that it will not recruit persons of certain ethnic or racial origin, which is likely to dissuade strongly certain candidates from submitting their candidature, and accordingly to hinder their access to the labour market, constitutes direct discrimination within the meaning of Article 2(2)(a) of the Directive. In that case

---

[38] Art 2(3). It has also been described in more general terms as the imposition of a detriment upon an individual. Bell (note 1 above) at 470.

[39] Note 18.

[40] Judgment para 24.

[41] Art 2(1).

[42] Case 129/79 *MacCarthys v Smith* [1980] ECR 1275; Case C-200/91 *Coloroll v Russell* [1994] ECR I–4389. Contrast with Case C-177/88 *Dekker* [1990] ECR I–3941.

[43] See *Waddington and Hendriks* (see note 1 above) at 42; Bell 'Anti-Discrimination law and the European Union' (see note 1 above) at 75.

[44] See note 18 above.

Firma Feryn was seeking to recruit fitters to install doors at its customers' houses. It placed a large 'vacancies' sign alongside its premises but made it clear in a public statement to the press that persons of Moroccan origin would not be recruited:

> By publicly stating his intention not to hire persons of a certain racial or ethnic origin, the employer is, in fact, excluding those persons from the application process and from his workforce. He is not merely talking about discrimination, he is discriminating.[45]

Indirect discrimination

28.32 Indirect discrimination occurs where an apparently neutral provision, criterion, or practice would put persons of a certain racial or ethnic origin at a particular disadvantage as compared to other persons unless that provision, criterion, or practice is objectively justified as being in pursuit of a legitimate aim and the means of achieving that aim are appropriate and necessary.[46] This definition is based on the criterion used in nationality discrimination[47] as opposed to gender discrimination and therefore avoids the need to rely on statistical evidence of disparate impact.[48]

Exceptions

28.33 There are three exceptions to the requirement of equal treatment:

(a) treatment based on nationality;
(b) genuine and determining occupational requirements;
(c) positive action.

Treatment based on nationality

28.34 Differences of treatment based on nationality are excluded.[49] The Directive is expressed to be without prejudice to provisions and conditions relating to the entry into, and residence, of third country nationals and stateless persons on the territory of the Member States and to any treatment which arises from the legal status of such third country nationals and stateless persons. This exception is probably designed to avert any challenge to the policies of the Member States on

---

[45] See note 18 above, Opinion of the Advocate General at para 16.

[46] Art 2(2)(b). See for example Case 41/84 *Pinna* [1986] ECR I–1 where an apparently neutral provision of French social security law which applied equally to French and non-French nationals was found to be more likely to disadvantage non-French nationals and hence to be contrary to the provisions on free movement of workers under Article 39 EC Treaty.

[47] *Pinna* (see note 46 above); Case C-237/94 *O'Flynn* [1996] ECR I–2617.

[48] Hepple (see note 1 above) at 25.

[49] Member States thus retain their exclusive competence with respect to the treatment under their national legal systems of third country nationals. This reflects the traditional approach of the Community.

work permits as being indirectly discriminatory. Whilst the Member States are in agreement about the application of the principle of equal treatment as laid down in the Directive, within their national territory, they do wish to retain control over the entry of non-nationals on to that territory. In other words, the principle of equality of treatment is to apply to those who are lawfully present and resident according to the legal system of each Member State regardless of their nationality.

Ascertaining whether discrimination has occurred because of nationality and therefore outwith the Directive, or race, which is covered by the Directive, may be problematic.[50] The dividing line between discrimination based on race and discrimination based on nationality is often unclear. Bell gives the example of a private sector employer who pays third country nationals less than other workers or who grants them less favourable conditions of employment, eg no entitlement to paid holidays. This, he argues, is a difference of treatment based on nationality but it may equally be indirect racial discrimination.[51] The ultimate burden of proof will in such cases generally fall upon the employer to prove that the difference in treatment is based on nationality rather than race and if he is unable to discharge that, racial discrimination will be presumed. This may act as a disincentive to such discriminatory practices in the first place.   **28.35**

Article 2(1) requires Member States when implementing the policy of equal treatment to 'promote equality between men and women, especially since women are often victims of multiple discrimination'.   **28.36**

D. Occupational Requirements

Member States may provide that a difference in treatment by reason of the nature of a particular occupation or activity or the context in which they are carried out, which is based upon characteristics related to racial or ethnic origin, shall not constitute discrimination where it is a genuine and determining occupational requirement. The objective of the discriminatory conduct must be legitimate and the required conduct must be no more than is necessary to attain that objective.[52]   **28.37**

---

[50] Brennan in Tridimas and Nebbia (see note 1 above) 530 at 380.

[51] Bell (see note 1 above). See also Hepple (see note 1 above) at 7 and Weiler: 'Thou shalt not oppress a stranger: on the Judicial Protection of the Human Rights of Non-EC nationals: a Critique' (1992) 3 EJIL 65; Lester: 'New European Equality Measures' (2000) PL 562 et seq.

[52] Art 4.

E. Positive Action

28.38 Member States are free to maintain or adopt specific measures to prevent or compensate for disadvantages linked to racial or ethnic origin.[53] Some guidance exists on the legality of measures of positive action in the gender discrimination area[54] from which it is clear that, since positive measures are an exception to the requirement of equality, they are subject to the principle of proportionality in the sense that they must be no more than is necessary to prevent or compensate for given disadvantages linked to racial or ethnic origin.

Victimization

28.39 Member States must adopt whatever measures are necessary to protect individuals from any adverse treatment or adverse consequences or reaction to a complaint or to proceedings aimed at enforcing compliance with the principle of equal treatment.[55]

Remedies and enforcement

28.40 Judicial or administrative remedies must be made available to all persons who consider themselves to have been the subject of discriminatory acts and these remedies must be available even if the relationship within which the unequal treatment is alleged to have occurred has ended.[56] The right to bring proceedings extends to associations, organizations, or other legal entities which have a legitimate interest in ensuring compliance with the Directive. Member States may determine which groups have a legitimate interest. But the right to institute proceedings is not autonomous; such entities have no right to bring proceedings in their own name. Proceedings can be undertaken only with respect to a particular complainant by such interest groups acting on behalf of or in support of that complainant. This implies that there must be an identifiable complainant and that such a complainant must acquiesce in the taking of proceedings.

28.41 In *Firma Feryn*[57] the ECJ found that Member States could give additional forms of redress over and above those prescribed by the Directive. Article 6(1) provides that Member States may introduce or maintain provisions which are more favourable to the protection of the principle of equal treatment than those laid down in the Directive. Article 6 sets out only minimum requirements. As the

---

[53] Art 5.
[54] Art 141(4) Directive 76/207 [1976] OJ L39/40; Case C-408/98 *Abrahamsson and Anderson* [2002] ECR I–5539 Judgment paras 55 and 56.
[55] Art 9; see C-185/97 *Coote* [1998] ECR I–5199.
[56] Art 7(1).
[57] See note 18 above.

Advocate General pointed out, Article 6(2) provides that the implementation of the Directive shall, under no circumstances, constitute grounds for a reduction in the level of protection against discrimination. Thus it is a matter for national law whether a public interest body may bring a legal action if it is not acting on behalf of a specific complainant, but the Directive does not require Member States to ensure that public interest bodies are recognized as having *locus standi* to bring judicial proceedings in the absence of a complainant who claims to have been the victim of discrimination.

The right to bring proceedings is subject to national time limits[58] taking into account the general rules governing effectiveness of remedies. Sanctions for breach of national provisions adopted to implement the Directive must be put in place by the Member States. Such sanctions, which may include the payment of compensation, must be effective, proportionate, and dissuasive.[59] In *Feryn*[60] the Court was asked what sanction might be considered to be appropriate for employment discrimination established on the basis of the employer's public statements. It was held that this was a matter for national law. The Directive does not prescribe a specific sanction but leaves the Member States free to choose between the different solutions suitable for achieving its objective. **28.42**

Where, as was the case in *Feryn*, there is no direct victim of discrimination but a body empowered by law seeks a finding of discrimination and the imposition of a penalty, the Court held that the sanctions imposed should also be effective, proportionate, and dissuasive. It went on to give guidance as to what those sanctions might be: **28.43**

> . . . those sanctions may, where necessary, include a finding of discrimination by the court or a competent administrative authority in conjunction with an adequate level of publicity, the cost of which is to be borne by the defendant. They may also take the form of a prohibitory injunction, in accordance with the rules of national law, ordering the employer to cease the discriminatory practice, and where appropriate, a fine. They may, moreover, take the form of an award of damages to the body bringing the proceedings.[61]

Apart from granting the claimant the right to bring proceedings for the enforcement of the principle of equal treatment, the Directive institutes a number of other enforcement mechanisms, aimed at the prevention of discriminatory conduct. First, it advocates the dissemination of information relating to the provisions of the Directive within the Member States;[62] secondly, it advocates **28.44**

---

[58] Art 7(1).
[59] Art 15.
[60] See note 18 above.
[61] See note 18 above Judgment para 39.
[62] Art 10.

fostering equal treatment in the workplace through the social dialogue;[63] thirdly, it requires Member States to encourage dialogue with appropriate non-governmental organizations;[64] and fourthly, under Article 13 Member States are required to designate a body responsible for the promotion of equal treatment. Such bodies must be competent to provide independent assistance to victims of discrimination in the pursuit of their complaints, to conduct independent surveys, and to make public reports and recommendations on any issue relating to discrimination. The powers given to entities to discharge these obligations are somewhat limited. No right is given to commence investigations into particular actions or patterns of discrimination or to initiate proceedings.

28.45 Meaningful enforcement thus lies primarily in the hands of the individual, which in the context of the Directive is not satisfactory; victims of racial discrimination may neither be willing nor able to commence legal proceedings to assert their rights. The individual and collective interests of those to which the Directive applies would be much better served by conferring enforcement powers on independent entities.

Burden of proof

28.46 Where a claim for equal treatment requires a claimant to adduce factual evidence, the burden of proving such evidence of unequal treatment shifts to the respondent who must show that there has not been any discrimination.[65] The burden of proof will not move to the respondent where the court or tribunal investigating the claim has a duty to ascertain the facts or where the proceedings are criminal in nature.[66]

28.47 In *Firma Feryn*[67] the Advocate General accepted the argument of the Commission that:

> . . . in circumstances where it is established that an employer has made the kind of public statements about its own recruitment policy that are at issue in the main proceedings, and where, moreover, the actual recruitment practice applied by the employer remains opaque and no persons with the ethnic background in question have been recruited, there will be a presumption of discrimination within the meaning of Article 8 of the Directive. It falls to the employer to rebut that presumption.[68]

---

[63] Art 11.
[64] Art 12.
[65] Art 8(1).
[66] Art 8(3) and (4). Article 8 echoes Article 4 of the Burden of Proof Directive, Directive 97/80 [1998] OJ L14/6.
[67] See note 18 above.
[68] Ibid para 23.

Part VIII

EQUALITY OF TREATMENT: RELIGION, DISABILITY, AGE, AND SEXUAL ORIENTATION

29

RELIGION, DISABILITY, AGE, AND SEXUAL ORIENTATION

A. Introduction

Directive 2000/78 establishing a general framework for equal treatment in **29.01** employment and occupation (the 'Framework Employment Directive')[1] is the subject of this chapter.[2] It is the second Directive adopted pursuant to Article 13 EC, the first being Directive 2002/43 implementing the principle of equal

---

[1] [2000] OJ L303/16.

[2] The Directive was required to be implemented by 2 December 2003. On 31 January 2008 the EC Commission sent reasoned opinions to 11 Member States requiring them to implement the Directive fully. The Member States concerned are: the Czech Republic, Estonia, Ireland, Greece, France, Italy, Hungary, Malta, The Netherlands, Finland, and Sweden. The main problems include national legislation being limited in terms of people and areas it covers; definitions of discrimination which diverge from those laid down by the Directive; lack of proper implementation of the obligation for employers to provide reasonable accommodation for disabled workers; and inconsistencies in the provisions designed to help victims of discrimination (for example the shift of the burden of proof; the protection against victimization; the right of associations to assist individuals with their grievances).

treatment between persons irrespective of racial or ethnic origin (the 'Race Directive'),[3] discussed in the previous chapter. Being based on Article 13 the Directive must be interpreted in the light of the goals pursued by Article 13 itself.[4]

29.02 The Preamble to the Framework Employment Directive emphasizes that equality before the law and protection against discrimination is a fundamental human right.[5] Reference is made in the Preamble to the Directive to a number of United Nations Conventions[6] and the European Convention on Human Rights. Convention No 111 of the International Labour Organization which prohibits discrimination in the field of employment and occupation is also referred to. Reference to such instruments may assist in the 'functional and dynamic interpretation' of the Directive.[7]

29.03 The purpose of the Directive, as expressed in Article 1, is to lay down a general framework for combating discrimination on the grounds of religion or belief, disability, age, or sexual orientation as regards employment or occupation. The Directive has been described as performing an 'exclusionary function': it excludes religious belief, age, disability, and sexual orientation from the range of permissible reasons an employer may legitimately rely on in order to treat one employee less favourably than another.[8]

B. Religion, Disability, Age, and Sexual Orientation

29.04 No definition or guidance is given of any of these concepts within Article 13 EC itself or in the Framework Employment Directive. Restraint has been urged in the interpretation of these key concepts. In *Chacon Navas*,[9] the Court adopted a restrictive attitude to the meaning of 'disability', drawing a distinction between it and 'sickness'. Advocate General Geelhoed stated that Article 13 and the Directive should be interpreted restrictively. The evolution and wording of

---

[3] [2002] OJ L180/22.
[4] Case C-303/06 *Coleman* Judgment of 17 July 2008 Advocate General Opinion of 31 January 2008 para 7.
[5] Recital 4.
[6] Universal Declaration of Human rights, United Nations Convention on the Elimination of All Forms of Discrimination against Women, United Nations Covenants on Civil and Political Rights and on Economic Social and Cultural Rights.
[7] Schiek: 'A New Framework on Equal Treatment of Persons in EC Law?' (2002) 8 ELJ 290–314 at 295.
[8] *Coleman* (see note 4 above) Advocate General's Opinion 31 January 2008 at para 17. See Pilgerstorfer and Forshaw: 'Transferred discrimination in European Law' (2008) 37 ILJ 384–93.
[9] Case C-13/05 [2006] ECR I–6467.

Article 13 reflected restraint on the part of the authors of the Treaty.[10] The detail of the Directive, particularly in Articles 5 and 6, suggested that the Community legislature was aware of the potentially far-reaching economic and financial consequences of the prohibitions set out therein. Moreover the essentially complementary nature of the Community's legislative powers required the 'definitions and delineations' set out in the Directive to be 'taken seriously'.[11]

The grouping together of a number of prohibited grounds of discriminatory treatment, into a single Treaty provision implemented by a single Directive, has been described as potentially: **29.05**

> . . . involving the risk of false consistency, in other words, that the attempt to shoe-horn four different grounds into a single legislative instrument will produce a model which is not wholly appropriate to any one or more of them.[12]

Whether this fear will actually be realized will only become apparent with the passage of time, as individuals and employers begin to grapple with the practicalities of implementing the Directive.   **29.06**

Possibly, for political reasons, it was not realistic to enter into any defining exercise. It is obviously easier to get agreement on one instrument encompassing a number of objectives not all of which would be acceptable singly to all Member States, but collectively they represent an acceptable package. This somewhat regrettable as it leaves a wide margin of discretion to the Member States in adopting transposition measures and ultimately, much to the hazards of litigation. The end result may be a widely differing application of the Directive throughout the Community.   **29.07**

Given that the Directive appears not so much to be a source of directly enforceable rights in itself, but rather a framework of objectives to be developed by the Member States within their own legal systems, and in accordance with national cultural and social norms, this could lead to a range of concepts which reflect those norms, and consequently differing levels of protection for the individual from Member State to Member State. This may affect not just his personal right not to be subject to discrimination but his ability to exercise his Community rights, such as the right to move within the Community as an economically active person, a recipient of services, or simply as a European citizen.[13]   **29.08**

Below we consider how these key concepts might be interpreted.   **29.09**

---

[10] Bell and Waddington: 'The 1996 Intergovernmental Conference and the Prospects of a non-Discrimination Treaty Article' (1996) 25 ILJ 320–26.
[11] See note 9 above. Opinion at paras 46 and 47.
[12] Ellis: *EU Anti-Discrimination Law* Oxford University Press 2005 at 33.
[13] *Definitions of Disability in Europe: A Comparative Analysis* European Commission 2002 at 3.

(1) Religion or belief

29.10 Religion or belief may be interpreted as going beyond traditional organized religions involving a belief in a divine being or a deity to 'other philosophical beliefs on major issues such as life, death and morality, akin to, but not amounting to a religion'.[14] It is unclear whether beliefs or lifestyle choices, such as pacifism, atheism, or vegetarianism, held by individuals but not involving a group or communal worship, are included in the concept of 'belief'.

29.11 Little guidance can be obtained from the European Convention on Human Rights, Article 9 of which asserts the right to freedom of religion including within this 'freedom to change religion or belief'. Article 9 has been interpreted broadly—but unsurprisingly—as extending beyond the major world religions to other groups such as Jehovah's Witnesses and the Pentecostal Church, both of which are identifiable as a form of religion.

(2) Age

29.12 Age is not defined in the Directive. Recitals 6 and 8 and of the Preamble refer to the 'elderly' and 'older workers' but this is in the context of other instruments, respectively the Community Charter of the Fundamental Social Rights of Workers and the Employment Guidelines 2002.

29.13 Article 6 of the Directive permits the Member States to provide that differences in treatment on the grounds of age may not amount to unlawful discrimination if they are objectively and reasonably justified by a legitimate aim. Such differences in treatment may include the setting of special conditions on access to employment and vocational training, employment and occupation for 'young people, older workers and persons with caring responsibilities'.

29.14 Article 6(2) permits the fixing for occupational social security schemes of different ages for admission or entitlement to retirement benefits, including the fixing under those schemes of different ages for employees and the use in the context of such schemes, of age criteria in actuarial calculations provided that this does not result in discrimination on the grounds of sex.

29.15 The wording of these provisions indicates that more groups than the elderly are envisaged in the Directive and that therefore 'age' should be interpreted broadly.

---

14 Ellis (see note 12 above) at 33.

(3) Disability

Chacon-Navas[15] considered the meaning of disability within the context of the **29.16** Framework Employment Directive. Ms Chacon Navas was employed by Eurest, a catering undertaking. On 14 October 2003 she was certified as unfit to work on grounds of sickness, and according to the public health service which was treating her, she was not in a position to return to work in the short term.

On 28 May 2004 Eurest dismissed Ms Chacon Navas. On 29 June 2004 she **29.17** commenced proceedings against Eurest maintaining that her dismissal was void on grounds of unequal treatment and discrimination. The referring court pointed out that Ms Chacon Navas must be regarded as having been dismissed solely on account of the fact that she had been absent from work because of sickness.

It referred two question to the ECJ, the first of which asked whether the Frame- **29.18** work Employment Directive conferred protection on a person who has been dismissed solely on account of illness.

The Court began by stating that the Directive conferred protection against **29.19** dismissal on grounds of disability. It then went on to consider what disability meant in the context of the Directive.

In the absence of any definition of the term 'disability', nor any express reference **29.20** in the Directive to national law for the purpose of determining its meaning and scope, the term had to be given an autonomous and uniform interpretation throughout the Community. The Court then looked to the Directive to see what disability might mean and concluded that:

> . . . 'disability' must be understood as referring to a limitation which results in
> particular from physical, mental or psychological impairments and which hinders
> the participation of the person concerned in professional life.[16]

In coming to this conclusion, the Court reasoned as follows: the legislature had **29.21** chosen a term which differed from 'sickness'; accordingly the two terms could not therefore simply be treated as being the same. The requirement to provide reasonable accommodation indicates that the Community legislature envisaged situations in which access to, and participation in, professional life is restricted over a lengthy period in time.

---

[15] See note 9 above.
[16] Judgment para 43.

29.22 The Court's reasoning is terse and leaves unanswered the fundamental point as to when sickness becomes disability. Sickness is usually a condition that is relatively short-term, as is indicated by the organization of cash sickness benefits in social security systems. The question is when does it develop into the longer term condition of disability? Many cases of disability begin as sickness. Where is the dividing line? One solution might be to look at welfare provision—when does entitlement for long-term disability benefits arise? In fact the Court might have been better persuaded to use entitlement to disability benefit under national social security systems as indicative of disability instead of attempting to define the concept in broad general terms. On the other hand, many disability benefits are of an income replacement nature and thus indicative of, and contingent upon, an inability to work. Consequently, their eligibility criteria may provide little guidance as to what constitutes disability in the employment context.

29.23 Advocate General Geelhoed dealt more extensively than the Court with the issues of what constitutes 'disability' for the purposes of the Directive and how disability is to be differentiated from sickness.

29.24 From his analysis it is apparent that the issue is complex: the concept of disability, he concludes, is 'an indeterminate legal concept' and is 'undergoing fairly rapid evolution'.[17] Whilst a uniform Community interpretation is necessary to determine the personal and substantial scope of the prohibition set out in the Directive, since otherwise the protection afforded by it will vary within the Community,[18] arriving at such a uniform definition is problematic:

> . . . in developing a uniform interpretation of the term 'disability' account should be taken of the . . . dynamic aspect of society's interpretation of the phenomenon of 'disability' as a functional limitation resulting from a mental or physical defect, the evolution of medical and biomedical understanding and the major contextual differences in the assessment of a wide variety of disabilities.[19]

29.25 Consequently, the Advocate General suggested that rather than finding more or less exhaustive or fixed definitions of the term 'disability', national courts should be provided with Community law criteria and a point of reference with which it can find solutions to the legal problems they confront. The convergent interpretation and application in the Community of the term 'disability' can thus be ensured without harming the open nature of the term.

---

[17] Opinion paras 57 and 58.
[18] The concept of disability differs widely throughout the Community. See *Definitions of Disability in Europe; A Comparative Analysis* European Commission September 2002.
[19] Opinion para 66.

He concluded by ruling that disabled people are people with serious functional **29.26**
limitations (disabilities) due to physical, psychological, or mental afflictions.
The causes of the limitations must be a health problem or a physiological abnor-
mality which is of a long-term or permanent nature. The health problem as a
cause of the functional limitation should, in principle, be distinguished from that
limitation. Consequently sickness which may cause a disability in the future
cannot in principle be equated with a disability. The position is otherwise if
during the sickness permanent functional limitations emerge. These must be
regarded as disabilities.

(4) Sexual orientation

Sexual orientation is not defined in the Directive. In addition to homosexuality, **29.27**
it could be interpreted as extending to heterosexual or bisexual persons; there is
no reason why it should be confined to homosexuality, the sole ground of sexual
orientation hitherto raised before the ECJ.[20]

C. Objective

The purpose of the Framework Employment Directive is to create, within the **29.28**
Community, equality for citizens in employment and occupation by combating discrimination on grounds of religion or belief, disability, age, or sexual
orientation.

Article 1 states that it is a 'general framework' for putting into effect the principle **29.29**
of equal treatment by the Member States.

Arguably this could mean that the Directive is not concerned with laying down **29.30**
the right to equal treatment itself, a conclusion which is possibly reinforced by
the wording of Article 13 which refers to 'combating discrimination', but with
setting out a number of principles to be given effect on a national level. If this is
the case, the Directive is not of direct effect.

However, Advocate General Mazak in *Palacios de la Villa*[21] stated that he had **29.31**
'. . . no doubt that the prohibition on the grounds of age as laid down in Directive
2000/78. is sufficiently precise and unconditional to satisfy the substantive
conditions for direct effect as regards the setting of a compulsory retirement
age'.[22] The ECJ did not address the issue in its judgment.

---

[20] See for example Case C-249/96 *Grant* [1998] ECR I–621.
[21] Case C-411/05 [2007] ECR I–8531.
[22] Ibid para 114.

(1) Implementation

29.32   The Directive was required to be implemented by 2 December 2003 or in the case of the 10 new Member States, by 1 May 2004, their date of accession. Luxembourg and Germany did not implement the Directive within the required deadline and as a result have been found to be in breach of their obligations under Community law by the ECJ.[23]

29.33   Member States were entitled to a further period of three years (ie until 2 December 2006 or 2 December 2007 as the case may be) to implement provisions on age and disability discrimination. The Directive challenges long-held assumptions about people's abilities and their place in society. The possibility of a further implementation period was deemed necessary to mitigate any adverse impact on the labour market that the obligation of equality of treatment might entail.

29.34   The Commission had to be informed, before the deadline for transposition, of any intention on the part of a Member State to avail itself of this extended implementation period.

29.35   Sweden, the United Kingdom, Germany, Belgium, and The Netherlands notified the Commission that they wished to avail themselves of the possibility of this further period of implementation. Denmark requested an extension of one year only for the implementation of the Directive. In January 2004 the Austrian government informed the Commission that four of its Länder wanted to make use of the additional implementation period. This request was refused as it gave no particular reasons why such an extension was required and the request was made well after the deadline for transposition. None of the 10 Member States which acceded to the Community on 1 May 2004 asked for an extension of the implementation period applicable to them.

29.36   The Court in *Mangold*[24] took a restrictive view of the obligations of Member States during the implementation period. It held[25] that Member States, during the period prescribed for the transposition of a directive, must refrain from taking any measures liable to compromise the attainment of the result prescribed by the directive. It is immaterial whether the rule of domestic law in question, adopted after the directive entered into force is concerned with the transposition of the directive.[26] Thus the Member States must be vigilant right across the

---

[23] Case C-70/05 *Commission v Luxembourg* Judgment 20 October 2005 (unpublished); Case C-43/05 *Commission v Germany* Judgment of 23 February 2006 (unpublished).

[24] Case 144/04 [2005] ECR I–9981.

[25] Following Case C-129/96 *Inter-Environnement Wallonie* [1997] ECR I–7411.

[26] Case C-14/02 *ATRAL* [2003] ECR I–4431.

legislative and regulatory landscape, lest the objective of a particular directive be compromised in any way.

In the case of Member States, which exceptionally enjoy an extended period for **29.37** transposition of a directive—which was the position of Germany in *Mangold*—no measures incompatible with the Directive may be adopted during the period allowed for implementation. And during that period there was an obligation 'progressively to take concrete measures for the purpose of there and then approximating its legislation to the result prescribed by the directive'.[27]

Mangold further held that in the case of age discrimination, since the right to **29.38** equal treatment derived from the general principle of non-discrimination as expressed in the various international instruments set out in the Preamble to the Directive and the constitutional traditions common to the Member States, its observance could not be conditional upon the expiry of the time allowed for the transposition of the Directive.

In those circumstances, it is the responsibility of the national court, hearing a **29.39** dispute involving the principle of non-discrimination, to provide the legal protection which individuals derive from the rules of Community law, in particular Article 6(1) of the Directive, and to ensure that those rules are fully effective, setting aside any provision of national law which may conflict with that law even where the period prescribed for the transposition of the Directive had not expired.

D. Minimum Requirements

The Directive lays down minimum requirements.[28] Member States may adopt or **29.40** maintain more favourable provisions than those envisaged by the Directive but they cannot rely on it to reduce levels of protection prevailing in the Member States at the time of the adoption of the Directive,[29] subject to an annual reporting requirement.[30]

In *Coleman*[31] the Advocate General found that there was nothing in either the **29.41** Directive or its recitals to indicate that the setting of 'minimum requirements' meant that the intervention of Community law in this area must be at its lowest level. He thus rejected the United Kingdom's argument to the effect that it was

---

[27] See note 23 above. Judgment para 72.
[28] Preamble, Recital 28 and Art 8(i).
[29] Art 8(2).
[30] Art 18.
[31] See note 4 above.

for the Member States to decide whether to prohibit discrimination by association in the field of employment or occupation.[32]

E. Horizontal Nature

29.42 The Directive is horizontal in nature,[33] in the sense that it is required to be implemented right across the marketplace. To maximize its efficacy, Member States are required to apply its provisions both to public and private bodies. The principle of equal treatment, as implemented by national law, binds both public and private law entities.

29.43 Any laws, regulations, and administrative provisions contrary to the principle of equal treatment are required to be abolished.

29.44 Provisions in contracts, collective agreements, internal rules of undertakings, or rules governing independent occupations and professions and workers' or employers' organizations which are contrary to the principle of equal treatment are required to be rendered null and void or capable of being declared null and void.[34] Thus collective agreements cannot be required to be set aside by a national court on the basis of their incompatibility with the Directive, unless national law obliges them to do so.

29.45 By making Member States responsible for the elimination of discriminatory structures at all levels in the marketplace, the rights set out in the Directive are effectively guaranteed on a horizontal as well as a vertical level thus 'ensuring a civil society which is inclusive and progressive rather than exclusive and particular'.[35]

F. Scope of Application

29.46 The Directive applies to all persons who exercise an economic activity, either in an employed or self-employed capacity, in the public or private sector, including public bodies[36] with respect to:

(a) conditions of access to employment, to self-employment, or occupation, including selection criteria and recruitment conditions, whatever the

---

[32] Opinion at para 24.

[33] But not in the effect; being a directive it has vertical direct effect only with the result that it cannot create obligations between private individuals.

[34] Art 16.

[35] Schiek (see note 7 above) at 294.

[36] Art 3(1).

branch of activity and at all levels of the professional hierarchy including promotion;

(b) access to all types and all levels of vocational guidance, vocational training, advanced vocational training, and retraining including practical work experience;

(c) employment and working conditions including dismissal[37] and pay;

(d) membership and involvement in an organization of workers or employers or any organization whose members carry on a particular profession, including the benefits provided by such organizations.[38]

The Directive applies within the areas of Community competence.[39]   **29.47**

Recital 14 of the Preamble to the Directive states that it is without prejudice to   **29.48**
national provisions laying down retirement age. This limitation on the scope of application of the Directive has been held in *Palacios de la Villa*[40] to be restricted to the right of Member States to determine retirement age and does not preclude the application of the Directive to national measures governing the conditions for termination of employment contracts where the retirement age thus established has been reached. Thus the Directive was applicable to national legislation which permitted the automatic termination of an employment relationship once a worker had reached the age of 65. Such legislation affects the duration of an employment relationship and the engagement of a worker in an occupation, by preventing his future participation in the labour force. It must therefore be regarded as establishing rules relating to 'employment and working conditions including dismissals and pay within the meaning of Article 3(1)(c)'.

G. Reasonable Accommodation

Disabled persons have the right to reasonable accommodation in the workplace   **29.49**
so as to have effective access to employment and training.[41]

At the time of the adoption of the Directive the concept of reasonable accom-   **29.50**
modation was largely unknown within the Community. Those Member States which had disability anti-discrimination legislation, that is the United Kingdom, Ireland, and Sweden, did recognize the obligation of reasonable accommodation

---

[37] See note 21 above at para 67, in which the Advocate General held that the setting of a compulsory retirement age was not to be equated with 'dismissal' within the meaning of the Directive.

[38] Art 3(1)(a), (b), (c), (d).

[39] Art 3(1). Article 13(1) operates within the limits of the powers conferred by the Treaty. The *ratione materiae* of both it and measures adopted under it is determined by the Treaty.

[40] See note 21 above.

[41] Art 5.

within their national legal systems but the other Member States and the accession states did not. The Directive itself gives little guidance on what reasonable accommodation may be taken to mean.

29.51   The general rule appears to be that employers must take appropriate measures to enable persons with a disability to have access to, participate, or advance in employment or to undergo training unless such measures would impose a disproportionate burden on the employer.

29.52   Guidance as to what are appropriate measures can be found in Recital 20 of the Preamble, which describes them as:

> . . . effective and practical measures to adapt the workplace to the disability, for example, by adapting premises and equipment, patterns of working time, the distribution of tasks or the provision of training and integration resources.

29.53   The reasonable accommodation obligation prohibits an employer from denying an individual with a disability an employment opportunity by failing to take account of his disability, in circumstances in which, were account taken of it and appropriate adjustments made to the work environment, he would have been enabled to do the work. This reflects a concept of equality which requires adaptation and change to meet the needs of the disabled employee.

29.54   The requirement of reasonable accommodation applies to all stages of the employment relationship. Thus at recruitment stage when comparing a job candidate with an impairment and one without such an impairment, the employer must assess the overall ability of the two candidates to carry out the work in question after taking into account any necessary reasonable accommodation which may be required to be made in respect of the candidate with the impairment.[42] An employee who develops a disability may have to be accommodated: he cannot be dismissed unless his dismissal is justified by the fact that he is not competent, capable, and available to perform the essential functions of his post, after reasonable accommodation has been made.[43]

29.55   What is a disproportionate burden, relieving the employer of the necessity to make a reasonable accommodation, is a question of fact to be determined in each case.

29.56   Accommodation measures will not be considered to be disproportionate where they are 'sufficiently remedied by measures existing within the framework of

---

[42] Waddington: *From Rome to Nice in a Wheelchair*. Europa Publishing 2006 at 40.
[43] See note 9 Judgment para 51.

the disability policy of the Member States concerned'. This would be the case if state aid were available to finance adjustments to the workplace.[44]

Achieving a balance between rights and obligations in this sphere may not be easy.[45] Assessing what proportionate reasonable accommodation might be is a two-step process; first it must be ascertained what accommodation is required and secondly whether it is reasonable in the circumstances to require an employer to make that accommodation. Reasonableness in this context will be a question of fact in each case and may involve the application of different criteria depending on the size and resources of the employer. A large undertaking might be expected to bear a heavier burden than a small undertaking with limited resources. **29.57**

Recital 21 of the Preamble to the Directive states that in determining whether a burden is disproportionate, account should be taken in particular of the financial and other costs to the undertaking in making the necessary accommodation, the scale and financial resources of the organization, and the possibility of obtaining public funds or assistance for the measures required. **29.58**

Advocate General Geelheod in *Chacon Navas*[46] added another subjective external (in the sense of being unrelated to the particular employment situation under consideration) criterion to the assessment of what is proportionate, in the context of a situation where a person's disability seriously restricts the pursuit of his employment or makes it impossible. The extent to which an employer can be required to accommodate such an employee involves an assessment of 'the accessibility of the disabled person concerned to other occupations or forms of business where his disability will be no obstacle or far less of an obstacle'. This implies a consideration of the employee's overall position on the labour market. **29.59**

H. Discrimination

The Directive prohibits direct and indirect discrimination.[47] Any instruction to discriminate against a person on any of the grounds to which the Directive relates constitutes discrimination.[48] Harassment in the sense of unwanted conduct taking place with the purpose or effect of violating the dignity of a person and of **29.60**

---

[44] See Commission Regulation 2204/2002 on the application of Articles 87 and 88 of the EC Treaty to state aid for employment [2002] OJ L337/3 which exempts from the requirement to notify, and deems compatible with the common market, state aid schemes for the recruitment of disabled persons the cost of adapting premises and equipment to their needs and the cost of providing staff for the assistance of disabled persons in the place of employment.

[45] Wells: 'The Impact of the Framework Employment Directive on UK Disability Discrimination Law' (2003) 32 ILJ 253 at 265–6.

[46] See note 8 above, Opinion para 83.

[47] Art 2(1) *Palacios de la Villa* (see note 21 above) Judgment para 50.

[48] Art 2(4).

creating an intimidating, hostile, degrading, humiliating, or offensive environment is deemed to be a form of discrimination.[49] An instruction to discriminate against a persons on any of the grounds set out in Article 1 is deemed to be discrimination.

(1) Direct discrimination

29.61   Direct discrimination is defined as meaning the less favourable treatment of one person over another in a comparable situation on one of the grounds specified in Article 1.[50] In *Mangold*[51] the Court found that a provision of German law permitting employers to conclude without restriction fixed-term contracts of employment with workers over the age of 52 'introduces a difference of treatment on the grounds directly of age'.[52]

29.62   In *Palacios de la Villa*[53] the ECJ found that national legislation which led to the automatic termination of an employment contract when a worker has reached retirement age 'must be regarded as directly imposing less favourable treatment for workers who have reached that age as compared with all other persons in the labour force. Such legislation therefore establishes a difference in treatment directly based on age . . .'[54]

29.63   *Coleman*[55] raised the issue of whether the Directive protects from discrimination and harassment persons who are not disabled themselves but are treated less favourably and harassed on the ground of their association with a person who is disabled.

29.64   Ms Coleman worked for a firm of solicitors in London as a legal secretary from January 2001. In 2002 she gave birth to a son who was severely disabled and required specialized and particular care. She was his primary carer. On 4 March 2005 Ms Coleman accepted voluntary redundancy, bringing her employment relationship to an end. Some months later she commenced proceedings before the Employment Tribunal alleging that she had been subject to constructive dismissal and that she had been treated less favourably than other employees because she was the primary carer of her disabled child and because of that treatment she had to stop working for her former employer. Her complaint was that

---

[49] Art 2(3).
[50] Art 2(2)(a).
[51] See note 24 above.
[52] Ibid Judgment para 57.
[53] See note 21 above.
[54] Ibid Judgment para 51.
[55] See note 4 above.

she had been treated differently than parents of non-disabled children in a number of respects.

The Employment Tribunal referred a series of questions to the ECJ, the essence **29.65** of which was whether the Directive, in particular Articles 1 and 2(1) and 2(a), must be interpreted as prohibiting discrimination on the grounds of disability only in respect of an employee who is himself disabled or whether the principle of equal treatment and the prohibition of direct discrimination apply equally to an employee who is not himself disabled but who is treated less favourably by reason of the disability of his child.

The ECJ held that the purpose of the Directive, as regards employment and **29.66** occupation, is to combat all forms of discrimination on grounds of disability. Following the opinion of the Advocate General it held that the principle of equal treatment enshrined in the Directive applies not to a particular category of person but by reference to the grounds referred to in Article 1 of the Directive, that is, religion or belief, disability, age, or sexual orientation. That interpretation was supported by Article 13 EC.

The fact that some provisions of the Directive, for example Articles 5[56] and 7(2),[57] **29.67** relate specifically to disabled persons did not mean that the Directive as a whole had to be interpreted strictly, that is to say, as prohibiting only direct discrimination on grounds of disability and relating exclusively to disabled people.

The Court also rejected the argument of the United Kingdom, Italian, and **29.68** Netherlands governments that it followed from *Chacon Navas*[58] that the scope *ratione personae* must be interpreted strictly. In view of Article 13 EC the scope of the Directive cannot be extended beyond discrimination based on the grounds exhaustively listed in Article 1 of the Directive, with the result that it cannot be extended to a case where a person was dismissed on account of sickness, but this did not mean that the principle of equal treatment and the scope *ratione personae* of that Directive must be interpreted strictly within those grounds.

He stated that the effect of the Directive was that it was impermissible for an **29.69** employer to rely on religion, age, disability, and sexual orientation in order to treat employees less well than others. It does not matter that the employee who is the object of the discrimination is not disabled herself. It is not necessary for

---

[56] Art 5 is concerned with the provision of reasonable accommodation in the workplace.

[57] Art 7(2) provides that with regard to disabled persons the principle of equal treatment is to be without prejudice either to the right of Member States to maintain provisions on health and safety at work or to measures aimed at creating or maintaining provisions or facilities for safeguarding or promoting the integration of such persons into the working environment.

[58] See note 9 above.

someone who is the object of discrimination to have been mistreated because of 'her disability'. The Directive applies if she was mistreated on account of 'disability' or presumably another ground of discrimination prohibited by the Directive.

29.70 Where an employee in a situation such as that of Ms Coleman suffers direct discrimination on the grounds of disability, an interpretation of the Directive limiting its application only to people who are themselves disabled:

> . . . was liable to deprive that directive of an important element of its effectiveness and to reduce the protection which it is intended to guarantee.[59]

(2) Indirect discrimination

29.71 Indirect discrimination is taken to occur where an apparently neutral provision, criterion, or practice would put a person having a particular religion or belief or a particular disability, a particular age, or a particular sexual orientation at a disadvantage compared with other persons unless that provision, criterion, or practice is: (a) objectively justified by a legitimate aim and the means of achieving that aim are appropriate and necessary; or (b) the employer is obliged, with respect to persons having a particular disability, under national law to take particular measures to provide reasonable accommodation for disabled persons in order to facilitate their effective employment.[60]

29.72 In the *Mangold* case[61] the Court found that the Directive did not in itself lay down the principle of equal treatment. The source of the principle prohibiting the forms of discrimination specified in the Directive:

> . . . being found, as is clear from the third and fourth recitals to the preamble to the directive in various international instruments and in the constitutions traditions common to the Member States . . . The principle of non-discrimination on grounds of age must thus be regarded as a general principle of Community law.[62]

29.73 This conclusion, which has consequences for the general effect of the Directive, in terms of whether it creates horizontal effects as well as vertical effects, as well as the point in time when those effects occur, has been the subject of academic criticism.[63]

---

[59] Judgment para 51.
[60] Art 2(2)(b).
[61] Case C-144/04 [2005] ECR I–9981.
[62] Ibid Judgment paras 74–75.
[63] Editorial Comments: 'Horizontal Direct Effect—A Law of Diminishing Coherence?' (2006) 43 CML Rev 1.

In *Lindorfer*[64] Advocate General Sharpston stated that it was reasonable to read   **29.74**
Mangold as referring to the general principle of equality:

> . . . the reference must surely be to the general principle of equality. The specific
> prohibition of age discrimination is, in both national and international contexts, too
> recent and uneven to meet such a description. The right to equality before the law,
> however, which may be seen as the ultimate source, is fundamental to the legal sys-
> tems of the Member States.

Some months later Advocate General Mazak in *Palacios de la Villa*[65] pointed   **29.75**
out that the various international instruments and constitutional traditions
common to the Member States to which the Court refers in *Mangold* enshrine the
general principle of equal treatment but not—except in a few cases, such as the
Finnish constitution—the specific principle of non-discrimination as such. He
concluded:

> . . . if the reasoning in Mangold were followed to its logical conclusion, not only
> prohibition on the grounds of age, but all specific prohibitions of the types of dis-
> crimination referred to in Article 1 of Directive 2000/78 would have to be regarded
> as general principles of Community law.
>
> . . . I do not regard as particularly compelling the conclusion drawn in Mangold as
> to the existence of a general principle of non-discrimination on grounds of age.[66]

It remains to be seen whether the Court will move away from or clarify its ruling   **29.76**
in *Mangold*.

I. Harassment

The concept of harassment, within the context set out in the Directive, is to be   **29.77**
defined in accordance with national law and practice. There will not, therefore,
be a uniform definition of harassment with the result that conduct which might
amount to harassment in one jurisdiction may not in another.

Coleman[67] was concerned with the limits of harassment. The Employment   **29.78**
Tribunal, South London asked the ECJ:

> Where an employer harasses an employee, and it is established that the ground for
> the treatment of the employee is that the employee has a disabled son for whom the
> employee cares, is the harassment a breach of the equal treatment established by the
> Directive?

---

[64] Case C-227/04 [2007] ECR I–6767.
[65] See note 21 above.
[66] Ibid Opinion at paras 96–97.
[67] See note 3 above.

29.79 The Court held that since harassment is a form of discrimination Article 2(3) of the Directive cannot be interpreted as being limited to the prohibition of harassment of people who are themselves disabled:

> Where it is established that the unwanted conduct amounting to harassment which is suffered by an employee who is not himself disabled is related to the disability of his child, whose care is provided primarily by that employee, such conduct is contrary to the principle of equal treatment.[68]

J. Victimization

29.80 Member States are required to introduce such measures as are necessary to protect employees against dismissal or other adverse treatment by an employer as a reaction to a complaint within the undertaking,[69] or to any legal proceedings aimed at enforcing compliance with the principle of equal treatment.[70]

K. Exceptions

29.81 The principle of equal treatment laid down by the Directive is subject to five exceptions. Additionally, Member States are permitted to make a number of derogations from some of its provisions. The Directive does not prevent any Member State from adopting specific measures to prevent or compensate for any damage linked to religion or belief, disability, age, or sexual orientation.[71]

29.82 Any exceptions or derogations are subject to the principle of proportionality.

29.83 With regard to disabled persons, the principle of equal treatment must not prejudice the right of Member States to maintain or adopt provisions on the protection of the health and safety at work or measures aimed at promoting the integration of the disabled into the working environment.[72]

29.84 As a general rule, the Directive applies without prejudice to measures laid down by national law in the interests of public security, public order, the prevention of criminal offences, and for the protection of health and the rights and freedoms of others.[73] No such exception figures in either the Equal Opportunities

---

[68] Judgment para 59.
[69] Art 2(2)(b).
[70] Art 11.
[71] Art 7(1). This provision reflects EC Treaty, Art 141(4) as interpreted in Case C-407/98 *Abrahamsson and Anderson v Fogelqvist* [2000] ECR I–5539.
[72] Art 7(2).
[73] Art 2(5).

Directive[74] or the Race Directive.[75] It appears to have been put in during the final negotiations of the text of the Directive, no evidence of it having appeared in prior drafts.

> ... It was thought necessary to prevent members of harmful cults, paedophiles and people with dangerous physical and mental illnesses from gaining protection from the Directive.[76]

A further rationale behind this provision may possibly be found in Recital 18 of the Preamble, which refers to the right of the armed forces and the prison and emergency services not to recruit or maintain in employment persons who do not have the required capacity to perform the function necessary to preserve the occupational capacity of those services, thereby putting at risk beneficiaries of those services. The breadth of the wording of this exception is a cause of concern: **29.85**

> It is ... an extremely broadly drafted provision, given that the Framework Directive covers only workplace discrimination. The ECJ will have to patrol its boundaries carefully.[77]

The Directive provides for two other specific exceptions to the principle of equal treatment: **29.86**

(i) it has no application to differences in treatment based on nationality or conditions relating to the entry and residence of third country nationals and stateless persons. The Directive is expressed not to have any impact on the legal status of such persons.[78] It therefore respects the confines of Article 13 EC: discrimination based on nationality remains subject to Article 12 EC and the rights of third country nationals to enter and remain in a Member state are within the exclusive competence of that state;

(ii) it does not apply to payments of any kind by state schemes 'or similar', including state social security or social protection schemes.[79]

In *Tadao Maruka*[80] the issue was whether a survivors' benefit paid under an occupational pension scheme fell within the scope of the Directive. The Court ruled that the Directive must be understood as excluding social security or social **29.87**

---

[74] Directive 76/207 [1976] OJ L39/40.
[75] See note 1 above.
[76] Ellis: *EU Anti-Discrimination Law* Oxford University Press 2005 at 291.
[77] Ibid.
[78] Art 3(2).
[79] Art 3(3).
[80] Case C-267/06 Judgment of 1 April 2008.

protection schemes which were not 'pay' within the meaning of Article 141 EC or payments of any kind made by the state with the aim of providing access to employment or maintaining employment. In that case the Court found that the characteristics of the survivors' pension in issue qualifies it to be classified as 'pay' within the meaning of Article 141 EC and therefore it fell within the scope of the Framework Employment Directive.

29.88 The Directive is without prejudice to national laws on marital status and the benefits dependent thereon.[81] In *Tadeo Maruko*, Mr Maruko was refused a widower's pension when his same-sex life partner died in January 2005. He and his partner had entered into the life partnership in November 2001. His claim was refused on the ground that the pension scheme did not provide for survivors' pension for life partners. Entitlement was confined to surviving spouses. In 2001 Germany altered its legal system to allow persons of the same sex to live in a union of mutual support and assistance which is normally constituted for life. Having chosen not to permit persons of the same sex to enter into marriage, which continued to remain a possibility only for those persons of different sex, Germany created for persons of the same sex an equivalent regime, the life partnership, the conditions of which were gradually made equivalent to those applicable to marriage. In these circumstances the ECJ held that the combined provisions of Articles 1 and 2 of Directive 2000/78 precluded legislation such as that at issue in the main proceedings under which, after the death of his life partner, the surviving partner does not receive a survivor's benefit equivalent to that granted to a surviving spouse, even though, under national law, life partnership places persons of the same sex in a situation comparable to that of spouses so far as concerns that survivor's benefit. It was for the referring court to determine whether a surviving life partner was in a situation comparable to that of a spouse who was entitled to the survivor's benefit provided for under the occupational pension scheme in question.

29.89 Member States can provide that the Directive does not apply to the following situations:

(a) the armed forces in so far as it relates to discrimination on the grounds of disability and age.[82] This derogation is broad in scope. It is intended to enable the Member States to safeguard the combat effectiveness of their armed forces. The Member States who avail themselves of this derogation have complete discretion to determine what constitutes 'combat effectiveness' and what is required to maintain it and accordingly to determine the employment rights of the disabled and the elderly. Given the record of some

---

[81] Preamble Recital 22.
[82] Art 3(1).

Member States in granting access to women to employment in the armed forces,[83] this is a matter of concern. That said, the exception to the right to equal treatment is subject to the general principle of proportionality which should provide some level of guarantee that national measures will go no further than a minimal erosion of the right of equal treatment in employment in the armed forces;

(b) differences in treatment on the grounds of age, provided there are objective reasons for the differential treatment and it is reasonably justified, within the context of national law, by a legitimate aim relating to employment policy, labour market, and vocational training objectives if the means of achieving those objectives are appropriate and necessary.[84] Such differences in treatment may include:

(i) the setting of special conditions on access to employment and vocational training, employment, and occupation, including dismissal and remuneration conditions for young people, older workers, and persons with caring responsibilities in order to promote their vocational integration or ensure their protection;

(ii) the fixing of minimum conditions of age, professional experience, or seniority in service for access to employment or to certain advantages linked to employment;

(iii) the fixing of a maximum age for recruitment which is based on the training requirements of the post in question or the need for a reasonable period of employment before retirement.

(c) the fixing, for occupational social security schemes, of differential ages for employees or groups or categories of employees for admission or entitlement to retirement or invalidity benefits including the fixing under those schemes of different ages for employees or groups or categories of employees. The use of age criteria in actuarial calculations does not constitute discrimination on the grounds of age provided it does not result in discrimination on the grounds of sex;[85]

(d) differences in treatment based on a characteristic required for a particular occupation. The characteristic in question must be a 'genuine and determining

---

[83] See paras 25.19–25.25 and 25.72–25.74.

[84] Art 6(1). See Case C-388/07 *Age Concern England* [2007] OJ C283/09 Opinion of Advocate General Mazak 23 September 2008. See the following cases pending before the ECJ: Case C-555/07 *Kucukdeveci* [2008] OJ C79/12; Case C-341/08 *Petersen* [2008] OJ C260/08; Case C-229/08 *Wolf* [2008] OJ C223/21; Case C-88/08 *Hutter* [2008] OJ C128/21.

[85] Art 6(2).

occupational requirement';[86] which has a legitimate objective and the difference in treatment to be justified must be proportionate to the attainment of that objective;

(e) occupational activities within churches and other public or private organizations the ethos of which is based upon religion or belief. In such cases a difference in treatment based upon a person's religion or belief does not constitute discrimination where by reason of the nature of these activities or the context in which they are carried out, a person's religion or belief constitutes a genuine, legitimate, and justified occupational requirement having regard to the organization's ethos. Such organizations can require individuals working for them to act in good faith and with loyalty to the organization's ethos.[87]

29.90 In *Mangold*[88] the Court held that a provision of German law whereby all workers who had reached the age of 52 years without distinction may, until the age at which they may claim their entitlement to a retirement pension, be offered fixed-term contracts of employment which could be renewed an indefinite number of times, could not be objectively justified. The age of the worker was the only criterion for the application of fixed-term contracts of employment. It had not been shown that that the fixing of an age threshold as such, regardless of any other consideration linked to the structure of the labour market or the personal situation of the workers concerned, was objectively necessary to achieve the vocational integration of the unemployed older worker, as had been argued by the German government. As a result of the operation of that law:

> This significant body of workers, determined solely on the basis of age, is thus in danger, during a substantial part of its members' working life, of being excluded from the benefit of stable employment which, however, as the Framework Agreement makes clear, constitutes a major element in the protection of workers.[89]

29.91 In the subsequent case of *Palacios de la Villa*[90] the Court considered a number of aspects of Article 6(1). It will be recalled that what was in issue in that case was a national provision which allowed the inclusion of compulsory retirement clauses in collective agreements, as part of a national policy aimed at promoting better access to employment by means of better distribution of work between the generations. Even though the objective was not referred to in the legislative provisions permitting such clauses in collective agreements, the Court found that

---

[86] Art 4(1).
[87] Art 4(5).
[88] See note 24 above.
[89] Judgment para 64.
[90] Case C-411/05 (see note 21 above).

'that alone was not decisive'. From this it may be concluded that a national employment policy of the kind envisaged by Article 6(1) need not be articulated in each and every measure which, although discriminatory within the meaning of Article 2 of the Directive, is seeking to implement that policy:

> It cannot be inferred from Article 6(1) of Directive 2000/78 that the lack of precision in the national legislation in issue as regards the aim pursued automatically excludes the possibility that it may be justified under that provision.[91]

However, it is necessary from the general context of the measure to enable its underlying aim to be identified.   **29.92**

Moving on to the substance of the measure the ECJ, following the stance it had adopted in *Mangold*,[92] held that Member States enjoyed a broad discretion in their choice, not only to pursue a particular aim in the field of social and employment policy, but also in the definition of measures capable of achieving it. The Advocate General stated in his opinion that only a 'manifestly disproportionate national measure should be censured' by the Court of Justice.[93]   **29.93**

In the case of the measure in issue in this case the Court found that it fell within the scope of Article 6(1). The compulsory retirement of workers who had reached a certain age was designed to create opportunities in the labour market for persons seeking employment. That was a legitimate aim of public interest which could not be called into question; it was amongst the objectives listed in Article 6(1) of the Directive and in accordance with the first indent of Article 2 EU and Article 2 EC, the promotion of a high level of employment is one of the issues pursued by both the European Union and the European Community. Furthermore the encouragement of recruitment constitutes a legitimate aim of social policy.[94]   **29.94**

> Therefore an objective such as that referred to by the legislation at issue must, in principle, be regarded as 'objectively and reasonably' justifying 'within the context of

---

[91] Ibid Judgment para 56 A similar issue has been raised in Case C-388/07 *The Incorporated Trustees of the National Council on Ageing (Age Concern England)*. See Opinion of the Advocate General of 23 September 2008 at para 41 i.

[92] See note 24 above Judgment para 63.

[93] Opinion of Advocate General Mazak at para 74 where he held that as a general rule it was not for the Court to 'substitute its own assessment of such complex issues for that of the national legislature or other political and societal involved in the definition of the employment and social policy of a particular Member State.' Advocate General Geelhoed in *Chacon Navas* (see note 8 above) put the point thus:'... the implementation of the prohibitions of discrimination of relevance here always requires that the legislature make painful, if not tragic, choices when weighing up the interests in question, such as the rights of disabled or older workers versus the flexible operation of the labour market or an increase in the level of participation of older workers. Not infrequently the application of these prohibitions of discrimination necessitates financial compensation, the reasonableness of which partly depends on available public resources or the general level of prosperity in the member State concerned.' Opinion at para 55.

[94] Case C-208/05 ITC *Innovation Technology Centre* [2007] ECR I–181 Judgment para 39.

national law' as provided for by the first subparagraph of Article 6(1) of Directive 2000/78, a difference in treatment on grounds of age laid down by the Member States.[95]

29.95   As to whether the means employed to achieve such a legislative aim were 'appropriate and necessary' the Court had this to say:

> It does not appear unreasonable for the authorities of a Member State to take the view that a measure such as that in issue in the main proceedings may be appropriate and necessary in order to achieve a legitimate aim in the context of national employment policy, consisting of the promotion of full employment by facilitating access to the labour market.[96]

29.96   Furthermore the Court held that the measures in issue could not be regarded as unduly prejudicing the legitimate claims of workers subject to compulsory retirement. These persons are entitled to financial compensation by way of a retirement pension at the end of their working life, the level of which cannot be regarded as 'unreasonable'.

L. Northern Ireland

29.97   Article 15 of the Employment Equality Directive lays down two exceptions to the principle of equal treatment with respect to employment in the police and the teaching professions in Northern Ireland. These exceptions are stated to be designed to promote peace and reconciliation between major communities in the province. Both exceptions are permitted only to the extent laid down by national law.

29.98   Article 15(1) provides that, in order to tackle the under-representation of one of the major religious communities in the police service in Northern Ireland, differences in treatment in the recruitment into the police services including support services do not constitute discrimination.

29.99   In order to maintain balanced opportunities in employment for teachers in Northern Ireland, Article 15(2) states that provisions on religion or belief in the Directive shall not apply to the recruitment of teachers in Northern Ireland.

---

[95] Judgment para 66.
[96] Judgment para 72.

M. Enforcement and Remedies

The Directive lays down a number of preventative measures. First, it advocates **29.100** the dissemination of information on the provisions of the Directive and other relevant provisions in the area of non-discrimination and, secondly, it encourages the social partners to foster equal treatment through the monitoring of workplace practice, codes of conduct, collective agreement, and good practice.[97]

The Directive also encourages dialogue with non-governmental organizations **29.101** with a view to promoting the principle of equal treatment.[98]

Judicial and administrative procedures (including, where appropriate, concilia- **29.102** tion procedures) are available to all persons who consider themselves wronged by failure to apply the principle of equal treatment even if the circumstances in which the alleged discrimination has occurred no longer exist.[99]

Associations, organizations, and other legal entities which have a legitimate **29.103** interest in ensuring compliance with the provisions of the Directive may engage in any judicial or administrative procedure established for the enforcement of obligations under the Directive, in support of a complainant or on his behalf and with his approval.

Any proceedings are subject to national time limits provided of course that such **29.104** limits are not such as to render the enforcement of rights under the Directive ineffective.[100]

In contrast to the Race Directive,[101] this Directive does not require the creation **29.105** or designation of an institution to promote equality in employment or matters related to the Directive. There is thus no mechanism whereby individuals wishing to assert their right may be assisted in doing so and no entity capable of conducting surveys or research being generally vigilant in ensuring the proper enforcement of the Directive.

N. Burden of Proof

The burden of proving discrimination under the Framework Equality Directive **29.106** is less exacting than that laid down in the Burden of Proof Directive[102] which, in

---

[97] Art 13.
[98] Art 14.
[99] Art 9(1).
[100] Art 9(3).
[101] See note 2 above.
[102] Directive 97/81 ([1998] OJ L14/6). See Case C-197/97 *ex parte Seymour Smith* [1999] ECR I–623.

order to establish indirect discrimination, requires that a 'substantially higher proportion' of men or women be affected by the alleged discriminatory rule or practice. This evidential rule has required indirect discrimination to be proved on the basis of statistical evidence.[103] The need to adduce statistical evidence is therefore avoided in the Framework Employment Directive as Recital 15 of the Preamble makes clear.

29.107 It states that indirect discrimination can be 'established by any means including on the basis of statistical evidence'. This move away from reliance on statistical evidence to prove indirect discrimination broadens the range of evidence which may be adduced to include qualitative as well as quantitative data.

29.108 The Directive lays down rules relating to the burden of proof comparable to those applicable in the case of complaints of gender discrimination. Where a person claiming a breach of the principle of equal treatment as laid down in the Directive relies on factual evidence in support of his claim, the burden of proving that there has not been a breach of the principle of equal treatment lies on the respondent. This rule does not apply to: (a) criminal proceedings; (b) proceedings in which it is for a court or competent body to investigate the case. In other words, the burden of adducing factual evidence is lifted from the claimant and placed on either the respondent or the person responsible for proving the allegation. Thus in the *Coleman*[104] case the Court held that should Ms Coleman establish facts from which it may be presumed that there has been harassment, the effective application of the principle of equal treatment requires that the burden of proof should fall upon the respondents to prove that there has been no harassment in the circumstances of the case.

---

[103] Case C-237/94 *O'Flynn* [1996] ECR I–2617.
[104] Note 2.

30

CONCLUSIONS

This book has set out the development of social and employment law and **30.01** policy within the European Community over the last half century. From a position where the Community institutions had little competence, the status of social and employment policy has gradually risen in stature. This has come about initially, as from the early 1970s, by virtue of the political will of the Member States to endow the Community institutions with some, albeit limited, measure of competence and then subsequently, as from the early 1990s, by granting the Community institutions and the social partners specific legislative powers and a defined role in policy-making. These developments have not come about consensually. Following the Treaty of Maastricht there was an awkward period in which the United Kingdom refused to accept the enhanced role given to the Community institutions and, as a result, provisions which ought to have formed part of the social chapter of the EC Treaty were instead consigned to a Protocol[1] whereby the Member States agreed, with the exception of the United Kingdom, to endow the Community institutions and the social partners with considerably increased powers. These powers were set out in the Agreement on Social Policy, attached to the Protocol. This uneasy state of affairs ended with the Treaty of Amsterdam, which in addition to incorporating the Agreement on Social Policy into Title XI of the Treaty, created a Title VIII on employment policy.

The Lisbon Treaty, as yet not ratified, raises the status of social policy within **30.02** the scope of the EC Treaty. It refers to the Community institutions as having 'shared competence'.[2] This marks a move away from the traditional hard-held view that Community competence and national competence should be clearly delineated, with, in many cases, the supportive or subsidiary role of the Community being emphasized.

---

[1] Protocol No 14 on Social Policy.
[2] Article 2C. Shared competence is defined in Article 2A.

30.03   A further enhancement of the status of employment and social law within the Community legal order has come about as a result of the recent judgment in the cases of *Viking*[3] and *Laval*,[4] where the ECJ held that since the Community has not only an economic purpose as well as a social purpose, the rights under the provisions of the EC Treaty on the free movement of goods, persons, services, and capital must be balanced against objectives pursued by social policy

30.04   In *Viking, Laval,* and more recently *Impact*,[5] the ECJ has held that even in areas where Community competence is expressly excluded by the EC Treaty such as Article 137(5), national competence is not exclusive: it must be exercised with due regard for Community rights. Although the Community cannot actively take measures in those areas to which competence is reserved to the Member States, that competence is not without the impact of Community law: Community law rights, such as the right of establishment, in issue in *Viking*, must be respected even if this means a curtailment of national law rights.

30.05   Apart from the gradual increase in the Community's legislative and policy-making competence over the past 30 years, the development of social and employment policy at a Community level owes much to the European Court of Justice, which has not hesitated to act robustly when interpreting and applying both EC Treaty provisions and legislation based on them.

30.06   From the original arid provisions of the EEC Treaty and early vague and imprecise legislative measures, a corpus of rights has been created which has had a huge impact on the lives of the people of Europe—a difference in the quality of their lives which, at least in some cases, their own governments were reluctant to sanction. For all the rhetoric—and considerable it has been—from politicians and law-makers, it is not from them that social Europe, such as it is, has derived. It has come from citizens themselves bringing legal proceedings the length and breadth of Europe, to assert their rights, and from a Court willing to assume the responsibility of putting flesh on often skeletal legal provisions to bring them to life in a manner which will fulfil the objectives for which they were designed.

30.07   Relying on the doctrine of the supremacy of Community law and the principle of direct effect, the ECJ has struck down provisions of national law which are incompatible with Community law and has held many provisions to be of direct effect with the result that Community citizens can rely on them as a source of rights which must be safeguarded by national courts. In protecting social and employment rights the Court has adopted an approach that is

---

[3] Case C-438/05 Judgment of 11 December 2007.
[4] Case C-341/05 Judgment of 11 December 2007.
[5] Case C-268/04 Judgment of 9 January 2008.

essentially functional. It has looked at the objective of the rules which are in issue before it and has interpreted them according to both what they are designed to achieve and wider Community objectives. Exceptions and derogations have been required to be proportionate to the objective which they seek to attain in the sense that limitations on rights must be both necessary and minimal. Provisions prohibiting discrimination have been held to include both direct and indirect discrimination. Indirect discrimination occurs where apparently neutral provisions applicable equally to two groups have in practice a disparate impact, with one group being more disadvantaged than another due to circumstances particular to them. Key concepts have been interpreted broadly to be fully effective.

Legislation adopted in the immediate aftermath of the 1974 Social Action programme, notably that on collective employment rights considered in Part IV, tended to be clear as to its objectives but somewhat opaque on how these should be achieved. This resulted in numerous references for preliminary rulings to the Court notably with respect to the Transfer of Undertakings Directive.[6] This Directive applies to any transfer of an undertaking, business, or part of a business to another employer as a result of a legal transfer or merger. Three concepts thus determine the scope of application of this Directive: none are defined therein. Moreover, the linguistic versions of the Directive vary, adding more confusion. As ways and means of doing business change, situations such as, for example, outsourcing and insourcing have raised issues which the original Directive did not address and which may not have been in the minds of the legislators at the time of its adoption. The Court has had to respond to these questions and in doing so has focused upon the objective of the Directive, giving its provisions the meaning best suited to protecting the employee. For example, in the absence of any definition of what constitutes a transfer of an undertaking, the Court has opted for a flexible interpretation designed to encompass a broad range of situations in which a change of employer takes place. It has held the Directive to be applicable whenever in the context of contractual relations there is a change in the natural or legal person who is responsible for carrying on the business in question and the economic activity carried on remains the same and the means to carry on that activity, be it manpower or assets or a mix of both, is transferred. **30.08**

In interpreting the Collective Redundancies Directive[7] the Court has also taken a pragmatic stance requiring consultation to be meaningful and to take place before any decision as to the possibility of mass redundancies takes place. **30.09**

---

6 Directive 2001/23 [2001] OJ L82/16. See Chapter 12.
7 Directive 98/75 [1998] OJ L225/16. See Chapter 11.

30.10 Community legislation on employment rights defines many key concepts by reference to national law. Whilst national law must be taken as it is found with the result that the extent and range of rights and obligations may vary from Member State to Member State, it may have to be amended in order to give effect to the objectives of a Community instrument. Thus for example, in *Commission v United Kingdom*[8] it was held that there was an obligation on the United Kingdom to put in place a structure necessary to achieve the appropriate consultation of workers required by the Collective Redundancies Directive: the fact that legislation referred to national law and practice did not mean that if there were no law or practice regarding the consultation of the workforce, that none need be established.

30.11 Likewise in the case of the Insolvency Directive,[9] the Court has held in *Robins*[10] that Article 8 of the Directive, which states in a general manner that the Member States 'shall ensure that the necessary measures are taken' to protect employees' entitlement to benefit under occupational pension schemes, imposed an obligation on Member States. Although it felt unable to define the extent of that obligation, it did find that that it did not imply an obligation to guarantee benefits in full and that the level of protection offered by the United Kingdom, the compatibility of which with Article 8 was in issue in that case, was inadequate.

30.12 As we have seen in Part VI, the influence of the ECJ on the development of the law and policy on gender discrimination in pay and employment has been considerable. There is abundant evidence of legislation, and even the EC Treaty itself, being led by case law. For example Article 141(4) EC, enacted by the Treaty of Amsterdam, was inspired by the *Kalanke*[11] case law. The concept of indirect discrimination developed by the ECJ from the early 1980s has now been incorporated into all the equal treatment directives.

30.13 As to the Court's interpretative approach to issues of equal pay and equal opportunities between men and women, this has been characterized by a strict interpretation of the scope of both Article 141 EC and the Equal Pay and Equal Opportunities Directives. It has refused to extend the concept of 'pay' to working conditions or state social security systems and held that Article 141 and the Equal Opportunities Directive were concerned with differential treatment based on sex only, a concept which it rules excluded sexual orientation. It has limited the right of equal treatment in the field of social security to those risks and benefits which are specified in the Equality of Treatment in Social Security Directive.

---

[8] Case 165/82 [1983] ECR 3431.
[9] Directive 80/987 [1980] OJ L283/12 as amended. See Chapter 13.
[10] Case C-278/05 [2007] ECR I–1053.
[11] Case C-450/93 [1997] ECR I–6363 discussed at paras 25.78–25.81.

It has thus refused to be persuaded to elasticize rights beyond the confines laid down by either the EC Treaty or legislation. At the same time it has insisted that rights conferred must be given full effect. A broad view has been taken of what constitutes 'pay', which has been defined as any consideration which a worker receives directly or indirectly in respect of this employment from his employer. In the case of social security systems the Court has focused on the risk to which a benefit is addressed, rather than on the nature of the benefit or to whom it is granted. The more recent case law on the Race Directive[12] and the Framework Employment Directive[13] has followed the same approach. A distinction has been drawn between disability, which has been held to fall within the scope of the Framework Employment Directive and sickness—even of a fairly lengthy duration—which has been held to be outwith the Directive.[14] *Coleman*[15] held that persons who are not disabled themselves may suffer discrimination by virtue of their association with a disabled person. The Race Directive has been interpreted broadly. Prohibited discriminatory acts must not be confined to those where there is an identifiable complainant; a public statement that persons of a certain racial or ethnic origin stand no chance of being recruited is an act of discrimination.[16]

This case law of the ECJ, which has done far more for social and employment **30.14** rights than any Treaty or legislative provisions, has been the subject of criticism.[17] The ECJ has been accused of judicial activism; of exceeding its competence of not confining itself to its proper functions of applying and interpreting the law. Is this justified?

Let us for a moment put ourselves in the Court's shoes faced with the questions **30.15** in the case law discussed in this work. Certainly in some, if not all, cases the Court's position has been difficult. It is obliged to respond to preliminary rulings: it cannot, when a national court or tribunal genuinely seeks help to resolve a dispute before it refuse such help. And if the provisions of Community law which

---

[12] Directive 2000/43 [2002] OJ L180/22 See Chapter 28.

[13] Directive 2000/78 [2002] OJ L180/22.

[14] Case C-13/05 *Chacon Navas* [2006] ECR I–6467.

[15] Case C-303/06 Judgment of 17 July 2008.

[16] Case C-54/07 *Firma Feryn* Judgment of 10 July 2008.

[17] For a sample of this literature, see Davies: '"Any Place to Hang My Hat?" or: Residence is the New Nationality' (2005) 11 ELJ 43–56; Dougan: 'Fees Grants Loans and Dole Cheques: Who covers the cost of Migrant Education within the EU?' (2005) 42 CML Rev 943–86; Fuchs: 'Free Movement of Services and Social Security—Quo Vadis?' (2002) 8 ELJ 536–55; Hailbronner: 'Union Citizenship and Access to Social Benefits' (2005) 42 CML Rev 1245–67; Hatzopoulos: 'A More Social Europe: A Political Crossroads or a Legal One Way? Dialogue between Luxembourg and Lisbon' (2005) 42 CML Rev 1599–635; Mather: 'The Court of Justice and the European Citizen' (2005) 11 ELJ 722–43; Simitis: 'Dismantling or Strengthening Labour Law: The Case of the European Court of Justice' (1996) 2 ELJ 156–76; Editorial Comments: 'The Court of Justice in the Limelight—Again' (2008) 45 CML Rev 1571–9.

it is required to interpret are skeletal, and hence difficult of practical application, it has no choice but to breathe life into them to make them workable.

30.16 Many of the matters discussed in this book which have been resolved through the judgments of the ECJ should never have been imposed upon that court. They are complex questions more appropriately solved through the legislative process which has the possibility of viewing matters from all appropriate angles and gauging the consequences, short- and long-term, of rights created and obligations imposed. Regulation through case law is often unsatisfactory. A particular issue is decided in the context of the legal and factual circumstances of the case in which it arises. And generally case law breeds case law, as rarely is an issue conclusively determined in one set of proceedings. The conclusion must be, therefore, that the Member States and the Community institutions themselves need to be more active in specifying precisely what are the limits of their respective competences. The treaty-making and legislative processes need to be open, not just in the interests of democracy, but in order to achieve a full appreciation of the consequences of proposals. Too much is done by too few behind closed doors. Mistakes are made, commitments are entered into in ignorance of their true extent, litigation begins in a court or tribunal which eventually comes before the European Court of Justice which hands down a judgment which has far-reaching consequences of which the Court may not have been aware and even if it was, could do little about. If the Member States are concerned at the extent of judicial activism of the ECJ, they have but to articulate their desires in the course of the legislative process in a clear and unambiguous manner, which has not—as this work has shown—always been the case. Possibilities do exist for treaty amendments; there is now adequate legislative competence to deal with social and employment issues. The effective use of both could alleviate the Court of an—at times heavy—interpretative burden; a development which it would welcome.

30.17 Turning now to the future, it is clear that the Community is facing a number of challenges to which an urgent response is needed. The three main challenges appear to be: the consequences of enlargement, which has widened the gap within the Community between the poorest and richest regions; the impact of globalization and the knowledge-based economy and the ageing of Europe's population. To these may be added technological change. These are serious challenges which, if not confronted in a positive manner, will have far-reaching consequences on multiple levels.

30.18 The enlargement of the European Community has increased the divide between the richest and the poorest regions, with the new Member States making up two-thirds of the least developed regions. Average EU per capita income has declined. Migration flows have increased within the Community, the dominant flow being from the new Member States to the older Member States. Whilst this has alleviated manpower shortages, it has led to concerns over social dumping, defined as low wage competition and low labour and social standards. There is a fear in the older Member States of a race to the bottom, a decline in salary levels and terms and conditions of employment. This has manifested itself in a general opposition to first the Constitution of Europe and subsequently the Treaty of Lisbon.

Migration following the enlargement of the Community to 27 Member States, **30.19** has overwhelmingly taken the form of the posting of workers, the movement of persons in the context of the provision of cross-border services. Such workers do not provide services in their own right. They are employed by the provider of services who in the course of that employment are sent by the service provider to work on a temporary basis in another Member State. The implications of the scale of such movement are manifold. For the sender Member State large-scale posting may result in a skills and labour shortage which hampers their development. For the recipient Member State there is the advantage of the availability of competitive services but this challenges the traditional home service provider.

The issues surrounding posted workers began to arise shortly after the accession **30.20** of Spain and Portugal to the EU. Following the *Rush Portuguesa*[18] case, under pressure from a number of typical host Member States, legislation was adopted to regulate the terms and conditions of posted workers. Contrary to expectations, matters have not gone smoothly since then. Tension remains between the typical service recipient country and the service provider Member States. This tension manifests itself in attempts to place restrictions on the provision of services. These issues—and the attempts to resolve them—are discussed in Chapter 23.

In late 2006 the Commission published a paper which captured the demographic **30.21** position within the Community and how the Commission believed it would evolve. The prognosis was troubling. In essence the Commission estimated that the working-age population will decrease by 48 million by 2050. The dependency ratio is set to double and will reach 51 per cent by 2050. This in effect means that the EU will change from having four to only two persons of working age for each citizen aged 65 years and above. The impact of the ageing population will affect the structure of the labour market, productivity levels, and economic growth. It will further affect welfare systems and public finances. Many of the current social and employment policies being pursued by the European Union are designed to overcome the adverse effects of the ageing population.

The Commission concluded that, given current trends, the total number of **30.22** persons in work was set to decrease by 30 million between the end of the decade

---

[18] Case C-113/89 [1990] ECR I–1417.

and 2050. This would in part be due to the low levels of employment of older workers. Early retirement levels, insufficient financial incentives to work offered by tax and social security systems, lack of access by older workers to training, and age discrimination within the workplace all contribute to the under-representation of older workers on the labour market.

30.23 On the basis of current policies, ageing will lead to greater pressures on public spending. The Commission estimates that the cost of pensions, health care, and services for the elderly could represent an increase of 10 per cent in public spending. These upward pressures will be felt from 2010 onwards and will become particularly pronounced between 2020 and 2040. In many countries public finances risk becoming unsustainable.

30.24 Whilst the Member States are taking steps to address these issues, the Commission is of the view that the complexity of the challenges of ageing requires an overall EU strategy.

30.25 It has therefore outlined five core policies which it believes the Community should pursue.

30.26 First, falling levels of population should be reduced. This can be achieved by a combination of measures operating on a national and a Community level. Universal access to assistance services to parents, in particular for the education and care of young children, should be offered and measures taken to balance private and working life through flexible forms of work. The Commission will work with the social partners on measures to improve the balance between the working, private, and family lives of men and women for example through parental leave and flexible working hours.

30.27 Secondly, the rate of employment must be increased. This can be done by reducing the segmentation of the labour markets, increasing the number of women in work, and increased flexibility in the labour market. An increase in the rate of participation in the labour market of men and women over the age of 55 years is necessary and can be achieved by removing incentives to exit the labour market at a relatively early age and by enabling older workers to remain economically active for longer. This necessitates promoting the good mental and physical health of workers and eliminating discrimination within the workplace on grounds of age. A third response to the demographic challenge is to improve the productivity of Europeans at work. The Lisbon strategy is designed to achieve this by bringing together in a coherent manner all the structural reforms which are likely to optimize European performance. The ageing population can contribute to productivity by creating new markets in goods and services which meet the needs of the elderly.

The fourth policy objective addressed by the Commission concerns the issue of **30.28** immigration. The decline in population means that the European labour market will need to attract a qualified labour force from outside.

The fifth challenge facing the Community is globalization. **30.29**

Globalization is perceived by some as an opportunity; an incentive to innova- **30.30** tions and growth. For others it is perceived as a threat to the values, institutions, and policies which have characterized Europe's post-war economic success and way of life, to what is often referred to as the European social model.

A recent study, carried out for the European Commission[19] concluded that the **30.31** EU as a whole will gain from globalization but the gains may not be evenly distributed across groups of individuals, regions, and the Member States. The gains will not accrue automatically; they will depend upon the successful adaptation to changes in the economic environment brought about by globalization and appropriate and judicious policy responses. Labour turnover can be expected to grow, putting a premium on the transferability and adaptability of skills and on flexibility in the workplace. Welfare reform is necessary first to cushion those who are marginalized and do not share in the gains from globalization and secondly, to bring about flexibility in the labour market: adequate income support during periods of transition in employment will encourage labour market fluidity. The study concludes that the challenge facing welfare provision is not about defending or opposing levels of social expenditure or casting doubt upon specific benefits or rules. Welfare systems need to be reconfigured so as to meet the challenges of globalization whilst at the same time remaining consistent with the values of the European social model.

These challenges require changes to the Community's labour markets and the **30.32** social protection systems of the Member States: they are common problems requiring a common solution and they are currently driving social and employment policy on a Community level at the moment.

The Community has put forward a number of proposals. The objective of these **30.33** proposals is twofold: to make labour markets more flexible and to get the economically active and the excluded onto those markets. The result, it is hoped, will be to raise the numbers in employment by making the labour markets more inclusive whilst at the same time making those markets more responsive to change thereby enabling the workforce to adapt to the challenges to the economic environment. Increasing levels of active employment will in turn ease the pressure on social

---

[19] Is Social Europe Fit for Globalisation: A study of the social impact of globalisation in the European Union. European Commission March 2008.

protection systems. Demand for benefit will decrease and potential beneficiaries will become net contributors.

30.34 The main tool being used by the EC Commission to increase the rate of employment is to combat discrimination in the workplace. Chapter 7 sets out the Commission's policy on the disabled; Chapter 28 discusses Community law and policy on the elimination of discrimination on grounds of race or ethnic orgin; Chapter 29 analyses the legislation prohibiting discrimination on grounds of age, disability, religion, and sexual orientation in the workplace. Although this legislation has been in place since 2000, there is concern at the level of implementation on a national level. The Commission is therefore actively engaged in ensuring the proper implementation of these Directives. In 2006[20] and 2008[21] it reported on the level of transposition of the Directives into national law, launching infringement proceedings where it was not satisfied that Member States had fulfilled their obligations. About half the Member States are concerned by these proceedings. The problems appear to relate to the failure to cover all the persons and areas covered by the Directives, definitions of discrimination that differ from those prescribed by the Directives, and inconsistencies in provisions to help victims of discrimination.

30.35 Despite these achievements the Community institutions have concluded that the European legal framework for tackling discrimination is not yet complete. The Commission has accordingly put forward a proposal[22] which will complete the process of giving full effect to Article 13 EC and bring to an end any perception of a hierarchy of protection, with discrimination in spheres of life outside the workplace being within the current legislative framework currently being prohibited only on the grounds of race. Discrimination on the other grounds specified in Article 13 EC is prohibited only in the workplace. The Commission's proposal builds upon the model used in existing directives. It reflects the current legislation with respect to the definitions of direct and indirect discrimination, harassment, and instructions to discriminate. Provisions on the role of equality bodies and the obligation for Member States to provide for proper redress against discrimination before the national courts are the same as those in the current legislation. The proposed directive applies to the provision of goods and services on a commercial level. The Commission felt that it would be disproportionate to extend the obligations in the proposed directive to individuals acting in a purely private capacity.

30.36 The proposed directive respects the diversity of European societies and consequently leaves issues such as the organization and content of education,

---

[20] COM (2006) 343 Final.

[21] COM (2008) 225 Final.

[22] Proposal for a Council Directive on implementing the principle of equal treatment between persons irrespective of religion or belief, disability, age or sexual orientation COM (2008) 420 Final.

recognition of marital or family status, adoption, reproductive rights, and other similar issues to be dealt with on a national level. A margin of flexibility is left to the Member States. For example rules which seem neutral but which in practice have a disadvantageous impact upon a group might be permissible if they are reasonable and pursue a justifiable aim.

Two policy initiatives are aimed at adapting the labour market to meet the chal-   **30.37**
lenges of globalization: (i) flexicurity and (ii) modernizing labour law.

At the European Council meeting of March 2006 the Commission, jointly with   **30.38**
the Member States and the social partners, was asked to 'explore the development
of a set of common principles on flexicurity' with a view to achieving more open
and responsive labour markets and more productive workplaces.[23] Flexicurity is
defined as a policy designed to bring about the flexibility of the labour markets,
work organizations, and employment relations on the one hand and security—
employment security and social security—on the other.

In June 2006 an expert group was set up by the Commission to review relevant   **30.39**
academic literature and practices in the Member States and to advise on precon-
ditions for flexicurity, various starting points, and flexicurity pathways. The
group reported in June 2007.[24]

On 27 June 2007 the European Commission published a communication on   **30.40**
flexicurity, in which it set out the policies it proposed to pursue to achieve
more open and responsive labour markets and more productive workplaces.[25]
The purpose of the Commission's communication is to encourage debate on the
common principles of flexicurity.

As part of this initiative in early 2008 the Commission set up its 'Mission for   **30.41**
Flexicurity', which spoke to businesses, employee organizations, social partners,
and national governments during the summer of 2008. The Mission's finding
and examples of good flexicurity practices will be published in December 2008.

In 2006 the Commission published a Green Paper the purpose of which was to   **30.42**
launch a debate within the EU as to how labour law could evolve to cope
effectively with the challenge of combining greater flexibility with the need to
maximize security for all—essentially a micro aspect of the flexicurity policy
discussed above.[26] More particularly the Green Paper wished to obtain views on

---

[23] Presidency Conclusions European Council 23/24 March 2006.
[24] Flexicurity Pathways: Turning hurdles into stepping stones. Report by the European Expert Group on Flexicurity June 2007.
[25] Towards Common Principles of Flexicurity: More and better jobs through flexibility and security. COM (2007) 359 Final.
[26] Modernising labour law to meet the challenges of the 21st century COM (2006) 708 Final.

whether a more responsive regulatory framework is required to support the capacity of workers to anticipate and manage change regardless of the form of their employment relationship.

30.43 The Green Paper points out that the traditional model of the employment relationship characterized by permanent full-time employment; employment relationships centred on the contract of employment but regulated—albeit differently from Member State to Member State—by law and the presence of a single entity employer accountable for the obligations imposed upon employers, is no longer the norm. Fixed-term contracts, part-time contracts, on-call contract, zero-hour contract, temporary agency workers, have become an established feature of the European labour markets. Given the increasing level of these forms of employment arrangements it might be necessary to examine the level of flexibility under more traditional contracts. Furthermore the Commission expressed the concern at the diversity of working arrangements. There is a concern that part of the workforce may get trapped in a succession of short-term low quality jobs which may leave them in a vulnerable position within the labour market. At the same time the Commission acknowledges that many such arrangements may provide a stepping stone to labour market entry.

30.44 The consultation process generated some 450 submissions, encompassing all stakeholders—national and regional governments, national parliaments, social partners, NGOs, individual enterprises, academics, lawyers, and private individuals were made in response to the green paper. Whilst they reflect a deep awareness of the challenges to the European labour market, the responses were of informative value only—there was little agreement on how to respond to the challenges set out in the Green Paper.[27] The conclusion was that although there was a difference of views on the nature and extent of potential action on an EU level, the consultation demonstrated a demand for improved co-operation in a number of areas and more information and analysis.

30.45 This is the position as we approach the end of the first decade of the twenty-first century. It is a time of great change both in Europe and on a global level. There are many unknowns but what is known is that we are facing a period of change which will have an impact both on our working and our social lives. We need to respond to this challenge in a positive, proactive manner. This requires a consensual approach on many levels and amongst all stakeholders. To be passive or defensive in the face of inevitable change can only be detrimental to the collective good.

---

[27] Outcome of the Public Consultation on the Commission's Green Paper COM (2007) 627 Final.

INDEX